W9-BRZ-699

TWENTIETH-CENTURY POPULISM

HD1773.A3S17 ST. JOSEPH'S UNIVERSITY STX
Agricultural discontent in the Middle We
3 9353 00167 5626

TWENTIETH-CENTURY POPULISM

Agricultural Discontent in the Middle West 1900-1939

76270

By
THEODORE SALOUTOS
and
JOHN D. HICKS

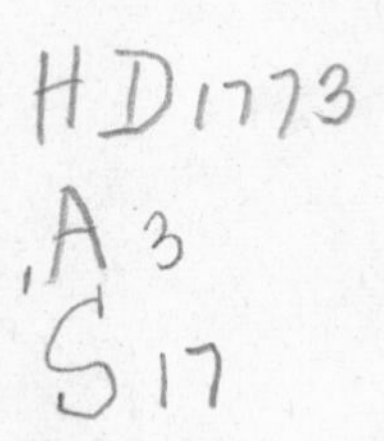

UNIVERSITY OF NEBRASKA PRESS · Lincoln

Copyright 1951 by the Regents of the University of Wisconsin
Library of Congress catalog card number 51-4287
Manufactured in the United States of America

Originally published as AGRICULTURAL DISCONTENT IN THE MIDDLE WEST 1900–1939

Bison Book edition reprinted from the 1951 edition by arrangement with the University of Wisconsin Press

TO

EDWIN BROUN FRED

PRESIDENT OF THE UNIVERSITY OF WISCONSIN

WHOSE INTEREST AND ENCOURAGEMENT

HELPED MAKE THIS BOOK A REALITY

PREFACE

THIS study originated in a series of seminars given by its senior author (Hicks) during the middle 1930's at the University of Wisconsin. At that time, neither the Old Deal nor the New Deal had reached satisfactory solutions for the farmers' ills, and the evidence of discontent was apparent on every hand. Since then the three Triple-A programs and the second World War have changed the situation materially, and the coming of the war has supplied a terminal date for our study. What the future may hold in store for the American farmer is by no means clear, but there is much evidence to support the opinion that neither the Republicans nor the Democrats will risk another Populist revolt by withholding the subsidies that now contribute so heavily to our agricultural income.

The center of agricultural discontent during the first four decades of the twentieth century lay in what we have called the western Middle West, or that part of the Middle West which is bounded on the east by Lake Michigan and the Indiana-Illinois boundary line. But the economic forces that contributed to the farmers' woes had little respect for state boundaries, so that it has seemed better to use in our title the more inclusive term, Middle West. Even that term, if restricted to the twelve north central states, is hardly adequate, but in common parlance the Middle West has come to include all of the central part of the United States, and thus defined, it suits our purpose reasonably well.

A considerable portion of this book was presented by the junior author (Saloutos) as a dissertation for the Ph.D. degree at the University of

Wisconsin in 1940. Since that time, however, the manuscript has been extensively revised and enlarged. As it now stands, Chapters I, II, and IV are primarily the work of Hicks, and the rest of the book the work of Saloutos. But we have consulted and advised together constantly, and we hope that the result is a continuous and unified narrative.

We are deeply indebted to the Committee on Research of the University of Wisconsin for its long-continued support of this project. Professor John D. Black of Harvard University read the manuscript, and favored us with many pertinent suggestions. Finally, we owe much to many libraries and many librarians.

THEODORE SALOUTOS
JOHN D. HICKS

University of California
September 15, 1950

CONTENTS

TWENTIETH-CENTURY POPULISM

Chapter I

THE REGION OF DISCONTENT[1]

IF AMERICANS were obliged to select a heartland for the United States, most of them undoubtedly would point on their maps to the twelve states of the Middle West, or as the census maps have it, the North Central states. Here lie the five states of the old Northwest—Ohio, Indiana, Michigan, Illinois, and Wisconsin—and beyond them in two neatly arranged tiers seven more—Minnesota, Iowa, and Missouri in the first tier and the Dakotas, Nebraska, and Kansas in the second. All of these states are far distant from the seas; they are heavily populated, except on their western and northern fringes, by the most "typical" of Americans; and they are capable of almost unlimited development, both agricultural and industrial. The exploitation of their riches is, indeed, already far along. On one census map after another, throughout the later nineteenth century and into the twentieth, the areas shaded to show acreage under cultivation, or crops harvested, or the production of wheat, or corn, or cattle, or swine, or dairy products reveal clearly the dominant role which this region has played, and continues to play, in the production of food. Here, too, lie the nation's richest deposits of iron ore and some of its richest coal fields. And into this sheltered haven industry also has marched with ever increasing tempo. Probably no other like-sized area could be found in all the world so capable of taking care of all its major needs.

1. This chapter follows in the main an article by John D. Hicks, "The Western Middle West, 1900–1914," *Agricultural History,* XX (April, 1946), pp. 65–77. Reprinted by permission.

It seems clear, however, that a distinction should be made between the eastern and the western Middle West. Exactly where the line of cleavage should be drawn to separate the two might well occasion considerable debate, but most observers would agree that the western Middle West lies wholly to the west of Chicago. One can even mark out a certain geographic unity here. While originally heavily timbered to the north and considerably less so to the south, this territory contains practically all the rich but treeless prairies, land at first spurned by the pioneers but later recognized as ideal for agriculture. Geologists eventually described this great expanse of prairie soils, which widens out westward like a wedge from the northern Indiana-Illinois border, as being among the richest in the world; furthermore, at about the ninety-sixth meridian the prairie soils shaded off into a still richer north-south zone, with a type of soil—the chernozem—so rich that it has been regarded as the ideal against which all others are measured.[2] The breaking plows have done their work, and these great flat or rolling stretches, for hundreds of miles westward from Chicago, offer a minimum of resistance to the farmers' will. On the northern and southern and far western borders of the western Middle West, however, nature has not been quite so kind. In northern Wisconsin and Minnesota the cut-over tracts left by the lumbermen are often sandy and barren. West of the one-hundredth meridian the rainfall is usually inadequate to insure crops without resort to irrigation. Down in southern Missouri the Ozarks have set expansive limits to what the farmer can do. Thus the political and geographic borders of the region do not precisely coincide, but the unity is there nonetheless.

The manner in which most of this western Middle West was opened to settlement offers yet another reason for its separateness. Except for the relatively small areas immediately bordering on the rivers or the lakes, its population grew as its railroad network grew. Most of the eastern Middle West was fairly well settled before the railroads appeared, but in the western Middle West, the exact reverse was true. To be sure, parts of Illinois, southern Wisconsin, eastern and central Missouri, and southeastern Iowa had a considerable population in advance of the railroads, but the era of really rapid settlement set in first during the 1850's as the Illinois Central, the Chicago and North Western, the Chicago and Rock Island, the Bur-

2. Fred A. Shannon, *The Farmers' Last Frontier* (New York, 1945), pp. 12–14.

lington and Missouri River, the Hannibal and St. Joseph, and a host of minor lines began to penetrate where water routes were too far distant for easy use. These and other railroads, helped along in most instances by federal grants of public land turned over to the states for the purpose, built even more feverishly after the Civil War, while great transcontinentals,

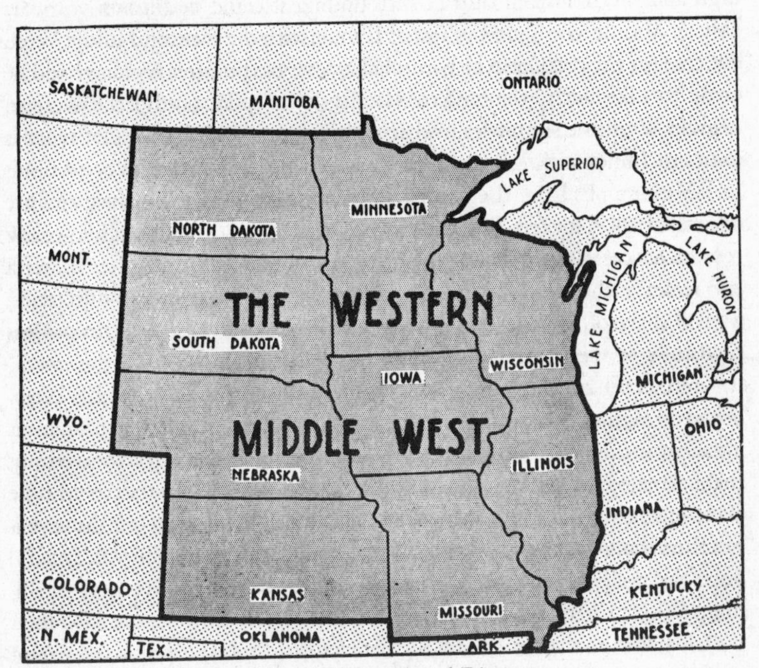

The Center of Agricultural Discontent

aided by land subsidies direct from the United States government, pushed their railheads ever farther and farther west. The western Middle West was thus from its infancy conditioned to railroads. Without them and the markets they opened up, its settlement would have been long delayed and in some portions could hardly have occurred at all.

Another factor tending to emphasize the difference between the eastern and the western Middle West was, and to some extent still is, the degree of industrialization to which each has attained. West of Chicago one finds few really large cities, and agriculture almost everywhere seems dominant. Except for Illinois, where Chicago heavily overweights the scales, as late as the census of 1920, more people in every state of this region still lived in the country, or in the country towns and villages, than in the city.[3] In the older Middle West as in Illinois, the exact reverse was true. If only Chicago and the industrial district surrounding it could be thrown with the eastern Middle West and the rest of Illinois with the western Middle West, the case for the predominantly rural character of the latter region would be complete. Similarly, the eastern Middle West quite outdid the western Middle West in the number and size of its factories. It is true that what is sometimes known as the second mill zone reached as far west as Saint Louis and Minneapolis,[4] but the greater proportion of the region's factories are bracketed by Chicago and Pittsburgh; except for a comparatively few remote outposts, the "black belt" of the manufacturing world leaves off a few miles to the west of Lake Michigan. And, if it makes any difference, a good share of the western outposts of the factory system exist to process foodstuffs or, perchance, to manufacture farm machinery.

There is yet another way in which the western Middle West has established its right to be considered a separate regional entity. Here numerous agrarian movements of reform have been born, here they have lived out their short spans of life, and here they have died. The western Middle West has behind it a long history of agricultural discontent. In the seventies the Grangers, cherishing a grievance against all monopolies in general but against the railroads in particular, captured legislative control of Illinois, Wisconsin, Iowa, and Minnesota and wrote into statute law their doctrine that the states might regulate railroad rates, even to the extent of fixing maximum charges. Following the Grangers came the Greenbackers, whose money reforms attracted followers in every section, but nowhere to quite the extent registered in the western Middle West. In the national election of 1876 Greenback presidential candidates polled over 54 per cent of their popular votes in the states of the western Middle West,

3. *Statistical Abstract of the United States,* 1943, p. 12. By 1930 Wisconsin and Missouri had joined Illinois as states with a predominantly urban population, although by very slender majorities.

4. Clifford L. Lord and Elizabeth H. Lord, *Historical Atlas of the United States* (New York, 1944), p. 157.

then only seven in number and not thickly settled at that. Four years later, with many more states offering Greenback tickets, the proportion was still 41 per cent.[5] After the Greenbackers came the Populist revolt. This movement, in its western manifestation, was strongest in the states bordering on the Great Plains—the Dakotas, Nebraska, and Kansas—but it picked up notable followings in both Minnesota and Iowa, and to the latter state it turned in 1892 for a presidential candidate.

In the twentieth century the gusty winds of reform continued to lash the western Middle West. The new crusades rarely struck with equal force in each of the nine states, but there were few periods in which one part or another of the region was not storm-tossed. The Wisconsin Idea got off to a good start early in the century. Hard on its heels came the Iowa Idea. Then, during and after the first World War, the Nonpartisan League upset the equanimity of all "right-thinking" people in North Dakota and Minnesota and to a lesser extent in neighboring states. In Congress the farm bloc, drawing heavily from all the states of the western Middle West, refused to permit the nation to forget the plight of the farmer. Here McNary-Haugenism originated, and here it found its most ardent supporters. Out of the same soil grew also the Farmer-Labor party of Minnesota, the Progressive party of Wisconsin, and many of the agricultural policies of the New Deal. From this region, possibly as a matter of appeasement, came seven of the nine secretaries of agriculture who held office during the first four decades of the twentieth century.

While agricultural discontent, both for the Middle West and for the United States as a whole, centered primarily in this region, economic forces have a way of straying at will across any such interior boundary lines as have been described. The plight of the corn farmer in Ohio and Indiana was not particularly different from the plight of the corn farmer in Illinois and Iowa. Wheat farming in Montana was a kind of projection of wheat farming in North Dakota, and similarly wheat farming in Kansas was much the same as wheat farming in Oklahoma. The Kentucky tobacco grower and the Wisconsin tobacco grower had much in common. Thus any investigation of the sources and consequences of farmer discontent in the western Middle West will frequently involve not only all

5. Based on Edward Stanwood, *A History of the Presidency* (Boston, 1898), pp. 383, 417.

the North Central states, but also, on occasion, some of their near neighbors as well. The term Middle West, however, if interpreted with reasonable elasticity, sets satisfactory limits to the scope of this study.

Obviously, anyone who wishes to understand the agricultural discontent of the Middle West must know something about the way of life that produced it. By 1900 American agriculture was "coming of age"; the era of pioneering was almost over, and each section had begun to realize what it could do best. While "general farming," defined by the census as that in which "no one source of income . . . represents so much as 40 per cent of the total value of products of the farm," was common throughout the Middle West, the tendency lay in the direction of some type of specialized farming particularly suited to the climate, soil, and location of the area concerned.[6] Indeed, the ordinary observer was surprised to discover that, in spite of the fact that nearly every farm grew a considerable variety of crops, there was an unmistakable tendency, region by region, to emphasize one crop above all others. It would overstate the case to compare the farm economy of the Middle West with the one-crop system of the cotton South, but in actual practice one of three principal activities absorbed the chief energies of most of these western farmers. Some of them grew corn, either to sell directly or to feed and sell as livestock; others devoted themselves mainly to the production of wheat; still others raised dairy cattle and made their living by selling milk and butterfat. Thus all three types of farmers, in spite of the numerous minor activities characteristic of most of the better farms, depended for their prosperity upon the marketing of a money crop.

The corn belt cuts a wide swath on any crop map of the United States. Centering in Iowa, all of which it includes, it extends westward into eastern Nebraska and southeastern South Dakota, northward into southern Minnesota, southward into northern Missouri, and eastward across northern and central Illinois on into Indiana and Ohio. In general, the corn farmer had much to be thankful for. He got a larger yield per acre for his labor than any other cereal grower, his crop season was long enough to keep him and his "hands" fully occupied most of the year, he had few problems of storage, and his marketing difficulties were minimum. If he

6. Foster F. Elliott, *Types of Farming in the United States,* U. S. Bureau of the Census (Washington, 1933), p. 48.

sold his corn directly, he found plenty of nearby purchasers who were ready to take it off his hands in order to feed it to livestock. Less than 20 per cent of the corn crop was shipped beyond the borders of the county in which it was raised. If he himself fed cattle or hogs, he was able to "condense" his freights. Ninety per cent of the corn crop, according to a common view, should never leave the farm on which it is grown. Every steer could conveniently carry a hundred bushels of corn to market, and in the thirty months of its normal life expectancy, it should consume also two or three acres of grass.[7] Livestock growers could always find plenty to complain about, but the packing houses to which they shipped were relatively close at hand, and in spite of the toll taken by the railroads and the commission men, profits were reasonably good.

Wheat was produced in many parts of the United States, but the greatest concentration of wheat growing was found in two large areas of the western Middle West. What came to be known as the hard spring wheat belt centered in North Dakota, but with a formidable extension in every direction—eastward into Minnesota, southward into South Dakota, westward into Montana, and northwest across the American border into the Canadian Northwest. Well to the south of this region lay another wheat-growing area, now commonly called the hard winter wheat belt, with Kansas as the center and overflowing into Nebraska, Colorado, western Oklahoma, and northern Texas. The growing of wheat had been a favorite frontier occupation, particularly after the thrust of population from the east reached the open prairies. Wheat is a highly concentrated crop, "storable," "haulable," and "salable" even under pioneer conditions. Furthermore, wheat culture thrives best on land plentifully supplied with humus, a condition present in most of the prairie states when the sod was first broken. There, too, the use of large-scale harvesting and threshing machinery was practicable. Pioneer farmers usually grew wheat as long as the soil produced a paying crop, then either moved westward to new prairie lands or gave up wheat growing for other and more complicated types of agriculture.[8]

As the twentieth century opened, the semiarid High Plains were begin-

7. *Wallaces' Farmer,* XXXVIII (February 21, 1913), p. 314.

8. Elliott, *Types of Farming,* p. 26; *Wallaces' Farmer,* XXXIII (October 2, 1908), p. 1179.

ning to set boundaries to the westward march of wheat. But a notable discovery had been made. Given modern milling conditions, the best bread wheats were not the soft wheats long favored by eastern farmers and millers but the hard wheats of high gluten content that could be produced only in regions of limited rainfall. This discovery, together with the introduction and improvement of turkey red, a variety of Russian hard winter wheat, had much to do with the rapid expansion of the hard winter wheat belt into western Kansas, the Oklahoma Panhandle, and northern Texas. As time went on, it became customary in the manufacture of bread flour either to use the hard wheats exclusively or to mix them with the soft winter wheats grown in Missouri, Illinois, and many eastern states. In times of shortage in the American hard wheat crop, millers sometimes felt obliged to import Canadian hard wheat, despite the tariff.[9]

There was a considerable difference in the methods by which spring wheat and winter wheat were produced. The spring wheat grower sowed his grain as early in the spring as he could and then harvested his crop from 100 to 110 days later. Winter wheat was sown in September or October and harvested the following June or July, thus requiring a ten-month season. In general, the winter wheat growers tended to be better farmers than the spring wheat growers, but the short work year was common to both. Conceivably, as one writer has put it, the wheat farmer could "put in a crop during a two- or three-week period in the fall or spring and harvest it in a like period during the summer or autumn; leaving at least ten months of the year free for vacation or other pursuits."[10]

The third principal type of economy upon which farmers of the western Middle West came to depend was the dairy industry. The rapid expansion of dairy farming was due principally to the demand of the great new urban centers for milk. Indeed, the new city population meant not only new milk customers, but as time went on it meant also more milk per customer. Educational campaigns changed the food habits of city dwellers and in particular taught them the virtues of the "perfect food," milk.

9. James C. Malin, *Winter Wheat in the Golden Belt of Kansas* (Lawrence, Kans., 1944), pp. 188–209, 254.

10. Edwin G. Nourse and Others, *America's Capacity to Produce* (Washington, 1934), p. 39; Theodore Saloutos, "Farmer Movements since 1902" (unpublished doctoral dissertation, University of Wisconsin, 1940), p. 3.

So great was the demand that means of transportation were devised to tap the milk supply a hundred, two hundred, or even three hundred miles from the city markets. In addition to milk for direct consumption, dairy farmers also sold butterfat to local creameries and comparatively small quantities of milk to ice cream makers, cheese factories, and condenseries. The production of butter and cheese began far back in the nineteenth century and antedated the urban era, but as with other food items, the increase in the number of city consumers greatly increased the demand.[11]

While cities inevitably furnished the principal market for milk, proximity to urban centers turned out to be only one factor in determining the location of dairy farms. The condition of the land mattered far less to the dairy farmer than to the grain grower, for a well-managed dairy farm tended to build up the soil rather than to deplete it. Naturally, therefore, where wheat growing or other types of general farming had robbed the soil of its fertility, dairy farming furnished a reasonable alternative. Rough and worn-out fields could be turned to pasture, and dairy farming produced an ample supply of fertilizer with which to stimulate the growth of feed crops. But the successful dairy farmer had to be a good farmer, intelligent as well as industrious and able to keep abreast of the rapid progress that scientific agriculture was making in his specialty.

The greatest concentration of dairy farming in the Middle West was in Wisconsin, northern Illinois, northwestern Iowa, and central and eastern Minnesota. Nearby lay the markets of Chicago, Milwaukee, St. Paul, Minneapolis, and numerous lesser cities. The urban influence, however, was less important in determining the location of dairy farms engaged principally in the production of butterfat. For this purpose some of the heaviest areas of concentration lay at a considerable distance from the large cities. There was, indeed, a considerable amount of dairy farming throughout the entire corn belt and even in the remoter grain-growing areas. It is also worth noting that the farmers of Wisconsin produced the milk that made that state for many decades the chief center of cheese manufacturing in the nation.[12]

11. Henry E. Alvord, "Dairy Development in the United States," U. S. Dept. Agri., *Yearbook*, 1899, pp. 381–402. See also *Wallaces' Farmer*, XXXIII (October 16, 1908), p. 1251.

12. Elliott, *Types of Farming*, pp. 44, 54.

The dairy farmer enjoyed certain substantial advantages over the grain grower. His work was less seasonal than that of any other farmer and provided employment for himself, his family, and his employees the whole year around. His profits, likewise, were fairly evenly distributed throughout the year, instead of coming in only at crop-marketing time. He had less to fear from high transportation charges, for his products were of small bulk in comparison to their value, and freight rates loomed correspondingly less important. His investment in land was moderate, and the stability of conditions under which he operated tended to make his credit good. What he asked of government was mainly low taxes, protection against substitutes, and aid in the never ending search for greater production at lower cost.[13]

It must not be forgotten that on most farms, whether in the corn belt, or in one of the chief wheat-growing regions, or in the area chiefly devoted to the dairy industry, there was generally a considerable amount of mixed farming. In the Middle West almost all varieties of cereal crops such as oats, barley, rye, and buckwheat were grown successfully. Milk and butterfat came from the same farms that also marketed swine and beef cattle. Fruits and vegetables were raised everywhere for domestic consumption and on a few truck farms for market. Potatoes were an important specialty in limited areas of Minnesota, Wisconsin, and Missouri. Sugar beets were raised in parts of Nebraska, tobacco growing achieved some importance in Wisconsin, and chickens, turkeys, geese, and ducks were universal. But in spite of these many side issues, the most important activities of farmers in the western Middle West centered on corn or corn and livestock, on wheat, and on dairy farming.[14]

Another circumstance, clearly apparent to the most casual observer, was the prevalence of the single-family farm. There were exceptions, of course, but in general the farmer of this region lived on his own or on rented land and carried on his farming activities mainly with such aid as he could obtain from his wife and children. The larger his crop of boys and girls

13. Benton H. Wilcox, "A Reconsideration of the Character and Economic Basis of Northwestern Radicalism" (unpublished doctoral dissertation, University of Wisconsin, 1933), pp. 33, 56.

14. See the appended map showing type-of-farming areas in 1930 in Elliott, *Types of Farming*.

old enough to help with the work, the better he was able to handle his labor problem. If he needed more help than his own family could give him, the hired man or hired hand, most probably the grown son of some other farmer, was introduced to supplement the family labor supply. If the farmer's wife, with the help of her own daughters, could not do all the work that fell to her lot, she sought the aid of a hired girl. Neither the hired man nor the hired girl was thought of as an inferior; in many instances the hired man became a son-in-law, and the hired girl a daughter-in-law. Working out as a hired man was a generally accepted method by which any young man without means obtained the start necessary to begin farming on his own.[15]

The ideal size of a family farm was traditionally 160 acres, and on the average the actual was not far from the ideal. This was the size of the farm allowed to each settler under the terms of the Homestead Act of 1862, but most of the farms in the Middle West had never been homesteads. The Homestead Act allotted 160 acres to each settler merely because a farm of that size had long been considered to be about right for one individual to operate. Eighty-acre farms were regarded as too small for economical farming: they required the same outlay for housing, work horses, and machinery as the larger farm but produced only half as much; they furnished more work than the farmer could do alone but not enough to justify his employing a year-round farm hand; and in the corn belt, where thrifty farmers expected about 90 per cent of their land to be tillable, the corn rows were likely to be too short.[16]

Farming was definitely a capitalistic affair and required a heavy investment. The size of the investment depended mainly upon the price of land, which varied from place to place and from time to time. A typical northwestern farm, according to one estimate, in 1910 would have represented an investment of $12,000. Of this sum about $1,400 would have been in buildings, $350 in machinery, and $1,400 in livestock—the rest, of course, in land.[17] Not every farm, by any means, was wholly free from mortgage, while in many cases chattel loans and store bills added ma-

15. Paul S. Taylor, "The American Hired Man: His Rise and Decline," U. S. Bureau of Agricultural Economics, *Land Policy Review,* VI (Spring, 1943), pp. 3–17.

16. *Wallaces' Farmer,* XXXIX (March 27, 1914), p. 540.

17. Wilcox, "Northwestern Radicalism," p. 23.

terially to the farmer's burden of debt. But the farm loan or farm mortgage was not necessarily an evidence of thriftlessness. It might, on the contrary, be regarded as a kind of evidence of prosperity. The wise farmer improved his buildings, bought new machinery, or expanded his acres even if to do so meant borrowing the necessary funds. Credit for the farmer was as necessary and proper as credit for any other businessman.

A burning problem throughout the entire Middle West was the steady increase in farm tenancy. "Nothing is more important to this country," said Theodore Roosevelt in 1907, "than the perpetuation of our system of medium sized farms worked by their owners. We do not want to see our farmers sink to the condition of the peasants in the old world, barely able to live on their small holdings, nor do we want to see their places taken by wealthy men owning enormous estates which they work purely by tenants and hired servants."[18] And yet, it seemed evident that something akin to the condition Roosevelt feared was coming about. Census statistics showed a steady increase in tenancy throughout the Middle West, and even more alarming, an increase which made tenancy more marked in this region than anywhere else in the United States except the South. In Iowa, for example, 76.2 per cent of the farms had been owned by their occupants in 1880, but thirty years later, in 1910, only 62.2 per cent were so owned. Furthermore, only half the farms of the state were operated exclusively by their owners.[19] Four years later, on the eve of the first World War, according to a reliable authority, almost 40 per cent of the farms in the corn belt were being cultivated by tenants. In parts of Illinois this proportion was no doubt well above 50 per cent, while in some of the newer and more sparsely settled sections it dropped to less than 20 per cent. But the long-cherished ideal, according to which each farmer owned his own farm and was thus accountable to himself alone, seemed farther from reality each succeeding year. If the tenant farmers were only organized, wrote one realistic observer, they could easily control elections and take over the state governments.[20]

18. *Wallaces' Farmer,* XXXII (October 11, 1907), p. 1145. On this subject in general, see W. J. Spillman and E. A. Goldenweiser, "Farm Tenantry in the United States," U. S. Dept. Agri., *Yearbook,* 1916, pp. 321–46.

19. *Thirteenth Census of the United States,* 1910, Vol. VI, *Agriculture,* p. 507.

20. *Wallaces' Farmer,* XXXV (November 4, 1910), p. 1494; XXXVII (March 8, 1912), p. 455; (June 28, 1912), p. 1019; XXXIX (March 27, 1914), p. 541.

There were two principal types of landlords. One was the retired farmer who, at perhaps sixty years of age, gave up farming and moved to town. Sometimes he rented to a son or son-in-law or nephew, and thus to a prospective heir, but in most cases he counted on enough from rent to take care of his needs. Thousands of these retired farmers had begun life as farm hands and had then become tenants, then farm owners, and at last retired farmers able to live on their rents and the interest on their savings. Many of them continued to take an active interest—frequently too active an interest for the tenant's peace of mind—in the farms they had left. Retired farmers often found that they had underestimated the expense of living in town and were inspired to drive new and harder bargains with their tenants, while in their communities they became "stationary" citizens, men who could be counted upon to vote consistently against better schools or city improvements on the sole ground that anything that might raise taxes was wrong.[21]

Another type of landlord was the investor, or as he was more likely to be called, the speculator. Farm land in the Middle West had for many years risen steadily in value and was thus considered by many investors to be safer than any bond, mortgage, or security on the market. Counting in the prospective rise in value of the farm, landownership seemed to promise a higher rate of return than any comparable investment. Investment-minded landlords, unlike the retired farmer, might know nothing whatever of farming, and some of them were totally unconscious of the need of keeping up the fertility of the land they owned. The worst of them seemed to "regard the farm as something like the old-fashioned coupon bond, from which they can clip coupons twice a year on the particular day and date on which they are due, whether crops are good or bad."[22]

While some farms fell to landlord-investors through the foreclosure of mortgages, there was another quite different cause of landlordism. Many prosperous farmers, convinced that land values had reached too high a figure, sold out their farms and moved north, west, or south to newer and

21. *Report of the Country Life Commission* (60 Congress, 2 session, Senate Document 705, serial 5408, Washington, 1909), p. 21.

22. *Wallaces' Farmer,* XXXIV (January 8, 1909), p. 40. See also E. H. Thomson and H. M. Dixon, *A Farm-Management Survey of Three Representative Areas in Indiana, Illinois, and Iowa,* U. S. Dept. Agri., Bulletin 41 (Washington, 1914).

cheaper lands. The number of Americans, mostly farmers, who left the United States for Canada exceeded 100,000 annually by 1911, while other thousands moved to the Mountain States, to the Pacific Coast, to the South, and even to Mexico.[23] These migrations were attended by far greater risks than most of the migrating farmers fully understood. Farming by irrigation or farming in an area of reduced rainfall involved new techniques, and while the land was cheaper, the man who purchased it was often poorer before he mastered them. Corn belt farmers who went west found out, usually only by experience, that beyond the ninety-ninth meridian conditions of corn growing were far less satisfactory than in the regions from which they had come. But they left in numbers just the same, and upon the land they vacated there often came tenants who were far less able to do the work than the men who had sold out. The time had come, said one editorialist, when Americans should settle down. "The farmers of the United States have been playing leapfrog over each other for over a hundred years, in fact, ever since the Revolution. . . . It is time for us to realize that the value of land depends more than anything else on the men who farm it."[24] But, at least as far as Iowa was concerned, all such pleas were in vain. That state lost steadily in farm population, and the census of 1910 even showed a decline in the total number of inhabitants.[25]

Rents paid by tenants varied. The prevailing rent in Illinois, according to one landlord, was half the corn, two-fifths the oats, and $5 an acre for meadow and pasture. In the corn belt states generally it was customary for the tenant to pay from one-third to one-half the grain he raised as rent. He was required, as a rule, to furnish all the necessary teams, implements, and seed, and in addition whatever labor was necessary to cultivate the land and keep it in good shape. He might also be expected to pay the

23. Senate Document 705, 60 Congress, 2 session, p. 49.

24. *Wallaces' Farmer*, XXXVIII (October 31, 1913), p. 1475. See also *ibid.*, XXXIX (July 24, 1914), p. 1044:

> "I never saw an oft removed tree,
> Nor yet an oft removed familee,
> That throve so well
> As one that settled be."

25. *Thirteenth Census of the United States*, 1910, *Abstract*, p. 24.

cost of threshing and to deliver the grain to the elevator free of charge. Owners who furnished teams or other equipment for their tenants took a correspondingly larger share of the crop. Cash rentals, which were very common, ranged from $2 to $5 or $6 an acre, depending upon the productiveness of the land. Sometimes land on which crops were raised was rented for a share of the crop, while meadow or pasture land on the same farm was rented at so much per acre. Cash tenants complained bitterly that their rents were raised much more rapidly than the rise in price of farm products justified and that they were certain to get a raise in rent if they exerted themselves to build up a farm in order to make it pay.[26]

While some landlords were benevolent and thoughtful, others cared little for their tenants' welfare. Most landlords insisted on a short-term lease, usually good for only one year. The tenants, landlords held, were an inferior lot as a whole and not to be trusted. The only way an owner could protect his farm was to be able to get rid of a poor tenant in the briefest possible time. The one-year tenant, however, condemned to uncertainty of tenure and to frequent moving, tried to get all he could out of the land while he was on it and to give to it the least possible attention in return. Rented farms were often distinguished by their poorly kept buildings, their deepening gullies, and their infertile acres. Landlords were frequently short-sighted along other lines also. They objected to making the improvements necessary to enable their tenants to farm at a profit. Or, if they consented grudgingly to erect buildings and fences and to lay tile for drainage, they might require the tenant to board the carpenters and other workmen free of charge, not to mention hauling in the needed materials and filling up the ditches after the tile had been laid.[27]

In quality the tenant farmers varied widely. In spite of the handicaps under which they labored, many of them were in reality good farmers. Some had once been farm laborers and by saving their wages had accumulated enough capital to start in as tenant farmers. Such persons expected to emerge eventually as farm owners and in many instances did so. A few had fallen in the economic scale, whether from bad luck or bad farming or bad management, and had become tenants where once they

26. *Wallaces' Farmer,* XXXIII (November 13, 1908), p. 1388; XXXV (September 9, 1910), p. 1184.

27. *Ibid.,* XXXIII (December 18, 1908), p. 1582.

had been owners. For many the climb from tenancy to farm ownership was a difficult, if not impossible, task to perform.[28]

The relationship between high tenancy and high land values was striking. According to the census of 1910 this parallelism was evident in two-thirds of the states in the Middle West. High-priced land that was held for speculative purposes was always for rent, and in these states there usually were tenants to take a good deal of it. By contrast, in the newer parts of Minnesota, North Dakota, and South Dakota, where there was land "begging for occupants," it had to be worked by the owner or not at all. The low tenancy rate in these parts held down the general average for those states, in spite of the speculation and tenancy in the older sections. This relationship between the value of land and tenancy was also found to exist in certain groups of counties within such a state, for example, as Illinois.

Likewise, there was a close tie between tenancy and the types of farming engaged in. According to the census of 1900 the tenant farmers of the Middle West had supervision of more than their proportional number of farms on which hay and grain were the principal products and a little more than half their proportion of the livestock farms. The tenants raised grain to sell, while the landowners usually raised it to feed to their livestock; they produced only three-fourths of their proportional share of hay and forage, and were even further behind the landowning farmers in the ownership of sheep. As for hogs, the tenants raised their full number. They grew only two-thirds of their share of wheat and exceeded by one-third their proportional share of corn. In some of the wheat-growing states, however, the tenants raised more than their share. With respect to corn, conditions were more nearly uniform throughout, although the tenants raised proportionately more than did the landowners. Vegetables, fruit, and tobacco usually were grown by the landowning farmers.

The character of the tenant farm itself was of some importance. The value of the farm per acre was about the same, but the buildings were

28. Senate Document 705, 60 Congress, 2 session, pp. 41–42; *Wallaces' Farmer,* XXXIV (January 1, 1909), p. 4; *Report of the Special Committee on Farm Tenancy* (75 Congress, 1 session, House Document 149, serial 10126, Washington, 1937). The validity of the "agricultural ladder hypothesis" is strongly attacked by L. F. Cox, "Tenancy in the United States," *Agricultural History,* XVIII (July, 1944), pp. 97–105.

likely to be worth about five-sixths as much as those on the farm occupied by its owner. The tenant had a little less than his proportional share of implements and farm machinery, in part because his need was less for such items as haying tools, corn binders, or milk separators. Hibbard pictured the tenant farmer in 1910 as one who was much younger than the landowner and as one who stayed on the same farm about a third as long. He was likely to have poor buildings and comparatively little grassland and livestock, and probably would be devoting his time to the raising of grain to haul to market, although he might feed much of his corn to hogs.

These conditions seem to indicate that the high price of land was not the sole reason for "the concentration of tenancy on the better land." The tenant farmer usually lacked the capital and was ill equipped to raise stock on a wider basis. He wanted returns that same year and not several years later. Usually the landlord gave him no encouragement to raise livestock because that would require a great deal of money to build the necessary barns, silos, and fences. Even if the farmer wanted to raise stock, he was likely to be discouraged by the fact that he would probably have to move soon. All this seemed to indicate that the tenant veered toward that type of farming for which he felt best fitted and which best met his needs. The one thing upon which the landlord and tenant were completely agreed was that they both wanted "prompt returns on the outlay."[29]

Critics of the farm tenancy system pointed out that the first and most important reform was to get rid of the one-year lease. They urged that the tenant be assured tenure as long as he farmed satisfactorily and also immunity from frequent and unreasonable increases in rent. The English system, which conceded the right of the tenant to whatever fertility he had put into the soil without being able to harvest it, was cited as an example for American landlords. In England, unlike the situation in the United States, a tenant could count on a virtually permanent lease and just treatment. Should the landlord grow careless with the tenant's rights, the tenant had the right of action at law for damages.[30]

29. B. H. Hibbard, "Tenancy in the North Central States," in T. N. Carver, ed., *Selected Readings in Rural Economics* (Boston, 1916), pp. 511–22.

30. *Wallaces' Farmer,* XXXVIII (April 11, 1913), p. 650; (October 10, 1913), p. 1372.

Granted that farm tenancy had undesirable social consequences, the soil depletion practices that prevailed throughout the nineteenth century can hardly be chalked up to tenancy alone. Farm owners as well as tenants were responsible for this. The extensive, as opposed to the intensive, type of farming that was practiced encouraged a "mining" of the soil, and the resulting exhaustion helped to bring down the yield per acre. "This lessening of soil fertility," declared the Country Life Commission appointed by President Roosevelt in 1908, "is marked in every part of the United States, even in the richest lands of the prairies. It marks the pioneer stage of land usage. It has now become an acute national danger, and the economic, social, and political problems arising out of it must at once receive the best attention of statesmen."[31]

And yet American agriculture in the first decade of the twentieth century, particularly in the Middle West, gave the appearance of great prosperity. "The value of the farm products," wrote Secretary of Agriculture James Wilson in his annual report for the year 1909, "is so incomprehensibly large that it has become merely a row of figures."[32] "There has never been a time," declared the Country Life Commission, "when the American farmer was as well off as he is to-day, when we consider not only his earning power, but the comforts and advantages he may secure."[33] According to another observer, "One American harvest would buy the kingdom of Belgium, king and all; two would buy Italy; three would buy Austria-Hungary; and five, at a spot-cash price, would take Russia from the czar."[34] In short, the farmers, tenants and landlords alike, were making money. Farm labor was fully employed and at what, for the times, were considered high wages. Prosperity showed itself in the improved character of farm homes, often surrounded by attractive lawns and gardens, in the multiplication of better barns and farm buildings, in the sanitary water supplies and plumbing equipment that farmers were beginning to enjoy, in the increasing availability of good reading matter on farm tables, and in the farmers' demand for better educational facilities

31. *Ibid.*, XXXIII (September 4, 1908), p. 1061; Senate Document 705, 60 Congress, 2 session, pp. 38, 41.

32. U. S. Dept. Agri., *Yearbook*, 1909, p. 9.

33. Senate Document 705, 60 Congress, 2 session, p. 21.

34. H. N. Casson, in *Wallaces' Farmer*, XXXIII (July 10, 1908), p. 871.

for their sons and daughters.[35] The case of the man who went through "the worst" in Kansas during the nineteenth century, but had become one of the stockholders and directors in the local bank, owned an automobile, and sent his children to college before the twentieth was far along was only one among many.

The prosperity of the American farmer during the early years of the twentieth century was due in large part to the high prices he was able to command for the commodities he had to sell. The Secretary of Agriculture, in his report for 1910, pointed out that if the year 1899 were regarded as 100, the value of farm products had risen as follows: 1900, 106.4; 1905, 133; 1907, 158.7; 1908, 167.3; 1909, 182.8; and 1910, 189.2.[36] Under these circumstances it seemed reasonable to assume that there was "good money for every man on good land who farms right." After 1910, the steady rise in farm prices was somewhat arrested, but compared to the low quotations of the nineties the farmers' receipts seemed excellent indeed. Wheat in 1914 brought around 80 cents a bushel, corn from 60 to 70 cents a bushel, butter from 25 to 30 cents a pound, and other farm prices in proportion. Such prices contrasted markedly with those of the nineties, when wheat sold for from 50 to 60 cents, corn for 25 to 30 cents, and butter from 12 to 20 cents.[37]

Attempts to explain the prevailing high prices were widely varied. Some, President Taft for example, held that the trouble was merely an increase in consumption without a corresponding increase in production, or as another phrased it, "Population has simply been increasing more rapidly than farm products; too many people in the town—too few on the farm."[38] Others noted that any greatly increased production seemed unlikely in the future, since practically the entire public domain had already been absorbed, while lands in the older sections were rapidly losing their fertility. The expansion of the corn belt seemed particularly improbable,

35. Senate Document 705, 60 Congress, 2 session, p. 20; *Wallaces' Farmer,* XXXIV (January 8, 1909), p. 40.

36. U. S. Dept. Agri., *Yearbook,* 1910, p. 10.

37. *Ibid.,* 1914, pp. 517, 529, 624; *Wallaces' Farmer,* XXXV (May 6, 1910), p. 745; (December 23, 1910), p. 1734.

38. Myron T. Herrick, *Preliminary Report on Land and Agricultural Credit in Europe* (62 Congress, 3 session, Senate Document 967, serial 6364, Washington, 1912–13), p. 5; *Wallaces' Farmer,* XXXVI (March 24, 1911), p. 542.

for the growing of corn, due to climatic reasons, was confined to an area already fully exploited. Furthermore, important new uses were being found for corn. Careful observers noted that the rising level of prices was by no means confined to the United States alone, and some of them argued that the increase in the world's supply of gold was partly responsible for price trends. The real trouble, they said, was that gold inflation had resulted in a steady decline in the purchasing power of the dollar.[39]

The high farm prices were deeply resented by the consumer public. Sometimes farmers were denounced as conscienceless monopolists who set the prices of the necessities of life to the disadvantage of every city dweller. Manufacturers claimed that the American farmer was lazy and inefficient. If only he would get busy and increase production, food would be cheaper, the wages of city laborers could be lowered, and the American manufacturer could the better meet foreign competition. But the farmers were disturbed only by the fear that the good prices might not last. Senator Porter J. McCumber of North Dakota voiced their sentiments when he said:

> We are now approaching a condition when the farmer is about to secure equality of remuneration, and the moment we reach toward that goal of justice a boycott is started against his products, both in the cities and in the National Legislature, by the introduction of bills designed to destroy his profits. . . . He is, however, receiving not one cent more for any article than he is justly entitled to, and in my candid opinion he is not receiving as much to-day as he is going to receive in the future, and in the very near future.[40]

But high prices for farm produce did not wholly explain the prosperity of the American farmer during the early years of the twentieth century. He was aided also by a phenomenal rise in the price of land. For the country as a whole, according to the census of 1910, land values increased during the preceding decade by 118.1 per cent. In states like Wisconsin and Minnesota, with a large proportion of cut-over timber land, the increase was less than this, but as the following percentages show, the advance was

39. *Ibid.,* XXXIV (October 1, 1909), p. 1219; XXXV (November 25, 1910), p. 1570; XXXVII (September 6, 1912), p. 1242.

40. *Congressional Record,* 61 Congress, 2 session, Vol. 45, Part II (1910), pp. 1479–80; *Wallaces' Farmer,* XXXV (March 11, 1910), pp. 431–32. See also *ibid.* (April 22, 1910), p. 679.

far greater in some of the states of the western Middle West: Wisconsin, 71.9; Minnesota, 82.2; Illinois, 104.1; Missouri, 107.9; Iowa, 123.0; Kansas, 189.0; Nebraska, 231.8; North Dakota, 321.3; and South Dakota, 377.1.[41] Numerous records of land sales backed up the census figures. Iowa lands that sold at from $10 to $30 an acre thirty years before were selling in 1908 at from $80 to $125. Lands six miles distant from a railroad that were worth only $3 to $5 an acre in the 1870's, and from $25 to $30 an acre in the 1880's, brought from $135 to $155 an acre in 1910. Farmers who had been able to hold onto their farms had thus accumulated wealth at a rapid rate, not so much from the prices for which farm products sold as from the rapidly appreciating value of the acres they owned. Mortgages that had occasioned the greatest anxiety a few years earlier could now be regarded as negligible. Whether he realized it or not, the average middle western landowner had made his money not so much from good farming as from the unearned increment that came with the ownership of farm lands. To a considerable extent, he was only a successful speculator.[42]

Explanations for the rise in land values were as varied as those which were advanced to explain the rising prices paid for farm products. Higher prices for grain, livestock, and dairy produce would of course tend naturally to boost land prices, but the increase in value of farm lands had quite outrun the increase in price of farm products. Nor could the rising price of land be ascribed to its increased productivity, for in spite of the best efforts of the proponents of scientific agriculture, the yield per acre had risen at best only a very little. Much was made of the supposed "disappearance of free land" on the theory that the supply of available land was being cut down just when the demand for it was greatest. Actually, there was much free land then available in the arid west, and a good deal of it was being taken up by homesteaders.[43] But lands that required expensive irrigation works to make them productive were hardly "free," while unirrigated lands were a bad gamble for most pioneers. Probably the demand for land really was up and the supply of good land down. Farms

41. *Thirteenth Census of the United States,* 1910, Vol. V, *Agriculture,* pp. 28, 79, and plate facing p. 44; Senate Document 705, 60 Congress, 2 session, p. 20.

42. *Wallaces' Farmer* XXXIII (September 4, 1908), p. 1061; XXXIV (December 31, 1909), p. 1704; XXXV (March 4, 1910), p. 369.

43. Fred A. Shannon, "The Homestead Act and the Labor Surplus," *American Historical Review,* XLI (July, 1936), pp. 637–51.

were worth more also because of the improvements their owners had made on them, the greater availability of markets, and the better roads and schools which they had paid for, and because of the world's increasing gold supply, which had inflated all prices. Undoubtedly, also, the speculative spirit was influential. Farmers, instead of depositing their savings in banks or investing in industrial stocks and bonds, bought more lands, knowing that land values were sure to rise. Speculators who had no interest whatever in farming bought land for the 6 or 8 per cent annual rise in value that seemed a certainty throughout the early years of the century.[44]

This picture of high prices and general agricultural prosperity contrasted oddly with the fact that farm population relatively, and in many communities actually, was on the decline. As already noted, the state of Iowa, one of the richest in the corn belt and one almost exclusively dependent on agriculture, showed an actual loss, a loss which amounted to .3 per cent in the population of the state as a whole during the years 1900–10. But in this state, as in many others, the most notable fact was the drift of the people from the farms to the towns and cities. Wherever the land was most valuable for agricultural purposes, it seemed that the decline in country population was most marked. Cities everywhere had grown. Iowa, in spite of its decrease in population, found that its principal city, Des Moines, had an increase of 39 per cent during the very decade when the population of the state as a whole was falling off.[45]

Several factors entered into the explanation of this exodus from the farms of the Middle West. Of fundamental importance was the increasing reliance upon agricultural machinery. With the new machines, fewer farmers could produce more goods. "A boy with four horses and a modern

44. Senate Document 705, 60 Congress, 2 session, pp. 20, 30, 40; *Wallaces' Farmer,* XXXVI (September 15, 1911), p. 1260; XXXVII (December 6, 1912), p. 1716.

An interesting formula has been worked out for the estimation of land values. To obtain the present value (PV) of a farm, divide the expected annual increase (a) by the expected rate of interest (r). Thus $PV = a/r$. If, however, the income of the farm is expected to increase, then the value of the farm will also increase. To measure this increase in land value for a given year, add to the present value the expected annual increase (i) divided by r^2. Thus $V = a/r + i/r^2$. John D. Black and Others, *Farm Management* (New York, 1947), pp. 737–38.

45. *Thirteenth Census of the United States,* 1910, *Abstract,* p. 68. See also *Wallaces' Farmer,* XXXV (November 4, 1910), p. 1493; (November 18, 1910), p. 1540; XXXIX (May 29, 1914), p. 851.

binder can cut and bind as much in one day as from ten to fifteen men could in a day in the time of his grandfather." But some blame lay also with the high prices that lands in the Middle West had begun to command. It was because of these prices that so many farmers sold out to their neighbors or to speculators and invested in farms located in newer areas where the prices were not so high. This movement of population did not lessen the nation's total farm population, but it did lessen the number of farmers in regions where land prices were excessively high. Most discussed of all the causes of rural decline was the lure of the city. Farm boys and girls were attracted by the higher wages and shorter hours that went with city jobs. They craved the excitement of city life, the superior comfort of city homes, and the variety of opportunities that the cities offered.[46]

It was this competition with the city that made the problem of farm labor so persistently acute. Farm labor, as those who really knew patiently explained, was skilled labor. A boy who had grown up on a farm knew many things that only years of experience could teach. When he left to work on the railroads, or in the factories, or in city stores, the loss to the farm was serious. Farm labor actually commanded very high wages, enough sometimes to enable the thrifty farm laborer to save from $200 to $250 per year. But so much of his pay came in board, shelter, heat, and washing and ironing that it was hard to make the farm boy see that the $20 and up he could earn on the farm was nearly all clear profit and not to be compared with the city wages from which he must pay high prices for board and room and for every service. Efforts to turn the tide of immigration farmward were not very helpful. The European immigrant, even if he had been a peasant, knew little of American farming methods and was practically useless on the typical American farm. Furthermore, he too liked the city better and generally preferred to stay there. As for unemployed city workers, they were apt to be a positive liability. If only an adequate supply of farm labor could be obtained, some said, crops could readily be increased by 25 per cent. "The greatest problem of the statesman of the future is to keep enough men on the land to make it produce the food required at prices the consumer can afford to pay."[47]

46. *Ibid.*, XXXIV (January 8, 1909), p. 43; XXXV (November 4, 1910), pp. 1467, 1493.

47. Senate Document 705, 60 Congress, 2 session, p. 42. See also *Wallaces' Farmer*,

The decline in rural population was a source of considerable worry to farm and city residents alike. Thoughtful observers sought long and earnestly for a remedy. Something must be done, they concluded, to improve "social conditions in the open country." The thesis almost universally accepted was that if the schools, churches, roads, home conveniences, and social activities of the farm could only be made to equal those of the city, there would be no further serious lack of people on the farm. The rural free delivery of mail and the party telephone line helped some but hardly enough to overcome the "isolation and utter barrenness" of country life. The need for good roads seemed obvious, but many landowners, fearful lest they have to foot the gigantic tax bill involved, were strangely skeptical. Besides, if the roads were improved, wouldn't the farmers use them mainly to go to town? What could be done to renovate the country church and make it a more satisfying social center? What could be done to promote the formation of social organizations comparable to the once active but now almost forgotten Grange? What could be done to provide sports and amusements in the country comparable with those so readily available in the city? Until answers for such questions as these could be found, it was idle to preach the gospel of back-to-the-farm. The matter of first importance was to keep the people on the farm who were already there.[48]

The status of the rural town was hardly better than that of the open country. Such local manufacturing activities as flour milling, wagon making, general blacksmithing, and tanning had once made each town a little industrial center. But establishments of larger capital, located at strategic points, had put most of the local manufacturers out of business. Even as merchandising centers the towns were running down. Sales direct to the farm from the factory or from mail-order houses cut in seriously on the profits of the small-town merchant. Retired farmers, with their chronic fear of taxes, kept civic improvements at a minimum. Boys and girls from the towns, no less than those from the farms, were hypnotized by the good wages and the bright lights of the city. The time had been

---

XXXIV (November 12, 1909), p. 1451; XXXV (February 11, 1910), p. 219; XXXVI (February 10, 1911), p. 214; XXXIX (July 3, 1914), p. 973.

48. Senate Document 705, 60 Congress, 2 session, p. 14; *Wallaces' Farmer,* XXXIV (October 22, 1909), p. 1338; XXXV (January 7, 1910), p. 2.

when the country town fronted toward the farm and was principally identified with rural life; now the town fronted rather toward the city, imitated the city, and, as fast as it could manage, moved to the city.[49]

What most concerned the public at large about the farm problem was the fear, duly re-enforced by the rising price of foodstuffs, that agricultural production would be unable to keep pace with the growth of the nation. The population of the United States had increased from 62,947,714 in 1890 to 75,994,575 in 1900 and 91,972,266 in 1910. And, whereas the rural population had constituted 63.9 per cent of the whole in 1890 and 59.5 per cent in 1900, it had dropped to barely 53.7 per cent in 1910.[50] Exports of foodstuffs from the United States had begun to show a steady decline. In 1900 the value of foodstuffs exported was set at $545,473,695; ten years later it was only $369,087,974, and formed but 21.59 per cent of the total domestic exports as compared with 39.8 per cent in 1900, 42.21 per cent in 1890, and 55.77 per cent in 1880. Meanwhile exports of meat and dairy products had declined to $143,000,000 in 1910 as compared with $254,000,000 in 1906 and an average of $222,000,000 during the preceding ten years.[51] Soon all this, and possibly much more besides, would be needed at home. "With our increasing population," said Theodore Roosevelt, "the time is not far distant when the problem of supplying our people with food will become pressing. The possible additions to our arable area are not great, and it will become necessary to obtain much larger crops from the land, as is now done in more densely settled countries." The same idea was expressed by W. C. Brown, president of the New York Central Railroad. "We must increase production per acre by more intelligent methods," he said, "or we must face the relentless certain day when we shall not produce enough to supply our own necessities." Viewing the situation still more pessimistically, James J. Hill of the Great Northern Railroad insisted that "in twenty-five years we shall face a nation-wide famine."[52]

49. *Ibid.*, XXXIV (January 8, 1909), p. 43; XXXVI (September 8, 1911), p. 1219.

50. *Thirteenth Census of the United States*, 1910, *Abstract*, p. 55.

51. U. S. Dept. of Commerce and Labor, *Reports*, 1910, p. 68. See also *Wallaces' Farmer*, XXXV (February 11, 1910), p. 236.

52. *Report of the National Conservation Committee* (60 Congress, 2 session, Senate Document 676, serial 5397, Washington, 1909), p. 7; *Wallaces' Farmer*, XXXV (February 11, 1910), p. 218; Ruth V. Corbin, "Federal Farm Credits, 1916–1936" (unpublished master's thesis, University of Wisconsin, 1936), p. 2.

In this present day of plenty such acute anxiety about the nation's food supply is difficult to understand, but in the early years of the twentieth century it did not seem unreasonable. The march of industrialization had promoted the growth of population to such an extent that there was in actual fact a relative shortage of food. This condition, to the considerable advantage of the farmer, was reflected in higher food prices. Thanks, at least in part, to the world's increasing supply of gold, there was a generally rising price level, but food prices were rising more rapidly than other prices. This was true not only in the United States, but in Europe as well, and in all other exporting countries. Not until the end of the decade was the balance between population and food supply sufficiently stable to put a check on the rising price of food.

Confident that the nation, if it was to continue to eat, must find some means of stimulating agriculture, publicists began to voice a demand for more effective agricultural education. Theodore Roosevelt, never very far from the head of any procession, urged the cause along. "We should strive in every way," he said, "to aid in the education of the farmer for the farm, and should shape our school system with this end in view."[53] A principal aim of this movement was to promote more scientific methods of farming, but efforts along this line were far from new. Ever since the creation of the Department of Agriculture in 1862, the federal government had participated actively in the scientific study of agriculture and in the dissemination of agricultural information. Colleges of agriculture, subsidized by land grants under the terms of the Morrill Act of 1862, existed in nearly every state not only to carry on direct instruction but also to maintain experiment stations for original investigation and extension divisions for projecting scientific findings beyond the campus to people on the farms. State departments of agriculture and private agencies also did useful educational work. Even so, critics could say that as yet "comparatively little really good farming has been done in the United States. . . . Speaking broadly, we have not even begun to really farm." Only by means of better farming, it was assumed, could the needs of the future for greater quantities of farm produce be met.[54]

53. *Wallaces' Farmer,* XXXII (October 11, 1907), p. 1145.

54. Edwin G. Nourse, *Government in Relation to Agriculture* (Washington, 1940), pp. 872–74; *Wallaces' Farmer,* XXXIII (June 26, 1908), p. 830.

But the believers in agricultural education had more in mind than merely the promotion of better farming methods. They wished also to convince farm boys and girls that farm life offered opportunities comparable with those of city life. Too many farmers still thought of education as a means of providing for their children an easier way of life than farming. As a result, the schools, even the agricultural colleges, some said, were educating farm youth away from the farm. Country schools needed a thorough overhauling. The one-room school with its underpaid, undertrained, and overworked teacher must go. Means must be found to provide for the transportation of children to larger, centrally located schools. Agriculture as a school subject must have an honored place in the curriculum, and teachers must be prepared to present it realistically, in terms applicable to the daily life of farm boys and girls. Prospective farmers must be taught to understand their "own soils, climate, animal and plant diseases, markets, and other local facts."[55] Perhaps an enlarged United States Bureau of Education should restudy all public educational activities and furnish more effective guidance to state and local authorities. All this was supposed not only to make the farmer into a better farmer but also to make him want to stay on the farm. Nevertheless, there was room for the word of warning voiced by an experienced observer:

> No matter how much money the government pours out to educate him, he [the farmer] won't be educated except as he educates himself; and his children can not be educated unless he provides better schools than he has now and better teachers than he has now, and takes a greater interest in the education of his own children than most farmers do. No amount of education laid at the farmer's door is going to do him any good unless he takes it with a relish, digests and assimilates it, and puts it actually into practice on the farm.[56]

And yet, taken as a whole, the picture of farm life in the western Middle West during the early years of the twentieth century was by no means discouraging. Agriculture had rarely enjoyed a higher degree of prosperity. Corn growers, wheat growers, and dairymen—farmers of every

55. Senate Document 705, 60 Congress, 2 session, p. 17; *Wallaces' Farmer*, XXXII (August 30, 1907), p. 940; XXXIV (August 20, 1909), p. 1025; XXXV (January 7, 1910), p. 7.

56. *Ibid.*, XXXVIII (January 17, 1913), p. 82. See also Senate Document 705, 60 Congress, 2 session, p. 56.

description—were doing very well. The prices farm products commanded were high, and the unearned increment that came from the increase in value of farm lands added a substantial quota to rural wealth. There were problems to worry about—the increase in tenancy, the shortage of labor, the drift to the city—but they were for the most part problems of prosperity, not of adversity. How could the farmers raise enough to feed the city dwellers? This was an opportunity and a challenge, not a reason for despair. Middle western agriculture was sound, or so, at least, many people believed. Farm mortgages were universally acclaimed as gilt-edged securities, and they commanded low interest rates. Even the federal government was hard at work to keep the farmer prosperous. It provided for agriculture free of charge extensive investigational services that non-agricultural industries had to provide for themselves, and it aided the cause of agricultural education generously.[57] Agricultural discontent was chronic and endemic, but for the moment, at least in the western Middle West, it had less than the normal reason for existence.

57. Nourse, *Government in Relation to Agriculture,* pp. 873–74.

Chapter II

FROM POPULISM TO INSURGENCY

IN SPITE of the prosperity of middle western agriculture during the years that preceded the first World War, the farmer's voice of protest was by no means stilled. During the late nineteenth century western agrarians had built up a philosophy of radicalism sufficient even to endure the acid test of good times. Their experiences with railroads, banks, middlemen, and manufacturers had made them convinced antimonopolists. They were by no means the first to hold antimonopoly views, for the ideas they expressed had often been cogently stated by eastern, or even European, theorists.[1] But the long struggle with frontier poverty, culminating in the Populist revolt, had instilled in many farmers' minds a deep-seated belief that the various combines through which big business operated must somehow be restrained. This attitude was due not to ignorance, but to experience. The farmers knew whereof they spoke. Nor did they have any doubt concerning the role the government must play in providing this restraint. Middle western agrarians were not socialists; on the contrary, they were, or at least they aspired to be, small capitalists. But their property-mindedness did not blind them to the fact that only the power of government could insure them against the unfair advantages of monopoly. They favored government regulation and control, or in extreme cases

1. This chapter follows in the main an article by John D. Hicks, "The Legacy of Populism in the Western Middle West," *Agricultural History,* XXIII (October, 1949), pp. 225–36. For a somewhat different point of view, see Chester McArthur Destler, "Western Radicalism, 1865–1901: Concepts and Origins," *Mississippi Valley Historical Review,* XXXI (December, 1944), pp. 335–68.

government ownership, only as a means of retaining for themselves the right to hold property and to do business on a reasonably profitable basis.[2]

It should be remembered that these rights, throughout the greater part of the western Middle West, were most imperiled by the railroads, and that it was against the railroads more specifically than against any other type of enterprise that the farmers aimed their principal reforms. The railroads had created the region; they had brought the population in; they were in close alliance or even partnership with other industries such as lumber, elevator, milling, and packing corporations; they were the chief exploiters of the farm population, which was obliged to pay them rates both coming and going. When the average middle western farmer living west of Chicago talked about monopolies and trusts, he was thinking primarily of the railroads. Even the towns and cities were peculiarly railroad-conscious. They had no other equally big businesses, and their very lives as trading centers depended upon the fairness, or sometimes the favor, with which railroad rate makers treated them.[3]

Implicit in the Populistic concept of government intervention in economic affairs was the assumption that the government itself should be truly representative of the people, that the long-established control of the "plutocrats" should be broken. The first task that the agrarian leaders set for themselves, therefore, was to capture for the people the machinery of government.[4] It was with this end in view that Farmers' Alliance and Populist candidates sought control of state governments, and that the Populist party nominated J. B. Weaver in 1892 and William Jennings Bryan in 1896 for the Presidency of the United States. Bryan's first defeat rang the death knell of Populism as an effective party organization and served notice on the people generally that the ousting of the "plutocrats" was to be no easy task. But the idea lived on. As Frederick Jackson Turner once phrased it, "Mr. Bryan's Democracy, Mr. Debs' Socialism, and Mr.

2. Benton H. Wilcox, "An Historical Definition of Northwestern Radicalism," *Mississippi Valley Historical Review,* XXVI (December, 1939), pp. 382, 394. This article sets forth the principal findings of the author's more elaborate study, "A Reconsideration of the Character and Economic Basis of Northwestern Radicalism" (unpublished doctoral dissertation, University of Wisconsin, 1933), hereafter cited as Wilcox, "Northwestern Radicalism."

3. Wilcox, "Northwestern Radicalism," p. 50.

4. John D. Hicks, *The Populist Revolt* (Minneapolis, 1931), pp. 405–6.

Roosevelt's Republicanism all had in common the emphasis upon the need of governmental regulation of industrial tendencies in the interest of the common man; the checking of the power of these business Titans who emerged successful out of the competitive individualism of pioneer America."[5] If this end was ever to be achieved, however, the people must somehow take over their government, and the desire to see this ambition achieved survived intact long after the disappearance of the Populist party.

Throughout the western Middle West, and to a considerable extent throughout the country as a whole, this legacy of Populism determined the course of political development during the opening years of the twentieth century. What reforms could be instituted to make sure that the people really governed? The movement for the direct primary, for the initiative and referendum, and for various other instruments of popular government grew naturally out of the soil prepared by the Populists. The campaign to limit the power of the speaker of the national House of Representatives was led by an outraged Nebraskan.[6] The activities of insurgents and progressives generally, culminating in the formation of the Progressive party of 1912, followed an evolutionary pattern easily connected with Populism. This is not to say that the only force that lay back of twentieth-century American radicalism was nineteenth-century middle western agrarianism. The contributions of the labor movement, of imported socialistic concepts, of a host of journalistic muckrakers must not be overlooked. But one extremely important ancestral line—a long and sturdy line—led back to a multitude of Granger-Greenback-Populist progenitors. As convinced antimonopolists, these reformers believed that the state must use its power to regulate and control the "trusts," most of which, in the western Middle West, turned out to be railroads. They believed, too, that if the state was to be charged with this responsibility, its power must be lodged firmly in the hands of the people. Probably they expected greater results from popular rule than was reasonable, but judged by any standards, they did accomplish a great deal. As a result of their efforts "something new had been brought into politics."[7]

5. Frederick Jackson Turner, *The Frontier in American History* (New York, 1921), p. 281.

6. George W. Norris, *Fighting Liberal: The Autobiography of George W. Norris* (New York, 1945), pp. 107–19.

7. Wilcox, "Northwestern Radicalism," p. 107.

Robert M. La Follette of Wisconsin was not a Populist, and the state which furnished the setting for his career was never Populist territory. Yet it would be hard to find another American of the period more thoroughly representative of Middle Western agrarianism or another state more receptive to the idea of governmental regulation of business. A conservative in his earlier years and almost a regular, La Follette had found his hopes for political advancement blocked at every turn by a party machine subservient to the state's industrial leaders. Taking his case to the people, he persuaded a majority of them, farmers for the most part rather than city dwellers, to back him in his war on the bosses. Undoubtedly he was aided in his efforts by the Old World background of many Wisconsin voters, men who were accustomed to a powerful government and now saw no harm in it as long as they could control it. But probably he was aided far more by the strong antimonopoly tradition which among Wisconsin farmers was much older than Populism and dated back to the Grangers. Above all, he furnished to the cause persistent, dynamic, intelligent leadership—something rarely found among the Populists.[8]

La Follette's acknowledgment of his debt to Grangerism is clear and explicit. Progressivism, he maintained, first "expressed itself in the rise to power of the Patrons of Husbandry," whose influence was brief but unique. The Grangers had succeeded in awakening Wisconsin farmers to the possibilities of cooperation; it had made them more sensitive to the abuses operating behind the political and economic scene. "As a boy on the farm . . . I heard and felt this movement of the Grangers swirling about me," wrote La Follette. "I suppose I have never fully lost the effect of that early impression."[9]

In spite of the inspiration he derived from the Grangers, La Follette's decision to lead a movement for agrarian reform did not materialize until he had gone down to defeat as a regular. When he stood for reelection to Congress in 1890, he was serving his third term as a Republican in the House of Representatives. Although showing some evidence of

8. Robert M. La Follette, *La Follette's Autobiography: A Personal Narrative of Political Experience* (Madison, Wis., 1913), p. 18; Theodore Saloutos, "The Wisconsin Society of Equity," *Agricultural History,* XIV (April, 1940), p. 79.

9. La Follette, *Autobiography,* p. 19.

independence, he was sufficiently satisfactory to the party leaders that he had been made a member of the important Ways and Means Committee, and in this capacity he had participated as a believing protectionist in the drafting of the McKinley tariff bill. His defeat for re-election to a fourth term was in part the culmination of a long period of agrarian discontent that swept scores of Republicans out of office throughout the Middle West. In Wisconsin, however, the Democratic landslide was greatly accelerated by the unpopular Bennett law, recently enacted by a Republican legislature.[10] This measure sought to promote a more stringent enforcement of the state's compulsory education laws, and the foreign elements—particularly German, Scandinavian, Irish, and Polish patrons of parochial schools—regarded it as a direct attack on their educational institutions. After his defeat, La Follette decided to confine his immediate political future to the state and began to formulate his plans. Once when asked how he could ever hope to create a truly progressive state out of a nondescript "foreign-born, foreign-bred, slow-moving population," he pointed confidently to the predominance of the agricultural population in Wisconsin and "the absence of great congested centres, which are always the stronghold of machine control through a corrupt combination of big business with municipal graft."[11]

La Follette's full realization of the need for reform probably dated from the day in 1891 when, as he implicitly believed, he was offered what amounted to a bribe by United States Senator Philetus Sawyer, a rich Wisconsin lumberman whose wishes in regard to state politics were generally respected. Out of this ordeal, the facts of which are still in dispute, La Follette emerged with a passionate conviction that he must take the lead in freeing his state from the corrupt influences which were "undermining and destroying every semblance of representative government in Wisconsin."[12] Believing that the mainspring of his reform movement would be found among the farmers, La Follette proceeded at once to ally himself with the outstanding farmer politicians of Wisconsin. Foremost among these was A. R. Hall, "the statesman of the hour immediately preceding the La Follette movement."[13] Hall was a former speaker of the

10. *Ibid.*, pp. 133–34. 11. *Ibid.*, pp. 222–23. 12. *Ibid.*, p. 164.
13. Albert O. Barton, *La Follette's Winning of Wisconsin* (Madison, Wis., 1922), p. 93.

Minnesota house of representatives who had migrated to Wisconsin, and had behind him a long background of agrarian protest. After 1890, when he was elected to the Wisconsin assembly from his new home in Dunn County, he became known for his earnest advocacy of anti-pass legislation, and by 1899 he had won the legislature to his way of thinking.[14]

With equal shrewdness La Follette also made friends with Nils Haugen, a popular Norwegian politician who, although a Republican, had won re-election to Congress in 1890. When Haugen unsuccessfully sought the governorship in 1894, La Follette supported him warmly, and the good feeling thus engendered was not forgotten by the Scandinavian contingent. The Scandinavian farmers, as La Follette well knew, were, next to the Germans, the largest foreign group in the state.[15]

Although La Follette lost in his first try for the Republican gubernatorial nomination in 1896, the returns showed that he had made notable progress in lining up the farmer vote. According to the *Wisconsin Farmer,* a leading farm journal, he was "a man in close sympathy with Wisconsin agriculture." "Such a chief executive," the editorial continued, "is greatly needed in Wisconsin at present. He should be a man, too, with brains and courage, a defender of the 'plain people' and not a tool of corporate interests, nor the choice of corporation lobbyists. . . . We believe that the Hon. R. M. La Follette is such a man."[16] The year following his defeat for governor, La Follette and some of his friends bought out the *Old Dane,* a newspaper for rural readers published at the state capital. Under a new name, the *State,* and with a tow-headed Norwegian, John M. Nelson, as editor, this journal soon became a power in Wisconsin politics.[17] Former Governor William Dempster Hoard, the founder of *Hoard's Dairyman,* was also a La Follette supporter, while two outside newspapers, the *Skandinaven* of Chicago and the *Tidende* of Minneapolis, both of which had many Wisconsin readers, gave him their blessing.[18]

14. La Follette, *Autobiography,* p. 221; *Blue Book of the State of Wisconsin,* 1897, p. 677.

15. Ernest W. Stirn, *An Annotated Bibliography of Robert M. La Follette* (Chicago, 1937), p. 23; K. C. Babcock, *The Scandinavian Element in the United States* (Urbana, Ill., 1914), pp. 166–68.

16. *Wisconsin Farmer* (Madison), July 24, 1896.

17. La Follette, *Autobiography,* pp. 190–91, 207–8.

18. Barton, *La Follette's Winning of Wisconsin,* pp. 55–57.

Meantime, La Follette had discovered in the direct primary an instrument through which the reforms he envisaged could best be accomplished. The direct primary idea, like so many others that the western agrarians found useful, was by no means new, although La Follette professed never to have heard of it until 1896. But whereas earlier efforts to apply this principle had been mainly abortive, La Follette, with the help of the recently adopted Australian ballot, hoped to make popular nominations a living force. The caucus and convention, he maintained, had been "prostituted to the service of corrupt organization." For these outmoded methods he would substitute "a primary election—held under all the sanctions of law which prevail at the general election—where the citizen may cast his vote directly to nominate the candidate of the party with which he affiliates, and have it canvassed and returned just as he cast it."[19] In season and out, during campaigns and between campaigns, he carried this program to the people of the state, and finally in 1900, with the direct primary as a principal issue, he was nominated and elected to the governorship. The completeness of his victory is evident from the fact that he had the unprecedented plurality of 100,000 votes. Beyond a doubt, it was the support of the farmers that had made this signal triumph possible.[20]

But the battle was not yet won. During his first term in office La Follette failed completely to carry a satisfactory primary law through the legislature and was obliged to bring the issue to the people again in his campaign for re-election in 1902. Once more the popular mandate was clear, and this time the legislature yielded, although the bill it finally passed contained a referendum clause designed by opponents of the primary to accomplish its defeat. But the thoroughness with which La Follette's propaganda had done its work was revealed in the election of 1904, when nearly 62 per cent of those who voted on the referendum gave the direct primary their support. At this same election La Follette won a third term.[21]

The first actual use of the primary system in Wisconsin came with the municipal elections of 1905; not until September, 1906, were primary nominations made for state and congressional tickets. Under the Wis-

19. Allen Fraser Lovejoy, *La Follette and the Establishment of the Direct Primary in Wisconsin, 1890–1904* (New Haven, Conn., 1941), p. 36.

20. *Ibid.*, p. 53; A. P. Wilder, "Governor La Follette and What He Stands For," *Outlook*, LXX (March 8, 1902), p. 631.

21. Lovejoy, *Direct Primary in Wisconsin*, pp. 78–79, 83, 90–91.

consin regulations separate primary ballots were provided for each eligible political party. Aspirants for party nominations qualified for a place on the ballot of their choice by obtaining the signatures of a specified number of voters, but each candidate was required to swear that he was a member of the party to whose nomination he aspired and that he would support the candidate who won the nomination for which he contended. Each voter at the polls was presented with a "separate ticket for each party all fastened together," from which he selected and marked one, depositing all others in a blank ballot box. The Wisconsin law, while not the first primary law to be passed, was reputed to be "the first state-wide law with fairly complete provisions for legal supervision."[22]

The direct primary, of course, was designed as a means to other ends, but the La Follette forces did not await its coming before attacking the special interests that had long dominated the state. At the same time that La Follette was promoting the primary elections bill, he was also urging upon the legislature a drastic reform in the method of railroad taxation. Under existing procedure, Wisconsin railroads paid an operating fee, assessed against their gross incomes, in lieu of other taxation. According to the Wisconsin Tax Commission, this meant that they paid only ".53 per cent. of their market value (based on the average value of stocks and bonds)," as compared with the 1.19 per cent paid by real property on its market value.[23] To remedy this condition, La Follette favored the taxation of railroad property on an ad valorem basis, the same as other property, and in 1903 he succeeded, despite the most frantic railroad opposition, in transforming his wishes into law. Nevertheless, every effort was made to be fair to the railroads. When it came to making the new assessment, not only was the market value of railroad stocks and bonds taken into consideration, but these figures were checked with engineers' estimates of the cost of replacement. As the reformers had foreseen, the railroads paid higher taxes. During the first six years the law was in operation the state took in from the railroads about four million dollars more tax money than the roads would have paid under the old system. Furthermore, expert

22. Charles E. Merriam and Louise Overaker, *Primary Elections* (Chicago, 1928), pp. 62, 402; William Francis Raney, *Wisconsin, A Story of Progress* (New York, 1940), pp. 289–90; *Laws of Wisconsin,* 1903, ch. 451, pp. 754–66.

23. La Follette, *Autobiography,* p. 243 .

state accountants searched the books of railroad companies for irregularities and compelled the payment of back taxes upon rebates, generously given but never reported as income.[24]

La Follette was not yet through with the railroads. Railroad rates within the state, he maintained, were unconscionably high. In a "message of 178 printed pages," presented to the legislature on April 28, 1903, he "furnished a final and unanswerable demonstration" that Wisconsin freight rates were from 20 to 69 per cent higher than corresponding rates in the neighboring states of Iowa and Illinois. With the freedom to levy rates they then possessed, La Follette quite plausibly maintained, the railroad companies could easily compensate themselves for higher taxes by passing the bill along to their customers. The proper course, then, was to provide for effective regulation by a railroad commission preferably chosen, so La Follette believed, by the governor. Eventually this reform, despite the usual violent opposition, reached the statute books. In making the appointments it called for, La Follette took pains to select men of broad experience and high standing. The result was that many unfair rates were reduced and many discriminations against communities and individuals discontinued.[25]

The La Follette reforms did not end with the railroads. Other public utilities, such as water, gas, electricity, and telephone corporations, were eventually brought under regulatory control, to their own great distress but to the equally great financial benefit of the public. A stringent Corrupt Practices Act made the use of large sums to influence the results of primary and state elections difficult. An antilobby bill required the official registration of all lobbyists, and even prohibited them from private communications with members of the legislature on matters of legislation. An inheritance tax and a graduated income tax greatly augmented the revenue of the state, enabling it to support educational and charitable institutions far more generously than ever before and also to build a new state capitol, mainly from current revenue.[26] A legislative reference library,

24. *Ibid.*, pp. 291–92; Raney, *Wisconsin*, pp. 290–91.

25. La Follette, *Autobiography*, pp. 280–85, 348–56.

26. *Ibid.*, pp. 297–98, 356–57. It should be noted, however, that during La Follette's administration the State of Wisconsin received a windfall of well over a million dollars from the federal government to cover interest and losses that came from the

designed primarily to furnish legislators with expert advice in the drafting of bills, was established, becoming a veritable hothouse for the growth of progressive measures.[27]

One result of this extensive program of legislation in Wisconsin was a split in the Republican party. Calling themselves "Stalwarts," the regular Republicans—those who saw nothing wrong, either with the old convention system or with the important part played in politics by great corporations—fought persistently against the measures advocated by the Progressives, and tried hard to discredit and defeat Progressive candidates. But the reforms adopted were too popular to be attacked successfully. The heat of controversy lived on, but in time the battle between Stalwarts and Progressives lost much of its meaning. The Stalwarts, generally speaking, came to accept the La Follette measures, and based their opposition on the contention that they alone, as efficient conservatives, were competent to administer them. Even when a Stalwart, Emanuel L. Philipp, was elected to the governorship in 1914, the conditions against which La Follette and his supporters had fought so valiantly were not permitted to return. The Progressives, on their part, were usually content with defending the reforms they had inaugurated, and advanced few new principles.[28]

The activities of La Follette in Wisconsin were speedily paralleled by similar activities on the part of other governors in nearly every other state of the western Middle West. As the direction of the political current became increasingly clear, men of outstanding ability did not hesitate to assume the role of reformer. "Do not fear the title of reformer," Governor Cummins of Iowa told an audience in 1902, "but put true meaning upon the word. The reformer who destroys is the enemy of mankind. The reformer whose cry is 'march on' is the benefactor of his race."[29] What the Populists had failed to develop by way of effective leadership, such

---

disposal of state Civil War bonds below par. This money was added to the general fund and used as if it were income. Raney, *Wisconsin,* p. 294.

27. Edward A. Fitzpatrick, *McCarthy of Wisconsin* (New York, 1944), pp. 43, 62–71.

28. Wilcox, "Northwestern Radicalism," pp. 110–14.

29. Johnson Brigham, "The Governor of Iowa, a Sketch of Albert Baird Cummins," *American Monthly Review of Reviews,* XXXIV (September, 1906), p. 295.

insurgents as La Follette and Cummins, acting through one or the other of the older parties, now provided in generous measure. Indeed, the contagion spread to the entire nation, and an era of reform set in which materially changed the character of state government in the whole United States.

In Iowa, Albert B. Cummins had found his aspirations for a political career blocked by forces similar to those which had fought so tenaciously against La Follette in Wisconsin. A Pennsylvanian by birth, Cummins had read law in Chicago, and in 1878, soon after being admitted to the bar, had opened a law office in Des Moines. He first attracted attention as chief attorney for the Farmers' Protective Association, which sought to break up an offensive barbed-wire combine. This combine, by the simple device of buying up all available patents and then closing competing factories, had succeeded in advancing the price of barbed wire to figures that were obviously exorbitant. For five years, beginning in 1881, through suit after suit, Cummins fought the farmers' battle, until at last he obtained a decision from the Supreme Court of the United States so favorable to his clients that the monopoly was broken.[30]

Cummins' growing interest in railroads led him to give up general practice and specialize in railroad law. His outstanding ability won him clients among the railroad corporations, but they "soon learned that they did not own him."[31] He was never willing to play the role of lobbyist, and as a member of the lower house of the Iowa legislature in 1888 he introduced a "long-and-short-haul" bill that was by no means pleasing to the carriers. During this session, under the leadership of Governor William Larrabee, an outstanding liberal, the legislature enacted a series of reform measures designed to facilitate the regulation of railroads by the state. Cummins participated fully in this program without losing his standing as a regular Republican, but his unwillingness to submit to their control cost him the confidence of the railroads. When he sought election to the United States Senate in 1894, and again in 1896, they branded him as undesirable and defeated him. The excellent showing he made in the

30. *Ibid.*, p. 293; E. W. Harrington, "A Survey of the Political Ideas of Albert Baird Cummins," *Iowa Journal of History and Politics,* XXXIX (October, 1941), p. 340 n.

31. Francis Ellington Leupp, *National Miniatures* (New York, 1918), pp. 105–6.

campaign of 1899, however, was described by the *Iowa State Register* as a "marvel," for he was opposed by "a railroad with millions backing the biggest 'boss' the state ever knew, and a half-dozen allied railroads with the shrewdest men in Iowa political life in their employ, half or more of the congressmen, the entire organization of the great Republican party of Iowa, most of the office holders and aspirants, an army of paid agents, hundreds of influential newspapers whose editors are repaying obligations incurred by accepting postmasterships, and scores of federal office holders whose salaries the nation had paid while they have spent three years in steady, continuous work for their benefactor."[32]

Finally in 1901 Cummins became a candidate for the Republican nomination for governor. His great object, he told one of his opponents, was "to bring the individual voter into more prominence, and to diminish the influence of permanent organization in the ranks of the party." Undoubtedly he had his eye on the United States Senate, but the road to that goal, he decided, lay through the governorship. In a vigorous campaign he denounced the undue influence that the railroads were exerting in the political life of the state and advocated, quite after the pattern set by La Follette in Wisconsin, that a program of primary elections be instituted in order to drive from power the corporations that ruled the state. To make his position doubly clear, he mentioned by name the railway representatives who had long dictated the policies of the Republican party in Iowa, and announced that his candidacy was definitely not by their request. In return for this impertinence they promised to "pound him into the earth," but by this time the people were ready for a change. As a result Cummins entered the nominating convention with a clear majority of the delegates, was nominated on the first ballot, and was later elected at the polls by a plurality of over 83,000 votes.[33]

The first concern of the reform governor, once he had taken office, was to bring the railroads of the state to book. Back in the days of the Farmers' Alliance, with Governor Larrabee in power, a railroad commission had been created, and notable advances had been scored in the establishment

32. Quoted in Fred E. Haynes, *Third Party Movements Since the Civil War, with Special Reference to Iowa* (Iowa City, 1916), pp. 442, 450.

33. *Ibid.*, pp. 451, 454; Harrington, in *Iowa Journal of History and Politics*, XXXIX (October, 1941), p. 347; Jonathan P. Dolliver, "The Forward Movement in the Republican Party," *Outlook*, XCVI (September 24, 1910), p. 167.

of railroad regulation, but some of the gains proved to be only temporary. As public interest in the subject relaxed, the railroads found ways and means to revive their influence. Railroad commissioners, for example, while elected officials, were nominated by railroad-controlled conventions, and they usually turned out to be far more effective in defending the wishes of the railroads than in looking after the interests of the public. Cummins thus found that much of the work done a decade earlier had to be done all over again.[34]

As La Follette was doing in Wisconsin, Cummins began by insisting that the railroads pay a fair share of the state's taxation burden. Railroad assessments, he had maintained during the campaign, should be made "upon the same basis as was applied to farms and city lots."[35] Familiar with every aspect of railroad finance, he was able to dominate the executive council of the state, through which railroad assessments were made. As a result, the total railroad assessment for the year 1902 ran to $4,041,556 more than it had in 1901. To facilitate further the correct evaluation of railroad property, a law of 1902 required that the railroads report to the executive council the net income they derived from business originating in Iowa and terminating in other states, or originating in other states and terminating in Iowa, or neither originating nor terminating in Iowa but carried across a part of the state. All these items were to be included in one lump sum. By the year 1906, railroad assessments in Iowa had been increased by $15,000,000. At the same time, similar increases were made in the taxable valuation of express, telephone, and telegraph companies.[36]

Had the railroad commission of Iowa been an appointive body, as in Wisconsin, rather than an elective body, it is probable that the effectiveness of railroad regulation in Iowa would have been far more marked. The elected commissioners were rarely well qualified for their responsibilities, and they were generally content to take action only on the complaint of citizens rather than on their own initiative. Of some importance was a measure passed by the Iowa legislature, late in the Cummins administration, which authorized the state railroad commission to represent the

34. Haynes, *Third Party Movements,* p. 444; *Wallaces' Farmer,* XXXV (May 27, 1910), p. 824.

35. Haynes, *Third Party Movements,* p. 453.

36. *Appletons' Annual Cyclopaedia,* 1902, pp. 723, 725; Brigham, in *American Monthly Review of Reviews,* XXXIV (September, 1906), p. 292.

people of the state before the Interstate Commerce Commission. When, in 1912, the railroads sought to increase their western rates by 5 per cent, the careful work of Iowa's Commissioner Clifford Thorne had much to do with the retention, at least temporarily, of the old rates.[37]

Although Cummins' record on regulatory legislation was hardly as striking as La Follette's, he managed to make himself thoroughly disliked by the railroads. Possibly his most important action on the railroad question was his veto of the Molsberry bill, through which an increase in the indebtedness of certain Iowa corporations was to have been made easy. The real purpose of this bill, according to former Governor Larrabee, was to turn the state into a "kind of New Jersey" by making the process of "manufacturing corporations" as easy as possible. This veto greatly intensified railroad hostility to the Cummins administration. When Cummins sought a second term, the Standpatters bided their time, but when he chose to violate the Iowa tradition against a third term and run for re-election in 1906, they came out against him in full force and nearly defeated him.[38] Before he left office he had been instrumental in placing on the statute books a two-cent passenger-fare law, a new freight-rate law, a law to limit the hours of railroad employes, and an anti-free pass law.[39]

The strenuous campaign of 1906 may have been the influence that brought Cummins to a really effective support of the direct primary. He had advocated the passage of such a law as early as 1903 and thereafter in his biennial messages of 1904 and 1906. "Wealth, and especially corporate wealth," he had stated in his first message as governor, "has many rights; but it should always be remembered that among them is not the right to vote . . . not the privilege to sit in political conventions or occupy seats in legislative chambers. Corporations, as such, should be rigorously

37. Harrington, in *Iowa Journal of History and Politics,* XXXIX (October, 1941), p. 370; *Wallaces' Farmer,* XXXII (April 19, 1907), p. 533; XXXIV (January 22, 1909), p. 98; XXXV (May 27, 1910), p. 824; XXXVII (February 16, 1912), p. 282.

38. A recent amendment to the constitution of Iowa had designated even-numbered years instead of odd-numbered years for the election of state officers, and had extended the terms of all incumbent officers for one year. Cummins' second term thus lasted three years—from January, 1904, to January, 1907.

39. Harrington, in *Iowa Journal of History and Politics,* XXXIX (October, 1941), pp. 349, 369–70. In his earlier days Cummins himself made free use of railroad passes, and even solicited them.

excluded in every form from participation in political affairs."[40] Cummins' drive for the direct primary in 1907 got results where his earlier efforts had failed. His opponents claimed that his interest in the reform was due in part to his desire to have an expression of the popular will in his impending candidacy for the United States Senate. If so, he must have been greatly disappointed, for when he entered the primaries in 1908 against the aging Senator Allison, he was defeated. Two months later, however, the subject was reopened by the death of Senator Allison, and after a special primary had endorsed Cummins' candidacy, he was at last chosen by the legislature to the office which he had coveted for so long. Meantime, he had recorded his ardent support of an amendment to the national Constitution which would require the election of United States senators by direct vote of the people.[41]

The direct primary was not, of course, the cure-all that many people had hoped it would be. When the time came for voting, the average citizen was likely to be apathetic, while the professional politicians worked without ceasing. Verdicts of the electorate were not always clear-cut. In the Iowa Republican primary of 1908, for example, the Standpat candidates for governor and senator were nominated, while Progressives won the nominations for lieutenant governor and numerous other state and legislative offices. But the results, in general, were good. No longer could it be said, as formerly, that "delegates to political conventions were selected by the railroad attorneys; were dead-headed [by free passes] to the places of meeting, and were then herded and voted by flocks"; or that "delegates were selected by dead-heads, hauled as dead-heads, herded like sheep, and voted as they were told." It is by no means demonstrable that the primary alone broke the back of the old railroad machine; in Iowa, as in Wisconsin, the first important victories of the Progressives were scored before the direct primary was instituted. But undoubtedly the primary system threw the bosses' noses still further "out of joint," and brought "true rule of the people" closer than it had ever been before.[42]

Cummins' interest in national politics clearly had much to do with the emphasis that he placed, while still governor, upon national affairs. One

40. Haynes, *Third Party Movements*, p. 456. 41. *Ibid.*, pp. 464, 467.

42. *Wallaces' Farmer*, XXXIII (June 19, 1908), p. 807; XXXVI (February 3, 1911), p. 162; XXXVII (June 7, 1912), p. 950.

subject that he stressed without ceasing was tariff reform. The Republican state convention of 1900, which contributed the "Iowa Idea" to the age-old tariff controversy, did not abandon the protective principle, but it did advocate "such changes in the tariff from time to time as become advisable through the progress of our industries and their changing relations to the commerce of the world." After endorsing "the policy of reciprocity as the natural complement of protection," the Iowa Republicans went on to advocate "any modification of the tariff schedules that may be required to prevent their affording shelter to monopoly." These last three words—"shelter to monopoly"—were the essence of the Iowa Idea. Neither the language of the platform nor the much-used term, Iowa Idea, were the work of Cummins, but they were both given wide publicity by his frequent public statements. His first and foremost objective, he maintained, was the prevention of monopoly. "I am not an advocate of a general revision of the tariff," he said in his first inaugural address, "but I stand for competition, the competition of the Republic if possible, but of the world if necessary. I regard the consequences of a monopoly, or substantial monopoly, in any important product, as infinitely more disastrous than the consequences of foreign importations."[43]

With reference to the railroads, Cummins again showed his consciousness of the national aspect of the problem. State regulation at best could be only partially effective; by the time a railroad was big enough to need regulation, it was too big for the states to regulate. As early as 1905 Cummins appeared before the Senate Committee on Interstate Commerce to argue for the greater protection of states and localities, as well as individuals, against rate discriminations. Both as governor and as senator he showed genuine interest in restraining railroad monopoly and promoting competition. The disappearance of competition, he believed, only opened the way to socialism.[44]

43. Haynes, *Third Party Movements,* pp. 452–54; see also George E. Roberts, "The Origin and History of the Iowa Idea," *Iowa Journal of History and Politics,* II (January, 1904), pp. 69–82. "It is, of course, not possible to give the farmer protection on very much," wrote the first Henry Wallace, "for tariffs never become operative, no matter what may be on the statute books, when products are shipped abroad in large quantities." *Wallaces' Farmer,* XXXIV (February 12, 1909), p. 221.

44. Harrington, in *Iowa Journal of History and Politics,* XXXIX (October, 1941), pp. 366, 370 n.

The leadership of Cummins in Iowa, like the leadership of La Follette in Wisconsin, revealed a widening rift in the Republican party. The opponents of reform were generally called "Standpatters," and they more or less accepted the designation, while the faction which supported Cummins assumed the more attractive label of "Progressives." In Iowa, no less than in Wisconsin, the reforms that the Progressives adopted were eventually accepted by the opposition, at least as necessary evils. Railroad domination of the Republican party was definitely broken, and the direct primary came to stay. If only Cummins' devotion to the cause of intrastate reform had been greater and his ambition for a career in national politics less, it is possible that he might have accomplished more as governor than he did. He was cautious and deliberate at a time when aggressive tactics would have paid good dividends; some of the most important reforms connected with his name were not put through until after his near defeat for a third term. "A La Follette," wrote Herbert Quick in 1906, "would have at least had the issues made up in less than five years."[45] It is quite possible that the antimonopoly, farmer-minded voters of Iowa were in their thinking well in advance of their leader.

It would have been strange indeed if so pronounced a movement for reform as was manifest in Wisconsin and Iowa had failed to affect Minnesota. Conditions in the three states were much alike, but effective leadership was essential, as the careers of La Follette and Cummins amply demonstrated, if the power of the vested interests was to be broken. Minnesota, ever since Populist times, had suffered from a dearth of able leaders. The men who won high office in the state, while ready enough to give devoted lip service to measures of reform, turned out all too frequently to be mere time-serving politicians, more interested in retaining office than in promoting the principles they preached. Not until the election of 1904, when John A. Johnson, a Democrat, won the governorship in spite of Minnesota's normal Republicanism, was any very genuine progress registered.[46]

Johnson had had no such struggle for political survival as had motivated both La Follette and Cummins, but he had a life story full of emotional appeal. He was the first native Minnesotan, it transpired, ever to hold

45. *Ibid.*, p. 383.
46. Wilcox, "Northwestern Radicalism," pp. 89–91.

office as governor of the state. His parents were humble Swedish immigrants, early settlers in St. Peter, where Johnson was born in 1861. His father, a blacksmith, was unfortunately too fond of drink to provide an adequate living for his family, and therefore young Johnson, because his earnings were needed, was obliged at thirteen years of age to leave school and go to work. Eventually he became interested in journalism, and as the editor of the *St. Peter Herald,* a country newspaper, he gained prominence in his own community. For a single term of four years, 1899 to 1903, he represented his district in the state senate, but his constituency was ordinarily Republican and by a narrow margin he was defeated for re-election.[47]

By this time Johnson had attracted considerable attention throughout the state, partly because of his great personal charm, which won him many friends, and partly because he had shown himself to be an independent thinker who could express himself effectively both in writing and in speaking. When John Lind, the most prominent Democrat in Minnesota, refused to be considered for the Democratic nomination for governor in 1904, the party leaders turned naturally to Johnson, and induced the convention to nominate him by acclamation. His election in the campaign that followed may be interpreted as a kind of popular protest against the petty factional strife and do-nothing tactics of Minnesota Republicans. While Theodore Roosevelt carried the state as Republican candidate for President by a margin of 216,651 to 55,187, the vote for Johnson was 147,992 and that for his Republican opponent only 140,130. Twice thereafter, in 1906 and again in 1908, Johnson won re-election by far more substantial majorities, in spite of every effort on the part of the Republican machine to displace him. His sudden death in 1909 cut short what might have developed into a brilliant career in national as well as state politics.[48]

Johnson was handicapped in his leadership by having to deal, throughout his three administrations, with legislatures opposed to him politically. More important, he could not even count on the support of a sufficient number of reformers to provide the necessary legislative majorities to put

47. William Watts Folwell, *A History of Minnesota* (4 vols., St. Paul, 1921–30), III, 275–76; Frank A. Day and Theodore M. Knappen, *The Life of John Albert Johnson* (St. Paul, 1910), pp. 52–114.

48. *Ibid.,* pp. 119–42; Folwell, *Minnesota,* III, 277–83.

through the reform measures he desired. His victories were therefore incomplete, but his interest in freeing the state from corporation control and in establishing popular government was fully demonstrated. The fact that the people stood by him in one election after another indicates that he felt the public pulse aright. And, with the spirit of reform riding high, Johnson did accomplish a great deal. Undoubtedly one of his greatest assets in obtaining a certain measure of support from Republican legislatures was the fear of the Republicans that the Democrats might get the credit for being more responsive to the current demand for reform than the Republicans.[49]

On the dominant problem of the railroads, Governor Johnson's contributions were somewhat less spectacular than those of La Follette and Cummins. A state railroad and warehouse commission already existed, but its members were reluctant to make full use of the powers they possessed. On one occasion, during the summer of 1906, Johnson was obliged to publicly demand action from the commissioners in order to induce them to so much as grant a request of the three principal railroads of the state to reduce their grain rates by approximately 10 per cent. "One speech of his," according to his biographers, "resulted in a voluntary reduction of ten percent. in certain classes of freight in northern Minnesota." Finally, after the subject of intrastate freight rates had been fully investigated, the legislature, by law, cut the rates on grain, coal, lumber, and livestock an average of 10 per cent. Other railroad measures enacted during Johnson's administration included a reciprocal demurrage law, "subjecting carriers to the same penalties for delay in furnishing cars as carriers impose upon shippers for delay in loading cars," an anti-pass bill, and a two-cent passenger-fare bill.[50]

The Johnson record of reform extended well beyond the railroad sphere. Johnson was deeply interested in the insurance problem, and induced the legislature to pass what "amounted to a code of life, fire, and marine insurance." He also signed measures extending the jurisdiction of the state bureau of labor, industries, and commerce; creating a depart-

49. *Ibid.*, p. 287.

50. Day and Knappen, *Johnson*, p. 159. See also R. W. Oppegard, "Governor Albert Johnson and the Reform Era in Minnesota" (unpublished master's thesis, University of Wisconsin, 1937), pp. 46–48, 52–67.

ment of banking; and permitting cities to own and operate such public utilities as street railways, telephones, water works, gas works, and electric light, heat, and power works. He had little to do, however, with the extension of the direct primary into Minnesota. Like many another state, Minnesota had long made some effort to control the party primaries through which delegates to conventions were chosen, but it took more advanced ground when, as early as 1899, its legislature passed an act for the use of the direct primary in Hennepin County only as a substitute for the customary caucus and convention nominations for city, county, judicial, school, and similarly nonpolitical offices. Two years later this act was extended to the entire state, thus making Minnesota the first state in the Union to require the universal, although strictly limited, use of the direct primary. But it was not until 1912, after the direct primary movement had gathered irresistible momentum, that the Minnesota legislature got around to the enactment of a direct primary law equally applicable to all state offices.[51]

In Missouri the reform governor was Joseph W. Folk. Unlike La Follette, Cummins, and Johnson, who rose to prominence mainly through rural support, Folk first made his name known as the chief law-enforcement officer of a large city, St. Louis. In this capacity, during the years 1901–2, he exposed and prosecuted a group of "boodlers," including the city boss, whose deals with corrupt business interests had cost St. Louis taxpayers princely sums. Twelve of the culprits were convicted and sent to jail. Folk then turned his attention to exposing grafting members of the state legislature and the state administration. The shocking conditions he revealed blasted numerous reputations and made Folk the logical candidate of the Democratic party, to which he belonged, for the governorship in 1904. Nominated less by the support of the cities, where frightened bosses did all they could to defeat him, than by the rural counties, where the spirit of reform was strong, he won the election handily in spite of the fact that the Republicans carried the state in the voting for President and for every other state office except governor.[52]

During his four years in office Folk used the executive power so effec-

51. Folwell, *Minnesota,* III, 287; IV, 366.

52. Lincoln Steffens, *The Shame of the Cities* (New York, 1904), pp. 101–43, and *The Struggle for Self-Government* (New York, 1906), pp. 1–39.

tively that reluctant legislatures were obliged to enact a large number of the reform measures for which the times called—laws for the more effective regulation of the railroads and public utilities, an antilobby law, a direct primary law, and a constitutional amendment making possible the use of the initiative and referendum. The Missouri constitution limited the governor to a single term of four years; thus Folk had no opportunity to run for re-election. His Republican attorney general, Herbert S. Hadley, who had successfully brought suit against three Missouri railroads for combination in restraint of trade and had won an important case against the Standard Oil Company, succeeded Folk as governor and continued in similar vein. Folk, perhaps unwisely, sought election to the United States Senate in 1908, but was defeated in the primary he had helped to establish by the veteran politician, William J. Stone. It is of some significance that Folk carried seventy-four counties to forty for Stone, and that the issue was settled by Stone's decisive victory in the cities. The country population remained loyal to Folk.[53]

What happened in all the other states of the western Middle West differed only in detail. No doubt, as time went on, governors sought consciously to imitate the records of such reformers as La Follette, Cummins, Johnson, and Folk. A reform attitude paid dividends; even the President of the United States, Theodore Roosevelt, had been quick to discover and exploit that fact. In South Dakota Coe I. Crawford turned his back upon his earlier career as railroad lobbyist, sought the Republican nomination for governor upon a platform that was strongly reminiscent of the La Follette demands in Wisconsin, and after a defeat in 1904 at the hands of the machine, won easily in 1906.[54] In Kansas a well-to-do businessman, Walter R. Stubbs, was impressed as a member of the legislature with the inefficiency of state government, and started out to do something about it. Eventually he realized that corporation control was the principal affliction from which Kansas suffered and became an ardent proponent of all the leading progressive reforms. After a decisive defeat by the machine in 1906, Stubbs won nomination and election to the governorship in 1908

53. Frank Warren Crow, "Joseph W. Folk and the Reform Movement in Missouri" (unpublished master's thesis, University of Wisconsin, 1937), pp. 58–84.

54. Doane Robinson, *Encyclopedia of South Dakota* (Pierre, S. Dak., 1925), p. 147.

and served two terms.[55] In North Dakota John Burke, a Democrat, was the reform leader. With the dominant political party, the corporations, and the leading newspapers of the state all against him, he was three times elected governor by excellent majorities—in 1906, 1908, and 1910.[56] In Nebraska, the reform leadership was less personalized, but two progressive Republicans, Norris Brown as attorney general and George L. Sheldon as a member of the state senate, gave some direction to the movement. Campaigning together in 1906 on a reform program, Brown went to the United States Senate and Sheldon was elected governor.[57] In Illinois, Charles S. Deneen, a Republican who held the governorship from 1905 to 1913, was certainly not a spotless reformer, but he at least worked energetically to establish the direct primary. When the supreme court, time after time, invalidated legislation designed to accomplish this end, he stumped the state "county by county, and ward after ward" to secure a law that the court would sustain. Only in 1912, on the fourth attempt, was such a law enacted.[58]

The reforms inaugurated by the legislatures of these states of the Middle West were by no means identical, but clearly marked trends are unmistakable. One type of legislation created, well in advance of most of the other states of the Union, a direct primary system of making nominations for office. This reform was fundamental, and throughout the western Middle West it literally revolutionized state government. Nor was there in this region any such backsliding and evasion as occurred in some of the eastern states. The change had come to stay; candidates were at the mercy of public opinion in a way in which they had never been before. Sometimes, but not always, the direct primary was supplemented by plans for direct legislation—the initiative and referendum. Honesty in politics was frequently sought by means of drastic antilobbying and corrupt practices acts. Direct primaries for candidates for the United States Senate became common, and in some instances a preferential vote, taken at the time of

55. Wilcox, "Northwestern Radicalism," pp. 87–88.

56. *Ibid.*, p. 94.

57. Albert Watkins, *Illustrated History of Nebraska* (3 vols., Lincoln, Nebr., 1905–13), III, 277.

58. Roy O. West, "Charles S. Deneen, 1863–1900," *Journal of the Illinois State Historical Society,* XXXIV (March, 1914), p. 11; Steffens, *Struggle for Self-Government,* pp. 74–78.

the regular election, bound the legislature to accept the candidate designated by the people at the polls. Presidential preference primaries for the selection of delegates to the national nominating conventions were also frequently provided, particularly as a result of the candidacy of Theodore Roosevelt against Taft for the Republican nomination in 1912.[59]

Along with these efforts to promote popular government came much legislation aimed at the political and economic supremacy of powerful business interests, particularly the railroads. Expansion of the prerogatives of railroad commissions, higher corporation taxes, maximum freight rates, two-cent passenger fares, and anti-pass laws were multiplied in state after state. It is no exaggeration to say that, for the most part, the peculiar hold that the railroads had long had upon the political life of the region was broken. Even the conservative reaction, which began in the western Middle West as early as 1912, and swept numerous standpatters and stalwarts back into office, was relatively unimportant, for the only way in which the conservatives could retain power was to outdo the progressives in their devotion to the new reforms.[60] The old Populist principle that if only the people could obtain control of their government, they could defend themselves adequately against the power of monopoly seemed in the process of being demonstrated.

The legacy of Populism could easily be traced also into the realm of national affairs. Such reforms as came to be associated with the name of Theodore Roosevelt were ardently supported by the agrarian leaders of the western Middle West, and to some extent, no doubt, were inspired by them. According to one enthusiast, Roosevelt was the "spokesman of the people, the expression and exponent of the reform spirit, the mouthpiece of an awakened conscience."[61] But the westerners wanted to go much farther than Roosevelt was willing to lead. As La Follette put it, "He acted upon the maxim that a half loaf is better than no bread. I believe that half a loaf is fatal whenever it is accepted at the sacrifice of the basic principle sought to be attained."[62] The insurgent movement of the

59. Merriam and Overaker, *Primary Elections,* pp. 62–63, 141–42; Wilcox, "Northwestern Radicalism," p. 107.

60. *Ibid.,* pp. 110–14.

61. *Wallaces' Farmer,* XXXIII (August 14, 1908), p. 976.

62. La Follette, *Autobiography,* p. 388.

Taft administration was even more obviously of agrarian origin. It was, indeed, mainly the work of senators and representatives from the Middle West—men who, according to William Allen White, "caught the Populists in swimming and stole all of their clothing except the frayed underdrawers of free silver."[63] The fight on Cannonism in the national House of Representatives was carried to a successful conclusion through the leadership of such middle western progressives as Norris of Nebraska, Nelson of Wisconsin, Murdock and Madison of Kansas, and Lindbergh of Minnesota. Aid came from some outside supporters, notably Poindexter of Washington and Fowler of New Jersey, but the credit for victory belonged primarily to the middle western agrarians.[64] The assault of the Senate insurgents upon the Payne-Aldrich tariff bill was almost wholly a contribution of the western Middle West. La Follette of Wisconsin, Clapp of Minnesota, Cummins and Dolliver of Iowa, and Bristow of Kansas were the outstanding leaders; only Beveridge of Indiana deserves comparable credit for the work the insurgents did in revealing the monopolistic intent of the Aldrich schedules.[65] In both houses of Congress the insurgents also fought for a graduated income tax, for conservation, for postal savings, for more vigorous railroad regulation, and against a type of reciprocity with Canada designed to benefit the industrial East at the expense of the agricultural Middle West.[66] The overwhelming approval of middle western farm constituencies of the program of the insurgents was repeatedly demonstrated at election time; not only were the radical leaders consistently returned to Congress, but old-guard conservatives were retired with great good will.[67] Eventually most of the reforms for which the insurgents stood found expression in the platform of the Progressive party of 1912, but the candidacy of Theodore Roosevelt blurred the issue and divided their forces. They could not very truly believe in

63. Kenneth W. Hechler, *Insurgency* (New York, 1940), pp. 21–22.

64. *Ibid.*, pp. 33–43.

65. *Ibid.*, pp. 83–91, 145.

66. *Ibid.*, pp. 146–219. Reciprocity with Canada, as proposed by the Taft administration, was, according to one middle westerner, a "jug-handled affair," wholly unsatisfactory to the friends of genuine reciprocity. It "assumes that the farmer owes the manufacturer a living." *Wallaces' Farmer*, XXXVI (March 10, 1911), p. 438.

67. Wilcox, "Northwestern Radicalism," pp. 106–8.

him, nor he in them.[68] But the statement of a close student of the subject that "Wilsonian liberalism and the New Deal were born of Insurgency" carries no appreciable discount.[69]

68. George E. Mowry, *Theodore Roosevelt and the Progressive Movement* (Madison, Wis., 1946), pp. 269–73.
69. Hechler, *Insurgency*, p. 221.

Chapter III

EARLY PHASES OF THE COOPERATIVE MOVEMENT

WHILE the early years of the twentieth century saw much evidence of the farmers' influence in politics, it must not be supposed that more direct methods of farmer action were overlooked. Chief among these was the development of farmer cooperatives, especially those designed for the marketing of dairy products, grain, and livestock. Long experience had convinced many farmers that too large a percentage of the prices ultimately paid by the consumer went to the middlemen and other handlers of farm produce rather than to the farmers themselves. According to one reliable estimate, the farmers' share of the consumer's dollar varied from 35 to 50 per cent, while the other 50 to 65 per cent went to transportation companies, wholesalers, and retailers. Small wonder that a subscriber wrote in to the editor of *Wallaces' Farmer:* "Had you not better take up the subject of how to market our produce, rather than to tell us all the time how to produce more?"[1]

Beginning in about 1900, cooperatives in the United States took a new lease on life, achieving their greatest successes, except for the strong movements in California and New York, among the dairy, grain, and livestock producers of Minnesota, Wisconsin, Illinois, and Iowa. In all these states the cooperatives showed remarkable increases in the numbers of

1. *Wallaces' Farmer,* XXXII (April 19, 1907), p. 534; XXXV (December 23, 1910), p. 1734; XXXVII (November 29, 1912), p. 1682.

cooperative organizations, the length of their membership lists, and the volume of their sales and purchases. The reasons for this development are complex and varied, including, among others, (1) a favorable trend in court decisions, (2) state and federal legislation for the legalization of cooperatives, (3) the demonstrated success of cooperative undertakings abroad as well as at home, (4) the desire of farmers to emulate the efficient methods of distribution achieved by business and industry, (5) the endorsement of cooperatives by prominent men in all walks of life, (6) the multitudinous activities of a variety of state and federal agencies, and (7) the hue and cry of untold millions—farmers and nonfarmers alike—for money-saving reforms in distribution.

Statistics provided by the federal government, although far from complete, indicate that during the late nineteenth century the greatest progress in the use of cooperatives had been made in the twelve north central states, nine of which comprise the western Middle West. By the year 1900 there were, mostly in these states, about 2,000 farmers' business organizations. Of these, nearly 1,600 were cooperative creameries or cheese factories, while about 100 were grain elevators and a similar number were devoted to the marketing of fruits. Of the 200 other farmer enterprises, some were engaged in the marketing of livestock or other farm produce and some were cooperative stores. The total business that these cooperatives transacted was estimated at only a little less than $200,000,000. As the years elapsed the volume of cooperative activities increased greatly, but the relative importance of the western Middle West as a cooperative center remained unchanged.[2]

The growth of cooperatives in the western Middle West owed a great

2. R. H. Elsworth, "A Quarter Century of Cooperative Development," *Cooperative Marketing Journal,* I (December, 1927), pp. 30–31; Federal Farm Board, *Statistics of Farmers' Selling and Buying Associations, United States, 1863–1931,* Bulletin 9 (Washington, 1932), pp. 7–9. For greater details on the status of cooperatives in different states and periods, see other studies of Ralph Henry Elsworth: *Development and Present Status of Farmers' Cooperative Business Organizations,* U. S. Dept. Agri., Agricultural Bulletin 1302 (Washington, 1925); *Agricultural Cooperative Associations, Marketing and Purchasing, 1925,* U. S. Dept. Agri., Technical Bulletin 40 (Washington, 1928); *Cooperative Marketing and Purchasing, 1920–1929,* U. S. Dept. Agri., Circular 121 (Washington, 1930); *Statistics of Farmers' Cooperative Business Organizations, 1920–1935,* Farm Credit Administration, Bulletin 6 (Washington, 1936).

deal to the long procession of farm organizations that flourished in this region—the Grangers, the Farmers' Alliance, the American Society of Equity, the Farmers' Union, the American Farm Bureau Federation, and numerous independent groups. The pioneer work was performed by the nineteenth-century orders, but their twentieth-century successors built upon the old foundations and exploited the same old farmer grievances. Mounting discontent over commission charges, dockage, grading, poor service, short weights, lack of competition among dealers, low prices, and the generally high marketing costs made the task of persuading the farmers that their salvation lay in the establishment of their own marketing machinery easy. From such a system they might hope to obtain a greater share of the consumer's dollar, a need particularly felt by all farmers who lived long distances from their markets and by small operators who were obliged to purchase and sell uneconomically in less than carload lots.[3] Immigrants such as the Norwegians, Swiss, and Danes of Wisconsin, Minnesota, and the Dakotas—many of whom were familiar with cooperatives in the Old World—often, but not necessarily always, responded favorably to propaganda for group action.[4]

While it is true that cooperatives had made their greatest progress in the western Middle West, the forces that had stimulated their growth were by no means solely confined to this region. Perhaps too great importance is attached, however, to the oft-cited example of the English consumers

3. The literature of this subject is extensive. See particularly E. G. Nourse, "Fifty Years of Farmers' Elevators in Iowa," *Iowa State Agricultural Experiment Station, Bulletin 211* (Ames, Iowa, 1923), pp. 236–51; E. G. Nourse and C. W. Hammans, "Cooperative Livestock Shipping in Iowa in 1920," *ibid., Bulletin 200* (1920) pp. 403–4; "Cooperation in Kansas," *Nineteenth Biennial Report of the Kansas State Board of Agriculture* (Topeka, 1915), pp. 154–81, 199–224; Henry H. Bakken and Marvin A. Schaars, *The Economics of Cooperative Marketing* (New York, 1937), pp. 2, 47–62 (especially pp. 49–51); P. R. Fossum, *Agrarian Movements in North Dakota* (Baltimore, 1925), pp. 51–83; Theodore Macklin, "Cooperation Applied to Marketing by Kansas Farmers," *Kansas State Agricultural Experiment Station, Bulletin 224* (Manhattan, Kans., 1920), pp. 7–8, 47–61; Herman Steen, *Coöperative Marketing* (New York, 1923), pp. 4–7; DeWitt C. Wing, "Trends in National Farm Organizations," U. S. Dept. Agri. Yearbook, *Farmers in a Changing World* (Washington, 1940), p. 964; Joseph G. Knapp and J. H. Lister, *Cooperative Purchasing of Farm Supplies,* Farm Credit Administration, Cooperative Division, Bulletin 1 (Washington, 1935).

4. Edward A. Ross, *The Old World in the New* (New York, 1914), p. 91.

who in 1844 had banded themselves together to form the Rochdale Society. Cooperative ventures, although generally unsuccessful, had been tried on this side of the Atlantic before the Rochdale group was organized, and at least one, a group of Wisconsin cheese producers, is credited with having achieved success as early as 1841 in the cooperative manufacture of cheese.[5] The Rochdale pioneers, important as they were in the history of cooperatives, were organized as urban consumers to economize on their purchases and not as sellers of farm produce. The success of their system rested upon two fundamental principles: (1) the acceptance of the prevailing market price in the sale of goods to patrons, and (2) the distribution of profits to members in proportion to the amounts of their purchases. Their program was woven of the same fabric as those of the Owenites, the Chartists, and the advocates of the Reform Bill of 1832. They were part and parcel of an urban movement bent upon rectifying or bettering the unfavorable situation of the unemployed or poorly paid urban workers rather than a rural movement seeking lower marketing costs and higher returns from farming.

The position of the Wisconsin cheese makers was more nearly typical of the producers of the western Middle West. They cooperated not "because of poverty and want" but rather to increase their profits.[6] Indeed, the farmers as producers and sellers and the consumers as purchasers and utilizers tended inevitably to gravitate toward opposite sides of the bargaining counter. The consumers, whether Rochdale pioneers or cooperators of a less distinguished line, were interested in purchasing their commodities at the lowest possible price, while the farmers who had banded

5. Steen, *Coöperative Marketing,* pp. 4, 156–57. Chapter 13 is entitled "America's First Coöperators." See also *Cooperation in Foreign Countries* (68 Congress, 2 session, Senate Document 171, serial 8397, Washington, 1925), p. xi. It was here reported that "The cooperative is of such magnitude and importance . . . that it challenges attention. More than 285,000 organizations in all parts of the world are connected with it." The number of people represented by cooperatives was placed at more than 30,000,000.

6. George J. Holyoake, *Self-Help by the People, The History of the Rochdale Pioneers* (London, 1900), pp. 2–3; Sydney R. Elliot, *The English Cooperatives* (New Haven, Conn., 1937), pp. 6–40. See also Henry W. Brown, *The Rochdale Pioneers; The Story of the Toad Lane Store, 1844, and the Origin of the Cooperative Union, 1869* (1931); Robert A. Campbell, "Coöperation in Wisconsin," *American Review of Reviews,* XLVII (April, 1913), p. 468.

together in cooperative marketing associations sought the highest possible returns.[7]

Whatever their foreign antecedents, the marketing cooperatives of the western Middle West had to face the practical, everyday problems that the American farmer confronted. He had troubles with railroads, with middlemen, and with financial institutions: cooperative associations had to deal with the same difficulties. Before they could succeed, there had to be much "experimentation in selecting, borrowing, adapting, contriving and fitting together devices, procedures and arrangements" into the kind of organization that would do the work required of it. So many elements of the modern business corporation had to be adopted that the cooperative which eventually appeared has been described as in outward form "a business corporation and in the end a mutual benefit society."[8] According to one authority, the marketing cooperatives had no "special techniques"—"they simply imitated the practices of the private business organizations with the important modification that the gains or advantages should accrue to those who participated in the enterprise." The fact that cooperative leaders often made reference to the efficient methods of distribution employed by American industrialists seems to indicate their very strong interest in trying to profit from these examples. Three principal characteristics emerged as the identification marks of a genuine cooperative: first, it must be democratically controlled; second, it must set reasonable limits on its capital; and third, it must distribute its earnings on the patronage basis.[9] But these characteristics alone would hardly have been

7. John Hanna, *The Law of Cooperative Marketing Associations* (New York, 1931), p. 4; Bakken and Schaars, *The Economics of Cooperative Marketing,* pp. 169–70. See also Steen, *Coöperative Marketing,* pp. 3–4. According to Steen, "The spectacular success of the Rochdale society led to the application of the Rochdale plan to agricultural coöperation. This was the case in Great Britain and Ireland, and through northern Europe, notably in the Scandinavian countries. It failed for farmers almost as completely as it had succeeded for the factory workers of Great Britain, and for a quarter of a century agricultural coöperation stood still in Europe. Then American farmers revived and perfected the old Swiss system of coöperative marketing and its success led to its general adoption in European agriculture."

8. Walton H. Hamilton, "Judicial Tolerance of Farmers' Cooperatives," *Yale Law Journal,* XXXVIII (May, 1929), pp. 938–39; W. S. Harwood, "Cooperation in the West," *Atlantic Monthly,* LXXXV (April, 1900), pp. 539–40; George Harold Powell, *Coöperation in Agriculture* (New York, 1913), pp. 10–12.

9. Bakken and Schaars, *The Economics of Cooperative Marketing,* pp. 146–47.

adequate to insure the success of a typical American cooperative. The American pattern generally combined good business practices with the Rochdale principles.

Nevertheless, every effort was made to find out what the English and European cooperatives were doing, and to adapt their methods to the needs of the movement in the United States. Commissions and individuals were sent abroad; data were collected; reports were submitted; and recommendations were made. But there is little tangible evidence that much of lasting importance resulted from these investigations. Inevitably they led to the holding of conferences, the passing of resolutions, and the depositing of materials in archives. But it was one thing to collect data and confer and resolve and quite another to influence the course of the cooperative movement.[10]

Probably more potent than the study of foreign procedures were the recommendations of President Theodore Roosevelt's Commission on Rural Life. The commission, besides emphasizing the need for cooperatives, called attention to the obstacles which impeded their growth, and designated the regions of undiversified one-crop farming as the place of their greatest need. The commission also urged upon the states the necessity of passing enabling legislation and upon Congress the desirability of promoting cooperatives in every way it could, particularly with respect to cooperative rural credits.

Naturally, the advocates of farmer cooperatives made good use of the

---

At the bottom of page 146 the authors cite "practices commonly used by American cooperatives [which] are not distinguishable from those of private business corporations." Melvin T. Copeland, interestingly enough, treats the topic of cooperative marketing under the broad general heading of "Marketing" in *Recent Economic Changes in the United States, Report of the Committee on Recent Economic Changes of the President's Conference on Unemployment* (2 vols., New York, 1929), I, 374–89.

10. *Agricultural Cooperation and Rural Credit in Europe* (63 Congress, 1 session, Senate Document 214, serial 6519, Washington, 1913); Senate Document 171, 68 Congress, 2 session; *Agricultural Cooperation and Rural Credit in Europe, Report of the American Commission* (63 Congress, 2 session, Senate Document 261, serial 6570, 2 vols., Washington, 1914); *Adaptation of the European Cooperative Credit System to Meet the Needs of the American Farmer—Report of the International Institute of Agriculture on the Conference Held at Nashville, Tenn., April 1912* (62 Congress, 2 session, Senate Document 855, serial 6178, Washington, 1912).

commission's findings. Farm groups and agricultural leaders saw to it that those phases of the report which favored cooperatives received wide circulation. There was nothing revolutionary or startling in these findings and recommendations; for the most part they only repeated charges and demands that farmers had been making all along. But the endorsement given to cooperatives by President Roosevelt and his commission did make a difference. The members of the commission—L. H. Bailey, Henry C. Wallace, Kenyon Butterfield, Walter H. Page, Gifford Pinchot, and Charles Barrett—were all well known in farm circles, and their warm approval of cooperatives helped place the hood of respectability upon them.[11]

The support given the movement by Sir Horace Plunkett, the prominent Irish cooperative leader, also lent prestige. Plunkett had come to the United States to regain his health, and had made the acquaintance of leaders all over the country. Even after his return to Ireland he was a frequent visitor to the United States. He exchanged views on cooperatives with President Roosevelt and with Gifford Pinchot. He also became acquainted with Charles McCarthy, the state legislative librarian in Wisconsin—a student of cooperation and a prominent figure in progressive Republican politics. Of his association with McCarthy Plunkett wrote, "I have had the privilege of assisting him to draft the Co-operative Law (which partly answers to our Industrial and Provident Societies and Friendly Societies Acts) for his State." Plunkett addressed the Wisconsin legislature in 1911 and again in 1913, and held conferences with "the Governor, with State officers, with the president of the University, and with the dean and faculty of the College of Agriculture." He subscribed heartily to the Roosevelt formula of "better farming, better business, better living," but urged that first emphasis be placed on the "better business" side of farming, because it was there that the farmers were most wanting.[12]

11. *Report of the Country Life Commission* (60 Congress, 2 session, Senate Document 705, serial 5408, Washington, 1909), pp. 128–37, 150. One of the recommendations of the commission was that the cooperatives might "establish prices and perhaps to control the production." This sounds like the work of Barrett.

12. E. F. Baldwin, "Two Leaders in Rural Progress," *Outlook*, XCVI (December 10, 1910), pp. 829–30; Horace C. Plunkett, "McCarthy of Wisconsin," *Nineteenth Century*, LXXVII (June, 1915), p. 1346; Campbell, in *American Review of Reviews*, XLVII (April, 1913), p. 468; Horace C. Plunkett, *The Rural Life Problem of the United States* (New York, 1910), pp. 86–87.

Unfortunately, the legal status of cooperatives in the United States was long the subject of heated controversy. Before the enactment of legislation specifically legalizing cooperatives, the practice of the farmers had been to organize as best they could under the corporation laws of their respective states. These laws, however, were designed for a different purpose and did not fit the cooperative need; moreover, they left the cooperatives open to the danger of prosecution under the antitrust laws, which forbade conspiracy in restraint of trade.[13] Farm organizations such as the Grange had long emphasized the need for constructive legislation on this subject, but their efforts to achieve a special status for horticultural and agricultural organizations did not at first achieve satisfactory results. In the case of *Loewe* v. *Lawler* (1908), when the United States Supreme Court was asked to invoke the Sherman Anti-Trust Act against labor organizations seeking higher wages and agricultural organizations striving for higher prices, the Court held unequivocally against the labor unions and the cooperatives. The act, it maintained,

> . . . had made no distinctions between classes. It provided that "every" contract, combination, or conspiracy in restraint of trade was illegal. The records of Congress show that several efforts were made to exempt organizations of farmers and laborers from the operations of the Act, and that all these efforts failed, so that the Act remained as we have it before us.[14]

This point of view caused the advocates of cooperatives much distress. Between 1890 to 1910 many attempts were made to prosecute the directors and officers of selling cooperatives. Indictments against such individuals were brought in five states under state antitrust laws, and in Louisiana an indictment was brought under the Sherman Act. While none of the defendants were convicted, as charged, of fixing prices, the farmers were left in grave doubt regarding the legality of their efforts to create and operate effective marketing cooperatives.[15]

13. H. W. Ballentine, "Cooperative Marketing Associations," *Minnesota Law Review,* VIII (December, 1923), p. 2. See also Hamilton, in *Yale Law Journal,* XXXVIII (May, 1929), pp. 938–39; Steen, *Coöperative Marketing,* pp. 3–4; Hanna, *Law of Cooperative Marketing Associations,* p. 4.

14. 208 U. S., 274, p. 301. See also Franklin J. Jones, "The Status of Farmers' Cooperative Associations Under Federal Law," *Journal of Political Economy,* XXIX (July, 1921), pp. 595–96; Knapp and Lister, *Cooperative Purchasing of Farm Supplies,* p. 24.

15. John D. Miller, "The Philosophical and Legal Background of the Cooperative

Fortunately, this unfavorable legal situation was not to endure unchanged. In spite of the stand taken by the Supreme Court, the weight of judicial opinion held that under the common law farmers had a perfect right to organize for collective marketing and purchasing. There was also a tendency to admit that the antitrust statutes "were enacted to correct abuses which had developed in the collective activities of other groups" and not among the farmers. While the *Loewe* v. *Lawler* decision was not the last of its kind, the view that eventually won out was that not all combinations restricting competition were necessarily illegal, especially if their object was to foster trade and increase business and not to "exercise improper control or unduly and unreasonably restrict competition." The test of illegality came to be whether they abused their power. By the time the Clayton Anti-Trust Act of 1914 was passed, farmer and labor organizations were strong enough to obtain the exemption of nonstock, nonprofit labor, agricultural, and horticultural organizations from the operation of the national antitrust laws. But the cooperative leaders were not satisfied with this victory; they also needed, and in some instances had already obtained, the specific and positive legalization of farmer cooperative associations organized for mutual benefit.[16]

Two states of the western Middle West—Wisconsin and Nebraska—took the lead in 1911 with the first really modern legislation on the subject of cooperatives. Needless to say, these laws were hardly the first statutes to deal with the problem. Minnesota, for instance, had passed a simple law on cooperatives as early as 1870, and had improved on it steadily thereafter. Likewise California and Alabama had "nonstock laws," and Kentucky had enacted a "pooling" statute. But the legislation of Wisconsin and Nebraska was more nearly fundamental than any that

---

Movement in the United States," The American Institute of Cooperation, *American Cooperation, 1935* (Washington, 1935), p. 16.

16. *Ibid.*, p. 15; Ballentine, in *Minnesota Law Review*, VIII (December, 1923), pp. 9–10; Jones, in *Journal of Political Economy*, XXIX (July, 1921), pp. 595–96; M. O. Tobriner, "Cooperative Marketing and the Restraint of Trade," *Columbia Law Review*, XXVII (November, 1927), p. 827. Frequently cited were two Iowa decisions which held that certain Iowa organizations were restraints in trade. *Reeves* v. *Decorah Farmers' Cooperative Society*, 160 Iowa 194 (1913), 140 Northwestern Reporter 844 (1913); *Ludoewese* v. *Farmers' Mutual Cooperative Co.*, 164, Iowa 197 (1914), 145 Northwestern Reporter 475 (1914).

had preceded it. Of the two laws, the Wisconsin statute was newer and broader in concept in some ways and had wider influence, serving eventually as the basis for similar legislation to be adopted in a dozen other states. It provided that any number of persons greater than five might organize for cooperative purposes; that the shares of each stockholder were not ordinarily to exceed one thousand dollars; that each stockholder was entitled to only one vote, which might be cast by mail; that dividends were paid in proportion to patronage; and that only associations living up to these provisions might designate themselves as cooperatives. The Nebraska law was mainly short and permissive, but it laid down the requirement that earnings be distributed "in part or wholly on the basis of, or in proportion to, the property bought from or sold to members, or of labor performed, or other service rendered to the corporation."[17]

The farmers, to qualify for the special treatment they obtained under these laws, had to satisfy the legislators of two things: first, that their associations and business agencies were not monopolies; and second, that the farmer's calling was unique compared with other businesses and hence was in need of special legislation to survive. There was an abundance of evidence on both points. It could easily be demonstrated that all efforts to perfect monopolies in the major agricultural industries were sure to meet with insurmountable difficulties. Open membership in the associations militated against monopoly. The inevitable tendency of millions of small producers to increase their output with the rise of prices also worked against monopoly. Lack of capital and problems of geography made monopoly practically impossible. As for the second point, farming was "different." Other industries enjoyed the benefit of concentrated production under single management in a factory system, whereas the farmer was isolated in his work. As a bargainer, the farmer was inexperienced; he was "ignorant of his fellow farmer's operations, of the quality, the grade, the character of the general crop, of his foreign and

17. Bakken and Schaars, *The Economics of Cooperative Marketing*, p. 272; Edwin G. Nourse, *The Legal Status of Agricultural Cooperation* (New York, 1928), pp. 46–47; Nourse, "The Growth of Cooperative Law," *Cooperative Marketing Journal*, I (December, 1926), p. 10; Hanna, *Law of Cooperative Marketing Associations*, pp. 31–33; B. H. Hibbard, "Agricultural Cooperation," *University of Wisconsin Agricultural Experiment Station, Bulletin 238* (Madison, 1914) [see pages 23–31 for a copy of the Wisconsin law of 1911].

domestic market, of general trading and credit conditions." His dependence on nature gave him little voice in any attempt to regulate the output. On these grounds supporters of agricultural interests based their plea for special treatment fitted to the farmer's "peculiar needs."[18]

Wisconsin and Minnesota also enacted legislation requiring the collection of information about cooperatives. In Minnesota, by a law of 1913, the department of agriculture of the University of Minnesota was required "to collect statistics and information in reference to cooperative associations among farmers and the management and methods of conducting such associations."[19] The Wisconsin legislation antedated this and was more ambitious. The Wisconsin State Board of Public Affairs, especially created for the purpose in 1911, was authorized, in conjunction with the Legislative Reference Library, to make a careful investigation of cooperation. "This investigation was made with three objectives in mind—first, to ascertain the extent and present status of cooperation in Wisconsin; second, to learn the causes for the success of existing cooperative organizations and causes for the failures of those that had not been able to withstand the struggle; and third, to see what lessons could be derived from abroad and how they could be applied here."[20] Possibly this action indicated an awareness of the fact that the responsibility for improving the business side of farming should not be left to sentimentalists, promoters, and more or less erratic farmers, but instead should be taken over by people who wanted to investigate the field in its entirety and to proceed along scientific lines.

The federal government gave slight attention to the farmers' marketing problems until the farmers themselves had taken the initiative in setting up their associations and had exerted considerable political pressure in their respective states. The Department of Agriculture, for the most part, had contented itself with impressing upon the farmers the necessity for bettering the quality of their produce and increasing it in quantity. Never-

18. Tobriner, in *Columbia Law Review,* XXVII (November, 1927), pp. 828–31; Tobriner, "The Constitutionality of Cooperative Marketing Statutes," *California Law Review,* XVII (November, 1928), pp. 25–26.

19. L. D. H. Weld, "Statistics of Cooperation among Farmers in Minnesota," *University of Minnesota Agricultural Experiment Station, Bulletin 146* (St. Paul, 1914), p. 3.

20. Campbell, in *American Review of Reviews,* XLVII (April, 1913), p. 470.

theless, the department had taken a few preliminary steps in the direction of improving the farmers' marketing conditions. It had gathered some information on the subject, had developed techniques for dealing with it, and had trained the necessary personnel for the study of the problem.[21] It had even made a study, in 1911–12, of a few cooperative cotton associations, and had furnished them with some suggestions for the improvement of the methods they employed in the handling and marketing of cotton. But with the creation of the Office of Markets and Rural Organization in 1913 there was a change of pace. Thereafter the collection of statistical information on cooperatives became a major undertaking.[22]

During these early years the state colleges of agriculture contributed even less than the United States Department of Agriculture to the growth of cooperative marketing, and, even harder to understand, they showed an astonishing indifference to the whole subject of agricultural economics. The guiding policy of the colleges of agriculture in the earlier days had been to make two blades of grass grow where only one had grown before and to apply "a knowledge of the laws of the 'natural' sciences to the practical operations of the farm." Of the state universities in the western Middle West, the University of Wisconsin was among the first, if not the first, to offer a course in the "Economics of Agriculture." This course, conducted by Professor William A. Scott "especially for agricultural students," was listed in the university catalogue as early as 1892–93.[23] Three or four years later, the Office of Experiment Stations of the United States Department of Agriculture sponsored a committee on instruction in agriculture which reported that rural economics should be recognized as a division of the science of agriculture. The treatment of the subject by the

21. J. T. Horner, "The United States Governmental Activities in the Field of Agricultural Economics Prior to 1913," *Journal of Farm Economics,* X (October, 1928), pp. 451, 458–59.

22. Chastina Gardner, *Cooperation in Agriculture,* Farm Credit Administration, Cooperative Division, Bulletin 4 (Washington, 1936), p. 5. See also Thomas Nixon Carver, "The Organization of Rural Interests," U. S. Dept. Agri., *Yearbook,* 1913, pp. 239–58.

23. *Catalogue of the University of Wisconsin,* 1892–93, p. 60. Two courses were listed for most of the years down to 1902–3: "Agricultural Economics," designed for students in the short course in the college of agriculture, and "General Course in Agricultural Economics." *Ibid.,* 1902–3, p. 94.

committee admittedly was crude and tentative, yet it did stimulate some interest.[24] In general, however, progress was slow. In 1903, one prominent rural educator observed that "beyond elementary work in economics, in civics, and occasionally in sociology, little opportunity is given students to study the farm question from its social standpoint. With few exceptions, these institutions offer no courses whatever in rural social problems, and even in these exceptional cases the work offered is hardly commensurate with the importance of the subject."[25]

When the colleges of agriculture did begin to act, it was in Wisconsin and Minnesota, where the cooperative movement had reached significant proportions, that the first serious beginnings were made. T. L. Haecker, of the University of Minnesota Agricultural Experiment Station, launched his campaign for the establishment of cooperatives as early as 1891, but it was not until 1908–9 that the University of Minnesota listed a course on the "Economics of Agriculture," dealing with such subjects as markets, prices, transportation, farm ownership, size, organization, and the labor system. In 1902–3 the University of Wisconsin offered a course in agricultural economics under the instructorship of Henry C. Taylor, thereby blazing a path for which its college of agriculture was to become justly famous. Taylor's book, *An Introduction to the Study of Agricultural Economics,* the first to bear in its title the term "agricultural economics," appeared in 1905. But in spite of its title, Taylor's text had no section dealing with marketing, rural finance, agricultural labor, wages, standards of living, cost of transportation, taxation, or related problems.[26] By 1911 Professor C. J. Galpin of the University of Wisconsin began his studies in

24. Alfred C. True, *A History of Agricultural Education in the United States, 1785–1925,* U. S. Dept. Agri., Misc. Publication 36 (Washington, 1929), p. 253.

25. Kenyon L. Butterfield, "American Agricultural Education," *Popular Science Monthly,* LXIII (July, 1903), pp. 257–58.

26. *Report upon the Survey of the University of Wisconsin: Findings of the State Board of Public Affairs and its Report to the Legislature* (Madison, [1915]), pp. 949–50; Andrew Boss, "Minnesota Agricultural Experiment Station, 1885–1935," *University of Minnesota Agricultural Experiment Station, Bulletin 319* (St. Paul, 1935), pp. 34–35; *The College of Science, Literature, and the Arts, 1908–1909,* University of Minnesota Bulletin (Minneapolis, May 26, 1908), p. 100; Edwin G. Nourse, "Agricultural Economics," in *Encyclopaedia of the Social Sciences* (15 vols., New York, 1930–35), I, 534–35.

the problems of rural Wisconsin, and two years later Professor B. H. Hibbard of the same institution gave the first extensive course in cooperation and marketing. That same year Professor George F. Warren of Cornell published a notable book entitled *Farm Management*. These three schools—Minnesota, Wisconsin, and Cornell—were well in the lead on these subjects. Most agricultural colleges, as late as 1914, had not even started to investigate them, or else had made only "a gingerly beginning, in abstract, general ways."[27]

Since cooperatives developed chiefly in regions specializing in the production of a particular commodity, it was hardly surprising that the first successful cooperatives to be found in any number were among the dairy producers. By the year 1900 no less than 549 dairy associations had been organized in the United States, most of them during the last decade of the century.[28] By 1915 the number of dairy cooperatives exceeded those of any other commodity. Minnesota then had more dairy associations than any other state; Wisconsin ranked second, and Iowa third; but by 1925 Minnesota and Wisconsin had changed places. In 1915 the Minnesota cooperatives had the most members, with those in Wisconsin and Iowa next in line; but by 1925, New York had jumped into the lead, with Minnesota, Wisconsin, and Pennsylvania following in the order mentioned. In 1915 Wisconsin ranked first in the amount of the cooperative business transacted, trailed by Minnesota, Iowa, and Michigan. But by 1925, Minnesota had moved into first place, New York into second, Wisconsin into third, and California into fourth. Most of the shifts in position that occurred during this decade can be accounted for by the relative growth of the cooperative marketing of fluid milk.[29]

The first organizations of dairy producers were effected in order to manufacture cheese and butter on a cooperative basis. As early as 1810, the dairy producers of Connecticut had made unsuccessful efforts to organize; and it appears on fairly good authority that it was a group of farmers in Rock Lake, Jefferson County, Wisconsin, who in 1841 first banded together to form a "cheese ring" to manufacture their cheese on

27. *Survey of the University of Wisconsin*, pp. 945, 947–49.
28. F.F.B., *Statistics of Farmers' Selling and Buying Associations*, p. 4.
29. Elsworth, *Agricultural Cooperative Associations*, pp. 36–37.

a cooperative basis. These "cheese rings," because they saved labor and commanded better prices for their product, soon began to appear in great numbers in Massachusetts, New York, and Wisconsin.[30]

Wisconsin made rapid strides as a cooperative cheese-manufacturing state. Favorable climatic and topographical conditions, a growing foreign demand, and the coming of Swiss immigrants helped the cheese industry off to a good beginning. The influx of the Swiss, beginning about 1845, into Green County and the adjoining parts of Iowa and Lafayette counties contributed greatly to the growth of cooperative cheese making, but the knowledge, skills, and habits of these people were not enough to reproduce the Swiss cheese industry. Superior Swiss cheese required a milk of higher quality than that used to make ordinary cheddar, limburger, or brick. When economic forces compelled an adjustment to geographic conditions, the cheese factories had to locate "on the highlands to the west and along the Lake Michigan shore counties to the northeast."[31] Furthermore, the "old dairy farm" system of production soon began to give way to the cheese factory, which was better equipped, reduced wastage and manufacturing costs, and produced a more nearly uniform product for market. Freed from the work of cheese making at home, the dairy farmer was now able to keep more cows and to give them better attention than ever before. It was estimated that in 1915 there were 718 cooperative and 1,211 private cheese factories in Wisconsin.[32]

Once the dairy producers had succeeded in manufacturing their cheese

30. *Cooperative Marketing* (70 Congress, 1 session, Senate Document 95, serial 8859, Washington, 1928), p. 7; for early data on cooperative cheese production in the United States, see Steen, *Coöperative Marketing,* pp. 156–57.

31. S. M. Babcock and H. L. Russell, "The Cheese Industry: Its Development and Possibilities in Wisconsin," *University of Wisconsin Agricultural Experiment Station, Bulletin 60* (Madison, 1897), pp. 5–6; H. C. Taylor and C. E. Lee, "Progress of the Dairy Industry in Wisconsin," *ibid., Bulletin 210* (1911), pp. 24–26. See also H. L. Russell, "Dairy Industry in Wisconsin," *ibid., Bulletin 88* (1901); O. E. Baker, "Agricultural Regions of North America," *Economic Geography,* II (October, 1926), p. 464; Glenn T. Trewartha, "The Green County, Wisconsin, Foreign Cheese Industry," *ibid.,* (April, 1926), pp. 292–308.

32. E. H. Farrington and G. H. Benkendorf, "Organization and Construction of Creameries and Cheese Factories," *University of Wisconsin Agricultural Experiment Station, Bulletin 244* (Madison, 1915), p. 3; B. H. Hibbard and Asher Hobson, "Markets and Prices of Wisconsin Cheese," *ibid., Bulletin 251* (1915), pp. 24–28 (see map on page 22).

cooperatively, they logically turned their attention to marketing it in the same way. In the beginning, the factories sold individually to country buyers who purchased on their own account or as representatives of dealers in central markets. As the industry developed, cheese boards sprang up at various points where buyers and sellers met, generally once a week, to transact business. The boards, in line with what happened in the purchase and sale of other commodities, established base prices for the purchase of cheese. Eventually the cheese board at Plymouth, Wisconsin, made up of important cheese dealers and producers, came to dominate the market and became the chief factor in determining the price of cheese in the United States.[33]

Equally important in Wisconsin was the cooperative marketing of butter. A survey conducted in 1914 by the Wisconsin State Dairy and Food Commission revealed that 380 creameries were cooperatively owned. Two years later these cooperatives represented 45 per cent of all the creameries in the state and paid the farmers better than three cents a pound more for their butterfat than the prices offered by the private creameries; they also paid their buttermakers $10 a month more than the wages current in the private creameries. The cooperatives were able to do this because they could command a higher price for their butter; also, they were in a better position than the private owners to control the quality of their cream.[34]

The development of the cooperative creamery movement in Minnesota was equally remarkable. In this state dairying began first to supplement, then to supplant the raising of wheat. As has already been noted, the name of Theophilus Levi Haecker loomed large in the history of Minnesota's dairy industry. Born of German immigrant stock in Ohio on May 4, 1846, Haecker moved with his parents to Dane County, Wisconsin, seven years later. Here he eventually acquired a reputation as a dairy farmer and made the acquaintance of William R. Taylor, the Granger governor of Wisconsin. Haecker became a leader in local Grange affairs;

33. Senate Document 95, 70 Congress, 1 session, p. 10; Steen, *Coöperative Marketing*, pp. 158–63.

34. B. H. Hibbard and Asher Hobson, "The Marketing of Wisconsin Butter," *University of Wisconsin Agricultural Experiment Station, Bulletin 270* (Madison, 1916), pp. 3–11, 66–69.

he joined in cooperative marketing and purchasing activities, helped organize a cooperative creamery and subsequently a cooperative fire insurance venture. As a clerk in the governor's office for seventeen years, Haecker developed a keen appreciation of public needs and became closely identified with a movement to promote a "more practical education" for the students of the University of Wisconsin's college of agriculture. In 1891, Haecker himself enrolled in the university's department of dairy husbandry, reputedly the first of its kind in the world. His superiors immediately recognized his practical knowledge of buttermaking; first he was made an assistant and later he was placed in full charge of "the home dairy work." That same year he went to the University of Minnesota as an instructor in buttermaking.

On moving to Minnesota, Haecker recommended that the farmers there make butter the main product of the state. In the manufacture of cheese, they would be unable to compete with Wisconsin, with its more advantageous freight rates. On Haecker's urging, the Minnesota dairy school placed its principal emphasis on high-quality butter and the control of conditions surrounding buttermaking. A short course was established to train the older men who were already engaged in the industry, while the full-school-year courses prepared the younger men. It is estimated that some 2,500 creamery operators, trained in the dairy division of the University of Minnesota, were influenced directly or indirectly by Haecker's training.[35]

Haecker knew the history of cooperative experiments in Wisconsin well, from Granger times on down, and was particularly impressed by the program of a Danish community at Clarks Grove in Freeborn County, Minnesota. With this as a model, he took steps to promote the cause of cooperative creameries throughout Minnesota. To answer requests for information, he prepared a bulletin, "Organizing Co-operative Creameries," which was published by the University of Minnesota Agricultural Experiment Station. This marked the beginning of a development which was not to stop until the Minnesota producers became nationally famous. When Haecker began to advocate cooperatives, there were probably not more than four cooperative creameries in Minnesota. Ten years later the

35. E. E. Edwards, "T. L. Haecker, The Father of Dairying in Minnesota," *Minnesota History*, XIX (June, 1938), p. 149–57.

number was almost double that of any other state and nearly one-third of the total in the country. In 1914, 42 per cent of the Minnesota farmers were patrons of the cooperative creameries, which comprised 72 per cent of all creameries in the state. Because of this situation, the butter industry in Minnesota was controlled by the farmers to a greater degree than in any other state. These cooperatives, after about thirty years of operation, formed the foundation for the Land O'Lakes Creameries, Incorporated, "probably the greatest butter marketing organization in the world."[36]

The cooperative movement among the dairy producers of Iowa was far behind those of both Wisconsin and Minnesota. Lacking the high quality of leadership which characterized the movements in these states, it endured a long period of trial and error. Nevertheless the Iowa dairy producers had certain common grievances which tended to bind them together. They were often kept waiting a full month before they learned the quality of the milk they sold and almost an equally long time before they knew what prices they were to be paid. If they objected to the price, there was little they could do about it; if there was any inaccuracy, waste, or dishonesty in handling their produce, all they could do was to complain, or go elsewhere and be treated worse. The cause for "nine-tenths" of the Iowa dairy farmer's dissatisfaction, according to one observer, was suspicion over the testing of his milk. Efforts to regulate the method of testing proved unsuccessful, and the discontented farmer, however groundless his suspicion, was on the alert for some means to redress the grievance he felt. Nor was this the only complaint. Sometimes the farmer suffered from insufficient competition among dealers, sometimes from excessive competition. Sometimes there was a lack of satisfactory outlets. The "one-price system" of paying for butterfat also caused great indignation. Often farmers producing high-grade cream received no premium whatsoever, a policy which naturally checked any incentive to improve the quality.[37]

Once the advantages of the cooperative creamery became apparent, whether in Iowa or elsewhere, promoters of various types began to invade

36. Boss, in *Minnesota Bulletin 319,* pp. 34–35; Weld, in *Minnesota Bulletin 146,* pp. 6–7.

37. Iowa Department of Agriculture, *Iowa Yearbook of Agriculture,* 1902, pp. 471–73; Frank Robotka and Gordon C. Laughlin, *Cooperative Organization of Iowa Farmers' Creameries,* Farm Credit Administration, Cooperative Division, Bulletin 14 (Washington, 1932), p. 1.

the field and plague the producers. Perhaps the situation in North Dakota during the first decade of the twentieth century was typical. Promoters, representing manufacturers of creamery machinery and equipment, encouraged farmers to build creameries in communities where not enough milk could be produced to support them. Real estate agents, eager to draw in settlers from the eastern dairy states, aided the promoters, regardless of the disaster that would inevitably follow. The promoters were merely interested in making cash sales, while the real estate agents cared little whether the creamery failed or succeeded, if only they could make land sales. Nearly 40 per cent of local creameries in North Dakota were built at the instigation of outside promoters. It should have occasioned no surprise that creameries established under such conditions failed. Out of 133 creameries established in the state between 1888 and 1923, not less than 107 failed, mostly because of the excessive competition between creameries for an inadequate supply of cream. Other trouble came from poor management, dishonest officials, and poor workmanship.[38]

Perhaps more representative of middle western agrarian discontent than the dairy farmers' cooperatives, and eventually more numerous, were the local grain-marketing associations. The organizations of these locals took on exceptional earnestness about 1900, and over the next twenty years nearly 4,000 of them were set up to receive and ship grain.[39]

The roots of the cooperative grain-marketing movement are to be found in the unfavorable marketing conditions which accompanied the expansion of wheat growing following the Civil War. During the seventies, the Grange had been instrumental in organizing a number of grain elevators, many of them cooperative, but largely because of mismanagement nearly all of them failed after a few years of operation. This left the country grain business in the hands of independent dealers who competed with one another fiercely, with disastrous results for many operators. Among the problems that perplexed them were overbidding for grain, dishonesty among weight masters and commission men on the primary market, and leaky cars which lost much of the grain en route to the market.

38. Alva H. Benton, "Marketing Dairy Products," *North Dakota Agricultural College Experiment Station, Bulletin 182* (Agricultural College, N. Dak., 1924), pp. 11–15.

39. F.F.B., *Statistics of Farmers' Selling and Buying Associations*, pp. 4, 43, 71.

To remedy this situation, the tendency was for a large number of dealers to join together in associations. By employing inspectors and grain masters to look after the interests of the group, they succeeded in checking many of the abuses. Once success was realized, the grain dealers did not always use their power to the advantage of the farmer. They made track buyers, for example, whom they had always looked upon with disfavor, the special object of their displeasure. Track buyers could quote higher prices for grain than other purchasers because they had little capital invested, paid no taxes, and stayed in business only while conditions were favorable. In one fashion or another the dealers' associations managed to squeeze them out.

Also of great importance in the grain trade were the activities of the commercial line companies, backed as they were by the abundant capital of exporters and commission firms and favored also by the railroads along which their elevators were located. Often the managers and large investors in these lines were stockholders or directors of the railroads that served them; hence the way was wide-open to special treatment, including cheaper rates. Line companies, when they chose, could make conditions intolerable for the independents. Sometimes they offered to buy an independent elevator outright, and if the owner refused, company officials might even threaten to build a new elevator and "run him out." Compelled to choose between financial ruin and compliance with the line companies' requests, hundreds of independents in the upper Mississippi Valley were obliged to choose the latter alternative.

Farmers soon detected a high degree of uniformity in the prices that the line companies offered them; only when local competitive conditions forced them to it did the line companies pay high prices. A. J. Hoskins, the price agent for a group of 39 elevator companies controlling from 900 to 1,000 elevators in Minnesota and the Dakotas, testified before the Interstate Commerce Commission in 1906 that he received from a committee representing the companies daily price quotations which he, in turn, communicated to the local elevators.[40]

The system of country grading and inspection of grain was another constant source of discontent. Local agents examined the farmers' grain

40. Oscar N. Refsell, "The Farmers' Elevator Movement," *Journal of Political Economy,* XXII (November, 1914), pp. 874–85.

for weed seeds, dirt, shrunken kernels, and other foreign materials, and then decided the allowance for dockage to be deducted. The method in common use was to pass a sample of the grain through a sieve and by a series of siftings to separate out the refuse. Weighing the grain to determine its grade was the next step; for this a "hand tester" or "test kettle" was used. Once the grade and weight had been determined, a price per bushel was offered.

According to the Federal Trade Commission, the highly competitive character of the country grain trade had forced many agents, seeking grain for their respective companies, to overgrade the grain offered them and then to resort to heavy allowance for dockage and underweighing in order to offset the overgrading. This became the practice especially when the farmer threatened to take his grain to a neighboring elevator. A sympathetic agent, often influenced by the deep-seated rural prejudices against the line company which he represented, or possibly by having himself been a farmer, or, as was very common, by having relatives who were farmers, was naturally tempted to overgrade the grain. And, since grading was largely a matter of individual judgment, the agent could hardly be taken to task for what he had done.[41]

But whatever favors were shown the farmer in the grading of his grain were generally more than offset by the system of cleaning grain that was customary. Farmers who cleaned their grain before hauling it to market had less of a problem than those who depended on the elevator for this service. Sometimes the dockage was returned to the farmer, who paid a charge for the cleaning of his grain; in other cases, the elevators performed the service gratis. Neither of these methods caused any difficulty, because in both instances the dockage was returned to the farmer. But there was trouble when the elevator kept the dockage and gave the farmer nothing for it. In defense of this practice it could be argued that the elevator was entitled to the dockage in compensation for the services it provided.[42]

The exact beginnings of the cooperative grain-elevator movement are unknown. It is well established that the Grange, the Farmers' Alliance,

41. *Report of the Federal Trade Commission on the Grain Trade* (7 vols., Washington, 1920–1926), I, 99–103; *The Application of Dockage in the Marketing of Wheat,* U. S. Dept. Agri., Farmers' Bulletin 919 (Washington, 1917), pp. 3–4.

42. F.T.C., *The Grain Trade,* I, 8–9, 204–6.

and the Farmers' Mutual Benefit Association were in the vanguard of the movement. Farmer elevators were in existence in Iowa during the sixties, in Kansas and Minnesota during the seventies, and in the Dakotas by the nineties.[43] Specific information on their existence in Wisconsin and Illinois is slight, yet the presumption is very strong that they were in existence in both states during these early years. In Iowa, where the grain-marketing activities were undoubtedly representative of those in other states, the earliest of the farmer elevators began its short career in Blairstown about 1867 or 1868, one or two years before the state Grange was established.

The majority of the early cooperative elevators were incorporated as regular stock companies, and the others as voluntary associations; there were few evidences of the payment of patronage dividends or the employment of other standard cooperative practices. There was a tendency, however, to limit the amount of stock issued and to restrict control to the organizers.[44]

The decline in the cooperative elevator movement, which set in following the first flush of Granger enthusiasm, revealed some serious defects in methods of organization and operation. The most common fault was insufficient funds, but some of the cooperatives failed because they had been set up in areas where a shift was in progress from wheat to livestock raising. An inadequate grasp of the complexities of the grain business, Granger politics, and rivalry for office added to the difficulties of the cooperatives, made competition with private grain dealers difficult, and contributed to the mortality rate.[45]

The spread of the Farmers' Alliance during the 1880's witnessed an earnest effort to re-establish the farmers in the grain business. This second period of cooperative activity found the private grain interests stronger and more firmly entrenched than ever before; it was, indeed, a period in which combinations both in industry and in transportation were the order of the day. Faced by stronger opposition, the cooperatives sought to adopt a stronger form of organization and to devise means to secure the

43. Nourse, in *Iowa Bulletin 211*, p. 236; *Nineteenth Biennial Report of the Kansas State Board of Agriculture* (1915), pp. 24, 155–56; Fossum, *Agrarian Movements in North Dakota*, p. 161. See also Senate Document 95, 70 Congress, 1 session, p. 54.

44. Nourse, in *Iowa Bulletin 211*, pp. 236–39.

45. *Ibid.*, pp. 239–40.

permanent support of their members. The most novel of the innovations was the "maintenance" or "penalty clause," which provided that any member who sold to a private dealer was required to compensate the cooperative elevator by paying into its treasury a specified sum, usually from one-half to one cent per bushel on all grain sold. At least four Iowa farmers' elevators are known to have adopted such clauses during the eighties and nineties: one in Marcus in 1887 and three others in Rockwell, Rockford, and Rock Valley in 1889, 1891, and 1892, respectively. The object of the penalty clause was to bind the farmers to their own elevators, and to some extent it seems to have succeeded. In spite of the continued opposition of the line companies and the hard times of the 1890's, the cooperative movement endured. In Iowa alone it has been estimated that between 1897 and 1903 from two to seven elevators were organized each year, despite the persistent and well-organized opposition.[46]

The success of the cooperatives in dealing with their opponents is well illustrated by events that transpired in Iowa following the organization in 1900 of the Iowa Grain Dealers' Association. This association provided for a union of forces between the independent dealers and the line companies, who together considered themselves entitled to the entire grain business. Through the association these two groups entered into agreements over prices and the sharing of all available business. But the farmer cooperatives were quick to retaliate. Meeting in Rockwell in November, 1904, the representatives of seventeen farmer elevators launched a counter-association known as the Iowa Farmers' Grain Dealers Association. The object of this new agency was to assist farmers who wanted to handle their own grain business in the formulation of suitable by-laws and in the adoption of sound methods of operation. The success of its propaganda is attested by the fact that the number of farmer elevator companies in Iowa grew from 30 in 1904 to 511 in 1921. Aid of various kinds was offered by the state association: legal advice, commercial information, an auditing service, information regarding competent managers, advice on the selection of elevator sites and the erection of buildings. As the farmer elevators grew in numbers, their bargaining strength won them better treatment from the railroads and from terminal purchasers. They also had a large part in the passage of the Iowa cooperative law of 1915. By 1913

46. *Ibid.*, pp. 241–46.

similar associations had been formed in six out of the nine states of the western Middle West. In the Nebraska state association, organized in 1903, grain and livestock producers joined forces to form the Farmers' Co-operative Grain and Livestock Association.[47]

Thus, despite all opposition, the farmer elevator movement continued to grow. From Illinois and Iowa it had spread into the Dakotas, Kansas, Minnesota, Nebraska, Wisconsin, and Indiana. Besides being engaged in the marketing of grain, some, but by no means all, of the farmer elevators handled coal, lumber, farm implements, bricks, drainage tile, flour and feed, binder twine, oils, kerosene, and gasoline. Some elevators also traded in livestock. In general, the establishment of a farmers' elevator at any given point meant a higher local price for grain, and as knowledge of this fact grew, the cooperative movement grew with it.[48]

With better control of their grain market assured, the farmers turned their attention increasingly to the great central terminal markets at Chicago, Minneapolis, Omaha, Kansas City, St. Louis, Duluth, and Milwaukee—the nerve centers of the grain business. Here were located the headquarters for all the large buyers and sellers, for the principal banks that financed the grain trade, and for the transportation companies that handled the grain. Here, too, were large accumulations of grain, stored in terminal elevators. Whatever the grievances of the farmers against the country system of grading, weighing, and cleaning, they were insignificant in comparison with those that might, and often did, arise on the terminal scene. With the growth in volume of cooperative business, the attitude of the terminal commission firms toward the farmer elevators tended to become more and more friendly. Commission firms that had formerly refused to do business with the cooperatives began to solicit their business eagerly, while those who had always been friendly to the farmers' movement flourished as never before. But the usual mixing, grading, and inspection practices at the terminals still gave rise to much farmer dissatisfaction, and the railroads were by no means free from the charge of discrimination.[49]

47. *Ibid.*, pp. 246–51. See also Refsell, in *Journal of Political Economy*, XII (December, 1914), pp. 977–78.

48. *Ibid.*, pp. 986–87.

49. *Ibid.*, pp. 978–79; Senate Document 95, 70 Congress, 1 session, p. 61.

The difficulties faced by farmer associations which tried to break into the terminal market before 1920 appear in the history of two such companies—the Equity Cooperative Exchange of St. Paul and the Farmers' Cooperative Commission Company of Hutchinson, Kansas. The Equity Cooperative Exchange of St. Paul, in spite of its name, was incorporated in North Dakota in 1911 and began its business operations in Minneapolis. There it became involved in endless difficulties with representatives and sympathizers of the Minneapolis Chamber of Commerce. It moved to St. Paul in 1914, where it set up a grain exchange and began to acquire a line of seventy or eighty local elevators scattered throughout the Dakotas, Minnesota, and Montana. Never a stable organization, the exchange experienced an endless procession of internal bickerings and litigation until it was forced into the hands of receivers in 1923. The second terminal marketing cooperative, the Farmers' Cooperative Commission Company, began operations in Hutchinson, Kansas, in 1915; in 1928, it claimed to own, operate, and control no less than fifty-four local companies and sixty country elevators. The company owned memberships on the boards of trade in Kansas City, Missouri, and in Wichita, Hutchinson, and Dodge City, Kansas. Both the Equity Cooperative Exchange and the Farmers' Cooperative Commission Company encountered their greatest opposition when they sought to obtain membership on boards of trade, for private dealers particularly resented the cooperative practice of disbursing patronage dividends. But eventually the farmers obtained state and federal legislation which prohibited boards of trade from discriminating in this way against cooperatives.[50]

Impressive as their accomplishments were, the grain-marketing cooperatives were probably not as effective as the associations formed for the marketing of livestock. In this activity the farmers of Minnesota, Wisconsin, Iowa, Nebraska, and Kansas were the pioneers. In these states the multiplication of local associations was most rapid during the years 1917 to 1920; in the latter year their volume of shipments attained record-breaking proportions. In Iowa alone on January 1, 1921, there were 610

50. *Ibid.*, pp. 61–63; Theodore Saloutos, "The Rise of the Equity Cooperative Exchange," *Mississippi Valley Historical Review,* XXXII (June, 1945), pp. 31–62; Steen, *Coöperative Marketing,* pp. 213–14; Senate Document 95, 70 Congress, 1 session, pp. 62–63.

livestock-shipping associations, plus 37 farmer elevators which bought and shipped livestock, thereby bringing the total up to 647. In Wisconsin the number in 1920 was placed at approximately 500 locals. The figures in Minnesota for 1919 show 655 locals in operation. More than one-fourth of the livestock shipped from the state of Iowa was handled by farmers' marketing organizations, while 75 per cent of the livestock sent into the South St. Paul market, and about 15 per cent of all that reached the Chicago market, was shipped by cooperative associations.[51]

In livestock marketing, as in grain marketing, both the Grange and the Farmers' Alliance had made important beginnings. Associations were organized in Iowa, Missouri, Nebraska, and Illinois during the years 1872 and 1873. Most of them were managed by agents of the Grange and operated mainly as selling agencies. As interest in the Grange declined, interest in the associations disappeared also, and few of these early cooperatives survived. Farmers' Alliance livestock cooperatives were active in Kansas, Nebraska, Iowa, and Missouri during the middle 1880's, but with the collapse of the Alliance and the growing farmer interest in politics, the livestock-shipping movement slackened.[52]

In the period from 1903 to 1920, the American Society of Equity and the Farmers' Union took the lead in furthering the livestock cooperative movement. Equity, directly or indirectly, was responsible for the establishment of associations at Postville, Iowa, in 1904, at Durand, Wisconsin, in 1906, and at Litchfield, Minnesota, in 1908. The Farmers' Union began its operations several years later in Nebraska, southern and western Iowa, Kansas, and Missouri. Iowa was ideally located for the movement to flourish. The state was surrounded by seven principal livestock markets and had within its borders, or close to them, eleven minor packing centers. Thus it could distribute its surplus hogs, cattle, and sheep to the various markets with the maximum of efficiency and a minimum of cost

51. E. G. Nourse and J. G. Knapp, *The Co-Operative Marketing of Livestock* (Washington, 1931), pp. 17–19; Nourse and Hammans, in *Iowa Bulletin 200,* pp. 404, 407; B. H. Hibbard, L. G. Foster, and D. G. Davis, "Wisconsin Livestock Shipping Associations," *University of Wisconsin Agricultural Experiment Station, Bulletin 314* (Madison, 1920), pp. 3–5; E. C. Johnson and J. B. McNulty, "Livestock Shipping Associations in Minnesota," *University of Minnesota Agricultural Experiment Station, Bulletin 302* (St. Paul, 1934), p. 3.

52. Steen, *Coöperative Marketing,* pp. 92–93.

and wastage. The earlier success scored in organizing cooperative creameries and grain elevators, plus the fact that local shipping associations were comparatively simple to organize and finance, helped promote their rapid progress.[53]

The chief incentive for the establishment of cooperative livestock shipping was the system of country buying then in use. The farmers complained bitterly of the wide margins of profit exacted by buyers, stockyards, and commission firms, the discriminatory nature of their prices, and their generally unfair trade practices. There was a strong conviction that marketing costs somehow had to be lowered. Before the local shipping associations assumed permanent form, it had been a common practice among farmers to join together in making up a carload shipment. Out of the success of these spasmodic and occasional efforts grew the decision to establish permanent marketing associations. In this instance, the association could be formed without either capital or plant. All that was needed was to assemble the livestock and ship it to market; the association itself assumed no risks by purchasing stock outright. Expenses were low, and an elaborate system of accounting was unnecessary.[54]

The advantages which the shipping associations offered the farmers best explain the rapidity of their growth. Livestock producers who shipped cooperatively got the market price, minus a minimum cost for marketing, and thus made larger profits. This was the case also in the handling of miscellaneous stock like canners or veals, when uniform shipments of stock could not be made. By shipping cooperatively, producers also became better acquainted with the market and the grades; they found it less difficult to get cars for shipments even in periods of shortages; they could ship their livestock whenever it was ready, without having to wait for a buyer to see it; they saved themselves much time and labor by the employment of a single manager; they obtained close to the market price for crippled livestock, which previously they had sold for half price; they learned that excessive losses from death, shrinkages, and injuries en route

53. Nourse and Knapp, *The Co-Operative Marketing of Livestock*, pp. 13–14; Nourse and Hammans, in *Iowa Bulletin 200*, pp. 403, 407–8; E. Dana Durand, "Cooperative Livestock Shipping Associations in Minnesota," *University of Minnesota Agricultural Experiment Station, Bulletin 15* (St. Paul, 1916), pp. 6–8.

54. Nourse and Knapp, *The Co-Operative Marketing of Livestock*, pp. 45–48; Durand, in *Minnesota Bulletin 15*, pp. 6–8.

to market could be avoided by not overfeeding their stock; they observed that better animals brought better prices, hence saw new value in scientific breeding; they got better treatment in the central market because of the larger volume handled; and finally, they enhanced the prosperity and the reputations of their local communities.[55]

The formation of local shipping associations in large numbers led naturally to the establishment of terminal livestock-marketing associations. And essentially the same reasons that induced the farmers to create local livestock cooperatives drew them into the terminal field. Here high commission rates, unfair discrimination in the services rendered, and the variety of prices paid spurred the livestock producers to compete with private firms.

The earliest farmer attempts to set up cooperative terminal agencies were by no means successful. One of the first such efforts was the American Live Stock Commission Company, organized in 1889. The shareholders in this company were the Farmers' Alliances of Kansas, Nebraska, and Missouri and the Kansas state Grange. Beginning operations in May, 1889, it soon had commission firms operating on the Chicago, Kansas City, St. Louis, and Omaha markets. With a paid-up capital of $25,000, by November 30, 1889, the company had some $40,494 in profits to divide among its stockholders. For the year which ended December 1, 1890, it collected more than $101,000 in commissions at the four markets and sold more than $2,500,000 worth of livestock. At first the Chicago manager was able to obtain a membership on the Chicago livestock exchange but this was soon lost, and without it the company was unable to operate in that center. The closing of the Chicago market was disastrous to the whole organization, and soon the other markets were also abandoned.[56]

Typical of other early failures was the Co-operative Live Stock Commission Company, organized under the laws of Colorado with a capital stock of $100,000. This company began business at Chicago and Kansas City on September 1, 1907, but speedily aroused the anger of the private firms by displaying a profit. The discriminations which followed led to

55. Hibbard, Foster, and Davis, in *Wisconsin Bulletin 314*, pp. 7–9.

56. C. G. Randall, *Cooperative Marketing of Livestock in the United States by Terminal Associations*, U. S. Dept. Agri., Technical Bulletin 57 (Washington, 1928), pp. 6–7.

a decline in its business and substantial financial losses. Eventually the company had to cease operations.[57]

Later efforts were more successful. Indeed, by the time the first World War broke out, the task of forming a cooperative of any kind had become far less difficult than in the formative years. This was due in considerable part to the provisions of the Clayton Anti-Trust Act and to the laws of the various states for the legal protection of cooperatives. The years 1915 to 1921 saw the formation of more farmers' cooperative associations than any like period either before or since. By 1921, according to one estimate, the number of such associations in the United States had reached a total of 12,000. Terminal livestock companies caught on in the new era along with the rest.

The Equity Cooperative Exchange established a terminal agency on the South St. Paul market in 1916, and two years later it began operations in Chicago. In 1917 the Nebraska Farmers' Union organized commission firms on the Omaha and the South St. Joseph markets; the following years Farmers' Union terminal agencies appeared in Sioux City, Iowa, and Kansas City, Missouri. Over the period 1917 to 1925, some twenty-five terminal agencies were established on a successful basis throughout the nation.[58]

One significant development that reflected the mounting interest in cooperatives was the government-sponsored credit system suited to the needs of agriculture.[59] Despite sharp differences over the actual credit needs of the farmers, there was a strong feeling that the existing credit institutions discriminated against them; that the farmers were in reality without organized credit; that they were obliged to pay interest rates that were far too high.[60] The Country Life Commission recognized this sit-

57. *Ibid.*, p. 8.
58. *Ibid.*, pp. 46–53, 101.

59. William I. Myers, *Cooperative Farm Mortgage Credit, 1916–1936*, Farm Credit Administration, Cooperative Division, Circular A8 (Washington, 1936), pp. 5–6.

60. Jesse E. Pope, "Agricultural Credit in the United States," *Quarterly Journal of Economics*, XXVIII (August, 1914), pp. 727–28. In critical vein, Pope wrote: ". . . there is an utter lack of adequate information as to the actual credit needs of the farmer and of the extent to which existing agencies are supplying them. . . . Credit agencies in great variety have come into being in the United States to meet the demands of an undeveloped, unstandardized agriculture. The evils of this lack of credit organization have been greatly exaggerated, but the time has probably come for more organization. . . ." *Ibid.*, p. 745.

ıation when it suggested that there be devised a method of cooperative credit through which the farmers could more easily secure loans on fair terms. The report of Senator Aldrich's National Monetary Commission contributed further to the same cause by presenting a favorable account of the German *Landschaft* system of farm-mortgage credit.[61] In addition, in 1912, President Taft called attention to the problem by asking the American ambassadors in Europe to investigate the cooperative credit systems in the countries to which they were assigned.

Perhaps more important than all this was the work of an investigating committee sent to Europe in 1912. In April of that year, the Southern Commercial Congress, mainly through the influence of David Lubin, eminent California agriculturalist, devoted a large share of its program to the rural-credits question. After some discussion the congress authorized "a commission of 70 delegates, representing 29 States and 4 Provinces of Canada," to visit Europe and report upon the cooperative credit systems there in use. This commission was joined by a congressional commission of seven set up in order to make a similar investigation. The result of their combined efforts was a joint report, but the congressional group carried its mandate a step further by submitting a draft of a proposed rural-credit bill based on the *Landschaft* system that had been operating in Germany for over a century and had been adopted more or less by England, France, and other European countries. The extent to which cooperative credit facilities had become a popular goal can be measured by the fact that in the campaign of 1912 the three principal political parties all gave this subject favorable mention in their platforms.[62]

Meanwhile, congressmen, eager to satisfy the demands of their constituents, had flooded the Sixty-third Congress with no less than seventy rural-credit measures. These proposals did not necessarily reflect the acceptance of European precedents; according to one authority, "when

61. James B. Morman, *Farm Credits in the United States and Canada* (New York, 1924), pp. 76–77.

62. Myers, *Cooperative Farm Mortgage Credit,* pp. 5–6. See also the preface of Myron T. Herrick's *Rural Credits, Land and Coöperative* (New York, 1915). Herrick discusses the German *Landschaften* in Chapters 5 to 9. Another study is found in Henry W. Wolff, *Co-operative Credit for the United States* (New York, 1917). See also Pope, in *Quarterly Journal of Economics,* XXVIII (August, 1914), pp. 728–29, for a criticism of the commission investigation on European rural credits.

one studies the measures in detail he discovers that instead of profiting by the experience of Europeans our legislators have proposed measures which these have avoided or abandoned." The measures introduced were varied in the extreme. One bill advocated that the national government make direct loans to farmers from funds obtained by the sale of government bonds. Another, assuming that farmers were in no position to conduct their own banking business, asked for the organization of land banks by would-be lenders, who could secure funds by selling the bonds of the banks. A third theory, the one brought back by the American commission, recommended the establishment of cooperative groups of farmer-borrowers who, through their associations, could secure loans from land banks deriving their original capital from the United States government. So marked were the differences, particularly over the last two proposals, that the whole matter had to be turned over to a joint subcommittee on rural credits, composed of members from both houses of Congress. The result of their deliberations was a compromise measure, known as the Federal Farm Loan Act, which became law on July 17, 1916. This law provided two types of rural credits. One was to be furnished by a system of Federal Land Banks, from which loans could be obtained only through cooperative farm-loan associations organized by borrowers; the other, by privately owned joint-stock land banks which could deal directly with individuals in need of funds.[63]

During the period of agricultural expansion that accompanied the participation of the United States in the first World War, the farmers of the nation thus had the advantage of excellent marketing cooperatives for dairy products, grain, and livestock, and a system of rural credits, based mainly on the cooperative principle. These developments may account in some measure for the success with which the farmers met the excessive demands made on them by the war; and they may also explain in part the land boom of the western Middle West that followed the war and the disastrous collapse which it suffered.

63. Myers, *Cooperative Farm Mortgage Credit,* pp. 5–6. Ruth V. Corbin, "Federal Rural Credits, 1916–1936" (unpublished master's thesis, University of Wisconsin, 1936), sheds much light on this general subject.

Chapter IV

THE IMPACT OF WAR

CERTAINLY no other section of the United States was less prepared than the Middle West for the news in August, 1914, that a general war had broken out in Europe. Nor was any section more convinced that the war was strictly Europe's war and not America's. Country dwellers from Chicago westward, while dependent to a degree on world markets for the disposal of their produce, knew little of what went on outside the United States and cared even less. Not a few of them, indeed, had migrated from the Old World to the New to get away from the turmoil and strife of Europe, with its emphasis on universal military training and its constant talk of war. No more convinced isolationists existed anywhere in America than these adopted sons and daughters and their descendants. Later, in opposing the entrance of the United States into the war, they were often less concerned about fighting against the nation of their origin than about having to fight at all. They thought that in migrating to America they had left all that behind.[1]

In commenting on the travail of Europe, *Wallaces' Farmer,* which well represented rural opinion in the Middle West, urged its readers not to take sides, but suggested at the same time that they make ready "to feed the nations." There was no thought that this American contribution should be a free offering; rather it was assumed that war trade would

1. Benton H. Wilcox, "A Reconsideration of the Character and Economic Basis of Northwestern Radicalism" (unpublished doctoral dissertation, University of Wisconsin, 1933), p. 139; *Wallaces' Farmer,* XXXIX (August 28, 1914), p. 1165.

bring American producers high profits. Reflecting smugly on the wisdom of Woodrow Wilson's policy of neutrality, the same journal held that the United States should take full advantage of the opportunity presented by the war to promote its national self-sufficiency; not only in agriculture but in industry and commerce as well the American nation should so fully develop its resources that in the future it would "be comparatively untouched by any like manifestation of madness and folly hereafter in any part of the world."[2]

The transition from a determined neutrality to a reluctant acceptance of the necessity for American intervention was made gradually and in some cases without full realization that it was being made at all. For a time middle western farmers seemed almost to ignore the fact that their new prosperity was due primarily to the war. They took comfort in the knowledge that the British navy would control the seas and so insure them a market for everything they could grow, but they overlooked the obvious inference that their incomes were closely linked with the continued successes of Allied sea power. They lauded neutrality, defended unpreparedness, and asserted insistently that the United States must keep out of the war at all costs. A few of them were even strongly pro-German and criticized freely the increasing favoritism for Great Britain and her allies shown by the American government.[3]

But at length the light began to dawn. When, in the spring of 1916, Wilson threatened to break diplomatic relations with Germany, *Wallaces' Farmer* inquired, "What hope is there for peace on earth if nations do not consider themselves bound by treaties they have signed, and by the international laws they have helped to make?"[4] By that time the same journal could face the added possibility that the United States would have to protect itself "by force of arms against all comers." Before the end of the year it had even begun to fear that Germany, in spite of her promises to Wilson, might reopen the submarine blockade. To Americans, no less than to Britons, it was now as plain as day that this would be a disaster of the first magnitude. Thus the involvement of the United States in the

2. *Ibid.* (September 25, 1914), p. 1284; (October 9, 1914), p. 1340.

3. *Ibid.* (September 11, 1914), p. 1221; XL (January 1, 1915), pp. 4–5; (June 4, 1915), p. 840; (October 8, 1915), p. 1316.

4. *Ibid.*, XLI (April 28, 1916), p. 664.

war, when it came, was by no means unanticipated. A few middle western farmers raised their voices in protest, but for the most part, like the editor of *Wallaces' Farmer,* they went along with the administration's policy. No doubt they believed at the beginning, as many others did also, that the United States could take the war comfortably, contributing only such naval activity as might be necessary to keep the sea lanes open. But eventually they left their pacificism and isolationism far behind.[5]

The role of producing whatever extra foodstuffs were needed by the fighting powers was accepted by American farmers without hesitation. The United States, wrote the editor of *Wallaces' Farmer,* must accept the "moral responsibility to feed the hungry people of the world."[6] Producers soon learned, however, that in time of war staple commodities such as wheat, livestock, and livestock products were in greatest demand, while such semiluxury foods as fresh fruits and vegetables tended to be forgotten. Furthermore, Great Britain needed American aid to overcome shortages arising from the wartime curtailment of her purchases from continental Europe. The British, for example, had depended a great deal on Denmark and the Netherlands for fats, but lack of feed for livestock in those countries, together with the grave hazards of overseas trade, kept shipments across the North Sea at a minimum. Likewise, the closing of the Dardanelles left the British short of Russian wheat. American farmers cheerfully did their best to make up all such deficits.

Probably the coming of the war had an even greater effect upon American agriculture than was generally recognized. In the three or four years immediately preceding 1914, food production had begun to catch up with the abnormal demands of urbanization. As a result, farm prices were leveling off, and, had there been no war, the price curve would probably have soon turned sharply downward. But the tremendous demands of war changed the situation completely. While the total volume of production soared sharply upward, achieving within a few years levels that might not have been reached for a generation in time of peace, prices not only tended to keep pace with production but in some cases to run far ahead. Also, drastic changes occurred in the American economy as the demands of war diverted farmers from their normal habits into new and more or

5. *Ibid.,* XLII (February 9, 1917), p. 236; (March 30, 1917), p. 564.
6. *Ibid.* (April 6, 1917), p. 604.

less unanticipated activities. Now and then a warning voice pointed out the dangers of such fundamental changes to meet a merely temporary emergency, but for the most part the food producers of America acted as if the changes made during the war would be permanent and gave little thought to the complications that were sure to arise when peace was restored.[7]

The entrance of the United States into the war speeded up tremendously the already abnormal demand for intensive food production. Assured by official propaganda that food would "win the war," farmers planted maximum crops and even brought into production much marginal or semi-marginal land—land that in normal times would not have been worked at all. According to one estimate, not fewer than 45,000,000 acres of new land were so opened up during the war decade. The policy of the government was to stimulate production, regardless of the consequences. With only a few exceptions, prices were allowed to rise in response to the pyramiding demand, and in addition to the incentive of high prices, government pamphleteers and publicists bombarded the farmers with appeals for greater production on patriotic grounds. With reasonably good weather conditions and the certainty of inflated prices, production went up amazingly. The average annual value of the American farm output from 1910 to 1914 was about six billion dollars, but by 1917 the take was thirteen billions, over fourteen billions by 1918, and nearly sixteen billions by 1919. For a year and a half after the end of the war the wave of farm prosperity continued. The obligation to feed the Allies had ceased, but the demands of war-ravaged Europe for American foodstuffs continued. And the productive powers of the American farmer remained intact.[8]

The greatest single crop demand on the United States was for wheat. In a sense this was nothing new, for heavy wheat shipments from the United States to Europe, particularly to England, were normal. Since the

7. A. B. Genung, "Agriculture in the World War Period," U. S. Dept. Agri. Yearbook, *Farmers in a Changing World* (Washington, 1940), pp. 278–80.

8. E. T. Meredith, "Report of the Secretary of Agriculture," U. S. Dept. Agri., *Yearbook,* 1916, p. 17; G. E. Mowry, "The Decline of Agriculture, 1920–1924, A Study in Economics and Politics" (unpublished master's thesis, University of Wisconsin, 1934), p. 6; Edwin G. Nourse, *Government in Relation to Agriculture* (Washington, 1940), p. 879; *Wallaces' Farmer,* XLII (April 6, 1917), p. 604.

British economy was geared to manufacturing rather than to agriculture, Great Britain had long imported greater quantities of wheat than did any other nation in the world. The leading port of entry for this commodity was Liverpool, and for years the Liverpool price of wheat had been recognized as the governing price for wheat, wherever it might be sold. Most of Great Britain's agricultural land had long since been turned into meadows and pasture, with possibly as little as 3 per cent of it in use for the growing of bread grains. After the war began, when the Russian wheat supply was cut off, there was much plowing up of ancient pastures—some of them hundreds of years old—and much replanting, but the main source of grain supply continued to be importation, principally from the United States, Canada, and the Argentine. Heavy British buying on the American market shot wheat prices upward with incredible speed. The wildest day ever witnessed on the Chicago exchange was the day that war was declared in Europe. By December, 1914, wheat was bringing about twenty-three cents per bushel more than at the same time the preceding year, and in spite of a bumper crop—Kansas alone harvested in 1914 almost twice as much wheat as the state had ever grown before—wheat prices continued to soar. By the spring of 1915 farmers at interior points were getting as high as $1.25 to $1.40 per bushel for all the wheat they could supply, and wheat exports from the United States were running to about $55,000,000 per month.[9]

The heavy demand and the high prices led naturally to a great expansion of wheat sowing in the fall of 1914 and the spring of 1915. During the decade that had preceded the war, the average annual acreage devoted to the growing of wheat had been about 48,000,000 acres, of which 30,000,000 had been in winter wheat and 18,000,000 in spring wheat. In the fall of 1914 the area sown to winter wheat was expanded by 5,000,000 acres, while in the spring of 1915 another extra 2,000,000 acres were sown to spring wheat. During the year 1915 over 60,000,000 acres of wheat were harvested, with a yield per acre that was phenomenally high. That year the United States produced more than a billion bushels of wheat, the greatest yield ever recorded up to that time and for many years to come.

9. *Ibid.*, XXXIX (August 14, 1914), p. 1110; (September 11, 1914), p. 1244; (October 16, 1914), p. 1496; (December 11, 1914), p. 1614; XLII (January 26, 1917), p. 138; Genung, in *Farmers in a Changing World,* p. 281.

Approximately one-fourth of this crop was sent abroad. So bountiful was the 1915 yield, not only in the United States but also throughout the world, that the price of wheat dropped to the prewar level of less than a dollar a bushel and remained low until the spring of 1916.[10]

Naturally this slump in price affected the acreage devoted to wheat in 1916. That year only 52,000,000 acres of wheat were harvested, and the yield—partly because of an epidemic of black rust—dropped to 636,000,000 bushels. But the war demands continued, and the price responded. By December, 1916, wheat was bringing the American farmer $1.60 a bushel, and predictions were made that if there should be another short crop the price would rise to $3.00. The effect of German resumption of submarine warfare early in 1917 caused a tremendous break in most American prices, including wheat, which dropped as much as fifteen cents a bushel; but the drop was not to last.[11] By April 1 wheat was up to $1.80, and following the entrance of the United States into the war a few days later, the rise was precipitate. Early in May, 1917, cash wheat touched the fantastic figure of $3.48 a bushel. It should be noted, however, that this sudden rise in price netted the actual dirt farmer very little, since at the time it occurred most available grain was already in the hands of speculators and distributors.[12]

The 1917 wheat yield was little or no better than that of 1916. Under authority of a sweeping Food Control Act, signed on August 10, 1917, the President set $2.20 as the minimum price for the 1917 crop. The law itself set a price of $2.00 a bushel on wheat for the 1918 crop, but gave the President authority to guarantee for a period not to exceed eighteen months whatever price he deemed necessary to ensure producers a reasonable profit. It was under the terms of this act that Herbert Hoover became Food Administrator and devoted himself assiduously to the encouragement of food production. But neither legislation nor presidential price

10. *Ibid.*, pp. 280–81.

11. *Ibid.*, pp. 281–84; *Wallaces' Farmer*, XL (July 9, 1915), p. 960; (November 12, 1915), p. 1505; XLII (February 9, 1917), p. 236; (May 25, 1917), p. 836; (August 3, 1917), p. 1096.

12. F. M. Surface, *The Stabilization of the Price of Wheat During the War and its Effect upon the Returns to the Producer* (Washington, 1925), p. 12; B. H. Hibbard, *Effects of the Great War upon Agriculture in the United States and Great Britain* (New York, 1919), p. 27.

fixing could control the weather, and the total harvest for the year was almost exactly the same as for 1916—only 650,828,000 bushels. Price fixing had come too late to ensure for all the crop the high return which the President had set. Estimates made by the Department of Agriculture indicate that the average price per bushel actually received by the American producer for his wheat in 1917 was $1.44.[13]

As noted, the Food Administration Act of 1917 set a minimum price of $2.00 per bushel for the 1918 crop in the hope that such a guaranteed high price would ensure the bountiful yield that the Allied war effort so greatly needed. The low yield of 1917 held American exports down to 138,000,000 bushels, and that figure was made possible only by the most drastic economies at home. In 1918 crop conditions were better, and the President, on June 21, 1918, used the authority given him in the Food Control Act to raise the minimum price, this time to $2.26. The net result was a harvest of 921,000,000 bushels, less by far than the bumper yield of 1915 but still a phenomenally high figure. Of this crop, 287,000,000 bushels were shipped overseas.[14]

Although the fighting part of the war came to an end officially with the armistice of November 11, 1918, the European demand for American wheat continued strong throughout 1919, and the government of the United States maintained its price guarantee to the farmers. As a result, the wheat sown was about 75,000,000 acres—the highest in all American history—and the yield came to more than 967,000,000 bushels. Of this crop about 220,000,000 bushels were exported. Strangely enough, the American farmer assumed that the wartime expansion of his wheat market abroad would continue indefinitely and made little effort to curtail production, either by abandoning marginal land or by shifting to other crops. In consequence, the wheat yield of 1920 was 833,000,000 bushels, a figure that was approximated, more or less, each year throughout the next decade. But neither the wartime market nor the European demand which had helped to sustain it continued long after the war. Furthermore, at midnight on May 31, 1920, the government guarantee on the

13. *Ibid.*, p. 29; Simon Litman, *Prices and Price Control in Great Britain and the United States during the World War* (New York, 1920), pp. 207–9, 219–21.

14. Surface, *Stabilization of the Price of Wheat*, p. 17; Genung, in *Farmers in a Changing World*, pp. 282–83.

price of wheat was removed and wheat dropped precipitately, thus laying among wheat farmers firm foundations for an era of discontent.[15]

The wartime boom in wheat was paralleled closely by a similar expansion of the corn-livestock industry. The heaviest items of meat export from the United States to Europe, both before and during the war, were pork and pork products, especially lard. With regard to these items the same as with wheat, the war did not so much serve to open up a new type of market for American produce abroad as to accentuate an already existing market. About 12 per cent of American pork and pork products had been shipped overseas in the prewar years, and during the war this proportion was approximately doubled. The average lard export from the United States to Great Britain during the five prewar years was about 450,000,000 pounds; by 1919 it was over a billion pounds.[16]

The effect of the acute wartime demand upon livestock producers was in most respects similar to its effect on the growers of wheat. But there were differences. A constant factor in the livestock industry that had no parallel in the wheat industry was the relation between the price of corn and the price of livestock, particularly hogs. If the price of corn rose more rapidly than the price of hogs, the tendency was for the farmer to sell his hogs rather than to buy expensive corn to fatten them. Corn prices were affected not only by the demand for feed, but also by the size and quality of the corn crop in a given year and by the export demand, which shot up considerably during the war period. Principally because of two bad years, 1916 and 1918, corn production during the war showed practically no increase over prewar years. There was some importation of Argentine corn, but this was more than offset by wartime exportation to Europe. As a result of these various factors, corn prices tended, from the feeders' point of view, to be abnormally high in proportion to the price obtainable for hogs. In the fall of 1914, for example, corn sold for nearly seventy-five cents a bushel, much too high a price to justify feeding it to hogs, which were then selling at the comparatively low price of about $8.00 per hundredweight. According to a well-established rule-of-thumb ratio current

15. *Ibid.*, pp. 283; *Statistical Abstract of the United States,* 1923, p. 181; F. M. Surface, *The Grain Trade during the World War* (New York, 1928), p. 459; E. G. Nourse, *American Agriculture and the European Market* (New York, 1924), p. 79.
16. Genung, in *Farmers in a Changing World,* pp. 286–87.

in farmer circles, for each hundred pounds of hog the producer should receive thirteen or fourteen times the average cost per bushel of the corn fed to the hogs. Hence, with seventy-five-cent corn, the price of hogs should have been not less than $9.75 per hundredweight rather than $8.00. One curious result of this imbalance was that more and more hogs were thrown on the market, thus keeping the hog price down.[17]

By the year 1916 the hog price had begun to rise, but the amount of pork and pork products available for shipment overseas was not nearly enough to supply the demand. With the entrance of the United States into the war and the creation of the Food Administration, every effort was made to remedy this situation. The Food Administration, however, made no attempt to fix livestock prices in a manner as forthright as it used in pegging the price of wheat. What it did instead was to enlist the cooperation of the middlemen. In this way it sought to assure a price of $15.50 per hundredweight for hogs, and to manipulate the corn-hog ratio in such fashion that the farmer would be ensured thirteen times the average cost per bushel of the corn fed into the hogs for each hundred pounds of hog ready for market. In the fall of 1917 the Chicago Board of Trade put a maximum price of $1.28 on all future deliveries of corn and refused to permit a higher price to be quoted.[18]

While the Food Administration found it impracticable to maintain the thirteen-to-one ratio, it did succeed in keeping hog prices at a reasonably high figure. In the fall of 1917 hogs averaged about $15 per hundredweight; by September, 1918, they reached $17.50; and by the summer of 1919 they stood at over $19. Although this was less than the farmers claimed they needed, it was enough to stimulate production. Exports of lard in 1917 had actually dropped below the figure for the year before, but in 1918 they rose by more than 47 per cent, and in 1919 by nearly 39 per cent more. Exports of such pork products as bacon, ham, and shoulders showed similar enormous gains. Here again the way was paved for a

17. *Ibid.*, p. 284; *Statistical Abstract of the United States*, 1920, p. 146; *Wallaces' Farmer*, XXXIX (September 18, 1914), p. 1256; XL (March 19, 1915), p. 480; XLI (February 25, 1916), p. 310; XLIII (April 12, 1918), p. 640; (October 11, 1918), p. 1466.

18. Genung, in *Farmers in a Changing World*, p. 286; *Wallaces' Farmer*, XLIII (March 15, 1918), pp. 484–85.

terrific collapse after the war, whenever the foreign demand for American supplies returned to normal.[19]

The beef cattle story repeats the corn-hog story with variations. Most important of the differences was the fact that the Argentine, rather than the United States, had been the chief source of supply for Europe before the war and no doubt would have continued in that capacity during the war but for the shipping shortage. With shipping at a premium, however, as the war wore on the short trip across the North Atlantic tended to overbalance the higher cost of United States beef, so that American exports of this commodity grew by leaps and bounds. Whereas total exports of beef from the United States had reached only 150,000,000 pounds in 1914, four years later the figure was 954,000,000. The increase in beef production necessary to make these figures possible was not accomplished without earnest effort. Beef cattle require pasture, and the tendency of the times, as already noted, was to plow up pastures and meadows, even in regions of inadequate rainfall, in order to plant wheat or other grain. Moreover, although Americans patriotically ate less pork during the war, their consumption of beef actually showed a per capita increase.[20]

While the Food Administration neither made a price guarantee, as in the case of wheat, nor designated a fair price, as with hogs, it did promise to do its best to see that the cattle growers were adequately remunerated. In its efforts to support the market, however, the Food Administration had always to keep an eye on the American consumer, whose cries of anguish as prices rose had strong political repercussions. Farmers claimed that in response to consumer protests the Food Administration actually urged the packers to keep their prices down, much to the disadvantage of the producer. Actually, beef prices advanced from an average of $6.24 in 1914 to $9.56 in 1919, while at the end of the war superior beef-steer cattle brought as high as $17.50 per hundredweight on the Chicago market. So stimulated, the cattle industry expanded in spite of all obstacles. When the war ended the number of beef cattle owned by American farmers had increased by 20 per cent. Just what was to happen when

19. Hibbard, *Effects of the Great War upon Agriculture,* p. 132; *Statistical Abstract of the United States,* 1920, p. 497.

20. Genung, in *Farmers in a Changing World,* pp. 287–88; *Wallaces' Farmer,* XLIII (March 22, 1918), p. 539; XLIV (April 11, 1919), p. 853.

the normal flow of beef from the Argentine to Europe began again, few seemed to consider.[21]

The dairy industry was in general less disturbed by the war than other major farm activities in the western Middle West. The first serious impact of war upon dairy farmers came during the years 1915 and 1916, when the price of milk failed to rise along with those of other commodities. Since the cost of producing milk had risen with the higher prices that had to be paid for feed and labor, the dairy farmers soon found themselves well along the road to bankruptcy. For this situation they blamed the distributors of milk, especially those in such metropolitan areas as Chicago and Des Moines, whom the farmers accused of setting prices regardless of the effect on the producers. Made desperate by this situation, some dairy farmers sold their cows and got out of business, but others made use of existing milk-producers' associations to force a rise in the price of milk. A climax was reached late in October, 1917, when the Milk Producers' Association, an organization of about 16,000 dairy farmers, threatened to stop the shipment of milk into the Chicago market unless the demand of the producers for $3.42 per hundred pounds was met. At this point the state food administrator decided to intervene by appointing an arbitration commission whose job it was to name the price to be paid the producer. This price was to be based on the cost of production plus a reasonable profit to the producer and the cost of distribution plus a reasonable profit to the distributor. Pending an investigation the producer was to accept $3.22 per hundred and the distributor was to retail it at 12 cents a quart. An agreement relative to price was reached only after a mass of data had been compiled on feed and labor costs. The prices per hundredweight first agreed upon to be paid the dairy farmers in 1918 were: February, $3.07; March, $2.83; April, $2.49; May, $2.04; June, $1.80. After further discussions the price to be paid for milk in March was raised from $2.83 to $3.10 per hundred, and the prices to be paid during the following months were to be based on figures published by the United States Department of Agriculture.[22]

21. Genung, in *Farmers in a Changing World,* p. 287.

22. Hibbard, *Effects of the Great War upon Agriculture,* pp. 136–45; *Wallaces' Farmer,* XLI (April 21, 1916), p. 633; XLII (August 10, 1917), p. 1104; (October 12, 1917), p. 1376; XLIII (May 24, 1918), p. 848; (August 2, 1918), p. 1104; XLIV

Eventually, particularly toward the end of the war, the prices of dairy products increased substantially, although in the case of milk and butterfat never in comparable degree with the prices of feedstuffs. By 1918 dairy products had registered an average increase of 70 per cent, while the farm price of butter had risen from 25 cents at the beginning of the war to 54 cents at its close. Even the high price of butter did not serve to keep up butter production, which declined during the last two years of the war in spite of heavy exports—34,000,000 pounds in 1919, compared with an average of 4,250,000 pounds in the five prewar years. Butter exports, however, were small in comparison with total production; only 2 per cent of the American output was sent overseas. Most important of the dairy industry products from the export point of view were cheese and evaporated milk. The demand for American cheese abroad increased the total export of that item during the war from an initial 1 per cent of the total amount manufactured to a final 12 per cent. Evaporated milk by the end of the war was exported to the extent of 853,000,000 pounds, nearly half the total produced in the United States and nearly fifty times the prewar export figures. Thus the dairy industry, whatever the complaints of the milk producers, was given a real lift by the war. The number of milk cows on farms increased during the war more than 8.5 per cent, and the total output of cheese, butter, and evaporated milk more than 7 per cent. As long as the high wartime wages lasted, the city population could and did buy milk and other dairy products in far greater amounts than formerly. But obviously dairy farming, while expanded by the war, was not overexpanded in like degree with the wheat, corn, and livestock industries. To the milk producers, the collapse of the boom, when it came, would therefore be less distressing.[23]

The farmers of the western Middle West, whose interests lay primarily in the production of these basic foodstuffs, undoubtedly took a heavy profit out of the war. Never before had American farmers received such prices. Yet they did not think of themselves as profiteers. One authority reported that from the 1917 crop the average farmer received not more than from seventy-five cents to a dollar an hour for his labor, while the 1918 crop,

(April 25, 1919), p. 944; (May 16, 1919), p. 1065; Litman, *Prices and Price Control,* pp. 256–59.

23. *Ibid.,* pp. 190, 256–61; Genung, in *Farmers in a Changing World,* p. 288.

because of his mounting expenses, netted him even less. Indeed, the farmers sometimes felt that they had a grievance, for the government had exerted its authority by intervening directly to control the price of wheat and indirectly to keep down the prices of hogs and other agricultural products. The cost-plus method—applied so generously to packers, shipbuilders, and contractors—had not been made available to the farmers. Nor was there any way to figure the loss in fertility that came from plowing up land to expand grain growing nor the damage done by short-term tenants, whose wasteful methods greatly depreciated the value of the farms they exploited. *Wallaces' Farmer,* fascinated by the cost-of-production problem on the farm, figured that the average cost per acre to produce a field of corn was $19 in 1917 and $23 in 1918, whereas during the period 1897 to 1906 it had been $10. Good farmers might spend as much as $40 an acre on their corn. All this was very well if the price was high enough and the yield was good, but at best the farmer took grave risks. The same journal held that western farmers who had made a profit of $18 per acre on their corn in 1917 probably made not more than $9 per acre on the 1918 crop, and the next year even less. As for net returns per hour of labor, the following calculations, while by no means entirely dependable, give some idea of what the farmer thought he was making.[24]

NET RETURNS PER HOUR OF LABOR[25]

	Iowa		North Central States	
	1917	*1918*	*1917*	*1918*
Corn	.98	.88	.92	.52
Wheat	1.26	1.08	.88	1.00
Oats	1.10	.58	.98	.68
Rye	.93	.77	.84	.40
Barley	1.63	.58	.72	.23
Potatoes	1.11	.44	.85	.65
Hay	.13	- .60	.77	- .05

Although most farmers seemingly failed to see the breakers ahead, a few warning voices were raised. The editor of *Wallaces' Farmer* repeatedly pointed out that prices were bound to drop at the close of the war and

24. *Wallaces' Farmer,* XLIII (November 29, 1918), p. 1741; (December 27, 1918), p. 1891; XLIV (March 14, 1919), p. 660.
25. *Ibid.,* XLIII (December 27, 1918), p. 1891.

urged the farmers to plan accordingly. If the descent down the price ladder could be made "a rung at a time," this sagacious observer was sure that all would be well. Otherwise, he feared, "someone will get pushed off." High war wages for labor, together with high prices for manufactured goods and high prices for agricultural produce, he argued, must all come down together. Certainly the farmer ought not to bear the first full brunt of price reductions all alone. In actual fact, except for a flurry of excitement at the time of the unexpectedly early armistice, prices remained good on most farm commodities throughout 1919 and on into 1920. The price of wheat was supported by law until May 31, 1920, but such guarantees as were given on hog prices were removed in the spring of 1919 without a serious price break. Hog prices averaged over $18 per hundredweight throughout the year 1919 and $14 in 1920. But by 1921 the average was only a little over $8.[26]

By this time the boom was over and the long depression in agriculture had begun. Beginning slowly in June, hard on the disappearance of the government guarantee on wheat, the descent down the price ladder gathered momentum as the season's abundant crops poured on the market. By November 1, 1920, farm prices were 33 per cent lower than the level of the previous year; by the next midsummer, they were down 85 per cent. On the other hand, the prices of what the farmer had to buy showed no such changes. According to one estimate, a given volume of farm produce would buy only 75 per cent as much in 1921 as it would in 1914. Individual items showed an even greater disparity. In 1919 one-fifth of a bushel of corn would buy a gallon of gasoline, but in 1921 the price equivalent was two bushels of corn. In 1919 six bushels of corn would buy a ton of coal, but in 1921 it took sixty bushels. The average price paid to the Nebraska producer for his corn in November, 1921, was twenty-five cents a bushel and prices as low as eleven cents were on record. Under these circumstances it was cheaper to burn corn for fuel than to buy coal, and many farmers did exactly that. Throughout the twenties and on into the thirties the farmers' travail continued. Rural standards of living went down, and many farmers, either from choice or from necessity, gave up

26. *Ibid.*, XLIV (January 17, 1919), p. 112; (January 24, 1919), p. 185; (March 14, 1919), p. 701; *Statistical Abstract of the United States*, 1923, p. 163.

the struggle. According to one estimate, the actual number of farms and farmers was reduced during these years by a million.[27]

Probably the factor which contributed more than any other to the deepness of this depression was the land boom that had accompanied the war prices. It was natural for the farmer, with a high income for almost the first time in his life, to pay off his debts, buy new machinery, improve his property, acquire automobiles, victrolas, and other articles he had long coveted. But it was a temptation, also, to buy more land, both as a means of increasing his profits and as a means of acquiring greater wealth by speculation. When new acquisitions, whether of land or of other property, were paid for in full, the chance of catastrophe was not so great. But when, as was so often the case, the purchases were financed in part by mortgages or made on the installment plan, the purchaser was merely gambling on the continuance of high prices. Some land transactions were the sheerest speculation, with down payments comparable to the smallest margins of stock market operations in 1929. According to an Iowa observer, "Half of the people here are either land agents or speculators in land. Most of the men have never been farmers, and never will be farmers. The game is to buy and sell, and many are boasting of making thirty and forty thousand dollars in a few months. And then they say the boom is just started."[28] Nearly 95 per cent of the land buyers in Iowa paid down in cash only 10 per cent or less, and nearly three-fourths of them paid only 5 per cent or less. The initial payment, however, was merely to bind the sale, and approximately one-third of the purchase price was normally expected by the next March 1, the date usually set for giving possession to a farm. Some farmers who sold out retired to live on their fortunes; others

27. Henry C. Wallace, "The Year in Agriculture," U. S. Dept. Agri., *Yearbook*, 1920, pp. 17–18; Archibald MacDonald McIsaac, "Whither Agriculture?" in J. G. Smith, ed., *Facing the Facts: An Economic Diagnosis* (New York, 1932), p. 290; F. M. Surface, *American Food in the World War and Reconstruction Period* (Stanford, Calif., 1931), p. 114; Warren S. Thompson and P. K. Whelpton, *Population Trends in the United States* (New York, 1937), p. 19; Mowry, "Decline of Agriculture," pp. 16–19.

28. *Wallaces' Farmer*, XLIV (June 20, 1919), p. 1256. See also Archibald M. Woodruff, Jr., *Farm Mortgage Loans of Life Insurance Companies* (New Haven, Conn., 1937), pp. 19–23; E. R. A. Seligman, *The Economics of Farm Relief* (New York, 1929), pp. 15–16.

bought more land, not only for themselves but sometimes also for their sons.[29]

Land prices began to rise as early as 1915 and continued the upward spiral until 1920. For the country as a whole, the price of land was up 40 per cent by the end of the year 1918 and up 70 per cent by the end of 1919, the worst year of the boom. Corn land, especially in Iowa and Illinois, made the most fantastic advances. In the former state the average price per acre had been $82.58 in 1910, but by 1920 it was $199.52; in Illinois during the same period, the rise was from $95.02 to $164.20.[30] Many individual purchases quite exceeded these figures. "Iowans believe," wrote one optimist in 1919, "that land is going higher, and that it can never be bought cheaper than at present. They buy therefore to avoid paying a higher price later on. They say there is but one corn belt to grow corn and hogs and the demand for these products is increasing and will continue to increase."[31] Inspired by such beliefs, purchasers paid as high as $300 or $400 an acre for some Iowa land and occasionally even $500. "Experts" were available to defend such prices as entirely reasonable. They maintained, with fair plausibility, that the price of land had been going up ever since the disappearance of the frontier and was bound to go up further. Corn land, they claimed, had risen during the past about $2 per acre for every cent of increase in the price of corn. Thus, in 1890 when corn brought 20 cents a bushel, corn land had sold for $30 an acre; in 1913, when corn brought 55 cents a bushel, the land that produced it had sold for $100 an acre; hence, they argued, with prices at $1 a bushel, the land should bring $190 per acre.[32]

To a very great extent the land boom, and the farmers' prosperity in general, was financed by rural banks. Loans from the Federal Farm Loan System were available, with rates of interest perhaps .5 per cent lower

29. *Iowa Yearbook of Agriculture,* 1919, p. 582; Woodruff, *Farm Mortgage Loans,* p. 22; L. C. Gray and O. G. Lloyd, *Farm Land Values in Iowa,* U. S. Dept. Agri., Bulletin 874 (Washington, 1920), p. 15.

30. *Statistical Abstract of the United States,* 1923, p. 140.

31. *Iowa Yearbook of Agriculture,* 1919, p. 583.

32. I. W. Wright, *Farm Mortgage Financing* (New York, 1923), pp. 9–13; John D. Black, *Agricultural Reform in the United States* (New York, 1929), p. 21; Freida Baird and Claude L. Benner, *Ten Years of Federal Intermediate Credits* (Washington, 1933), p. 29.

than had been customary before its advent and with the longer period for amortization of the loan. Life insurance companies also had an abundance of money on hand for real estate loans. But the local small-town bankers, many with huge surplus deposits that they were eager to put to work, literally pressed money upon the not unwilling farmers and speculators. New banks were established by men who knew next to nothing about banking, often by retired farmers with their wartime profits as capital. From 1914 to 1920 more than 1,700 new banks began operations in eleven typical agricultural states. Often two or three banks appeared where one would have been enough.[33]

With money from so many sources so easily obtainable, the farmers of the boom-stricken area were tempted further and further into debt. Mortgages on farms in the western Middle West increased over 128 per cent during the decade that ended with the year 1920. According to the United States Department of Agriculture, in 1915 the banks of the country "had outstanding to farmers, loans on personal and collateral security to the amount of $1,609,970,000." By 1918 this figure had grown to $2,506,814,000, and in 1920 to $3,869,891,000. Much farmer borrowing was for other purposes than to buy land, although all such debts were an ultimate charge on the land and what it could produce. Farmers who might have paid off old debts when prices were good often borrowed money in order instead to gain for themselves the living standards of city dwellers. More and more, the farmers bought washing machines, electric sweepers, radios, and automobiles. They sent their children to college. They improved their houses and built new ones. To the rural bankers, loans for all such items seemed reasonable and the cash was in the till or could easily be obtained from the Federal Reserve Banks. Few seemed to realize that a change in policy on the part of the Federal Reserve System might easily dry up the farmers' credit or to understand the problems inherent in such an eventuality.[34]

Both farmers and bankers should have known that the spending spree could not last forever. The high valuations set on farm land were not in

33. *Ibid.*, pp. 25–26; *Wallaces' Farmer*, XLIV (May 16, 1919), p. 1064; Woodruff, *Farm Mortgage Loans*, pp. 23–24.

34. *Statistical Abstract of the United States*, 1923, p. 146; Black, *Agricultural Reform*, p. 37; Woodruff, *Farm Mortgage Loans*, pp. 25–29; Baird and Benner, *Ten Years of Federal Intermediate Credits*, p. 25.

reality justified by its earning power, even in the years of prosperity. Perhaps an occasional superior farmer might make his farm pay a reasonable percentage on the investment, but the ordinary farmer did well to realize as much as 3 per cent. As a matter of fact, to the great distress of the small-town bankers and the farmers who had borrowed from them, the Federal Reserve Board did reverse the policy of credit expansion that had been standard during the war. In its sixth annual report the board stated its new policy: "The expansion of credit set in motion by the war must be checked. Credit must be brought under effective control and its flow once more regulated and governed with careful regard to the economic welfare of the country and the needs of its producing industries."[35]

Possibly the farmers might have staved off the worst effects of the depression a little longer by additional borrowing, but with this alternative denied them and with the cost of production up and prices down, great numbers of them were obliged to dispose of their land. The high boom prices of real estate came tumbling down. Many who were obliged to sell realized only enough to pay their debts and came out of the ordeal as tenants on the farms they once had owned. Others lost their farms through bankruptcy proceedings. Those who were able to hold on to their land found its value alarmingly diminished. Suppose, for example, a man had purchased a farm for $20,000 during the last year of the boom, with a mortgage of $10,000 on it. By 1928 his farm would have shrunk in value to about $14,000, while the mortgage would probably have remained the same. Thus the farmer's equity would have declined from $10,000 to $4,000. And how could a $4,000 investment support a $10,000 mortgage?[36]

Naturally the collapse of land values fell with devastating effect upon the small-town bankers who had put up the money to back the real estate boom. Too many of these bankers had lent without discrimination, and the so-called "frozen assets" on which they blamed their troubles were in reality practically worthless. Often they had lent to individuals whom they knew to be doubtful risks, and some of them had even ignored sound banking policy by lending altogether too much money to a few favored customers. The epidemic of bank failures began as early as 1920 and continued throughout the decade. The lowest number of such failures came

35. *Ibid.*, pp. 30–31.
36. Black, *Agricultural Reform*, p. 17; Woodruff, *Farm Mortgage Loans*, p. 56.

in 1922, with 367 for the country as a whole, and the highest in 1926, when there were no fewer than 976 suspensions, mostly in the small towns and country districts. Aid from the Federal Reserve Banks and other credit sources enabled many bankers to delay the final reckoning for a time, but in an alarmingly large number of cases the collapse could only be postponed. As a result of these failures, many farmers who had resisted the temptation to make speculative land purchases suffered along with the culpable. Some of them lost all of their savings; when they had owned bank stock, they were also subject to heavy assessments that became a lien on their property. Indeed, the general demoralization that inevitably accompanies a series of bank failures left almost no individual in all the Middle West untouched. In the place of the boom psychology that had accompanied and succeeded the war, the whole agricultural population suffered from an atmosphere surcharged with gloom.[37]

The gradual loss of the European wartime markets contributed heavily to this state of mind. Predictions had been common during the war that the food demands of Europe on American producers in the postwar period would greatly exceed the volume of the prewar years. Perhaps the general currency of this idea served to stimulate European production; in any event, European crop yields, at least outside Russia, mounted rapidly after the war came to an end. All the land was still there, even if some of it had been fought over, and its fertility was undiminished. After demobilization there was no longer a labor shortage. With a few simple tools and the will to work, European farmers were soon able to bring the land into full production again. The huge wartime purchases by European governments, paid for with money lent by the United States, were speedily discontinued, and normal trade routes, such as had previously brought so much Argentine beef to Europe, were as speedily resumed. During the war the United Kingdom had imported 50 per cent of its fresh beef from the United States; by 1923 imports from America had fallen to about 5 per cent. Wheat from Canada, the Argentine, and Australia was available for European purchase in ever increasing volume and at discouragingly low prices. European consumers during the war had

37. William Howard Steiner, *Money and Banking* (New York, 1933), pp. 275, 283; Fred L. Garlock, "Bank Failures in Iowa," *Journal of Land and Public Utility Economics,* II (January, 1926), pp. 48–66.

learned to eat less or differently, and the per capita consumption of some staples after the war refused to rise. Strained credit relations, mounting tariff barriers, and the almost universal aim among nations for economic self-sufficiency—each played a part in holding American exports to Europe at a minimum.[38]

Nor was the American market all that it might have been. The per capita consumption of cereals in the United States, with the exception of rice, had long been on the decline. During the first quarter of the twentieth century the consumption of wheat flour had diminished by 20 per cent; corn meal over 60 per cent; rye flour about 60 per cent; and barley, which had been used chiefly in the manufacture of beer, nearly 90 per cent. The eating habits of the people seemed in some respects to be permanently changed by the war, although there was probably little or no actual decline in calorie consumption. With many the substitution of other foods for bread and meat—"Hooverizing"—had become a habit. Restrictions on the use of wheat flour were lifted by 1919, but public eating places did not always return to the practices of serving extra slices of bread free of charge, nor housewives to their earlier recipes. The per capita consumption of meat and meat products had likewise declined, although after the war ended there was a considerable rise in the use of pork and milk. Sugar, and to a lesser degree vegetables, also showed increases. For this condition inflationary prices—the high cost of living—bore some responsibility; so also did the brief industrial depression of the early twenties which, while it lasted, seriously curbed the purchasing power of city laborers. Dieting, particularly by women interested in achieving more stream-lined figures, was sometimes blamed, but could hardly have had much effect. Altogether, according to one economist, "Instead of population pressing upon food supply, food supply is pressing upon population."[39]

The American farmer had other troubles in addition to a limited market. Taxes continued to rise at an alarming rate all through the postwar decade. For the country as a whole the farmer in 1913 had paid 55 cents

38. C. A. Wiley, *Agriculture and the Business Cycle* (Madison, Wis., 1930), pp. 128, 168–78; Nourse, *Government in Relation to Agriculture,* pp. 881–82.

39. O. E. Baker, "Changes in Production and Consumption of our Farm Products and the Trend in Population," *Annals of the American Academy of Political and Social Science,* CXLII (March, 1929), pp. 117, 123, 127, 131; Wiley, *Agriculture and the Business Cycle,* pp. 114–15, 165; Seligman, *Economics of Farm Relief,* p. 24.

in taxes for each $100 in real property, but by 1932 he was paying $1.50. From 1913 to 1929 the rise had persisted, year after year, with the single exception of 1918, when there had been a drop from 58 to 57 cents. Real estate values, in terms of the 1913 level, stood at 160 per cent in 1920, 114 per cent in 1929, and 87 per cent in 1932. But taxes in the same years stood at 209 per cent, 241 per cent, and 189 per cent of the 1913 figures. In Iowa alone taxes rose from $96,000,000 in 1920 to $110,000,000 in 1930—a $14,000,000 increase in a decade when prices were going steadily down.[40]

The rising cost of doing business was another headache for the farmer. Farm wages, according to the most trustworthy estimates, had risen from the prewar level by the index figures of 101 in 1914, 239 in 1920, and 170 in 1927, while the prices of the things the farmer had to buy had shown a similar ascending curve. With his earnings down and consumers' goods, equipment, and wages still up, the farmer's struggle to keep solvent grew harder year by year. Transportation costs provided still another heavy item of expense. Freight rates, after two preliminary boosts of 5 per cent and 15 per cent respectively in the region east of the Mississippi and north of the Potomac, were increased by 25 per cent for the country as a whole in 1918. This meant for most of the western Middle West a total increase of about 50 per cent. Still another increase occurred in August, 1920. Meanwhile, although farm prices also had been rising, even faster than the freight rates, the break in prices came just before the last major advance in rates took place. Sharp protests on the part of the rate payers brought from the railroads a voluntary reduction of 10 per cent on the shipment of farm commodities in January, 1922, followed shortly thereafter by a general cut of 10 per cent; but absolutely essential transportation costs still took a formidable share of the farmers' profits.[41]

Numerous necessary readjustments in farming methods made another heavy dent in the farmer's budget. New and expensive machinery was available, and the farmer who lacked it was at a serious disadvantage.

40. *The Farmers' Tax Problem* (73 Congress, 2 session, House Document 406, serial 10126, Washington, 1934), p. 10; J. O. Babcock, "The Farm Revolt in Iowa," *Social Forces,* XII (March, 1934), p. 369; McIsaac, in *Facing the Facts,* p. 290; G. F. Warren and F. A. Pearson, *The Agricultural Situation* (New York, 1924), p. 32.

41. *Ibid.,* pp. 1–5; J. C. Folsom, "Relief from Farm Labor Costs," *Annals of the American Academy of Political and Social Science,* CXLII (March, 1929), pp. 196–201; H. Gabriel, "Transportation Rates and Facilities," *ibid.,* p. 147.

Horses and mules on many farms, and for that matter in the cities also, were being replaced in considerable part by tractors, trucks, and automobiles. Acreage previously required to raise hay and oats for draft animals was increasingly set free for other purposes. It was estimated in 1929 that not less than twenty million acres had thus been made available for the production of food crops. But the farmer had to buy both the trucks and tractors and the gasoline or kerosene to run them. He also, unless he expanded the number of his cattle and hogs, lost the natural fertilizer that his draft stock had produced and had to depend more and more on expensive commercial fertilizer. Better methods of farming, better breeds of livestock, better types of seed grain, and more attention to diversification—all preached persistently by the Department of Agriculture and the state colleges of agriculture—might bring an increase in agricultural production, but for even his best efforts the farmer seemed to be only worse off financially each suceeding year.[42]

An economist divided the farmers who failed in the postwar depression into four groups.[43] First, there was the farmer, usually a young man, who purchased his land, livestock, and equipment at the high price prevailing during the years 1918 to 1920. He had to pay the penalty for misjudging prices. A second group consisted of farmers who purchased cattle, sheep, and hogs for feeding purposes early in 1920. These farmers fed to their livestock grain which they might instead have sold for a high price. A third group, principally the farmers of North and South Dakota and certain sections of Minnesota and Montana, failed because of their one-crop systems and their frequent short crops. Many of these farmers had taken up wheat raising under the stimulus of high wartime prices. The land upon which they farmed was often marginal and would have required the talents of the most efficient farmers to produce good crops. Montana's heavy proportion of failure was, in part, a reflection of misfits' attempting to farm nonagricultural and marginal lands. In the areas of heaviest failure in that state, 51 per cent of those who went on the land

42. Seligman, *Economics of Farm Relief,* pp. 20–22; Nourse, *Government in Relation to Agriculture,* p. 881; Baker, in *Annals of the American Academy,* CXLII (March, 1929), p. 117.

43. David Friday, "The Course of Agricultural Income during the Last Twenty-Five Years," *American Economic Review, Supplement,* XIII (March, 1923), pp. 156–57.

were without previous farming experience, and 30 per cent had no capital.[44] Among them were men from sixty-three occupations other than farming. "There were two circus musicians, a paper hanger, a sailor, a seagoing engineer, two wrestlers, two barbers, a cigar maker, a race horse man, a bricklayer, an undertaker, a deep-sea diver, six old maids, a milliner, and a professional gambler." The fact that such people exposed themselves to the hazards of a single crop increased the risk they took. A fourth group of farmers failed because of their inefficiency. Their production costs were simply too high.[45]

For a while the postwar depression in agriculture was paralleled by a similar depression in industry, business, and finance. After the spring of 1920 industrial production fell off rapidly and price levels began to sag. By the end of the year, wage cuts were common and unemployment had become a serious problem. The year 1921 was dark for industry and agriculture alike, but for most business activities other than farming the depression was fading out by the end of 1922 and recovery was beginning. Thereafter, from 1923 to 1929, the nation's business, except for agriculture and a few industries, experienced a long period of steady expansion, marred only by a few minor setbacks. Iron, steel, and coal production mounted steadily, trade revived, and a veritable boom developed. The seemingly insatiable demand of the American public for automobiles, radios, electric washing machines, electric refrigerators, and the like, accompanied by a widespread use of installment buying and supported by an equally insistent demand for housing, made for a general appearance of prosperity, at least for most of the nonfarm population. Much of this prosperity eventually turned out to be more illusory than real, for the position of organized labor was weak and unemployment was slowly but surely growing in some industries. But the bulk of the nonfarm population and its leaders believed that a permanent plateau of prosperity had been reached, and the farmers were envious.[46] Speaking in Paris in the

44. John H. Rich, *The Economic Position of Agriculture in the Northwestern Grain Areas* (Minneapolis, 1922), p. 7.

45. Friday, in *American Economic Review, Supplement,* XIII (March, 1923), pp. 156–57.

46. Reginald C. McGrane, *The Economic Development of the American Nation* (Boston, 1942), pp. 547–49; George Soule, *Prosperity Decade, From War to Depression, 1917–1929* (New York, 1947), pp. 107–26, 208–28, 275–84.

fall of 1918, Senator James Hamilton Lewis of Illinois had declared, "We are going to hear from the farmers as never before. They will tell us that their profits have been limited and their businesses regulated during the war, while others have been getting rich because of the war, without restraint. This protest of the farmer will be a big factor two years hence."[47] The senator was right, but if he could have foreseen that the farmer was soon to find himself in a state of depression with most of the city population in a state of prosperity, he would have expanded his rhetoric. The country would indeed hear from the farmer.

47. *Wallaces' Farmer,* XLIII (September 20, 1918), p. 1329.

Chapter V

THE AMERICAN SOCIETY OF EQUITY

THE EXCESSIVE individualism of the American farmer has long been a subject of extensive historical comment. Frederick Jackson Turner lost no opportunity to emphasize this characteristic in his studies of the American frontier. American individualism, Turner believed, was itself largely a frontier product, since in every frontier region each pioneer farmer had to work out his own salvation with a minimum of assistance from his fellow men. The decline of subsistence farming and the rise of production for sale made extensive alterations in the farmer's way of life, for under the new conditions he was as much a businessman as a producer. Contacts with the outside world for such necessities as credit, transportation, marketing, and merchandising were unavoidable. And yet each farmer preferred to stand aloof from every other farmer as much as he dared. In a sense, as has often been noted, each farm, even in thickly settled areas, was in itself a little frontier, and each farm boundary a kind of frontier line. Farmers were obliged most of the time to work alone or in family units, not shoulder to shoulder with other workers after the fashion of factory operatives. Their contacts with other farmers, at least from the point of view of the city dweller, were few and far between. They looked with the suspicion of rivals at what went on across their fences in their neighbors' fields. Every farmer thought of himself, in a sense, as a competitor with every other farmer; and such, indeed, he tended to be.

Thus the task of organizing the farmers in their own defense was formidable in the extreme. As small producers, each standing alone, they were deplorably weak in bargaining power, but they clung tenaciously to their independence and resisted with all their might those same possibilities for united action that so intrigued the men with whom they had to deal. Their business adversaries, perhaps because they were fewer in numbers, less isolated, and on the whole better educated, got together. City laborers joined forces in powerful unions to fight for what they believed to be their rights. But the discontented farmers, faced by similar circumstances, were reluctant to organize. Often they preferred flight to the nearest frontier, as long as the frontier remained, or even flight to the city in search of a job. Only when times grew excessively hard were they willing to surrender a small portion of their independence to achieve something resembling a united front.[1]

During the late nineteenth century two such periods of stress and strain—one in the seventies and the other in the late eighties and the early nineties—actually drove the farmers together, at least in certain portions of the Middle West and the South. The first period of distress produced the Granger movement; the second, the Farmers' Alliance and Populism. But as soon as agriculture prospered again, these organizations fell apart. By the early twentieth century the Grange had reverted to the status of a cultural and educational body, as its founders had originally intended it to be; furthermore, it had shifted the center of its activities to the northeast, and was strongest in New England and the Middle Atlantic states.[2] As for the Farmers' Alliance, it had evaporated into thin air, while Populism, whatever ideas of political reform it might have contributed to the older parties, had lost its status as an independent movement.

The economic disorders of the 1920's were sufficiently acute to bring into prominence another group of agricultural organizations. Most of these orders, however, dated well back into the prewar years, and some of them had already had short periods of vigorous activity. The prosperity of the early twentieth century was by no means equally distributed, and

1. On this general subject see W. S. Harwood, "Coöperation in the West," *Atlantic Monthly,* LXXXV (April, 1900), p. 540; J. R. Elliot, *American Farms* (New York, 1890), p. 125; C. Vincent, "Cooperation Among Western Farmers," *Arena* XXXI (March, 1904), p. 287.

2. K. L. Butterfield, "The Grange," *The Forum,* XXXI (April, 1901), p. 233.

areas of considerable discontent could be found at any time. Moreover, for farmers who faced the fact that such prosperity as they enjoyed stemmed far too much from rising land values and far too little from the sale of produce, there were also ample grounds for worry at any time. Some farmers were learning, too, as the cooperative movement abundantly attests, that they could accomplish much more when many stood together than when each man stood alone.[3]

One of the earliest of the twentieth century farm orders to achieve some degree of prominence was the American Society of Equity, which was founded in Indianapolis on December 24, 1902. The man who claimed full credit for the founding of Equity, and for the plan of action by which the order hoped to better the lot of the farmer, was James A. Everitt, publisher of an Indianapolis journal known as *Up-to-Date Farming and Gardening*. Everitt also owned a feed and seed business by means of which he augmented his income from printing and publishing and increased his contacts with the farmers. He claimed, however, to spend much time in thought; indeed, his every waking moment, he said, was given over to "originating ideas and revolving plans in my brain." In time an anti-Everitt faction arose in Equity which asserted that Everitt was no more the founder of the order than he was the author of the Bible. This faction pinned its faith to W. L. Hearron of Carlinville, Illinois, from whom it claimed Everitt had filched all his best ideas, but the fact remains that Everitt's newspaper, together with a highly emotional volume entitled *The Third Power,* which he published in 1903, were principally responsible for launching the organization.[4]

Everitt thought of himself as a strictly practical man, and, as he saw it, the object of his order was primarily to contribute to the farmers' profits.

3. Gerald Goldstein, "The Economic Basis of Agrarian Unrest in the Progressive Period" (unpublished master's thesis, University of California, 1948).

4. James A. Everitt, *The Third Power* (Indianapolis, 1903), pp. 246–47; R. H. Bahmer, "The American Society of Equity," *Agricultural History,* XIV (January, 1940), pp. 33–35; J. L. Nash, "Building a Farmers' Monopoly," *World Today,* XIII (July, 1907), p. 717; *Wisconsin Equity News* (Madison), June 1, 1908, p. 13; *ibid.,* June 10, 1912, pp. 1–2; Robert Lee Hunt, *A History of Farmer Movements in the Southwest, 1873–1925* (College Station, Texas, 1935), pp. 104–8; American Society of Equity, *The Plan of the American Society of Equity* (Indianapolis, n.d.), p. 1 [pamphlet].

What he had in mind was essentially a gigantic holding movement. Why shouldn't the farmers set prices themselves instead of allowing "the captains of industry, the promoter, the underwriter, the labor leader, and the grain gambler" to dictate to them? By devising some simple machinery for setting prices, and by keeping farm produce off the market unless and until these prices could be obtained, Everitt was certain that the farmers could not only secure relief from the ill effects of monopoly; they could themselves, in fact, become the greatest of all monopolists.[5]

Everitt was much concerned with the necessity of holding down the "visible supply" of any given commodity, for it was this "visible supply" which in relation to the demand tended at any given time to fix the price. He believed that wherever possible the farmers should provide storage facilities for their own crops on their own farms. If forced to it, however, they could "put up granaries, elevators or warehouses to hold their products, or build cooperative cold storage plants to hold their fruit, etc." But he was chary of the business complications that resulted from joint-stock companies, or even cooperatives after the Granger pattern. The farmers should keep out of all business except the farming business as completely as possible. All they need try to do was to put farming itself "on a safe profitable basis," with benefits for the farmer "equaling those realized in other business undertakings."[6]

The violent fluctuations in prices from which the farmers continually lost while the speculators gained, Everitt believed to be entirely unnecessary. The farmers could change all this if only they would stop dumping the bulk of any particular commodity on the market at harvest time. What they needed was some method of feeding the market with a twelve-month supply on a twelve-month basis. Everitt was sure that this could be done if only a fraction of the producers—the more intelligent ones—would join forces. He had no notion that all the nation's wheat growers, for example, could be persuaded to hold their wheat off the market. But if the organized farmers could control no more than half the total amount of wheat normally exported, he insisted, they would be in a position to set

5. Everitt, *The Third Power,* third edition (1905), p. 35; fourth edition (1907), p. vii.

6. *Plan of the American Society of Equity,* pp. 2–3; Bahmer, in *Agricultural History,* XIV (January, 1940), p. 37.

a just and equitable price. As he saw it, a million farmers working together through a single agency could control the surplus and assure the producers the fair prices they ought to have. Some of Everitt's ideas even foreshadowed McNary-Haugenism. He believed that the farmers, by standing firm in their demand for a high selling price, could take full advantage of tariff protection. "What is the use of having a tariff," he asked, "if it don't benefit the wheat growers? Farmers get together and make this tariff effective."[7]

In his obsession with price control as the one sure remedy for the farmers' ills, Everitt tended to close his eyes to the related problem of how to limit production. In his earlier statements he clearly had both problems in mind. "If it was possible," he wrote in 1901, "to control and limit the production of our chief farm crops, within the action of the farmers themselves, it would be possible to control prices." But eventually he reasoned himself into the belief that there would be no need to worry about surplus production. The American people were consuming more food all the time, and they would need still more in the future. Soon they would be able to consume all the foodstuffs the farmers could possibly produce. All that was really needed was careful and systematic marketing of the available supply. Some of his statements indicate that Everitt envisaged something closely akin to Henry A. Wallace's "ever normal granary":

> Every person has noted that a season of scarcity usually follows a season of plenty, or in case of a bountiful crop one year the next is likely to be much shorter. With profitable prices fixed for each farm crop, it will soon be very easy for farmers to hold their grain over to make up for shortages that are bound to exist. Thus the seasons of plenty will help out seasons of scarcity.[8]

Had Everitt lived a few decades later, it is possible that his services as an agricultural expert might have been in great demand. He would certainly have found much that was familiar to him in the parity concept. Beginning with the premise that "farmers are under neither legal nor moral obligation to feed the balance of the world at an unprofitably low

7. *Plan of the American Society of Equity,* p. 3; Everitt, *The Third Power,* third edition, pp. 284, 291; fourth edition, p. 275; Bahmer, in *Agricultural History,* XIV (January, 1940), p. 37.

8. Quoted, *ibid.,* pp. 35–37.

price," Everitt argued that it should be possible to "remove agriculture from the list of uncertain industries and place it on a basis of certainty for prices equal to that enjoyed by the best regulated manufacturing or commercial enterprises." Farming had become a business and it was high time that farmers behaved as businessmen. Other businesses had discarded competition in their quest for profits and had sought to "control the market." They entered without scruple into combinations "to limit output, to lift prices, to regulate wages, and to 'work' the government." It was up to the farmers to adopt similar methods; they were just as much entitled to fix prices as the manufacturers were—more so, indeed, since agriculture was the most important segment in our economy. "We might survive the loss of our steel mills, but if our farms were to quit producing the country would go to ruin. Why should not the farmers be supreme? And if they strive for something less than supremacy—namely mere parity with the rest of our people—ought they not to be encouraged?"[9]

The structure and control of Equity was highly centralized, at least from its beginning until the house cleaning of 1907. The official publication, *Up-To-Date Farming,* remained in the private control and ownership of Everitt; in fact, a subscription to the "official paper" was considered adequate to bring one the full benefits of membership. For all practical purposes, the national union consisted of a seven-man board of directors, which was supposed to be in constant session. One did not have to belong to a local union, but locals of ten or more members might be organized by persons of "good moral character" who paid a membership fee of $1.50 and annual dues of $1.00. Those under twenty-one or over seventy-five and the wives of farmers were admitted free and paid no dues.[10]

Everitt and his paper, aided by the national board of directors, were supposed to shape the marketing policies of the society and to serve as a clearinghouse for agricultural information. A crop-reporting service was an integral part of the marketing program. The secretaries of locals were required to obtain annual reports on their crops from all members, although the precise nature of these reports was not specific. On the basis

9. *Plan of the American Society of Equity,* p. 1; Everitt, *The Third Power,* third edition, pp. 6, 9, 23–24, 71; fourth edition, p. vii.

10. Bahmer, in *Agricultural History,* XIV (January, 1940), pp. 38, 40; *Plan of the American Society of Equity,* p. 1.

of information so obtained, the board of directors, each of whom was supposed to be an expert in some line of agriculture, was to study the demands of the nation and then place what it considered to be an equitable price on each commodity. Ideally, there should also be held annually "a convention of wheat growers, of corn raisers, of cotton planters, of tobacco raisers, of fruit growers, of livestock men—of every great agricultural interest" to consider the supply, demand, market, and price and all other questions that affected the industry. Such "equitable prices" as were set by the board of directors were also referred to as "minimum prices," below which the farmers were urged not to sell. "There need be no fear," wrote Everitt, "that buyers will be out of the market long, because the world must have your goods all the time."[11]

The name Equity had something appealing about it. It was synonymous with justice, equality, parity, fairness, righteousness, and honesty. The order was also referred to as the "American Square Deal Association," no doubt after the "Square Deal" of Theodore Roosevelt.

An analysis of the backgrounds of twelve men prominent in early Equity councils reveals precisely what one would expect. All claimed to have had farming experience of one kind or another, vocational or avocational. Three had had teaching experience and one had been a member of Congress. At least five claimed to have attended or to have graduated from college. Two had had newspaper experience and one had been a customs collector under two different presidents. A number had been members of the Farmers' Alliance and the Populist party. One who was to assume an important role was an osteopath who had "an active interest in religion and politics, [and] sociology, believing heartily in the philosophy of Jesus Christ, the Fatherhood of God and the Brotherhood of Man; [and] that we are our brother's keeper."[12]

As might be expected with such leadership, the membership and organizing policies of the Equity Society were highly defective. Apparently Everitt had had little experience as an organizer before his founding of the order. The membership dues of one dollar, really the subscription price of his paper, was far too small a sum to cover the costs of organizing; yet

11. *Ibid.*, pp. 1–2; Everitt, *The Third Power,* third edition, pp. 231–32, 273–77.

12. *Ibid.*, fourth edition, pp. 214–15; *Wisconsin Equity News,* February 10, 1912, p. 1; *Equity Farm Journal* (Indianapolis), I (November, 1908), p. 6.

Everitt expected to recruit a million members, and with their support to usher in an era of profitable prices by the control of marketing. But even at this nominal fee the farmers were slow to respond. Equity obtained only about twenty or thirty thousand members during its first few months of existence, which was far short of the several hundred thousand which Everitt had anticipated. Hoping to speed up the drive for membership, Everitt lowered the rates, first to fifty cents and then to twenty-five, but all to no avail. He had hoped, too, also in vain, that these reductions would curb rumors that he was building up his fortune at the expense of the society.[13]

What membership figures are available are incomplete and perhaps unreliable. In 1906, one estimate placed the number at 200,000, but it appears unlikely that the society had more than 100,000 members at its peak. In 1907, the number was placed at 60,000, and in October, 1908, at 26,259. By the latter year state organizations, which were no part of the original scheme, had been formed in Arkansas, Illinois, Indiana, Kansas, Kentucky, Michigan, Minnesota, Nebraska, New York, North Dakota, Oklahoma, South Dakota, Virginia, and Wisconsin, but Equity attained its greatest strength in Kentucky, Wisconsin, Minnesota, the Dakotas, and Montana.[14]

During the early years the price-setting activities of Equity revolved chiefly around wheat and tobacco. Wheat appears to have had primary place on the agenda. In 1903 Everitt distributed the first of a series of "Dollar Wheat Bulletins" urging the farmers to hold their wheat for a dollar a bushel. The following year he asked them to demand $1.20 a bushel. At the same time he also appealed to the southern farmers to hold their cotton, but the cotton growers apparently preferred to join organizations with a southern background, such as the Southern Cotton Association or the Farmers' Union, and paid little attention to Equity. In 1904, an organization of tobacco producers was established in Lynchburg, Virginia, largely under the influence of Equity, and late that same year the society began to attract attention in the tobacco fields of Kentucky and

13. Everitt, *The Third Power,* third edition, pp. 280, 284; *Wisconsin Equity News,* June 10, 1912, p. 2.

14. *Indian-Arbiter* (Ada, Okla.), March 1, 1906, p. 12; *Equity Farm Journal,* I (November, 1907), p. 2; (October, 1908), p. 9; (January, 1908), p. 9.

Tennessee. By 1907, some headway was reported, also, among the spring wheat producers of the agricultural Northwest and the tobacco fields of Wisconsin.[15]

Meanwhile some sentiment had developed in favor of "direct trade between the producers and consumers" so that "organized farmers and organized laborers" could cooperate more effectively. In the hope of fulfilling this ambition, nine farmers representing Equity appeared on November 14, 1906, before the national convention of the American Federation of Labor in Minneapolis. Plans were discussed "to effect an honest, quick and practical means of exchange of the products of the farm and also the products of organized labor as identified by the 'Union Label.'" The ultimate result of this meeting was the short-lived International Equity Exchange.[16]

The leader in this movement was M. Wes Tubbs, national secretary of Equity, who had grown increasingly skeptical of Everitt's crop-holding, price-fixing program and believed that more could be accomplished by orthodox methods of cooperative marketing. Through Tubbs' efforts, three joint-stock cooperatives were organized in Chicago, Detroit, and Scranton, Pennsylvania. In each city the local federation of labor supported the idea on the theory that union members would be able to save money by dealing directly with the producers through an exchange. Tubbs finally got a charter in New Jersey for the International Equity Exchange, which was designed to act as a holding company for local exchanges. Tubbs hoped eventually to develop an extensive system of country shipping exchanges for the use of the farmers, as well as city exchanges for the storage and shipment of farm produce. Perhaps his scheme was no less chimerical than Everitt's, at least in the extent to which he believed it could be made effective.[17]

Naturally this development was viewed by Everitt with the greatest misgivings, for the founder of the order had committed himself to the

15. Everitt, *The Third Power,* third edition, pp. 220–23; fourth edition, pp. 226–29; *Western Tobacco Journal* (Cincinnati), XXXI (November 14, 1904), p. 1; XXXII (January 16, 1905), p. 2; (March 13, 1905), p. 1; (November 27, 1905), p. 2; (October 23, 1905), pp. 1–2.

16. *Equity Farm Journal,* I (May, 1908), p. 5; International Equity Exchange, *The Farmers' New Marketing System* (Madison, Wis., 1908), pp. 16–22 [pamphlet].

17. Bahmer, in *Agricultural History,* XIV (January, 1940), pp. 53–54.

principle that the total energies of Equity should go toward price fixing and he was now particularly absorbed in trying to fix the price of wheat Everitt had considerable evidence to show that his propaganda had been making good progress in the wheat-growing areas, especially in North Dakota, where a state organization had been set up and a grain growers branch was contemplated. Under these circumstances, he deplored the distraction that Tubbs' activities provided. Furthermore, he had been opposed all along to joint-stock business cooperatives of the type that Tubbs had organized. The way was thus wide-open for a violent split in Equity, and at the national convention of 1907 the split came.[18]

There was more to the opposition to Everitt than a mere difference of opinion on principle. Tubbs and others were concerned over the way in which Everitt sought to dominate the society; some had even suggested that the order should be rechristened "The American Society of Everitt." And there were other charges, even more disturbing. Everitt was accused of mishandling the funds of the national organization. He had apparently made no effort to separate the accounts of the seed store, the printing establishment, and Equity, which were all in his building. Auditors who examined the organization records, which were handled by Everitt's own bookkeeper, found them "all mixed up, the seed business, the printing plant and the society's own accounts, and it was simply impossible . . . to straighten [them] out." Many felt that at the very least, Everitt had been conducting his business in a manner unbecoming the head of a farmers' organization.[19]

A subject of particularly bitter contention was the fifty-year contract which Everitt had negotiated with the society for publishing its official paper. Irritation over this situation came to a head because of mounting complaints that Everitt had refused to publish material that certain members had submitted to him. A group of investigators later reported that the contract was not binding because Everitt, an executive of Equity and thus party of the first part, could not "sign a contract or make a contract" with himself as an individual, the party of the second part. In other words, Everitt could not legally enter into a contract with himself. When mem-

18. *Ibid.*, pp. 54–55.

19. *Annual Meeting of the North Dakota State Union of the American Society of Equity* (Devils Lake, N. Dak., November 19, 1907), pp. 28–30.

ers of the society asked him what he would take for his paper, he priced t at $75,000, an exaggerated price which naturally was rejected.[20]

Whatever the truth of the matter may have been, the convention of 1907 deposed Everitt and elected a new slate of officers headed by C. M. Barnett of Kentucky as president. Completely unreconciled to the change, Everitt organized a short-lived rival order, the Farmers' Society of Equity, as a spite move, obviously designed to drain the original Equity of its membership. Bitter warfare, with violent charges and countercharges, followed, to the detriment of both the orders. Many farmers continued to subscribe to *Up-To-Date Farming,* thinking that they were paying dues to the American Society of Equity, while others, who had grown disgusted with the turn of events, refused to have any further dealings with either body.[21]

The departure of Everitt from the presidency marked a sharp break in the policies of the Equity. Plans for controlling production were gradually relaxed and greater stress was placed on cooperative marketing and buying. Also, the organization became highly decentralized, as opposed to the earlier practice of centering authority in Indianapolis. The result was an unwieldly collection of state and commodity organizations, theoretically but not practically bound to the parent body, with a common name and common enemies, but influenced in their various activities more by local interests than by a general agricultural program. In fact, the American Society of Equity, as a national organization, had suffered mortal wounds from which it never fully recovered.

An early manifestation of the new spirit of autonomy in Equity occurred during the wars waged by the tobacco producers of Kentucky and Tennessee against the tobacco trust. This episode, in which Equity played a leading role, marked the last, as well as the most conspicuous, effort of the society to put its production-control and price-fixing policies into operation. It was also a classic illustration of the possibilities open when a group of agriculturists band together in an effort to exact fair prices from a giant corporation.

By 1900 the American Tobacco Company, or the "tobacco trust," as it

20. *Ibid.,* pp. 35–36.

21. *You Have Been Deceived and Betrayed By Your Trusted Representatives* (Indianapolis, 1907), p. 28 [pamphlet]; *Equity Farm Journal,* I (October, 1908), p. 7; III (February 1, 1910), p. 12.

was more commonly called, had reduced the growers of tobacco to a hopelessly unsatisfactory bargaining position. This condition was no doubt promoted considerably by the infiltration into the tobacco areas of an army of illiterate tenant farmers who raised tobacco on share leases with no other hope of betterment than what they might obtain by an increase in their acreage.[22] This situation exactly suited the trust, which was not satisfied with its control of the manufacturing and marketing processes, but expected also to dictate the prices paid for tobacco to the original producers. The resulting low prices, coupled with high living and production costs, created among the tobacco growers a situation of acute poverty and distress.[23]

Some of the tobacco producers had felt the need of organizing well before Equity appeared on the scene and had discussed plans for the organization of a "farmers' tobacco trust" as early as 1901. Agitation for controlling production became more common during 1903 and 1904. By 1904 agitators were urging the farmers to "grow no more tobacco," or to "cut down the crop to half," or to "grow only 25 per cent of a crop." Equity appears to have received serious mention for the first time in 1904, and Equity members seem to have taken an important part in the holding movement of 1905 that resulted in substantially higher prices. But such groups as the Dark Tobacco Growers' Protective Association, the Burley Growers' Association of Kentucky, and no doubt others—all with similar ideas—had either preceded Equity or were contemporaries of it.[24]

The object of Equity, when it appeared on the scene, was to consolidate

22. *Report of the Commissioner of Corporation on the Tobacco Industry,* Part I, *Position of the Tobacco Combination in the Industry* (3 parts, Washington, 1909–15), pp. 14–15; John L. Mathews, "Agrarian Pooling in Kentucky," *Charities and the Commons,* XX (1908), p. 193.

23. *Hearings on the Bills for the Relief of Tobacco Growers* (59 Congress, 2 session, Senate Document 372, Vol. VI, Washington, 1907), p. 42; Anna Youngman, "The Tobacco Pools of Kentucky and Tennessee," *Journal of Political Economy,* XVIII (January, 1910), p. 36; H. C. Filley, *Cooperation in Agriculture* (New York, 1929), pp. 246–471.

24. *Western Tobacco Journal,* XXVIII (January 14, 1901), p. 1; XXX (January 5, 1903), p. 1; (February 2, 1903), p. 2; (February 9, 1903), p. 2; (April 27, 1903), p. 2; (May 11, 1903), p. 4; (May 18, 1903), p. 1; XXXI (January 14, 1904), p. 4; (February 29, 1904), p. 2; (August 22, 1904), p. 2; XXX (April 22, 1903), p. 2.

or absorb all these local groups. In 1906 it took the lead in a "forty-day whirlwind campaign" to obtain pledges from the farmers not to dispose of their crop at the prices offered by the trust. This campaign succeeded so well that on January 2, 1907, according to one report, about 58 per cent of an estimated 92,000 acres planted to tobacco for the year was pledged to the newly organized Burley Tobacco Society.[25]

Even more aggressive action was planned for the 1907 crop. Equity officials sought to "produce a short crop and sell it for a long price." They also suggested that tobacco factories be established in the event that the American Tobacco Company failed to purchase the 1906 and 1907 crops. On July 11, with some 103,000 acres out of an estimated 135,000 planted reportedly in the pool, representatives of the tobacco associations from Wisconsin, North Carolina, South Carolina, Pennsylvania, and other states planned a meeting with representatives from Ohio, Indiana, and Kentucky to organize a tobacco association covering the entire country. In the fall of 1907, the Burley Society formally announced that it would attempt to eliminate the 1908 crop altogether.[26]

Despite the various methods employed to facilitate organization, difficulties of the most trying character arose. The unfavorable system of land-tenure system, the indifference of the slow, lethargic, and incompetent farmer, the financial disabilities of most producers, and the financial strength of trust opposition impeded action. Fortunately, both the Planters' Protective Association and the Burley Society received considerable assistance from their few well-to-do members, as well as from equally sympathetic warehousemen in Louisville and Cincinnati who saw their business menaced.[27]

Perhaps more irritating than even the expected trust opposition was the attitude of the independent farmer who refused to join the association,

25. *Wisconsin Equity News,* June 1, 1908, p. 4; *Western Tobacco Journal,* XXXIV (January 7, 1907), p. 1; Everitt, *The Third Power,* fourth edition, p. 289.

26. *Western Tobacco Journal,* XXXIV (March 18, 1907), p. 1; (May 13, 1907), p. 7; (July 15, 1907), p. 1; (November 4, 1907), p. 1.

27. Youngman, in *Journal of Political Economy,* XVIII (January, 1910), pp. 40–41; John L. Mathews, "The Farmers' Union and the Tobacco Pool," *Atlantic Monthly,* CII (October, 1908), p. 484; *Wisconsin Equity News,* June 1, 1908, p. 5; R. Bache, "The Great Tobacco Strike," *Technical World,* VI (1907), p. 604; Youngman, in *Journal of Political Economy,* XVIII (January, 1910), p. 43.

either because he was convinced that it offered no hopes for betterment, or because he suspected the organizers, or because he was already enjoying the benefit of higher prices. Pooling members deeply resented the tendency of the occasional independent, or "hillbilly," as he might be called contemptuously, to cash in on the higher prices the holding movement had achieved. Why should one producer join the organization, pay fees, and endure hardships while another who refused to cooperate sold at a fancy profit?[28]

Aroused by this situation, some of the tobacco growers finally decided to employ force in order to achieve conformity. Their "night riders" used the whip or even the rifle on independents or farmers who "talked too much"; they brutally assaulted tobacco buyers, they set fires, sowed plant beds with salt or grass seed, and even dynamited machinery. One terror-stricken farmer found a grave dug in the midst of one of his plant beds.[29]

The effects of these acts of violence on the tobacco country were devastating. As selling tobacco independently of the farmers' association became dangerous, neighbors became suspicious of one another and terror prevailed everywhere. Courts of law were paralyzed by perjury, packed juries, or fear on the part of witnesses to testify against known marauders. Hundreds of farmers left the tobacco areas in search of homes elsewhere. So widespread was the disorder that in 1907, the secretary of the Kentucky Board of Fire Underwriters cautioned residents of the affected areas that "unless confidence can be restored, the companies will refuse indemnity to all handlers of tobacco."[30]

While innumerable obstacles had threatened to defeat the elimination program in 1908, in actual fact the acreage devoted to tobacco was held at a low minimum. In the Burley country the estimated acreage fell to 18 per cent of normal, and in the dark-tobacco country also sharp reductions

28. *Wisconsin Equity News,* June 1, 1908, p. 6; Mathews, in *Atlantic Monthly,* CII (October, 1908), pp. 489–90.

29. Youngman, in *Journal of Political Economy,* XVIII (January, 1910), p. 45; C. M. Meacham, *A History of Christian County, Kentucky* (Nashville, 1930), pp. 346–48; J. C. Miller, *The Black Patch War* (Chapel Hill, N. C., 1936), pp. 16–17.

30. E. A. Jonas, "The Night-Riders: A Trust of Farmers," *World's Work,* XVII (February, 1909), p. 11217; Marie Taylor, "Night Riders in the Black Patch" (unpublished master's thesis, University of Kentucky, 1934), p. 38.

were effected. Western market receipts which in 1889 were placed at 300,000 hogsheads had dwindled to about 110,000 in 1909.[31]

After long-drawn-out negotiations, on November 19, 1908, the American Tobacco Company and the Burley Tobacco Society finally consummated what was considered the largest tobacco transaction in history. Between 60 and 70 million pounds of Burley changed hands for a cash consideration of between 12 and 13 million dollars. According to the agreement, the company was to buy 75 per cent of the 80 million pounds in the 1907 pool at an average price of 17 cents a pound, totaling about $10,000,000, and 75 per cent of the estimated 13 to 15 million pounds of the 1906 crop at an average of between 20 and 21 cents a pound, bringing an additional $2,000,000. This left the pool still in possession of 25 per cent of the Burley crop, which became an exciting subject of discussion. Some believed that it was being held for the independent manufacturers who had been the allies of the Burley and Equity societies; others maintained that the American Tobacco Company had wanted the remaining 25 per cent to squeeze the independents out of business.[32]

Once the tobacco deal had been completed, accounts of the anxious moments experienced by both sides during the pooling period began to be told. The Burley Society, so the story ran, had to contend on the one hand with the American Tobacco Company and its untold millions of dollars, while on the other hand it faced impending demoralization in Equity ranks. Had the war lasted sixty days longer, the pool would probably have disintegrated. The tobacco company also had its problems. Its reserve stocks had dwindled; the 1908 crop was small and the big demand from independent manufacturers had caused alarm for the company's future supplies. Then, too, the activity of Thomas J. Ryan, the dominant spirit of the company, had been an important factor. He wanted peace and harmony restored because of the "effect and influence such action might have with the government in its prosecution of the Tobacco Trust as an illegal combination in restraint of trade."[33]

31. *Ibid.*, p. 23; E. H. Mathewson, *The Export and Manufacturing Tobaccos of the United States*, U. S. Dept. Agri., Bureau of Plant Industry, Bulletin 244 (Washington, 1912), pp. 47–48, 250–51; Filley, *Cooperation in Agriculture*, pp. 25–51.

32. *Cincinnati Enquirer*, November 20, 26, 1908.

33. *Ibid.*, November 21, 1908.

By 1909 the Equity movement was on the decline in Kentucky and Tennessee. Dissatisfaction had developed over the prices which the farmers received; the possible benefits of production control were disputed by many growers who had taken part in the farm strike of 1908; and the administrative policies of Equity and its subsidiary organization had become matters of heated controversy. Some believed that with the price rise of 1908, the marketing troubles of the tobacco growers were at an end, but tobacco production took an upward swing in 1909, as usual after a good price year, and with it, the marketing problem reappeared. For many Equity left bitter memories, and they wanted no more of it. Still, the farmers had something to show for their troubles. They had cooperated in building a number of warehouses; they had obtained better grading methods and a tobacco factory; and they had demonstrated the potentialities of organized action.[34]

Meanwhile, Equity was slowly but surely rooting itself in Wisconsin and the spring wheat regions of the agricultural Northwest. It was here that the society gained its greatest strength; in fact, such local organizations as the Wisconsin Society of Equity and the autonomous Equity Cooperative Exchange dwarfed the national organization into insignificance. Equity began its activities in Wisconsin in 1903, expanded rapidly, and by 1920 could claim a paid-up membership of 40,000. At first, the Wisconsin Equity sought higher prices for farm products by a voluntary curtailment of the output, but later it encouraged the growth of cooperative marketing and purchasing associations and sought legislation favorable to these ends.[35]

As in Kentucky and Tennessee, the Wisconsin Equity was influenced by various local developments, both economic and political. It attracted its first substantial support in the wheat-growing river counties of the

34. *Western Tobacco Journal*, XXXVI (June 28, 1909), p. 7; (July 19, 1909), pp. 1–2; (July 26, 1909), pp. 1–2; (August 2, 1909), p. 4; (July 19, 1909), pp. 1–2. Also B. H. Hibbard, *Marketing Agricultural Products* (New York, 1921), p. 238; Filley, *Cooperation in Agriculture,* pp. 251–52; Youngman, in *Journal of Political Economy,* XVIII (January, 1910), p. 42.

35. Everitt, *The Third Power,* fourth edition, pp. 269–70; J. G. Thomson, *The Rise and Decline of the Wheat Growing Industry in Wisconsin* (Madison, Wis., 1909), pp. 82, 99.

upper Mississippi Valley, where agricultural discontent was an old story.[36] Here the Scandinavian element was strong, and blood ties tended to supplement the economic unity which stemmed from the common problems experienced by grain growers. Many farmers in this area had strong reminiscences of the Granger and Populist campaigns, particularly those waged by the great Minnesota orator, Ignatius Donnelly. Their minds were thus well prepared for the propaganda put out by Equity organizers and La Follette supporters alike. Both groups were antimonopolistic in philosophy. To La Follette and his followers, monopoly and graft were the principal corrupting influences in government; to the Equity leaders, these same forces—in the form of middlemen, boards of trade, bankers, and railroad interests—were responsible for the depressed agricultural prices. Both were fighting on a common ground but were utilizing different methods of attack.[37]

Another contribution to the growth of the organization came from the Wisconsin tobacco farmers, who suffered no less than the farmers of Kentucky and Tennessee from an "antiquated" and "unscientific" system of marketing. Because of its interest in these difficulties, Equity had penetrated into the tobacco areas of the state to such an extent that, according to the *Milwaukee Journal,* it had won complete control of the tobacco production in the important Edgerton area by 1907 and could threaten to eliminate the entire crop the following year. Within a year the tobacco farmers had built or leased a substantial number of tobacco warehouses in the southern and southwestern part of the state, but their attempt to duplicate the feat of the tobacco farmers of Kentucky and Tennessee by eliminating the crop and "letting the demand catch up with the supply" ended in failure.[38]

36. *Equity News* (Madison, Wis.), December 1, 1915, p. 234.

37. Robert M. La Follette, *La Follette's Autobiography: A Personal Narrative of Political Experience* (Madison, Wis., 1913), pp. 18–19; A. P. Wilder, "Governor La Follette and What He Stands For," *Outlook,* LXX (March 8, 1902), p. 631; Henrietta M. Larson, *The Wheat Market and the Farmer in Minnesota, 1858–1900* (New York, 1926), pp. 249–50; André Siegfried, *America Comes of Age* (New York, 1927), pp. 287–88.

38. "Cooperative Tobacco Marketing in Wisconsin," Wisconsin State Department of Markets, *Bulletin,* Vol. IV, No. 4, pp. 8–9; *Milwaukee Journal,* October 26, 1907; *Wisconsin Equity News,* May 1, 1908, p. 6.

Once the Wisconsin Society of Equity was under way, it began to level a barrage of criticism against the state agricultural college. The school was as obnoxious from the farmer's point of view, Equity critics said, as the middlemen, the grain gamblers, and the corporations. As far as the average farmer was concerned, the university was a "cold-storage institution of dead languages and useless learning which costs several millions of bushels of wheat each year." Furthermore, the college of agriculture was too "productive-minded." Its traditional policy was to encourage the farmers to increase production on the theory that agriculture, like industry, had to be made as efficient as possible. Equity leaders insisted that this attitude on the part of the college not only failed to better the farmers' position, but actually hurt them because of the heavy surpluses which it promoted. According to one Equity spokesman, who insisted that the society had no desire to "cross swords" with the college, there was pertinence in the thought that peach growers were interested not so much in Bordeaux mixture, while peaches were rotting, as they were in selling their products at profitable prices.[39]

Equity critics also charged that the college offered courses which were not only far removed from the economic needs of future farmers but actually made students lose their taste for rural life. Thus as a result of their college experience, farm youths drifted to the city instead of returning to the farm. The same critics held that professors of agriculture lacked practical farm experience and were unsympathetic with farm difficulties. The college of agriculture remained aloof from farm organizations and did nothing to help solve the farmers' marketing problems. Indeed, why should one not assume that it was actually doing the bidding of the corporations?

The *Wisconsin Equity News* made innumerable demands for a legislative investigation of university courses and university expenditures. When it was announced in 1909 that the university baseball team was planning a trip to the Orient, this journal remarked protestingly: "It is time for the investigation. Also, for the passage of laws that will protect the public

39. Frederick C. Howe, *Wisconsin: An Experiment in Democracy* (New York, 1912), p. 164; C. A. Lyman, "The Cooperative Society in Wisconsin," in National Conference on Marketing and Farm Credits, *Marketing and Farm Credits, 1915* (Madison, Wis., 1916), pp. 41–42.

by placing officials who will authorize and permit such useless waste of the people's money in the institutions at Mendota [the state insane asylum] or Waupun [the state penitentiary]." A few months earlier, when students preparing for the consular service petitioned the university authorities for courses in Chinese and Japanese, the Equity publication demanded that the requests be turned down. These were "special" and purely "personal professions," it held, "from which the general public will derive no benefit whatever."[40]

Finally in 1914, the state board of public affairs, much to the satisfaction of the Equity authorities, began an investigation of the university, including the college of agriculture. The resulting *Survey of the University of Wisconsin,* whatever the animus which inspired its compilers, contained much valuable information and gave a clear insight into the thinking of various groups. It set forth the facts concerning the teaching of agricultural economics and rural problems, including marketing. It pointed out, deprecatingly, that the Wisconsin college of agriculture was "more than forty years old before it began to teach the distribution and marketing of farm wealth in general, and to study Wisconsin market problems in particular." These facts could not be disputed, but it was also true that the Wisconsin college of agriculture was one of the few such institutions in the nation to offer courses in agricultural economics at all.[41]

The state board, in the course of its investigations, found that many times the college authorities held opinions at variance with the "definite" and "positive" demands of certain farmer groups. It admitted, however, that the college staff "opposed" or "held aloof" from many such proposals because they were deemed "violative of economic, social or civic law." It conceded also that the farmers' complaints were "apt to be crude, unwise, and ineffective in the proposed principles and methods of action."

> The college cannot be expected to head an agrarian revolution for distributive justice. If it were proper to do so, it is beyond reason to expect it. It is not recorded in history that fat men, lawyers, and college professors ever headed a

40. *Wisconsin Equity News,* May 10, 1908, p. 6; August 10, 1909, p. 10; August 25, 1909, p. 5.

41. *Report upon the Survey of the University of Wisconsin: Findings of the State Board of Public Affairs and its Report to the Legislature* (Madison, [1915]), pp. 942–45.

riot. Teachers are conservative by nature, with courage very like that of Burns' field mouse. . . . [The college] cannot be allied with farm organizations or devote itself to class propagandism; but it can put freely at the service of students, farmers, farm leaders and their organizations the knowledge that is needed for wise action.[42]

No doubt all this Equity pressure had some effect. For example, the Wisconsin college of agriculture presently took pains to study the history of cheese from producer to consumer, and the state board of control formulated plans for a more efficient system of marketing.[43]

The Equity Society, besides putting pressure on the college of agriculture, also exerted influence on the state legislature. The first major legislative measure to attract the attention of the organization was a bill seeking additional funds to build and maintain a state-owned binder-twine plant which was expected not only to manufacture twine for the farmers at lower prices but also to net the state a profit. A bill providing the necessary funds for such a plant was introduced in the legislature of 1909, but, much to the disgust of the Equity leadership, it was defeated. This was enough to grind the wheels of discontent, and Theodore Roosevelt's words, "Farmers Must Organize," became suddenly popular. A thorough analysis of the strength of Equity influence in the Wisconsin legislature brought out the fact that the assemblymen in and adjoining the organized Equity territory voted for the binder-twine bill, while those in and around the unorganized territory voted against it.[44]

That Equity was also interested in other progressive measures is evident from the demands it made during the state election campaign of 1910. The Wisconsin society favored more stringent education laws; completion of the binder-twine plant; conservation of natural resources; enactment of employers' liability and industrial insurance; establishment of a state commission to study living costs and the difference between the prices received by the farmers and those paid by the consumers; encouragement of coöperative buying and selling; extension of the scope and authority of the dairy and food commission; improvements in the registration, primary,

42. *Ibid.*, pp. 947–49.

43. R. W. Campbell, "Coöperation in Wisconsin," *American Review of Reviews*, XLVII (April, 1913), p. 470.

44. Wisconsin State Board of Control, *Biennial Report*, 1911–12, pp. 10–11; *Wisconsin Equity News*, July 25, 1909, pp. 4–7; *ibid.*, June 10, 1909, p. 10.

and general election laws; passage of a corrupt practices act and initiative, referendum, and recall measures; and the sale of the remaining public lands to actual settlers on long-term contracts.[45]

The Wisconsin legislature of 1911 was one of the most remarkable in the history of the state. Included among its long list of progressive accomplishments were measures providing for an industrial commission, workmen's compensation, state life insurance, an income tax, limitations on the labor of women and children, a state binder-twine plant, a cooperative-marketing law, and a state board of public affairs. Highly gratified with the accomplishments of the session, the *Wisconsin Equity News* boasted that the legislature had fulfilled its platform pledge to the farmers; and the following year the executive board of the order announced that in the past two years Equity had received more political recognition than ever before.[46]

The Wisconsin Society of Equity was not content with a merely political program; it was also active in promoting the organization of local cooperative associations. It helped create the Sheboygan County Cheese Producers' Federation, later known as the Wisconsin Cheese Producers' Federation, although a Plymouth farmer named Henry Krumery, who only later became a member of Equity, was mainly responsible for its growth.[47] But perhaps the biggest Equity accomplishment was the organization of local cooperative livestock-shipping associations. The first of these was organized at Durand in 1906, but the years of greatest activity along this line came during the period from 1912 to 1916. Individual associations began business with approximately thirty members; but in well-organized areas such as Pierce County, membership lists included as many as three or four hundred farmers. In 1917, the Ellsworth Equity Cooperative Association reported 520 members and claimed to be the largest in the state.[48]

45. *Ibid.*, September 25, 1910, pp. 9–10.

46. Milo M. Quaife, *Wisconsin, Its History and Its People, 1634–1924* (2 vols., Chicago, 1924), II, 36; *Wisconsin Equity News*, June 25, 1911, pp. 4–5; *ibid.*, October 25, 1912, p. 1; National Conference on Marketing and Farm Credits, *Marketing and Farm Credits*, pp. 39–40; Edwin G. Nourse, *Legal Status of Agricultural Cooperation* (New York, 1927), p. 46.

47. *Equity News*, September 1, 1915, p. 129; Henry Krumery, *A Blow at the Cheese Trust* (n.p., n.d.), pp. 7–8 [pamphlet].

48. Edwin G. Nourse and Joseph G. Knapp, *Co-Operative Marketing of Live-*

While the Equity Society was entrenching itself in Wisconsin, the spring wheat growers were beginning to organize under its leadership in Minnesota, the Dakotas, and then in Montana. This was accomplished mainly through the Equity Cooperative Exchange, the first cooperative terminal marketing agency of importance in the United States. Later, a livestock-marketing firm was added. Generally speaking, the organizers of the exchange operated on the theory that local cooperative marketing reform, desirable as it was, did not and could not provide relief from the abuses that existed on the terminal market.[49]

The grievances of the spring wheat growers against the grain merchants were of long standing, and when Equity projected itself into the struggle it simply followed in the footsteps of the Grangers, the Alliancemen, the Populists, and other promoters of the cooperative grain-marketing movement. In graphic style Equity leaders denounced the grain merchants for depressing prices, underweighing, undergrading, and heavily assessing the farmers for foreign material in their grain. The mixing of lower-grade wheat with that of a higher grade and selling the mixed wheat as the higher grade was termed a fraud. The railroads, the bankers, and the Minnesota State Grading and Inspection Board were considered enemies of the farmers.[50] The railroads were charged with both denying cars when needed and exacting heavy tolls when the cars were furnished. The bankers and other agencies financing the movement of grain were "usurers." The Minnesota State Grading and Inspection Board was assailed as the tool of "speculators," "grain gamblers," "vultures," "pilferers," "bandits," "pirates," "thieves," "crooks," and "the Grain Combine." All this, when reduced to the smallest common denominator, became the

---

stock (Washington, 1931), pp. 12–16; B. H. Hibbard and Asher Hobson, "Cooperation in Wisconsin," *University of Wisconsin Agricultural Experiment Station, Bulletin 282* (Madison, 1917), p. 17; *Equity News,* May 1, 1917, p. 10.

49. For a statement by the head of the Equity Cooperative Exchange explaining why farmers had taken to the terminal market, see the *Equity Farm News* (Fargo, N. Dak.), January 1, 1912, p. 13.

50. L. D. H. Weld, "Cooperation in Minnesota," *Papers and Proceedings of the Seventh Annual Meeting of the Minnesota Academy of the Social Sciences* (Minneapolis, 1914), VII, 57–58; *Report of the Federal Trade Commission on the Grain Trade* (7 vols., Washington, 1920–1926), III, 154–61 [see page 161 for the arguments of the grain trade]; *Minnesota Leader* (Olivia), December 17, 31, 1921.

Minneapolis Chamber of Commerce, which to many grain growers was the perfect symbol of graft and corruption.[51]

To evaluate fairly the charges and countercharges made by the farmers and the grain trade is no simple task. Much of the printed material is highly emotional. Granted that many charges were probably true, others exaggerated, and still others half true, the fact is that many farmers believed the charges. Because of this, they readily joined first the Equity Cooperative Exchange and then later the Nonpartisan League. As so frequently noted, what people believe to be true is often more important than the truth itself.

The mere launching of an attack against the Minneapolis Chamber of Commerce, which to the farmers was a monopoly, greatly accelerated the growth of the exchange in the northwestern grain-growing area. Here La Follette was popular and the progressive movement was strong. George S. Loftus, James A. Manahan, Benjamin Drake, and Magnus Johnson, influential leaders with the exchange at one time or another, represented varying shades of the progressive viewpoint in politics. *La Follette's Magazine* published numerous articles favorable to the exchange marketing program, while Equity publications gave much space to La Follette. Thus the exchange represented something broader than mere terminal marketing reform.[52]

The marketing program of Equity was aided, no doubt, by the presence of large numbers of Scandinavians in the spring wheat area. The Scandinavian Transportation Company, organized during the late 1860's, was

51. *Equity Farm News,* December 1, 1911, p. 15; *Interstate Commerce Commission Reports* (Washington, 1908), XII, 563–64; *Montana Equity News* (Great Falls), September 14, 1916; W. E. Davis, "Fighting the Grain Combine," *La Follette's Magazine* (Madison, Wis.), VI (January 17, 1914), p. 3; *La Follette's Magazine,* V (December 13, 1913), p. 5; *ibid.* (December 20, 1913), p. 5; *Equity Cooperative Exchange, Proposed Farmers' Terminal Elevator, St. Paul, Minnesota* (n.p., n.d.), inside back cover; Charles E. Russell, "The Revolt of the Farmers," *Pearson's Magazine,* XXXIII (April, 1915), pp. 417–27; *Coöperators' Herald* (Fargo, N. Dak.), October 24, 1913; March 6, August 7, 1914. For a more critical account of the financing of grain shipments by bankers and commission firms, see F.T.C., *The Grain Trade,* III, 183–96.

52. *The New International Year Book,* 1912, p. 476. La Follette won the first presidential primary election in North Dakota in 1912. Somewhat typical were the remarks appearing in the *Coöperators' Herald* for March 6, 1914, and July 23, 1915.

probably the first cooperative marketing organization in Minnesota. There is reason to believe that during the Equity period more cooperative stores, creameries, and elevators existed among the Scandinavians of the Northwest than among the native Americans. Among the Scandinavians progressive views in politics were also strong.[53]

Significantly, Equity sentiment had penetrated into the Edmonton, Alberta, area as early as 1905, but had made slight headway there because the Canadian farmers were reluctant to affiliate with a strictly American organization. The grain growers of western Canada, however, with grievances similar to those suffered south of the border, had appealed to their government for aid and had obtained substantial assistance in the establishment of cooperative elevators. All this was watched with the greatest interest by the American farmers, who made it a point to compare the prices obtained by the Canadian cooperatives at Winnipeg with the prices paid for grain in Minneapolis. Whenever higher prices prevailed in Winnipeg, the natural assumption was that the attitude of the Canadian government made the difference, and Equity enthusiasts placed the blame for the lower prices paid on the Minneapolis market on the Minneapolis Chamber of Commerce.[54] Whether the facts warranted such an assumption is beside the point. The Equity farmers believed it to be true.

The immediate forerunner of the Equity Cooperative Exchange was the short-lived Minnesota Farmers' Exchange, the spring wheat counterpart of an abortive national movement for reform on the terminal markets. The Minnesota exchange, established in 1902, was incorporated for $500,000, but speedily found that it could not hope to dispose of any grain it might obtain without a seat on the Minneapolis Chamber of Commerce. But all efforts by the exchange to purchase a seat on the chamber proved futile. Chamber representatives claimed that membership was denied the exchange on grounds of insolvency, a charge which the exchange leaders heatedly denied. And so the Minnesota Farmers' Exchange accomplished nothing, except to build up farmer sentiment against the

53. Larson, *The Wheat Market,* p. 104; Edward A. Ross, *The Old World in the New* (New York, 1914), p. 91.

54. Louis A. Wood, *A History of Farmer Movements in Canada* (Toronto, 1924), pp. 199–201; Harald S. Patton, *Grain Growers' Cooperation in Western Canada* (Cambridge, Mass., 1928), pp. 114–17; *Hearings on Grain Exchanges* (63 Congress, 2 session, House Resolution 424, Washington, 1915), pp. 180–91.

chamber. All this information was at the disposal of the Equity representatives who assembled in Minneapolis on May 30, 1908, to organize the Equity Cooperative Exchange.[55]

There were other preliminaries. The first phase of Equity operations in the northwest probably began on May 25, 1903, with the circulation of Everitt's series of "Dollar Wheat Bulletins" urging farmers to withhold their wheat from market until the price of one dollar per bushel could be obtained. Many northwestern farmers accepted this advice, and when necessary even constructed new warehouses and granaries in which to store their wheat. Much to their joy they found that the price of wheat did rise to the dollar level, a development for which Equity leaders immediately assumed full credit. Next year Equity sponsored another "hold-your-wheat" campaign, but without the favorable results claimed in 1903. Other similar attempts followed, and in 1907, according to Equity statistics, some thirty million bushels of wheat had been pledged; but the program as a whole was a failure. The chief obstacles to success were the futility of the plan, poor leadership, dissension at national headquarters, and the lack of a satisfactory method for the financing of pooling members. Despite these failures, the hold-your-wheat program was not altogether without results. By recruiting ten or twelve thousand Equity members in North Dakota alone, the leaders of the movement had paved the way for the much more important program of cooperative marketing.[56]

With the organization of the Equity Cooperative Exchange in 1908, the grain-marketing program in the Northwest entered its second phase. The "grain growers' division" of the American Society of Equity had plans to organize the grain growers of the country on as many terminal markets as possible, but it was only in the spring wheat country that the program materialized. By this time it was abundantly clear that organizing local farm associations and establishing state service and educational organizations to aid the farmers in cleaning, grading, and storing their grain were not enough. Much as these achievements might improve local marketing

55. *Co-operators' Guide* (Indianapolis), IV (February, 1911), p. 4.

56. Nash, in *World Today,* XIII (July, 1907), p. 717; Chelsa C. Sherlock, *The Modern Farm Cooperative* (Des Moines, 1922), pp. 14–15; *Equity Farm Journal,* I (May, 1908), p. 10; *Devils Lake* (N. Dak.) *Inter-Ocean,* June 28, 1907; Hibbard, *Marketing Agricultural Products,* pp. 232–33; Herman Steen, *Coöperative Marketing* (New York, 1923), p. 212.

conditions, they did nothing toward the reform of conditions on the terminal market. What was needed was a farmers' terminal marketing firm that would receive grain shipped on consignment, or, better still, could be fed by a chain of local cooperatives with ample storage facilities. With such a setup the farmers could clean, condition, transfer, and store their grain at a minimum of risk and expense, and thus retain control of their grain from the time it left the farm until it was sold on the terminal market.[57]

The exchange marketing program was significant in that it sought to organize the farmers on the basis of the crop produced. By so doing its leaders were pursuing a realistic course, for experience had revealed that the "farming class" was a heterogeneous group consisting of farmers with differing and frequently antagonistic interests and that the success of a marketing organization depended primarily on bringing together producers of the same crops who had the same problems. The farmers could also, should the need be felt, organize as consumers to purchase feed, seeds, fertilizers, machinery, farm implements, and general farm supplies.[58]

Unfortunately, such a plan of organization was hardly designed to promote good relations between the American Society of Equity and the Equity Cooperative Exchange. Sharp differences developed between the parent order and its offspring over aims and objectives, policies, jurisdiction, and finances. The Equity Cooperative Exchange was interested solely in the problems of the spring wheat grower, while the American Society of Equity claimed an interest in all farmers—"the grain grower, the stock feeder, the dairyman, the tobacco grower, the fruit grower, the cotton grower." The exchange was realistic and opportunistic, while the Equity Society was idealistic and altruistic. The former saw no reason why it should submit to policies that did not directly and immediately benefit the grain producers, while the latter asked that commodity and regional interests be submerged for the general welfare of the farmers as a class.

57. *Coöperators' Herald,* October 10, 1913, and April 17, 1914; *Equity Farm News,* January 1, 1912, p. 13. See Lionel Smith-Gordon, *Cooperation for Farmers* (London, 1918), pp. 190–93, for a good, brief discussion on the pros and cons of local and terminal marketing operations.

58. George Harold Powell, *Coöperation in Agriculture* (New York, 1913), pp. 5–10, 18–23; Chris L. Christensen, *Farmers' Cooperative Associations in the United States. 1929,* U. S. Dept. Agri., Circular 94 (Washington, 1929).

These conflicting philosophies were responsible for many of the rifts and cleavages within Equity ranks.[59]

Although the exchange was organized in 1908, it was not until 1911 that it was incorporated under the laws of North Dakota for the purchase and sale of grain on consignment. Its executives included John M. Anderson, former member of the North Dakota legislature who headed the exchange until 1922, as president; A. A. Trovatten, a grain solicitor, employed to drum up business; and Pliney E. Cooper as agent and sales manager. The sales of the exchange were small between the years 1908 and 1912, amounting to only 805 cars for the period, and out of these, 681 were reportedly sold through members of the Minneapolis Chamber of Commerce. Cooper's services with the exchange ended on August 1, 1912, when George S. Loftus became sales manager. This marked the beginning of the third and perhaps the most spectacular phase in the history of the exchange.[60]

Loftus was more a reformer than a business manager. He came to the exchange as an aggressive and uncompromising foe of the organized grain trade and as a seasoned campaigner for La Follette progressivism. He hardly fitted the requirement of an expert trained in the principles and practices of cooperative marketing. His chief qualification was that, in season and out of season, he fought for and represented the point of view of the small shipper. Like the farmers among whom he worked, Loftus was a great admirer of Senator La Follette. He was an artful platform speaker, and his mastery of farmer psychology brought farmers from miles around to hear him denounce the "grain combine." Naturally Loftus was cordially hated by the organized grade trade, which regarded his elevation to office as tantamount to a declaration of war against the Minneapolis Chamber of Commerce.[61]

59. *Plan of the American Society of Equity,* p. 20; Everitt, *The Third Power,* third edition, p. 277; *Equity Farm Journal,* I (December, 1907), p. 4; (May, 1908), p. 5.

60. House Resolution 424, 63 Congress, 2 session, p. 340; C. U. Pierson, *The American Society of Equity* (Casselton, N. Dak., 1909), pp. 1–2 [pamphlet]; *State of North Dakota Legislative Manual,* 1907, p. 370; *Federal Trade Commission Decisions* (Washington, 1926), VII, 145.

61. Equity Cooperative Exchange, *Cooperation in Marketing of Grain* (Minneapolis, n.d.) [pamphlet].

Meanwhile, the chamber of commerce had been maintaining a vigilant eye over the activities of the exchange and had been girding itself for future action. There were some merchants who believed that the exchange, if allowed to go on unchecked, would provide the nucleus for a powerful cooperative movement. The thing to do, therefore, was to destroy it in its infancy. This task was assigned to John G. McHugh, secretary of the Minneapolis Chamber of Commerce, a man who had been associated previously with the Winnipeg Board of Trade and had been active against the Canadian cooperatives. Undoubtedly the decision to turn McHugh loose against the exchange was a mistake from the point of view of the chamber of commerce, for it was all that was needed to spur the Equity leaders into action.[62]

The clash between the chamber and the exchange became the subject of a series of legislative inquiries during the session of 1913. A Minnesota house committee, sympathetic with the exchange, began its investigations first; thereupon the grain trade, aroused because of the activities of the house, instigated an investigation by the senate, which reputedly was more favorable to the interests of the private merchants. The public, as a result, was treated to the spectacle of seeing two rival groups seeking to substantiate their known convictions. Neither group conducted an impartial investigation, but each, with some accuracy, accused the other of being unfair.[63]

Early in 1914, Congressman James A. Manahan, the counsel for the Minnesota house committee, introduced a resolution in the national House of Representatives calling for a congressional investigation of the grain trade. The resolution was adopted, and a congressional committee was appointed which included, besides Manahan himself, J. Campbell Cantrill, former president of the Kentucky Society of Equity, and I. L. Lenroot of Wisconsin, whose progressive leanings were already well known. Little,

62. Paul Fossum, *Agrarian Movement in North Dakota* (Baltimore, 1925), p. 83; F.T.C., *Decisions,* VII, 145.

63. *Minnesota Journal of the House,* 1913, pp. 1748–57; House Resolution 424, 63 Congress, 2 session, pp. 397–401; *Minnesota Journal of the Senate,* 1913, pp. 231, 285. For a newspaper account of the senate and house committee investigations, see the scrapbook of Benjamin Drake, in the private possession of Benjamin Drake of Minneapolis.

if anything, came from this probe other than a considerable amount of publicity for the exchange.[64]

By late 1914 the exchange had plunged into the campaign to erect a state-owned terminal elevator in North Dakota, a campaign which dated back to the days of the Farmers' Alliance and the Populists. The elevator issue was put to a popular vote in 1912 and again in 1914. Each time it passed with a decided majority. Legislation also had been enacted for the financing of the project, while the state board of control had been authorized to investigate the subject and to present plans to the legislature for the building of the state elevator.[65]

The board of control began its investigations by visiting terminal elevators in the United States and Canada and interviewing government officials, grain merchants, bankers, business leaders, and cooperative leaders. Among those consulted were representatives of the Minneapolis Chamber of Commerce, the Duluth Board of Trade, and the Equity Cooperative Exchange. But instead of presenting plans as it had been ordered to do, the board of control became critical of the project. It recommended strongly against the state's erecting such an elevator and advised that if the state insisted on doing something of the sort, it would be better to lease an elevator and try out the scheme at the lowest possible cost.[66]

The exchange, in anticipation of the unfavorable report, prepared a lengthy statement of its own to present to the North Dakota legislature, and in cooperation with other Equity groups it called a mass meeting of farmers to assemble in Bismarck at the time the board of control was to make its recommendations. The exchange statement criticized the board for failing to interview people who were best qualified to present the Equity point of view. It defended participation by the exchange in the controversy on the ground that it was a North Dakota corporation, 90 per cent of whose members paid taxes to the state. Such an elevator, the ex-

64. J. E. Boyle, "The Agrarian Movement in the Northwest," *American Economic Review,* VIII (September, 1918), p. 513.

65. John D. Hicks, *The Populist Revolt* (Minneapolis, 1931), pp. 287–89; Herbert Gaston, *The Nonpartisan League* (New York, 1920), pp. 40–41; Fossum, *Agrarian Movements in North Dakota,* p. 87; Andrew A. Bruce, *Non-Partisan League* (New York, 1921), p. 57.

66. *North Dakota Journal of the House,* 1915, pp. 165–69.

change claimed, would stimulate competition, bring higher prices, provide farmers with adequate storage facilities, aid them in their cleaning and drying operations, and, in short, provide them with many of the benefits that the Canadian farmers already enjoyed. With the failure of the North Dakota Board of Control to act on the measure, St. Paul became the desirable spot for the location of this elevator because of its strategic situation at the head of the Mississippi River, its admirable transportation facilities, its willingness to contribute to the success of the venture, and its well-established reputation of friendliness to the farmers' cause.[67] The subsequent efforts of the North Dakota farmers to secure a terminal elevator are closely interwoven with the history of the Nonpartisan League, and will be considered in the next chapter.

The bitter campaigns in behalf of a terminal elevator which the Equity Society was waging in North Dakota against the Minneapolis Chamber of Commerce no doubt helped the organization to spread westward into Montana. This state lies beyond the boundary of the western Middle West, but since in its farming activities it was becoming a kind of projection of North Dakota, its interest in the Equity Society is worth noting briefly. Montana, in 1914, was still a booming pioneer state about to complete the transition from a cattle-raising to a grain-growing economy. Rising grain prices and bumper crops promised to make grain growing a veritable bonanza. Montana's prospects had lured thousands of immigrants from the Dakotas, Minnesota, Canada, and other grain-growing areas. With easy credit provided by eastern mortgage companies and middle western bankers, loan agents were familiar people. So, too, were automobile and tractor salesmen. New towns, churches, schools, and roads appeared. Land values soared, and so did debts; but the favorable climate, the breaking of much fresh sod, and the European war helped many to conclude that prosperity had come to stay.[68]

The influx of new population, together with bumper crops and high wheat prices, which enabled farmers to pay dues, accounted largely for

67. *Ibid.*, pp. 932–35; *Pioneer Press* (St. Paul), February 3, 4, 1915; *Bismarck Daily Tribune*, January 31, 1915.

68. Bureau of Agriculture, Labor and Industry, *Montana Resources and Opportunities* (Helena, 1933), p. 75; *Coöperators' Herald*, July 23, 1915; *Montana Resources and Opportunities*, pp. 74–75.

the rapid growth of the Montana Equity from a membership of 200 in 1914 to 6,000 in 1916. By 1917 the *Montana Equity News* claimed 12,000 subscribers, 60,000 readers, and an Equity membership of about 15,000.[69]

The complaints of the Montana farmers were similar to those of their neighbors in Canada, Minnesota, and the Dakotas. They had also watched with interest the campaigns of the Canadian growers and those of the Equity Cooperative Exchange. Many of the newly arrived settlers had belonged to the Equity Society in the older states to the east or to the cooperative organizations in Canada to the north. Oddly enough, the Montanans seemed to display a greater interest in the Canadian movement than they did in the exchange.[70]

Besides protesting against the unfavorable wheat market, Montana farmers also registered complaints against the high cost of farm supplies and consumer goods and the dominating influence of the mining corporations in the state government. To fight against these conditions Equity promoted the establishment of cooperative marketing and purchasing associations, consumer stores, and cooperative credit and insurance companies; it agitated for lower railroad rates and a reformed tax system, and finally it undertook a persistent courtship of organized labor. But most of this activity was in vain. Successive crop failures, factionalism, declining wheat prices, and the postwar reaction eventually placed the Montana Equity in its grave. By 1918 it had yielded its leadership as a farm order to the Nonpartisan League.[71]

During and immediately following World War I, the activities of the Wisconsin Society of Equity and the Equity Cooperative Exchange were apparently headed for newer and loftier heights, but this appearance was

69. *Montana Equity News,* February 23, March 22, July 19, 1917; *Great Falls Tribune,* June 15, 1917.

70. Patton, *Grain Growers' Cooperation in Western Canada,* pp. 114–17; *Montana Equity News,* February 22, November 15, 1917; April 25, 1918; J. M. Mehl, *Cooperative Grain Marketing,* U. S. Dept. Agri., Bulletin 937 (Washington, 1921), pp. 1–5.

71. *Montana Equity News,* August 24, 1916; January 4, 11, March 1, 1917; *Nonpartisan Leader* (Fargo, N. Dak.), January 28, 1916, p. 4; *Great Falls Tribune,* January 10, February 18, May 16, 1917; Louis Levine, *The Taxation of Mines in Montana* (New York, 1919), pp. 10–14; *The Nation,* CVII (November 2, 1918), pp. 507–8; *Montana Equity News,* May 24, August 16, 1917; May 2, 1918; August 10, 1919.

illusory. In point of fact these two remaining segments of Equity strength were soon to founder on the rocks of disaster.

In Wisconsin, the demand for direct political action surpassed the earlier enthusiasm for cooperatives. Early in 1917 the Nonpartisan League had attracted the attention of some of the politically minded members of the Wisconsin Society of Equity. On March 22 about two hundred farmers representing eighteen counties assembled in Marshfield and, after marked differences over the best methods of organization, finally decided to demand immediate affiliation of the Equity with the League. Another meeting held in Wausau the same year indicated that a well-groomed political machine would be ready for the elections of 1918.[72]

Chief aspirant for the leadership of the political movement was James N. Tittemore, already three times an unsuccessful candidate for Congress. Despite the avocational character of his farming activities, he spoke eloquently and profusely of the need for "farmers to represent farmers," and presented himself as one ideally qualified to lead the "soil-tilling fraternity" to victory. Tittemore set for himself the task of getting 50,000 members for the Wisconsin Equity, and by combining rhetoric, politics, religion, and sophistry, he came close to attaining his goal. He spoke of Lincoln and his efforts to preserve the American homestead, of his own birth in a log cabin, of his rise from telegraph boy to traffic manager of a railroad, of how the farmers were being "skinned" by the railroads, and of the hope for emancipating the farmers by taking to direct political action. This ushered in one of the most uproarious periods in the history of the organization.[73]

Rumors of a farmer-labor alignment assumed new proportions in 1918 after an announcement to the effect that the Nonpartisan League would not present a slate until two years later. An organization, temporarily known as the Wisconsin Farmers' Progressive League, called a meeting for May 1 to decide on the platform, the candidates, and the party through which the new political alliance was to function. Enthusiasts sought to

72. *Wisconsin Leader* (Madison), September 11, 1920; *Equity News,* March 1, 1917, pp. 720, 726; *Organized Farmer* (Milwaukee), April 26, 1917, p. 5.

73. *Evening Wisconsin* (Milwaukee), May 2, 1918; *Equity News,* January 1, 1918, p. 259.

allay the fears of the apprehensive by the argument that "conditions are now different." [74]

On May 1 approximately five hundred delegates representing Equity, the Nonpartisan League, and organized labor met in Madison to nominate a slate headed by Tittemore. Merlin Hull and John J. Blaine, both prominent in progressive circles, were nominated for secretary of state and attorney general, respectively. These endorsements were made without party designation.[75]

The *Milwaukee Leader,* the daily Socialist publication, suspicious of the Madison gathering, sent a special representative to determine the motives behind the meeting. According to his report, certain prominent Equity men were the "guiding spirits" in the movement, and the meeting was merely the beginning of a drive to place Tittemore in the governor's chair. Tittemore was accused of willingness to use any party to satisfy his ambitions and even of appropriating his platform from the "immediate demands" of the Socialist party in order to bait it with "a program, luscious and appetizing." [76]

Like the La Follette reformers before them, the Tittemore supporters decided to cast their lot with the Republican party. But they pushed their program and their candidates in every part of the state. The *National Equity News* helped the cause along by filling its pages with campaign promises. Whether Tittemore had completely alienated himself from the political affections of the Nonpartisan League is uncertain, but he did try to capitalize on what League sentiment existed in the state. But all this was in vain. Tittemore was defeated in the Republican primaries by the incumbent, Emanuel Philipp, who got 72,000 votes against 45,000 for the "ambitious Equitarian." In the general elections, only John J. Blaine, the nominee for attorney general, was elected.[77]

Shortly after this election, the Wisconsin Equity became involved in

74. *Milwaukee Daily News,* April 6, 1918; *National Equity News* (Madison, Wis.), April 18, 1918, pp. 1, 7.

75. *Organized Farmer,* May 30, 1918, p. 9; *National Equity News,* May 2, 1918, p. 4.

76. *Milwaukee Leader,* May 3, 1918.

77. *National Equity News,* September 12, 1918, pp. 6–7; *Blue Book of the State of Wisconsin,* 1919, p. 93.

internecine warfare. The year 1919 found the state and national organiza tions embroiled in controversies over postwar issues, politics, and finances The Red issue also was injected into the struggles and dissensions.[78] De spite the numerous factions, however, the aggressive Tittemore prepared t seek the Republican nomination for governor again in 1920. But this tim the Nonpartisan League entered the campaign with a ticket of its own in reality a La Follette progressive slate under new political clothing The League lost no time in exposing the political machinations of Titte more, who had urged it to organize in Wisconsin and had then turned against it to satisfy his own interests. The League ticket, incidentally, wa headed by John J. Blaine, who had been elected attorney general on th Tittemore ticket in 1918.[79]

Once again Tittemore waged an aggressive campaign, and once agai he was defeated. This time he received only a little more than half a many votes as in 1918, while of the six candidates for the nomination, h received the fewest votes. He failed even to secure the votes of the Equit members and their families, upon which he had so greatly relied. From this time on his activities in the Equity became negligible; in fact, hi exit was about as hurried as was his entrance.[80]

The successor of Tittemore to the state presidency of the Wisconsi Society of Equity was E. C. Pommerening, Tittemore's first lieutenan Functioning after the fashion of his master, this youthful would-be ad ministrator supplanted the Tittemore mania for politics with his ow mania for cooperatives, setting up enterprises with a fantastic swiftnes that sapped the organization of its remaining strength. Placing a rankin official on a political ticket and using Equity resources to promote hi candidacy was bad enough, but the promotion of a succession of coopera tive failures was even worse. Pommerening's policy brought down upo the society the rising wrath of the older members and furnished the op position with a much-appreciated opportunity to denounce it as a racket.

78. *Wisconsin Equity News,* November 27, 1919, p. 9.

79. *Wisconsin Leader,* November 6, 1920; *Organized Farmer,* September 1 1920, p. 20.

80. *Ibid.,* p. 2.

81. *Equity News,* December 15, 1920, p. 8; December 22, 1920, p. 3; *Wisconsi Leader,* January 29, 1921; *Wisconsin State Journal* (Madison), October 21, Novem ber 29, 1921; *Capital Times* (Madison), November 4, 1921.

Equally turbulent was the course pursued by the Equity Cooperative Exchange. Much of the crusading fervor of the exchange subsided after its departure from Minneapolis in 1914, and this, coupled with the rising wartime demands for farm products, brought a growth in its business activities. In 1914, it organized the St. Paul Grain Exchange, a "non-stock membership corporation" that was expected to become a sort of farmer-managed and controlled chamber of commerce.[82]

The St. Paul Grain Exchange required that all grain be sold through its members, who in turn charged a commission of one cent a bushel to sellers and shippers. Buyers, however, could make use of its facilities without purchasing through a broker and without having to pay a commission. This, exchange leaders said, made St. Paul an open market. The Equity Cooperative Exchange held two seats on the St. Paul Grain Exchange.[83]

In 1916, the exchange expanded its activities into livestock marketing, then into wool marketing, and finally into the cooperative purchasing of farm supplies. It entered the livestock-marketing field on the South St. Paul market. Its leaders had become convinced that the successes experienced in organizing local cooperative associations in Wisconsin, Minnesota, and upper Iowa warranted expansion into the terminal market. This move was noteworthy for two reasons: first, this was the forerunner of a series of similar commodity organizations sponsored by the Farmers' Union, the Farm Bureau, and numerous independent groups in the Middle West; and second, it brought to a head a standing controversy among the several Equity organizations on the policy of terminal marketing. The question at issue was whether farmers should continue to endorse those private terminal firms which had handled the livestock of the local associations in the past, or whether they should give their exclusive support to a farmer-owned and controlled agency. The establishment of the terminal agency indicated the predominance of the latter view.[84]

Business began on the South St. Paul market in October, 1916, and two years later a branch was established in Chicago. However, events soon

82. F.T.C., *Decisions,* VII, 137.

83. *Non-partisan Leader,* August 17, 1916, p. 6; *Minnesota Leader,* October 9, 1920.

84. Nourse and Knapp, *The Co-Operative Marketing of Livestock,* pp. 12–14, 106–7; *Organized Farmer,* January 24, 1919, p. 10.

convinced even the most enthusiastic exchange supporters that their terminal livestock-marketing operations were either ill advised or mismanaged, or both.[85]

The war years witnessed a rapid growth in the grain business of the exchange. New elevators were built or acquired, the number of stockholders was increased, and the financial reports presented favorable accounts of the progress of the organization. By midyear of 1922, the exchange owned eighty local elevators—fifty-two in North Dakota, two in South Dakota, and twenty-six in Minnesota. The exchange also operated twelve local cooperative elevators for farmer groups that either were unable financially to operate themselves or else preferred to operate as part of a large marketing organization.[86]

The stockholders' report for 1922 hinted that the financial condition of the exchange was not so healthy as previously claimed. Then, in the following year, the ugly rumors that circulated were confirmed. The capital stock of the exchange had been impaired to the extent of $750,000; money that had been obtained from the sale of the grain in the pool of 1923 had been diverted to the general business of the exchange; and a substantial amount of pool money had not been paid to the stockholders. Some fifteen elevators were located in territory that was not essentially grain-producing.[87]

Poor business leadership was the most important single reason for the decline of the exchange. Beginning with the time when one of its managers did not know enough to keep his personal accounts separate from those of the company, through the period when the business policies of the exchange had oscillated between "applied Christianity" and progressivism in politics, down into the unhealthy expansion of the war period the history of the exchange was one long procession of errors.

Psychologically also the management of the exchange was handicapped

85. *Equity News,* March 1, 1915, p. 714.

86. *Montana Equity News,* April 17, 1919; Ralph L. Harmon to Austin P. Haines, September 9, 1919, in the possession of R. L. Harmon of South St. Paul. See also H. B. Price, "Farmers' Cooperation in Minnesota, 1917–1922," *University of Minnesota Agricultural Experiment Station, Bulletin 202* (St. Paul, 1923), p. 35.

87. Equity Cooperative Exchange, *Statement by the Board of Directors* (Fargo, N. Dak., 1922), p. 3; Equity Cooperative Exchange, *Twelfth Annual Stockholders Convention, January 16–17–18, 1923.*

Its leadership was composed of agitators who were ill prepared for business management. It was more interested in war against the Minneapolis Chamber of Commerce than in the adoption of sound business policies. Resistance against the attacks of the chamber of commerce was easy, but the creation of an alternative marketing system was hard. The livestock agency was operated inefficiently; frequently complaints were registered about the poor handling of grain; sales were entrusted to subordinates while the leaders were busy quarreling with one another or else were attending to other matters than business. All this, coupled with the depression which hit the farmers in the early twenties, sent the organization sagging. In 1923, the exchange was finally placed in the hands of receivers, but not without challenge on the part of those who believed that with better management it could have kept going.[88]

The Equity suffered from the fact that it was a loosely knit, in fact regional, organization; only in the period from 1902 to 1907, when the control of the society was vested in Everitt, was there any trace of a central authority. At various intervals its strength was concentrated in Kentucky and Tennessee, Wisconsin, the Dakotas, Minnesota, and Montana. Its greatest strength was gained in Wisconsin, although the extent of the marketing operations of the Equity Cooperative Exchange cannot be overlooked. The influence of the national body never was strong; for the most part, it only struggled to keep itself alive. It would be a mistake to assume that Equity ever at any time acquired the status of a national movement. Eventually the Farmers' Union absorbed the remnants of the Equity, first in the agricultural Northwest and finally in Wisconsin.

But in spite of its unfortunate experiences, Equity left its mark. Under its leadership numerous local grain- and livestock-shipping associations were created, and the farmers were taught the need for a more efficient handling of their produce. Some of its leaders became identified with the Nonpartisan League and took an important part in the League's work, and men like Myron W. Thatcher and others who later assumed positions of leadership in the strong cooperatives built by the Farmers' Union in

88. *St. Paul Daily News,* October 4, 7, 1922; *Courier-News* (Fargo, N. Dak.), January 19, 1923; *Fargo Forum,* February 10, 1923. See also File 150484, *Emil Piper et al.* v. *Equity Cooperative Exchange,* Ramsey County Courthouse, St. Paul, Minn.

the upper Mississippi Valley obtained much of their early training with the old Equity Cooperative Exchange. It was upon the ruins of this last agency that the business program of the Farmers' Union was built. Equity agitated, sometimes successfully, for better grading standards, better warehousing, and better credit facilities; it brought pressure to bear on educational and governmental agencies to devote more attention to problems of marketing and distribution.

Chapter VI

THE NONPARTISAN LEAGUE BEGINNINGS[1]

THE NONPARTISAN LEAGUE was organized in North Dakota in 1915, and was thus a contemporary of the Equity. It differed sharply from the older society in a number of ways: it originated in the region where it was to score its greatest successes; it placed chief emphasis on political as opposed to economic action; and it was deeply influenced by the Socialist movement and by organized labor. Like the Equity, however, it was organized in an era of rising farm prices, and it appealed most to the discontented spring wheat growers who lived in the northern part of the western Middle West. Eventually the League helped decimate the ranks of the Equity, but when the League, in turn, went into a decline, the Farmers' Union, an order more like the Equity than like the League, moved in to fill the vacuum. Throughout these years the example of the Canadian wheat farmers, who had successfully carried their fight against the organized grain trade to a sympathetic government, greatly influenced the action of the American farmers across the border.[2] Mindful, also, of the success with which organized labor waged war against unemploy-

1. This chapter is reprinted in the main from Theodore Saloutos, "The Rise of the Nonpartisan League in North Dakota, 1915–1917," *Agricultural History,* XX (January, 1946), pp. 43–61.

2. Harald S. Patton, *Grain Growers' Cooperation in Western Canada* (Cambridge, Mass., 1928), pp. 114–17; Louis A. Wood, *A History of Farmers' Movements in Canada* (Toronto, 1924), pp. 199–201.

ment, low wages, poor working conditions, and long hours, the North Dakota farmers were moved to adopt similar methods in their struggle against low farm prices, high transportation rates, unfavorable marketing conditions, and monopoly.

It will be recalled that the burning issue in North Dakota politics by the year 1914 had become the farmers' demand, strongly supported by the Equity Society, for a terminal elevator. In this same year, however, Louis B. Hanna, a conservative, had contrived to win the governorship. Hanna had waged his campaign largely in opposition to extravagance in government, and promptly made it clear that he intended at all costs to prevent the erection of the greatly desired terminal elevator.[3] Equity leaders were certain that the governor would have the support of the state board of control, which was scheduled to make a report on the subject, and they feared the legislature would also be hostile. They therefore called the annual convention of the North Dakota Society of Equity to assemble in Bismarck, the capital, at the time early in February, 1915, when the legislature was expected to have the elevator project under consideration.[4] They also extended an invitation to the Farmers' Union, then a comparatively new organization in the state, to take part in the February convention, to fraternize, and to exchange views on questions that confronted the farmers.[5] When this convention met, it came out strongly in favor of a terminal elevator, and its representatives drew up a bill to present to the legislature.[6] Representatives of the city of St. Paul were on hand to inform the farmers that their city would aid them if the elevator were located there. A feature of the convention was the march to the capitol to present the demands of the farmers, most prominent among them being the construction of a state-owned terminal elevator.[7] When the conven-

3. Andrew A. Bruce, *Non-Partisan League* (New York, 1921), pp. 57–58.

4. Herbert E. Gaston, *The Nonpartisan League* (New York, 1920), p. 43; *Bismarck Daily Tribune,* January 31, 1915; *Pioneer Press* (St. Paul), February 3, 4, 1915; *Non-partisan Leader* (Fargo, N. Dak.), September 23, 1915, pp. 5–6.

5. *Coöperators' Herald,* January 1, 1915, p. 4. The Union reported charters authorized for forty-two local chapters in North Dakota in 1914. Farmers' Educational and Cooperative Union of America, Tenth Annual Session, September 1–3, 1914, *Minutes,* pp. 18–19.

6. *Pioneer Press,* February 5, 1915.

7. *Coöperators' Herald,* February 5, 1915.

ion adjourned, some of the Equity leaders decided to remain in Bismarck until the elevator issue had been decided.

Among the speakers at an Equity rally held the night before the elevator issue came to a final vote was George S. Loftus, the pugnacious sales manager of the Equity Cooperative Exchange and a seasoned campaigner against the organized grain trade. Whether Loftus labored under the pains of an illness that shortly proved fatal or whether he had become unduly embittered because of the unfavorable report of the board of control is unknown, but the effects of his talk were generally conceded to be detrimental to the Equity cause.[8] Like Senator La Follette, whom he admired, Loftus called the roll of the legislature and in vicious and abusive language denounced those who he suspected would vote against the measure. A number of legislators were in the audience, and his acts unquestionably compelled some wavering members to vote against the measure.[9] It was killed in the lower house by a vote of 64 to 40 on the grounds that the state was not in a financial position to support the project.[10] Some Equity followers predicted that they would return two years hence, but the executive committee of the Equity Cooperative Exchange, meeting in Fargo shortly thereafter, voted to proceed with plans to finance an elevator to be owned by Equity farmers, relying on the city of St. Paul for the donation of a site.[11]

Other farm leaders, however, did not acquiesce in the decision of the legislature. The report was that the resentment of the farmers had been growing, stimulated by such accounts as the one shortly circulated to the effect that in the course of the debate over the elevator bill, Treadwell Twitchell, a leading opponent of the measure, had angrily told the farmers to "Go home and slop the hogs!"[12] Twitchell and his associates de-

8. James E. Boyle, "The Agrarian Movement in the Northwest," *American Economic Review,* VIII (September, 1918), p. 513.

9. William Langer, *The Nonpartisan League* (Mandan, N. Dak., 1920), pp. 13–14. See *Bismarck Tribune,* February 14, 1915, for excerpts from North Dakota newspapers denouncing the activities of Loftus prior to the vote on the elevator bill. See also the *Co-operative Manager and Farmer* (Minneapolis), IV (March, 1915), pp. 29–33, for hostile accounts of Equity activities.

10. *Pioneer Press,* February 21, 1915.

11. *Ibid.,* February 22, 1915.

12. Gaston, *The Nonpartisan League,* p. 43; Bruce, *Non-Partisan League,* p. 59; Charles Edward Russell, *The Story of the Nonpartisan League* (New York, 1920),

nied the charge, but whether it was true is immaterial; many of th farmers believed it and it spread like wildfire.

Leadership, at least in the beginning stages, has always played an im portant part in the organization of reform movements.[13] It was a tremen dous factor in the origin and development of the Nonpartisan League The driving force in the new movement was Arthur C. Townley, one c the most gifted farm organizers as well as one of the most colorful per sonalities in agrarian history. His ability to organize farmers and collec dues had caused many of his adversaries to dub him "After Cash Town ley." He had attended the historic Equity convention in February, 1915 but not in the capacity of delegate or leader; no doubt he was contemplat ing the idea of organizing a farmers' political movement of his own whe the psychological moment presented itself.[14] Townley had an interest i the plight of the farmer because he himself had been an unsuccessfu farmer and was reputedly in debt to the extent of $100,000. Nor was sc cialistic talk strange to him, for he had been recruiting members for th Socialist party of North Dakota.

The radicalism of Townley, in all probability, was influenced by th unsettled surroundings in which he found himself. North Dakota was young state, having been admitted into the Union in 1889, and its man ethnic groups, which were tenacious in their adherence to Old Worl traditions, made it seem like the polyglot nations of Europe.[15] Accordin to the 1910 census, there were 156,158 foreign-born whites, representin twenty-five nationalities and 27 per cent of the population at the time. A equal number of natives born of foreign parents raised the total foreig element of the state to well over 50 per cent. Furthermore, only a smal fraction of the native Americans were born on North Dakota soil, an

---

p. 107; *Co-operative Manager and Farmer,* IV (March, 1915), p. 21. The last pub lication, a supporter of Twitchell, described him as a resident of North Dakot "since the real cow boy days." Another publication charged that he came to Bismarc "to be the king bee of the progressive movement" but was defeated for speaker an went over to the opposition camp. *Industrial Freedom,* I (June, 1915), p. 19.

13. Richard Schmidt, "Leadership," *Encyclopaedia of the Social Sciences* (1 vols., New York, 1930–35), IX, 282–87.

14. Gaston, *The Nonpartisan League,* p. 45.

15. N. C. Abbott, "Social Center Development in North Dakota," University o North Dakota, *Quarterly Journal,* II (July, 1912), p. 355.

carcely any two families had come from the same part of the United tates. The restlessness and change so characteristic of pioneer life had ot been outgrown. A decade later, in 1920, it was reported that 86 per ent of the people of the state lived either on farms or in towns of less han 2,500. The 1920 census showed that, of a population of 648,872, some 15,009, or 79.6 per cent, were native-born and the remaining 131,863, or 0.4 per cent, were foreign-born. Of the latter, some 38,190 were born in Norway, 29,617 in Russia, 15,550 in Canada, 11,960 in Germany, and 0,453 in Sweden. The rest of the foreign population came from various arts of Europe.[16]

Townley was born in a region of northwestern Minnesota not unlike North Dakota. He attended the high school in Alexandria, Minnesota, nd as a student he had become interested in debating and other forensic ctivities and had displayed an interest in religious, political, and economic issues. He taught school for a while but soon tired of the routine of the classroom and set out for the West in search of livelier pursuits.[17] His talent for organization first showed itself as he tried his luck at farming in the extreme western part of North Dakota near the Montana border, a submarginal farming area.[18] Since working with horses was too slow or him, he persuaded his neighbors to pool their resources and buy a steam tractor and plows. This was soon followed by other innovations, or he had always displayed impatience with doing things on a small scale. After forming a farming syndicate with neighbors, Townley withdrew when the prospects for a good crop looked slim and allowed the other members to divide the seed and equipment and take their chances. Heavy

16. *Statistical Abstract of the United States,* 1921, pp. 61, 73; *Fourteenth Census of the United States,* Vol. III, *Population,* 1920, p. 764.

17. Gaston, *The Nonpartisan League,* pp. 46–48.

18. Macy H. Lapham and Others, *Soil Survey of Western North Dakota,* U. S. Dept. Agri., Bureau of Soils (Washington, 1910), pp. 27–28. During the years 1892–1906 the acreage devoted to the production of wheat in North Dakota rose from 2,868,729 acres to 5,992,000 acres, with a total production in 1906 of nearly 58,000,000 bushels. The increased production was due mainly to agricultural expansion in western North Dakota. "In local districts and under unusually favorable conditions a yield of from 35 to 40 bushels per acre is sometimes harvested. The average yield is, however, much lighter, the average yield per acre for the State during the fifteen-year period cited above being 12.6 bushels. A yield of from 12 to 15 bushels per acre is usually considered profitable."

rains soon followed, however, and as a result those who had been associ ated with him prospered.

After spending a year wandering to the Pacific Coast, Townley returne to North Dakota to try raising flax in the Golden Valley, where return from farming were very high.[19] During two fairly successful seasons, h expanded his holdings beyond what might be termed sound economi practice, and soon came to be known as the "flax king." Land agent pointed him out as a successful farmer, but this reputation was short-lived his third farming year, 1912, proved disastrous. The payments on the ad ditional land and machinery that he had purchased could not be mad for the season was dry, the harvest small, and the prices low. Townle himself attributed his failure to the speculators and the "grain gamblers, and disclaimed any responsibility on his part for his mishaps. This poin of view soon found its way into the "campaign of education" of the Non partisan League. Inefficient farm management and weather hazards a causes for small crops, low prices, and small incomes had no place i Townley's thinking. The farmer was not at all responsible for the condi tions under which he farmed.

Townley's failure at farming drove him headlong into the Socialis camp. North Dakota was a state fertile for the spreading of discontent an the sowing of Socialist propaganda. Commercial wheat farming ha brought the farmer into direct relation with the organized grain trad financial institutions, the railroads, and the town merchants.[20] Agricultura discontent was accentuated by the semiarid conditions prevailing in large part of the state, for the farmers were not familiar with the existin climatic hazards, or else they were indifferent to them and to the need of diversified agriculture to insure some income regardless of weather con ditions.[21] The Socialists capitalized on these conditions; they held meet

19. Gaston, *The Nonpartisan League,* pp. 49–50.

20. James E. Le Rossignol, *What is Socialism?* (New York, 1921), pp. 239–40 Meyer Jacobstein, "The Aldrich Banking Plan," University of North Dakot *Quarterly Journal,* III (January, 1913), pp. 154–56.

21. Wheat farmers repeatedly were warned against the disastrous consequence of single-crop farming. In 1889, for instance, Dakota farmers were advised: "The is money in gardening, in poultry and eggs, in butter and cheese, and a score of othe things which seem trifling to a man who harvests 3,000 or 4,000 bushels of dolla wheat, but supposing there is a hot wind, a lack of rain or a frost? The man wh

ngs, sold literature, and canvassed the farming areas for membership.[22]

The Socialist party of North Dakota was a fairly well organized unit rom 1908 to 1914, despite the predominance of agricultural population n the state, and the party's influence was greater than its membership igures would indicate. As early as 1908 it had adopted a platform embodying the chief features of the Nonpartisan League, calling for state-owned elevators and mills, credit banks, and a system of state-owned and operated hail insurance. At Minot, a center of radical activities, the Socialists published the *Iconoclast,* which repeatedly urged the farmers to organize for political action.[23] It saw the American Society of Equity movement as a step in the direction of socialism but hardly sufficient to achieve the goal the Socialists desired. "We recognize the Equity as well as every other radical organization or movement, no matter what its name or label as a social force, and therefore a part of the great process of social evolution which will result in the eventual socialization of the na-

---

puts all his eggs in one basket is liable to go smash." Frank H. Hagerty, *The State of North Dakota, The Statistical, Historical and Political Abstract* (Aberdeen, S. Dak., 1889), p. 61.

The dairy commissioner's report for 1910 indicated that the failure to practice diversified farming in the state was not because of ignorance or indifference, but because of conditions that were difficult to overcome. The commissioner said, "When we consider the early settlement of this state at a time when it was possible to secure large tracts of land either by purchase at a nominal price, or through governmental regulations, and realize that the great majority of farmers have large farms, that diversified farming means building fences, barns, arranging for pastures and foods for live stock, that it calls for better and a higher grade of help, that it means more labor must be added to the farm, that there will be no months of leisure, and that the size of the farm practically prohibits their handling it in the most approved methods advocated by scientific agricultural experts, we realize more fully what it means for the grain farmer to take up diversified farming. It is not wholly prejudice, but a condition, that confronts them. . . ." *Biennial Report of the Dairy Commissioner to the Commissioner of Agriculture and Labor,* 1910, p. 8.

22. Arthur Le Sueur, "The Nonpartisan League" (unpublished manuscript in the Minnesota Historical Society), p. 2; *Iconoclast* (Minot, N. Dak.), July 17, 1914. Beecher Moore was a pioneer Socialist in North Dakota.

23. *Ibid.* See Frederick E. Haynes, *Social Politics in the United States* (Boston, 1921), pp. 204–8, for the distribution of political strength of the Socialists in the nation. Minot was the headquarters for the North Dakota Socialists. *State of North Dakota Legislative Manual,* 1913, pp. xxiii, 265–67. See also Le Sueur, "The Nonpartisan League," pp. 1–2.

tion's industries. It is the quintessence of jackassable stupidity to ignore any of the intermediate stages in the development of the social progress."[24] Experience soon pointed out that the Socialist program was more popular than the party itself, and quite appropriately so; the Farmers' Alliance had agitated for some of the same measures a couple of decades earlier.

In time the Socialists provided for an organization department within their party which made it possible for non-Socialists to join without having to sign "the red card of terrible reputation." The establishment of the department proved that the party itself did not appeal to the farmer but that its platform did. Socialist propaganda emphasized, among other things, that the farmer as an individual had certain duties to perform if he was to better himself; he had to learn to manage efficiently, to work diligently, to initiate state-owned mills and elevators, to launch cooperative associations, to practice diversified farming, and to use every other available opportunity to free himself from the "dominant" economic forces that ruled him.[25] The Socialist argument, in other words, placed some of the responsibility for the plight of the farmer on the farmer himself. This argument did not augur well for the welfare of the party. The farmer who attended a Socialist meeting and then went home to his tumbledown house, his uneducated children, his ragged, overworked wife, his weedy fields, and his rusty and outmoded machinery and then applied the doctrines he had heard would not have a comfortable feeling, for he could not escape from some measure of responsibility for his condition.[26]

24. *Iconoclast,* June 25, 1915.

25. Henry P. Richardson, "Scientific Organizing and the Farmer," *International Socialist Review,* XV (March, 1915), pp. 554–58, discusses Socialist organization problems among North Dakota farmers. The North Dakota Socialists used automobiles to contact farmers before the Nonpartisan League was organized.

26. In 1912 the Socialist party received 7.9 per cent of the state's total vote. It was surpassed by Oklahoma, Nevada, Montana, Washington, California, Idaho, Oregon, Florida, Arizona, Ohio, Wisconsin, Texas, Minnesota, and Utah in the order listed. The total Socialist vote in 1912 was 897,011, which was 5.9 per cent of the total national vote. In the presidential election of 1916, North Dakota was surpassed in Socialist strength by Oklahoma, Nevada, Florida, Wisconsin, Idaho, Washington, Arizona, Montana, and Texas. *The American Labor Yearbook,* 1917–18 (New York, 1918), pp. 336–37. In 1914 the membership of the Socialist party in Montana was 1,589; in North Dakota, 1,644; and in Minnesota, 4,965. In 1915 it was, respectively, 1,057 and 1,107 and 3,542. *Ibid.,* 1916, pp. 95–96. One source says: "Ameri-

In 1914 Townley volunteered to serve as an organizer for the organization department of the Socialist party to help test out the differences in popularity between the party and its platform. Supplied with plenty of Socialist literature and an automobile with which to travel from place to place, he held meetings arranged for him by headquarters, sold the literature, and took pledges from farmers who joined the organization department, not the Socialist party. When cash was not available, he accepted postdated checks.[27] Monthly dues of $1.00 were to be paid, and the platform and the candidates of the organization were to be supported.

Townley's success was almost instantaneous. In less than three months he had four organizers at work—men who, it was claimed, were members of the Socialist party. There is still a difference of opinion, however, on whether Townley himself was actually a member. The expenses of the organizers were paid from the receipts for the literature, from contributions, and from the thousands of pledges received. But this experiment, was short-lived, for at the Socialist convention in 1915 the state committee recommended the discontinuance of the work of the organization department. The committee charged that such a program was inconsistent with the future welfare of the party and the farmers and pointed out that the organization department had as many members as did the party itself, the main difference being that the members of the latter were educated on the subject of socialism, while those of the former were not.

When the Socialist party refused to permit Townley to continue organizing, he felt that he had been poorly treated. Consequently, when A. E. Bowen, an associate, recommended that they organize a nonpartisan organization having nothing to do with the Socialist party, Townley was immediately impressed with the idea.[28] Townley and Bowen were both

---

can Socialism seems . . . to have its chief strength, not in the manufacturing centers, but in those Western states where mining and farm tenantry prevail." *Ibid.*, 1917–18, p. 338.

27. Le Sueur, "The Nonpartisan League," p. 4; J. D. Bacon, *A Warning to the Farmer against Townleyism as Exploited in North Dakota* (Grand Forks, N. Dak., 1918), p. 11.

28. Le Sueur, "The Nonpartisan League," p. 5; *Milwaukee Leader*, July 29, 1916. One Socialist leader charged: "The Socialist organization of North Dakota is today a travesty and a farce. The red-card organizers of the league are yet 'comrades' and control the Socialist Party."

credited with being the "midwives" of the Nonpartisan League, and although the statement to the effect that Townley stole the Nonpartisan idea from Bowen frequently circulated, it was the organizing genius of Townley that placed the new organization on its feet.[29]

Political action appeared feasible to the farmers at the time because it held out promises that were not to be achieved readily by other, slower means. Besides, the rate at which North Dakota farmers were joining the organization department of the Socialist party indicated that a new movement was on foot; all that was needed was the leadership. The grievances of the farmers against the organized grain trade were well known, and the psychological moment for the new movement had already presented itself.

Organization of the Nonpartisan League began shortly after the memorable Equity meeting of February, 1915. At this convention Townley renewed his acquaintanceship with F. B. Wood, a highly respected and admired Equity leader whom he had met in the course of his work for the Socialist party. Conversations between the two shortly followed, and Wood later admitted that he "had told Townley that he could come to our farm when spring broke and I would help him get started." Townley, however, could not wait until spring, and the two talked the matter over again. This time Wood's two sons sat in; and the following morning Townley and Howard Wood, one of the sons, "started out with a team and bobsled to call on the neighbors. The Farmers' Nonpartisan Political League of North Dakota had begun organizations. . . . Howard Wood furnished the introductions. Townley did the talking. It was an arrangement that later became a standard of methods in League organization work." Howard Wood, the convert, became the "booster" in the township, accompanying the organizer to "break the ice with his neighbors." The League reportedly enrolled twelve members the first day.[30]

Soon the Ford car was introduced into the League's organizing operations in order to cover wider stretches of territory. That Townley was preparing to deal the state a political blitzkrieg in a day when such terminology was unknown soon became apparent. Organizers and members

29. S. R. Maxwell, *The Nonpartisan League from the Inside* (St. Paul, 1918), p. 44.

30. Gaston, *The Nonpartisan League,* pp. 56–58.

were cautioned to keep their membership confidential, "to keep all knowledge of the movement from the leeches who sucked their blood," and the work proceeded without organized opposition.[31] One newspaper was quoted as saying:

> It is being rumored . . . that a number of strange characters are operating in this part . . . whose business is not definitely known. It is claimed, however, by those who profess to know, that they are organizing a farmers' political league of some kind or other. They go about in Ford cars, leaving town early in the morning and returning late at night. They tell no one their business voluntarily and when the question is put directly to them, reply that they are selling washing machines. It is needless to say that the farmers of this community are too intelligent and prosperous to be taken in by any wild-eyed scheme of a political nature and certainly if they want washing machines our enterprising merchants have plenty of them to sell. If, however, farmers are approached or pestered on any new proposition which they do not understand thoroughly, we urge them not to sign any papers or make any pledges or promises until after they have consulted with their banker or with the editor of this paper. Beware of gold-brick agents.[32]

The methods employed in organizing the League represented a curious blend of socialism and high-pressure salesmanship. Farmers were advised to do as "big business" did when it came to organizing for politics. League leaders pointed out that "big business" was "absolutely nonpartisan and well-financed; it operated politically through the dominant parties or in any other way that comes in handy." They cited the case of Jay Gould, who, when asked what his politics were, replied, "In Democratic states I am a Democrat; in Republican states I am a Republican, but I am always for the Erie Railway." [33]

The League propaganda was "intended to shock and startle and stir up" both the reader and the listener and represented "the farmer as an upright and down-trodden member of society and Big Business as the vil-

31. [James Frost], *Townley & Co. and the Nonpartisan League* (Beach, N. Dak., 1918), p. 31. See also J. W. Brinton, *Wheat and Politics* (Minneapolis, 1931), pp. 36–37.

32. O. M. Thomason, *The Beginning and the End of the Nonpartisan League* (n.p., 1920), pp. 105–6.

33. As quoted in *Nonpartisan League Methods and Principles* (Waco, Texas, n.d.), p. 10 [booklet].

lain."[34] Arguments were advanced to substantiate reasons why the farmers should control the political life of North Dakota. To a degree, they resembled those of the French physiocrats, who strongly upheld the superiority of agriculture over other forms of economic activity. League leaders pointed to agriculture as the basic industry, "the most important industry under the shining sun. Emperors, Kings, Ministers, Presidents, Parliaments, Congresses, great generals, mighty armies with monster guns and forests of bayonets and mountains of shot and shell, are down on their knees before the man with the hoe. Yet, he has had but little direct voice in affairs of government that determine his weal or woe. Men who can hardly tell the difference between a cotton boll and a chrysanthemum, are expected to legislate for the most vital industry of all. . . ." The League demanded "proportional occupational representation" as a means of eliminating the imposter from public life. It was maintained that a representative of the farmers, with a knowledge of the views of that economic group, would be more likely to legislate in accordance with the needs of the farmers than one representing a variety of economic interests. It was not "sleek, smooth-tongued, bay-windowed fellows that looked well, talked well, lived well, lied well" who could best run the government. The case of the North Dakota farmers was but one instance where "the farmers had been vainly begging a bunch of wind-jamming, poker-playing, booze-fighting politicians for legislation to protect them against the flour-mill trust and the grain gamblers. . . ." If the farmers of North Dakota constituted 83 per cent of the population, they said, why should they not "control 83 per cent of the government."[35]

Greater confidence was obtained among the farmers by limiting the organization to actual tillers of the soil and later by encouraging practical cooperation with organized labor. Office seekers were to be eliminated by nominating as candidates for public office a farmer, a wage earner, or anyone else "tried in the field of unselfish service." Campaign expenses were to be financed with fees that were high enough to cover the costs, the candidates in turn being tied to the farmer organization in the same manner that the candidate from big business was tied to the business interests.

34. John M. Gillette, "The North Dakota Harvest of the Nonpartisan League," *Survey,* XLI (March 1, 1919), pp. 759–60.

35. *Nonpartisan League Methods and Principles,* pp. 14–15.

That the actual administration of the League would be highly centralized was accepted as axiomatic almost from the very beginning. It was dominated by a committee of three that was democratic in form but despotic in practice.[36] Townley was chairman of the committee, the other two members being William Lemke and F. B. Wood. Tenure on this committee was indefinite since there was no provision for the election of successors. The opposition made much of this centralized control, but Townley's replies placated the rank and file, temporarily at least, and typified his ability to obtain their confidence. "Are not the milling interests organized and ably led by a few men?" he asked. "And the interests that manufacture agricultural machinery? And the railroads? Does anybody know of a single great interest in this country that is not highly organized?"[37]

The actual organizing of the farmers was one of the most dramatic aspects of the League, for it had gathered together one of the most artful groups of radical writers and speakers the nation had ever seen. They were thoroughly saturated with radical doctrines, techniques of indoctrination, and large-scale organization methods. In knowledge of mass psychology they were unsurpassed. They were capable of finding the least common denominator among their farmer listeners; they adopted few themes, and they repeated them untiringly. Townley, in particular, was a man of striking physical appearance, boisterous in talk but rich in expression; and the League leaders in general were capable of pointing out the enemy to the farmers in simple fashion. In North Dakota the League encountered no difficulty in arousing the farmers against their traditional foes—the railroads, the financial interests, and the press. League leaders ably fed the passions of the farmers by telling them exactly what they wanted to hear.

In contacting the farmers the League's organizers were instructed to ascertain the particular interests of the farmer and to talk about them instead of necessarily the League program, to agree with everything the farmer said, and to condemn everything he disliked. This approach is epitomized in a former League leader's account of Townley's instructions.

36. *Nonpartisan League; Origin, Purpose and Method of Operation, War Program and Statement of Principles* (n.p., n.d.), pp. 10–11; James Manahan, *Trials of a Lawyer* (Minneapolis, 1933), p. 221.

37. *Why Should Farmers Pay Dues?* (St. Paul, n.d.), p. 7 [booklet].

"Make the rubes pay their god-damn money to join and they'll stick—stick 'til hell freezes over." Organizers were drilled on how to "organize" the farmer in his barn yard; how to "surround the rube," one man in front and one on each side, facing him, and all urging him to join. . . . "Find out the damn fool's hobby," taught Townley, "and then talk it. If he likes religion, talk Jesus Christ; if he is against the government, damn the democrats; if he is afraid of whiskey, preach prohibition; if he wants to talk hogs, talk hogs—talk anything he'll listen to, but talk, talk, until you get his god-damn John Hancock to a check for six dollars."[38]

In short, the tricks of the accomplished salesman and the orator were put into full swing by an ably trained group of radicals advocating a Socialist program. Many of the grievances they aired were no doubt highly exaggerated, but they achieved the desired end of increasing membership. In many rural areas strong appeals were made to the antipathies of farmers toward town merchants and business interests. Even national feeling and racial pride were used; organizers were instructed "to put a soft pedal on all the Wilson stuff" when organizing in German communities.[39] Mass meetings and large picnics were arranged to supplement the work of the organizers and sometimes to pave the way for them in new territory. Whether League organizers approached the farmer in his barn or whether they addressed him in public meetings, the expression "Go home and slop the hogs" was used with increasing effectiveness.

A potent factor in the early successes of the League was the Nonpartisan League press, which, according to one writer, furnished "a significant case study in the use of propaganda by a highly class-conscious pressure group." Nowhere within the organization, with the possible exception of the speaker's platform, were the gifts of expression better demonstrated than in the columns of the League press.[40] League writers warned the members not to trust the existing press; they were skilled in the techniques of indoctrination, and "with astute realism they anticipate[d] a wave of opposition from newspapers within and without the state. . . ." Charles Edward Russell, the noted Socialist publicist and editor of the *Non-partisan Leader,* the official organ, warned against "tainted news,"

38. Manahan, *Trials of a Lawyer,* pp. 219–20.

39. Maxwell, *The Nonpartisan League from the Inside,* pp. 82–85.

40. Joseph H. Mader, "The North Dakota Press and the Nonpartisan League," *Journalism Quarterly,* XIV (December, 1937), pp. 321–23.

"poisonous news," and the "poisoned special article." An early issue of the *Non-partisan Leader* cautioned: "The greatest advantage the interests and corporations have is their control over the press. That is where the first great danger lies before your organization. Beware of it; it is the greatest power in the world, the most subtle, insidious, poisonous, the hardest to detect and the hardest to defeat." [41] When the opposition press unleashed its attack upon the League, the skill and ingenuity of its journalists were well demonstrated in the retaliatory tactics. Little time was lost in portraying big business as the mortal enemy of the farmer in both cartoons and articles.[42] Feature articles were written in praise of government ownership, particularly in Australia and New Zealand. Editorials were written simply; they were graphic and presented to attract attention. Cartoons generally carried the point across.[43]

The organization work was in high gear by the close of 1915, and it is estimated that the League conducted five to six hundred meetings during the winter of 1915–16. By February, 1917, some 30,000 members were reported enrolled, and about three-fourths of the state was organized.[44] Shortly after the organization work of 1915, preparations were made for the 1916 election by calling precinct meetings to assemble on February 22, 1916, and elect delegates to a state convention.[45] These meetings were to be held at the regular polling places in each precinct, unless other arrangements already had been made. Parallels were drawn between the acts of the North Dakota farmers of February, 1916, and the American Revolution of 1776. "The conditions under which the people . . . in 1776 suffered . . . are only unlike in degree to the present conditions which the farmers are suffering in North Dakota." [46]

The meetings were well attended in each of the 2,000 precincts of North Dakota, and delegates were elected to legislative and district conventions.[47] The district conventions nominated candidates for both houses of

41. *Non-partisan Leader,* September 23, 1915, p. 7; October 21, 1915, p. 4.
42. F. A. Teigen, *The Nonpartisan League* (St. Paul, 1918), p. 45.
43. Gillette, in *Survey,* XLI (March, 1919), pp. 759–60.
44. *Literary Digest,* LIV (January 20, 1917), p. 115.
45. *Non-partisan Leader,* January 27, 1916, p. 5.
46. *Ibid.,* February 10, 1916, p. 6.
47. *Literary Digest,* LIV (January 20, 1917), p. 115; *Non-partisan Leader,* March 2, 1916, p. 3.

the legislature and delegates to a state convention which met at Fargo on March 29 and 30. The League candidates were as follows: for governor Lynn J. Frazier of Hoople, graduate of the University of North Dakota to run in the Republican primary; for lieutenant-governor, Albert Stenmo of Merrifield, Grand Forks County, graduate of the University of North Dakota, to run in the Republican primary; for secretary of state, Thomas Hall, the incumbent, to run as a Republican; for auditor, Carl R. Kositsky of Bismarck, secretary of the state tax commission and a Burleigh County commissioner, to run as a Republican; for treasurer, P. M. Casey, vice-president of the North Dakota Society of Equity, to run as a Democrat; for attorney-general, William A. Langer of Mandan, state attorney for Morton County, to run as a Republican; for superintendent of public instruction, N. C. MacDonald of Valley City, graduate of the University of North Dakota and state inspector of consolidated schools, to run on the nonpartisan school ballot; for commissioner of insurance, S. A. Olsness, a farmer at Cheyenne in Eddy County, to run as a Republican; for commissioner of agriculture, John Hagan of Deering in McHenry County, a graduate of Valparaiso University in Indiana, town supervisor for eleven years and a farmer, running on the Republican ticket. Candidates for railroad commissioners were Charles Bleick of Elgin, Morton County, an active Equity and Farmers' Union man and a graduate of the Nebraska School of Agriculture; M. P. Johnson of Tolley, Renville County, president of the North Dakota Society of Equity; and Sam Aandal, a farmer from Litchville, Barnes County—all running on the Republican ticket. Those running for the bench of the supreme court were Luther Birdzell, former state tax commissioner and professor of law in the University of North Dakota; J. E. Robinson, a Fargo lawyer; and R. H. Grace, lawyer from Mohall—all three running on the nonpartisan ballot in the primaries.[48]

As announced, League officials and organizers were not permitted to accept a nomination for state office, the theory being that the office should seek the man and not the man the office.[49] Furthermore, only farmer members had seats in the convention in which candidates for posts ranging from representatives in the state legislature to governor were endorsed. County politics were of no concern to the League.

48. *Ibid.,* April 6, 1916, p. 3.
49. *Nonpartisan League Methods and Principles,* p. 12.

The nomination of Lynn Frazier for governor represented an ingenious piece of politics, for, according to his sponsors, he was "a plain farmer, with no political record which they could misrepresent." [50] At the time of his nomination Frazier was forty-one years old. He was a native American and a farmer—"not an imitation farmer nor a town farmer, either," for he worked the land his father had been farming since 1881. Frazier, like Townley, was born in Minnesota, his parents moving to Pembina County, Dakota Territory, in 1881. There the father built a sod house, and when Frazier graduated from high school at the age of seventeen, he and his brother took up the task of running the farm, their father having died the previous year. Having developed an ambition to become a professional man, Frazier taught school for two years and saved enough money to enter the Mayville Normal School. He completed his course in one year, graduating in 1895 with the school's first class. After teaching school for another two years, Frazier entered the University of North Dakota at Grand Forks. There he displayed qualities as a student and an athlete, his main sport being football. Frazier was the "square blocky type, ideal for a center in those days of driving line rushes." He was football captain for two years and graduated in 1901 with a good scholastic record and many honors bestowed upon him by his classmates. Meanwhile, the brother in charge of the family farm had died, and consequently Frazier had to give up all ideas of a profession and return to the "prosaic work of being a farmer." [51]

If Townley and Lemke were unaware of the wisdom of their choice of Frazier as the "political pontiff" of the League, they were soon convinced of it. Upon his nomination Frazier was immediately labeled the "modern Cincinnatus" who was "called from the plow to head his people and to govern a great commonwealth." [52] He was "blessed by the substantial figure and confident pose of a statesman. He looked like a bishop. But Farmer Frazier was at that time untrained and inexperienced as a public speaker." Townley and Lemke then assigned him the job of meeting the farmers and selling himself with his "wholesomeness and unassumed solidity." Public meetings were widely advertised and usually

50. *Where the People Rule* (n.p., n.d.), p. 6 [pamphlet].
51. *Non-partisan Leader,* April 6, 1916, pp. 3, 5, 6.
52. *Ibid.,* April 27, 1916, p. 7.

held out of doors. Farmers drove miles to hear him. "He stood before them, sunburned and baldheaded. His voice was firm and persuasive. He spoke briefly and the tired farmers loved him." [53]

Townley and other League leaders emphasized the need for victory in the primary election by painting lurid pictures of the consequences that would follow the defeat of League candidates:

If the farmers and their friends lose . . . North Dakota will be drained to the limit of her ability to pay. Homesteads will be mortgaged and lost. As in the past, horses, machinery and household goods will be sold under the hammer and the tillers of the soil will be turned out of their homes. Merchants will go broke because the farmers can not pay their store bill. Heavy mortgages, high interest, low prices, will force long hours of toil. Wives, mothers and sisters will work in the field. Children will be kept out of school summers to plow, seed and harvest, and kept at home winters for lack of money to pay the way through high school or college. All will be debt and drudgery. Mothers and fathers will die from overwork and worry while yet they should be young.

Meanwhile we will yield up tens of millions of the earnings of our wives and daughters and mothers and fathers and brothers to the greedy masters of trade and finance in the East—millions that they do not need and can not use—millions that should be spent in North Dakota to make happy and prosperous a great people in a great state—millions that should be spent by North Dakota farmers with North Dakota business men to the greater advantage of both.

All this—as in the past—*if we lose.*[54]

Frazier, despite his lack of political experience, displayed all the earmarks of one willing to learn; furthermore, there was something appealing about his inexperienced campaigning. "Public speaking like this is out of my line, I must admit," he said. "I am not a politician, but I can milk and slop hogs and fill the bill on the farm." [55] "[When told that] I was chosen to lead the farmers' ticket to victory, I thought that they had made a mistake." This approach appealed to the farmers, and the *Non-partisan Leader* made much capital of the fact that his speeches were "unadorned with flourishes."

A novelty of the campaign that caused amazement among the experienced politicians was the chartering of a special train, the "Frazier

53. Manahan, *Trials of a Lawyer,* pp. 221–22.
54. *Non-partisan Leader,* June 1, 1916, p. 1.
55. *Ibid.,* April 13, 1916, p. 16.

Special." This type of campaigning was not, however, the invention of the Nonpartisan League. In 1908 the Socialist presidential candidate, Eugene V. Debs, was carried to all parts of the country in the "Red Special." [56] The chances are that the League leaders borrowed this idea from the Socialist party, whence many of them had come. The "Frazier Special" was scheduled to stop at all important points in North Dakota during the last week of the campaign, which closed on June 28, primary day.[57] It carried the League candidates and it was intended to give the farmers a chance to hear the case of the farmers. A series of picnics were arranged with five-, ten-, and fifteen-minute speeches by the candidate for governor and his party. An opportunity was also given the prospective voters to board the "Frazier Special" and ride from their home station to the nearest mass meeting by simply purchasing a ticket. Business offices, stores, and shops were closed in honor of the occasion in some of the towns, including New Rockford, Jamestown, Valley City, Bottineau, and Minot.[58]

Frazier, running true to form, defeated four candidates in the primaries and received a larger vote than the opposition candidates combined.[59] In fact, the League "swirled" into the campaign and "tore it wide open." All its candidates were nominated on the Republican ticket with the exception of P. M. Casey, its choice for treasurer "whom the Democrats obligingly nominated." [60] A Mandan newspaper, upon hearing of the nomination of Frazier, asked: "Who in Hell is Frazier, and Where in Hell is Hoople?" [61] As a result of the League showing, both the Republican and Democratic parties adopted programs largely in accord with the League platform.[62]

Originally, the League had announced that it would support only candidates for the state executive, judiciary, and legislative offices, but it di-

56. Haynes, *Social Politics in the United States,* pp. 196–97; McAlister Coleman, *Eugene V. Debs* (New York, 1930), pp. 244–48; David Karsner, *Debs* (New York, 1919), pp. 190–91.

57. *Non-partisan Leader,* June 15, 1916, p. 8.

58. *Ibid.,* July 6, 1916, p. 5.

59. Brinton, *Wheat and Politics,* p. 37.

60. *Literary Digest,* LIV (January 20, 1917), p. 115.

61. Brinton, *Wheat and Politics,* p. 37.

62. *Non-partisan Leader,* November 30, 1916, p. 5.

verted sufficiently to support Porter McCumber for re-election to the United States Senate. Officially, the League endorsed no candidates for county offices or for the Presidency; secretly, according to report, it endorsed Woodrow Wilson, although Lynn Frazier was for Charles Evans Hughes.[63]

In the November election the League again achieved a thunderous victory by capturing every elective state office but one and electing three justices who had endorsed the League program for state-owned utilities to the supreme court.[64] Of the 107,000 votes cast, Frazier received 87,000, or 80 per cent.[65] The farmers, however, forgot to "remember Casey," the League candidate for treasurer, who ran on the Democratic ticket. The League gained control of every branch of the government except the senate, the majority in the house being 85 per cent. North Dakota presented the anomalous situation of having elected a Republican governor over the Democratic candidate by a vote of four to one and a Republican senator over a Democrat by an overwhelming majority and yet having given the Democratic presidential candidate a safe majority.[66]

The postelection comments were amusing. Nonpartisan leaders pronounced the results as the beginning of "a peaceful revolution" that had "found its place of incubation in the Northwest states."[67] One correspondent pointed out that "ten months ago Governor Frazier was unknown outside of his own precinct," and another queried whether "slopping hogs is the right sort of training for anyone charged with the grave duties of state's chief executive." The wonder of the election was that the League had "dipt into its first political campaign," before it was a year old; "even more astonishing" were the results when one considers North Dakota's "magnificent distances." Well over 80 per cent of its population was scattered on farms that could be reached for the most part only by a personal canvass.[68]

63. *The New International Year Book,* 1916, p. 496; *Non-partisan Leader,* November 2, 1916, p. 8.

64. *Literary Digest,* LIV (January 20, 1917), p. 115.

65. *Non-partisan Leader,* January 18, 1917, p. 7.

66. *Ibid.,* November 16, 1916, p. 3; *Literary Digest,* LIV (January 20, 1917), p. 115; *The New International Year Book,* 1916, p. 496.

67. *Non-partisan Leader,* February 22, 1917, p. 3.

68. *Ibid.,* January 4, 1917, p. 2; *Literary Digest,* LIV (January 20, 1917), p. 115.

League leaders had hopes of encouraging a migration of farmers to North Dakota, largely because of the legislative program that they expected to place in operation, but the opposition, which was regaining its balance, was doing everything to prevent the realization of such expectations.[69] Arguments used both in defending and in attacking the League were immersed in personal animus, lost tempers, and heated words. The cry of socialism was, by far, the most popular charge against the organization, the attack being led by Jerry Bacon, an implacable foe of the League, and his *Grand Forks Herald*.[70] Local bankers in all probability were encouraged by the large financial institutions upon which they were dependent to resist the League. Opposition leaders feared that the success of the League program would jeopardize property values and the credit structure of the state. They claimed that North Dakota mortgages and other securities that previously had been easy to sell would become a drug on the market.[71] The *Minneapolis Journal* asserted: "Capital won't invest," "men with money are afraid," "confidence is shaken. . . ."[72] There was no question that past profits and privileges were imperiled. Local merchants, largely through the pressure of wholesalers, jobbers, and manufacturers and a personal fear for their business future, also attacked the League violently. Business interests in general saw in the League program the possible creation of machinery for the manufacturing of state-owned products in state-owned mills, packing houses, and factories and the eventual establishment of state-owned stores that threatened their very existence.[73]

Besides lining up the business interests of North Dakota against the League, the opposition assailed the political and economic theories of the movement. At times it claimed that it was not opposed to the League

69. *Non-partisan Leader,* November 23, 1916, p. 16; November 30, 1916, p. 16.
70. *Ibid.,* February 22, 1917, p. 4.
71. Bacon, *A Warning to the Farmers,* p. 7.
72. Quoted in *Non-partisan Leader,* July 27, 1916, p. 11.
73. Teigen, *The Nonpartisan League,* pp. 44–45. The *Non-partisan Leader,* February 24, 1916, p. 6, said that the farmers and businessmen had many things in common and that their interests were identical. "But many business men have got themselves in bad with the farmer because in matters political, in matters relative to high interest rates, railroad robbery and grain gambling, they have been only half-heartedly with the farmer, if with him at all. Indeed, many of them align themselves with the political tricksters, and the schemers who prey upon the farmer."

itself, but only to its leaders and candidates.[74] What became of the money that the League collected was a question frequently asked by its adversaries.[75] Nonpartisan leaders were dubbed as "red Socialists," "expert hypnotists," "gold brick vendors," "world revolutionaries," "atheists," "I.W.W.'s," "dynamiters," "free lovers," "carpetbaggers," "home wreckers," "Huns," "traitors," "noisemakers," "theorists," "dilettantes," "dreamers," "beautiful phrasemakers," "swivel-chair reformers," "mild-eyed poets," "sweet-mouthed flatterers," "mountebanks," "confidence men," "anarchists," "charlatans," "agitators," and "visionaries."[76]

The charge was advanced that North Dakota would become an "agrarian dictatorship." It was claimed that the League was a "virulent infection . . . carrying death dealing germs into the vitals of our state. . . . With progress stopped industrial and commercial stagnation will ensue and the human family will deteriorate like angle worms in a tin can with too little dirt to cover or feed them." It was also charged that the program would make North Dakota a "mecca for Ne'er-Do-Wells" and thus open its doors to the "thriftless," "shiftless," and criminal.[77] Had the opposition charged that the League was an organization in which the few decide and the many follow, it would have made a more pointed criticism.[78]

The first real test of opposition to the League program was destined to come from the North Dakota senate. Of the total of 49 senators, 24 were holdovers from the previous session; and of the 24 newly elected, 18 were endorsed by the League, 14 being Republicans and 4 Democrats. In the lower house the strength of the League was impressive, 81 being elected by the League and 32 by the opposition.[79]

74. Bacon, *A Warning to the Farmer,* p. 25.

75. Thomason, *The Beginning and the End of the Nonpartisan League,* p. 185; Charles Merz, "The Nonpartisan League," *New Republic,* XXII (May 12, 1920), pp. 333–38; Maxwell, *The Nonpartisan League from the Inside,* pp. 58, 62, 71; Gillette, in *Survey,* XLI (March, 1919), p. 755.

76. Independent Voters' Association, *Townleyism's Future in North Dakota* (Fargo, N. Dak., 1919), pp. 7, 12, and *Voters' Guide* (Fargo, 1920), p. 6; *Nonpartisan Leader,* February 8, 1917, p. 15; Maxwell, *The Nonpartisan League from the Inside,* p. 58; *Daily Journal Press* (St. Cloud, Minn.), October 11, 1919; Thomason, *The Beginning and the End of the Nonpartisan League,* pp. 113, 185, 192, 200; *Trade Unionism and Townleyism* (n.p., n.d.) [leaflet].

77. Independent Voters' Association, *Voters' Guide,* pp. 5, 9, 11.

78. *Non-partisan Leader,* March 9, 1916, p. 2.

79. *Ibid.,* November 30, 1916, pp. 5, 12.

Frazier, in his inaugural address, besides recommending the adoption of the League's industrial program, advocated reduction of the legal interest rate, minimum wages for workmen, better roads, civil service for state employees, development of the local coal beds, better rural schools, state aid for rural education, and a nonpartisan ballot.[80] Most of the bills embodying these proposals were freely discussed in League caucuses held nightly at the Northwestern Hotel, and the men who were best qualified to introduce the bills in the legislature were selected. The legal committee of the League assisted in framing the bills.[81]

The first major task was to amend the constitution in order to provide a legal basis for state-owned utilities and for their financing. The issuance of bonds for such purposes was blocked by the constitution.[82] Several ways were open for constitutional changes. The 1917 legislature could have submitted proposed amendments to the 1919 legislature which, if passed, would then go to the people for a referendum vote. The main objection to this method was that it would take three or four years. The legislature could also have called a constitutional convention—an expensive process—to frame a new constitution and then submit it to the people for approval. A third means was the submission of a constitution by the legislature, or by a representative body elected by the legislature to do so, to the people to accept or reject. This last method called for only one election. Since the constitution was silent on the matter, it remained for the legislature to determine the best and most efficient procedure.

The hostility of the senate to any constitutional changes was shown immediately. Few League supporters were given important committee assignments. Of the forty committees appointed, the League held the majority in only six, an arrangement that was totally out of proportion to its actual strength in the senate.[83] The major committees, including those concerned with banks and banking, education, insurance, the judi-

80. *Ibid.,* January 11, 1917, p. 5.

81. *Ibid.,* January 18, 1917, p. 9.

82. *Ibid.,* January 11, 1917, p. 7. The following comment was a typical League explanation for the constitutional amendment: "It was adopted when North Dakota was a frontier settlement and long before its position as the greatest granary of the country was ever suspected. The state was like a man trying to get around in a suit of clothes made for him when he was a boy." Charles Edward Russell, *In and Out of the Yoke* (n.p., n.d.), p. 28.

83. *Non-partisan Leader,* January 11, 1917, p. 10.

ciary, livestock, public lands, railroads, rules, taxes and tax laws, and ways and means, were packed with holdover senators.

A new constitution was embodied in house bill 44, called the farmers' bill of rights, and a special election was "to give the voters an opportunity to pass upon a modernized code of government."[84] The provisions of the constitution were far-reaching, and included authorizations other than those permitting state-owned utilities, state hail insurance, and the exemption of farm improvements from taxation.[85] Among other things, the proposed constitution included the following provisions: state-wide prohibition; the election of state and county officers every four years rather than biennially in order to economize and also to prevent state issues from being influenced by national affairs; the short ballot, permitting the election of the governor and one or two other executive officers—the rest to be appointed by the legislature; the meeting of the legislature every two years so that there would be no holdover senators; the investment of state funds within the commonwealth in order to make possible extensive loans to farmers at reasonable interest rates; an increase in the bonded-debt limit of the state to $500,000 to permit the construction of state-owned projects; a four-fifths vote by the supreme court to declare laws unconstitutional; petitions for the recall of public officials to require the signature of 10 per cent of the voters; and the adoption of the Torrens system of land registration, "one of the up-to-date things in government."[86]

It was no secret that the defeat of house bill 44 would be considered a mortal blow to the League, for it embodied the chief features of the industrial program. As expected, the opposition to the bill was strong. It was assailed as unconstitutional, socialistic, "sudden, revolutionary, unprecedented"; it was charged that its enactment would encourage irre-

84. Charles Merz, "Political Revolt in the Northwest," *New Republic,* XIII (November 10, 1917), pp. 44–45.

85. *Non-partisan Leader,* January 18, 1917, pp. 5, 20.

86. *Ibid.,* p. 5. There was already precedent for the establishment of state-owned enterprises in North Dakota. State bonds previously had been issued to build and equip the state bindery plant. In fifteen years, according to League officials, the principal and interest were paid out of the net earnings. A tax was not levied to finance the plant, which was paid for in fifteen years. Furthermore, North Dakota farmers were reportedly saved about a cent on each pound of twine. *Ibid.,* January 25, 1917, p. 5.

ponsible people to seize office, go on a wild spending orgy, and plunge he state into debt.

When the strength of the opposition was felt, Townley decided to carry he fight directly to the farmers at scheduled meetings, addressing them n a conversational tone, and in many instances appealing to them by name.[87] In one case he asserted: "There is nothing in the federal constitution that forbids it, nothing in the state constitution and nothing in your constitution, I am sure. I'll tell you whose constitution it doesn't agree with. It doesn't agree with the constitution of those who have been making this extra dollar a bushel profit out of Feed D wheat. . . . They alk about a debt limit to protect you. There is no limit now to the ability of the trusts to put you into debt. I am for a debt limit. Sure! I am for a imit to the power of the plunderbund to rob you."[88]

In the house the opposition to the bill was led by A. G. Divet, who lost no time in informing League leaders who had challenged him to a debate that he would not humiliate himself by debating the bill with "an anarchist, discredited socialist, or I.W.W. worker, with which you are so richly endowed, seeking only an occasion to rant about his own particular grievances against God and society." John Baer, the League cartoonist, meanwhile had been caricaturing Divet as the "shepherd of the people" with "cramps—in the head" and as a "lackey for big interests."[89]

House bill 44 was passed by the house on January 26, after five days of "invective, cajolery, and constitutional arguments. . . ." League leaders charged that the bill was opposed by lawyers, not farmers, who engaged n dilatory tactics by repeating trivial motions, by demanding roll calls on trifling matters, and by offering amendments they knew would be voted down. In the end the bill was passed by a vote of 81 to 28, with four not voting; six legislators not endorsed by the League voted for it, and five endorsed voted against it.[90]

It was not until house bill 44 reached the senate that it encountered real opposition. Senate antipathy to the measure was displayed early in the

87. Bacon, *A Warning to the Farmer,* p. 19; *Non-partisan Leader,* January 25, 1917, p. 8.
88. *Ibid.,* February 1, 1917, p. 20.
89. *Ibid.,* February 8, 1917, p. 10; February 15, 1917, p. 5.
90. *Ibid.,* February 1, 1917, pp. 5, 7.

session when an outright repudiation of its features was demanded, but suddenly the tactics of the opposition were revised, with the introduction of a bill providing for constitutional changes by the method that necessitated a special election to be followed by two regular elections. This was the procedure the League had sought to avoid because of the delays involved. The change in opposition tactics was intended to serve a twofold purpose. The opponents, sensing the popularity of the League's program with the farmers, could say that they were for the program but not the League's leaders; and by postponing enactment of the bill, it was hoped that the ardor for the measures would pass after the first flush of enthusiasm. The League repeatedly urged the farmers to exert pressure on senators known to be against house bill 44, but despite League efforts the upper house succeeded in postponing action indefinitely by a vote of 29 to 20. One senator endorsed by the League voted for the delay, while two not endorsed by the League voted against it.

Some League members accepted the defeat of house bill 44 as "a piece of luck," for had it passed, some members "might have expected the immediate arrival of the farmers' millenium." The failure of the new constitution afforded the Nonpartisan Leaguers a breathing spell, an opportunity to warn their followers not to expect too much, and a chance to get the new constitution adopted by a petition to the people.[91]

Other proposals introduced in the 1917 legislature included the following: repeal of the "Better Farming Law" and distribution of the accumulated funds; compulsory notification by mortgagors before foreclosure; permission to subpoena witnesses by telephone, telegraph, or mail; uniform interest rates before and after maturity, with all contracts to the contrary to be null and void; authorization of a tax levy on land for creating a hail-insurance fund; a scaling-down of the legal rate of interest for any indebtedness; limited woman suffrage; setting aside the third Friday in January as "state temperance day" to be observed in public schools; compelling farmers to rotate their crops; and a call for a constitutional convention. There was a series of bills designed to provide "an evening up of opportunities between country and town," and others provided for the construction of a $200,000 terminal elevator wherever the Equity Cooperative Exchange wanted it built and its subsequent transference by

91. Merz, in *New Republic,* XIII (November 10, 1917), p. 45.

ale to the Equity. Still another bill required physicians and surgeons to keep prominently posted a list of all their charges and fees, and surgeons who removed appendixes, tapeworms, or the like were to send the removed parts to the medical school of the University of North Dakota, which, in turn, would forward to the patient a certified report to aid him in auditing his doctor bills.

A bill termed the "Old Gang" elevator bill, calling for a $300,000 appropriation to be raised by direct taxation, was vetoed by Governor Frazier, who described it as "a fake bill," the purpose of which was to discredit state ownership and defeat the farmers' purposes.[92] The objections to this bill were particularly strong because it provided for only one small elevator; its taxing features would have been a burden to the state; it would not have been re-enforced with a flour mill or any other state-controlled marketing unit; furthermore, it would not prove of any substantial service to the grain producers, and finally it would give the enemies of the League an opportunity to declare state ownership a failure.

The important board of regents bill, known as house bill 65, called for the abolition of the existing board and the establishment of a new one. It was strictly a League bill which, according to the League, was in line with the purpose of placing the agricultural college in the hands of a board that was friendly to the farmer. The League was particularly in opposition to the old board because of the investigations that had resulted in the dismissal of John Worst, who was then also the superintendent of public instruction, from the presidency of the college of agriculture.[93] Besides eliminating the salary of the commissioner of agriculture, League leaders claimed that leaving the superintendent of public instruction as head of the entire system would have brought about unity in the state administration of education. The League charged that Governor Hanna had appointed the board of regents on March 2, 1915—two days before there was any law providing for the establishment of such a body. In the course of this controversy the members of the board refused to relinquish their posts, and their actions were upheld by the senate, which defeated the bill by a vote of 26 to 17. Another measure, house bill 174, provided for the

92. *Non-partisan Leader,* March 8, 1917, p. 5.

93. *Ibid.,* January 25, 1917, p. 11; February 22, 1917, p. 22. The office of commissioner of education was created by the 1915 legislature.

transfer of the farmers' institutes from the control of the agricultur
college to the state agricultural commission, with special instructions t
deal with the marketing of farm products.[94]

Despite the failure of the League to obtain passage of house bill 44,
was successful in fulfilling some of its campaign pledges. The newl
created office of state inspector of grains, weights, and measures wa
empowered with authority to regulate the weighing and grading of grair
Farm improvements were partially exempt from taxation by the enact
ment of a law permitting such improvements to be assessed at 5 per cen
of their true valuation, while the property of banks, railroads, and "th
lesser agents of Big Business" was assessed at 30 per cent of its actual valu
Another act prevented railroads from discriminating against cooperativ
elevators when supplying them with cars, while still another placed
new cooperative corporation law in operation. Limited woman suffrag
was granted; a public welfare commission was organized to look into th
conditions of female and child labor; evening schools were established fo
adults; the inheritance tax on large fortunes was raised to 15 per cent; an
the compulsory school age was raised to seventeen.[95]

League claims in the field of education were particularly noteworthy
When the League came into power in 1916, it was said that only one farn
child of every four finished the eighth grade and only one of every te
enrolled in high school. The average attendance was 65 days, the averag
rural school year being 150 days. City schools had a term of 180 days an
a 90 per cent attendance.[96]

Since the new superintendent of public instruction was a League man
it was quite natural that changes were made. One complaint against th
old course of study was that nowhere was the word "dockage" used. Sinc
it was a common word in the grain business, the new superintenden
placed it in the new course of study along with such words as "musi
and calisthenics." Studies of farm accounts and public ownership wer
introduced in the seventh grade. The eighth-grade teacher, among othe
things, had to have an appreciation of "the benefits of eliminating al

94. *Ibid.*, March 8, 1917, p. 8.

95. Merz, in *New Republic,* XIII (November 10, 1917), p. 45; Gillette, in *Survey*
XLI (March, 1919), p. 758.

96. Merz, in *New Republic,* XIII (November 10, 1917), pp. 71–72.

ınnecessary middlemen and selling in the open market." There were also ıumerous other curricular qualifications required in "making farm chil-ɫren into militant economists."

Higher requirements were demanded of new teachers. Legislation made ›ossible an easier access to medical inspection for rural schools; free trans-›ortation was provided for children living more than two and a quarter niles from school. If the child had not graduated from the eighth grade, ıe was compelled to go to school until he was seventeen. Opportunities for chooling were also provided for adults. Rural schools were standardized nd consolidated; it was claimed that more than a hundred consolidated chools were added to the state list during the ten months the League was n control. As expected, a friendly legislature also provided more money or rural education.

Besides passing some two hundred and fifty-four laws in the legislative ession of 1917, the League also indicated definitely that it sought the upport of labor. League members introduced bills that were asked for ınd endorsed by the North Dakota Federation of Labor. A number of ninor bills were passed, but major measures, such as bills for working-nen's compensation and minimum wages and hours for women and :hildren, were defeated.[97]

The year 1917 witnessed the first serious attempt on the part of the Nonpartisan League to grow nationally—particularly by expanding into Minnesota, "the gateway of finance and business to the Northwest."[98] Organization work began in Minnesota early in 1917, when "a battalion of automobiles" used in organizing North Dakota was placed at the lisposal of the Minnesota organizers. Between eighty and ninety cars, each driven by trained organizers and supervised by experienced super-ntendents, were placed in the hands of an executive committee of five armers from five counties. By March, 1917, the League claimed 12,000 nembers in Minnesota, but hardly had the League started its activities here when a rival "Nonpartisan League of Minnesota" was organized by

97. *Nonpartisan League Methods and Principles,* p. 20; *Non-partisan Leader,* March 8, 1917, p. 23.

98. A. K. Horwill, "The Nonpartisan League," *New Republic,* XVIII (April 5, 1919), p. 304. See also Ray McKaig, "The New Minnesota Despotism," *Public,* XXI (April 13, 1918), pp. 465–67.

five men representing wealthy lumbermen and merchants of Minneapolis and St. Paul.[99]

The legitimate League invaded Minnesota by publishing a pamphlet, *Facts for the Farmer,* the purpose being to reveal to Minnesota farmers how they were being robbed by the "land grabs" of corporations, the unequal system of taxation, elevator men, millers, "grain gamblers," and "manipulators of the butter and egg markets and unconscionable meat packers." The pamphlet also charged that government in Minnesota was a one-sided affair. Of the 67 members in the senate in 1917, only 9 were farmers; and of the 130 members in the lower house, only 38 were farmers. It asserted that the business, financial, and professional groups comprised only one-tenth of the population of the state, but held three-fourths of the legislative seats and all major state offices. On the other hand, the combined population of farmers and workers, comprising nine-tenths of the population, held but one-fourth of the legislative seats and no state offices.[100] A second pamphlet, *Facts Kept from the Farmer,* appeared in September and attempted to show that "the huge investments of the big financial and corporate interest for political campaigns and the insidious efforts of such combinations . . . [were deceiving] the people by means of 'good will campaigns.'" Wide circulation was given these pamphlets through the mails.

Many League leaders, especially those in Minnesota, believed that the organization could grow nationally only with the aid of organized labor, and consequently a determined bid was made for labor's support. While it was true that a fusion of agrarian and laboring forces was brought about in North Dakota, the growth of the League there was due primarily to the predominant agricultural population of the state. In Minnesota, where there were three large cities—Minneapolis, St. Paul, and Duluth—and the

99. William Watts Folwell, *A History of Minnesota* (4 vols., St. Paul, 1921–30), III, 554. The rival league issued a paper, the *Nonpartisan,* beginning in August, but it survived only until December. It expressed sympathy for the plight of the farmer but attacked Townley as the exponent of socialism. The "fake" league published two large issues of a paper called *On The Square,* distributing a great number at a cost of $50,000. Some 50,000 copies of another pamphlet, *America First,* were circulated, as well as tons of other anti-League literature. The "fake" league, it was claimed, spent about $500,000.

100. *Facts for the Farmer* (St. Paul, 1917), pp. 132–33.

vote of agriculture and labor was more evenly distributed, the situation was more typical of that of other states. Cooperation between agriculture and labor at the ballot box was essential if the League was to grow nationally.

The proposed alignment of agriculture and labor threw a scare into the camps of the Republican and Democratic parties, but the entrance of the United States into the war and the radical doctrines propagated by the League leaders gave the opposition its much-desired opportunity. League theories made it almost impossible for the League to avoid criticizing certain aspects of the policies of the federal government. Its leaders, for example, had objected to the manner in which the nation was organizing for war.

> It was natural that an emergency structure should build, not around the isolated farmer, but around the industrial captain whose leadership is almost the only sort that exists locally, around the grain-buyer, the banker, the miller in whom the farmer saw his economic and political opponents, more to be feared than any distant autocracy. A grain-buyer, suspected of using a short scale, declares that this is a war for universal participation in the world's good things. . . . Liberty bonds have not the best chance of being taken quickly when their salesman is a local banker suspected of having done his best to block the enactment of a state rural credits law.[101]

The charges of Townley typified the attitude of the League toward the war; he described it as a rich man's war, and informed those who were sending their boys across the water that they "must pay the steel trust added, ever-increasing millions of profit to keep your boy from being destroyed after he gets over there."[102]

Added reason for attacking the League was supplied by the conference of producers and consumers held in St. Paul in September, 1917. The League called this conference primarily to enlist the support of labor. Among the speakers was Senator Robert M. La Follette, whose subject, "The People's Fight," was intended as an appeal for reduced living costs. He had promised not to say anything disloyal, but after his speech got under way he became bolder and bolder, and among other things lamented

101. "The Farmer and the War," *New Republic,* XIII (November 3, 1917), pp. 8–9.

102. Franklin F. Holbrook and Livia Appel, *Minnesota in the War with Germany* (2 vols., St. Paul, 1928–32), II, 45.

"the decline of truly representative government" and other "things" which Townley later said "we didn't invite him there to discuss." La Follette charged that America's declaration of war had been unnecessary and demanded that the present generation pay the cost of the war not by the sale of bonds but by taxation. He also accused the wealthy, who controlled the government, of tabling "the proposition to tax wealth. . . ."[103]

Although the pronouncements of La Follette and the subsequent repercussions of his speech overshadowed the purpose of the meeting, the implications of the proposed alignment were not to be minimized, for it moved a step closer to the organization of the farmer-labor party that was in the process of formation. The conference favored price fixing "so that the rich speculator and the powerful trust may be compelled to bow to the same level rule as the toiling farmer and wage-worker," emphasizing the point that if the profits in articles of daily consumption cannot be passed on to the consumer, the Food Administration should "seize and operate storage elevators, flour mills, bakeries, cereal and breadstuffs factories for the benefit of the people." Representatives from ten state federations of labor were present at this conference of producers and consumers, the total number of union men represented being between 1,500 and 2,000.[104]

Townley was not slow in pointing out the political possibilities of such an alliance. "The farmers control 35 per cent of the vote of this country; labor controls about 27 per cent; a combination of these two elements would make itself felt throughout the nation."[105] At times the relations between the two groups were close. State federations of labor in North Dakota, Minnesota, Idaho, Wisconsin, and other states endorsed the League. Later, when the North Dakota industrial program was launched, the Chicago Federation of Labor and the Minneapolis Trades and Council Assembly voted to deposit their funds with the Bank of North Dakota.[106]

103. *Ibid.*, pp. 46–47. See also *Report of Minnesota Commission of Public Safety* (n.p., n.d.) for the commission's action against the League pursuant to La Follette's remarks.

104. Eleanor Taylor, "Farmer and Factory-Hand," *Survey,* XXXVIII (September 29, 1917), p. 565.

105. *Ibid.*

106. *Non-partisan Leader,* February 22, 1917, p. 6; January 27, 1919, pp. 10–11; June 23, 1919, p. 11; August 4, 1919, p. 3; *Wisconsin Leader* (Madison), July 31, 1920.

In the beginning the Nonpartisan League had attempted to capitalize on the differences existing between town and country. Consequently the opposition among city people was not surprising, for they found themselves excluded from the organization. They felt that the League as a political power would benefit the farmer at their expense. Limiting the organization to farmers was a strong point in the beginning, but as time elapsed it became a source of weakness.[107]

The outcome of the conference of producers and consumers in St. Paul was exactly the opportunity that the opposition was waiting for, and it was the signal for a general assault against the League, especially in Minnesota. Storms of protest arose. Both La Follette and the League were charged with pro-Germanism, treachery, partnership with the Kaiser, and the other crimes against the country. La Follette was threatened with a trial and expulsion from the United States Senate. Among the most vigorous opponents of the League was the Minnesota Public Safety Commission, of which Judge John F. McGee was the dominating personality and only one of the many Minnesota citizens believing that what the state needed was a few "necktie parties." McGee was quoted as stating that "a Nonpartisan League lecturer is a traitor every time. In other words, no matter what he says or does, a League worker is a traitor."[108] Other prominent citizens also accused League leaders of disloyalty and of obstructing the draft.

League leaders tried hard to refute the accusations of disloyalty by asserting their Americanism. North Dakota leaders pointed to the speaker of their senate, who was an American of New England stock; to the speaker of the house, who came to North Dakota from the South, and to many others of foreign stock who were American-born. If what the farmers of the Nonpartisan League produced was a European product, so were the Declaration of Independence, the federal Constitution, the United States Congress, and the deeds of countless numbers of prominent Americans who had been influenced by European thought. The activities of the League were compared with Shays' Rebellion, the American Revolution, Populism, Wat Tyler's Revolt, the Lollard movement,

107. Arthur Warner, "The Farmer Butts Back," *The Nation,* CXI (August 28, 1920), pp. 240–41.

108. George M. Stephenson, *John Lind of Minnesota* (Minneapolis, 1935), pp. 334, 336, 338.

and numerous other struggles of English-speaking peoples who had revolted against the domination of government by commerce and industry. League leaders pointed out that they were not trying to exclude others from the government but merely attempting to persuade the farmers to pool their votes and use them "to elect representatives who would carry out their political and industrial programme." Everything the League had attempted was "peculiarly and distinctly American"; the farmers had obtained control of the Republican party in North Dakota by legal means, and they had nominated and elected officers who legislated in accordance with the wishes of the majority of the citizens of the state. If organizing a state bank was un-American, so were the acts of Alexander Hamilton, who drew up plans for the first Bank of the United States, and those of George Washington, who supported it. Furthermore, there were numerous cases of states and municipalities being engaged in business activities similar to those proposed by the League. The State of Louisiana owned and operated the Port of New Orleans, including cotton warehouses and a grain elevator; King County, Washington, owned and operated the Port of Seattle, which, besides having storage and elevator facilities, provided for packing fish, baling hay, and processing foodstuffs. It was neither political nor industrial autocracy, neither communism nor socialism, but democracy that was "in the saddle" in North Dakota.[109]

The League attributed the disloyalty charges hurled against it largely to misquoting of its speakers by newspapers and to other similar abuses which in effect amounted to a denial of constitutional rights. The League cited a series of patriotic acts as refutation of the charge of disloyalty.[110] Before the opening of the third Liberty Loan drive, the League had wired the Secretary of the Treasury, William G. McAdoo, offering the services of its organization to the national cause, to which offer McAdoo had replied: "I welcome the assistance of the farmers of the great Northwest in this patriotic service to the country." North Dakota, a state fully controlled by the League, was the first to oversubscribe its quota by 100 per cent, despite the drought of 1917. It had also oversubscribed the first and

109. W. G. Roylance, "Americanism in North Dakota," *The Nation,* CIX (July 12, 1919), pp. 38–39. North Dakota furnished 18,595 men to the armed forces, or 2.12 per cent above the national average. *State of North Dakota Legislative Manual,* 1919, p. 441.

110. *Nonpartisan League Methods and Principles,* pp. 48–50.

second Liberty Loan bond quotas; and Montana, reported to have had the largest League membership in proportion to its population, was the second state to oversubscribe. It was further claimed that the farmers of Montana, Minnesota, and North and South Dakota—the four great spring wheat states—had increased their wheat acreage by 52 per cent. "The League farmers do not prove their loyalty by merely waving flags; they do not wear their patriotism just on their coat lapels—they carry it in their hearts." Thousands of League farmers were said to have had Red Cross acres; their wives had Red Cross hens and Red Cross circles. More than 550 leases were written by the North Dakota Council of Defense, placing some 100,000 acres of idle land under cultivation to produce additional crops valued at $500,000. The council also aided in meeting the serious labor shortage.[111] North Dakota furthermore claimed that its draft costs were among the lowest in the nation.[112] Governor Frazier, since the start of the war, had issued at least twenty-five proclamations urging the people to stand behind their government. "Every state official from the governor down [had] pledged at least 10 days of manual labor in the harvest fields instead of a vacation." The League also had approved Wilson's Fourteen Points.[113] On August 10, 1920, H. G. Teigan, the secretary of the League, had written Upton Sinclair that "on the whole we had very little trouble with the national government."[114]

One of the best means of refuting the arguments of the opposition was to cite what the League had accomplished in North Dakota in a legislative sense. The drought and the black rust in 1916 and 1917 had left the farmers in the western and central portions of the state prostrated financially. The increasing demands of the nation for more food production had resulted in the mortgaging of their land, livestock, and heavy machinery. Representatives of the North Dakota Council of Defense and the state bankers' association frankly admitted that the banks were unable to meet the credit needs of the farmers. Thus, when the farmers failed to receive aid from the federal government, Governor Frazier called a special session of the legislature to consider the feed and seed problem and other needs

111. *State of North Dakota Legislative Manual,* 1919, p. 433.

112. *The Nonpartisan League, Loyal or Disloyal?* (n.p., n.d.) [leaflet].

113. *Non-partisan Leader,* February 17, 1919, p. 5.

114. H. G. Teigan to Upton Sinclair, August 10, 1920, in the Minnesota Historical Society.

of the state. This special session, the second in the history of the state, convened on January 23, 1918. As a result, an act was passed which permitted counties where the seed and feed situation was acute to issue bonds and lend the proceeds to farmers. The amount which any county could issue was limited to 5 per cent of the assessed valuation of the property in the county, from which six or seven million dollars was to be raised.[115]

115. John T. Frederick, "A Legislature That Works," *New Republic,* XIV (February 23, 1918), pp. 105–7. *State of North Dakota Legislative Manual,* 1919, pp. 296, 371. The "Seeding and Feeding Act" entrusted the sale of over $3,000,000 in bonds to the commissioner of agriculture and labor.

Chapter VII

THE NONPARTISAN LEAGUE EXPANSION AND DECLINE[1]

THE SUCCESSES of the League in North Dakota called striking attention throughout the nation to the program of state socialism for which it stood and aroused the fears of conservatives everywhere. When it became clear, during the year 1917, that League leaders were intent on a program of expansion, and that they meant also to win the full cooperation of organized labor, the opposition drew tightly together and fought back earnestly, although, as indicated in the last chapter, not always fairly. But the determination of League leaders to carry their program forward was undimmed, even by the irrelevant and generally untrue charges of pro-Germanism which they so often had to face. They found farmers in all the Middle West who were receptive to their arguments. Some of them had in turn supported the Grange, the Alliance, the Populists, and the Equity; for all such the appearance of the League had the effect of reviving old political principles and giving to them a new significance. Expansion into Minnesota was facilitated by the close ties between the farmers in the western part of the state and those in eastern North Dakota. A combination of political, economic, racial, and psy-

1. This chapter follows in the main an article by Theodore Saloutos, "The Expansion and Decline of the Nonpartisan League in the Western Middle West, 1917–1921," *Agricultural History,* XX (October, 1946), pp. 235–52. Reprinted by permission.

chological ties likewise expedited the spread of the League into Wisconsin, Iowa, South Dakota, Montana, and other neighboring states.

The political campaign of 1918 got under way in Minnesota, as in North Dakota, with the staging of local meetings on February 22—Washington's birthday. Delegates named at these conventions were to meet in district conventions for the purpose of nominating delegates to the state convention. Simultaneously, plans were made to get out as much of the vote as possible by staging whirlwind membership drives. No pains were spared in organizing Minnesota. Two hundred and sixty Ford cars were purchased at a cost of $130,000; the most capable organizers were summoned from Colorado, Nebraska, South Dakota, Wisconsin, Iowa, Oklahoma, Kansas, Texas, Montana, and Idaho, adding some 150 organizers to those already in the state. At one time Minnesota farmers were said to be joining the League at the rate of a thousand a day.[2]

In the Minnesota primaries, for governor the League supported Charles A. Lindbergh, the "original lone eagle" and former congressman who had represented the district around Little Falls. He was described as one who "never wore the corporation collar." In Congress he had voted against declaring war on Germany—an unfortunate act in view of the fact that the League had been accused of disloyalty. Lindbergh also was opposed by many Catholics, against whom he had shown hostility. While a member of Congress, he had introduced a resolution asking for congressional investigation of the political activities of the Catholic Church in America. He charged that Roman prelates "in all lands and at all times have been the ally of oppression," implying that "Big Biz" and the Catholics were closely allied.[3]

The League set out to gain control of the dominant party in Minnesota as it had done in North Dakota. Since Minnesota elected the members of its legislature by a nonpartisan system, the League was not confronted

2. *Non-partisan Leader* (Fargo, N. Dak.), March 4, 1918, pp. 11, 17; S. R. Maxwell, *The Nonpartisan League from the Inside* (St. Paul, 1918), p. 13; James W. Witham, *Fifty Years on the Firing Line* (Chicago, 1924), p. 101.

3. Robert Kingsley, "Recent Variation from the Two-Party System as Evidenced by the Nonpartisan League and the Agricultural Bloc" (unpublished master's thesis, University of Minnesota, 1923), p. 29; *Catholic Bulletin* (St. Paul), June 15, 1918 [leaflet in Minnesota Historical Society]; Lynn and Dora B. Haines, *The Lindberghs* (New York, 1931), pp. 221–23.

with any party-affiliation difficulties in endorsing its candidates. The League did no work in Minneapolis, St. Paul, and Duluth, the three large cities of Minnesota, for it endorsed no candidates from city districts.[4]

The opponents of Lindbergh concentrated on the election of J. A. A. Burnquist as the Republican candidate for governor. The candidacy of Fred Wheaton, the Democrat, never personally a strong contender, was further weakened by the open endorsement of Burnquist by several prominent Democrats and also by the support given the Republicans from several bipartisan anti-League organizations. Of the latter, the most prominent was the America First association, formed in the summer of 1917. During the last week of May and the first week of June, the newspapers of the Twin Cities carried daily appeals to the Democrats to enter the Republican primaries "to save the State from Socialism," and with some degree of success. Old party lines already had given way to "a pro-League and anti-League grouping." Lindbergh had written a book "whose bungling expressions on the war came home to roost . . . , when published by the opposition during the campaign." He was defeated in the primaries but received 150,000 votes, or three times the number of members the League had in Minnesota at the time.[5] The results of bipartisan voting were obvious. The Democrats, who had polled 93,112 votes in 1916, cast only 32,649 votes in the primaries, while the Republicans, who never had tallied more than 200,000 votes in the primaries, this time received 349,951. With the aid of labor the League nominated 80 out of 130 members to the lower house, and 42 out of 67 members to the senate. The League carried 30 counties, mainly those along the North Dakota border.[6]

The defeat of Lindbergh gave the third-party advocates within the League their opportunity, for the elements favoring such an alignment had gathered strength. Nominating petitions were circulated to place candidates in the general elections on a "farmer-labor" ticket.[7] Only three

4. Kingsley, "Recent Variations from the Two-Party System," p. 29.

5. Austin P. Haines, "The Nonpartisan League and the Loyalty Issue," *New Republic,* XVI (September 14, 1918), p. 188; Herbert E. Gaston, *The Nonpartisan League* (New York, 1920), p. 261.

6. Kingsley, "Recent Variations from the Two-Party System," pp. 30–31; *Nonpartisan Leader,* July 29, 1918, p. 2.

7. Ray McKaig, "The Nonpartisan League and Its Independent Press," *Public,* XXII (January 4, 1919), p. 13.

candidates, however, were so listed. D. H. Evans—a Populist, an old-time Democrat, and a banker—was named for governor, and Tom Davis and Fred E. Tillquist, both insurgent Republicans, were put up for attorney general and warehouse commissioner, respectively. But this eleventh-hour farmer-labor party failed. League nominees, who had claimed the majority of the districts in the primaries, were defeated in the general election. In the house the farmer-laborites mustered only 26 votes against 105 for the opposition; in the senate about 15 out of 67 senators voted with them, but of these the farmer-laborites had elected only 10.[8]

One result of the League's defeats was the impression of its leaders with the need for more effective organization. The drive for a larger membership began shortly after the 1918 political campaign. Great emphasis was also placed on the need for more effective cooperation between labor and agriculture at the ballot box. In July, 1919, the Working People's Nonpartisan and Political League of Minnesota, which became the town and city branch of the League, was organized, absorbing various trade unions and other League sympathizers who were ineligible for membership in "the farmers' league."

In Nebraska, as in Minnesota, the League was given an unceremonious reception. No candidates were put up for state executive offices, but attempts were made to elect legislative and county officers.[9] Even the powerful Nebraska Farmers' Union had passed resolutions the year previous strongly condemning the policies of the League.[10] One report had it that a Nebraska organizer "was taken by an armed mob, in the dead of night, to an island in the Platte River, where one end of a rope was tied around his neck and the other thrown over the limb of a tree. He was given his life only on his promise to sell his League automobile, give the money to the Red Cross, and himself enlist in the United States army."[11] Suit was brought against members of the state's council of defense, which had ordered the League to cease organizing Nebraska and "had prohibited it from holding a State convention for the purpose of nominating a State

8. Kingsley, "Recent Variations from the Two-Party System," pp. 30–32.

9. Frank G. Moorhead, "The Non-Partisan League in Politics," *The Nation,* CVII (October 5, 1918), pp. 364–65.

10. *Nebraska Union Farmer* (Omaha), August 8, 1917, p. 1.

11. Moorhead, in *The Nation,* CVII (October 5, 1918), p. 364.

icket." The League charged the council with "insisting that no new political parties shall be organized, but that the members of the League shall vote for either one or the other candidates of the two principal parties. . . ." The case was finally compromised; the council promised to cease its opposition if the League withdrew its paid organizers from the state, secured a new manager, and ceased circulating copies of Woodrow Wilson's *The New Freedom*.[12]

In Kansas, the League did not consider entering the state elections until 1920, but it did indicate its preference for Governor Arthur Capper for the United States Senate. Capper had shown his sympathies for the League when the federal Department of Justice asked him to investigate charges of disloyalty within the organization by reporting that "the League was comporting itself in accordance to law and the war needs of the nation." This probably was partly responsible for Capper's carrying all the 105 counties in the primary election. Again, when the League was required to present written references from two well-known residents in order to rent offices in Topeka, Governor Capper and Tom McNeal, editor of *Capper's Farmer,* came to its assistance.

South Dakota appeared to be more friendly to the League, but the vote received in the primaries by Mark P. Bates, a farmer, as its candidate for governor on an independent ticket was not very encouraging. The antagonism present in the other middle western states apparently did not exist there, and League meetings prohibited in Minnesota were frequently held across the state line in South Dakota.[13] Early in 1918, the League made known the fact that it was not prepared to enter the Wisconsin campaign until the elections of 1920 and left the field open to the independent farmer ticket led by the president of the Wisconsin Society of Equity.[14] In Iowa, the League claimed a membership of 15,000 in the fall of 1918

12. *Ibid.,* pp. 364–65; Elmo Bryant Phillips, "The Non-Partisan League in Nebraska" (unpublished master's thesis, University of Nebraska, 1931). See also the *Non-partisan Leader,* February 25, 1918, p. 12.

13. Moorhead, in *The Nation,* CVII (October 5, 1918), p. 365; *Non-partisan Leader,* August 19, 1918, pp. 3, 14; *Wisconsin Leader* (Madison), January 15, 1921; "Townley in Kansas," *Literary Digest,* LXVIII (March 12, 1921), pp. 17–18; *Minnesota Leader* (Olivia), March 26, April 9, 1921.

14. *National Equity News* (Madison, Wis.), April 25, 1918, p. 11; *Non-partisan Leader,* May 20, 1918, p. 16.

and also announced that it would not be ready for political action in that state until the fall of 1920. James M. Pierce, the publisher of the *Iowa Homestead,* was forced to resign his post as a member of the state council of defense because of his League sympathies. In Montana, the League nominated forty out of ninety-five members of the lower house and fourteen members of the upper house.[15] It claimed considerable success in organizing the state of Washington, and showed particularly keen interest in the Idaho campaign. Unlike the League in North Dakota, which dominated the Republican party, the Idaho League gained control of the Democratic party and nominated H. F. Samuels for governor. Two congressmen and two United States senators endorsed by the League were also nominated; one of the senators endorsed was William E. Borah.[16]

The general election of 1918 made the League triumph of 1916 in North Dakota more secure.[17] All state officers were re-elected with increased majorities; majorities were obtained in both houses of the legislature; two more congressmen were elected; and League-endorsed candidates were elected to the supreme court and the railroad commission. In Minnesota and South Dakota, League candidates displaced those of the Democratic party as the leading opponents of the Republicans; but in Idaho the League showing was not what its members had anticipated, and only the state treasurer and superintendent of public instruction were elected from its candidates.

League triumphs in several legislatures were registered, but in no case did the League obtain the majorities gained in North Dakota. In Minnesota, the combined farmer-labor forces in the upper house numbered fifteen and in the lower house thirty-six; in Montana sixteen League members were elected to the lower house and four to the senate; in Idaho, six League-endorsed senators and ten League-endorsed members of the lower house were elected.[18]

Now that the League had captured complete control of North Dakota, it was only logical for it to seek passage of the industrial program which

15. *Ibid.,* September 30, 1918, p. 4.

16. Moorhead, in *The Nation,* CVII (October 5, 1918), p. 365; *Non-partisan Leader,* August 5, 1918, pp. 8–9, 14; September 23, 1918, p. 3.

17. For a vote tabulation, see *State of North Dakota Legislative Manual,* 1919, p. 283.

18. *Non-partisan Leader,* November 25, 1918, p. 4.

had been blocked by the conservative senate in 1917 on the theory that the state lacked the constitutional authority to engage in industrial activities.[19] The new legislature immediately busied itself ratifying all the proposed constitutional amendments required to obtain the constitutional authority needed.

Correspondence exchanged by Arthur Le Sueur, legal counsel and personal adviser to A. C. Townley, and Frederic C. Howe, writer and exponent of progressive legislation and platforms, throws light on the procedure used in the early stages. On April 22, 1918, Howe wrote to Le Sueur that he was expecting "to begin gathering material for the legislative program of the League early in May."[20] Howe was planning to acquaint himself with "the material in the libraries" and then "go to the country in order to get away from the distractions of the city, and . . . remain there for a considerable time familiarizing [himself] with the . . . achievements of Australia, Denmark and some of the more progressive legislation of our own states." He added:

> The underlying idea I have in mind is the economic and political freedom of the state not only from exploiting but from the unnecessary distributing agencies that now control the economic and the political life of the state.
>
> This involves shifting distribution to the producers, acting either through political or cooperative agencies. It also involves shifting political control to the producers. In other words, I have in mind a producers' commonwealth in which privilege in all of its forms will be either exercised or reduced to a position of service within the state.
>
> In so far as it is economic it should, in my opinion, where possible, be worked out along quasi-cooperative rather than state-socialistic lines in order that the program will not be jeopardized with every election.
>
> I should not be so fearful of state socialism if the political machinery were better adjusted to our purposes or if the producing classes had more cohesive training, as they have in some European countries. In addition, there are substantial ethical reasons for emphasizing the cooperative as opposed to the state-socialistic motive.

On July 8, 1918, Le Sueur informed Howe that Townley had agreed

19. Gilbert W. Cooke, "The North Dakota Industrial Program" (unpublished doctoral dissertation, University of Wisconsin, 1936), pp. 17–18.

20. F. C. Howe to Arthur Le Sueur, April 22, 1918, in the Minnesota Historical Society. All letters cited hereafter are in this depository except as noted.

that "we should have some of your time to aid in working this out" and described the Howe plan as "a very comprehensive outline for work; I think more comprehensive than we would care to tackle at this time."[21] League officials, according to Le Sueur, inquired "when and how much time you can give us . . . what we want of Mr. Frederic C. Howe is that he recognize the fact that . . . he is one man in the United States who can and ought to be of tremendous service in carrying out the practical program that we are driving at. . . . Mr. Townley has assured me that even if we have to sell our hides to cover the cost it must and will be covered and tell you to come."[22]

Despite the efforts made to obtain the aid of Howe, it became quite apparent in subsequent correspondence that he had become involved in other reform projects, and consequently was not instrumental in drawing up the final plans for the League's industrial program. Generally speaking, the legislation of the League was framed by attorneys and others in its employ. These men acted in the same capacity as did the legislative representatives of the Canadian government in the provinces. The men engaged in shaping the legal and economic phases of the industrial program were W. G. Roylance, a former college professor; William Lemke and W. A. Day of the legal staff of the League; A. C. Townley; and Walter Thomas Mills of California, a League lecturer.[23]

The League's industrial program was passed in its entirety by the 1919 legislature. The legislation provided for the establishment of an industrial commission to head the state industries; the organization of the Bank of North Dakota to finance the industries; the construction of a mill and elevator and cheaper homes for farmers and laborers; compulsory state hail insurance;[24] authorization for an experimental creamery; exemption of all improvements from the general property tax; the issuance of ten million dollars in bonds for rural-credit loans, plus bonds for financing the state bank and the state mill and elevator. The industrial commission, the all-important agency empowered to direct the entire industrial program (with the exception of the hail insurance plan), was a body com-

21. Le Sueur to Howe, July 8, 1918.

22. Le Sueur to Howe, July 23, 1919.

23. Cooke, "The North Dakota Industrial Program," p. 18.

24. See Gilbert W. Cooke, "North Dakota Hail Insurance, 1911–36," *Journal of Business,* XI (1938), pp. 277–307.

osed of the governor, the attorney general, and the commissioner of griculture, who held their posts ex officio.[25] Particularly powerful was the overnor, who had full veto power over any act of the commission.

The League had no intention of levying new taxes to start the new inlustries. Each industry was expected to finance its own way; the credit f the state was to be used to endorse the industrial bonds of each indusry authorized to begin operation, the purpose of this credit plan being o provide each industry with money when it was needed. It was mainained that thousands of small businesses were forced into bankruptcy at his time by the larger concerns not merely because these larger concerns vere operated on a sounder basis or were able to operate more safely from he business standpoint, but because the larger organization was a more rofitable customer of the bank and hence more likely to receive a loan.[26]

Opposition to the industrial program came from two directions: from ormer League members who had rebelled against the leadership and olicies of the organization, and from the traditional foes of the League. One of the most outspoken foes of the program was Arthur Le Sueur, ormerly an adviser to Townley and a League "brain truster." Similar opposition came from W. G. Roylance, another ex-League adviser.

Le Sueur, in attacking League policies and leadership, outlined the rocedure followed in placing the industrial program in operation. Le Sueur and Roylance had gathered "data of state-owned and operated inlustries from the ends of the earth" and prepared "legislation for carry-

25. Cooke, "The North Dakota Industrial Program," pp. 19–20. The main proviions of the act were as follows: ". . . Manage, operate, control, and govern all utiliies, industries, enterprises and business projects, now or hereafter established, wned, undertaken, administrated or operated by the State of North Dakota, except hose carried on in penal, charitable or educational institutions. To what end it shall ave the power, in the exercise of its sound judgment is hereby directed: (a) to determine the location of all utilities and industries. (b) to acquire by purchase, lease, or eminent domain all necessary property rights, and to equip, maintain and repair and alter same. (c) to employ a manager and all help for each utility. (d) to remove and discharge all persons when the public interest requires it. (e) to fix the buying rice of all things bought and the selling price of things sold. (f) to make rules, egulations, and by-laws for all industries. (g) to procure the necessary funds for such industries, by negotiating the bonds of North Dakota. (h) to conduct investigaions on all matters connected with the industries."

26. *Nonpartisan League; Origin, Purpose and Method of Operation, War Program and Statement of Principles* (n.p., n.d.), p. 16.

ing [the] ideas . . . gathered from this research." This was completed by November, 1918, and submitted to League officials for consideration in the early part of December, 1918.[27] "The policy followed in drawing up this legislation for the establishment of the bank and the mills and elevators," according to Le Sueur, "was to *Take These Institutions As Far Out of Politics As Possible.* When these bills were turned over to the officials of the League for study and suggestion, objections were brought out, and other bills based upon an exactly opposite policy were drawn up. . . . The policy was *Keep The Bank and The Industries Tied to Politics For The Sake of Political Success.*" These industries could have been operated either through the "political state" or through the industrial commission; in practice they were managed by a political body, the industrial commission.

Le Sueur pointed out several weaknesses in the industrial program as finally organized, among the foremost being that it would make for "instability." A League defeat in the elections would place the entire program in the hands of its enemies, who would lose little time in emasculating it. A shift in opinion on the part of a small group of a fickle electorate could change the whole industrial policy. In short, there would be "no stability, no sense of confidence in the future of the enterprises, a condition which is absolutely essential to industrial building." American political psychology would make it difficult to retain a friendly administration in office for more than two or three terms.[28]

Another shortcoming was that further inefficiencies would result from the standpoint of management. The three members of the industrial commission had very wide powers granted them not because of their proficiency but merely because they happened to hold ex-officio posts. The men serving on the commission were also ex-officio members of other state bodies—the banking board, the board of education, and the workmen's compensation board. These men did not carry on active management of these enterprises but employed "experts" to perform this function; yet these duties were important, and critics of the industrial commission

27. Arthur Le Sueur's manuscript in the industrial program, November 30, 1920, in the Minnesota Historical Society.

28. Arthur Le Sueur, "The Nonpartisan League: A Criticism," *Socialist Review*, IX (November, 1920), p. 193. Le Sueur was officially connected with the League until April, 1919.

maintained that its members could not do full justice to all their responsibilities. It was impossible for the commission to make contracts for longer than two years, and the political character of the administration would tempt it "to lay the blame for any failure on the hired managers." As set up, the commission could discharge "at will with or without cause," the result being the erection of "a powerful political machine" and "the attendant evils of the spoils system, bureaucracy, and incompetency." For example, the majority of the industrial commission, which operated the bank, also comprised the banking board, to which reports of the bank's activities had to be made.[29]

The greatest opposition to the League came from the traditional foes of the organization, who capitalized greatly on the arguments of Le Sueur. First they resorted to the courts and finally to the press and the ballot box. An injunction was obtained to prevent the floating of the bond issue, but the state supreme court in *Green* v. *Frazier* held that the laws in question provided "an ample and complete method for the payment of both principal and interest of the bonds . . . and are in entire harmony with the provision of Article 182 of the Constitution as amended. . . ." In the case of *Langer* v. *Hall*, the court decided that the bonded indebtedness of the state could be increased, declaring that "the state could issue $2,000,000 of bonds in excess of the existing debt and that they would be within the debt limit." In *Sargent County* v. *State of North Dakota*, the court held that "the Bank of North Dakota, as an agency of the sovereign power engaged in the banking business, has a distinct status separate and apart from the state itself; this status permits it to function as a distinct and separate agency of the sovereign power."[30] Another suit filed in the federal district court, the suit of the "forty-two taxpayers," charged that the industrial program was a deprivation of their property rights under the Fourteenth Amendment of the federal Constitution. The court, presided over by Judge Charles F. Amidon, supposedly a League sympathizer, held that the industrial program was not a deprivation of property rights.[31]

29. *Ibid.*, pp. 194–95. See also the *Grand Forks Herald*, December 30, 1919; Oscar Anderson to Le Sueur, December 26, 1920; Wallace Campbell to Le Sueur, December 24, 1920.

30. Quoted in Cooke, "The North Dakota Industrial Program," pp. 21–23.

31. *Ibid.*, p. 23. See also *Scott* v. *Frazier*, 258 Fed. Rep. 676 (1919), and Hugh E.

This decision was frequently cited as legal evidence that the League program was constitutional.

The failure to crush the League program by court action did not deter the opposition from making preparations for the elections of 1920. Dissension within the League provided the opposition with much-needed ammunition and did the League irreparable damage. Among the rebelling leaders were M. P. Johnson, former president of the North Dakota Society of Equity, and Theodore G. Nelson, "Two-bit Nelson" according to his enemies, former president of the grain growers' department of the American Society of Equity and an important factor in the early activities of the Equity Cooperative Exchange. These Equity men had been more interested in the cooperative movement than in the industrial program of the League, but they were swept into the League columns by the first flush of enthusiasm. Opposition organizations like the Good Government League, caricatured as the "Goo-Goo League" by League leaders, and later the Independent Voters' Association furnished most of the opposition in the general election of 1920 and especially in the recall election of 1921.

"The real revolt against the League's hierarchy came in 1919, when the attorney general, William Langer, the state auditor, Carl Kositsky, and the secretary of state, Thomas Hall, raised the standard of revolt. All of these men had formerly been members of the League and had been elected by its suffrage. Even since their rebellion they have never claimed to be opposed to the organization as an organization, nor have they at any time renounced their allegiance to its original industrial program." [32] Their two chief arguments of opposition were the mismanagement of funds and the growing burdens of taxation. Once again it was demonstrated that the League program was acceptable, even though its leadership was not.

Another unfortunate development from the standpoint of the League, a development which was used by both sides for all that it was worth politically, was the Scandinavian-American Bank case.[33] The Scandina-

---

Willis, "North Dakota's Industrial Program and the Law," *Survey,* XLV (December 18, 1920), pp. 418–19.

32. Andrew A. Bruce, *Non-Partisan League* (New York, 1921), p. 200.

33. Gaston, *The Nonpartisan League,* pp. 303–12.

vian-American Bank of Fargo, a North Dakota corporation used primarily as a financial agency for the League and its subsidiary organization prior to the establishment of the Bank of North Dakota, had, among other things, lent money to the League on postdated checks which the organization had accepted in payment of membership dues. The Scandinavian officials, it was asserted, repeatedly had refused an audit of its books, but an examination was finally ordered by the board of bank examiners, two of whose three members were the dissenting League officials, William Langer and Thomas Hall. The examination revealed that the bank had some $75,000 in postdated checks among its assets, had exceeded its authorized lending limit, and was totally insolvent. As a result, the bank was ordered closed and a receiver appointed. League officials immediately sought to rally the aid of the farmers to the bank and succeeded in so doing; yet the fact remained that this was but another in the series of blows that led to the collapse of the League.

More trouble was in store for the League in the elections of 1920, caused mostly by its disaffected leaders. William Langer, in seeking the Republican nomination for governor, came within a few thousand votes of defeating Lynn J. Frazier, whose strength was largely in the eastern and more prosperous counties. Two other rebelling members, Carl Kositsky and Thomas Hall, were nominated for state auditor and secretary of state. The opposition also nominated John Steen, a Republican, as state treasurer, and two others for the railroad commission. Majorities were won by opposition candidates A. M. Christianson for the supreme court and Minnie Nielson for superintendent of public instruction. Indications also were that the conservatives were to gain control of the lower house of the legislature. E. F. Ladd, the League candidate, defeated Ansel J. Gronna for the Republican nomination for the United States Senate, despite the fact that Gronna was a member of the League. Gronna's defeat also brought dismay to the progressives.[34]

In Minnesota, it appeared for a time that the League finally was to have its day. The primaries gave J. A. O. Preus, the Republican, 44 per cent of the total vote, and Henrik Shipstead, the Nonpartisan nominee, for whom an airplane campaign was conducted, 41 per cent.[35] The other four

34. Bruce, *Non-Partisan League*, pp. 212–13.

35. *Ibid.*, p. 214. For accounts of the airplane campaign, see the *Minnesota Leader*, May 8, 1920; *Non-partisan Leader*, May 31, 1920, p. 4.

candidates obtained the remaining 15 per cent. League strength was largely confined to the new, sandy, and sparsely settled counties, while older, more prosperous, and better-cultivated counties were still found in the conservative column. Nonpartisans were successful in Montana, where they nominated their candidate for governor in the Democratic primary. In Wisconsin and Colorado, their candidates were nominated on the Republican ticket.[36] The strength of the League in Wisconsin, as expected, was due largely to the La Follette movement rather than to the League itself; there the League merely consisted of La Follette Progressives dressed in new political attire.

In spite of the League's show of strength in the primaries, however, all signs pointed to a return to power of the conservative forces in the fall elections. In Minnesota, the conservative triumph was decisive. The Republicans, despite the close call experienced in the primaries, defeated Shipstead and the remainder of the League candidates for state offices, and even elected their candidates to the supreme court. The conservatives were assured of complete control of both houses of the legislature. It was claimed that the failure of farm women to vote (the Nineteenth Amendment had just been adopted) was largely responsible for the poor showing made by the League. A shrewd move on the part of the Republicans was their pledging support to the cooperative movement. This probably played an important part in dividing the votes of the farmers. The loss of Minnesota was a serious blow to the League, for it had maintained hopes of capturing the solid vote of the farmers, the labor unions, the Socialists, and other radical Minnesota elements. Indeed, the gubernatorial candidate of the Working People's Nonpartisan League had withdrawn for the purpose of presenting a united front in support of Shipstead, and from all appearances the Socialists of Minnesota delivered their votes to the League.

In Montana the League, despite its success in nominating its candidate for governor on the Republican ticket, was defeated in the final election by a coalition of Republicans and Democrats. The same thing happened in Colorado; but in South Dakota, in a three-way race between Republicans, Democrats, and Nonpartisans, the League finished second. Wisconsin received much attention, but the success of J. J. Blaine and the re-

36. Bruce, *Non-Partisan League*, pp. 213–15.

mainder of his ticket in that state was more of a Progressive victory than a League triumph.

In North Dakota, particularly stiff opposition was met in returning Lynn J. Frazier to the governor's office. The regular Republicans had agreed to support the Democratic candidate, J. F. T. O'Connor, who came within 4,630 votes of defeating Frazier. The opposition was successful in electing its candidates for superintendent of public instruction, secretary of state, state treasurer, a justice of the supreme court, four out of six district judges, two members of Congress, and enough members in the lower house of the legislature to control it. Control of the upper house by the conservatives was lost by one vote. Important to the League, however, was its success in securing the passage of ten measures brought up by initiative which it had sponsored. The triumph of E. F. Ladd, League candidate for United States senator, was attributed chiefly to his personal popularity and to the fact that he was running as a Republican in a Republican presidential year.[37]

By and large, the position of the League was becoming more and more insecure. The strong reactionary feeling that set in with the close of the World War unquestionably was one reason for the League defeats, and bipartisan combinations against the League furnished another. The failure of women to vote in sufficient numbers in rural areas and other places where League sympathy existed also cost the League votes. Also, the desire of the people to rebuke the Democratic party was detrimental to the League where its candidates ran as Democrats. Nevertheless, in several states the League supplanted the Democratic party as the chief rival of the Republicans. Republican candidates in all states where they were opposed by the League got smaller majorities and pluralities than did the remainder of the Republican ticket. On the basis of the gubernatorial vote, the League candidates in 1920 received more than 1,200,000 votes, compared with 230,000 in 1918.[38]

Meanwhile, a powerful new opposition force known as the Independent Voters' Association had been making its strength felt against the Non-

37. *Ibid.*, pp. 216–24.

38. C. R. Johnson, "The Nonpartisan League Defeated," *The Nation*, CXI (December 1, 1920), p. 614; Oliver S. Morris, "The Nonpartisan League," *ibid.* (December 22, 1920), p. 733.

partisan League in North Dakota. This association was the spiritual and organic successor of the Good Government League, the earlier short-lived opponent of the League. The I.V.A. was organized in the summer of 1918 in Griggs and Steele counties for the supposed purpose of studying the problems of government. Work began at Cooperstown on December 9, 1918, and the organization was placed on a permanent basis at a conference held in Bismarck in January, 1919. Toward the close of the legislative session, another state-wide conference was held; an executive committee was appointed, and the decision was made to place eleven of the measures passed by the legislature up to the people for a referendum vote. Seven of the measures were to be voted upon without change, while alterations were proposed for the other four. The association also organized campaign communities in forty-three of the fifty-three counties.[39]

In the elections of 1920, the Independent Voters' Association circulated a "voters' guide," sponsored chiefly by a Republican-Democratic-I.V.A. joint campaign committee that supported the anti-Townley candidates.[40] Party lines were eliminated as far as possible; independent Republicans and Democrats were asked to bury the hatchet for the time being to present a "compact front against the particular brand of politics" known as "Townleyism." The association pledged itself "to the practising of greater economy, home rule by home people, loyalty to the state and nation, strict enforcement laws, stabilizing of credit and an equitable distribution of the tax burden by taxing all property wherever it is found in proportion to its value." Changes were proposed in the laws governing the Bank of North Dakota to "make it impossible not only to misuse the funds on deposit . . . but also to use the bank as a political club over political enemies and as a means to reward political friends." It demanded a "fair and unbiased examination of the bank's affairs by elected officials"; limitation of "real estate mortgage loans by the Bank of North Dakota to actual farmer residents"; and passage of legislation authorizing "the publication of all private legal notices affecting local property and people and their interests, in local papers thus giving the citizens of every country town

39. Independent Voters' Association, *Townleyism's Future in North Dakota* (Fargo, N. Dak., 1919), p. 65.

40. Independent Voters' Association, *Voters' Guide* (Fargo, N. Dak., 1919), pp. 3–10.

and its tributary territory, a right to use local resources for the purpose of maintaining in their midst, one or more independent newspapers." A law was also asked restoring to the office of superintendent of public instruction many of the records, duties, and powers that had been taken away from it by the board of administration.

In this election the opposition to the League, having failed in its attempt to devise an original and alternative program, had accepted in effect a platform that approved the principles of the League, demanding a fair trial for the industrial program, with some changes in the law and administration to make it "workable and efficient" and to "drive the leaders of the League from the public crib." The public's acceptance of this program adopted from the League was one reason that the I.V.A. captured control of the lower house.[41]

But the I.V.A., despite its glowing promises, had made plans to emasculate the industrial program, as its attack on the bond issue soon demonstrated. The $17,000,000 bond issue had been authorized by the legislature of 1917, and after having been attacked in the state and federal courts, was finally upheld as constitutional by the United States Supreme Court. A compromise agreement was arranged between the independents and the League with the hope of helping the industrial commission dispose of the bonds; but the compromise was broken when a committee of bankers who, in consideration for financial aid, demanded that the state "not . . . enter . . . any more Socialistic enterprises," meaning in effect that the bank was to become nothing more than a rural-credits institution. Failure to float this bond issue was immediately charged to the opposition of the I.V.A. H. G. Teigan wrote a fellow Leaguer: "The I.V.A.'s saw that if the deal went through and six million dollars of North Dakota bonds were sold their political prospects would not be any too rosy in North Dakota. Consequently the bankers refused to go on with the negotiations until things settled down . . . somewhat. Just when the settling down will take place I am sure I do not know."[42]

Shortly after the elections of 1920, investigations of the industrial commission by senate and house committees followed. The house committee,

41. Oliver S. Morris, "What is Happening in North Dakota," *The Nation*, CXII (March 9, 1921), pp. 367–68.

42. H. G. Teigan to O. M. Thomason, February 27, 1921.

dominated by the independents, found some "minor irregularities" but nothing serious, while the senate committee, controlled by the League, found "the enterprises properly conducted."

The Bank of North Dakota was causing difficulties to both the League and the independents. The latter felt especially menaced not by what the bank was doing, but by what it was likely to do under its broad powers, which included establishing branch banks and accepting deposits. At the same time, the law initiated and enacted by the lower house making it optional for local government officials to deposit funds with the Bank of North Dakota was causing the League considerable trouble. This law meant that the League was to lose the funds of counties, cities, and school districts where officials hostile to the League had been elected. The bank ignored this act by failing to heed the demands of hostile communities for their funds, and some counties actually brought suit to collect. This, plus the refusal of the business interests to take the bonds, added to the "financial stringency," since it came in a period of deflation, low farm prices, and repeated crop failures. One observer noted: "Business in the State is disorganized and banks are getting into worse instead of better condition. The State industrial program is held up, and the legislature continues deadlocked. Political feeling is bitter and intense beyond description."[43]

The League charged that because the Bank of North Dakota would not guarantee the bankers that it would not extend its operations to include the broad powers granted, the independents had resorted to more drastic measures. This was noted in the numerous schemes for delay and obstruction. Attempts were made to force the resignation of William Lemke, the much-feared attorney general. Compromise measures were proposed which were intended to cripple the League program. Laws were sought to make the legal deposit of public funds in the Bank of North Dakota equal only to its combined capital and surplus, thus making it impossible to give financial aid to the industrial commission. Another bill sought the appointment of the industrial commission by the governor instead of by the people. The industrial program was to be limited to the completion of the home buildings already undertaken and the mill and

43. Morris, in *The Nation,* CXII (March 9, 1921), pp. 367–69.

elevator already under construction at a total expense of $250,000 and $1,000,000 respectively. Finally, the bank was to be abolished after a period of liquidation.[44]

Opposition reached a climax in 1921, when a series of proposals was referred to the voters with a petition for the recall of the entire industrial commission. Five of these measures pertained to the industrial program, being by and large a crystallization of the obstructionist tactics pursued by the independents.[45] Real strength was displayed by the League opponents in the first recall election on a state-wide basis ever conducted in the nation. The man groomed for the governorship by the independents was R. A. Nestos, who had been seriously considered for the candidacy in 1920 but had been passed over for William Langer with the hope that the ex-Leaguer would be successful in turning the tide against the League. Nestos was selected by the independents at a convention held at Devils Lake in March, 1921, having been nominated by J. F. T. O'Connor, the Democratic gubernatorial candidate in 1920.[46] Nestos, a lawyer and Sunday school teacher from Minot, had been seeking public office for years; furthermore, he was a Norwegian by birth and came from the western part of the state, which was predominantly Nonpartisan in its sentiments.[47]

Besides carrying the names of the candidates for the three major state offices, the ballots also contained six measures brought up by initiative which were backed by the independent forces and on which the voters were asked to vote Yes or No. These six initiated measures called for the nomination and election of state and county officers, congressional candidates, and party committees without party designation; a public depository law; an amendment to the industrial commission law; a rural-credits act; and the dissolution of the Bank of North Dakota. Three constitutional amendments were likewise submitted: one, sponsored by the independents, asked for a reduction of the state debt limit; the other two,

44. C. R. Johnson, "The Struggle in North Dakota," *New Republic,* XXVI (March 9, 1921), p. 43.

45. Cooke, "The North Dakota Industrial Program," p. 26.

46. *Minneapolis Tribune,* November 24, 1921.

47. Oliver S. Morris, "The Vote of the North Dakota Farmers," *The Nation,* CXIII (November 9, 1921), pp. 535–36; "North Dakota's Political Twister," *Literary Digest,* LXXI (October 22, 1921), pp. 12–13.

submitted by the last legislature, proposed to increase the salary of legislators to $500 a year and to consolidate the offices of county judge and clerk of court in counties with a population under eight thousand.[48]

The recall election, much to the surprise of the League, brought about the defeat of both Governor Lynn J. Frazier and Attorney General William Lemke. This League defeat meant the transfer of control of all important boards, except the board of administration, to the independents. The independents had gained control of the industrial commission, which in turn controlled the Bank of North Dakota, the mill and elevator association, and the home-builders' association. Changes in the offices of governor and attorney general also shifted control of the board of school and university lands. The League, however, managed to retain control of the board of administration, which was charged with the supervision of all state institutions, the only change here being the substitution of Joseph A. Kitchen, the new commissioner of agriculture and labor, for John N. Hagan, a League member.

Other boards and commissions passing to the independents were the auditing board, the banking board, the depositors' guarantee-fund commission, the board of equalization, the printing commission, the budget board, the motor-vehicle registration department, the tax department, and the pool-hall inspection department, which, among other things, had become a valuable political institution of the League. Curiously enough, the voters defeated all the initiated measures intended to destroy the industrial commission, but at the same time they elected a new commission opposed to the program. From then on, the program was under the domination of the I.V.A., and it was not until 1933 that the forces which had fought for the program were placed in complete control of the state enterprises.[49]

The strength of the opposition was centered mainly in the eastern part of the state, and the reasons for the recall of the League officials were strikingly similar to those accounting for the League defeats in 1920—

48. *Minneapolis Journal,* October 28, 1921; *Minneapolis Tribune,* October 28, 1921; "North Dakota's 'Recall' Puzzle," *Literary Digest,* LXXI (November 19, 1921), p. 10.

49. *Minneapolis Journal,* November 2, 1921; Cooke, "The North Dakota Industrial Program," pp. 26–27; H. G. Teigan, "Recalling the Farmer Governor," *Labor Age,* X (December, 1921), pp. 9–10.

namely, the depression that was sweeping the country, the strength of the anti-League propaganda, the mistakes of the League officials in administering the industrial program, the general national trend against the party in power, and poor management of the campaign. Among the mistakes committed by the League were those revolving about the conduct of the home-builders' association program and the losses accruing from operations of the state-owned mill. "Houses were built at a greater cost to the state than was permitted by law and as contracted for with the owners. Then, too, the small losses suffered by the state-owned mill at Drake did the League administration some damage." The losses made by the mill were said to be due mainly to the decline in the price of wheat during the fourteen months previous. Other failures, such as the Equity Packing Plant, with large losses to the stockholders, and the failure of a number of cooperative stores organized by League members no doubt had influenced voters to favor the recall of League candidates.[50]

Governor Nestos, in his inaugural address, repeated the campaign pledges of the independents to reduce state expenses and to seek to attract outside investors to North Dakota. He promised that his administration would proceed cautiously in its tasks; an immediate survey of the business of the state and the conditions of the industrial program would be made; state credit would be restored, the number of public employees would be reduced, and the Grand Forks state mill and elevator project would be completed. "It is the hope and purpose of the incoming administration," he said, "to forget as far as possible the differences and discords of past campaigns and to view the present situation in the state calmly and dispassionately and with but one thought and purpose in mind, that of serving honestly the best interests of the citizenship of our state.[51]

There were other forces besides the Independent Voters' Association and the numerous reversals suffered in the management of League enterprises that were contributing to the disintegration of the League. Among them were the internal dissension already mentioned; the agricultural depression; the indifference of Senator Robert M. La Follette, who, in all probability, looked upon the League as a rival to the Progressive move-

50. See *Consumers' United Stores Company* (Fargo, N. Dak., n.d.) [pamphlet]; Teigan, in *Labor Age,* X (December, 1921), pp. 9–10.

51. Quoted in the *Minneapolis Tribune,* November 24, 1921.

ment and consequently to his personal leadership; the rise of other farm organizations that were helping divide and confuse the farmers of the Northwest; and, to a lesser degree, the hostility of the Socialist party.

Liberal and radical groups have had a notorious record of open hostility and differences of opinion among themselves over the methods to be used and the goals to be sought, the case of the Nonpartisan League being no different in this respect. The League from the very beginning was accused of being a Socialist organization, but the Socialist Party of America had other ideas and expressed itself very clearly on the League issue in a resolution adopted at the St. Louis convention in 1917. The Socialist party repudiated any attempted affiliation with the League on the ground that the latter was interested in acquiring political power for a "certain division of the industrial class of the United States," while "the historic mission of the Socialist Party was the emancipation of the working class." State Socialist organizations were warned not "to fuse or to compromise," and were urged to "maintain in the utmost possible vigor the propaganda of Socialism, unadulterated by association of office seekers. . . ." Finally, the Socialists believed: "The Social Revolution, not political office, is the end and aim of the Socialist Party. No Compromise, No Political Trading."[52]

Other basic arguments were advanced against the League. The Socialist party was interested in the welfare of city people as well as that of the farmers, but since the League consisted primarily of farm owners, the interests of the League farmers were "in conflict with those of agricultural workers and their actions in the long run must be dictated by their interests." The League, in effect, it was reasoned, would be opposed to state insurance for agricultural workers, to old-age and unemployment insurance, to fixing maximum prices on farm products, and to the compulsory sale of such produce. During the war, the Socialist party said, League representatives in Congress succeeded in inserting minimum sale prices for wheat in the Food Control Act so that the consumer would be compelled to pay at least $2.00 per bushel for wheat. Victor Berger, the Socialist congressman from Milwaukee, in a speech delivered in Minneapolis early in 1920, reminded his listeners: "Did the Nonpartisan League by stealing the livery of the capitalist class [think] they could do some-

52. *A Political Guide for the Workers* (Chicago, 1920), pp. 82–83.

thing for the workers and farmers. Six men voted to unseat me in Congress after I was elected by the workers. . . . The Nonpartisan cowards, Sinclair and Baer, voted to lynch me. I understand in St. Paul they elected another man, Keller, who also voted to lynch me."[53] What more "conclusive evidence" was required to show that "the League program is not socialism?" Was the League not composed of rich farmers "thirsting for political power?" Did it not represent the "bourgeoisie" as opposed to the "proletarian" movement? Did the League not have old and conservative aims? Would it not be found allied with reactionary political and economic forces?

Efforts were made to bring these groups together. Particularly active in this respect was W. C. Zumach, a Socialist who later went over to the Nonpartisan League in Wisconsin and repeatedly tried to arrange conferences between Socialist leaders such as Mayor Daniel W. Hoan of Milwaukee and Victor Berger and representatives of the League. Zumach wrote Teigan, the national secretary of the League, that he was pushing the "get-together" idea with the hope that as many Socialists as possible would be able to sit in with the Nonpartisans. "Of course I'll see to it that only the fellows with the right ideas will take part in the conference so that no time or energy will be dissipated." He admitted, however, that there were still in the Socialist party "a few 'nuts' that love to roll their 'R's' especially in the word revolution."[54] A meeting finally was arranged, but hope of reaching an understanding was dispelled before the meeting had come about when League congressmen showed their antipathy or indifference to Berger by voting to expel him from Congress or by being conveniently absent when the vote was taken. Zumach expressed the views of the Socialists when he wrote Teigan:

> But I'm disgusted with the showing of League congressmen on the expulsion vote. I'm heartsick for I see all hopes of getting together knocked in the head. I could not and would not ask our boys to make common cause with such representatives. Do you expect that labor of Wisconsin will consider you people as safe guardians of their interests? Not if I know the Labor movement of

53. Quoted in *Answering the Socialist Charge* (n.d.), a leaflet in the Minnesota Historical Society.

54. W. C. Zumach to H. G. Teigan, October 15, 1919; October 22, 1919; Teigan to Zumach, October 23, 1919; H. G. Teigan to Martin Teigan, October 26, 1919.

Wisconsin. They know the principles and issues involved in this fight and they are behind Berger.

My God! how could these men vote to unseat Berger? Is not Townley in the same fix? Has he not been several times indicted? Has he not been found guilty of sedition and sentenced? Has not the League itself been branded by these same powers as disloyal, seditious, and everything else that is bad? I myself saw Congressman Baer driven from Rice County, Minnesota because he was branded as disloyal. Do these men hold these seats in Congress because they are considered safe by Big-Biz while Berger is driven out?

Zumach pleaded with Teigan to see to it that the League took a stand on this matter, if the Socialists and the League were to get along. "You simply must clean your house of this stain."[55]

Teigan replied that he did "not believe that we should conclude that a combination of forces in Wisconsin is impossible. After all the League organization in Wisconsin does not belong to us here at the National office, neither is it in any way responsible for the acts of a North Dakota congressman. All that we have done in Wisconsin, as in other states, is to build the organization. The farmers who have enlisted in the movement there own the organization after it has been built."[56]

The action of League congressmen in helping to unseat Berger was perhaps explained in a letter by Teigan to an inquirer concerning the League's position on national issues:

The National Nonpartisan League has not concerned itself very much with National matters. In fact its concern with these things has been so small that at times we have forgotten about having representatives at the national capitol. As a consequence these men were never advised as to what was the desire of the organized farmer in the Berger matter. Thus, both Baer and Sinclair were left to act on their own initiative as is the case with them, on most other propositions that have come before Congress.[57]

Later Teigan summarized the League relationship with the Socialist Party of America in a letter to F. Thoeneman of Kiel, Germany, in December, 1921:

55. Zumach to H. G. Teigan, November 14, 1919.
56. Teigan to Zumach, November 18, 1919.
57. Teigan to O. E. Smith, July 7, 1920.

> The Socialist Party . . . has not been particularly friendly to our movement although it is more so now than was the case some years ago. The good work done by the League in North Dakota and which was attempted by our legislators in other states had a rather convincing influence upon the Socialists as to the honest intentions, at least, of the League and its leaders.[58]

Although the opposition of the Socialist party to the "opportunistic" program of the League was well known, the position of Senator Robert M. La Follette was not exactly clear. La Follette never had issued a clear-cut statement concerning where he stood with respect to the League, yet his attitude toward the organization was all-important. The La Follette movement was a psychological counterpart of the same forces that were crystallized into the organization of the League; furthermore, some of his most enthusiastic supporters were in the states in which the League had its largest membership. La Follette's stand on the war at the conference of producers and consumers in St. Paul in September had endeared him to the most ardent League admirers. Still, his pronouncements there and elsewhere could not be considered ipso facto evidence that he had become an integral part of the movement. W. C. Zumach, who had become the office manager of the Wisconsin branch of the League, probably had the La Follette camp in mind when he wrote to Teigan: "Various forces whom we have counted upon as our friends are becoming fearful of League power, and are interested in seeing the League relegated to a position of impotency."[59]

The Progressive forces in the fall of 1920, according to Zumach, "were under the impression that the League was plentifully supplied with money, and that we were in a position to put up a big campaign." Such, however, was not the case. "The League financially and otherwise was in a most deplorable position."[60] In the Wisconsin senatorial race, certain Socialists and Leaguers tried to obtain La Follette's support for Frank Weber, a Milwaukee Socialist leader and labor organizer, but with little success. The Socialist sympathies of La Follette were too well known. James Thompson, the La Crosse Progressive, was his choice.[61] In October,

58. Teigan to F. Thoeneman, December 6, 1921.
59. Zumach to Teigan, January 5, 1920.
60. Zumach to Teigan, September 27, 1920.
61. Teigan to Zumach, September 30, 1920. Bitter feelings existed among Progres-

1920, when an attempt was made to secure the campaign services of La Follette in Minnesota, he refused on the ground that the Thompson campaign was occupying much of his time. This campaign meant "a great deal to him personally. There can be no question that the foundation is being laid for a bitter fight against the re-election of Senator La Follette two years hence. Should Thompson be victorious in this fight it would, of course, give La Follette a tremendous advantage."[62] La Follette's aid was sought largely because of his influence with the Scandinavian and German voters, his stand on the war having made him very popular with the latter group.[63] Furthermore, it was felt that an appearance by La Follette in the Twin Cities would lead to a press attack on him because of his war record, and thus redound to the benefit of the League. That the League in Wisconsin in 1920 was in a disorganized state and dependent largely upon the strength of La Follette was attested to by Emil Pladsen, the Wisconsin secretary and manager of the Nonpartisan League, in a letter to Teigan: "We are at our wits end in the matter of devising some real practical and efficient plan for getting the state re-organized."[64]

Shortly thereafter, these same League leaders expressed the view that La Follette was "doubtful as to the stability of the League." Zumach also felt that La Follette was uncertain of the political wisdom of tying up with the League:

> It seems to me that they [the Progressives] have adopted a policy of watchful waiting to see whether the League will succeed in its re-organization. From conversations I have had with the Senator, I am sure that he is favorable to the idea of a new party; in fact, he told me some time ago that he would attempt during the next year to lay the foundation of such a new party. Conferences of Progressive Senators, Congressmen, newspaper men and prominent leaders have already been held to discuss this very proposition; at least, so the Senator informed.
>
> I am quite certain that the Senator's ambition is to become a candidate for the presidency of the United States, and that his only hope in so doing is to

sives because of Berger's opposition to the candidacies of Blaine and Thompson. The small showing of the Progressives in Milwaukee was attributed to Berger's influence. Zumach to Teigan, September 27, 1920.

62. Zumach to Teigan, October 13, 1920.

63. Teigan to Zumach, October 11, 1920.

64. Emil Pladsen to Teigan, October 29, 1920.

have a new party. I know that he was intensely interested in the convention of the forty-eighters in Chicago last summer, and was ready to head the new party as its candidate. This was conditioned upon the adoption of a platform acceptable to the Senator. You know the results of this convention, and I believe a splendid opportunity for the foundation of a new party was lost.[65]

Somewhat typical of the division existing among liberal groups was the situation then prevailing in Wisconsin. Pladsen, in writing to Teigan, described it quite accurately:

There is a meeting to be held in Madison tomorrow called by the People's Reconstruction League; La Follette is slated to speak there. With this People's Reconstruction League and the United Farmers of America, Farm Bureau, La Follette Progressive League, and the Equity Society, putting on a membership drive together with some little organization here in Dane County known as the Tax-Payers League, and considerable talk about organization work by the Farmer-Labor Party, it will be a matter of running the gauntlet between all these different organizations.[66]

Equally discouraging to the League in Wisconsin was "the extremely reactionary attitudes of the administration. It is beginning to seep through into the consciousness of the people at large, the real League members and progressives, that the speech that a certain gentleman made last summer with reference to the Non-Partisan League program, 'I stand with both feet upon that program' was mere political camouflage." [67] The conservatism of the state administration reflected the views of a substantial portion of the population. League officials pointed out that "conditions in the northwest part of the state are better than over in the lake shore district." [68]

Briefly, it can be stated that La Follette, like many other liberal leaders, looked upon the League as a rival. Congressman J. H. Sinclair of North Dakota informed Teigan: "The Senator takes a broad national view of the whole progressive movement, and feels that a greater cooperation should be had among the various progressive groups . . . he hopes that the

65. Zumach to Teigan, February 16, 1921.
66. Pladsen to Teigan, March 24, 1921.
67. Pladsen to Teigan, June 24, 1921.
68. Teigan to Pladsen, June 27, 1921; Pladsen to Teigan, June 24, 1921.

League in going into new territory will study the conditions that prevai there and combine its efforts with the progressive forces there, rathe than to supplant or antagonize them."[69] La Follette was reportedly mucl offended by the defeat of Senator Gronna by E. F. Ladd.[70] Teigan in formed Sinclair that he would "like to see some move made to adjus matters in North Dakota with Senator Gronna. It is a lead pipe cincl that if things were fixed up with Gronna, the League would have eas sledding in the Flickertail State." [71] Gronna had been a faithful followe of La Follette during the war, and La Follette felt very grateful for hi aid.[72]

It would be difficult to assess accurately the effects on the League o the growing coolness of the La Follette forces and the open hostility o the Socialists. These developments, particularly the Progressive stand helped divide and confuse the farmers, who had come to look upon th League and the Progressives as being pretty much the same thing. Yet couple of years later, when La Follette made his bid for the Presidency these elements and numerous others united behind the Progressive banner

More tangible in its effect on the League were the rival farm organiza tions which appeared and threatened its position not only in North Dakot but also in Minnesota, Iowa, Wisconsin, and many other states wher the League had displayed some semblance of vote-getting power. Th organization most powerful in the early twenties was the American Farn Bureau Federation, which was born in Chicago in the fall of 1919. I made a tremendous appeal to the farmers of the Middle West. Generall speaking, the federation appealed to the more conservative elements which were opposed to the League. Its real display of power was in state in which the League failed to obtain a strong membership.

County agent work in Iowa, the forerunner of the Farm Bureau move ment there, had started in 1912, when the first farm bureau was organizec in Iowa County. When the United States entered the war, the number o counties in which county agents were at work had increased to twenty four, largely as a result of the attempt to stimulate food production.[73] Ir

69. J. H. Sinclair to Teigan, July 15, 1921; Teigan to Sinclair, July 20, 1921.
70. Sinclair to Teigan, July 13, 1921; July 21, 1921.
71. Teigan to Sinclair, July 20, 1921.
72. Sinclair to Teigan, July 13, 1921.
73. *Iowa Farm Bureau Messenger* (Waterloo), November 5, 1919; Barton Mor-

)ecember, 1918, at a meeting held in Marshalltown to organize a state ederation, seventy counties responded to the invitation. Financial assist-nce from both the federal and state governments, plus the cooperation of Iowa State College, were powerful aids in the organization work.[74] Membership in the Iowa Farm Bureau Federation fluctuated; on De-cember 1, 1920, the membership was placed at 92,000; on September 1, 1921, it was given as 124,000; but on September 15, 1921, the member-hip was placed at 60,250, and the number of county farm bureaus at 100.[75]

The North Dakota Farm Bureau Federation was organized in January, 1921, when both the Nonpartisan League and agriculture were beginning to flounder in the depths of depression. In 1921 thirty-five counties were reported organized, with a total of 23,679 members; the "paid-up" mem-bership on September 14, 1921, was 7,705. Although the North Dakota Farm Bureau shortly became involved in financial difficulties, it neverthe-less contributed to the confusion of the depressed farmers, who already had faced several years of crop failures, low prices, and a variety of ag-ricultural reforms, plus disillusionment over the accomplishments of the League. Less aggressive, but equally important, was the Wisconsin Farm Bureau, which claimed a membership of 12,548 and a paid-up member-ship of 5,015 in September, 1921. Eighteen county farm bureaus had been organized. Montana had no farm bureau membership on December 1, 1920, but in September, 1921, a membership of 7,200 was claimed, with thirty counties organized. Minnesota, the state which the League had tried desperately hard to organize, reported a membership of 72,000, of which 39,000 were paid up. Seventy-eight county farm bureaus were or-ganized. The Minnesota Farm Bureau to this day has remained one of the most prominent of the entire movement. A good foothold was also ob-tained temporarily in Nebraska, where a paid-up membership of 19,082 was claimed in September, 1921. The South Dakota Farm Bureau was

---

gan, *A History of the Extension Service of Iowa State College* (Ames, Iowa, 1934), pp. 34–40.

74. C. R. Dudley to D. Davis, February 17, 1938, in the office of the American Farm Bureau Federation, Chicago.

75. American Farm Bureau Federation, *Report of the Executive Secretary to the Third Annual Meeting, Atlanta, Georgia, November 21–23, 1921*, p. 29.

organized in February, 1919, at South Dakota State College, and on September 15, 1921, when a paid-up membership of 11,237 was reported there were thirty-nine county farm bureaus organized.[76]

Equally menacing to the Nonpartisan League was the Farmers' Union which was making a strong bid to obtain a large membership in the Middle West. The opposition to the League program in Nebraska and Kansas was demonstrated in the latter state by the Kansas Farmers' Union, which campaigned openly against the "subversive doctrines" of the League. The Farmers' Union, however, made greater progress in organizing in even such strongly pro-League states as Montana and North Dakota than did the American Farm Bureau Federation. By the end of the twenties, the Farmers' Union had become the largest farm organization in both of these states.[77]

League leaders who were quick to realize that the League had about run its course and who were eager to capitalize on what remained of the organization had become interested in the formation of a farmer-labor party. Chief advocate of this new movement was H. G. Teigan, secretary of the Nonpartisan League. Opposed to this farmer-labor alignment was the "balance-of-power" formula of A. C. Townley, president of the League, who urged that "support be given to such candidates of any party as were regarded as desirable, thus controlling the balance of power." [78] This was simply the old device of selecting reform candidates through the old parties.

Teigan had been espousing the third-party move for some time prior to the League defeat in the recall election. On November 10, 1919, he wrote Zumach that he was "going to Chicago for the 22nd to act as a sort of unofficial delegate at the Labor Party convention"; but a week later Teigan wrote to his brother in Chicago that "in as much as the League

76. *Ibid.*, pp. 29–31; *Fargo Forum,* December 4, 1922; *Early Organization of the South Dakota Farm Bureau Federation* (n.p., n.d.), p. 1.

77. For accounts of the Farmers' Union, see the following booklets: Northwest Division, *The Farmers' Educational and Cooperative Union of America* (St. Paul, [1930]); *North Dakota Farmers' Union* (Centuria, Wis., 1936); *Montana Farmers' Union* (Jamestown, N. Dak., 1937).

78. "The Nonpartisan League Fights On," *The Nation,* CXIV (June 14, 1922), p. 711. See also *Minnesota Farmer-Labor Convention, Proceedings,* 1923 (St. Paul), p. 24; *Minnesota Leader,* February 25, 1922.

could not officially participate, it would be unwise to have any unofficial representative in attendance."[79]

Teigan again stated his views on the idea of a third party in a letter to H. W. Laidler, a prominent American Socialist writer. Laidler had addressed a letter to Townley which read in part: "We are particularly desirous of finding out what changes in tactics, if any, you believe that the labor movement and the minor political parties should make if they are to do their most effective work."[80] Teigan, in replying for Townley, who was not in the habit of answering correspondence, said: "In my opinion, a change in the political tactics of the labor movement is absolutely necessary to offer any hope of success. A political party, organized along the lines of the British Labor Party, looks to me as offering the best means of political expression for the working class. The Farmer-Labor Party is a good start in that direction, though it may need a little 'revamping,' so to speak, to make it more workable."[81] A. W. Ricker, who later joined Townley as editor of the *Farm Market Guide,* official organ of the National Producers' Alliance, summarized the two divergent views developing within the League as "one the practical—trying to get something of the campaign—the other—the Utopian—building a party. Party building at this time is impractical—The country is in a state of flux—."[82]

Much uncertainty prevailed regarding the future of the League while Townley was serving six months in jail on charges of disloyalty and sedition. Many had hoped that the jailing of Townley would make a martyr of him and thus revitalize the League. Meanwhile Teigan had been campaigning for a farmer-labor party. In January, 1922, he wrote to one D. C. Dorman that labor was opposed to the balance-of-power plan, stating that it had functioned along those lines for a number of years and received nothing from it, and adding that "Gompers . . . is a balance of power man." The Minnesota Nonpartisan League reportedly favored the balance-of-power idea, but it was considered unwise to pursue the plan if labor

79. H. G. Teigan to W. C. Zumach, November 10, 1919; Teigan to Martin Teigan, November 17, 1919.

80. H. W. Laidler to A. C. Townley, November 22, 1920. This information was gathered for the *Socialist Review,* which was sponsoring a symposium on the "Lessons of Recent Elections."

81. Teigan to Laidler, November 26, 1920.

82. A. W. Ricker to Teigan, September 13, 1922.

refused to follow suit. "To have the League going one direction and labor another would mean a split in their forces which could not be compensated for no matter how successful the balance of power plan might work out in the state." [83]

On the day that Townley was released from jail, his associates had planned a huge banquet to which liberal leaders from the Twin Cities area were invited. Townley was to be the honor guest. The balance-of-power plan was still uppermost in his mind, and contrary to the advice of some League leaders who had gone over to the farmer-labor idea, he insisted on advocating his own views. Reports were that his suggestions were received coldly. At any rate, Townley tendered his resignation as president of the League in May, 1922, but offered to stay as supervisor of the national organization.[84]

Both the nation and the Minnesota Nonpartisan League accepted Townley's reorganization plan, recommended before his resignation, for separating the political and organizational activities of the League. The national committee also announced that it had approved of Townley's idea to reduce membership fees from $18 for two years to $6.50 or $7.50 for the same period, depending upon the organizational problems of the various states. In Minnesota, the state committee approved a new fee of $6.50; in other states, where the work was more costly, the $7.50 fee was adopted.

Judging from the tone of his letter of resignation, Townley had been losing faith in the political formula for agricultural relief:

> I have finally reached the conclusion that a strong, active and numerous membership in each state is the only basis upon which political and economic success can be built, and that in striving for the election of candidates we have lost sight of the important things. In other words we have devoted almost all our force and energy to seeking the election of our selected candidates and have neglected the re-enrollment of old and securing new members.
>
> And finally and most important of all, I have concluded that this neglect of enrollments and failure to give it first attention was due to the fact that in each state we have been endeavoring to carry on both political and economic func-

83. Teigan to D. C. Dorman, January 13, 1922.

84. *Wisconsin State Journal* (Madison), March 26, 1922; *Minneapolis Star,* May 12, 1922. H. F. Samuels of Idaho, chairman of the state committee of Idaho and League candidate for governor of that state in 1920, was chosen temporary president of the League.

tions through one set of executives. It is my opinion that this work of enrolling members is a business function, requiring specialized training, and is inevitably bound to be neglected and fail, if required of men who are at the same time engaged in the business of looking after the political activities of the league.[85]

The withdrawal from power of such leaders as Townley meant that the organization which had appeared with dramatic swiftness in 1915 was about extinct. Townley himself was perhaps the most important of the few individuals who in the early days had applied to political organization the methods of high-pressure salesmanship. The key to the rapid growth of the League, perhaps, was not its proposed remedies for financial and political problems, but rather the large-scale application of the techniques of oil-stock salesmen. As a result, the political organization formed was financed from the bottom up by the rank and file rather than from the top down.

Repeated charges of mismanagement were hurled against Townley, but at no time were they substantiated. There were, however, strong evidences of looseness in financial bookkeeping and also an absence of real responsibility on the part of the bulk of the membership. Perhaps one of the strongest indictments was the readiness of the League's leadership to embark on new ventures without the necessary experience and personnel. Especially trying were the effects of the depression, beginning in 1921, when the League found it impossible to continue organizing on the commercial basis which had proved so successful in earlier years. An annual income of some seven million dollars dwindled; large sums of postdated checks could not be collected; its newspapers were sold one by one; and the League as an organization had to cease functioning.

The charge that an organization had to be built upon an economic base was perhaps correct; otherwise movements like that of the League and the Populists would fade out completely, as the latter did in the nineties. Mass movements are of temporary duration unless founded upon an economic organization that functions every day of the year; they must have strong local units; they cannot be maintained if they are to perform vital functions only once every two years.

Despite these shortcomings in organization, all the things the League campaigned for were not in vain. "As in all movements," wrote one au-

85. *Ibid.*

thority, "some of the leaders sold out. Republican and Democratic candidates stole the League's thunder by promising or half-promising the same thing the League endorsed candidates pledged, and they were running on the same ticket. Nonpartisan methods were obviously a failure, and the remaining members of the League decided to try something else." The visible machinery of the League, in large measure, had melted away, but League sentiment persisted in the minds of hundreds of thousands of farmers in North and South Dakota, Minnesota, Wisconsin, Nebraska, and other states in the Northwest and Far West. As long as the price of wheat remained low, this viewpoint was likely to be a factor of political significance.[86]

86. "Minnesota, the Nonpartisan League, and the Future," *The Nation,* CXVII (August 1, 1923), p. 102. A former editor of the *Non-partisan Leader,* Charles Edward Russell, gave his explanation of the League's decline in his book, *Bare Hands and Stone Walls* (New York, 1933), pp. 343–44.

Chapter VIII

THE FARMERS' UNION

THE Farmers' Educational and Cooperative Union, or as it was more commonly called, the Farmers' Union, was a contemporary of the Equity and the Nonpartisan League. Founded in Raines County, Texas, in 1902, it was during its earlier years active only in the South, but when it had passed its peak in that region, it sought survival by expansion into such states as Kansas, Missouri, Illinois, and Nebraska, where other farmer organizations had so far failed to attract many supporters. It also flirted, unavailingly, with Equity, hoping for a merger of the two organizations. The greatest successes of the Union were achieved after the Equity and the Nonpartisan League had spent their force, when the Union penetrated effectively into Wisconsin, Minnesota, the Dakotas, Montana, and a number of other states. Under its auspices many cooperative grain elevators, livestock-shipping associations, and consumer stores were organized. It appealed most to the type of farmer who failed to respond to the more conservative programs of the Farm Bureau, another contemporary, and the Grange. Its own program was more radical and aggressive than that of any other farm order of the time, with the possible exception of the Nonpartisan League.

The founder of the Farmers' Union, Isaac Newton Gresham, like the founder of the Equity, was a newspaperman. "Newt" Gresham was born in Florence, Alabama, on February 20, 1858, and got his start in agricultural reform as an organizer for the Farmers' Alliance in Alabama and neighboring states. Later, as a Populist, and then as a Bryan Democrat, he continued to brood on the farmers' ills, and found expression for his views in a local paper which he began to publish in 1900 at a little town named Point in Raines County, Texas. Gresham thought that a new farm order which would avoid the political involvements that had wrecked the original Grange and the Alliance might succeed in really doing something for the farmers. Finally, in 1902, he succeeded in establishing the first Farmers' Union local at Smyrna, not far from Point. Smyrna was the center of a chronically unprosperous agricultural district, and the farmers of the area proved to be ripe for organization. Wisely, Gresham kept the cost of joining the Union down to an initiation fee of one dollar and dues of only five cents a month. No matter how poverty-stricken they might be, the hard-pressed Raines County farmers could, and did, join up. With what little money came in from members and what he could borrow in addition, Gresham pushed the work of organization along. As modest success came his way, he employed other organizers on a fee basis, and within four years not only locals but state organizations as well had appeared in six southern states, with another half-dozen in process of formation. Membership was open to farmers and farm laborers and to the professional classes who served them. According to one estimate the Union had 200,000 members by 1905.[1]

There was nothing especially novel in the original demands of the Farmers' Union. Its purposes were first expressed as these:

To secure equity, establish justice and apply the Golden Rule.
To discourage the credit and mortgage system.
To assist our members in buying and selling.
To educate the agricultural classes in scientific farming.
To teach farmers the classification of crops, domestic economy and the process of marketing.
To systematize methods of production and distribution.
To eliminate gambling in farm products by the Board of Trade, Cotton Exchanges and other speculators.
To bring farming up to the standard of other industries and business enterprises.
To secure and maintain profitable and uniform prices for cotton, grain, livestock and other products of the farm.

1. William P. Tucker, "Populism Up-to-date: The Story of the Farmers' Union," *Agricultural History*, XXI (October, 1947), pp. 198–201. On the Texas origins, see also Robert Lee Hunt, *A History of Farmer Movements in the Southwest, 1873–1925* (College Station, Texas, 1935), pp. 44–77.

To strive for harmony and good will among all mankind and brotherly love among ourselves.[2]

During the earliest years the Farmers' Union was not only an effective vehicle for the expression of farmer protests, but it also made some progress with cooperative ventures, particularly in the marketing of cotton. Less successful were its efforts to establish cotton warehouses and to control the price of cotton by securing voluntary pledges for acreage limitations. Nevertheless, by 1905, a national organization was devised, and with the death of Newt Gresham the next year a new and far more able leader took his place.[3]

Gresham's successor was Charles S. Barrett, of Union City, Georgia, a man of some influence who for more than two decades as national president of the Farmers' Union was its principal spokesman and promoter. Barrett was born on a farm in Pike County, Georgia, the son of a prosperous farmer, and received a good education. But his sympathy for the underprivileged led him to join the Farmers' Alliance in its time, and later, when he had heard of the Farmers' Union, to make a trip all the way to Texas to find out about the new order. On his return he promptly organized the Georgia state Union, and became its first president. Under his leadership the Union grew rapidly in numbers and influence, and Barrett himself became a man with an important future. After he took over the presidency of the national organization, his home—Union City, Georgia—grew from a tiny hamlet into a sizable center of Union activities, with a fertilizer plant, an implement factory, and various other cooperative projects to attest its importance. Barrett also spent much time in Washington and won fame as the "friend of presidents." Theodore Roosevelt made him a member of the Country Life Commission, and almost every president from Roosevelt to Hoover honored him with an appointment of one kind or another. He attended the Paris Peace Conference as the representative of fourteen American farm organizations, and described this assignment as "the most interesting and most thrilling

2. Charles S. Barrett, *The Mission, History and Times of the Farmers' Union* (Nashville, 1909), pp. 103–7.

3. Tucker, in *Agricultural History*, XXI (October, 1947), pp. 200–1; *Report of the Commissioner of Corporations on Cotton Exchanges*, Part V (60 Congress, 1 session, House Document 912, serial 5322, 5 parts, Washington, 1908–9), pp. 340–59.

experience of my life." Much of the success of the Farmers' Union, both in the South and elsewhere, must be credited to Barrett's persistent and enthusiastic leadership.[4]

The decline of the Union in the South was due in no small part to the almost hopeless backwardness of the southern cotton farmers. As a class they were illiterate, suspicious, and unprogressive. The cooperative organizations that were founded in their name were badly managed and insufficiently patronized. Efforts to hold cotton off the market for higher prices generally turned out badly. Conscious of these shortcomings, the southern leaders of the Farmers' Union hoped to bring new life into the order by expansion into the western Middle West. This was the obvious purpose of the Farmers' Union members who attended the Farmers' Cooperative Business Congress held in Topeka, Kansas, late in October, 1906. During the congress there was much talk of the need for uniting the agricultural interests of the South and the West. Surely some plan could be devised whereby they could help each other obtain higher prices for their products. The hope was also expressed that through the Farmers' Union some system of "direct exchange" between farmer and consumer might be devised. Perhaps as a means to this end, the congress emphasized the need for the "enactment of a uniform law authorizing and regulating the organization of cooperative societies." Somehow, it maintained, the farmers of the nation should achieve the same right to name the price of their products that the manufacturers of iron, cloth, and other commodities had to name theirs.[5]

During these years Farmers' Union leaders made every effort to emphasize the appeal of sectional interests. According to one editor, the Union provided the best hope not only for uniting the farmers of the South and West, but also for bringing them independence from the East. "It must be the destiny, the proud privilege of the South and West to give our Nation industrial and financial freedom, for the Republic of the Fathers must not perish from the face of the earth." A convention of grain and livestock producers, dominated by Union sympathizers, as-

4. *Farmers' Union Herald* (South St. Paul, Minn.), May, 1935; Tucker, in *Agricultural History,* XXI (October, 1947), p. 200.

5. *Oklahoma Farmer* (Oklahoma City), October 31, 1906; *Kansas City Journal,* October 25, 1906.

sembled in Springfield, Missouri, on May 12 and 13, 1909, to devise a program of action satisfactory to both the West and the South. It urged the establishment of cooperative meat-packing plants, cooperative elevators and storage warehouses, and, wherever practicable, cooperative commission firms. Also, it favored the adoption of some plan to limit the amount of grain placed on the market. The announcement of this program was, in effect, not only an attempt to promote better relations between the West and the South, but also a frank confession, according to Charles Barrett, the national president, that the Union had "reached the height of its usefulness in the South" and had turned for new conquests to the North and West.[6]

Organizations in a state of decay are known to refer to their numbers and achievements as a means of bolstering their morale; hence it is not surprising that the Union, as it unfolded its program for western expansion, emphasized the size of its membership and the extent of its business activities in the South. The Union boasted the fantastic figure of 2,000,000 members in 1909, which, if it had been true, would have made it the largest farm organization in American history. It claimed that it was active in twenty-seven states, and that it operated several thousand cooperative warehouses and gins. A year later it asserted that business organizations affiliated with or sponsored by its national body had transacted a total of about $100,000,000 worth of business.[7]

The first serious efforts of the Union to penetrate into the western Middle West were made in the states of Illinois, Missouri, and Kansas. Union work in Illinois was based upon the Farmers' Social and Economic Union, which was organized in Somerset Township, Jackson County, on April 27, 1900. A few weeks later, on May 17, 1900, this organization was chartered by the state. From Illinois it spread into Missouri, where it was known at first as a Temporary National Union, but in April, 1906, it was consolidated with a segment of the Farmers' Mutual Benefit As-

6. *The National Co-operator and Farm Journal* (Fort Worth), January 22, 1908; Barrett, *The Farmers' Union,* pp. 125, 236; *The Farmers' Union* (Salina, Kans.), June, 1909; *Fort Smith Elevator,* May 14, 1909; *Farmers' Union News* (Union City, Ga.), May 19, 1909.

7. *Mississippi Union Advocate and Southern Farm and Home* (Winona, Miss.), April 7, 1909; *St. Louis Globe-Democrat,* May 7, 1910.

sociation and the local Farmers' Relief Association under the name of the Farmers' Union. That year McDonald, Dunklin, and Barry counties in Missouri each claimed about 1,000 Union members, and Newton County about 1,500. State-wide organization of the Missouri Farmers' Union was achieved at West Plains on March 22, 1907, and in 1908 the number of locals in the state was placed at 615, with a total membership of 16,836.[8]

During these early years Kansas was probably the most important center of Union activities. Organizational work began on a wholesale basis following the Topeka meeting of the Farmers' Cooperative Business Congress already mentioned. Since the Union was considered the largest and most powerful farm organization at the time, the congress pledged its support to the extension of the Union program into the unorganized western states. Promptly accepting the challenge, the executive committee of the Union, in a meeting following the adjournment of the congress, voted to place organizers in Kansas, Iowa, Nebraska, the Dakotas, and other states. This action appears to have brought results. In 1907, the Kansas Union had some 4,000 members and 85 locals. Equity members were reported coming into the Union fold in droves. In April, 1908, Kansas claimed 8,000 members. About the same time, the *Farmers' Union,* the official organ of the Kansas branch, began publication.[9]

The rapid growth of the organization attracted the attention of William Allen White, who observed that it was encountering the same reception that the Alliance had received back in 1889 and 1890. The Union grew most rapidly, he noted, in the fifth and sixth congressional districts, where agricultural conditions were least satisfactory. "It is a queer movement," wrote White, "and one that politicians should consider, who think the Republican party in Kansas can do anything whether the people like it or not. The earth has buckled up in a Kansas earthquake before and it may be just possible that the signs are favorable to another upheaval."

8. Barrett, *The Farmers' Union,* pp. 235–42, 250–51; *Indian-Arbiter* (Ada, Okla.), June 7, 1906.

9. *Topeka Daily State Journal,* October 24, 1906; *Kansas City Journal,* October 25, 1906; *Topeka Daily State Journal,* October 25, 1906; *Southern Mercury United With Farmers' Union Password* (Dallas), February 28, 1907; *The Farmers' Union,* April 3, 17, 1908.

But these political anticipations never materialized, although in 1920 some 120,000 men and women in Kansas wore the Farmers' Union insignia.[10]

The Union, as part of its expansion program, sought to absorb the American Society of Equity. If this could be done, optimists claimed, the combined membership of the two organizations would reach the fantastic total of 5,000,000 members. Such a merger became one of the chief topics for discussion at a conference held in St. Louis during May, 1910, but so far as formal action was concerned, all such hopes failed to materialize for many years.[11]

The St. Louis convention, judging from the prominent names carried on its program, had attracted significant attention. Heading the list of notables was President William Howard Taft; others less prominent, yet important, were Secretary of Agriculture James Wilson, William Jennings Bryan, Robert M. La Follette, former Governor J. W. Folk of Missouri, Samuel Gompers, president of the American Federation of Labor, and Clarence Poe, editor of the *Progressive Farmer* of North Carolina.[12]

One topic that seemed to interest the delegates was the possibility of forming a new party, with the members of the farmers' organizations and the labor unions as a nucleus. Among those who emphasized such a need was Jacob Coxey, of "Coxey's Army" fame, who argued that many of the old Populists who had gone into the Socialist party were not satisfied with its doctrines and were anxious to form a new political alignment. Barrett was quoted as being in agreement with the Coxey proposal, but Samuel Gompers, true to the balance-of-power policy of the A.F.L., did not concur. The resolutions finally adopted by the convention represented only a résumé of past demands: the elimination of speculation in farm commodities; the abolition of unnecessary middlemen; the establishment of postal savings banks and a system of parcel post; the extension of farm demonstration work; the drainage of swamp lands; the building of good

10. *Emporia Daily Gazette*, February 2, 1907; Stuart Blythe, "Is Kansas the Greatest Cooperative State?" *Country Gentleman*, LXXXV (September 11, 1920), p. 13.

11. *St. Louis Globe-Democrat*, May 3, 7, 1910.

12. *Ibid.*, May 2, 1910; *Farmers' Union News*, May 25, 1910. According to the latter source, President Taft was received "coolly."

roads; and support for labor unions "to the end that their rights and liberties, with our own, shall be preserved."[13]

Next in importance to the Kansas branch of the Union during these early years was the Nebraska organization, whose membership had a greater tendency to be permanent than that of most other states. The first Nebraska local was organized in Antelope County on May 29, 1911, by O. F. Dornblaser of Texas, a protagonist extraordinary of the theory that the cost of production should determine agricultural prices. The Nebraska organization grew steadily in Antelope, Knox, and Pierce counties and, with a total of 245 locals and 5,000 members, formed the Nebraska division of the Union at Fremont in 1913. By 1915, the membership reported was 11,000, and four years later, 37,286. The number of locals by 1928 had reached 1,524, but of these only about 1,000 were active. The troublous late twenties and thirties, as might be expected, witnessed heavy fluctuations in Union membership.[14]

The first publication of the Nebraska Union, the monthly *Bulletin,* appeared in February, 1914, with a circulation of 5,000, and the *Nebraska Union Farmer* came out in April of that same year, with C. H. Gustafson as editor. One of its earliest recommendations was that the federal government devote more time and money to the farmers' problem of distribution, particularly by encouraging cooperative buying and selling. By November, 1915, the paper claimed a reading list of 22,000.[15]

There was nothing especially novel in the state legislative demands of the Nebraska Union. Perhaps the resolutions adopted in its 1915 convention were representative of the attitude of its membership. The convention urged the calling of a state constitutional convention, the legalization of the Torrens system of land registration, the formulation of a suitable rural-credits system, lower freight rates, nonpartisan primary elections,

13. *St. Louis Globe-Democrat,* May 2–5, 1910.

14. *Nebraska Union Farmer* (Omaha), January 10, 1917; O. F. Dornblaser, *The Only Way* (Columbus Junction, Iowa, 1934), p. 7; Farmers' Educational and Cooperative Union of Nebraska, *The Farmers' Union* (Omaha, 1928?), pp. 1–3; *Nebraska Union Farmer,* February, 1915; *ibid.,* January 27, 1926; F.E.C.U. Nebraska, *The Farmers' Union,* pp. 2–3. See also *Secretary's Annual Report, 1930, Farmers' Educational and Cooperative State Union of Nebraska* (also reports for 1934 and 1938).

15. *Nebraska Union Farmer,* November 24, 1915; F.E.C.U. Nebraska, *Bulletin,* No. 1, February, 1914.

the completion of the binder-twine plant in the state penitentiary, and state ownership, operation, and control of telephone and hydroelectric utilities. These demands, although in part radical enough, represented nothing more than a recapitulation of earlier farmer resolutions. The convention's stand on the qualifications that should be required of rural teachers, however, was neither customary nor forward-looking. It opposed any legislation which might require country school teachers to be high school graduates on the theory that teachers' qualifications might better be measured by their ability to pass "a creditable examination" before their respective county superintendents than by their having had a secondary education. The convention also opposed the granting of pensions to school teachers, holding that they had "no more right to a pension than the man who has spent the best part of his life tilling the soil."[16]

As time elapsed, a strong element which was against government aids of all types blossomed forth within the Nebraska Union. During the twenties, for instance, it registered strong protests against all bills before Congress "for the relief of the farmers"; against the creation of any new state bureaus, boards, and commissions; against the enactment of a federal child-labor amendment; and against government price fixing of all forms. While it endorsed the plea of "equality for agriculture," this equality, it held, was to be achieved not by the establishment of a government-sponsored mechanism to make effective the tariff on farm products, but by lowering the excessive protection on manufactured and other nonagricultural products. By 1933, because of the seriousness of the depression, these antipathies toward government controls had vanished, and the Nebraska state convention endorsed federal legislation intended to bring the farmers "cost of production" for the products they had to sell.[17]

Meanwhile, repeated warnings were made of the need for safeguarding the agricultural interests from the "political farmers" and nonproducers. L. S. Herron, editor of the *Nebraska Union Farmer,* pointed to the calamities that had befallen the Grangers, the Alliancemen, and other groups which had heeded the "siren call" of politics. Even though the

16. *Ibid.* (no bulletin number), January, 1915.

17. *The American Labor Yearbook,* 1926 (New York, 1926), p. 229; *Nebraska Union Farmer,* January 27, 1926; January 25, 1933.

Nebraska Union did not enter "the hurly-burly of political campaigns," it did adopt legislative recommendations and encouraged its members to vote for candidates who promised to support them. It also opposed such measures as it considered to be detrimental to agricultural interests and agitated earnestly for cooperative legislation.[18]

If legislation was of secondary importance to the Nebraska Union, the spread of cooperative sentiment and the building of cooperative associations were not. In fact, many Nebraskans believed that this promised the best means for bringing "greater equality and prosperity for the farmers." Cooperatives, according to Herron, had the healthful effect of encouraging the type of competition that held profit-seeking business in check. It followed, then, according to this line of reasoning, that cooperatives, free competition, and conceivably the breaking up of the large corporate units into small ones had more to offer agriculture than did any other formula.[19]

This antistatist philosophy, coupled with a well-defined superiority complex, gave to the Nebraska Farmers' Union a conservative aggressiveness which made it contrast markedly with the other state organizations of the Farmers' Union and with the parent organization itself. While all the various units favored cooperatives, most of them, including the national, leaned heavily on the hope of legislative action and urged government assistance as the chief means for the relief of agriculture.

This difference in point of view often made relations between the Nebraska Union and the national Union anything but harmonious. Many Nebraskans were unhappy that their Union belonged to the national organization at all. They were proud of their success in business, and they believed that the voting in the national conventions should be changed to give to the Nebraska unit a greater voice in national affairs. The Nebraska Union even threatened, in 1920, to withdraw from the national unless there could be devised a fairer basis for voting, but it left to the state board the question of deciding whether to pay dues and send delegates to the national convention. This question came up again in 1934 when the national Union suspended the Nebraska Union for failure to pay dues and then filed suit in Douglas County, Nebraska, to recover

18. *Ibid.*, February 24, 1915; August 24, 1932; F.E.C.U. Nebraska, *The Farmers' Union*, pp. 3–4.

19. *Ibid.*; *Nebraska Union Farmer*, April 27, 1932.

$4,095.85, plus interest, in back dues. When the parent unit lost, it appealed to the Nebraska supreme court, which decided that the members of the Nebraska Union were also members of the national organization and hence subject to its by-laws.[20]

More typical of farmer opinion than the antistatist, free-competitive-society philosophy of certain elements within the Nebraska Farmers' Union was the militant, strongly pro-government-aid, revivalistic, oftentimes doctrinaire attitude of some of the other state bodies. These views were far more representative of the psychological and economic status of the depressed farmers than were the unusual notions expressed by the conservative members of the Nebraska Union.

The typical Union member of the western Middle West displayed a belligerent attitude toward the existing agricultural colleges, toward the daily press, and toward professional politicians. Politicians, for instance, were accused of accepting an obvious untruth when they extolled the farmers as constituting the "backbone of the nation." There was no evidence in support of such a statement. If these politicians were really interested in the farmers' welfare, they should do more than talk, and join an organization which advocated bringing farmers "cost of production" for their products. The agricultural colleges were likewise accused of feeding the farmers a big "dose of bunk." Of what use were admonitions to "become more efficient, produce more" at a time when the domestic surplus was great and foreign markets were scarce. The press contributed its share to this chaotic state of affairs by telling the farmers that "the cow, the sow and the hen, have worked overtime," and that their products "sold through cooperative marketing organizations" would solve farmer problems. This kind of talk was designed to keep "the farmer confused and joining all sorts of associations, from cabbage to cream, and gets him out of the hole not at all."[21]

Milo Reno, the stormy leader of the Iowa Farmers' Union, was venomous in his attacks against the typical agricultural college. His thrusts were

20. *Ibid.*, January 28, 1920; *National Union Farmer* (Oklahoma City), December 1, 1932.

21. *Farm Market Guide* (Minneapolis), May-June, 1926. Compare this militant stand against the agricultural college in later years with that taken previously. See *48th Annual Report of the Board of Agriculture, The Missouri Year Book of Agriculture* (Columbia, 1916), p. 317.

representative of the extremist views that prevailed during the depth of the agricultural depression. He charged that the agricultural colleges deliberately distracted the attention of the farmers from the real solution of the farm problem and conditioned them to "accept the lowly position of the peasant." He heaped unlimited ridicule upon the bulletins sent out by Iowa State College, some of them instructing farmers' wives on how to make undergarments for their children out of feedsacks.[22]

Reno had nothing but scorn for the "stuffy" college professor. He stated that the "stuff" that the "ancient professor" handed out to his students was not going to be of any use to them in the immediate future. "The theories of advanced economics aren't going to be worth a damn in the next two or three years in solving the practical problems that confront us." Reno, according to one account, carried on an extensive correspondence with a prominent professor who had stated in his textbook that there were fourteen basic industries. This, Reno said, was wrong. To Reno, agriculture was the one and only basic industry, because it was concerned with the procurement of food for human consumption; throughout the course of history, man had been able to get along without every other industry, but not without the producers of food.[23]

Union antagonisms toward existing economic institutions resulted in orgies of emotional denunciation. Agriculture was a meek lamb sitting alongside the lion of big business. Speculators operating on grain exchanges were nothing more than racketeers of "a higher . . . mentality and character" who were on the loose. "We permit a gambling game to run in our grain exchanges which takes millions from suckers where slot machines take cents." John A. Simpson, the most militant of Farmers' Union national presidents, castigated the capitalist system after the fashion of a prophet, and heaped unlimited praise on cooperatives. The capitalistic system, like the doings of the devil, he said, was based on "selfishness, greed, avarice," and led to "theft, robbery, murder, suicide and war," while the cooperatives were of "Christian origin instead of the devil," were based on "service instead of profit," and had as their attributes "unselfishness and the brotherhood of man."[24]

22. *Iowa Union Farmer* (Columbus Junction), January 11, 1933.

23. *Des Moines Register,* January 27, 1934.

24. *Farmers' Union Herald,* March, 1927; April 6, December 31, 1931; August, 1933.

Equally violent was the Union opposition to the county agents and the Farm Bureau. The Bureau was nothing more than a "gentlemen farmers'" organization sponsored by the United States Department of Agriculture, the chamber of commerce, the agricultural colleges, and the local businessmen; it worked hand in glove with the county agents, who did an excellent job in misleading farmers into breeding better stock, improving the quality of the soil, and raising more produce.[25] Simpson declared it to be an agency "ruled by Chicago grain merchants and Washington politicians." Reno claimed it was brought into existence to prepare the farmers for the postwar deflation, to check radicalism, and to enslave the farmers with "lollypops, calf-clubs, pig-clubs, farmer's institutes . . . to override and destroy the fundamental principles of our Republic." Union folks, according to the *Iowa Union Farmer,* "believe in good farmers, good homemakers and healthy boys and girls, better pigs, and better calves, but we are more concerned about farmers being placed on an equilibrium with other groups of society, which means nothing less than a protected price, the equivalent of our cost of production."[26]

The benefits promised and objectives sought, although often confused and inconsistent, were significant. At least one eloquent testimonial was delivered in behalf of the cooperative commonwealth. "And when all business is cooperatively owned there will be no profit system left, neither rich nor poor, and in place of the profit system will come the cooperative commonwealth." On another occasion, the *Farmers' Union Herald* referred to the Union as an industrial, not a craft, union because it took in all farmers—tenants and owners alike—regardless of the size of their operations. The Union sought "economic justice" for the farmers by resisting those who used them as "saddle horses." Getting rid of their exploiters, "big and little," was just "a phase of the class struggle," which made mandatory the building of a "red blooded, class conscious, fighting farm organization."[27] The Union was "officered and manned by farmers," published its own paper, was freed from domination by "commercial clubs, county agents, or the agricultural college." Only thus would the

25. *Farm Market Guide,* April 20, 1926; *Farmers' Union Herald,* March, 1927.
26. *Des Moines Tribune,* January 16, 1931; *Iowa Union Farmer,* March 25, September 9, 1931.
27. *Farmers' Union Herald,* July, 1935; December, 1936; October, 1928; September, 1929.

farmers be able to graduate from the "sucker class," and to cease "hewing wood and carrying water" for their exploiters as they had been doing for centuries. The educational program of the Iowa Union was based on "two fundamentals—Cost of Production plus a reasonable profit, and the doctrine of real Co-operation."[28]

Once headway had been made in Nebraska, Kansas, and Iowa, it was only natural to expect the Union to penetrate into the Dakotas, Minnesota, and Wisconsin. In fact, representatives of the Equity Cooperative Exchange of St. Paul appeared before the annual convention of the national Farmers' Union as early as 1922 to extend to it an invitation to organize the farmers of the agricultural Northwest. More serious consideration was given to this possible merger with the Equity Cooperative Exchange after the Des Moines meeting of May 12, 1925, which had assembled for the specific purpose of uniting the farmers in their campaign for farm relief. Early that year the nearly defunct National Producers' Alliance announced that it had started to coordinate its work with the Equity exchange and the Farmers' Union. On November 16 and 17, the Alliance committee which had considered the merger proposal with the Union indicated that it had reached an agreement on four points: (1) the need for creating a single powerful farm organization capable of demanding a fixed price based on "cost of production"; (2) the establishment of more effective marketing machinery; (3) the adoption of a name that would be descriptive of such objectives; and (4) recognition of the fact that the Farmers' Union, which had spread into the Mississippi Valley but was ineffectively organized in Wisconsin, Minnesota, North Dakota, and Montana, was the organization best qualified to achieve these objectives. Merger was acceptable to the Alliance if the Union gave assurances that "cost of production" would serve as the base for determining price and if it proceeded to organize the Northwest farmers. Barrett responded by reminding the Alliance that the Union was organized with "cost of production" as its guiding principle, and that Union representatives had sponsored the call for a "cost of production" conference to assemble in Des Moines on May 12.[29]

28. *Farm Market Guide*, May-June, 1926; *Iowa Year Book of Agriculture*, 1927, pp. 352–53.

29. *Nebraska Union Farmer*, March 22, 1922; *Farm Market Guide*, February, December, 1925.

The next step was to absorb the Equity Cooperative Exchange. The way was prepared for this at the annual convention of the exchange in Fargo on January 16, 1926. At this meeting Barrett appeared and pleaded for "one solid organization of farmers." Later a joint convention of Equity and Alliance delegates adopted a series of strongly worded resolutions urging businessmen, labor, Congress, the tariff beneficiaries, and the speculators in farm products to take cognizance of the plight of the farmers and to join in the demand that the federal government come to the farmers' aid. One way to help them, the convention believed, was to raise the tariff on wheat, flax, and butter. The convention also adopted a merger resolution which read in part, "Whereas . . . agriculture is engaged in a titanic struggle with the interests who are bent on reducing the farmer to the level of a peasant . . . it is essential that all our forces unite for a defense of our economic rights."[30]

This marked the final step in the merger and the beginning of a concerted effort by the Union to organize the farmers of the agricultural Northwest. The new Union was heralded as "a real dirt farmers' organization." All funds received by the national body from these states were to be used for organizing and for the *Farmers' Union Herald,* the official publication of the northwest states. The national body and the Iowa Union each pledged $500 for organizing activities.[31]

Thus fortified, the national Farmers' Union created in 1927 the Northwest Committee to facilitate organization work. That year efforts were concentrated primarily on North Dakota because of the good prospects of success in that state. North Dakota, as a large producer of wheat and flax, presented a maximum need for building a terminal marketing agency; it was also a great livestock producer, although most North Dakota livestock was marketed through noncooperative agencies. Furthermore, the state of North Dakota had already been familiarized with the farmers' program of reform by the Nonpartisan League. Little attention was devoted to Wisconsin and Minnesota, presumably because of the want of money and organizers. In Wisconsin, indeed, there were reversals, due in part to a secession movement, which resulted in the establishment of a new state organization without the approval of the national board.

30. *Fargo Forum,* January 16, 1926; *Farm Market Guide,* February, 1926.
31. *Ibid.,* December, 1925; February, 1926.

As a result of the organized drive in the Northwest, the year 1927 saw the establishment of a North Dakota Farmers' Union, which claimed a paid-up membership of over 8,000, and also a slight membership gain in Minnesota. Further Union accomplishments included the growth in patronage of the livestock department in South St. Paul; the creation of a life insurance company and a property insurance company in North Dakota; and finally, the organization of the Farmers' Union Exchange, Inc., functioning in a small way but growing nonetheless.[32]

An even greater increase in Union activities took place in 1928. A training school for organizers was established, and five field organizers, together with more than fifty local organizers, were put to work. Membership during the year was placed at 20,505. The livestock department had a force of ten organizers who worked systematically to build up and consolidate the membership about shipping points and to form the members into livestock-shipping associations. The grain department had five men in the field capable of arranging local meetings. By November, 1928, Minnesota had enrolled 2,796 members and Wisconsin, exclusive of the secessionists, had 1,735. Four organizers were put to work in the latter state to overcome the effects of factionalism. The future of the Union in Wisconsin appeared to depend largely on the ability of the Farmers' Union Central Exchange to cater to the dairy producers, who were well organized on the marketing side but totally unorganized in purchasing.[33]

The Union, in the course of its expensive organizing activities in the Northwest, incurred an unspecified deficit. This prompted the recommendation that the earnings of the Northwest business organizations be used to finance organizational work rather than to pay the customary patronage dividends. According to the *Farmers' Union Herald,* "Our members clearly understand this policy and warmly approve it, realizing that the end aimed at in cooperative buying and selling is conditioned on large scale organization. By no other means will we ever be able to acquire bargaining power either in the marketing of products or the purchase of commodities used on the farm." Much criticism was leveled at the Northwest Committee for this policy, but the *Farmers' Union Herald* in defense simply inquired how else a farm organization might be built.[34]

32. *Farmers' Union Herald,* November, 1928.

33. *Ibid.*

34. *Ibid.,* November, 1928; February 17, 1930.

Even more progress was reported in the Northwest between the national conventions of 1928 and 1929. During this year serious efforts were made to bring Minnesota into the "Union sisterhood." Minnesota was described as the most difficult state to organize because of the presence there of many small, unfederated, and unrelated cooperatives which resisted centralized authority. Many farmers thought that there were enough organizations in the state the way things were; many had had unpleasant memories of wheat, potato, egg, and poultry pools which had failed; the opposition of the established grain interests to the erection of farmer-owned and controlled grain-marketing organizations was also strong. In Wisconsin, the membership passed the 6,000 mark and there were five county bodies and locals functioning in thirteen counties. Late in 1930 the Union, according to Northwest sources, had enrolled nearly 60,000 members and "added three stars to the Union flag."[35]

It came as no surprise that the growth of the Union in the Northwest and the organizing tactics employed there aroused the ire of the conservative Nebraska Farmers' Union, which had nothing but contempt for the organizing techniques of the Northwest Committee and its leadership. A. W. Ricker, editor of the *Farmers' Union Herald,* an ex-Producers' Alliance man, ex-Nonpartisan Leaguer, ex-Socialist, ex-Populist, and ex-Farmers' Alliance man, sought to reduce the conflict between the two groups to the least common denominator. The Northwest group, he insisted, saw the farm problem as one of controlled marketing, with the farmers' goal the power to bargain for prices as organized labor bargained for wages; but the Nebraska group saw it only in terms of "prune and vinegar peddling," *i.e.,* cooperative marketing and buying.[36]

Herron, the editor of the *Nebraska Union Farmer,* took issue with this description. He accused Ricker of drawing heavily on his imagination. "If there was any battle . . . over the issue of price-fixing versus toll-reducing co-operation, it was waged in the minds of Mr. Ricker and his colleagues. . . . The real issue was whether the Reno-Northwest Committee machine should dominate the organization and re-elect Barrett and Davis as convenient rubber stamps." Price fixing was "the pet obsession, or at least the big talking point, of the Reno-Northwest Committee

35. *Ibid.,* February 3, December 15, 1930.
36. *Ibid.,* November, 1927.

group"; in fact, it was the theory on which the Farmers' Union was founded in Texas. For years Union committees had been appointed to estimate the "cost of production" and to name prices for cotton and other farm products. Membership in the cotton states, where this theory had been widely accepted, had vanished into thin air, while in those states where a program for "toll-reducing cooperation" had been established, the membership of the Union had increased. If Nebraska was one of those states which went in for the "prune and vinegar peddling" to which Ricker had referred so slurringly, it had nevertheless done rather well. "We have peddled some vinegar, besides other groceries, a lot of twine, farm machinery, fencing, seeds, feeds, oils, gasoline, paints, work clothing, and other supplies too numerous to mention." This had saved Nebraska farmers substantial sums of money. Ricker, on the other hand, was associated with at least two other organizations over the past ten years, *i.e.*, the Nonpartisan League and the Producers' Alliance; the last was a price-fixing venture that never got beyond the dues-collecting stage, and it was "a bit unbecoming and presumptuous" for him "to assume the role of godfather to the Farmers' Union."[37]

This flare-up between the editors of the two Union papers was part and parcel of the mounting opposition to Charles S. Barrett, the national president since 1906, and A. C. Davis, the national secretary. Barrett without question was a man with many political ties and great influence in Washington. On this account, no doubt, he had managed to be re-elected president year after year, despite the fact that neither his state of Georgia nor for that matter the whole South was any longer of consequence in the Union. The organization, during his tenure, had spread from the South into the Middle West, and had changed its program from holding products off the market for a fixed price to cooperative marketing and purchasing, although lip service was still given to "cost of production" and fixed prices.[38]

For a time, C. H. Gustafson, the president of the Nebraska Farmers' Union from 1913 to 1922, had loomed as the chief antagonist of Barrett; in fact, a story circulated to the effect that he had threatened either to unseat Barrett at some future national convention or else lead his Nebraska

37. *Nebraska Union Farmer,* December 28, 1927.
38. *Ibid.,* April 24, 1935.

Union out of the national organization. This threat came to naught when Gustafson later was forced to resign as president of the Nebraska organization because he accepted a position with the Farm Bureau-sponsored United States Grain Growers, Incorporated.[39]

By the middle twenties, the leadership in opposition to Barrett had passed into the hands of John A. Simpson, the president of the Oklahoma Farmers' Union and a rising influence within Union circles. In 1927, Simpson had recommended to the national convention, the recommendation coming in the form of a constitutional amendment, that in the future the presidency and the secretaryship be nonsalaried positions to be filled by individuals who were also state presidents at the time they were elected. During the debates on the amendment Milo Reno, who later sided with Simpson, came to the defense of Barrett. In the end the Simpson amendment failed; 45 votes were cast for it and 59 against it. Illinois, South Dakota, Nebraska, and Oklahoma voted for the amendment, and Iowa, Montana, California, Idaho, Washington, Oregon, Georgia, Minnesota, North Dakota, Missouri, and Arkansas were against it. The states which favored the Simpson amendment voted for E. M. Pollard of Nebraska for national president. These states even suggested a boycott of the national convention the following year, a threat of no mean consequence, since they paid half the national revenues. The *Nebraska Union Farmer* agreed with Simpson that it would be a waste of time, money, and effort to have the national Union continue under the leadership of Barrett and Davis, who were nonetheless re-elected in 1927; Barrett, however, announced that he would not be a candidate for re-election.[40]

Apparently this announcement by Barrett was hardly adequate to placate the insurgent states, for on January 9, 1928, they assembled in Des Moines to reform the national Union. The rebelling states included Oklahoma, Nebraska, South Dakota, Illinois, Minnesota, and a faction in the Wisconsin Union. Nebraska was anxious to elect as president someone who had an understanding of the problems of the corn-raising states. Simpson, who was too ill to attend this convention, sent a statement censuring the national administration for failing to build up the Union and for accepting

39. *National Leader,* January 23, 1922; *Minnesota Leader* (Olivia), July 29, 1922.
40. *Des Moines Register,* November 17, 18, 1927; *Nebraska Union Farmer,* November 23, 1927; April 24, 1935.

money from states that did not have the membership they represented themselves to have; the fictitious members, he claimed, gave to such states delegates which they did not deserve and increased the vote in support of the incumbents. It was also charged that the national administration promoted dissension by ruthlessly "pushing" into other states with business enterprises of doubtful cooperative character.[41]

In 1928, C. E. Huff of Kansas was elected president and James O'Shea of Montana, secretary-treasurer; but these results were achieved only after a near revolt by delegates from Oklahoma and Nebraska. The insurgents, according to the *Farmers' Union Herald,* had demanded majority control of the board of directors, which was denied them. As a result, they remained out of the national Union "until within the last thirty days, when they came back one by one, Nebraska being the last." Two of the states had refused to pay dues unless they obtained three seats on the national board, or majority control.[42]

Obviously, two distinct schools of farm relief had developed within the Union. One group had pinned its faith on the power of the farmers to work themselves out of the agricultural dilemma by encouraging the growth of cooperative marketing and purchasing associations and by seeking what legislation was necessary to insure the cooperatives a free hand. The other group saw the value of cooperatives, yet felt that the ramifications of the farm problem were so gigantic that it would be impossible to rehabilitate agriculture without federal assistance; the power of the federal government had to be utilized to stabilize farm prices and to protect cooperatives against unfair discrimination. This latter group had its largest following among those who produced staples, the prices of which were greatly affected by world competitive conditions.[43]

As a matter of fact, cooperative marketing and purchasing associations had always occupied a conspicuous role in Farmers' Union activities, and in the earlier years nearly everything else had been subordinated to teaching farmers "the business side of farm life." It was then sound Union doctrine that economic wrongs would be corrected through neither "the

41. *Ibid.,* January 25, 1928.

42. *Des Moines Register,* November 23, 1928; *Farmers' Union Herald,* November, 1928.

43. *Oklahoma Union Farmer* (Oklahoma City), December 1, 1924.

rantings of politicians" nor "the cultivation of the esthetic tastes of individuals," but only by "the application of practical business methods," meaning, mainly, cooperative buying and selling.[44]

Information about the earlier business activities of the Union in the western Middle West is fragmentary. But in 1913, Union-sponsored cooperatives were operating in the states of Illinois, Missouri, and Kansas. In Illinois, business associations catered to the diversified agricultural interests of the farmers. Kansas reported eighteen cooperative associations that handled farm products for Union members and purchased supplies in wholesale quantities; they paid dividends that ranged from 10 to 25 per cent. In Missouri, there were 11 mercantile houses, with a combined capital stock of $150,000, in addition to 125 smaller stores located in various parts of the state and an unspecified number of creameries.[45] In South Dakota, during 1919–20, there were reported seventy cooperative elevators, stores, telephone companies, flour mills, and creameries.[46]

The cooperative movement in Nebraska achieved more sizable proportions. In 1917 there were a total of 75 elevators, 15 stores, 1 creamery, and about 125 buying and shipping associations. By 1928 the number had increased; there were 250 cooperative elevator associations, 200 cooperative stores, and an unspecified number of cream and produce stations. Most of these were still functioning, even though a number had fallen victims to deflation, inexperienced management, and the failure to adopt cooperative principles. Their practice was to charge the prevailing prices. At the end of the year, after paying the interest on capital stock and setting aside a sum for the sinking fund, the profits were returned to the members in proportion to the trade that they had given the association.[47]

One of the first business agencies to be established by the Nebraska Union was the Farmers' Union state exchange, which began business operations in May, 1914. This business association was owned and con-

44. *48th Annual Report, The Missouri Year Book of Agriculture,* p. 317.

45. *Farmers' Educational and Cooperative Union of America, What It Is and What It Is Doing* (n.p., n.d.), pp. 31–33.

46. *F. E. and C. U. of America, Supplement "A" To What It Is Doing* (n.p., [1917]), pp. 21–24.

47. F.E.C.U. Nebraska, *The Farmers' Union,* p. 4; *F. E. and C. U. of America, Supplement "A,"* pp. 21–24.

trolled by the entire membership, and was capitalized from the fees and dues that the members had paid into the state Union. The state exchange handled groceries, clothing, machinery, engines, cream separators, twine, oil, salt, coal, lumber, cement, posts, fencing, flour, feed, hay, produce, and numerous other items, and supplied goods to the cooperative stores, elevators, buying and shipping associations, and Union locals, as well as to members directly. In 1915 the exchange claimed to have done a business of $319,882; the following year it reported almost a million dollars' worth of business, and by 1928 it was operating ten branch retail stores. Besides making purchases for members at a saving, the exchange forced competitors to hold down their prices.[48]

Grain marketing became another concern of the Nebraska Union. Associations organized by it adhered more strictly to the cooperative principle than did the older farmer companies. The National Grain Commission Company, which was formed by the Union, obtained a seat on the Omaha Grain Exchange.[49]

The Nebraska Union sought to organize only creamery stations in the beginning, but discrimination by the old-line creameries soon forced it to establish a cooperative creamery. Local creameries had never been successful in Nebraska because they failed to obtain a sufficient quantity of cream. This accounts for the decision to set up a regional cooperative creamery covering a territory large enough to supply the necessary volume. The first such creamery was established in Fremont, and later others were organized in Superior, Aurora, and Fairbury. It was claimed that these creameries increased the price for butterfat paid to farmers from three to four cents a pound, while patronage dividends ran the profits of patrons up an additional two or three cents a pound.[50]

Cooperative gasoline stations began to appear in 1925, and three years later there were forty-five of them in Nebraska. The earliest of these associations were said to have brought savings of as much as eight cents a gallon. This forced the old-line distributors in the state to bring down their prices from four to six cents per gallon. In May, 1927, the Nebraska Farmers' Union Cooperative Oil Association was organized, which in turn made the Farmers' Union state exchange its buying agent.

48. *Ibid.;* F.E.C.U. Nebraska, *The Farmers' Union,* pp. 11–12.
49. *Ibid.,* p. 5. 50. *Ibid.,* pp. 8–9.

In 1918, the Farmers' Union Co-operative Insurance Company of Nebraska was organized. At the end of 1927, after a little more than nine years of operation, this company had about 6,000 policy holders and $33,840,323 worth of insurance in force on all kinds of farm property.[51]

Remarkable success was scored also in the organization of livestock-shipping associations; and here, more notably than in other commodities, great strides were made on the terminal market. The Nebraska Union tried in 1917 to purchase a membership on the Omaha Livestock Exchange, but its application was turned down on the grounds that the Union, contrary to exchange rules, paid patronage dividends. The only thing left to do was to form a cooperative firm independent of the exchange, and on April 2, 1917, such an organization was established. By the third month it was on a paying basis, although when an attempt was made to incorporate the firm in 1920, the farmers failed to respond to the proposal to buy stock. Originally, the practice of the cooperative exchange was to pay patronage dividends to Union members only, but this soon was modified to include non-Union members. A plan was finally devised whereby those who did not belong to the Union gained membership in cooperatives by paying an annual fee of one dollar. This policy prevailed from August, 1922, to February, 1924, despite some confusion over the role that these "dollar members" were to play in the management of the firm.[52]

As the business of the Omaha cooperative exchange grew, the Nebraska Union entered into arrangements in 1924 with the Iowa and South Dakota Unions to operate the firm jointly. Later, the Colorado and Montana Unions entered into similar arrangements; but the Nebraska Union maintained the dominant voice in the business policy of the exchange and in effect controlled it.[53]

A similar agency was established in South St. Joseph by September, 1917. Like the Omaha firm, it at first paid dividends only to those who were actually Union members, but this policy was modified to provide payment to such members of shipping associations as might send their

51. *Ibid.*, p. 12.

52. C. G. Randall, *Cooperative Marketing of Livestock in the United States by Terminal Associations,* U. S. Dept. Agri., Technical Bulletin 57 (Washington, 1928), pp. 46–48.

53. *Ibid.*

livestock to the agency. In 1924, the Farmers' Unions of Nebraska, Kansas, and Iowa, the Missouri Farmers' Association, and the Missouri Farm Bureau joined forces with the Nebraska Union to operate the firm, and still other state groups joined later. By 1926 the number of shippers who made use of the agency was placed at 8,000, representing no less than 200 local associations.[54]

A third agency, the Farmers' Union Live Stock Commission, was established by the Nebraska Union in 1918 at Sioux City, Iowa. As happened elsewhere, a number of other organizations soon entered into an agreement to operate the Sioux City firm jointly. These associates included the Farmers' Unions of Nebraska, South Dakota, and Iowa, the national Farmers' Union, and the Farmers' Cooperative Society of Sioux Center, Iowa. As a result of the cooperative, the commission rates at Sioux City were reduced by 1925 to about one-third the former charges. Over the period 1924–26, the Sioux City house handled more than 500,000 head of livestock, valued approximately at from $12,000,000 to $16,600,000. This business represented between 11 and 12 per cent of the total receipts at Sioux City in each of the three years. In 1926, the company had about 8,000 shippers. An attempt was also made to operate a house in Sioux Falls, but this was short-lived.[55]

The business activities of the Kansas Farmers' Union also were among the most prominent in Union circles. The total business operations were placed, in 1921, at about $300,000,000. The Kansas Union's activities included 600 cooperative elevators, 200 retail stores, and 300 cream and produce stations—a total of 1,100 enterprises with a combined capital of $15,000,000.[56]

There were five district organizations affiliated with the Kansas Union: the livestock commission, the jobbing association, the auditing association, the hail insurance company, and the fire insurance company. The jobbing association held a membership in the Kansas City Board of Trade and the livestock commission in the Kansas City Livestock Exchange. According to Union officials, the profits and savings realized by these associations totaled about $30,000,000 over a period of thirteen years. The 1,100 local cooperative enterprises fell into four categories: produce

54. *Ibid.*, p. 50. 55. *Ibid.*, p. 52.
56. *Oklahoma Union Farmer*, June 15, 1922.

stations, retail stores for consumers, grain-marketing elevators, and county-unit cooperative business associations. The 300 produce stations—usually small enterprises with 20 or more members and a paid-up capital ranging from $1,000 to $5,000—handled cream, eggs, butter, and other farm commodities. The annual business of the average produce station ranged from $5,000 to $25,000. Many of these stations were operated in connection with retail stores. The demand for retail stores apparently was great. Membership in these stores ran anywhere from 50 to 300, while the capital invested in them ranged from $15,000 to $300,000.[57]

An elevator, if it was to be successful financially, required from $12,000 to $35,000 in paid-up capital, not less than 300 members, and an annual shipment of 85,000 bushels of grain. In addition to grain, most elevators handled coal, feed, flour, salt, fruit, and vegetables—all purchased in carload lots and sold to members. Many elevators and retail stores carried farm implements, oil, and gasoline. As a rule, 8 per cent interest was paid on the invested capital and the cooperative dividends averaged about 6 per cent.[58]

In the county-unit cooperative business associations the shareholders varied in number from 400 to 2,000 and the annual business turnover from half a million to between three and four millions. Any such enterprise usually had associated with it from four to twelve elevators, several retail stores, and all the necessary produce stations within the county. The entire business was in charge of a board of directors and one general manager.[59]

The Farmers' Union Jobbing Association was the first state-wide cooperative association undertaken by the organization in Kansas. It was organized in June, 1914, and began business operations in Kansas City, Kansas, in May, 1915. This association marketed grain, hay, produce, and poultry for its members; it also sold to local associations and, under certain conditions, to individual members such items as coal, feed, salt, flour, syrups, oils, tires, soap, rough clothing, groceries, and other articles. It attempted to specialize in carload-lot shipments. During the summer of 1918 this association made contracts with six great farm-machinery manufacturers and in 1922 it was reported to be doing a business of a million dollars annually.[60] The jobbing association held two seats on the grain

57. *Ibid.* 58. *Ibid.* 59. *Ibid.* 60. *Ibid.*

exchange and one on the hay exchange. It asserted that it did $4,000,000 worth of business in 1923 and that in 1924 it had consigned to it more wheat than came to any other firm in Kansas City, Missouri. Its livestock business, which amounted to about a million dollars annually, was likewise the largest enjoyed by any firm on the Kansas City market, and its insurance business alone amounted at the time to about $40,000,000.[61]

A livestock commission firm was authorized by the Wichita convention in January, 1918, and began its business operations in Kansas City, Missouri, on October 14, 1918. It was chartered under the laws of Kansas in July, 1919. The agency was also given representation on the market-practices committee, which established trading rules and regulations in that market. It was the custom to set aside 10 per cent of earnings for the reserve fund and to pay 8 per cent dividends on stock before distributing any patronage dividends. By the end of 1926, it had transacted a total business of $63,811,013 for its customers. Over the period 1924–26 more than 1,000,000 head of cattle, hogs, and sheep were sold, and more than 78,000 head of stockers and feeders were purchased.

In 1923, the Kansas City firm opened a branch on the Wichita market, beginning with a cash investment of $3,000 furnished by the Kansas City office. During the first three years of operation, the total livestock handled was between 60,000 and 65,000 head, valued at nearly $2,000,000.[62]

The Kansas Farmers' Union Auditing Association audited accounts for different business activities over the state, as well as the records of the livestock firm, the jobbing association, the bank, and the state Union.

A novel feature of the Kansas Farmers' Union was a cooperative bank. This institution was not merely a credit union, but rather a "real bank of its own, state-wide in character, organized explicitly to provide members of the Farmers' Union with banking services to fit their own peculiar needs." The establishment of such a bank had long been a topic for discussion before it materialized in 1924. A committee had surveyed the activities of various labor-union banks in order to find out, if possible, how well a similar financial cooperative would suit the needs of the Kansas farmers. When the doors of the Farmers' Union Bank were thrown open on July 1, 1924, in Kansas City, it received $35,000 in deposits on the

61. *Oklahoma Union Farmer,* November 15, 1924.
62. Randall, *Cooperative Marketing of Livestock,* pp. 53–55.

first day. By May, 1925, the bank claimed to have had $500,000 entrusted to its care, but nevertheless it turned out to be a short-lived affair.[63]

During and immediately after the first World War, the Iowa Farmers' Union experienced a tremendous spurt in business activities. The cooperative store became especially popular. These stores were of two types: branch stores, owned and controlled by the state exchange, and the independent locals. There were 125 of the latter under the control of the state exchange. Many stores appear not to have cooperated with the central organization any too well, if the numerous purchases which they made from traveling men who represented the old-line warehouses can be considered a criterion.[64]

The Iowa Farmers' Union also undertook a variety of cooperative marketing and purchasing activities during the 1920's. It acquired livestock firms in Chicago and South St. Paul, and it entered the insurance business in 1922 with the establishment of the Farmers' Union Mutual Life Insurance Company, a company which, by 1929, was operating in nine states. By that same year the Farmers' Union Mutual (Fire) Insurance Company had approximately $55,000,000 worth of insurance in force, and was chartered to do business in Iowa, Illinois, North Dakota, and Missouri. The Farmers' Mutual Automobile Insurance Association, chartered in 1928 to operate in Iowa and North Dakota, specialized "in a full-coverage policy or protection against all manner of hazards incident to automobile operation—collision, public liability, property damage, tornado, theft, fire, hail, etc.—all in one policy." The Farmers' Union Service Association handled "practically every commodity necessary to the farm—from farm machinery of every description to food products, stock feeds, radios and automobile accessories." The annual volume of business conducted by this association in 1929 approached a million dollars. At that time the Farmers' Union Co-operative Oil Association had in operation no less than thirty-one bulk and filling stations located in all sections of Iowa, with new stations opening every week.[65]

Equally remarkable was the progress of the cooperative program among the farmers of the northwest states. Here, as in other Farmers' Union

63. *Missouri Farmer* (Columbia), May 15, 1925.
64. *Nebraska Union Farmer*, November 24, 1920.
65. *Iowa Year Book of Agriculture*, 1929, pp. 352–56.

states, grain, livestock, oil, and farm and household supplies were han
dled successfully and in growing quantities by cooperatives.

One of the first major business enterprises of the Farmers' Union in
the Northwest was acquired full grown when the Iowa Farmers' Union
took over the old livestock branch of the Equity Cooperative Exchange
in South St. Paul, and then transferred its ownership to the Unions of the
northwest states. The volume of business transacted by this firm never
was great, yet it attracted much attention because of the policy it adopted
with reference to patronage dividends and because of its quarrel with the
Central Cooperative Livestock Commission Association, also of South
St. Paul.

It will be recalled that the Northwest Committee had announced that
the patronage dividends which it normally would pay to its patrons would
be withheld to promote the organizational and educational activities of
the Union. Patronage dividends were also employed, in part, to pay for
the building purchased from the defunct Equity Cooperative Exchange
When this policy went into operation in 1926, the immediate effect was
a drop in the patronage of the firm, especially among those farmers who
shipped to the agency but did not belong to the Union.[66]

The quarrel between the Union house and the Central Cooperative
represented a good deal more than the rival ambitions of two competitive
firms. The Central Cooperative, supported as it was by the Minnesota
Farm Bureau and the extension division of the University of Minnesota,
adhered to the basically different point of view from that held by the
Farmers' Union and accepted by its agency. The Union maintained that
the solution to the farm problem would best be reached by one centraliz-
ing force—in this case the Union—to which all the different commodity
organizations should belong. The Central, on the other hand, was simply
a single commodity organization and was content to operate by itself
alone. The Union insisted that the farmers would obtain a better price
for their goods only when they, as producers, were strong enough to
control the flow of their commodities and so to fix their own prices. The
Central, while conceding that such a situation might be ideal, maintained
that it would be impossible to achieve. The Union agency, by virtue of
the fact that it was the successor to the Equity house, the oldest marketing

66. *Farmers' Union Herald,* June, 1927.

terminal in the country, maintained that there was no need for the Central Cooperative on the South St. Paul market; it charged that the Central was in fact a mere duplication of existing marketing facilities and impeded the solution of the farm problem.[67] To this charge the Central replied that the Union livestock agency was inefficient and bankrupt and was operated by promoters; in contrast, the Central was incorporated under the cooperative laws of Minnesota, and had been organized and managed strictly as a cooperative by producers tributary to the St. Paul market, not by outsiders who were only remotely interested in the marketing problems of the area. Further, the Central claimed that, starting in 1921 with only $27,000 capital, it had handled over a five-year period—1922 to 1927—some 99,381 carloads of livestock for 125,000 producers at a saving of over $200,000 annually, whereas the more expensive Union house had handled only 14,361 carloads for a correspondingly smaller number of shippers. The Central was on friendly terms with the other Farmers' Union houses, had established public confidence by having its books audited monthly by public accountants, had not spent its profits on promotion but had returned them to the shippers, and had no interest in joining a general farm organization unless by so doing it could be of additional service to its members.[68]

Grain marketing was high on the list of Union activities in the Northwest. The first major effort materialized with the organization of the Farmers' Union Terminal Association, which was built upon the ruins of the old Equity Cooperative Exchange. Originally this institution was known as the Equity Union Marketing Association, but in 1926 the name was changed to the Farmers' Union Terminal Marketing Association.[69] Its business in the first year, 1925–26, totaled 1,500,000 bushels; during the second year, 1926–27, 8,000,000 bushels; and during the third year, 1927–28, 8,000,000 bushels. The grain of its affiliated members and elevators was distributed through the Minneapolis-St. Paul and Duluth-Superior markets. In 1930, by virtue of its handling more than 15,000,000 bushels of grain annually, it claimed that it was the largest cooperative

67. A. W. Ricker, *The Farmers' Union and Its Enemies* (n.p., n.d.), pp. 1–4 [pamphlet].

68. *Co-operative Shipper* (South St. Paul), May, 1928; January, 1930.

69. Northwest Division, *The Farmers' Educational and Cooperative Union of America* (St. Paul, [1930]), p. 15 [booklet].

grain-marketing association in the United States. In 1930 its officers announced the distribution of $35,000 in patronage dividends—the first time in the agricultural Northwest, they said, that a grain cooperative had paid patronage dividends.[70]

Various factors account for the success of the Farmers' Union Terminal Marketing Association. The years 1926–29 were ones of relatively good times for the grain growers of the Northwest, and business was plentiful. Also, the association profited greatly from the favorable reputation of the national president of the Farmers' Union, C. E. Huff, who was a popular figure in the Northwest and a warm supporter of the Federal Farm Board after its organization. Later, indeed, he became president of the Farmers' National Grain Corporation, established by the F.F.B. Under the circumstances, it is not surprising that the association could claim to be the largest cooperative grain-marketing organization affiliated with the Federal Farm Board. In 1931 it announced its intentions of sponsoring legislation in Minnesota providing for the issuance of negotiable receipts for grain stored on farms similar to that enacted in 1929 by North Dakota and Montana, and eventually of campaigning for the same type of legislation in South Dakota, Texas, Oklahoma, Kansas, and Nebraska.[71]

It is possibly worth mentioning, also, that the scope of activities permitted to the terminal association was unusually broad and, as its critics pointed out, "utterly lacking in humility." It was organized for the purposes—

(1) Of engaging in the business of buying, selling, marketing, manufacturing, handling and dealing in any and all products produced or consumed in the general business and occupation of agriculture in the broadest acceptation of the term;
(2) Of engaging in any activity in connection with the marketing, manufacturing, selling, harvesting, drying, processing, grading, storing, handling or utilization of grain and grain products received from its members, or the by-products of the same;
(3) Of engaging in any activity in connection with the purchasing, hiring, or use by members of supplies, machinery, equipment, and other articles of commerce;
(4) Of entering into marketing contracts with its members for the purchase

70. *Incorporation Articles, By-Laws, Sketch, Personnel and Financial Status of Farmers' Union Terminal Association* (St. Paul, [1930]), p. 3 [booklet].
71. *Ibid.*, pp. 14–15.

of all or any specified parts of the agricultural products grown or produced by such members from year to year;

(5) Of borrowing money from any source and investing its reserve and making advances or lending money to members of the association and others upon adequate security and of taking collateral for any such loans or advances . . . ;

(6) Of purchasing, leasing, or otherwise acquiring real property, and of building, constructing, purchasing, renting or otherwise acquiring any buildings, warehouses, store rooms, work shops, elevators, mills, and machinery, and any other kind of property necessary or useful, or that may be deemed profitable or convenient in carrying on the business of this corporation;

(7) Of purchasing, buying, selling, transferring, owning and utilizing the capital stock or bonds of other corporations;

(8) Of doing all other acts and things that a natural person may lawfully do in manufacturing, buying, selling and dealing in any agricultural products or any merchandise consumed or used by men engaged in agriculture.[72]

The Farmers' Union Terminal Marketing Association even acquired holding-company status in 1927, when it organized a Delaware corporation known as the Farmers' Union Exchange. The terminal association owned all of the stock of the exchange and its board of directors elected the directors of the exchange. The purpose of the exchange was to conduct the merchandising activities of the Union in the Northwest, and exchange profits were either devoted to educational and organizational activities or absorbed into the treasury of the terminal association. The merchandising activities of the exchange were confined to staple items used by the farmers in large quantities, such as gasoline, oil, greases, all kinds of feeds, fertilizer, twine, coal, fencing, tires, seed, grain loaders, scales, flour and other food provisions. In 1927, the exchange handled about 600,000 pounds of binder twine; in 1928, over 5,000,000; and in 1929, nearly 7,000,000. Such items as coal and binder twine were handled on a brokerage basis by the exchange. From 1927 to 1929, coal was shipped to the exchange by rail from eastern Kentucky, West Virginia, and southern Illinois. Arrangements were made with an Ohio salt company to pack salt under a Farmers' Union brand and to ship it to points in Wisconsin, Minnesota, North Dakota, and Montana. Similar arrangements were made with the United States Rubber Company to ship tires to Union members at mail-order prices. In 1928 a feed-mixing plant was acquired

72. *Ibid.*

to prepare dairy rations, calf meal, pig meal, poultry feeds, and minerals which enabled the exchange to sell these feeds at wholesale prices, and in 1929 the exchange began the merchandising of seed.[73]

Union bulk-oil stations were first organized in the Northwest either in the fall of 1928 or in the spring of 1929. The first two bulk-oil associations were erected in Minot and Williston, North Dakota. To promote the interests of these oil companies, the Farmers' Union Petroleum Association of North Dakota was formed, and similar associations for Minnesota, Wisconsin, and Montana followed rapidly. In 1930 there were twenty-nine such Union stations in North Dakota and ten in Montana.[74]

The oil business had reached such dimensions by the summer of 1930 that it was considered advisable to set up a new Farmers' Union Central Exchange, Inc., under the cooperative laws of Minnesota and to disband the old Farmers' Union Exchange. Fortified with an advance of $75,000 from the Farmers' Union Terminal Association, a new exchange began to operate, with the business of no less than fifty local oil cooperatives. By the end of 1934, the sale of lubricating oils had been extended to more than two hundred affiliated cooperatives and the business operations of the exchange approached the million-dollar mark. By 1935, the Central Exchange had built its own compounding plant for lubricating oils.[75]

The business organizations set up by the Northwest Committee were subjected all the while to severe criticism by the Nebraska Union. The Farmers' Union Exchange was described as being non-farmer-controlled because not one of its three incorporators was a farmer. There was a provision in its articles of incorporation which stipulated that the corporation could begin business with ten shares of stock without nominal or par value. This, the *Nebraska Union Farmer* said, was a favorite trick of the "trusts," whose aim was to cover up their tracks and hide their profits. Also, it was argued that too much arbitrary power was vested in the board of directors and nothing was said in the articles of incorporation about the annual meetings of stockholders. Nor for that matter was anything said about the "one man, one vote" principle, the limiting of stock dividends, or the disbursal of patronage dividends. "This document does

73. Northwest Division, *The F.E.C.U. America,* pp. 24–29.

74. *Ibid.*

75. *Set-Up, History, Growth and Development, Farmers' Union Central Exchange, Inc.* (South St. Paul, Minn., 1936), pp. 4–5 [pamphlet].

not contain a single cooperative feature," wrote the *Nebraska Union Farmer*. "It is strictly an old line document, even more autocratic than the articles of incorporation of most joint-stock companies."[76]

In defending the incorporation of the Farmers' Union Central Exchange, and also of the Farmers' Union Publishing Company, both of which were incorporated under the laws of Delaware, the *Farmers' Union Herald* said that this was the simplest procedure to follow. The State of Delaware permitted a corporation to operate with a minimum of $1,000 capital, while many states required as much as $10,000. If the Farmers' Union Exchange had been organized under the cooperative law of Minnesota it would have been impossible for the Farmers' Union Terminal Association to be the owner of the exchange, because it was impossible for one cooperative to own another. It was possible, however, for a cooperative to own a corporation.[77]

In further defending its actions, the *Farmers' Union Herald* pointed out that the three incorporators had transferred their stock to the Farmers' Union Terminal Association on the same day that it was issued. Likewise, cooperation was permissible under the old corporation laws; the fact that a cooperative was not incorporated under the cooperative laws of a state did not necessarily mean that the cooperative spirit was lacking. Though this latter statement was true enough, it was hardly a satisfactory explanation for the long list of criticisms hurled against the Northwest business enterprises, both by Union and non-Union sources. Later, when all Union enterprises were organized under the necessary cooperative statutes, the basis for these complaints was removed.[78]

It is evident that despite the earlier "apostolic" and at times doctrinaire zeal of its leaders, the Union was by no means the radical organization that its language made it out to be. It sought, with a limited degree of success, to teach farmers that they could live within the capitalist system. The emotional and strongly phrased language employed in condemning the existing order was but a means used by the Union for selling itself to depressed farmers who did not respond to other appeals. This

76. *Nebraska Union Farmer,* March 13, 1929; J. W. Brinton, *Wheat and Politics* (Minneapolis, 1931), pp. 149–52.

77. *Farmers' Union Herald,* June, 1929; September, 1929; February 17, 1930; Ricker, *The Farmers' Union and Its Enemies,* pp. 9–11.

78. *Farmers' Union Herald,* May, 1928.

enabled it to enroll members in areas where other groups had failed. I 1934, it was observed that ". . . the Farmers' Union now has propertie running into the millions. In Nebraska its annual business is second onl to the Union Pacific Railroad. In North Dakota, its gasoline business i second only to the Standard Oil. Its executives are men whose keennes and intelligence would startle the urban dweller, accustomed to thin of the farmer as an economic illiterate."[79]

The Farmers' Union Central Exchange had built up a business, throug affiliated local cooperatives, which amounted by the end of the 1930's t almost $5,000,000 annually. Farmers' Union cooperatives could be devise by this time to meet almost any emergency. When the Farmers' Nationa Grain Corporation withdrew from active service on May 31, 1938, th Farmers' Union Terminal Association took over. Within a year after it organization, it had affiliated 83 new cooperative elevators, bringing th total of such subsidiaries up to 220. More than 250 locals marketed thei grain through this association. In 1940 it was pronounced the larges grain-marketing cooperative in the world.[80]

In spite of its rather considerable successes, the Farmers' Union itsel was never a well-integrated body. A national president once described i as "a loose federation of state organizations." As to type and function there were almost as many different patterns as there were state organizations. In Alabama the organization was principally one of sharecropper and tenant farmers; in Ohio it was composed of farm owners who di not belong to the Farm Bureau; while in California, although it wa mainly inactive, it participated through some of its members in the ultra-conservative Associated Farmers.[81]

The attitude of the Farmers' Union toward labor, with a few minor exceptions, was persistently friendly throughout this period. The Union expressed its gratification in 1937 because the national convention of the C.I.O. had endorsed the cost-of-production principle. Again in 1940, the Union thanked organized labor for the support which it had given to farm legislation. The Union asked farmers and workers to join hands

79. R. H. Peters, "The Farmer's Way to Recovery," *The Forum and Century,* XCI (April, 1934), p. 233.

80. U. S. Dept. Agri. Yearbook, *Farmers in a Changing World* (Washington, 1940), p. 955.

81. *Farmers' Union Herald,* January, 1941.

so "that the program affecting the common people of America shall be executed with Democratic and not with dictatorial bureaucratic and fascistic methods and controls."[82]

The continued aggressiveness of the Farmers' Union was well attested by the resolutions adopted by its national convention in 1937. At this meeting the delegates affirmed their belief that "we, as an organized group, must unite upon a militant program of action—that we must adopt a positive rather than a negative attitude toward the solution of problems confronting our industry." Unless a program of positive action should be adopted, "America will become the victims of fascism and dictatorship, the prey of war lords and munition makers; a shackled and Desecrated Ghost of Democracy." The farm problem was only a part of the larger economic problem which confronted the nation and which was bound to become more serious. "A profit system must be predicated upon the theory of scarcity, which necessitates controlled production and controlled distribution for the specific purpose of price-fixing." The sole hope for the maintenance and safeguarding of democracy was the building of "a system of cooperative business, owned by producers and consumers," that would strive for potential abundance for all, instead of "controlled production and controlled distribution for the specific purpose of price-fixing." To achieve these ends, the Union recapitulated its demands of previous years.[83]

Historically, the policy of the Union was to seek "cost of production." This was enunciated in convention after convention. In 1937, the national convention went on to say that "since the cooperative movement is of necessity slow in its growth, we, being practical people, recognize that we have an immediate problem; a problem which cannot wait for its solution upon the slow growth of the cooperative movement, a problem which society as a whole, expressed through the Congress, must temporarily solve through the medium of Legislative Enactment."[84]

82. Farmers' Cooperative and Educational Union of America, *National Legislative Program and Resolutions Adopted at the Thirty-third Annual Convention, November 16–18, 1937* [in Oklahoma City], pp. 3, 6–7.

83. *Ibid.*

84. *Ibid.*, p. 5. But it should be noted that in 1939 M. W. Thatcher, chairman of the insurgent Farmers' Union Legislative Committee in Washington, opposed this principle. Thatcher said that "cost of production" was "a grand idea—but it

Throughout the New Deal years, the northwest tier of states maintaine
a legislative committee in Washington under the leadership of Myron W
Thatcher, a keen student of the grain market and a lobbyist of no smal
stature. This was openly acknowledged as a sectional type of representa
tion, although as time elapsed, sentiment developed for the establishmen
of "a national Farmers' Union legislative fund" and the abandonmen
of this sectional representation. On the national scene, the Union claime
partial credit for the crop insurance scheme of 1933, through whic
A.A.A. benefit payments were paid on seeded acreage, and also for th
establishment of a drought-area cattle-buying fund in 1934, which covere
western Wisconsin, Minnesota, North Dakota, South Dakota, and easter
Montana. The Union helped save the Resettlement Administration i
1935 after the House had killed appropriations for its continuance; agai
that same year it fought to prohibit the sale of the farmers' stored grai
by private groups. It worked in 1936 for the Commodity Exchange Ac
and in 1938 for wheat crop insurance and the tenant purchase progra
under the Bankhead-Jones Act. It took responsibility in 1939 for cro
insurance premiums and for the ruling which permitted expanded fla
acreage without penalties. It was likewise instrumental in securing during
the years 1939–40 the transfer of the Farm Credit Administration to the
Department of Agriculture, the halting of foreclosure proceedings, and
the institution of generally more lenient policies toward debtors.[85]

---

would not work"; it would lead to inflation and higher living costs. "What the Farmers' Union wants is—parity!" M. W. Thatcher, *Pay Check for the Wheat Farmer, Crop or No Crop* (St. Paul, [1939]), pp. 22–23 [booklet].

85. *Farmers' Union Herald,* January, 1941.

Chapter IX

THE AMERICAN FARM BUREAU FEDERATION

THE RISE of the American Farm Bureau Federation in 1919 marked the entry into the agricultural scene of a farmers' organization that was strikingly different from and even hostile to the Nonpartisan League, the Farmers' Union, and the Equity. It was the most ambitious attempt ever made to organize the farmers of the country into a superorganization. The temper of the times reveals that the Bureau came into being for other reasons, however, than that of seeking to organize the farmers from the bottom up. The cooperative movement, as already observed, was thriving, and the need for coordinating the local units was great. The social and industrial unrest that followed in the wake of the war created alarm in many quarters. Most farmers in the country were not members of any general farm organization. (The Grange and the Farmers' Union were the only two farmer organizations of importance; the Equity was very weak, and while the Nonpartisan League was still strong, signs of decline were apparent to the shrewd observer.) Commercial and financial interests as well as government officials and educational leaders who saw the need for a strong farmer organization were unwilling to encourage any of the existing movements. They wanted a body that was conservative, stable, and better financed—organized along safe and sane lines and hence more in keeping with American tradition. The feeling was that this new superorganization could best be built around the county agents

Even though the Farm Bureau gained a large membership in oth parts of the country, its leadership and its legislative and economic d mands were just as reflective of the sentiments of the western Midd West as of those of any other section of the country, if not more so. It membership, its cooperative buying and selling associations, and its o ganizational activities in general, over the period from 1920 to 1933, we more permanent and numerous in Illinois, Iowa, and the adjoining stat than in most other areas. Bureau spokesmen from the western Midd West took a leading role in the McNary-Haugen movement of th twenties. Other evidences of this regional influence are shown in th facts that Chicago became and remained the headquarters of the nation organization and that two of the first three national presidents were fro Iowa and Illinois.[2]

The Farm Bureau can hardly be credited with originating the idea o federating existing farm groups into one major body. There were vario attempts at it, at least two major ones just before the American Far Bureau was organized—the Farmers' National Headquarters and th National Board of Farm Organizations. Neither of these originated i the western Middle West even though both sponsored legislation th had found great support there. But both, by trying to bring about federation of existing farm groups, were seeking to do for agricultur what the American Federation of Labor years ago had done for labo Also, by virtue of their being more or less a part of the progressive mov ment of the pre-World War I period, both found themselves complete out of step with the conservatism of the postwar era.

The Farmers' National Headquarters came into being in 1910, whe a number of state organizations "of progressive or radical tendencies

1. B. H. Hibbard, "American Farm Bureau Federation," *Encyclopaedia of th Social Sciences* (15 vols., New York, 1937), VII, 105–6; Orville M. Kile, *The Far Bureau Movement* (New York, 1921), pp. 54–93, 233–43; *Iowa Farm Burea Messenger* (Waterloo), February 7, 1920.

2. DeWitt C. Wing, "Trends in National Farm Organizations," U. S. Dept. Agr Yearbook, *Farmers in a Changing World* (Washington, 1940), pp. 963–64. For historical résumé of the most powerful of the state associations, see *The Illino Agricultural Association Record,* XIX (January, 1941) for an account of twenty-fiv years of activities. See also Ralph Russell, "Membership of the American Far Bureau Federation, 1926–1935," *Rural Sociology,* II (March, 1937), pp. 29–35.

net in Washington to establish a "temple of agriculture" to furnish "the itting representation of the great foundation industry of agriculture at he nation's capital." Since 1910 was a high-water mark in the campaign of the insurgents against the stalwart Republicans in Washington, it is conceivable that the organization of the Farmers' National Headquarters could have been part of this agitation. Also, one must not overlook the fact that the creation of a national headquarters in Washington was expected to bring about a program based on the demands of the farmers themselves rather than upon those groups who sought to "uplift" the farmers without consulting them. When the American Federation of Labor occupied its Labor Temple, the idea of a temple of agriculture in Washington gained popularity.

Once the Farmers' National Headquarters was established, an office was opened in Washington and the *Farmers' Open Forum* became the official paper of the body. Before the United States had entered the war, it had agitated for the establishment of a parcel post system, the direct election of United States senators, and the Federal Farm Loan Act. During and after the war, it favored government ownership and operation of the merchant marine, the railroads, and the natural resources of the nation. Obviously, it favored a program that differed radically from that which the American Farm Bureau Federation was to sponsor.[3]

A rival body, the National Board of Farm Organizations, was formally organized in Washington in 1917 to bring unity to the various farm groups, to promote and give publicity to matters of common interest to them, and also to build a "temple of agriculture" at a cost of $1,250,000.[4] According to one source, this board was expected to function after the fashion of the United States Chamber of Commerce and to be of some service to congressmen who had no good way of gauging farmer opinion. This board also had a program for affirmative action, but it was less militant than that of the Farmers' National Headquarters. It favored an amendment to the Clayton Anti-Trust Act to facilitate the attempts of farmers at "collective bargaining"; it favored the appointment of a practical farmer as secretary of agriculture; and it contemplated some action against government control of food prices. Though its claim would be

3. James E. Boyle, *Agricultural Economics* (Philadelphia, 1921), pp. 287–89.
4. *The New International Year Book*, 1919, p. 27.

hard to prove, it did say that it represented one-third of the farms of th country and that it had plans to create a fund of $8,500,000 to carry o its work.[5]

Precisely what happened to the National Board of Farm Organization is uncertain, but the fact is that it was completely obscured by the ris of the more aggressive American Farm Bureau Federation. The Burea sponsored a program that highly reflected the postwar reaction; it wa built upon well-organized county units and state federations, was muc better financed than any previous attempt to organize the farmers, em ployed methods that were used by business interests, and gave definit evidence of becoming one of the most powerful pressure groups that th country had ever known.

The fear of radicalism, industrial unrest, labor disturbances, and th prospects of a farmer-labor alignment, remote though it was, were fore most among the reasons for the formation of the national organization A long list of public statements, resolutions adopted in conventions, an printed material supports these fears of radicalism. For instance Henry J Sconce, president of the aggressive Illinois Agricultural Association—th farm bureau in Illinois—in his keynote address in the meeting in Chicag on November 12 and 13, 1919, described the first national meeting o the state farm bureaus as a timely one because of the need for taking actio against the industrial unrest that had been plaguing the nation since th armistice. "Is it any wonder," he asked, "that production has dwindled an the cost of living has so greatly increased? . . . It is our duty in creatin this organization to avoid any policy that will align organized farmer with the radicals of other organizations. The policy should be thoroughl American in every respect . . . a constructive organization instead of destructive organization."[6] Early in January, 1920, James R. Howard, th first president of the American Farm Bureau Federation, called attentio to the conflict between capital and labor and the need for organized agri culture to strike a balance of power between the two: ". . . Capital, whic is ever monopolistic in tendency and inclined to be oppressive, is oppose to an organized labor which is becoming very defiant and very domineer ing in its demands upon the general public. Apparently there is no hop

5. *Nation's Business,* VII (November, 1919), p. 17.
6. Kile, *The Farm Bureau Movement,* pp. 116–17.

that capital and labor will come to an amicable understanding without the intervention of some outside organization of sufficient power and influence to act as a balance wheel." "Patriotism," Howard said, "ought to be as vital a part of our existence today as when we were fighting the Huns. Patriotism should be taught in the schools, and the American flag should float over every school house in the country today as it did two or three years ago."[7] And he believed that a farmer-labor party was "an economic and political impossibility."[8]

Perhaps nothing aired the atmosphere that surrounded the Bureau better than did the resolutions enacted by it in 1919. They stated that "a large factor in the high cost of living is the curtailment of production through short hours, lessened efficiency of labor and strikes," placed the Bureau "unqualifiedly in sympathy with the government's determination to suppress radicalism," and offered the aid of the federation to the effort "to rid the country of Bolshevism and other anarchistic tendencies."[9] The state farm bureaus that assembled in Chicago on March 3 and 4, 1920, to ratify the work of the November meeting re-emphasized their "unwavering faith in and full support of the Constitution of the United States," denounced those "who have distressed and bewildered the country by ill-advised and un-American virtues and beliefs of the yesterdays," hailed the American Legion as "one of the most important factors in the life of America," assailed the Farmers' National Council as the ally of "the radical element of the industrial world," and condemned the lag in production brought about by strikes for shorter hours and better wages.[10] In 1921 President Howard again warned: "There is too much radicalism, or going off 'half-cocked', using a common vernacular, among farmers of this country."[11]

Even though the fear of a farmer-labor alignment haunted many leaders, there appears little to justify these apprehensions. The economic position of the average farmer militated against such a union. The farmer

7. *Iowa Farm Bureau Messenger,* February 7, 1920.

8. *Ibid.,* January, 1923.

9. American Farm Bureau Federation, *Resolutions of November 14, 1919, and March 4, 1920* (Chicago, 1920) [leaflet].

10. *What Is The American Farm Bureau Federation?* (Chicago, 1920) [pamphlet].

11. *Milwaukee Journal,* June 10, 1921.

was both a laborer and a capitalist. Because he performed menial tasks for long hours and small returns, Marxists, liberal politicians, labor leaders, and intellectuals assumed that the interests of the farmers and laborers were alike. But, as one farm economist wrote, ". . . these are scarcely comparable social groups." "The farmer is to be compared with the small business man of the city—the retail merchant; or with the city man with a profession—the small city lawyer, doctor, or teacher; or with the city man with a trade—the carpenter or plumber."[12] The Wisconsin Council of Agriculture carried this point a little further: "In addition to working long hours, he . . . the farmer . . . has a large investment in land, buildings, livestock, machinery, and other equipment. He is a business man carrying large inventories. He must take chances on the markets that gyrate with the weather and world-wide conditions. As an individual, he is the world's greatest producer of new wealth, under the most speculative conditions and on the narrowest margin."[13]

Besides the fact that the average farmer had a substantial amount of money invested in property, there also was his psychological attitude that militated against the formation of a farmer-labor coalition. Under normal conditions, the farmer felt superior to labor and often displayed an indifference toward it. He was likely to regard labor unionism as something with which his "capitalist brother" had to contend. His unfriendliness to "cults, and isms and new-fangled notions" made him suspicious of such "urban phenomena." During periods of low prices, as in the postwar depression, such differences transformed themselves into open hostility. At these times the farmer had no difficulty in detecting the means by which his interests conflicted with those of labor. He sensed a conflict arising from the buyer and seller relationship. Each group sought to buy the other's commodities at the lowest possible price and sell its own at the highest. Shorter working hours and higher wages meant higher living costs and higher production costs for the farmer. The fact that there was some relation between large labor incomes and large farm incomes did not necessarily interest him. In times of strikes the farmer could easily find his market affected adversely. Finally, "Manufacturers and middlemen,"

12. John D. Black, *Agricultural Reform in the United States* (New York, 1929), p. 49.

13. Wisconsin Council of Agriculture, "Farmer-Labor Relationship," *Hoard's Dairyman*, LXXXIII (June 10, 1939), p. 319.

as one student wrote, "have long drummed into his ears, that high industrial wages are the cause of the high prices he pays for his shoes, clothing, agricultural implements, and automobiles."[14]

Equally important as a factor in the growth of the American Farm Bureau Federation was the county-agent system, which played an important role in its organizing activities.[15] The county agent had been brought into existence by the Department of Agriculture chiefly for the purpose of teaching Texas cotton farmers how to combat the boll weevil.[16] Once his usefulness was demonstrated, the idea spread into the adjoining states. From there it spread into the North and West, where the problems that faced the farmers were different from those in the South. Here farming was more advanced and diversified. More farmers owned their farms. The problem of Negro tenancy was absent, and the most urgent needs were for more efficient methods of production and distribution. Livestock and fertility problems needed special attention. Incidentally, this is a good illustration of how movements originating in one section of the country came to a juncture with similar developments in another section.

Another agency to become involved with the county-agent movement and to play a pioneering role in the farm-bureau movement was the chamber of commerce of Binghamton, New York. On March 1, 1911, the chamber organized the first county farm bureau, a fact which the enemies of the organization never forgot.[17] Time and time again this was cited as evidence that the organization was dominated by the commercial and financial interests of the country.[18]

The Binghamton Chamber of Commerce was prompted to act partly by the report of the Country Life Commission, which had been appointed by President Theodore Roosevelt, and partly by the visit of

14. Ellen Sorge, "Farmer-Labor Relationships in Wisconsin" (unpublished term paper, University of Wisconsin, 1938), pp. 6–7.

15. Kile, *The Farm Bureau Movement*, pp. 71–93.

16. M. C. Burritt, *The County Agent and the Farm Bureau* (New York, 1922), pp. 153–54; Gladys Baker, *The County Agent* (Chicago, 1939), pp. 25–27; A. C. True, *A History of Agricultural Extension Work in the United States, 1789–1925*, U. S. Dept. Agri., Misc. Publication 15 (Washington, 1920), pp. 60–65.

17. Burritt, *The County Agent and the Farm Bureau*, pp. 155–61.

18. A typical example is that of Dale Kramer, *Truth About the Farm Bureau* (Minneapolis, 1937) [pamphlet].

Secretary of Agriculture James Wilson to southern New York, where he observed agricultural conditions and expressed concern over the rate at which farms in that locality were being abandoned. This caused the campaign to set up an agency to extend to the farmers the same opportunities that businessmen enjoyed. In its efforts the chamber got the aid of the Delaware, Lackawanna and Western Railroad. The road went so far as to plan a demonstration farm along its lines, but following an alternative proposal by W. J. Spillman of the United States Department of Agriculture, this plan was abandoned and a resident county agent hired instead. After a series of conferences, the Department of Agriculture and the railroad company agreed to finance the project, and the state college of agriculture was to "give advice and encouragement."[19]

The response of the farmers to the first agent was hardly encouraging. It was largely his personality and the aid of successful community leaders that enabled him to overcome the prejudice and indifference of the farmers. Many farmers had a hard time trying to figure out why the chamber of commerce should want to come to their aid; in fact, they had been told that such agencies usually "skinned" them. Besides, many felt that it was not better methods of production that they needed to know more about but how to get more money for what they produced.[20]

The pattern for organizing and financing the Binghamton County Farm Bureau was repeated by numerous other groups in the western Middle West, as well as in other parts of the country. Some states like Minnesota, North Dakota, Wisconsin, and Illinois passed legislation allowing county supervisors affiliated with the county farm bureaus or with the development associations formed by certain business groups to raise money to be used by these organizations. But before county funds would become accessible, certain local funds had to be raised. In general, this procedure was followed: a meeting of businessmen and prominent farmers of the county was called. An association would be formed, either independently or under the auspices of the commercial club or chamber of commerce. Members were charged a nominal fee. Additional funds came from bankers, railroads, and other business groups interested in the agricultural development of the county. This, plus financial aid from the

19. Burritt, *The County Agent and the Farm Bureau,* pp. 160–61.
20. *Ibid.,* p. 162.

United States Department of Agriculture, provided "a comprehensive plan for financing such an organization."[21]

One of the earliest such programs to be launched in the western Middle West was that of the Better Farming Association of North Dakota.[22] It came about because the efforts of Seaman A. Knapp in the South had impressed certain business leaders in North Dakota who were anxious to develop a similar program in their state. The association began its operations in the state on November 15, 1911. During the year ending November 30, 1912, the association had received more than $52,000 from counties, districts, railroads, wholesale houses, and the North Dakota Bankers' Association. Shortly, the agricultural college supplanted the Better Farming Association in the supervision of the work, but the general plan was retained.[23]

The Better Farming Association of North Dakota also had much to do with the beginning of county-agent work in Minnesota. The West Central Development Association gave much support to the movement. Donations of various sizes came from bankers, businessmen, farmers, the Office of Farm Management in the United States Department of Agriculture, and the Minnesota Farm Institute. The large part played by the business interests of Minnesota and North Dakota caused many farmers to become openly hostile to it, and the Equity was an outspoken critic.[24]

Obviously, the railroads and bankers financing county-agent work were prompted by ulterior as well as altruistic motives. Many railroads operated miles of lines through areas which they were anxious to develop. Besides encouraging settlers to purchase their lands, they conducted demonstration farms, staged cooperative experiments, employed agricultural experts to advise farmers, and published and distributed literature.

Commercial institutions depending on agriculture also made generous contributions to demonstration work. Among the greatest contributors were Sears, Roebuck and Company, the International Harvester Com-

21. Robert H. Moulton, "Revolutionizing Farm Methods," *Outlook*, CXII (October 26, 1916), pp. 993–96.

22. F. P. Stockbridge, "North Dakota Man Crop: the Work of Tom Cooper," *World's Work*, XXV (November, 1912), pp. 84–93.

23. True, *A History of Agricultural Extension Work*, pp. 75–76, 85–86.

24. *Ibid.*, pp. 92–93; *Coöperators' Herald* (Fargo, N. Dak.), I (June 12, 1914), pp. 1, 3.

pany, and the Chicago Board of Trade. Sears, Roebuck and Company, the Chicago mail-order house, provided $1,000,000 for experts to advise and demonstrate in a hundred counties throughout the United States, and the International Harvester Company is said to have earmarked another million to be spent in agricultural extension work under the supervision of Professor P. G. Holden, formerly of Iowa State College. The Chicago Board of Trade also reportedly set aside $1,000,000 for the improvement of agricultural methods through a system of county agents.[25]

The federal government probably would have been slower in extending financial help had it not been for the earlier efforts of the mercantile firms, the chambers of commerce, and the railroads. The passage of the Smith-Lever Act in 1914 committed the federal government to the aid of the county agents. Money provided by the federal government was to be matched by state grants and spent and administered through the state agricultural colleges.[26] By 1917, a strong extension program had been worked out in nearly every state.

When the United States entered the first World War, the demand for food and the need for manpower placed heavy responsibilities on the agents to increase production and conserve food. Many new "emergency agents" were appointed. Crop and livestock production was stepped up; seeds and tractors were obtained for farmers; farm labor was supplied; new county farm bureaus were created. By 1918, the county farm bureaus had made rapid strides in the North and West.[27]

Once the value of the county agent had been established, the need for federating these county units into state organizations became obvious. The forming of state bodies was expected to coordinate the work of the county organizations, to enable them to discuss their mutual problems, to profit from the experiences of one another, and to give the farmers "a power and influence in state and nation commensurate with the importance of agriculture. . . ." State farm bureaus had been organized before the entrance of the United States into World War I. The Missouri Farm Bureau, organized in March, 1915, was the first state organization. By the fall of 1918, they had been formed in ten or twelve states, and after

25. *The New International Year Book*, 1912, p. 20.

26. Burritt, *The County Agent and the Farm Bureau*, pp. 169–70; True, *A History of Agricultural Extension Work*, pp. 100–15.

27. *Ibid.*, p. 134.

the American Farm Bureau Federation was organized, the state farm bureau movement received even greater stimulus.[28]

Also important as a factor in contributing to the rise of the American Farm Bureau Federation was the mounting strength of the cooperative movement. Many cooperative grain elevators and livestock groups of a local character had made their appearance over the period from 1895 to 1920. In Wisconsin, Minnesota, and Iowa local cooperative grain- and livestock-marketing associations had originated through the efforts of the Equity and numerous independent groups. The Equity Cooperative Exchange had gone to the extent of building a chain of eighty local elevators to feed its terminal marketing agency in South St. Paul, and later opened livestock-marketing firms there and in Chicago. In Nebraska and Kansas the Farmers' Union had laid the foundations for some of the most extensive marketing associations in existence. In Missouri, the Missouri Farmers' Association, under the leadership of William Hirth, was building a formidable array of firms, with a total membership put at 34,242. Throughout the western Middle West the Farmers' National Grain Dealers Association was striving to federate the service and educational activities of local grain cooperatives. The state farm bureaus also sought to coordinate the local agencies.[29]

In their first meeting the farm bureaus of the Middle West made known their intentions to use the newly formed federation as a means for solving the marketing problems of the farmers on a national cooperative-marketing basis. But they encountered opposition to this aim. Representatives from southern, eastern, and western states favored an educational program rather than one "designed specifically to bring about improved business and economic conditions." On the convention floor the advocates of a

28. Burritt, *The County Agent and the Farm Bureau,* pp. 233–35.

29. Henry H. Bakken and Marvin A. Schaars, *The Economics of Cooperative Marketing* (New York, 1937), p. 67; Edwin G. Nourse and Joseph G. Knapp, *The Co-Operative Marketing of Livestock* (Washington, 1931), pp. 12–17; H. B. Price, ed., *The Marketing of Farm Products* (Minneapolis, 1927), p. 100; Stuart Blythe, "Is Kansas the Greatest Cooperative State?" *Country Gentleman,* LXXXV (September 11, 1920), pp. 13, 48; Maurice H. Weseen, "The Co-operative Movement in Nebraska," *Journal of Political Economy,* XXVIII (June, 1920), pp. 477–98; *Missouri Farmer* (Columbia), XII (September 15, 1920), p. 20; *Cooperative Marketing* (70 Congress, 1 session, Senate Document 95, serial 8859, Washington, 1928), pp. 60–61; Kile, *The Farm Bureau Movement,* p. 115.

strong educational program expressed fear over the launching of this program of "radical commercialism," while the supporters of the co-operative-marketing proposal feared that the easterners would combine with other sections of the country to block "the things which the Midwest thought most essential to the economic readjustment of agriculture." Henry C. Wallace, editor of *Wallaces' Farmer,* voiced the sentiments of the western Middle West when he said, "This federation must not degenerate into an educational or social institution. It must be made the most powerful business institution in the country."[30]

Despite the existence of older farm organizations such as the Grange, the Farmers' Union, the Equity, the Missouri Farmers' Association, and numerous independent commodity groups, not to mention the Non-partisan League, the fact remains that the bulk of the farmers of the nation were not members of a general farm organization. Except for the Grangers, the combined membership of the others, substantial though it might have been, was hardly impressive. The Farmers' Union had passed the peak of its power, as had the Equity, which never was a strong organization. The Missouri Farmers' Association was strictly a state body, and before too great an elapse of time, the League was to be on the brink of disaster.[31] Equally important was the fact that the Bureau appealed to the type of member that could hardly have been receptive, for a very long period at least, to the type of program sponsored by the Farmers' Union, the Equity, or the League.

Meanwhile, sentiment had been shaping for the formation of a national organization. Early in 1919 S. L. Strivings, the president of the New York Farm Bureau Federation, called a meeting of state farm bureaus to meet in Ithaca, New York, on February 12 for the purpose of providing the nation "with some sane organization thoroughly representative of agriculture" and to take advantage of the farm bureau movement, which offered the greatest possibilities in developing a program to reach the farmers of the country. The meeting was held and a committee was selected to outline the best methods for bringing the national organiza-

30. *Ibid.,* p. 123.

31. Edward Wiest, *Agricultural Organization in the United States* (Lexington, Ky., 1923), pp. 398, 476–78; *Missouri Farmer,* XII (September 15, 1920), p. 20; see also Chapter VII, pp. 194–218.

tion into existence. Finally, arrangements were made to hold a meeting in Chicago on November 12 and 13, 1919.[32]

The November meeting brought to the surface differences over policies to be adopted. There were present some 500 delegates from thirty-six states. Of these 220 were from Illinois, 32 from Iowa, 16 from Indiana, and anywhere from 1 to 8 representing each of the other states. The issues included matters of representation, finances, the name to be adopted, and whether the organization was going to be commercial and legislative or strictly educational in character.

Perhaps most easily settled was the question of the name. While the Illinois delegates proposed that the organization be called the National Farmers' Association, it was the name American Farm Bureau Federation that was finally adopted.[33]

A considerably thornier problem, however, revolved about the matter of whether the policy of the newly formed group was to be commercial and legislative or exclusively educational. Harvey J. Sconce, the president of the Illinois Agricultural Association, stressed the lurking dangers of radicalism and the need for better farm management and more efficient methods of distribution. S. L. Strivings of New York pointed to the divergent agricultural interests of the farmers, which made it difficult for them to be coordinated into a national body, and asked that special consideration be given to the building of a structure that would help stabilize the nation and promote loyalty and sanity.[34] James R. Howard, the president of the Iowa Farm Bureau and later of the national federation, believed that the differences of the agricultural interests of the nation were superficial at best and that the need of the farmers was for an organization that struck out from the shoulder. In the end the views of the western Middle West generally prevailed. According to the preamble, the object of the organization was "to correlate and strengthen the farm bureaus of the several states and to promote, protect and represent the business, social, economic, and educational interests of the farmers of the nation."[35]

32. True, *A History of Agricultural Extension Work,* p. 160; Kile, *The Farm Bureau Movement,* p. 113.

33. True, *A History of Agricultural Extension Work,* p. 161.

34. Kile, *The Farm Bureau Movement,* pp. 116–18.

35. *Chicago Daily Tribune,* November 14, 1919.

The issue of representation also was a touchy one. The voting strength of the various sections was always taken into account when an important question arose. The Middle West had more members present, but the other states had more votes. After much discussion the question of representation was settled by allowing one director for each state and an additional director for each additional twenty thousand members.

Equally delicate was the matter of finances. Those who favored a strong business program sought large fees and a large budget. Illinois, for instance, wanted "a financial program that would insure success." A Kentucky delegate said: "Kentucky is not here to support any penny-wise-and-pound-foolish policy. The national work is of a magnitude and scope that requires money. We do not want any ten cent policy. . . ." Those who wanted an educational organization opposed large fees on the ground that they would be a constant temptation to launch commercial enterprises. A California delegate declared that too much "vision" and "too much money" wrecked farmer organizations.

Events came to a climax when it appeared that the Illinois delegates were going to bolt the convention and form a midwestern organization, and a compromise was reached on finances as well as on representation. A temporary organization was also set up with James R. Howard serving as president, and the final plans for launching the organization were deferred until after the ratification meeting of March 3 and 4, 1920.[36]

The resolutions adopted by the November convention, though distinctly conservative, were a fair reflection of the attitudes of farmers on issues of state and national policy. The convention declared its "independence of affiliation with any commercial, labor, or industrial organization," and expressed a "cooperative attitude toward all movements promoting the welfare of the American institutions." It was pointed out that farmers' profits came from the "unrestored fertility taken from the soil," from the long hours of labor and the "unpaid labor of women and children," which were "legitimate factors" in determining the cost of production and facts which the nonfarmers had to take into account when they considered agricultural policy. A short-lived endorsement was that farmers were entitled to a just profit based on cost of production. The system of tenancy that was rapidly fastening itself on the farmers of the nation

36. Kile, *The Farm Bureau Movement*, pp. 119–20.

was condemned. The rights of every class of people to organize for its material benefit and of every American citizen "to the free and unhampered privilege of disposing of his labor or products thereof as he may individually require" were upheld. Relief from monopoly was also asked for; this, it was said, could be had through the "enforced publicity" of the business records of corporations and the adoption of a "just graduated income tax law" rather than by an undue interference with economic laws.

The convention would hardly have been complete without the adoption of resolutions. The policy of the government in protecting the public through "regulative legislation" was approved. Regulation was asked for "all purveyors of foodstuffs" in a manner that would be fair to the producer, the consumers, and industry alike. Government ownership of public utilities was opposed, and a demand was made for the return of the railroads to private control. Economy in public expenditures was demanded, as was the incorporation under federal charter of all corporations doing interstate business; likewise, incorporation in the state in which their principal business was located was asked of all other corporations. A request was made for an increase in the maximum loan obtainable by farmers through the Federal Land Banks. The agricultural extension agents were praised, and the American Legion was extolled because of its efforts to rehabilitate returning veterans. Also, in the Legion the federation saw "a soldier citizenry for law and order, a guarantee that civil and religious liberty shall be maintained in the land." The returning soldiers were welcomed with the statement that "no gift of the people is too good for them." Again, a firm stand was taken against radicalism, and the aid of the government was asked in preventing such outrages "against the Flag and the Citizens" as those committed in Centralia, Washington, in the heart of the lumber country, where a parade of overseas veterans was fired upon from an I.W.W. hall, four men being killed in the episode.

When the November convention adjourned there were feelings of disappointment among the representatives from the western Middle West. The *Prairie Farmer* reflected this in saying: "Instead of being born of the enthusiastic vision of big service to the business of American agriculture with which many of the delegates were inspired . . . [the bureau] was born of the suspicion and conservatism which others brought to the meeting." Nevertheless, it was conceded that an organization was born and that many of the imperfections about which the delegates from the western Middle West complained would be removed by March.

When the March meeting assembled, the delegates from the other sections of the country had come closer to the views of the delegates from the western Middle West. Sentiment for cooperative marketing had gained considerable ground. Also, the convention agreed that each state should pay into the national treasury fifty cents for each member enrolled in a county farm bureau. Twenty-eight states ratified the constitution that gave to the national organization $200,000, minus the expenses contracted before March 3, with which to begin operations. Two of the three most prominent officers elected were from the western Middle West—James R. Howard of Iowa, president, and John W. Cloverdale, also of Iowa, secretary. Gray Silver of West Virginia became the Washington representative.[37] In effect, the farm bureaus from the western Middle West scored impressive triumphs in matters of policy, finances, and election of officers.

The resolutions adopted in March were substantially the same as those of November, with the exception that the demand for "cost of production" had been replaced with the plea for a tariff to give to agriculture "equal consideration with other industries."[38]

If there were any doubts about the influence of prominent commercial and financial interests on the organization of the American Farm Bureau Federation, there definitely were none when it came to the methods that were employed by it, the salaries it paid, the publicity releases it issued, and the legislative pressure it exerted.

Early in 1920, a department of organization came into existence to help the state farm bureaus launch membership drives. Special field men were also employed to tend to particular organizing problems whenever they presented themselves.[39]

37. American Farm Bureau Federation, *Resolutions of November 14, 1919, and March 4, 1920.*

38. B. H. Hibbard, *Marketing Agricultural Products* (New York, 1921), pp. 263–64.

39. American Farm Bureau Federation, *Report of the Executive Secretary to the Third Annual Meeting, Atlanta, Georgia, November 21–23,* 1921, pp. 8, 13.

Distinctly businesslike was the creation of the department of information to keep the general public "sympathetically informed" about the Farm Bureau. This department kept "the closest possible co-operative relationship" with the publicity departments of the state federations. The latter, in turn, were expected to localize the publicity materials coming from the national headquarters and to build up efficient publicity departments.

The department of information was divided into various divisions with special duties to perform. The news service, one of the subdivisions, issued the *Weekly News Letter,* which summarized the work of the federation. In addition, the *Weekly News Bulletin* was issued to the agricultural press and to weekly publications in those territories in which the state federations did not have publicity directors. News releases were issued several times each week to the Associated Press, the United Press, the International News Service, the Universal News Service, the Newspaper Enterprise Association, Scripps-McRae, and the Publishers' Autocaster Service Company. The editorial service, another subdivision, assembled information and collected figures of interest to editorial writers on agricultural problems. The feature service furnished and distributed to magazines, newspapers, and county farm bureaus special articles written by Bureau leaders. A publishing department printed pamphlets, reports, and other publications of the federation. A project was also undertaken to publish, through a reputable publishing firm, a series of Farm Bureau books. A farm films service, indeed novel for those days, was established through an arrangement with the Illinois Agricultural Association to take advantage of motion pictures as an educational medium. Upon failing to obtain bona fide farm films from established firms, a Farm Bureau motion picture division was established. Complete information on this novel experiment is lacking, but it is known that a number of pictures, a series of newsreels and animated cartoons were produced.[40]

The department of cooperation was charged with the study of cooperative methods both here and abroad, with a view toward evolving standard forms and procedures for cooperative agencies. This department worked closely with the Farmers' Grain Marketing Committee of Seventeen, the Livestock Marketing Committee of Fifteen, the Farmers' Dairy Commit-

40. *Ibid.,* pp. 9, 37–38.

tee of Eleven, the Wool Growers' Committee, the Sugar Beet Growers' Committee, and other commodity groups appointed from time to time. One of the big objectives of the department of cooperation was to unite the local commodity cooperatives into a national marketing program.[41]

Other divisions included the legal and transportation department, the financial department, and legislative department. The first sought to better the quality of service furnished by the railroads to the farmers, to prevent excessive freight rates, to study the problems of railroad regulation, and to obtain a better allocation of freight cars for the farmers. The second collected dues, made settlements with the state federations, and tended to the usual routine of bookkeeping and accounting. Extremely important, and by no means to be minimized, were the activities of the legislative department in Washington. This office kept in touch with legislative matters, compiled statistics and information on legislation that affected agriculture, and arranged for hearings on bills affecting farmers' interests.[42]

Likewise, far more typical of the methods of large business than of the general run of farm organizations were the salaries paid to the officials and the budget appropriations made. The salary of President James Howard was placed first at $15,000 and later at $12,500; that of the vice-president was fixed at $25 per day and expenses while working for the Bureau. The secretary and the Washington representative drew at first $12,000 and then $10,000 a year. For 1920, the national body was reported to have had funds amounting to about $200,000.[43]

The growth of its membership in 1920 and 1921 was meteoric. On March 4, 1920, the national organization claimed a membership of 456,000, with twenty-eight affiliated state federations. On June 1, 1921, the membership was 1,052,114 and the states belonging to the national organization totaled forty-three. About half a dozen states—Iowa, Illinois, Ohio, Texas, Michigan, and Indiana—claimed more than half the membership. Of these six states, the membership of the first two was to remain consistently large.[44]

41. *Ibid.*, p. 9.

42. *Ibid.*, pp. 9–10.

43. R. P. Crawford, "The Farmer Organizes," *American Review of Reviews*, LXI (June, 1920), pp. 632–34.

44. *American Farm Bureau Federation Weekly News Letter*, June 2, 1921; Russell, in *Rural Sociology*, II (March, 1937), p. 33.

Bureau members, the rank and file, were hardly the land moguls that their enemies made them out to be. Common sense would tell anyone that the claim that the membership of the American Farm Bureau Federation in 1921—well over a million—consisted mostly of large landowners was ridiculous. There never were that many large landowners in the country; and if there had been, the chances are that they would have known better than to organize on such a basis.

These charges were popularized by those who either had nothing but contempt for the conservative leadership or were unaware of or indifferent to the fact that the average American farmer was conservative. Bureau leadership was far more representative of the American farmer than its left-wing critics cared to admit. They would have been far nearer the truth had they said that the Bureau did not have as many substantial farmers belonging to it as did the Grange, but that it had far more than did other groups. But even this was a far cry from its being an organization of and by large landowners and farmers.[45]

No doubt there is much truth, however, to the charge that the Bureau had admitted into membership many who had had "no sympathy with the working farmer and his problems. Men with political ambitions who happen to own some land, conservative men of wealth whose money is mainly invested in farm property and professional men of the extension-worker type have seized important positions in the organization and have to some extent dictated its policies."[46]

Cooperative marketing, and to a lesser degree cooperative purchasing, always formed a prominent part of Bureau activities. This was especially true during the period from 1920 to 1924, when cooperatives were looked upon by the Bureau as the big hope of the farmer. After that time the Bureau veered off in the direction of McNary-Haugenism and the equalization-fee principle, but even so, it never failed to encourage the cooperative movement.[47]

The concern of the American Farm Bureau Federation with large-scale marketing began to take concrete form early in 1920 with the appointment of marketing committees. Three of these stood out: the Farmers'

45. Hibbard, in *Encyclopaedia of the Social Sciences,* VII, 106.
46. *Iowa Farm Bureau Messenger,* January 1, 1924.
47. Wing, in *Farmers in a Changing World,* pp. 964–65.

Grain Marketing Committee of Seventeen, the Farmers' Livestock Marketing Committee of Fifteen, and the Farmers' Dairy Committee of Eleven. The first two were the most important.[48]

Grain marketing was first on the agenda. President Howard called a conference of grain growers to meet in Chicago on July 23, 1920, to erect more efficient marketing machinery. About five hundred delegates representing state farm bureaus, the Grange, the Farmers' Union, the Equity, the United States Department of Agriculture, and numerous other agencies responded.[49] A more trying period for the launching of a grain-marketing program could hardly have been selected. Farm prices had already started to fall; freight rates were high; industrial production had started to lag; labor costs were very burdensome; and the governmental guarantee on wheat and other commodities had been removed. The task was a Herculean one.[50]

Besides the gathering clouds of depression, there were problems of an internal nature with which the marketing conference had to deal. Various groups that were represented were hesitant about losing their individuality, while others with their own plans for large-scale grain-marketing associations did not want them jeopardized. For example, the Nebraska Farmers' Union, because of its success in cooperative marketing, wanted "preferential treatment." So did the Equity Cooperative Exchange, with its string of grain elevators throughout the agricultural Northwest and its terminal marketing facilities, and the Missouri Farmers' Association, which was destined to become the largest independent state farmers' organization in the country, and the Farmers' National Grain Dealers Association, which served as the coordinating, educational, and service agency for state associations throughout the western Middle West. When President Howard denied the National Board of Farm Organizations, representing largely the Farmers' Union, with Charles Barrett as its chairman, the right to name half of the marketing committee, it bolted the conference.

48. Kile, *The Farm Bureau Movement,* pp. 148–64, 165–66.

49. *Ibid.,* pp. 149–50.

50. Report of the Joint Commission of Agricultural Inquiry, *The Agricultural Crisis and Its Causes,* Part I (67 Congress, 1 session, House Report 408, serial 7922, 4 parts, Washington, 1921–22), pp. 61–62; see Table E–2 for the relative wholesale prices of groups of commodities and of specific commodities, by months, 1919–21. *Ibid.,* pp. 180–82, 224; U. S. Dept. Agri., *Yearbook,* 1921, pp. 2–13.

Besides these rival ambitions, there were conflicting views regarding the course that the national marketing program should take. Some wanted an arbitrary price-fixing program based on the principle of "cost of production plus a reasonable profit." Others sought the abolition of private grain exchanges and the building of public warehouses to serve public needs. Still others had only hazy conceptions of the principles of cooperative marketing.

By far the most popular demand was for cooperative marketing. The representatives of the Farmers' Grain Dealers Association expressed their satisfaction with the local cooperative marketing association, and asked that more progress be made along these lines. Taking direct control of the marketing function, it was felt, would hardly increase materially the profits of the producers. It was argued that, because of the volume handled, greater savings could be realized through better handling, shipping, marketing, weighing, grading, cleaning, drying, and selling methods.[51]

More radical was the marketing plan of Aaron Sapiro. He favored fastening monopolistic control over the wheat crop, a plan that he had been working on since his entry into the legal profession. Before his ties with the American Farm Bureau Federation, he had been building up a reputation as a cooperative-marketing authority in California. His plan operated from a legalistic base. Farmers who raised a particular crop were to form an association and pool their crops; the pooling member was to bind himself by contract to deliver his products to the association for a period of years, usually five.[52]

Sapiro was undoubtedly influenced by Harris Weinstock, the director of the California State Marketing Commission, to whom he was related by marriage. Weinstock had hopes of integrating the marketing activities of the California producers into a single marketing agency. He, in turn, was influenced by David Lubin, his half-brother and business partner for many years and also the founder of the International Institute of Agriculture in Rome. Weinstock had been to Europe in 1913 as a member of the American commission that visited Europe to study cooperation and agricultural credit and had even formulated a plan to establish "a national

51. Kile, *The Farm Bureau Movement,* pp. 149–51; H. C. Filley, *Cooperation in Agriculture* (New York, 1929), p. 148.

52. *Ibid.,* p. 149; Kile, *The Farm Bureau Movement,* pp. 150–51.

marketing commission with state and local organizations for disseminat ing information and stabilizing the movement of produce. . . ."

Sapiro often discussed the marketing problems of the farmers wit both Weinstock and Lubin. He had served as counsel for the Californi State Marketing Commission. As counsel, he took the records of th California cooperatives and analyzed them. He selected those features o the cooperatives which he believed were responsible for success an devised his model plan, also known as the California plan.[53] This is wha he brought before the Chicago grain-marketing conference in July, 192

Sapiro repeatedly emphasized the point that if it was to succeed, th marketing association to be formed had to gain title to most of the whea in the country. "You won't start this thing unless you have 51 per cen of the wheat in the nine most important wheat states tied up under thi system. When you get 51 per cent of the nine most important wheat state tied up you can go ahead and nothing can stop you." The convention di not adopt his entire program, but there were many who subscribed to i as later events proved.

There were other phases to this Sapiro plan, none of which were orig inal with him. The association had to devote itself exclusively to busines and to the principle of "one man, one vote." Directors were to be electe by districts. Payments for crops were to be made from a pool, so tha growers of like quantity, kind, grade, and quality would get the sam price. The association had to be in a position to finance the farmer a harvest time, when he needed credit the most, and was "not to star operations before a set minimum of business is assured, so it will hav enough of a given crop to be able to meet necessary overhead, without to great a burden on any one bushel, etc." The contracts with the member provided a penalty for those who did not deliver the pledged crop. Abov all, the organization had to "hire the best men possible to run the associa tion; expert sellers to do the selling, railroad men to handle the traffi problems, lawyers to do the legal work, and bankers to look after th finances."

Merchandising methods were hardly overlooked. Crops had to b graded and packed to attract the consumer. Advertising methods had t

53. Edwin G. Nourse, *The Legal Status of Agricultural Cooperation* (New York 1928), pp. 94–95.

be used to find new markets. The flow of products to market had to be regulated in order to make the supply equal the demand. Individual selling was to be avoided, and products were to be sold at the point of consumption rather than at the point of production.[54]

After two days of discussion, the conference advised President Howard to select a committee which was not to exceed seventeen members to investigate grain marketing and to form plans for cooperative grain marketing through one or more central organizations of grain exchanges. The selection of the committee was from more than 150 available men, the overwhelming majority of whom came from the states of the western Middle West. Some of the men appointed to the committee had a practical knowledge of cooperative grain marketing; unfortunately, a few could hardly "distinguish between things which were practical and those which were only spectacular."[55]

The committee spent nearly seven months studying marketing. Visits were made to Canada to study the activities of the United Grain Growers, Limited, and to California, where the citrus fruit industry had built a successful marketing system. The best-informed men in the grain trade, both those opposed to cooperative marketing and those favorable to it, were interviewed. Among those consulted were Julius Barnes, grain exporter and head of the United States Grain Corporation during the World War; Bernard M. Baruch, New York financier and chairman of the War Industries Board; Leslie F. Gates, president of the Chicago Board of Trade; G. Harold Powell, manager of the California Fruit Growers' Exchange; and Huston Thompson, chairman of the Federal Trade Commission.

A marketing plan was finally agreed upon in a meeting held in Kansas City on February 17, 1921. The next step was to explain the plan to the various farm groups and to have them elect delegates for a convention to be held in Chicago on April 6, 1921.

The recommendations made at the April 6 meeting were nothing more than a résumé of past demands. The old grievances against the marketing system and the organized grain trade were repeated. It was

54. Aaron Sapiro, *Co-Operative Grain Marketing* (Chicago, 1920) [a pamphlet published by the Illinois Agricultural Association; it has in it the address delivered by Sapiro before the Chicago conference of July 23 and 24, 1920].

55. Filley, *Cooperation in Agriculture*, p. 150.

reported that 72 per cent of the wheat coming onto the market wa
marketed within ninety days after it was harvested. It was hoped tha
the farmers, through their marketing agencies, would mix, regrade, an
condition grain, because these were profitable operations and ones fron
which the farmers would benefit. The need for a system of unbiase
crop reporting, more direct sales, and more efficient use of transportatio
and warehousing facilities was emphasized. The boards of trade an
chambers of commerce came in for serious criticism because they denie
membership to cooperatives on the pretext that patronage dividends is
sued by cooperatives were rebates, and congressional legislation grantin
cooperatives membership in these agencies was accordingly requested

The organization that the committee recommended to be establishe
was the United States Grain Growers, Incorporated, a nonstock, nonprofi
association made up exclusively of grain growers. Each member had t
pay a ten-dollar fee and sign a contract to sell his grain through th
national agency for a period of five years. Existing local cooperative
were to be used wherever they were operating, and new ones were to b
organized when needed. The United States Grain Growers was to provid
the terminal and warehouse facilities, a finance and export corporation
and a market news service. The types of contract to be used were twofold
one between the grower and the local agency, and the other between th
local agency and the national body. The members could sell their grai
individually through their local association for cash, by consignmen
to the national agency, or by taking advantage of any of the pooling
methods that existed. Penalties were provided for those who failed t
deliver their products as provided by the contract; defaulting whea
growers were to be assessed ten cents a bushel, refractory flax grower
twenty cents, and other types of producers six cents a bushel.[56]

The greatest dispute centered about the pooling issue. Those wh
wanted a compulsory pool argued that unless the control of all grai
was put into the hands of the sales agency, the benefits would be negli
gible. C. V. Gregory, editor of the *Prairie Farmer,* was a strong supporte
of the compulsory pool, as were the hard-pressed farmers of the agricul
tural Northwest. Its opponents insisted that the general public woul
react unfavorably to a compulsory pool on the grounds that it would b

56. Kile, *The Farm Bureau Movement,* pp. 153–64.

a monopoly. Clifford Thorne, the general counsel of the Farmers' National Grain Dealers Association, questioned the legality of the compulsory pool and expressed the belief that the courts could easily consider this a case of restraint of trade. It was also feared that the farmers would not be inclined to compulsory pooling. The issue was settled by a vote of 61 to 38 against the compulsory pool, which was in line with the views of the more conservative members of the Committee of Seventeen.[57]

Once the grain-marketing conference of July 23 and 24 was provided for, plans were also made for a similar meeting of livestock producers. The latter met in Chicago on October 8, 1920, after a call had been sent out by President Howard to the Farmers' Union, the Equity, the Grange, the state farm bureaus, independent livestock-shipping associations, and other interested groups. As a result of this conference, Howard was authorized to appoint a Committee of Fifteen to consider all phases of cooperative livestock marketing. On January 3, 1921, the personnel of the Livestock Marketing Committee of Fifteen was announced.

This committee had on it several members of general farm organizations, but the majority of them were either chiefly interested in livestock production or in animal-husbandry work in agricultural colleges. The committee met in Chicago on February 23, 1921, and elected C. H. Gustafson of Omaha as its chairman and H. W. Mumford of the University of Illinois as its secretary-treasurer. The object of the committee, according to Gustafson, was to "get the livestock business back on a sound basis and keep it there." Emphasis was to be placed on better prices and "orderly marketing."

The committee labored for six months and announced its tentative plan in mid-August. Later the plan was presented to the ratification conference held in Chicago on November 10 and 11. Fifty-three delegates from fifteen states assembled at this meeting, most of them from the Farm Bureau, with a considerable representation of delegates from shippers' and feeders' organizations.

As in other Farm Bureau meetings, sectional grievances came to the surface, and again the views of the representatives of the western Middle

57. *American Co-operative Journal* (Chicago), XVI (April, 1921), p. 4; *ibid.*, (June, 1921), p. 4; *North Dakota Leader* (Fargo), May 21, 1921; Filley, *Cooperation in Agriculture*, p. 156.

West prevailed. Those from the range states called the committee's plan a "Corn Belt scheme" that hardly fitted their requirements. Their industry was in a bad state, and they needed immediate relief. Livestock-shipping associations and better marketing machinery were not what they wanted. The majority of the members of this conference were from the corn-hog area, however, and therefore the National Producers' plan, designed primarily for the hog market, went into effect. It called for a system of terminal livestock commission associations with a central administrative organization, the livestock commission associations to be supplied by producing members bound together through local cooperative shipping associations.

There were two other points of controversy: the relation of the newly organized system to existing livestock-marketing associations, and also its relation to the general farm organizations. Opponents of the committee's plan insisted that the organization should grow from the bottom up and not from the top down, as had been recommended. But supporters of the plan replied that their marketing machinery was going to be built around the individual farmer, and their views were sustained by a margin of 28 to 22, chiefly because of the votes of Farm Bureau delegates from Indiana, Illinois, and Iowa.

As Nourse and Knapp wrote, the arguments of the supporters of the committee's plan to the effect that their proposal "was built on the individual farmer was hardly less than rubbing salt in the wounds of the leaders of the cooperative shipping movement." Shippers from already established local associations in Iowa and Minnesota were hardly enthusiastic about dismantling their associations or turning them over to the state farm bureau federations. Representatives from these states had come to the conference with the idea that whatever marketing organization came into existence would be based "strictly on commodity lines" and not be attached to any general farm organization. Leaders from Wisconsin, Kansas, and other states said that when and if a national livestock-marketing plan came into being, it should come about because the local associations had expanded into the terminal market. One Kansas delegate remarked that the adoption of the committee plan would bring about something "little short of revolution and murder in Kansas" because of the strong pro-Farmers' Union sentiment that prevailed there and the success which that order had had in building terminal marketing agencies.

Farm Bureau delegates vigorously protested against these arguments and in the end they won out. Farmers' Union delegates, much to their disgust, discovered that when the committee recommended that the local associations join up with a state-wide farm organization, "it meant joining the Farm Bureau in their respective states and not the Farmers' Union or Equity." The prevailing sentiment behind the plan of the committee was best summed up by the Iowa leader who said: "Well, the Farm Bureaus are expected to pay all the cost, so why in the deuce shouldn't they control?"[58] Though this sentiment was perhaps valid enough, the fact was that a flare-up was ignited which was to persist throughout the twenties and well into the Federal Farm Board era.

If the American Farm Bureau Federation originally had placed its chief reliance on cooperative marketing, the evidence is that by 1924 its faith had shifted to surplus-control measures. Surplus controls appear to have first received serious consideration during the summer of 1923, when the Bureau proposed that the farmers withhold two million bushels of wheat from market as an emergency measure. It was hoped that the farmers would make use of the Intermediate Credit and Warehouse Acts passed by the Sixty-seventh Congress. According to this legislation, the Secretary of Agriculture could rule that a farm storehouse or granary could become a bonded warehouse and thus permit the farmer to put his surplus wheat into his own bins, lock up the door, and turn over the keys to a government agent. He would then receive a warehouse receipt on which he could borrow money from the Intermediate Credit Bank. That fall, the American Farm Bureau Federation went on record as being opposed to government price fixing of agricultural commodities, emphasizing the point that the surplus wheat question was an economic and not a political problem.

Early in 1924 the executive committee of the American Farm Bureau Federation endorsed the amended McNary-Haugen bill that provided for an export corporation to dispose of the agricultural surpluses. It based its action on the theory that agriculture, the most basic industry in the country, suffered from low prices because of unfair trade practices, from market-sharing agreements among the major nonfarm producers, from

58. Nourse and Knapp, *The Co-Operative Marketing of Livestock*, pp. 124–39.

discriminatory tariffs, embargoes, and other high-cost factors. This proposed export corporation could supplement the cooperative-marketing associations. More important was the fact that the export corporation could be used to ship surpluses in wheat, livestock, cotton, and other commodities abroad; what losses were sustained could be charged up to the entire crop. This bill was based on a modified plan proposed earlier by George N. Peek which had been discussed by Henry C. Wallace in his annual report.[59] In effect, this marked the start of a campaign that reached a peak in 1927 and 1928.

As a result of its aggressive program, it came as no surprise that the Farm Bureau aroused the antipathies of the older farm organizations, as well as of other groups. The Bureau exposed itself to such attacks partly because of its professed friendliness with those business and financial groups that many farmers had been taught to view with suspicion and distrust.[60]

One group to lash out against the Bureau was the Nonpartisan League. Some of its spokesmen openly charged that the federation had come into being for the very purpose of checking the League. They accused the Farm Bureau of being in "an unholy alliance" with the country bankers. Stories circulated in the rural communities to the effect that bankers renewed Farm Bureau memberships and even deducted dues from the farmers' bank accounts without consulting the farmers. Henry G. Teigan, secretary of the national Nonpartisan League and later congressman from Minnesota, said that in his state those in control of the Farm Bureau were reactionaries in politics.[61] Another argument was that no genuinely farmer-financed and controlled farm organization could afford to maintain palatial headquarters and pay its officers the salaries that the American Farm Bureau Federation did. No "dirt farmer" would tolerate such expenditures.

Senator Robert M. La Follette of Wisconsin accused some Bureau leaders of having conspired with railroad, coal, steel, and lumber in-

59. A.F.B.F., *Weekly News Letter,* June 18, 1929, p. 2.

60. *The American Labor Yearbook,* 1926 (New York, 1926), p. 335; *Minnesota Leader* (Olivia), July 15, 1925.

61. A.F.B.F., *Report of the Executive Secretary,* 1921, p. 8; Henry G. Teigan to H. L. Keeler, February 8, 1921, in the Minnesota Historical Society.

terests not to make any vigorous efforts to repeal the guarantee section of the Transportation Act of 1920.[62]

The Equity listed a variety of reasons for opposing it: the Chicago Board of Trade gave $1,000 to each of the first hundred county farm bureaus that were organized (hence all benefiting from such sources were held suspect); the Farm Bureau endorsed the Esch-Cummins Law; it received money, the Equity alleged, from packers who opposed "any real packer control"; it baited labor; it endorsed the ship-subsidy bill; it failed to endorse a progressive federal inheritance tax to pay off the war debt; it "favored better credit facilities to farmers when it knows that what farmers need is not merely more credit, . . . but a fair price to enable him to get out of debt"; it was trying to crush other farm organizations; and county agents told farmers that they had to be members of the Farm Bureau in order to get help from the United States Department of Agriculture.[63]

One individual attacked the Bureau because he thought it was wrong to have "a separate organization for almost every farm leader of ability and opinion." The Bureau was a hybrid organization, "being neither a true farmers' association nor a government agency." County farm bureaus were subsidized by federal funds, county funds, and membership fees while the state and national organizations were supported entirely by the membership. This made for a "controlled farmer opinion." The boards of directors of the county farm bureaus were governed by the extension service of the Department of Agriculture. This limited their powers and was unfair and discriminatory to farmers who supported the county organizations. It was unfair for farm organizations to receive funds from the federal government. Union labor, for instance, had never benefited from such sources and it was not right for farm organizations to do so.[64]

Charles S. Barrett, the president of the national Farmers' Union and chairman of the National Board of Farm Organizations, early labeled the Farm Bureau as being a "new and powerful assistant government

62. *Christian Science Monitor,* December 22, 1921.
63. *Equity News* (Madison, Wis.), July 15, 1923, p. 14.
64. R. J. Leth, "What's Wrong with the Farm Bureau?" *Wallaces' Farmer,* XLVII (July 21, 1922), p. 858.

in Washington." This "assistant government," declared Barrett, "has one advantage over the Constitutional government. It is more effectively trained for its work. It is an association of specialists. Eminent men and women who know all the legislative, administrative and bureaucratic avenues, streets and alleys in Washington belong to this interesting and patriotic collection of men and women."[65]

The Farmers' Union was an outspoken critic of the Farm Bureau. From the beginning it always considered the Bureau as an auxiliary of the chamber of commerce, big business, and the agricultural colleges.[66] Since the Bureau admitted businessmen into membership, said the Union, it had absorbed the businessmen's point of view regarding the solution of the farm problem, which was contrary to the best interests of the farmer.

Another bone of contention was the affiliation of the Farm Bureau with the county agents. Such a tie was held to be unfair. It gave to the Bureau a distinct advantage when it came to getting new members. Some of the money provided for the support of the county agents was furnished by Farmers' Union members in the form of taxes, and these sums were being used in a manner held detrimental to the best interests of the Union.[67]

Naturally, Bureau spokesmen came to the defense of their ties with the county agents. It was claimed that the county farm bureaus were organized especially for the purpose of helping the county agents. "There were other farm organizations in the field [at the time the American Farm Bureau Federation was organized] but they were not created to do extension work. A secret, fraternal farm organization, or one engaged directly in business, clearly was not equipped to cooperate with the Extension Service."[68]

The relationship between the Farm Bureau and the county agents was explained in another way: county agents were organized, along with the county farm bureaus, chiefly for the purpose of stimulating the productive efficiency of the farmers. At the time of their inception, the Farmers' Union and the American Society of Equity were bitterly assail-

65. *New York Times,* May 15, 1921.

66. *Farm Market Guide* (Minneapolis), May-June, 1926.

67. *Farmers' Union Herald* (South St. Paul, Minn.), May, 1929; March, 1927; December 21, 1931.

68. American Farm Bureau Federation, *The Extension Service and the Farm Bureau Movement* (Chicago, [1939]) [mimeographed]; *Nation's Agriculture,* XIV (July-August, 1939), p. 16.

ing such a policy. These two organizations were demanding the withholding of crops from market, production controls, and later cooperative marketing. In effect, they were condemning the proverbial policy of making two blades of grass grow where only one had grown before, the policy which the government, the agricultural colleges, and the county agents originally had adopted as the means of bettering the economic position of the farmers. Thus the traditional policy of the Union and Equity formed another bond between the Bureau and the county agents, for their program of attacking the existing marketing mechanism could not have done other than to arouse the opposition of some of those agencies which had given financial and moral support to both the farm bureaus and the county agents in the beginning and to unite them behind these two new groups.

Despite the backwardness of the county agents in tackling the distributive aspects of farming, the Farm Bureau had a distinct advantage because of the early ties. During and after the war, when the farm bureaus in the western Middle West were paying more attention to marketing, the close relations between the farm bureaus and the extension service had already been established. Neither the government nor the commercial interests behind the new marketing program were prepared to endorse organizations which had been in the field earlier. If the county agents and the county farm bureaus had been successful in demonstrating their efficiency in stimulating the productive capacities of the farmers, conceivably they could do the same with respect to marketing. Why change from tried and acceptable leadership to the erratic and untried of other organizations?

In one respect the actions of the American Farm Bureau Federation may be compared with those of the two major political parties, which appropriated reform issues popularized by third parties. While the Farmers' Union, the Grange, and the Equity agitated for cooperative marketing reform, the county agents and farm bureaus for the most part were clamoring for increased agricultural production. The American Farm Bureau Federation was organized about this program of increased production, yet at the same time it pledged itself to tackle the problem of distribution. In this way it gained considerable support from both sides, but as with all compromises it alienated the affections of some of its early benefactors and well-wishers.

Chapter X

THE COOPERATIVE MOVEMENT

1920-32

THE YEARS 1920 to 1932 will go down as among the greatest in the history of cooperative development. Once the postwar depression had hit, the farmers, their spokesmen, politicians, and others joined in the hue and cry for more efficient methods of selling. As a result, from 1920 to 1924 there was staged the most intensive campaign for the building of cooperative marketing associations that the nation had known. About 600,000 farmers took part in this program. Even though these activities were hardly confined to the western Middle West alone, the leadership of the region cannot be denied. Enabling legislation, political pressure, leadership, and financial aid, much of it originating in the region, along with government support of various kinds, played a big role in this growth. After 1924 the enthusiasm for cooperatives temporarily waned; but once the Agricultural Marketing Act of 1929 was put on the statute books and the depression struck the farmers with greater force, the cooperative movement was given greater stimulus by the government than ever before. With the coming of the Triple A there followed a period of readjustment, but the leadership of the western Middle West in cooperatives was as strong as ever. In 1934–35 almost 55 per cent of the marketing associations and 45 per cent of the membership were found in seven of these states.[1]

1. R. H. Elsworth, *Statistics of Farmers' Cooperative Business Organizations, 1920–1935,* Farm Credit Administration, Cooperative Division, Bulletin 6 (Washington,

The second decade of the twentieth century, as already seen, had witnessed a remarkable growth in cooperatives. State bureaus of marketing, agricultural experiment stations, federal bureaus, and the publicity departments of the countless associations spread the merits of cooperatives far and wide. Commissions appointed to study the cooperative movement abroad helped to popularize it, and the United States Department of Agriculture aided by devising a model bill that was used as a guide by a number of states in drawing up legislation from 1917 to 1921. Published works on agricultural marketing by men such as G. Harold Powell, Louis D. H. Weld, and John Lee Coulter appeared which helped prepare the farmers and the general public for the next wave of cooperative growth.[2]

The year 1920 was a high point in cooperative organization. More cooperatives were formed that year than during any previous time. In the American Farm Bureau Federation conferences of 1919 and 1920, the representatives from the western Middle West won out in the battle to decide whether the policy of the Farm Bureau was to be strictly one of promoting agricultural education or one of launching a program of "commercial radicalism."[3] Another sign of rising sentiment was the periodic references that were made by the Republicans to the benefits of cooperative marketing and credit associations.[4]

The events of 1920 were merely an indication of what was to follow; much legislation was passed, investigations were staged, and important conferences were held. Congress, amidst the agitation of the farm bloc, the strength of which was great in the western Middle West, and the

1936), pp. 8, 16–17; "Congress and Cooperative Marketing," *Congressional Digest*, IV (October, 1925), pp. 255–87.

2. Porter R. Taylor, "What State Marketing Agencies have Accomplished in Ten Years," *Eighth Annual Meeting, Proceedings of the National Association of Marketing Officials, Chicago, 1926*, pp. 57–63; Henry H. Bakken and Marvin A. Schaars, *The Economics of Cooperative Marketing* (New York, 1937), p. 289; L. D. H. Weld, *The Marketing of Farm Products* (New York, 1916); George Harold Powell, *Coöperation in Marketing* (New York, 1913); John Lee Coulter, *Cooperation Among Farmers* (New York, 1911). For a convenient summary of those publications which helped propagandize the cooperative movement, see Chastina Gardner, *Cooperation in Agriculture*, Farm Credit Administration, Cooperative Division, Bulletin 4 (Washington, 1936).

3. Orville M. Kile, *The Farm Bureau Movement* (New York, 1921), p. 115.

4. *Republican Campaign Textbook, 1920*, p. 128; "Harding on Agriculture," *New Republic*, XXIV (September 22, 1920), p. 84.

recommendations of both the Joint Commission of Agricultural Inquiry and the National Agricultural Conference, in 1922 enacted the Capper-Volstead Act, which legalized cooperative marketing associations and defined the terms under which producers engaged in interstate commerce could organize. The Capper-Volstead Act, referred to as "the Magna Carta of Cooperative Marketing," bore the names of two representatives from the western Middle West, Senator Arthur Capper of Kansas and Representative Andrew Volstead of Minnesota. In 1922 Congress also passed the Grain Futures Act, which sought to protect cooperatives from discrimination at the hands of boards of trade and chambers of commerce. Financial help was provided by extending the life of the War Finance Corporation and by passing the Intermediate Credits Act of 1923. The Purnell Act of 1925 made available more funds for marketing research. In 1926 Congress created the Division of Cooperative Marketing in the Bureau of Agricultural Economics, which proved to be of great help to the cooperatives. Added moral support came from a report of the National Industrial Conference Board and the Business Men's Commission, which recommended the establishment of cooperatives to stabilize farm prices and to aid agriculture. Finally in 1929 the Agricultural Marketing Act was passed.[5]

The personal equation was also a factor. One of the most ardent exponents, as well as the very personification of the promotional phases of the cooperative movement, was Aaron Sapiro. Sapiro, unlike other farm leaders, did not support the McNary-Haugen program. Instead, he preached the cooperative gospel with an evangelical vehemence. His activities began on the Pacific Coast and then spread eastward. He helped organize tobacco growers in the South, wheat growers in the western Middle West, broom-corn raisers in Oklahoma, milk producers in the Chicago area, potato growers in Maine and Minnesota, and grain growers in Canada. In 1923 he was made general counsel for the American Farm Bureau Federation. Despite the fact that he won his greatest following in the South, his influence was felt in the western Middle West.[6]

5. Federal Farm Board, *Cooperative Marketing of Farm Products,* Bulletin 10 (Washington, 1932), pp. 21–22; Wilson Gee, *American Farm Policy* (New York, 1934), pp. 30–34; *Cooperative Marketing* (70 Congress, 1 session, Senate Document 95, serial 8859, Washington, 1928), pp. 392–93.

6. Silas Bent, "Three City-Bred Jews That the Farmers Trust," *Outlook,* CXXXIV

Sapiro, besides speaking eloquently of the need for organizing commodity associations, also stressed the need for cooperative legislation and even drafted a measure, a Standard Marketing Act, which he believed would meet the needs of the farmers. He helped popularize the nonstock feature in cooperative organization, something that had been placed on the statute books of California as early as 1895. In 1921 measures based on the experiences of Sapiro in California and Oregon were passed in Arkansas, Idaho, Texas, Arizona, Kansas, Montana, North Carolina, North Dakota, Washington, Georgia, Alabama, and Kentucky. It is to be observed that a substantial amount of cooperative legislation had been passed in the western Middle West before the appearance of Sapiro.[7]

Despite the whirlwind methods of organization that he recommended and the confusion that resulted from differences of opinion, Sapiro helped popularize the centralized type of cooperative association that had grown roots in California. The Capper-Williams bill introduced in Congress during the spring of 1924 embodied the centralized and integrated type of marketing structure that he espoused. The bill sought to create a federal marketing board consisting of seven members who would work out a plan to handle and sell farm products on a commodity basis. If passed, the measure would have placed the control of marketing in the hands of the central government.[8]

The Republican farm program, which was of great aid to the cooperative movement, also reflected this trend toward the more centralized type of marketing organization. Coolidge, who was forever preaching that farm conditions were about to "resume normalcy," favored a high protective tariff and the growth of cooperative marketing. He believed that the government "must encourage orderly and centralized marketing. . . ."

(August 8, 1923), pp. 553–56; Aaron Sapiro, "True Farmer Coöperation," *World's Work,* XLVI (May, 1923), pp. 84–96; M. Crowell, "Nothing Could Keep This Boy Down," *American Magazine,* XCV (April, 1923), p. 16; F. C. Linderman, "Sapiro the Spectacular," *New Republic,* L (April 13, 1927), pp. 216–18.

7. Edwin G. Nourse, *The Legal Status of Agricultural Cooperation* (New York, 1928), pp. 99–101; Bakken and Schaars, *Economics of Cooperative Marketing,* pp. 272–73; *Monthly Labor Review,* XX (February, 1925), pp. 192–202.

8. For a critical analysis of the problems involved, see John D. Black and H. Bruce Price, "Cooperative Central Marketing Organization," *University of Minnesota Agricultural Experiment Station, Bulletin 211* (St. Paul, 1924). *Congressional Digest,* III (May, 1924), p. 264.

Cooperation in production, finance, buying, and marketing had to be encouraged "to the utmost practical development."[9] Herbert Hoover, his Secretary of Commerce, saw eye to eye with him in this, while Henry C. Wallace, who had served with Hoover under both Harding and Coolidge, had more faith in surplus-control measures and McNary-Haugenism. The successor of Wallace, William M. Jardine, former president of Kansas State College, was very much in accord with the administration viewpoint. Jardine believed that farming should be treated as a business. He proposed to lend government money to farmers and their cooperatives and thus aid the cooperatives to market their crops advantageously rather than dumping them on the market at ruinously low prices. Jardine told the farmers that their marketing machinery had to be built "along the same lines that industry and other lines of business have found to be effective."[10]

In the presidential campaign of 1928, Hoover renewed his faith in cooperative marketing and vigorously denounced the equalization-fee principle of the McNary-Haugen bill.[11] His promise was translated into legislation with the passing of the Agricultural Marketing Act of 1929. This was the most important single piece of legislation ever enacted in behalf of cooperative marketing. It called for the creation of a federal farm board, the appointment of committees to advise on marketing, and the setting up of a revolving fund of $500,000,000 to help cooperatives and to engage in price-stabilization operations.[12]

The aid given the cooperatives by the Republicans was one of the few achievements of the otherwise lethargic administrations of Harding, Coolidge, and Hoover. But it appears that when the Republicans com-

9. Gee, *American Farm Policy,* p. 38; "President Coolidge Outlines Agricultural Policy," *Congressional Digest,* IV (October, 1925), p. 261.

10. John D. Black, "Progress of Farm Relief," *American Economic Review,* XVIII (June, 1928), p. 268; George Soule, "Herbert Hoover, Practical Man," *New Republic,* LIII (December 28, 1927), p. 159; James E. Boyle, "Our Three Wallaces," *American Mercury,* XXXIV (March, 1935), p. 321; "Secretary Hoover Analyses Waste in Marketing," *Congressional Digest,* IV (October, 1925), p. 262; Russell Lord, *The Wallaces of Iowa* (New York, 1947), pp. 230–58, 261–62; *Outlook,* CXXXIX (February 25, 1925), p. 286; "Dr. Jardine's Farm Prescription," *Literary Digest,* XC (September 25, 1926), pp. 12–13.

11. Lord, *The Wallaces of Iowa,* pp. 275–80.

12. See Ellis A. Stodyk and Charles West, *The Federal Farm Board* (New York, 1930), for an early analysis of the act and the problems facing the Farm Board.

mitted themselves to the cooperative movement, they did so not because of any particular love for it, but because it was thought to be the least offensive of the numerous proposals advanced for the relief of the farmers. They realized that something had to be done to appease the farmers, especially those of the western Middle West; but whatever relief plan was adopted had to be as inoffensive to the industrial interests as possible. The McNary-Haugen proposal, export debentures, domestic allotment plans, inflation of the currency, price fixing, and other similarly radical measures were out of the question. Republicans, as well as others, realized that cooperative marketing was a "perfectly valid longtime policy, but comparatively futile as a measure for immediate relief."[13] If one took Republican orators seriously, the depression was going to be short-lived; meanwhile, the cooperative movement could be used as a talking point. When the depression failed to lift, the Republicans, for the want of a more satisfactory remedy, had nothing but larger and better doses of cooperatives to offer.

One of the most conspicuous phases of the cooperative movement during the twenties dealt with wheat pooling.[14] Obviously, these pools tried to do for their farmer members what the salt pool, the wire pool, the plate pool, the gunpowder pool, the envelope manufacturers' pool, and numerous other pools had tried to do for industrialists and manufacturers during the seventies and eighties. The forming of these agrarian pools also displayed a lag in the thinking of the farmers, who tried to put into operation what the industrialists, who were in a more favorable position to accomplish their end, had failed to do some half-century earlier.

The pools had hoped to strengthen the bargaining position of the producers. Obviously, the average wheat farmers were small individual operators who were at a competitive disadvantage. To overcome this, a pool would be formed and a manager would be hired and given complete control of the storing and selling of the farmers' wheat. The farmers usually bound themselves to the pool for a period of five or seven years.

13. Gee, *American Farm Policy,* p. 43. See also Henry E. Erdman, "Possibilities and Limitations of Cooperative Marketing," *Annals of the American Academy of Political and Social Science,* CXVII (January, 1925), pp. 217–26.

14. Elsworth, *Farmers' Cooperative Business Organizations,* p. 57; see also Chapter IX on pooling in H. C. Filley, *Cooperation in Agriculture* (New York, 1929), pp. 114–26.

It was believed that such associations would not only overcome some of the evils of competition but also would make it possible for the producers to control the wheat market. The plan also called for the formation of a national pool and the eventual joining of forces "with an international pool, including Canada, Argentina, and Australia."

Perhaps what the wheat pools had attempted to do was best expressed by their leaders and advisors. For instance, in 1922 George E. Duis, president of the North Dakota wheat pool, said to a convention of wheat growers in Kansas City: "The ultimate aim of the wheat growers is to put a price tag on a bushel of wheat." Frank O. Lowden, chairman of the National Wheat Growers' Advisory Committee, was quoted as saying: "If we were organized we would direct our wheat as the steel industry controls the flow of its steel. We would say to our mills: 'Our wheat costs us so much; there is not any more than is needed for consumption; if you want to grind our wheat, you must pay our price.' That is what everybody else does." As it was so aptly stated by another, the poolers proposed "to do for wheat exactly what the U. S. Steel Corporation does for steel."

The methods used in organizing these pools seemed to follow a set pattern. Usually a big meeting was held; speeches were made; whirlwind membership campaigns were staged; often long, legally worded contracts were entered into by farmers who neither read nor understood the contents of the documents they signed; and an official organ was issued carrying the familiar arguments against the middlemen, the grain merchants, and the bankers.[15]

Even though the industrialists were the first to resort to pooling in wholesale fashion, it can hardly be said that the farmers were unfamiliar with it. It had been tried as early as the seventies, if not earlier. It also had been practiced during the World War years, and was credited in large part with the high prices received during that period. It appealed especially to those farmers who lived in areas where the cooperative-elevator movement was weak. Once the depression struck, it was natural for them to look to pooling as a means for resisting low prices.[16] Many

15. James E. Boyle, "The Farmers and the Grain Trade in the United States, An Interpretation of the Present Pooling Movement," *Economic Journal,* XXXV (March, 1925), pp. 14–20.

16. J. T. Horner, "The United States Government Activities in the Field of Agricultural Economics Prior to 1913," *Journal of Farm Economics,* X (October, 1928),

believed that the depression would be short-lived and that such a program was as feasible as any.[17]

Equally pertinent to the wheat-pooling movement were various other forces beyond the political boundaries of the western Middle West. Congress, for instance, because of the pressure from farm leaders and politicians and the influence of Secretary of Agriculture Henry C. Wallace, gave the pooling movement encouragement. The coffee-valorization plans of the Brazilian government, the attempts to control the production of sugar in Cuba, the activities of the California raisin growers, the Canadian wheat pools, and the evangelizing efforts of Aaron Sapiro stimulated pooling. By 1927 the pooling movement had passed its peak, but it was estimated that about one million farmers were still under contract to deliver goods to associations which would pool and sell them at the proper time.[18]

The wheat-pooling movement of the twenties had its inception in the western Middle West and on the Pacific Coast. One of the first of these organizations was the Washington Wheat Growers' Association, incorporated in August, 1920. The Idaho Wheat Growers' Association was incorporated the following month. In 1921 associations were also formed in Oregon and Montana, and after that it became apparent that these four groups were to be merged. The result was the Northwest Wheat Growers, Associated. As long as the Northwest Wheat Growers had confined its activities to the Pacific Northwest, it was unnecessary for it to operate through an organized grain exchange, but when it reached into North Dakota, as it did in 1922, it had to find such an outlet. A seat was bought on the Minneapolis Chamber of Commerce.

Meanwhile the National Wheat Growers' Association was functioning in the Southwest. It had its beginnings in the western Middle West, hav-

---

pp. 451–52; Filley, *Cooperation in Agriculture,* p. 126; Herman Steen, *Coöperative Marketing* (New York, 1923), p. 212.

17. Jesse E. Pope, "The Holding Movement in Agriculture," in Jacob H. Hollander, ed., *Economic Essays Contributed in Honor of John Bates Clark* (New York, 1927), pp. 243–46.

18. Arthur Capper, *The Agricultural Bloc* (New York, 1922), an account of the farm bloc by one of its members; Lord, *The Wallaces of Iowa,* pp. 249–58; Pope, in *Economic Essays in Honor of John Bates Clark,* pp. 245, 272; Harald S. Patton, *Grain Growers' Cooperation in Western Canada* (Cambridge, Mass., 1928); Bakken and Schaars, *Economics of Cooperative Marketing,* p. 273.

ing been organized in May, 1920, in Hutchinson, Kansas, in the attempt to keep wheat prices up after the government guarantee was removed on June 1, 1920. Its marketing contracts were similar to those of the Northwest Wheat Growers except that provisions had been made to curtail the acreage of wheat if necessary. In the fall of 1920 an abortive wheat strike was staged, but despite this the organization at the end of 1920 still boasted a membership of fifty thousand, extending from Texas to North Dakota.

During the next two years the National Wheat Growers' underwent a series of changes in its structure and marketing program. Originally, it had in it many radicals and was a loosely knit affair, but in time many of these elements were eliminated. Finally, in 1922 the National Wheat Growers' merged with the Northwest group to form the American Wheat Growers, Associated.

The latter began its marketing operations in August, 1923, with its headquarters in Minneapolis. According to the plan, the United States was divided into three selling zones, with agencies in Minneapolis, Duluth, Spokane, Seattle, and Portland. The Northwest Wheat Growers, Associated, became the selling agency for the Washington, Oregon, Idaho, and Montana associations. The American Wheat Growers, Associated, became the selling agency for the North Dakota Wheat Growers' Association and a number of other associations. Obviously, the purpose of the American Wheat Growers was to establish a national wheat-marketing agency.

Experience soon proved that these national agencies and the numerous state associations formed were to be short-lived. By and large, operations began before an adequate supply of wheat had been signed up; the marketing activities took in wide and often remote areas; associations were unable to enforce their marketing contracts; mortgaged wheat was exempted; local points of contact had not been established; and the pooling of wheat was undertaken in a period of declining prices.[19]

An equally ambitious phase of the cooperative movement was the launching of large-scale terminal grain-marketing agencies. Beginning with the creation of bodies such as the United States Grain Growers, In-

19. Senate Document 95, 70 Congress, 1 session, pp. 64–66; Steen, *Coöperative Marketing*, pp. 216–18; Filley, *Cooperation in Agriculture*, pp. 127–29.

corporated, the Grain Marketing Company, and finally the government-sponsored Farmers' National Grain Corporation, spokesmen for the farmers gave evidence of their belief that large-scale marketing methods were applicable to grain. Meanwhile, terminal marketing associations on a smaller scale were being organized. Some four or five were in existence before 1920; but by 1935 the number had grown to twenty-six, twenty-three of which belonged to the Farmers' National Grain Corporation.[20] Apparently, the consolidations in industry and business had encouraged agriculturists to seek similar economies in their marketing operations.

The United States Grain Growers, sponsored by the American Farm Bureau Federation Committee of Seventeen and organized in 1921, as of that date was the most ambitious project ever devised for the marketing of grain. It had hoped to bring about higher prices by creating "a highly centralized organization with facilities for holding grain off the market."[21]

The enthusiasm of the sponsors of the U.S.G.G. was not shared by all; in fact, its creation was met with mixed feelings, mostly of skepticism and downright pessimism.[22] The critics pointed to the various forces with which the company would have to contend; it could do little or nothing about world competition, the independent farmer, the legal and financial problems that would inevitably arise, and the general ineffectiveness of "voluntary action." The president of the Minnesota Farmers' Grain Dealers Association, for instance, advised that if the U.S.G.G. was to succeed, it would have to have the services of the most experienced merchants and financiers in the world, who were not to be found in the ranks of the farmers. With forthrightness he asked, "[Why] agree to sell your grain for a period of five years through an untried agency, the ability of which is to be demonstrated?" Was it possible that a board of twenty-one producers who were omniscient enough to determine grain prices

20. Ward E. Fetrow, *Cooperative Marketing of Agricultural Products,* Farm Credit Administration, Cooperative Division, Bulletin 3 (Washington, 1936), pp. 50–51; Elsworth, *Statistics of Farmers' Cooperative Organizations,* pp. 57–59.

21. B. H. Hibbard, "The Extent of Cooperative Marketing Among Farmers To-day and the Results Secured by Cooperative Associations," *Annals of the American Academy of Political and Social Science,* CXVII (January, 1925), p. 204.

22. "A Farmers' Union to Balk the Grain Gambler," *Literary Digest,* LXIX (April 30, 1921), p. 13.

that were governed, more or less, by world conditions could be brought together by the U.S.G.G.? Were the officers who were to head the company worthy of the fat salaries that they were to receive? Also, could not an organization employing such policies, in view of the lack of enabling legislation at the time, be found guilty of violating the federal antitrust laws?[23]

Unfortunately, the history of the U.S.G.G. was one of complete, in fact scandalous, failure; still, the main outlines of its career are worth tracing. Controversies over policy, poor management, intrigue, and opposition rounded out its course and emphasized the very practices that farmers' marketing associations had to avoid if they were to succeed.

Differences over policy broke out from the start. Nearly all the members of the board of directors had been members of the Committee of Seventeen and the ratification conference, and their differences found their way into the management of the company. This brought it face to face with differences over pooling, the principles and practices of cooperation, and the means that were to be used to aid the United States Grain Growers to become powerful. The conservative members, especially those experienced in the cooperative grain-elevator business, wanted the company to grow slowly and economically, but the radicals wanted the immediate construction of a superorganization that would dominate the American grain market. One director went to the extent of sending telegrams to numerous grain solicitors offering them jobs at salaries ranging from $6,000 to $7,500 per year; when five men reported for duty, it was discovered that the majority of the members of the executive committee had known nothing about the offers.

Despite the fact that the United States Grain Growers was one of the best-advertised companies in the country, one board member proposed an even greater advertising campaign. One proposal called for the rental of a building at $70,000 per year, another for the purchase of a twenty-two-story office building in the heart of the Chicago Loop district "to be prepared for rapid expansion."

The salaries paid invited more trouble. To many it appeared extravagant to pay the president a salary of $16,000 per year, the treasurer $15,000,

23. Charles Kenning, *Question Book Regarding Proposed Grain Marketing Plan of the Committee of Seventeen as Compared with Grain Marketing System* (n.p., n.d.), pp. 1–2.

and the secretary $12,000. Loud protests arose and in due time downward revisions were made.

The membership of the organization grew, but so did its expenses and problems. Money was borrowed from farm bureaus, country elevators, and other sources. Practically everything that was accomplished was the result of a compromise between the conservatives, who favored a slow and economical progress, and the radicals, who wanted a large-overhead organization. Expense was a secondary matter to the latter group. The conservatives felt that the resources of the organization were being dissipated, while the radicals were critical of the lack of progress.

At the first annual meeting of the United States Grain Growers, these differences flared into the open. When the conservatives saw the unused office space and the list of unpaid employees to whom the company owed thousands of dollars, they demanded an explanation. A group of the dissatisfied delegates and their friends held a meeting the night before the convention was to assemble and formulated plans. Board members were called in and questioned; a determination to clean house followed; men who were responsible for the "extravagant" policies were not to be re-elected.

During the convention little was heard about cooperative grain marketing; it was a political affair, with most of the time being spent on securing control of the convention. When the treasurer's report was completed, events came to a head. A deficit of $102,524 was shown; doubtful assets were listed as $141,000; current liabilities totaled $336,080; the membership stood at about fifty thousand.[24]

To many it had become apparent that too much time had been spent in compromising. One faction led by the Illinois Agricultural Association notified the president of the company that the funds borrowed from the association had to be repaid at once. It was further evident that a new board of directors would have to be elected "in whom everyone would have complete confidence," and that a sales agency would have to be established soon if the company was to be saved. President C. H. Gustafson was re-elected and his supporters, who won control, promised to have the sales agency in operation in ninety days.[25]

24. Filley, *Cooperation in Agriculture*, pp. 152–55; Steen, *Coöperative Marketing*, pp. 220–23.

25. *American Farm Bureau Federation Weekly News Letter*, March 23, 1922,

Criticisms of the company, nevertheless, continued to pour forth. The *American Co-operative Journal,* conservative spokesman for the state farmers' grain dealers associations, pointed out that the U.S.G.G. had failed to obtain the support of the local cooperative elevators. The managers of these elevators felt either that their activities had been unduly interfered with or that they had been completely ignored. They were unwilling to give up their hard-earned positions to this proposed super marketing organization. They had taken a states' rights attitude.

This same journal emphasized that only 1 per cent of the fifty thousand grain growers who had signed contracts with the U.S.G.G. had elected to use any of the several pooling methods. The cooperative elevators, in particular, were opposed to pooling. Since the company had been purged of the radicals and was in the hands of conservatives, the *American Co-operative Journal* advised that progress and larger profits could be had by improving the methods of cleaning, weighing, grading, and storing grain. It also felt that the American Farm Bureau Federation had to give more help. The Farmers' National Grain Dealers Association likewise had to take a more active part, because its grain dealers were men of experience who had elevators in twelve states and had been working together in solving their problems since 1903. The Farmers' Union, which was doing a large business in Nebraska, Kansas, Oklahoma, and Colorado, also had to be taken into consideration.[26]

Regardless of the promises of the new board, the president, and the conservative counsel, things had gone too far for the organization to succeed. News of the chaotic state of affairs within the company had been spread far and wide. Creditors, often egged on by ousted officers, pressed their claims; new members were hard to obtain and revenues dropped. When the new board failed to erect the sales agency within the promised time, it resigned and a new board assumed charge. The new group of officers inherited a debt of almost $300,000 which had been built up

---

pp. 1–2; *Minnesota Farm Bureau News* (Central Edition, Grand Rapids), March 1, 1925; Steen, *Coöperative Marketing,* p. 221; Filley, *Cooperation in Agriculture,* p. 155.

26. "The United States Grain Growers, Inc.," *American Co-operative Journal* (Chicago), XVII (April, 1922), pp. 2–3.

largely by overhead costs, high salaries, and general extravagance.[27] To solve the financial problem of the organization, there was appointed an advisory committee made up of Bernard M. Baruch, the New York financier; Alexander Legge, president of the International Harvester Company; and Frank Wetmore, president of the First National Bank of Chicago.[28] But even with the additional aid and advice that the company received, it was unable to discharge the obligations incurred during the first year.

The marketing activities of the U.S.G.G. were short-lived. Early in November, 1922, it began marketing grain on the Minneapolis Chamber of Commerce through the manager of the United States Grain Growers' Sales Company of Minneapolis, a subsidiary organization.[29] In Chicago its efforts in this respect were not so fortunate. On November 14, 1922, the Chicago Board of Trade rejected the membership application of E. H. Cunningham, which was to have been the first step in establishing a sales agency for the U.S.G.G. The Capper-Tincher Act, which prohibited boards of trade and chambers of commerce from rejecting the membership applications of cooperatives that dispensed patronage dividends, had been temporarily suspended by an injunction which restrained the Secretary of Agriculture from enforcing it. The Chicago Board of Trade, in rejecting the application, informed the applicant that the farmers would be admitted when they came in "the regular way."

In short, the United States Grain Growers was doomed. The modified plan probably would have had a better chance to survive had the com-

27. Filley, *Cooperation in Agriculture,* pp. 154–55; Steen, *Coöperative Marketing,* p. 221.

28. A.F.B.F., *Weekly News Letter,* August 10, 1922, p. 1; *Minnesota Farm Bureau News,* March 25, 1925.

29. A.F.B.F., *Weekly News Letter,* November 16, 1922, p. 1; *Minnesota Farm Bureau News,* May 1, October 1, 1923; Senate Document 95, 70 Congress, 1 session, p. 69. When the U.S.G.G. failed, a number of the state farm bureaus financed the United States Grain Growers' Sales Company to handle its grain on the Minneapolis Chamber of Commerce. Late in 1922 the Equity Cooperative Exchange and the North Dakota Wheat Growers' Association affiliated with it. This was of short duration because of differences in marketing policy. In 1923, or thereabouts, the United States Grain Growers' Sales Company became the property of the Montana Wheat Growers' Association and the Minnesota Wheat Growers' Cooperative Marketing Association.

pany had the needed operating capital and had it been free from debt. A small amount of grain was handled, but it was insufficient to net profits and liquidate debts. The refusal of the Chicago Board of Trade to admit it on the exchange floor unquestionably hindered its marketing program, but its unsound financial condition was no doubt a major cause for its collapse.[30] Also, not to be lost sight of was the fact that the company was organized at a time when grain prices were falling. When the United States Supreme Court declared the Capper-Tincher Act constitutional, those who felt that the "grain-growers plan" had not been given a fair trial decided to start anew. This element was successful in launching the Grain Marketing Company.[31]

The Grain Marketing Company met a similar fate. From the start, opposition to it was strong. The members of the Chicago Board of Trade opposed it; so did the McNary-Haugenites, who viewed the company as a distinct threat to their program; wheat pool leaders looked upon it as a rival, as did most farm organizations, which felt that "it was no child of theirs." Spokesmen for the farmers, men like Henry C. Wallace and Frank Lowden, opposed it. Its bitterest enemies "left no stone unturned"; they demanded government investigations, appeared before blue-sky commissions, and charged it with not being "a true cooperative." But the American Farm Bureau Federation and some of the state farm bureaus supported it.[32]

The history of the Grain Marketing Company appears to have followed a pattern familiar to cooperative failures. In 1924 several Chicago elevator companies agreed to sell to the new company their fixed assets and grain, amounting to $16,000,000 and $10,000,000 respectively. What aroused the suspicions of many was the fact that the men who sold their properties to the company were generally considered hostile to the cooperative movement.[33] The explanation offered for the acts of these merchants was that

30. A.F.B.F., *Weekly News Letter,* November 16, 1922, p. 1.

31. *Ibid.,* August 9, 1923, p. 1; Filley, *Cooperation in Agriculture,* pp. 156–57.

32. B. F. Goldstein, *Marketing: A Farmers' Problem* (New York, 1929), p. 240; "Exit the Grain Marketing Company," *Saturday Evening Post,* CXCVIII (October 3, 1925), p. 30; "Why a $26,000,000 Marketing Project Won't Work," *Literary Digest,* LXXXCI (August 8, 1925), p. 59; Filley, *Cooperation in Agriculture,* pp. 157–59; Senate Document 95, 70 Congress, 1 session, pp. 69–70, 312–13.

33. *Saturday Evening Post,* CXCVIII (October 3, 1925), p. 30.

the "rising tide for cooperative marketing" was going to drive the private grain traders to the wall. Their reasoning ran something like this: "The farmers have got the cooperative bug. It's going to break us. Why not organize a farmers' cooperative marketing concern, and sell to the farmers our elevators before they build warehouses of their own. We know that the farmers will never pay large enough salaries to get the brains necessary to handle such a monstrous corporation and eventually the company will fail. The cooperative idea will die, and we'll get our elevators back." [34]

Whatever the motives were, the fact is that the Grain Marketing Company was on the road to failure from the start. Very little of its stock was sold. Funds were lacking. Wheat growers, in particular, failed to buy stock in it. Also, in order to qualify under the state and federal laws for cooperative associations, the company had to be farmer-owned and do as much business for its members as it did for the outsiders. This it failed to do.[35]

It appears that the company functioned until the latter part of June, 1925, but then its difficulties rose to the surface. The options to purchase the properties expired and the terminal facilities were returned to their original owners. Charges and countercharges followed. In 1926 the question was turned over to an arbitrator, who reported a fraud of $2,700,000.

Public opinion was shocked when the award of the arbitrator was announced. The bitterness of the farmers grew. There quickly rose a demand, especially in Illinois, to punish the guilty parties and to take safeguards against similar acts in the future. An appeal was also made to the Illinois legislature, and in 1927 the speaker of the house appointed a committee to investigate grain warehousing in Chicago and look into the causes for the failure of the Grain Marketing Company. This led to the uncovering of other fraudulent acts.[36]

The third major attempt at large-scale marketing reform, the Farmers' National Grain Corporation, differed from the other two by virtue of its longer life and by its being a government-sponsored agency. It came into being in 1929 shortly after a call was sent to farm groups to meet in Chicago to organize a national marketing agency. There were in the

34. F. Boselly, "The Armours Betray the Farmers," *The Nation,* CXXV (August 31, 1927), p. 196.
35. *Saturday Evening Post,* CXVIII (October 3, 1925), p. 30.
36. Goldstein, *Marketing: A Farmers' Problem,* pp. 241–56.

country at the time about 4,000 local grain-marketing associations, eleven state farmers' grain dealers associations, eight wheat pools, and twelve terminal marketing agencies. In response to the invitation, some fifty-two delegates representing thirty-five associations, including the American Farm Bureau Federation, the Farmers' Union, the national Grange, and the Farmers' Equity Union, an offshoot from the American Society of Equity, met in Chicago on July 26 and 27. The result was the organization of the Farmers' National Grain Corporation, the first of the national marketing associations to be established under the Agricultural Marketing Act of 1929. The Farmers' National was organized in a manner that allowed marketing associations, wheat pools, terminal agencies, and cooperative elevators to join. Only associations that could qualify under the terms of the Capper-Volstead Act were eligible for membership. It could buy and sell grain and own and operate both terminal and local associations.[37]

Even though a discussion of the Farmers' National and the grain-stabilization operations logically falls under the chapter on the Federal Farm Board, the importance of the organization to the cooperative movement cannot be overemphasized. The Farmers' National intended to make the local cooperatives more efficient, to bring producers the benefits of centralized control, and also to give to them the returns from terminal-elevator operations. It was felt that the Farmers' National would attract a sufficiently large volume of grain, encourage loyalty on the part of members, and furnish leadership, able management, and adequate capital.[38]

It was plain from the start that the ambitions of the Farmers' National would exceed those of both the United States Grain Growers and the Grain Marketing Company. In 1929–30 it provided aid to cooperatives to help them make greater advances to member associations for their grain than would otherwise have been possible. Cooperatives thus were enabled to make advances to members totaling about 90 per cent of the value of the wheat, based on current prices. But this was felt to be inadequate. Therefore in October, 1929, loans were extended up to the full value based on market prices. When wheat prices collapsed in February, the Grain

37. Federal Farm Board, *Cooperative Marketing Makes Steady Growth,* Bulletin 8 (Washington, 1932), pp. 8–9; Deane W. Malott and Boyce F. Martin, *The Agricultural Industries* (New York, 1939), p. 262.

38. F.F.B., *Cooperative Marketing Makes Steady Growth,* p. 9.

ʾtabilization Corporation was set up to buy wheat from the cooperatives, vithhold it, and thus lend support to the market.[39] By June 30, 1930, the net holdings (deducting some sales—mostly for export) were about 5,000,000 bushels. According to report, the Grain Stabilization Corporaion and the cooperatives affiliated with it held control of a quantity of wheat equal to about "one-half of the visible supply of wheat." By July , 1931, the holdings of wheat totaled 257,000,000 bushels.[40]

When the New Deal took office, the activities of the Federal Farm Board were curtailed, and the next year wheat-stabilization operations eased. Meanwhile, a policy was begun to dispose of the local elevators of the Farmers' National, and in 1935 the federal government took them over as security for the advances that had gone unpaid. The operations of the corporation ceased in 1938.[41]

Somewhat more successful than the large-scale grain-marketing agenies were the cooperative livestock firms on the terminal markets. The first of the more recent attempts was made by the Equity Cooperative Exhange in 1916 in South St. Paul. In 1918 the exchange opened a second irm in the Chicago market. Unlike the Farmers' Union houses, neither of these two firms got off to a good beginning. Both got into difficulties rom the start because of faulty management. Gains and losses from livetock-marketing operations were pooled with those from grain marketing. Naturally, this caused resentment among the livestock growers, who saw heir profits go toward the support of less profitable enterprises. Besides his poor policy, there were corruption and dissension in management, lissatisfaction among shippers, and opposition from the private livestock nterests, all of which helped to keep these agencies in an exhausted conlition. The position of the South St. Paul firm became more untenable vith the coming in 1921 of the highly efficient rival firm, the Central Cooperative Commission Association.[42]

Meanwhile, the Farmers' Union had begun to establish a creditable eries of agencies on several terminal markets. The Nebraska Farmers'

39. Malott and Martin, *The Agricultural Industries,* p. 262.

40. Food Research Institute, Stanford University, *Wheat Studies,* XII (March, 936), p. 252.

41. Malott and Martin, *The Agricultural Industries,* p. 262.

42. Edwin G. Nourse and Joseph G. Knapp, *The Co-Operative Marketing of ivestock* (Washington, 1931), pp. 106–9.

Union took the lead in this, largely because of the influence of C. H. Watts, a prominent cattle grower and livestock dealer. The Farmers' Union Livestock Commission was organized in Omaha on April 1, 1917. This firm began business with the modest sum of $2,000, which it had borrowed from the Nebraska Farmers' Union. But when it applied for membership on the Omaha Livestock Exchange it was denied because it issued patronage dividends.

This ban failed to check the growth of the Omaha firm. After eighteen months of business it had surpassed all but one of the fifty commission houses on the Omaha market, and by the end of the second fiscal year, it had showed a profit of 56 per cent. The Nebraska Farmers' Union, after making payments into a sinking fund and deducting other expenses, returned to its shippers forty-six cents on every dollar it had received in commissions. From 1921 on it was the leading firm on the Omaha market.

This was merely the beginning of the Farmers' Union livestock-marketing program. A second agency was set up at St. Joseph, Missouri, just six months after the Omaha house began business. In August, 1918, a third agency was established by the Nebraska Union on the Sioux City, Iowa, market; and in October of the same year, a fourth house was opened with the cooperation of the Kansas Farmers' Union. Late in 1919 a fifth firm began operations in Denver under the joint sponsorship of the Nebraska and Colorado Unions. In 1922, when the Iowa Farmers' Union bought the Equity houses on the Chicago and South St. Paul markets the number of houses jumped to seven. The Farmers' Unions of Iowa and Missouri had also acquired an interest, along with the Missouri Farmers Association, in a firm in St. Louis. The building of these agencies encouraged Union spokesmen to think in terms of building a national sale organization, the Farmers' National Cooperative Livestock Marketing Association, which never materialized.[43]

Obviously the Farmers' Union had made considerable headway in both the local and terminal marketing of livestock before the American Farm Bureau Federation began to project itself into the field. Once the latter had made known its plans to establish the National Livestock Producers Association system, through the efforts of the Committee of Fifteen, a clash between the two was imminent. This committee, much to the con-

43. *Ibid.*, pp. 109–16.

sternation of the Farmers' Union, sought to dominate the cooperative livestock-marketing trade regardless of the older agencies that already were in the field. When the Farmers' Union houses refused to merge with it, complications developed.

This opposition did not stop the Committee of Fifteen from sponsoring its producers' system with vigor. Its first energies were directed to the East St. Louis market as early as August, 1921, three months before the livestock plan of the committee had been ratified. No cooperative commission firm had yet been established on this market, the only important unorganized one, but the Missouri Farmers' Association had been preparing to do so for quite some time. The Missouri Farmers' Association had perfected such a plan as early as 1920, but withheld it until legislation was passed that would permit cooperative terminal associations to disburse patronage dividends. When the legislation was finally passed in 1921, the Missouri Farmers' Association decided to carry out its plan to erect an East St. Louis agency; and when the Farm Bureau Committee of Fifteen announced its intentions, both the Farmers' Union and the Missouri Farmers' Association took exception and proceeded to organize their firm, which began operations on November 16, 1921.

The producers' house, sponsored by the Committee of Fifteen, began its business activities on the same market on January 3, 1922. This inevitably led to an exchange of harsh words, but in due time it was found out that an ample supply of livestock was available for both firms. By the end of the sixth week, the producers' house was one of the most important firms on the East St. Louis market.

For the remainder of 1922 the producers' group concentrated its attention on its East St. Louis house. A period of five months elapsed before another agency was established. The reasons for the delay were to permit the controversy between the Missouri Farmers' Association and the producers' association to cool off, to place the East St. Louis house on a successful footing, and to consider carefully all other markets before another location was selected.

The fears of the older organizations, however, were not stilled. William Hirth, the president of the Missouri Farmers' Association, charged that the producers' group contemplated entering the Kansas City, Omaha, Denver, and St. Joseph markets, places in which the Farmers' Union had been operating. This was denied by the president of the National Livestock Producers' Association, but instead of quieting the fears of the rival bodies, the denial caused them to strengthen their forces on those markets to prove that they were functioning efficiently. It was not until it became evident that there was room for both houses on the East St. Louis markets and that both Equity and Farmers' Union territory were safe from invasion that the Union groups quieted down.

On May 15, 1922, a producers' house was organized in Indianapolis, and on June 25 another agency began business in Peoria, Illinois. Since no other farmers' organization was competing on these two markets, trouble was avoided. On June 19, an agency was located in Chicago, the site of a rival Farmers' Union house, but the size of the Chicago market prevented any serious conflict from developing. On November 1, two more producers' agencies were opened in Buffalo and Forth Worth. By the end of the first year, 1922, six producers' houses were functioning.

During 1923, the second year of the producers' group's existence, terminal commission associations were established in Kansas City, Sioux Falls, Cleveland, Oklahoma City, Evansville, and Pittsburgh. On going into the Kansas City market, they again entered Farmers' Union territory. Here the Union accused the Farm Bureau of seeking to "rule or ruin." The producers' association denied the charge, replying that the Farmers' Union firm in Kansas City was inefficient and that the livestock market there could be remedied only by establishing a producers' agency. Efforts to reconcile these two groups failed. The producers' house, however, failed to measure up to its expectations. Factional warfare, difficulties in setting up an efficient organization in a highly competitive market, and discrimination by the Kansas City Livestock Exchange impeded its progress.

Further disputes between the Farmers' Union and the Farm Bureau groups flared up in the Sioux Falls area, for the Farmers' Union, having its agency in Sioux City, was well organized in this area; but a "temporary amalgamation" between the two gave the producers' group a foothold and on March 15, 1924, the Sioux City Producers' Commission Association started business. When the National Livestock Producers' Association, the parent organization for the producers' group, merged with the National Livestock Marketing Association, the national agency set up by the Fed eral Farm Board in 1930, it had commission houses in St. Louis, Indianapolis, Chicago, Peoria, Buffalo, Kansas City, Cleveland, Evansville, Pittsburgh, Sioux City, Cincinnati, and Detroit.[44]

The producers' group, although it did not radically increase the profits of its members, did bring benefits to them. It helped improve business methods; it gave the livestock producer more bargaining power; it saved patrons money, improved service, and obtained for them better credit facilities. It also agitated for a tariff on livestock and meats and for the enactment of packer-control legislation, both of which were considered helpful to livestock producers. This association was active in farm-relief legislation, particularly in the support of the Cooperative Marketing Act of 1926 and the Agricultural Marketing Act of 1929.[45]

Several months before the marketing plan of the Committee of Fifteen had been ratified, the Central Cooperative Livestock Commission Association was incorporated in South St. Paul in May, 1921. The Central was an independent firm, not being affiliated with any general farmers' organization. It received no aid from the Committee of Fifteen, but it did get help from the Minnesota Farm Bureau and the extension division of the University of Minnesota.

The Central had been brought into being by livestock producers around the South St. Paul area who had long felt the need for marketing reform. These producers had seen the hostile relations between the Equity Cooperative Exchange livestock agency and the private merchants. This, along with the ineffectiveness of the Equity firm, had a demoralizing effect on the producers. But this attitude of apathy soon changed to one of direct action. In 1921 the "open market law" was passed which made boycotts and discriminatory practices against cooperatives illegal. This encouraged the livestock producers to organize, and the result was the Central Cooperative Livestock Commission Association. It began business on August 8, 1921.[46]

44. *Ibid.*, pp. 140–56.

45. *Ibid.*, p. 274.

46. Edwin M. Gaumnitz, "Marketing Livestock at South St. Paul," in H. B. Price, ed., *The Marketing of Farm Products* (Minneapolis, 1927), pp. 131–32; *Cooperative Shipper* (South St. Paul, Minn.), VII (March, 1927), p. 2; Central Cooperative Association, *Central Cooperative Association* (South St. Paul, Minn., 1946) [leaflet].

The record of the Central was nothing short of spectacular. Before it began business, W. A. McKerrow, a man who had organized many local shipping associations in Minnesota, was hired to secure the affiliation of roughly 220 local groups. Each one of these locals subscribed for a $25 membership and one $25 share of stock for each fifty cars of livestock handled annually. "An agreement, but no contract, was reached, as a result of which the associations promised to ship to the Central." Some of the best salesmen on the South St. Paul market were also hired before beginning business.

The rapid success of the Central was due to the preliminary preparations and to the fact that it met a long-felt need of the farmers. From the start it charged commission rates that were 25 per cent lower than those of the regular firms and showed large profits despite these differences. This also helps explain why the company got more consignments during the first month of its existence than did any of the other thirty-eight firms on the South St. Paul market, and why five months after its beginning it was handling about 25 per cent of the livestock coming on the market. This success let loose a flood of harmful propaganda against it, which, in turn, prompted the management to encourage the signing of contracts between the locals and the Central.

By 1922 the Central appears to have brought about some degree of stability to the South St. Paul market. The extent of its influence is hard to measure but it seems that the wild fluctuations of past years had been somewhat curbed. In 1927 one student wrote that "on some days other commission agencies do not sell any livestock until they have learned the Central's opening price. This is especially true in selling hogs, of which the Central often controls forty per cent of the daily receipts."[47]

In the spring of 1925, some 631 shipping associations owned stock in the Central. Twenty years after its founding, it had 593 shipping associations in Minnesota, Wisconsin, the Dakotas, and Montana as members. Over the period 1921 to 1939 the Central had gross sales amounting to more than $465,000,000 and paid back more than $1,900,000 in patronage dividends.[48]

47. Steen, *Coöperative Marketing,* pp. 110–11; Gaumnitz, in *The Marketing of Farm Products,* p. 133.

48. *Minnesota Farm Bureau News,* May 1, 1925; Central Cooperative Association, *20 Years of Working Together* (South St. Paul, Minn., 1941), pp. 5, 45.

As in the case of grain and livestock, once the local dairy cooperatives ad shown their value, the next step was to organize regional marketing sociations. Progress was made in the marketing of fluid milk and manuictured products, including cheese and butter.

The attempt to organize fluid-milk marketing associations was noth-g new. Such associations, weak and isolated though they were, existed uring the last decades of the nineteenth century. Still, one must look the World War years to find the first successful large-scale associations. mong the first to organize were those in the Chicago, New York, and oston areas. During the nineteenth century the idea appeared among the astern producers and then spread into the Middle West, but the methods nployed later were popularized by the producers of the Chicago area. heir chief weapon, the strike, was borrowed from organized labor.

The thing that drove the producers together was the low price of milk. appears that from the latter part of 1912 to the end of 1915, milk prices ere almost invariably higher than those of other commodities; but the ear 1916 showed that a wide disparity had developed. Using the years 910 to 1914 as the base, milk prices late in 1916 were more than thirty oints lower than were those of all other commodities. In the spring of 917 milk prices dropped to even lower levels, with no relief in sight. he first reaction of the milk producers was to turn to the existing coperatives for relief.[49]

The producers of the Chicago area were the first to act. In the spring f 1916 there were about 13,000 producers supplying milk to Chicago, bout 2,600 of whom belonged to the Chicago Milk Producers' Associaon. It is claimed that 52 per cent of the townships adjoining this area ere about 70 per cent organized, that over 65 per cent of the farms were perated by tenants, and that some 56 per cent of the producers were oreign-born.

In 1916, producers for the Chicago market asked $1.55 per hundred ounds for 3.5 per cent milk, an increase over the past year, to which the istributors replied by offering $1.33½ per hundred. This was rejected y the producers, who decided instead to withhold their milk from the arket. In about one week their prices were met and the strike was over.

49. Hutzel Metzger, *Cooperative Marketing of Fluid Milk*, U. S. Dept. Agri., echnical Bulletin 179 (Washington, 1930), pp. 1–9.

From the Chicago area the strike spread into southern Illinois. The the farmers asked $1.40 for 3.5 per cent milk sent to the St. Louis marke But although a strike was called, it failed because the producers were u able to restrict the supply of milk sufficiently to enforce their demand The distributors managed to beat the strike by getting milk from no striking farmers and condensery districts outside the area and even b hauling it in from great distances.

By September, 1916, stories of the success of the organized dairymen ha reached the members of the Dairymen's League of New York, and leader of the Chicago dairymen was asked to come to New York. H helped to arouse the enthusiasm of the farmers there and they set a ne price of $2.05 per hundred for 3 per cent milk. After a couple of month distributors handling 65 per cent of the milk were reported to have m the League prices; the other distributors gradually fell in line and th strike was at an end. Meanwhile, the strike idea had spread among pr ducers in New England, New York, Pennsylvania, and Ohio.

The strikes staged by the milk producers during the years 1916 t 1920 were fairly successful, despite their temporary effects. They helpe focus attention on the sources of the cities' milk supplies and told th public that the farmers had to have a fair price. They were responsib for the increases in retail prices paid by the consumers, and they helpe strengthen the cooperative ties of the producers. It is worth noting th the resistance of the consumers to these price increases was less than might have been because of the general rise in price levels.

The only strike of importance during the twenties was that of the Pur Milk Association of Chicago in 1929. Once under way, a committee re resenting the public was appointed to probe the strike. Interestingl enough, the investigating committee advised price increases to the pr ducers. The producers had demanded $2.85 per hundred, but the distr butors were willing to pay only $2.50 for 3.5 milk. The distributors chos to ignore the committee's recommendations. A strike was called that wa later put into the hands of an arbitrator. The arbitrator put the price a $2.64 for the first three months and ruled that the distributors were to pa one cent per hundred pounds to the Pure Milk Association on all mil received; the distributors also were bound to reject milk from producer who were not members of the association. Perhaps the big difference b

ween this and other strikes was that the consumers favored price in-
reases for the producers.[50]

Among the first of the large-scale fluid-milk-marketing associations, nd a typical one, was the Twin City Milk Producers' Association which perated in the Minneapolis and St. Paul area. Before the association came nto being in 1916, there were local groups in the adjoining counties. For nstance, in Washington County, Minnesota, there was the Woodbury Milk Producers' Association, with 175 members, that had been marketing he milk of its patrons for the past three years; and there were similar rganizations doing business in Hennepin, Dakota, and Rice counties. These associations had made efforts to better the market, but without sucess. Eventually this brought about a reaction. Farmers in Hennepin County began complaining about this treatment to the county agent, K. A. Kirkpatrick, who finally decided to call together the producers nd distributors to settle their differences. As usual, the attitude of the dealers was one of indifference.

This prompted Kirkpatrick to get in touch with agents and leaders in nearby communities and to begin organizing them in preparation for a central organization. On September 1, 1916, after much discussion, the Twin City Milk Producers' Association was formed "to protect the rights of the dairymen in the twin cities area." It was recommended that "producers get for their milk at least 50% of the highest prevailing prices in he Twin Cities, F.O.B. their farms or shipping points," the price to be based on milk meeting the legal standards set by the state. A sliding scale, based on the butterfat content of the milk, was recommended.[51]

Originally, the Twin City Milk Producers' Association was organized as a bargaining association; it was incorporated early in 1917 and began to handle the milk of its members that spring, but the next year the entire bargaining plan was given up.

In 1930 the association drew its milk from within a radius of forty miles. Of the ninety-six creameries and cheese factories within this area, fifteen were owned and operated by the association. One would have the impression that the association was in a position to exercise monopoly control, but the total milk production in this forty-mile radius was about five

50. *Ibid.*, pp. 11–13.
51. Twin City Milk Producers' Association, *Annual Report, 1920,* pp. 12–14.

times the amount needed in the cities. Within an eighty-mile radius there was about twenty times the amount that was needed for fluid-milk consumption.[52]

Late in 1919 and on beyond the mid-twenties, a series of changes were made in the form of the organization. In 1919 a single share of stock which originally had a par value of one dollar then had a book value of $6.50. At the same time an increase was ordered in the capitalization from $50,000 to $500,000 and in the par value of the stock from $1 to $50 in order to make it possible for the association to purchase factories that were owned by the local groups. In 1922 the capitalization was raised to $1,000,000 and again in 1926 to $3,000,000.

Beginning in 1919 the association enjoyed a period of good prices. They were as follows:

1919	$3.05	1925	$2.37
1920	2.82	1926	2.29
1921	1.97	1927	2.47
1922	2.16	1928	2.53
1923	2.50	1929	2.45
1924	2.12	1930	2.02

But from 1931 on there followed a period of low prices. That year the average price was $1.52, and the next year it was $1.12. Other creameries crowded into the Twin Cities area and promised to sell at lower prices than did the association. One creamery made a contract on the basis of thirty cents per hundred less than the association price. This led to a milk war in 1933. In January the price to the distributors was ninety-five cents a hundred, in February eighty-four cents, and in March sixty cents. At this time milk in Minneapolis sold at a retail price of five cents a quart at home. Fortunately, the members remained loyal to the association and within a short time all milk-market customers had returned to the association for their supply and had made long-term contracts. This was a turning point in the history of the organization.

Other milk markets had encountered similar difficulties, but with the coming of the New Deal, marketing agreements were entered into. The Twin City Milk Producers' got one for its market. The first marketing

52. Metzger, *Cooperative Marketing of Fluid Milk*, pp. 81–82.

agreement provided for a price of not less than $1.42 a hundred for 3.5 per cent milk and a retail price of eight cents a quart. Late in November, 1933, this was changed to provide for a minimum price of $1.70 a hundred, and there were other changes after that as well.[53]

Another Twin Cities cooperative, the Franklin Cooperative Creamery Association, was organized by producers, milk-wagon drivers, and some distributors who did not cooperate with the Twin City Milk Producers' Association. This association retailed milk and began its operations in March, 1921, with eighteen wagons. About a year and a half later it operated 130 wagons and delivered half the milk in Minneapolis.[54]

Another type of cooperative dairy association was that dealing with manufactured products, such as butter and cheese. Large-scale associations handling these products were built where the local creameries were the most numerous. In 1934 some 1,079 local cooperative creameries operating in Wisconsin, Minnesota, and Iowa produced about 68 per cent of the butter turned out by the nation's cooperatives. Cooperative cheese factories also had made their greatest progress in the western Middle West. Almost two-thirds of the total production of American and foreign types of cheese were manufactured there. Other states, in the order of their importance from the standpoint of volume, were Minnesota, Illinois, and New York.[55]

One of the first and most successful of these dairy associations, and also the largest, was the Land O'Lakes Creameries, Incorporated, a federation of local associations located largely in Minnesota, Wisconsin, and the Dakotas. The first step taken by local cooperative creameries toward this end came in 1919, when county associations were established in Houston and McLeod counties in Minnesota. The next year even more effective county organizations were set up. By the end of 1920, fifteen counties in Minnesota and one in Wisconsin had formed county cooperative associations. The annual output of butter manufactured by the 226 creameries belonging to these county associations amounted to about forty million pounds.

Next the dairymen began to talk of improvement, standardization,

53. Twin City Milk Producers' Association, *Annual Report, 1920*, pp. 12–17, and *Annual Report, Twenty-Fifth Anniversary Number* (St. Paul, 1941), XXV, 42–43.

54. Filley, *Cooperation in Agriculture*, pp. 283–84.

55. Fetrow, *Cooperative Marketing of Agricultural Products*, pp. 23–24.

and marketing of cooperative-creamery butter through a more central association of these local units. In 1921 matters were helped along by the organization of the Minnesota Department of Agriculture, which was staffed with men who were sympathetic with the problems of the local cooperatives. First the idea was to establish a state-wide organization, but the shortcomings of an organization based on such political boundaries were obvious. No state-wide association was in existence, and there was no body of experience from which to draw. The marketing plan proposed was accepted by representatives from over 330 cooperatives who came together in June, 1921. The name Land O'Lakes was adopted for all butter scoring 93 or better, and in 1926 the name of the marketing association was changed from Minnesota Cooperative Creameries Association to Land O'Lakes Creameries, Incorporated.[56]

The central agency usually received products from local associations on a consignment basis and then repacked them under the trade name and sold them. Savings were also made possible for members through the cooperative purchasing of creamery supplies, by emphasizing quality of product, and by shipping goods in large quantities. Field men helped encourage more efficient creamery operation. In 1934 the association sold about eighty million pounds of butter, a large part of which went to eastern markets, and in addition Land O'Lakes now handled cheese, cream, casein, milk powder, and poultry products.[57]

Another type of cooperative dairy organization was the producers centralizer association, usually operating within a radius of 200 miles or more from the manufacturing plant. This type of association was usually found in regions where dairying was a side line and cream shipments were small. Such agencies were established by the Farmers' Equity Union in Orleans, Nebraska; Aberdeen, South Dakota; and elsewhere. These associations marketed their butter through the Chicago Equity Union Exchange, which began business operations in 1928.[58]

56. *Land O'Lakes Creameries, Incorporated, Its Organization, Nature and History* (Minneapolis, 1934), pp. 19–27; A. W. McKay and C. H. Lane, *Practical Cooperative Marketing* (New York, 1928), pp. 151–63; see also Deane W. Malott, *Problems in Agricultural Marketing* (New York, 1938), pp. 227–33, for a discussion of the sales policy of Land O'Lakes.

57. Fetrow, *Cooperative Marketing of Agricultural Products,* p. 26.

58. McKay and Lane, *Practical Cooperative Marketing,* pp. 168–69; Filley, *Cooperation in Agriculture,* pp. 298–99.

The most conspicuous example of a large-scale cheese-marketing association was the Wisconsin Cheese Producers' Federation Cooperative. This helped develop more effective sales programs for the marketing of cheese produced by cooperatives in Wisconsin and southeastern Minnesota. Its history goes back to the formation of the Sheboygan County Cheese Producers' Federation in Wisconsin in 1913. There were forty-three member factories in the federation at the time, but its activities expanded. Later the name was changed to the Wisconsin Cheese Producers' Federation and in 1928 to the National Cheese Producers' Federation. In 1929 the federation controlled about 60 per cent of the Swiss-cheese production of Wisconsin and about 30 per cent of the limburger production. The next year the federation was recognized as the regional marketing agency of the Federal Farm Board; late in 1934 it became a member of the Land O'Lakes Creameries; and the following year it adopted the name of the Wisconsin Cheese Producers' Federation Cooperative.[59]

Besides the marketing of grain, livestock, and dairy products, there were some developments in the marketing of potatoes and tobacco. The campaign to market potatoes cooperatively in the western Middle West reached its peak in Minnesota. In 1920 falling prices prompted the growers to organize the Minnesota Potato Growers' Exchange, a federation of local shipping associations representing about 10,000 growers in Minnesota, North Dakota, and South Dakota. Unfortunately, difficulties faced it from the very beginning. Prices received during the greater part of the first year were low when compared with those that buyers had offered growers earlier that year. Careless sorting and grading, the transaction of a small volume of business, the vesting of too much authority in the locals, and disorderly marketing simply added to the general dissatisfaction.

In 1923 the Minnesota Potato Growers' Exchange was reorganized and set out to remedy some of the past mistakes. This time the locals were ignored. The central body entered into contracts directly with the individual growers. But again disaster descended upon the group. Problems that

59. William Kirsch, "The History and Accomplishments of the Wisconsin Cheese Producers' Federation," Wisconsin Department of Markets, Vol. VI, *Bulletin No. 5* (1925); Senate Document 95, 70 Congress, 1 session, pp. 9–12, 627–65; Fetrow, *Cooperative Marketing of Agricultural Products*, pp. 23–24; R. W. Bartlett, *Cooperation in Marketing Products* (Springfield, Ill., 1931), pp. 75–78.

were peculiar to Minnesota and the industry were not anticipated. Th
fact that there were three separate potato-raising districts in Minnesot
each with distinctly different marketing problems was either ignored
completely overlooked. Returns from the sale of potatoes grown in th
eastern part of the state were used to buy warehouses and to pay fo
storage of potatoes in the other districts. This made the eastern growe
unhappy. Their potatoes came on the market first and they wanted pa
ment as soon as they were sold.

More trouble was created for the exchange because of the attempt th
had been made to finance the organization out of the first year's crop. Th
promotional expenses exceeded $80,000. This increased the general dissati
faction. Faulty accounting methods and a bumper crop in 1924 adde
to the woes of the exchange. Finally in 1925 the board of directors decide
to release the growers from their contracts and the exchange ceased t
function.[60]

More successful were the efforts of the cigar-leaf producers in th
neighboring state of Wisconsin. Here, too, it was low prices that force
the growers to organize the Northern Wisconsin Cooperative Tobacc
Pool. Once the organization was incorporated in the spring of 1922,
launched a campaign to control a minimum of 75 per cent of the tota
crop based on the 1920 acreage. About 7,200 growers signed pledges. Th
contract was a purchase-and-sale agreement noncancellable prior to Jun
1, 1927, after which it was to run from year to year terminable on June
of any year on thirty days' notice. Available figures indicate that durin
1922–23 more than 67 per cent of the state's total production was delivere
to the pool; during 1923–24 better than 64 per cent was delivered; an
during 1925–26 more than 58 per cent.

An attempt was made by some of the dissatisfied growers to end th
pool, but early in the spring of 1927 the decision was made to continue it
About 20,000,000 pounds of tobacco was pledged to the pool under th
new contract. Good management and wise policies made possible th
handling, processing, and selling of the tobacco at satisfactory prices
Perhaps the type of farmers that the pool appealed to and their economi

60. H. B. Price, "Farmers' Cooperation in Minnesota, 1917–1922," *University o Minnesota Agricultural Experiment Station, Bulletin* 202 (St. Paul, 1923), pp. 35–40 Senate Document 95, 70 Congress, 1 session, pp. 303–5.

position had something to do with the success of the pool. Another fact of some account was that there were more companies manufacturing cigars than there were producing most other tobacco products, hence greater competition and better sales opportunities.

By 1934 membership in the association had dropped to 7,700. By that time tobacco production had also dwindled in the state. Simultaneously the demand for cigar leaf had fallen off and the stocks of the association had grown.[61]

Of greater significance were the activities of the Missouri Farmers' Association in the field of cooperative marketing. The M.F.A. differed from the average cooperative in that it was involved in the entire gamut of marketing—the handling of grain, livestock, poultry, dairy products—and in making purchases of farmers' needs. The M.F.A., the state body, served as the coordinating, integrating, and educational force, with hundreds of affiliated associations.

Beginning with the organization of the first farm club in 1914 in Chariton County, Missouri, there were organized hundreds of local clubs, scores of county associations, and finally the M.F.A., the central body. William A. Hirth, the founder and head of the state body, advised the farmers to enlist from 200 to 300 members at each selling point in order to insure the success of the local association. The pooling of purchases seems to have accompanied the formation of a local farm club. As soon as 1,000 or 1,200 farmers were organized around different points, the farmers set up a county association and maintained an exchange that was intended to bring buyers and sellers together.

By 1920 hundreds of business associations were sponsored by the M.F.A. In June of that year the association controlled about 75 grain elevators, some 125 producer exchanges, and about 100 livestock-shipping associations. By 1924 the array of business agencies appeared even more formidable, and this despite the fact that the farmers were undergoing hard times. There was the Farmers' Livestock Commission Company at the National Stockyards in East St. Louis, which was organized in 1921 and received thousands of cars of livestock annually from the 300 or 400 local shipping associations and from private shippers as well, scattered through-

61. *Ibid.*, p. 200; Chris L. Christensen, *Farmers' Cooperative Associations in the United States, 1929,* U. S. Dept. Agri., Circular 94 (Washington, 1929), p. 43.

out the state. During 1923 the company handled 13,104 carloads of livestock, with the sales from these totaling $16,674,153 and the patronage dividends paid out amounting to $152,323.

Another firm, the Farmers' Union Livestock Commission at Kansas City and Chicago, was operated jointly by the Farmers' Union and the Missouri Farmers' Association, while still another, the Farmers' Union Livestock Commission at St. Joseph, was operated by the Farmers' Union, the Farm Bureau, and the M.F.A. These three firms, along with the Farmers' Livestock Commission Company at East St. Louis, handled a total of 46,655 carloads of livestock in 1923. The savings from their business operations totaled $386,896.75, which was paid back to the producers.

Early in 1924 the Missouri Farmers' Association established its own terminal egg-marketing sales agency in Chicago and another was in the process of being launched on the New York market. It was estimated that about 1,200 carloads of eggs would be marketed by the end of 1924. These eggs were shipped from the ten cold-storage plants of the association, which, in turn, were supplied by the produce exchanges scattered throughout the state. The report was that this phase of business activities had succeeded beyond all expectations because of the high quality of the products put on the market.

Another recent development was the establishment of the Producers' Grain Commission Company on the St. Louis market to market the grain of the various local associations. Plans also were devised to establish creameries and butter sales agencies to market the millions of gallons of cream which were handled annually by the produce exchanges and which, because of the want of such farmer-owned facilities, had to be sold through the existing butter-manufacturing agencies.

Besides these millions of dollars' worth of eggs, livestock, grain, and cream sold annually, there were more than five hundred carloads of live poultry and more than a million pounds of wool, seeds, and other miscellaneous products of the farm. Hundreds of thousands of dollars were also saved for members through the cooperative wholesale purchase of feeds, fertilizer, salt, and other merchandise.[62]

Organizations for the cooperative purchasing of farm supplies, though

62. Theodore Saloutos, "William A. Hirth and the Missouri Farmers' Association," *Missouri Historical Review,* XLIV (October, 1949), pp. 1–20.

known to the Grangers and other farm groups during the seventies, made the greatest strides after the first World War. Their growth was stimulated by the growing need for the type of farm supplies that technology had made necessary, the farm depression of the twenties, the high cost of supplies, and the relative ease with which purchasing cooperatives could be started. Again, it was the states of the western Middle West that took the lead in this. In 1939 Minnesota, Wisconsin, and Iowa had percentages of 45.5, 28.9, and 28.3 respectively of farms that reported cooperative purchases. Washington, North Dakota, Nebraska, South Dakota, and Idaho followed with 26.5, 25.8, 23.7, 23.5, and 23.5 per cent respectively.

Purchasing associations formed before 1916 handled chiefly groceries, clothing, and farm supplies. But after that the associations provided more specialized services, stocking such supplies as feed, seed, fertilizer, farm equipment, and petroleum products.[63]

The cooperative purchasing of petroleum products also gained headway in the western Middle West during the twenties. By 1928 the greatest strides appear to have been made in the rural areas of Minnesota, Nebraska, and Illinois. This progress was due largely to the fact that the oil business lent itself readily to the cooperative plan. Only a few lines were handled and the cost of the sales was small in comparison to the value of the business transacted.[64]

The first cooperative oil association is said to have been founded in Cottonwood, Minnesota, by members of the state farm bureau in 1921. In the same year farmers in Casco, Wisconsin, formed the second cooperative oil association.[65] In 1926 the Midland Cooperative Oil Association, the first wholesale agency to distribute gasoline, oil, kerosene, and grease, was organized. By 1930 the Midland had eighty-eight affiliated cooperative oil associations in Minnesota and fifty in Wisconsin.

The handling of petroleum products cooperatively spread into Illinois and Nebraska; state associations were formed in Minnesota and Nebraska

63. Joseph G. Knapp, *The Rise of Cooperative Purchasing,* Farm Credit Administration, Cooperative Research and Service Division (Washington, 1942), pp. 3–10 [mimeographed].

64. "Cooperative Purchasing of Gasoline and Motor Oils," *Monthly Labor Review,* XXVI (March, 1928), pp. 565–66.

65. "Cooperative Oil Associations in Minnesota," *ibid.,* XXV (December, 1927), p. 1287.

in 1927 and in Illinois in 1928. In 1929 the Farmers' Union Central Exchange of South St. Paul embarked on its oil program, and in the same year the Consumers' Cooperative Association of North Kansas City, Missouri, then known as the Union Oil Company, was organized. Although the chief item in the trade of the latter was petroleum products, it also started to handle other consumer goods.[66]

An unimportant but unique type of rural cooperative venture in the western Middle West was the cooperative burial association. In 1936 there were between forty and fifty such associations in operation in Iowa, Minnesota, and South Dakota. The largest of these was the Minnesota Valley Burial Association, with a membership of about 1,200. In Iowa the State Federation of Burial Societies included ten societies. Experience showed that a local society in order to have a good beginning had to have assets worth about $5,000 and a membership of 500, each paying $10. The manager of the association, generally the undertaker, received a salary. Savings were paid back to the families having funerals during the year in proportion to the prices paid. A lower-priced funeral cost $97 and a more elaborate one $172. In 1936 the Minnesota Valley Burial Association conducted eighty-six funerals at an average cost of $214. In 1936 the United States Bureau of Labor Statistics estimated that forty-two associations, with a membership of 27,000, did an annual business of $170,000.[67]

66. R. K. Froker and J. G. Knapp, *Farmers' Purchasing Associations in Wisconsin*, Farm Credit Administration, Cooperative Division, Bulletin 20 (Washington, 1937); H. A. Cowden, "Oil and Gasoline Cooperatives," *Annals of the American Academy of Political and Social Science*, CXCI (May, 1937), pp. 109–12; Ellis Cowling, *Cooperatives in America* (New York, 1938), p. 123.

67. O. E. Burley, *The Consumers' Cooperative as a Distributive Agency* (New York, 1939), pp. 114–15; James Myers, Jr., *Cooperative Funeral Associations*, The Cooperative League of the United States (New York and Chicago, 1946) [pamphlet]; see pages 37–38 for a list of the various cooperative funeral associations in the country.

Chapter XI

THE FARM BLOC

1920-23

As conspicuous as the rapid growth of the cooperative movement and the rise to power of the American Farm Bureau Federation was the political role played by the farmers during the early twenties. In this they were hardly novices, as the experiences of the Grangers, the Populists, and the Nonpartisan League had earlier shown. As seen, the Republicans, who had made a clean sweep in the elections of 1920, had no farm program to offer, despite the fact that the depression was in full swing by the time that Harding took office. In 1920 it was foreign policy and not the agricultural problem that had held the political spotlight. But once the seriousness of the depression began to be felt, the farm problem attracted the attention of a growing number of congressmen and senators, who pressed the administration for action. This agitation took two forms. One group, comprised of progressives, liberals, and radicals of various shades, sought social reform, and favored the establishment of a new political alignment patterned after the British Labor party. A second group, more pragmatic but equally ambitious, the "farm bloc," taking a leaf from the book of other pressure groups, launched an independent program of bipartisan action.[1]

1. Fred H. Haynes, "The Collapse of the Farmer-Labor Bloc," *Social Forces,* IV (September, 1925), pp. 148–56; E. D. Graper, "The American Farmer Enters Politics," *Current History,* XIX (February, 1924), p. 817; Arthur Capper, *The Agricultural Bloc* (New York, 1922).

In politics the term "bloc" is applied to a group of legislators who are strong enough to pass laws favorable to their interest and by the very same token to prevent the passage of measures held to be harmful. Their strategy is both offensive and defensive. Usually party lines are discarded and the combined strength of the bipartisan forces often is adequate to "tip the legislative scales in their favor."[2]

Bloc politics was nothing new to the American political scene when the farm group formed. We had had silver blocs, tariff blocs, big-business blocs, a Pacific Coast bloc, an irrigation bloc, an ex-servicemen's bloc, and even a "baby congressmen's" bloc. The big difference between the farm bloc and the other interest groups was that the latter did not operate openly and as such in the congressional debates, but secretly "through the manipulation of the regular party machinery." As for the farm bloc, its leaders openly stated that it represented the agricultural interests and came forward with "a distinct program outside the regular legislative program of either party." To many, this was not only a novel departure from our traditional two-party system, but also a distinct threat to it. Events soon proved that these apprehensions were unwarranted.[3]

The basic assumption of farm bloc theorists was that the prosperity of agriculture was fundamental to the prosperity of the nation and hence it was necessary to raise farming to a status of equality with industry.[4] To be sure, this was to be the basic theme of the McNary-Haugenites, of the Federal Farm Board, and also of the Triple A.[5] The time had come when it was politically expedient to demand parity for agriculture.[6]

Bloc leaders were insistent that the machinery of the federal government had to be employed to end discrimination against farmers. It had been used for the benefit of industry, finance, and commerce, and it was only just that it be used for agriculture. If Congress gave protection to

2. *Congressional Digest,* I (June, 1922), p. 4; *ibid.* (March, 1922), p. 18.

3. "The Farm Bloc—A Peril or a Hope?" *Literary Digest,* LXXI (December 24, 1921), p. 10; "Bloc Against Bloc," *The Nation,* CXIV (January 18, 1922), p. 58; Phillips Bradley, "The Farm Bloc," *Journal of Social Forces,* III (May, 1925), p. 714.

4. Arthur Capper, "The Agricultural Bloc," *Outlook,* CXXX (February 1, 1922), p. 176.

5. *Congressional Digest,* III (May, 1924), pp. 270, 276; see opening paragraphs of the House Committee on Agriculture Report on House Resolution 1, *ibid.,* VIII (May, 1929), p. 140.

6. John D. Black, *Parity! Parity!! Parity!!!* (Cambridge, Mass., 1942), pp. 53–54.

American manufacturers, it was incumbent that the same be done for agriculture. If Congress established a banking system that was helpful to the business and commercial interests of the nation, then it was the duty of Congress to do the same for the farmers. If Congress failed to respond, bloc spokesmen were justified in taking the initiative to press for such action.

Bloc leaders were on the watch for cries of favoritism and special privilege. They insisted that since agricultural prosperity was essential to national prosperity, the enactment of the desired legislation would be beneficial to the entire nation and not merely to favored sections or industries.

Nor was the emphasis that they placed on legislation to be construed to mean that the sole hope for the farmer was to be focused in the passage of remedial legislation. But it was to be interpreted to mean that the co-operation of the executive and legislative branches could hasten the return of a healthy agriculture.[7]

The farm-bloc program came into being because the Republicans had failed to offer a satisfactory agricultural plan in the special session that had been called by Harding. The regular Republicans wanted tax and tariff revision, while the western representatives were interested chiefly in cooperative legislation, liberal credit facilities, and the regulation of the packers.[8] The crisis came on July 5, 1921, when the regulars tried to adjourn Congress without having taken the desired action. The rebellious westerners, pressed for action by their constituents, succeeded in postponing the adjournment of Congress by the narrow margin of 27 to 24. This was the first outward act of defiance to regular leadership and definitely pinned on the agrarians the name "farm bloc."[9]

The leadership in the formation of this bloc was furnished by the American Farm Bureau Federation, acting largely through its Washington representative, Gray Silver, dubbed the "Silver Eel" by some. Silver, a former member of the West Virginia senate and an able lobbyist, had been watching the progress of farm legislation during the closing session of the Sixty-sixth Congress, and reported back to Farm Bureau

7. Capper, in *Outlook*, CXXX (February 1, 1922), pp. 176–77.

8. J. G. Welliver, "Agricultural Crisis and the Bloc," *American Review of Reviews,* LXV (February, 1922), p. 159.

9. Graper, in *Current History,* XIX (February, 1924), p. 819.

headquarters on what had been taking shape. By the time the Sixty-seventh Congress was to assemble, the condition of agriculture had grown progressively worse. The Farm Bureau, Silver, and others, fully aware of the need for a positive program of action, called together a group of men who assembled in the Washington office of the federation. This was on May 9, 1921. Most prominent of those present were Senators William S. Kenyon of Iowa, an able floor leader but no organizer, Arthur Capper of Kansas, an able organizer but a weak floor leader, and Ellison D. Smith of South Carolina. Later, a meeting of this group took place in the Chicago offices of the federation.[10]

The number of senators belonging to the bloc varied. Some thirty-odd members belonged to it at one time or another, but the chances are that the effective number at any one time probably was not more than twenty-six or twenty-seven. In the House the membership was even more fluid. Ninety-five or ninety-six congressmen, under the leadership of L. J. Dickinson of Iowa, were recognized as being strongly agrarian in their sentiments, while some twenty others were regarded as sympathetic.[11] Even though southerners figured prominently in farm-bloc activities, the fact seems to be that the program largely originated in the western Middle West, having grown out of the special desires of the senators and representatives from this area. In this the grain growers of the Middle West had the strategic position, and they created an alliance with leaders from the Far West and the lower South based upon the common economic need for agricultural relief.[12]

The tactics employed by these two groups varied. The members of the Senate bloc held regular meetings to which cabinet members and experts were invited to speak. In the House the bloc functioned through key men in the state delegations and on important committees.

The program of the bloc appears to have been shaped largely by the Senate group acting with Silver. A few joint meetings were held with the House members, but the real leadership was furnished by Kenyon while he was a member of the Senate and later by Capper and Smith.

10. John K. Barnes, "The Man Who Runs the Farm Bloc," *World's World,* XLV (November, 1922), pp. 51–59.

11. Bradley, in *Journal of Social Forces,* III (May, 1925), pp. 715–16.

12. E. Pendleton Herring, "Farm Bloc," *Encyclopaedia of the Social Sciences* (15 vols., New York, 1937), VI, 103.

The resolutions that were passed in the annual sessions of the American Farm Bureau Federation, which were drawn up from the results of polls that were conducted by Silver, helped to keep close ties between the farmers and the bloc.

On the offensive these agricultural spokesmen were especially potent. Between July 5 and August 25, when the special session finally adjourned, five measures were passed that were of direct interest to agriculture. These included a packer-control bill, the Futures Trading Act, legislation lengthening the life of the War Finance Corporation in order to help farmers find foreign markets, and two acts relating to the Federal Farm Loan System which increased the capital of the board and the interest rate on farm loan bonds to 5½ per cent.[13] These measures bore out the convictions of one observer who said that the farm bloc "is aggressive and cohesive and knows precisely what it wants and how to get it."[14]

A prime goal on the farm-bloc agenda was legislation to regulate the packers and the stockyards. Agitation for legislation of this type had been waged for some years and had grown out of the low prices that the livestock growers had received for their animals. The meat packers had also incurred the wrath of consumers, who charged that they paid too much for their meat, but the truth of the matter is that the demand for regulation had come mostly from the producers, who complained of low and fluctuating prices.[15]

A feeling of distrust toward the meat packers had grown with the outbreak of the European war and the rising cost of living. The farmers in particular felt that they were denied a just price. Hence in 1915 a conference was called in Chicago to help bring about an understanding between the industry and the livestock growers. Livestock men, packers, wholesalers, and retailers were represented. The meat packers, unfortunately, were not there in person. Instead there was an agent representing them who did much listening and very little talking. This the producers took as a slight, because they had come there with the full expectation that the meat packers would appear in person to explain why livestock prices had not risen as they had expected.

13. Bradley in *Journal of Social Forces,* III (May, 1925), pp. 715–16.

14. *Literary Digest,* LXXI (December 24, 1921), p. 102.

15. "A Bill to Make the Packers Be Good," *Literary Digest,* LXVIII (February 5, 1921), pp. 10–11.

The demand for an investigation of the industry grew. After some controversy, the President ordered the Federal Trade Commission to investigate the industry from the "hoof to the table," as someone put it, to determine whether or not there were any "manipulations, controls, trusts, combinations, or restraints out of harmony with the law or the public interest."[16] As the investigation proceeded, the clamor for reform mounted. In so far as the press, the public, and the politicians were concerned, the meat packers were chiefly responsible for the high cost of living.[17]

Shortly after the Federal Trade Commission had completed its investigation and made its recommendations, bills were introduced in both houses authorizing the President to acquire and operate the large stockyards which the commission had recommended to be taken over. Two of the proposals provided for government acquisition and operation of the larger stockyards, while one, the Kenyon bill, strictly a war measure, treated the meat-packing business as a public utility.

The meat-packing industry also became a prime concern of the "red-baiting" Attorney General, A. Mitchell Palmer. Finally, at the request of the packers, a conference was arranged between their representatives and Palmer, who stipulated that the packers must agree to "go out and stay out directly and indirectly, from all the lines of business unrelated to the meat business, and in addition must submit to an enforceable injunction against any act that would constitute a violation of the Sherman Anti-trust law. . . ." Eventually this led to the drawing-up of the Packers' Consent Decree, which had the effect of congressional legislation on the subject but with one major difference: by cleaning up the packing industry from within, this decree was intended to forestall the passage of the more drastic legislation that had been recommended by the Federal Trade Commission.

But agitation for legislation to regulate the packers persisted despite the decree, and the result was the enactment of the Packers and Stockyards Act in 1921. This measure provided that packers engaged in interstate commerce were prohibited from resorting to unfair, discriminatory, or deceptive practices, manipulating or controlling prices, or otherwise

16. G. O. Virtue, "The Meat-Packing Investigation," *Quarterly Journal of Economics,* XXXIV (August, 1920), pp. 626–30.

17. "Packers State Their Case," *Literary Digest,* LXIII (October 4, 1919), pp. 14–15.

creating a monopoly and restraining commerce. Commission merchants, yard dealers, and those engaged in stockyard services were required to establish reasonable rates. The Secretary of Agriculture was empowered to enforce this act, subject to court appeal and a heavy fine for its violation.[18]

The reaction to this measure was pretty much what would have been expected. Those who wanted more stringent controls said that it would not bring down prices because it was "vague in the extreme" and totally inadequate to cope with the problem that it was intended to solve. One packer pointed out that the measure would have little effect on prices, because it was not the meat packers that depressed their prices, but the inefficient system of marketing under which the farmers operated.[19]

The act was enforced with a certain degree of success, but not without some resistance. Late in 1921 the Chicago livestock interests unsuccessfully tried to restrain its enforcement.[20] In 1923 two cooperative firms filed suit with the Packers and Stockyards Administration, charging that members of the Kansas City Livestock Exchange discriminated against them because of their refusal to sell or purchase livestock from them. In 1924 after some bitter controversy, the Secretary of Agriculture signed an order notifying fifty-six commission firms and thirty traders to cease discriminating against at least one cooperative firm. This supports the observations of two authorities who said that the cooperatives, with few exceptions, were well treated by the packers and the stockyards but not by the private commission firms and livestock exchanges.[21]

Other actions of the Packers Administration reveal the character of the work it performed. It helped to end the practice of discrimination by private firms against traders and buyers who bought and sold livestock of the cooperatives. It helped the cooperatives find open competitive markets. Hearings were also conducted at Omaha, Sioux City, and Kansas City, where the books of many private commission firms were investigated

18. *The Packers' Consent Decree* (71 Congress, 3 session, Senate Document 324, serial 9347, Washington, 1931), pp. 21–26.

19. "Uncle Sam to Control the Packers," *Literary Digest,* LXX (July 2, 1921), p. 16.

20. *The New International Year Book,* 1921, p. 23.

21. Edwin G. Nourse and Joseph G. Knapp, *The Co-Operative Marketing of Livestock* (Washington, 1931), pp. 150, 158.

by government auditors who sought to find out what the average cost of doing business was. A comparison of the figures of the private companies and the cooperatives placed the farmers' agencies in a very favorable light. Obviously, the cooperatives had injected much vigor into the enforcement of the Packers and Stockyards Act.[22]

Equally important to the farm bloc was the passing of legislation to regulate the grain exchanges of the country. Movements of this type had been on foot since the days of the Grangers. For the most part they succeeded in forcing the grain exchanges to clean house on their own, as the Packers' Consent Decree was intended to do, thus checking the passage of regulatory legislation.[23] But this time there was no escape; the Futures Trading Act was passed. This put a prohibitive tax of twenty cents a bushel on speculative transactions such as "puts and calls," "bids," "offers," "indemnities," and "ups and downs" and on grain sold for future delivery except when the transactions were made by owners of the grain through certain authorized contract markets. These authorized contract markets were placed under the supervision of the Secretary of Agriculture, who, along with the Secretary of Commerce and the Attorney General, had the power to punish violators by revoking their privileges.[24] In 1922 this act was declared unconstitutional by the United States Supreme Court.[25]

Tariff protection was another aim, but it was not brought to the fore by the farm bloc. Although this movement gained greater momentum later, some of the farm-bloc spokesmen, in cooperation with a western tariff bloc, kept protectionist sentiment alive by insisting that the same policy that had been used to build up industry had to be applied to agriculture. Also, they remonstrated that foreign products had to be kept out if the American farmers were to survive.[26]

It was logic such as this, before the farm bloc took form, that was behind the emergency tariff bill that was introduced in Congress during the closing days of the Wilson administration. The bill met a hostile reception.

22. *Ibid.*, pp. 189, 241, 244.

23. Herman Steen, *Coöperative Marketing* (New York, 1923), p. 211.

24. *The New International Year Book*, 1921, p. 23.

25. U. S. Dept. Agri., *Yearbook*, 1922, pp. 48–49; G. O. Virtue, "Legislation for the Farmers: Packers and Grain Exchanges," *Quarterly Journal of Economics*, XXXVII (August, 1923), pp. 693–704.

26. Capper, *The Agricultural Bloc*, pp. 105–7, 148.

It was assailed as "vicious class legislation," "fragmentary, faulty, and lopsided," "a meaningless sop to the farmers," "a crude, impractical, and dangerous procedure" that had been evolved without any hearings or the benefit of expert testimony, the sole effect of which was going "to raise the price of a barrel of flour, a loaf of bread, or a mutton chop. . . ." One had sympathies for farmers whose harvest in 1921 was worth $5,000,000,000 less than it had been the year before, but what would it do to the salaried classes and the wage earners who would have to foot the bill if such legislation were passed? The evidence seemed to be that wages were being reduced in the textile and the iron and steel industries on the grounds that living costs had been falling. One could hardly be reasonable in demanding that food and clothing prices go up while wages were being slashed.[27]

One of the strongest arguments against tariff legislation like this was that it would fail to find new markets for farm products. In fact, nations like Argentina and Canada and several European countries had already been talking about reprisals against the United States. On March 3, 1921, President Woodrow Wilson with statesmanlike vision vetoed the bill.

> If we wish to have Europe settle her debts, governmental or commercial, we must be prepared to buy from her, and if we wish to assist Europe and ourselves by the export either of food, or raw materials, or finished products, we must be prepared to welcome commodities which we need and which Europe will be prepared, with no little pain, to send us. Clearly this is no time for the erection of high trade barriers. It would strike a blow at the large and successful efforts which have been made by many of our great industries to place them on an export basis. It would stand in the way of the normal readjustment of business conditions throughout the world, which is as vital to the welfare of this country as to that of all the other nations.[28]

Shortly after Harding was inaugurated as President, a second emergency tariff bill was introduced; and this time the Republicans, in full control and committed to a policy of protection, made the measure law. In November the act was extended until other provisions were made by law.[29]

Rural credit became another major concern of the farm bloc. This, of

27. "Doubtful 'Aid' for the Farmers," *Literary Digest,* LXVIII (January 8, 1921), pp. 12–13.
28. Quoted in Wilson Gee, *American Farm Policy* (New York, 1934), pp. 25–26.
29. *The New International Year Book,* 1921, p. 23.

course, came as no surprise in a period of low prices and forced liquidation, of deposit withdrawals and depleted reserves. Livestock raisers, cotton producers, wheat and dairy farmers, and cooperative marketing associations alike faced trying financial conditions.

The first move was to revive the lending powers of the War Finance Corporation. This was done early in 1921 to promote foreign trade. But when this failed to achieve the desired ends, pressure was exerted for added legislation. While the Joint Commission of Agricultural Inquiry was trying to find out what was needed in the way of permanent legislation, Congress, because of farm-bloc pressure, amended the provisions of the War Finance Corporation, authorizing it to extend further loans.

The War Finance Corporation, in passing on loans, had exercised the most careful surveillance. Even though it was authorized to make loans up to the exent of a billion dollars, the loans of the corporation at their highest point amounted to only $201,000,000. This was a negligible sum when compared with the more extensive loans made under the liberal credit policy of the Federal Reserve Banks, which received bitter protests from the farmers who were caught short at the time that the credit-expansion policy was curtailed. The Iowa country bankers were but one group to protest against the war agency because of its rigid security requirements.

The advances that were made by the corporation, for the most part, were used to convert frozen credits into liquid assets. In Iowa 60 per cent of such advances were to be used for this very purpose and the rest were employed to renew past-due notes of the farmers. Only a very small percentage of the funds went for new credit. But in 1921 and 1922, when cooperatives were finding it hard to get funds, the War Finance Corporation was of great help. The required capital was advanced with the understanding that the cooperatives were not to use it for "speculative withholding to create an artificial scarcity for the sake of higher prices." After the War Finance Corporation had showed a willingness to advance funds to the cooperatives, local bankers also displayed a willingness to do so. The money that the corporation provided was a timely help, but by no stretch of the imagination was it to be assumed that it was to serve as a permanent rural-credits agency.[30]

30. Freida Baird and Claude L. Benner, *Ten Years of Federal Intermediate Credits* (Washington, 1933), pp. 38–52.

Besides liberalizing the facilities of the War Finance Corporation, there were changes in the Federal Land Bank System. Once the Supreme Court upheld the constitutionality of the Federal Farm Loan Act, new bond issues were floated, and lending operations were resumed. Still another change was an act authorizing the Secretary of the Treasury to place additional deposits in the Federal Farm Loan Banks to provide them with capital, pending the issuance of land bank bonds. Authority was also granted to raise the interest to be paid on land bank bonds from 5 to 5½ per cent, until June 30, 1923, hoping that this would make the bonds more marketable and thus help make the Land Bank System of greater use.[31]

What sympathies one had toward the farm bloc were pretty much a matter of "occupation and geography."[32] Opposition toward it was great in prominent financial and commercial circles, and President Harding and his administration were opposed to it. What had stirred up this opposition was the unwillingness of the westerners to vote for lower surtax rates.[33] Bloc tactics were hypocritically denounced as "un-American" and "a vicious European practice," especially by those who had been in the habit of receiving legislative favors.[34] Otto Kahn, a New York banker, was reportedly organizing a committee of businessmen to fight the demands of farm representatives in Congress and in the state legislatures.[35] A New York congressman introduced a bill aimed to outlaw all blocs, combinations, or agreements organized by congressmen who represented special or sectional interests.[36] New Hampshire-born Secretary of War John W. Weeks, a banker and broker by profession, saw in the bloc a real menace to American institutions. But one eastern paper, the *New York Globe,* took issue with Weeks, charging that he objected not so much to the bloc itself as to the fact that farm spokesmen finally had perfected a device that others had used with some success. After all, "Secretary Weeks has never

31. *The New International Year Book,* 1921, p. 23; Clara Eliot, *The Farmers' Campaign for Credit* (New York, 1927), pp. 74–75.

32. *Literary Digest,* LXXI (December 24, 1921), p. 10.

33. Graper, in *Current History,* XIX (February, 1924), p. 821; J. D. Beck, "The Farmers' Bloc," *La Follette's Magazine,* XIV (January, 1922), p. 3; Bradley, in *Journal of Social Forces,* III (May, 1925), p. 717.

34. *World's Work,* XLIII (December, 1921), p. 164.

35. Beck, in *La Follette's Magazine,* XIV (January, 1922), p. 3.

36. *The Commercial and Financial Chronicle,* CXIII (December 24, 1921), p. 2646.

evinced any alarm over the business bloc, which is active. His dismay arises from the fact that a new political power threatens the sway of his own group. . . ."[37]

Action to relieve the farmers also had been taken in other quarters. An October order of the Interstate Commerce Commission slashing freight rates on grains, grain products, and hay carried in the region between the Mississippi River and the Pacific Coast was followed by reductions in other parts of the country. Late in 1921 the Senate ordered the Federal Trade Commission to investigate the export prices paid to the grain growers. Secretary of Agriculture Henry C. Wallace kept pressing his demands for more research in the marketing of farm products, and President Harding, in his message to Congress in December, told the representatives that the main remedy for the relief of the farmers was to be found "in distribution and marketing."[38]

By this time the wheels had been well greased for legislative action. In December, 1921, Representative Sydney Anderson of Minnesota, the chairman of the Joint Commission of Agricultural Inquiry, which had been appointed earlier in the year, handed the first report of his committee to the President. On December 30 the President, now more sensitive than ever to the seriousness of the crisis, sent a letter to Wallace asking him to call the conference which he had been so insistent upon, but which both Hoover and Mellon had been dead against, to consider the plight of the farmers. It was suggested that "such a conference might divide itself into two parts: One to give consideration to our present day difficulties which, though temporary, are serious and need effective attention; the other part, a survey of the future in an effort to determine upon general policies, having in view the maintenance of production, the greatest possible use and at the same time the conservation of our agricultural resources, and the more complete coordination of our agricultural, manufacturing and general business interests."[39]

The first National Agricultural Conference met in Washington from January 23 to 27, 1922. All in all, there were 336 delegates and 20 different

37. *Literary Digest,* LXXI (December 24, 1921), p. 10.

38. *The New International Year Book,* 1921, pp. 23–24.

39. *Ibid.,* pp. 23, 27; Report of the Joint Commission of Agricultural Inquiry, *The Agricultural Crisis and Its Causes,* Part I (67 Congress, 1 session, House Report 408, serial 7922, 4 parts, Washington, 1921–22).

farm organizations present from 37 states. Some 80 farmers representing 30 states attended, as well as 84 representatives from agricultural organizations, 67 from businesses related to agriculture, and 18 women delegates. A few economists and "other scholars" were invited.[40]

Among those present was the nationally prominent economist, Richard T. Ely, who observed among other things that the delegates in general had a better grasp of economic issues than had the delegates to similar bodies in the past. Some of the "freaks" who had been in the habit of frequenting conventions were there, but they did not equal the number of those of earlier days:

> To be sure, we heard the old-time oratory and exhortations, to effect mighty combinations in order to smite the farmers' enemies "hip and thigh," to overthrow their evil machinations, and to press forward to achieve those things which would make the farmers prosperous, the implications being that there could be no doubt about measures which would restore prosperity and that only selfish and evil minded groups of powerful "interests" prevented the achievement of the desired ends. We heard the old familiar talk that the farmer does not fix his prices, while those whom he deals with fix their prices . . . we saw here and there that bird of prey, the demagogue in politics . . . but he evidently failed to reap any considerable harvest from this conference.[41]

The work of the conference was divided among twelve committees. When the committees finished their deliberations they made recommendations—most of which were not new—to Congress, the farmers, and the President. Congress, for instance, was advised to investigate means for stabilizing the dollar, to provide short-term credit if necessary, to continue the work of the War Finance Corporation, to amend the Federal Reserve Act to provide for an agricultural representative, to consider crop insurance, to ban tax-free securities, to restore the power of state railway commissions, to complete the Muscle Shoals project, to develop the St. Lawrence–Great Lakes Waterway, and to pass cooperative legislation.

40. Richard T. Ely, "The National Agricultural Conference," *American Review of Reviews,"* LXV (March, 1922), p. 271; Samuel Gompers, a member of the conference, wrote: ". . . the real farmers were not there, only those who exploited farmers. . . ." See Gompers, *Seventy Years of Life and Labor* (2 vols., New York, 1925), II, 521. For Wallace's views, see H. C. Wallace, *Our Debt and Duty to the Farmers* (New York, 1925), p. 521.

41. Ely, in *American Review of Reviews,* LXV (March, 1922), p. 271.

The farmers also were urged to cut their overhead costs, to diversify their crops, to adjust their production to the demands of the market, and to organize to advance their interests.

There were several other significant recommendations. One was the often repeated assertion that there could be no national prosperity unless capital and labor bore "a just share" with agriculture in the readjustment. Another, which soon received serious consideration, was that the President and Congress had better take steps to "re-establish a fair exchange value for all farm products." This was talking the language of McNary-Haugenism and parity. But price fixing and the issuance of more paper money as remedies were rejected, as was the Hoover-inspired proposal to have the Bureau of Markets transferred from the Department of Agriculture to the Department of Commerce.[42]

Next on the agenda were legislation defining and legalizing cooperatives engaged in interstate commerce, a new measure to regulate the grain exchanges of the country, authority for the placing of a "dirt farmer" on the Federal Reserve Board, the building of a protective wall around agricultural products, and the re-extension of the life of the War Finance Corporation.

One of the most important measures passed was the Capper-Volstead Act. This act removed all doubts about the legality of cooperative marketing associations engaged in interstate commerce by exempting them from prosecution under the antitrust laws. Unlike the Clayton Act of 1914, this allowed the farmers to organize marketing associations either with or without capital stock, provided that no member had more than one vote regardless of the amount of stock or membership capital he owned and provided that the dividend payments of the association did not exceed 8 per cent. Another important clause forbade associations incorporating under its provisions to handle products for nonmembers in excess of those handled for their own members.[43]

Another very important act, the Fordney-McCumber Tariff of 1922, which was in line with the protectionist sentiment of the postwar era, put many heavy duties on farm products, as did the Emergency Tariff of

42. *Ibid.*, p. 273.

43. *Cooperative Marketing* (70 Congress, 1 session, Senate Document 95, serial 8859, Washington, 1928), pp. 334, 392–93; *Congressional Digest,* I (March, 1922), p. 9.

1921. There were duties of thirty cents per bushel on wheat, three cents per pound on beef, two and a half cents per gallon on milk, eight cents per dozen on eggs, fifty cents per hundred on potatoes, and twenty-four cents per pound on scoured wool.[44]

Demands for added credit facilities were very strong during 1922. A sharp controversy revolved around the structure of this permanent rural-relief agency, but even at that some steps were taken to bring aid. Most important was the act extending the powers of the War Finance Corporation for another year. Another act of March 20 made available $1,500,000 for the purchase of seed grain in areas of crop failure. Under these provisions about twelve thousand loans in amounts of less than $300 were made to farmers in the Dakotas, Montana, Idaho, and Washington.[45]

An amendment to the Federal Reserve Act provided for the placing of an agricultural representative on the Reserve Board. Farm spokesmen accepted this as proof that agriculture was finally beginning to get treatment equal to that enjoyed by commerce and industry. Such a step had been advanced by those who felt that the postwar policies of the Federal Reserve Board had been guided by people who had no idea what effect its deflationary policy was going to have on the farmers. But evidence proved that the board had not adopted a discriminatory policy against agriculture, as farm leaders had long charged.[46]

Once the Supreme Court had declared unconstitutional the measure that had been passed in 1921 to regulate the grain exchanges, Congress was faced with the task of passing a new law. This was to be the Grain Futures Act of 1922, which was no different from the unconstitutional Futures Trading Act except that it was based on the power of Congress to regulate interstate commerce rather than on its power to tax.

Meanwhile, bloc tactics had started to assume different dimensions. The congressional elections of 1922 injected new life into the progressive ranks. Toward the end of the Sixty-seventh Congress a progressive bloc was formed, and into this passed many, if not most, of the old bloc members. This new bloc was formed in December, 1922, when the economic fortunes of the farmers had taken a turn for the better, and consisted of

44. F. W. Taussig, "The Tariff Act of 1922," *Quarterly Journal of Economics*, XXXVII (November, 1922), pp. 4–9.

45. *The New International Year Book*, 1922, p. 24.

46. Capper, *The Agricultural Bloc*, pp. 123–24.

thirty-two Senate and House progressives, including both Republicans and Democrats and one Farmer-Laborite. Enlisted in its ranks were such political warhorses from the western Middle West as La Follette of Wisconsin, Norris of Nebraska, Capper of Kansas, Frazier and Ladd of North Dakota, Brookhart of Iowa, and Shipstead of Minnesota. The program that it adopted was strictly a progressive one. It asked for the extension of the direct primary to the nomination of the President and Vice-President of the United States, for the direct election of these two officers without the electoral college, the passage of an effective corrupt-practices act, and the immediate release of all free-speech prisoners convicted under the wartime espionage laws.[47]

The leaders of this insurgent group, amidst the queries of onlookers, insisted that this was merely a protest against the policies and the personnel of the Harding administration and not a third-party movement. Still, the third-party implication was there. The appeals that the bloc made gave to it an ominous note. The support of the American Federation of Labor was solicited on the grounds that it favored legislation to protect labor, and the help of the farmers was also sought on the grounds that it favored the growth of cooperative marketing associations and legislation to stabilize prices.[48]

Little was to be expected from this group in the Sixty-seventh Congress, since the session was due to end in about three months. Yet its influence was felt. Its avowed purpose was "to drive special privilege out of control of the government and restore it to the people." To achieve this end there were created "special committees composed of members of the Senate and House cooperating with men of affairs and experts, to prepare and submit from time to time during this and the next Congress, practical and constructive plans for dealing with . . . Agriculture, labor, railroads, shipping, natural resources, credits, taxation, and amendments to the Constitution looking to the abolishment of the electoral college and the earlier meeting of the newly elected Congress."[49]

President Harding, bent upon stealing the thunder of the progressive

47. *The New International Year Book*, 1922, p. 24.

48. "Will the 'Insurgent Tail Wag the Party Dog?'" *Literary Digest*, LXXVI (March 31, 1923), p. 7.

49. "Big Possibilities of the Progressive Bloc," *Literary Digest*, LXXV (December 16, 1922), p. 7.

bloc, announced on the very same day that this group met in Washington that his administration would promptly take up legislation for further relief of the farmers. It was expected that certain of the progressive demands, such as the restoration of excess-profits taxes, would be ignored, but those which had formed the basis for the bloc program and had tempted some of the newly elected senators to fall into the progressive fold were expected to become part and parcel of the administration program.[50]

This soon became evident in the rural-credits campaign of 1923. The progressives were only partly responsible for this legislation. Republicans and Democrats who were not affiliated with the progressive cause contributed to its passage. Perhaps they had been prompted to vote for it because of the November elections and the fear that unless the farmers were placated, they would go over into the progressive columns en masse.[51]

The big difference between the credit demands of the early twenties and those of previous years was that the demands of the later years were for the purpose of keeping farm prices up rather than of stimulating production as in the earlier ones. Farmers had been complaining persistently that the lack of credit was one of the basic causes for low prices, a condition which they felt had been aggravated by the policies of the Federal Reserve Board. If only credit agencies were established that were peculiarly adapted to the special needs of the farmers, the deflationary spirals that they had earlier experienced would disappear.

The Joint Commission of Agricultural Inquiry had devoted an entire volume to the study of farm credits. It found that the complaints of the farmers that the Federal Reserve System had inaugurated a deflationary policy were not justified, but their demands for short-term credits were. The commission found that the lack of short-term credit was due largely to the fact that bank credit was extended usually for periods of six months or less. The reason that banks would not extend credit for a longer time was that the Federal Reserve Bank would not discount paper with a longer maturity period. Neither could mortgage companies handle loans of this type; their procedure was too cumbersome for it. The commission

50. *Literary Digest,* LXXVI (March 31, 1923), p. 9.

51. John W. Owens, "The Progressive Bloc," *New Republic,* XXXIV (March 14, 1923), p. 61.

also drafted a rural-credits bill that was later introduced in Congress as the Lenroot-Anderson bill.

Other investigations were launched by Senate and House committees, but the grievances that these agencies found were also pretty much the same as those presented by the commission: the lack of short-term credits, high interest rates, and the want of reliable sources from which the farmers could borrow.

If there was a general agreement on the short-term-credit needs of the farmers, there certainly was no such agreement about the means through which this aid was to be had. Not even bloc members could agree on that. Numerous bills had been introduced in Congress in 1922, conservative and radical, revolving chiefly around such proposals as amending the Federal Land Banks, extending the life of the War Finance Corporation, and increasing the credit facilities of the Federal Reserve Banks. In the end, the controversy narrowed down to one between the Lenroot-Anderson measure, sponsored by the Joint Commission of Agricultural Inquiry, and the Capper-McFadden bill, drawn up by Eugene Meyer, Jr., the managing director of the War Finance Corporation, and based largely on his experiences with this agency.

The Capper-McFadden bill was based on the assumption that the Federal Reserve System could be made to meet the needs of every type of farming except livestock raising, if the Federal Reserve Banks were allowed to discount paper on a nine-month instead of a six-month maturity basis, and if small rural banks with capital of less than $25,000 were allowed to join the system. As for the requirements of the livestock industry, they could be satisfied by specially created credit institutions.

The Lenroot-Anderson bill, on the other hand, was based on the assumption that the Federal Reserve System was incapable of providing for the intermediate needs of the farmers. It sought the creation of separate institutions connected with, yet independent of, the Federal Land Bank System. The initial capital for these banks would be provided by the United States Treasury and the funds for its operating expenses would be furnished by the sale of tax-free securities.

Strong differences existed over the relative merits of these two measures. The Capper-McFadden bill was strongly supported by the livestock industry and the cooperative marketing associations, while the Lenroot-

Anderson measure had the support of the American Farm Bureau Federation, the Grange, and the national Farmers' Union.

The general farm organizations felt that the Capper bill would be unsatisfactory to the needs of the general run of farmers, while the Lenroot bill was expected to furnish funds at lower rates of interest because the credit agencies set up under its provisions would have the privilege of issuing tax-free securities. The provision that loans would be extended from six months to three years was held to be a very satisfactory one. These two features in particular attracted the support of most of the farm organizations and the agricultural press. Wallace supported the measure, as did Hoover, who, despite this, believed that the credit needs of the farmers were being greatly exaggerated.

The Agricultural Credits Act of 1923, the bill that was finally passed, was an omnibus measure that took in features of the Capper and Lenroot bills and a lesser-known measure, the Strong bill. The act of 1923 was passed because the time was short and the political exigencies great. About all that Congress could do was to connect the several measures "end to end with only a little attempt at smoothing off the edges." Despite this it was passed in the closing hours of the Sixty-seventh Congress with great majorities.[52]

The Agricultural Credits Act set up two fundamentally different systems of farm credit: the Federal Intermediate Credit Banks, a government-owned, operated, and controlled system; and the National Agricultural Credit Corporations, private agencies which did not operate under government auspices but nonetheless were authorized by the national government and received financial support from it.

Twelve Intermediate Credit Banks were established in the same cities as the twelve Federal Land Banks. The Federal Farm Loan Board was given supervision over them, subject to the provisions of the Agricultural Credits Act. In this manner it was felt that the organization could be kept up at very little expense in periods when the demand for their services was small and expanded when the demand for short-term credits

52. Baird and Benner, *Ten Years of Federal Intermediate Credits,* pp. 67–82; Claude Benner, *The Federal Intermediate Credit System* (New York, 1926), pp. 103–23; G. C. Henderson, "The Agricultural Credits Acts of 1923," *Quarterly Journal of Economics,* XXXVII (May, 1923), pp. 518–22.

was great. Funds were to be furnished by the Secretary of the Treasury, who was directed to subscribe to capital stock in these banks, but not in excess of five millions for each bank. Additional funds were to be provided by authorizing the Intermediate Credit Banks to issue and sell collateral trust debentures. These banks were not to make loans directly to the farmers; the latter formed associations and then secured loans from the Intermediate Credit Banks without the help of commercial banks. Funds were to be made available for "any agricultural purpose or for raising, breeding, fattening, or marketing livestock."[53]

The Agricultural Credits Act also provided for the National Agricultural Credit Corporations. Their paper was first discounted by the Intermediate Credit Banks following an amendment to the act in 1925. These credit agencies were set up to meet the special needs of the livestock industry and were subject to federal control; the Comptroller of the Currency had the same power over them that he had over the national banks. But the use of these agencies was limited. After ten years of the Agricultural Credits Act, only three National Agricultural Credit Corporations were established, and only one of these was intended to serve as a permanent agency. The other two were emergency corporations organized to enable Iowa farmers to withstand the ruinously low corn prices of 1926. After the emergency had lifted both corporations went into voluntary liquidation.[54]

Other legislation was passed, too. In 1923 there was an extension to the Warehouse Act of 1916 increasing the number of commodities for which the federal government would issue licenses to warehouses. The "filled milk" bill also became law, thus outlawing in interstate commerce the shipment of milk whose fat content had been replaced in part or in whole with vegetable oil.

There were other measures for which there was some prospect of passage but which failed of enactment. These included the "truth-in-fabrics" bill, the numerous proposals to use Muscle Shoals for the manufacture of fertilizers, and the Purnell bill, which sought to increase financial assistance to agricultural experiment stations.[55]

53. Baird and Benner, *Ten Years of Federal Intermediate Credits*, pp. 83–93.

54. *Ibid.*, pp. 93–103.

55. *The New International Year Book*, 1922, pp. 24–26; Bradley, in *Journal of Social Forces*, III (May, 1925), p. 716.

All in all, the record of the farm bloc was both aggressive and impressive. Despite the fact that farm organizations, cooperatives, congressional representatives from farm districts, and others had sought similar measures at an earlier time, these demands reached a fruition point during the heyday of the farm bloc. Because of its leadership, farm convention after farm convention adopted strikingly similar resolutions. If the farm bloc did not originate the ideas behind the legislation, it certainly furnished the drive needed to pass it.[56]

In addition, these bloc tactics gave the administration as well as the nation something to think about. For one thing, they made Congress and the administration more conscious of agricultural demands than they would otherwise have been and later forced them to take some of the wind out of the sails of the progressive bloc. They also brought to the fore the need for a better "integration of the various and often clashing interests of the nation."[57] Curiously enough, too, the farmers found themselves at political flood tide at a time when their numbers had reached the lowest point in history. The *New York Times* was wrong in taking the farm bloc lightly but perhaps correct when it predicted that the bloc would come to pass as did "the Wheel, the Brothers of Freedom, the Society of Equity, the Farmers' Alliance, the Greenbackers, and other shadows."[58]

56. Barnes, in *World's Work,* XLV (November, 1922), pp. 51–59.
57. Bradley, in *Journal of Social Forces,* III (May, 1925), p. 718.
58. *Literary Digest,* LXXI (December 24, 1921), p. 10.

Chapter XII

THIRD-PARTY IDEOLOGIES

1920-24

LESS successful than the farm bloc but nonetheless an important phase of agrarian unrest in the western Middle West was the launching of third parties that were based on farmer-labor cooperation. Such programs for political action were spearheaded by elements within the Equity Society and the Nonpartisan League, the La Follette Progressives, liberals of various shades, and labor leaders who felt that the time was ripe for an American counterpart of the British Labor party. The Farm Bureau, as was to be expected, came out against this movement in unmistakable terms; the two major parties also viewed it with misgivings and conservatives everywhere fought it, but the farmer-labor challenge was to remain a vital force as long as farmers and labor had common grievances. The Farmer-Laborites went down to defeat in the national elections of 1920, but they also took some comfort in the victory of Ladd in North Dakota and the showings of Brookhart in Iowa and Shipstead in Minnesota. In 1922 the re-election of La Follette, along with the senatorial victories of Shipstead, Brookhart, and Howell in Nebraska and gubernatorial triumphs of progressives in Wisconsin, Nebraska, and Kansas, gave the progressives and Farmer-Laborites fresh courage. The victory of Magnus Johnson in Minnesota in the following year also was encouraging. The climax was finally reached in 1924 when La Follette bolted the Republican party to head an independent ticket.

Even though this movement gained its greatest adherents in the western Middle West, it can hardly be said to have been peculiar to that section, nor to the United States for that matter. There were interesting parallels in England, and in Canada farmer-laborities had considerable success with their third-party movement. They were victorious in the provincial elections of Ontario and Alberta, and in the Dominion elections of 1921 they became the official opposition, holding 65 of the total 235 seats. In England an organization similar to the Farm Bureau was found in the National Farmers' Union, which claimed 100,000 members. In 1921 it announced that it had gained the entire support of sixty-seven members of Parliament, and the support of ninety-eight others with reservations, for its program of agrarian legislation.[1]

The rise to power of the British Labor party had suggested to a vocal minority that a similar movement might well develop in the United States and take an active role in the postwar reconstruction. They felt that labor and farm organizations could form the nucleus for such a movement, conduct a program of education, and draft a plan for action. These elements felt that the conditions that led to the formation of the British Labor party were also present in the United States, except that there was no body like the Fabian Society functioning here, "studying social and economic problems and developing a constructive program for the future, comparable to 'Labor and the New Social Order,' adopted by the British Labor Party in 1918."[2]

For a time it appeared as if the Nonpartisan League were going to blossom forth into a national movement with the active political assistance of organized labor. In September, 1917, a conference of producers and consumers had been held in St. Paul, presumably for the purpose of enlisting the support of labor, with representatives present from ten state federations of labor. A. C. Townley, the president of the League, was quick to point out the political possibilities of such an alliance: "The farmers control 35 per cent of the vote of this country; labor controls about 27 per cent;

1. Phillips Bradley, "The Farm Bloc," *Journal of Social Forces,* III (May, 1925), p. 718. See also Paul F. Sharp, *The Agrarian Revolt in Western Canada* (Minneapolis, 1948).

2. Fred E. Haynes, "The Collapse of the Farmer-Labor Bloc," *Social Forces,* IV (September, 1925), p. 155.

a combination of these two elements would make itself felt throughout the nation."[3]

In the Minnesota primaries of 1918, trade unionists supported the Nonpartisan League. In its convention that year the Minnesota Federation of Labor resolved to call a farmer-labor conference, which met and nominated candidates for governor, attorney general, and railroad and warehouse commissioner. Though defeated, the Farmer-Labor party officially was established as the second party in the state.[4]

Once the war was over, hopes for a national third party in 1920 mounted. One of the first moves in this direction was in the forming in 1919 of the American Labor party, which was to be rechristened the Farmer-Labor party. Others interested in a new party included the Committee of Forty-Eight, the American party of Texas, the Single Tax party, the Nonpartisan League, the American Constitutional League, the Private Soldiers and Sailors League, and the Chicago Federation of Labor. But the militant trade-unionist element, which succeeded in adopting a program for nationalization, alienated most of the early supporters. La Follette withdrew from the new party because the platform it adopted was too radical; the Forty-Eighters bolted the ranks for pretty much the same reason; and even Hearst's *New York American* became cool to the point of suggesting its disintegration when it became known that its first concern was not "how to promote effective American opposition to foreign entangling alliances." The convention in desperation had to turn to Parley Parker Christensen of Utah, a nonentity, as presidential candidate.[5]

The Farmer-Labor party was doomed to defeat. It was faced with the usual difficulties that normally confronted third parties. It lacked finances and organization. Few farmers supported it. La Follette, the Socialists, the Leaguers, and others ignored it. To make matters worse, its standard bearer was a colorless figure, his vote being far less than that of Eugene V. Debs, the Socialist, who polled 900,000 votes. In Minnesota, South Dakota, and far-off Washington the Farmer-Labor party claimed second place.

3. Quoted in Eleanor Taylor, "Farmer and Factory-Hand," *Survey*, XXXVIII (September 29, 1917), p. 565.

4. *American Labor Yearbook*, 1919–20 (New York, 1920), p. 289; *Minnesota Farmer-Labor Convention, Proceedings*, 1923 (St. Paul), pp. 23–24.

5. "Birth of the Farmer-Labor Party," *Literary Digest*, LXVI (July 24, 1920), p. 12.

By all odds this was not a third but a "fifth" or "sixth" party, as its critics said.[6]

Similar farmer-labor sentiment had been developing in the states. Early in 1920 the Wisconsin Federation of Labor invited the Equity, the Committee of Forty-Eight, the Nonpartisan League, and the Socialist party to discuss the prospects of uniting the liberal forces for a common program of political action. Later the Brotherhood of Locomotive Engineers and the Brotherhood of Railway Trainmen were also invited. But little was accomplished in the way of a fusion. The liberal votes were captured by the League candidates who really were nothing more than La Follette Progressives in new guise.[7]

Equally unsuccessful, but more encouraging, were the efforts of Farmer-Laborites in several states of the western Middle West. In Minnesota the Farmer-Laborites had pinned their hopes on Henrik Shipstead, a second-generation Norwegian born in the United States. His father had left Norway too early to join the radical movement there, but came to the United States in time to join the Farmers' Alliance. Henrik, the son, studied dentistry and practiced for some years in western Minnesota before settling in Minneapolis. As one observer wrote, young Shipstead "practised dentistry by day and read books at night on economics, sociology, and history." He ran for the state legislature in 1916 and in 1918 was defeated for Congress by Andrew Volstead, but two years later he came within 7,000 votes of capturing the Republican nomination from J. A. O. Preus. Upon his defeat in the primaries, he decided to run as an independent in the finals and polled some 281,000 votes against 416,000 for Preus.[8]

In Iowa Farmer-Laborites were building their hopes around Smith W. Brookhart. Brookhart had been a member of the progressive movement that Senator Albert B. Cummins led in the state, but he broke with Cummins over the railroad question and sought to unseat his former boss in 1920 when he ran for re-election. Rumor had it that Brookhart had been

6. *Ibid.;* Fred E. Haynes, *Social Politics in the United States* (Boston, 1924), p. 108.

7. *Report of the Twenty-Eighth Annual Convention of the Wisconsin Federation of Labor,* p. 116.

8. Chester H. Rowell, "La Follette, Shipstead, and the Embattled Farmers; What's Happening in Wisconsin and Minnesota, and Why," *World's Work,* XLVI (August, 1923), p. 415.

brought out by the late James Pierce, radical farm journalist in the state. In the campaign, support was obtained from the state federation of labor, the Farmers' Union, and the remnants of the Equity. "Although no formal alliance has developed between farmers and laborers . . . Senator Cummins was unable to campaign in his usual vigorous fashion and his connection with the passage of the Transportation Act of 1920 exposed him to the hostility of both groups."[9] Brookhart polled 97,000 votes against 115,000 for Cummins. Obviously, Brookhart was going to be the "leader of any radical movement which might follow at a later election."[10]

In 1922 one of the first hopeful signs for the progressive cause was La Follette's winning of the Republican nomination to succeed himself in the United States Senate. This was significant, because many things had happened. The World War had intervened since the last election in 1916. La Follette, because of his opposition to America's entry into the war and to the draft law, had been repudiated by many of his former supporters. Once the war was over, this "super-patriotism" was converted "into economic conservatism and pacifism into economic radicalism." This was apparent in the campaign of 1922. The "super-patriots" and friends of the open shop put up the Reverend Dr. William A. Ganfield, the president of Carroll College of Waukesha, who ran as a "bone-dry" in a state in which the thirst for beer was great. He was badly beaten. In the election La Follette won by a thumping 289,000 majority, and Governor John J. Blaine was re-elected by 317,000, compared with his own 118,000 two years earlier.

The La Follette triumph was due to more than one factor. The German vote, which had become more pro-LaFollette than ever before, supported him in great numbers; and the Scandinavians, radically bent on economic questions, were also behind him in sizable force. The farmers were traditional La Follette supporters. Agrarian discontent was evident in Wisconsin as in other states, except that the dairy farmers were not so hard hit as other farmers. They were less given to radicalism, partly because they were too busy for politics and partly because they sold their products in a more highly processed condition and hence were less subject to

9. Haynes, in *Social Forces,* IV (September, 1925), p. 153.

10. Chester H. Rowell, "Brookhart, Howell, and 'Brother Charley' Bryan," *World's Work,* XLVI (August, 1923), p. 481.

manipulations by speculators. "Farmers generally were disquieted with the failure of both parties to offer constructive remedies, but this disgust did not extend to La Follette and Blaine, even though they did not at the moment offer much more. The farmers were satisfied that their hearts were in the right place."[11]

In the neighboring state of Minnesota the forces of the Nonpartisan League, the influence of La Follette, low returns for farmers, and the support of organized labor helped to unseat Frank B. Kellogg, a Republican, and elect Henrik Shipstead on a Farmer-Labor ticket. Kellogg once had been a Roosevelt "trust buster" of sorts, but since then had become a lawyer of national reputation, having among his clients the steel, milling, and lumber interests, which, of course, were no asset to him politically. Kellogg also made the mistake of traveling about in a Pierce Arrow with a chauffeur. From 1920 to 1922 he tried to play the "re-election game" by joining the farm bloc and supporting demands that were popular with the farmers.

But in 1922 the home-grown radicalism of Shipstead had greater appeal. While Kellogg covered the country in his Pierce Arrow, Shipstead made the rounds in a Ford. Instead of speaking from behind floodlights, he spoke to crowds of picnic-goers. Farm people, who were accustomed to the continental Sunday, had the habit of going to church in the morning and holding picnics in the afternoon. Shipstead made political capital of this. He attended them, spoke to the farmers on serious economic questions, and passed the hat around "for tires and gasoline." From the start, the antiwar vote was inclined toward him, but it was surely delivered to him by La Follette, who invaded the state to campaign for him after he himself had been assured of the Republican nomination in Wisconsin. Shipstead, in so far as the antiwar elements were concerned, had a good war record, not because of what he had done but because he was affiliated with the League and had had his house painted yellow during the war.[12]

The tide against Kellogg was irresistible. Capper had come into Minnesota to campaign for him and antagonized the progressives because of it. Vice-President Calvin Coolidge also entered the state in his behalf and

11. Rowell, in *World's Work*, XLVI (August, 1923), pp. 409–12; *Chicago Daily News Almanac and Yearbook*, 1923, p. 731; *The New International Year Book*, 1920, p. 758.

12. Rowell, in *World's Work*, XLVI (August, 1923), pp. 416–17.

had no effect. Then came the big "potato catastrophe." The farmers, with a record crop on hand, faced a car shortage and prices so low that it was unprofitable for them to dig the potatoes. Wheat brought only eighty cents a bushel. Add to this coal and railroad strikes and one can readily understand why talks such as the one delivered by Coolidge about "improved agricultural conditions," "reduced taxes," and "prosperity" fell flat.[13]

In the North Dakota elections of 1922 there was a swing both to the left and to the right; the first sent the well-known Leaguer, Lynn Frazier, to the United States Senate, and the other returned R. A. Nestos, the conservative, to the office of governor. One observer noted that undoubtedly this "did represent in part a violent oscillation in the opinions of some people on fundamental issues." Another commented that the state had gone radical in 1920, conservative in the recall election year of 1921, and seemingly both conservative and radical in 1922. The election of Lynn Frazier sent him to Washington to join E. F. Ladd, who had been elected in 1920. This put the state in the anomalous position of having a conservative government at home and radical representation at Washington.

The results in the senatorial race arose from situations woven deep into the history of the state. In 1920 Ladd defeated Senator Albert J. Gronna for the Republican nomination. Gronna himself was a progressive of the Roosevelt variety and also an enemy of Alex McKenzie, a state political boss of many years' standing. Both Gronna supporters and League insurgents attributed the Ladd triumph to a political deal whereby the League would not put up a candidate against Porter J. McCumber, who was coming up for re-election in 1922.

But when 1922 came around, strong League elements, opposed to the political deal made by Townley with McKenzie, who had since died, put up Lynn Frazier "with a whoop." McCumber, besides being faced with the League candidate, had other hurdles to jump. There were the familiar low wheat prices and hard times. Then, too, McCumber suffered from the fact that he had been in office for a long time. "His long residence in Washington had made him a comparative stranger at home. The farmers accused him of having acquired the Eastern viewpoint and were not impressed by the report of the greatness of the national position.

13. M. M. Hedges, "The Liberal Sweep in the West," *The Nation,* CXV (November 22, 1922), p. 54.

'What good does that power do North Dakota'? they said. The dignity of the chairman of the Senate's chief committee was probably less imposing among his own constituents than anywhere else in the world. The Conservatives, on the other hand, charged McCumber with having played for re-election by flirting with the Senate farm bloc. . . . Also, in twenty-four years in office McCumber had accumulated the usual enemies, while his aloofness had prevented him from acquiring a corresponding number of militant friends. . . ."[14] McCumber also had taken a prominent hand in the shaping of the Tariff Act of 1922, which sent tariff schedules sky-rocketing to a new high. This was something that many progressives would not allow his constituents to forget.

Iowans, normally less iconoclastic than the people of Wisconsin, Minnesota, and North Dakota, did not hesitate to elect an aggressive radical like Smith W. Brookhart to the Senate. The German vote, prohibition, and the World War had a hand in this uprising. "But the common bases of revolt were the low price of farm products and the high price of everything else; high freight, high taxes, and opposition to the Esch-Cummins Law, to the Federal Reserve Board, to ship subsidy, and to 'Wall Street' influences generally."

Brookhart captured the seat that had been vacated by Senator William S. Kenyon, who became a federal judge. The old-guard Republicans, instead of putting up a real leader with a real policy, bungled things by allowing four regular candidates to divide the vote among themselves in the primaries. Brookhart, "the cowhide radical," got 42 per cent of the votes, was nominated and finally elected.[15]

In Nebraska, a more radical state than Iowa, two progressives were elected, one a Republican senator and the other a Democratic governor. The new senator, R. B. Howell, an "educated gentleman" with less shocking views and mannerisms than Brookhart, defeated Senator Gilbert N. Hitchcock by a majority of 72,085. Local factors played a role in this election as they did in Iowa.

The new Nebraska governor was Charles W. Bryan, the brother of "the perennial W. J." "Charley" Bryan had a long, checkered career. He had been an Omaha cigar-store operator; an advisor, secretary, and "man

14. Chester H. Rowell, "The Political Cyclone in North Dakota," *World's Work*, XLVI (July, 1922), pp. 265–67.

15. Rowell, in *World's Work*, XLVI (August, 1923), pp. 478–81.

behind the scenes" for his brother; manager of *The Commoner,* the Bryan sheet; mayor of Omaha; and city commissioner of Lincoln before becoming governor. As governor, he would not hesitate to sit on his desk "with his hat on . . . and talk to you with the utmost naturalness. . . ."[16]

In Kansas a farmer-labor combination put Jonathan Davis, a Democrat, in the governor's position. This was unusual for a state that was as "rock-ribbed Republican" as Kansas. Harvey J. Allen, the outgoing Republican officeholder, who could not succeed himself, had aroused various elements in the state. A big factor in this was Allen's calling the legislature into special session to pass a law that created an industrial-court commission devoid of judicial functions and also forbade the calling of strikes in the three basic industries—transportation, coal mining, and the production of food. Bitterness and name-calling resulted. Strikes continued despite the law. Davis, "a person of no renown," at least so it was claimed, but who had the reputation of wearing overalls, milking cows, and sowing and reaping, had voiced opposition to the industrial court; he said that it had failed and many Kansans apparently believed him. Obviously, the farmers played a great role in this triumph, because some 65 per cent of the people in the state lived on farms. On the whole, the state was devoid of large factory towns and the problems of urban labor. Farmers were restless because of low wheat prices and the failure of the outgoing administration to lower taxes.[17]

The Democrats were quick to interpret the results of 1922 in an encouraging light, while progressives saw them as a mandate to go ahead with their program.[18] La Follette's statement was this:

> Can you not understand this wonderful movement which is sweeping over the Middle West? . . . It is organized because there is a belief among the people that there is a power that puts them at a disadvantage by controlling the market price of everything they buy. They have appealed to the Democratic Party; they have appealed to the Republican Party, and they have appealed in vain for relief, for legislation to break the power that took out of their toil just what tribute it pleased.[19]

16. *Ibid.,* pp. 482–84; *New York Times,* July 13, 1924.

17. Charles B. Driscoll, "Kansas Cleans Up Governor Allen's Mess," *The Nation,* CXV (December 6, 1922), p. 600; Haynes, in *Social Forces,* IV (September, 1925), pp. 153–54.

18. *Christian Science Monitor,* November 8, 1922.

19. Quoted in Rowell, *World's Work,* XLVI (August, 1923), p. 412.

After the elections, the progressive movement appeared in two forms. One, headed by William E. Borah of Idaho, sought to block the passage of the ship-subsidy bill. Borah had also warned that a third party would sweep the nation unless the Republicans mended their ways, and George Norris of Nebraska seconded him. A second group, consisting of two wings of the progressive factions, in and out of Congress, planned conferences for December to formulate plans for political action.[20]

On December 1, progressives met in Washington. La Follette, the chairman of the People's Legislative Service, called this meeting. The feeling on the part of many prior to the conference was that the meeting would be torn asunder by rival ambitions. La Follette, it is claimed, avoided the danger by limiting it to organizational matters and to the discussion of general issues. Specific issues were left to special committees chosen from all progressive factions. The plan was to use the long vacation of Congress, following the short session, to study the questions on which legislation was sought.[21]

On December 11, the Conference for Progressive Political Action assembled in Cleveland for its second meeting that year. This group had held its first convention in Chicago on February 20–21, to gear the progressives for the congressional elections that fall. It was attended by representatives of agriculture and labor and liberals and progressives of various stripes who had resolved to elect senators, congressmen, and state and local officials who were pledged to "the principles of genuine democracy in agriculture, industry and government." This conference had also appointed a committee of fifteen to call a meeting after the elections to mobilize the progressives for political action. The avowed purpose of this next conference was to perfect plans to wrest the government from those who would establish "an absolute tyranny and plutocratic dictatorship" and restore it to the people to whom it rightfully belonged.[22]

The tools and the equipment that were necessary for the building of a new third party were available when the second Conference for Progressive Political Action met; but the delegates, it appeared to one observer, were not sure whether they wanted to build "a church or a pig-sty." Un-

20. *Christian Science Monitor,* November 15, 1922.

21. John W. Owens, "The Progressives," *New Republic,* XXXIV (March 14, 1923), pp. 61–62; *The Nation,* CXV (November 29, 1922), p. 565.

22. *The American Labor Yearbook,* 1923–24, p. 149.

like similar conventions in the past, there was "no hymn-singing . . . no sense of battling at Armageddon. If there has been, the conference anthem would have had to be: 'We don't know where we're going, but we're on our way.' . . ." The conference moved slowly because it was not sure whether the Republicans would nominate La Follette in 1924, and also because the railroad men who dominated it were afraid that the radicals would take over the movement. This same observer also commented on the restrained temper of the delegates. Most of the labor representatives "were comfortable-looking and gray-haired, obviously men of prominence in their communities. They stayed at the best of hotels, and plainly saw no reason why they should not be expected to do so. . . ."[23]

With the elections and the progressive conferences over, the strategy and the tactics that the progressive bloc hoped to employ in the Sixty-eighth Congress became of more than passing interest. The strength of the bloc in the lower house was placed at about sixty, which progressives hoped would be enough to nullify the Republican majority. Into this had gone many House members of the old farm bloc. Again, as was to be expected, the backbone of this new bloc was furnished by representatives from the western Middle West. There were pledged to it ten men from Wisconsin, seven from Minnesota, five from Iowa, four from Kansas, three each from Illinois and Nebraska, two each from California and New York, and one each from North Dakota, South Dakota, and Michigan.

The strategy of the progressives, as understood at the time, was not to bolt the Republican party, but to resist all efforts to pack the Interstate Commerce Commission, the Ways and Means Committee, and to some extent the Rules Committee to make it impossible to suppress desirable or to promote undesirable legislation. Some considered this La Follette strategy as timely because of an oligarchy that appeared to have sprung up around the Steering Committee, the Speaker, and the chairman of the Rules Committee. Significantly, this progressive minority challenged the administration fully nine months before the new session of Congress convened. It was even hinted that this possibly could have the effect of

23. "The Bricks of the New Party," *The Nation,* CXV (December 27, 1922), p. 707.

avoiding another leaderless Congress, as the Sixty-seventh Congress was, or of accentuating a similar hapless demonstration.[24]

La Follette resented having his group called a bloc. It was simply men from both parties who came together to discuss the issues before the nation in the spirit of true progressives. To La Follette, progressivism was a gradual process that avoided the extremes of conservatism and radicalism:

> Progressivism is moving forward one step at a time and dealing with specific problems as they present themselves, rather than trying to formulate a panacea or cure-all for the troubles of the world.
>
> This method of approaching great problems of government clearly distinguishes the Progressives from both the revolutionists and the reactionaries. The revolutionists are ready to tear down everything in order to apply certain formulas which they have concocted. The reactionaries, whether they call themselves Republicans or Democrats, are determined either to stand still or move backward. The idea of progress checks and terrifies them.
>
> The Progressives . . . abhor a dictatorship of the plutocracy as much as a dictatorship of the proletariat.[25]

The next major event on the progressive agenda was the special election in Minnesota in 1923 that sent Magnus Johnson, the Farmer-Laborite and "a real dirt farmer," to the United States Senate to fill the unexpired term of the deceased Knute Nelson. His victory gave new confidence to the progressives and added to the balance-of-power tactics of the La Follette bloc in the Senate.

Johnson, a Swede by birth, was no stranger to the progressive movement. He was "a full-fledged glass-blower" before coming to the United States. For a time he worked in the lumber camps of the West and then settled down to farm in Meeker County, Minnesota. He was active in the Equity. He served for a time in the Minnesota legislature. In 1922 he ran against J. A. O. Preus for the Republican nomination for governor and came within about 14,000 votes of defeating him.

His "strange mixture of sense and nonsense," as one observer noted, lent color to the progressive movement. He spoke English with a marked

24. "Will the 'Insurgent Tail Wag the Party Dog?'" *Literary Digest,* LXXXVI (March 31, 1923), p. 8.

25. Quoted in "The Progressives—What They Stand For and Want," *Saturday Evening Post,* CXCV (March 10, 1923), pp. 27, 162, 165.

Swedish accent, often posed for photographers in overalls, had a voice that was "variously compared to a fog-horn and a radio 'loud speaker,'" boasted that he would behave like a common man and never wear a dress suit. Many had expected him to become a target for cartoonists and the comic strips, but his friends assured critics that Johnson was "bombproof" to such attacks. By his own admission big men in the Senate did not frighten him in the least. On occasions he said that his experiences in the state legislature had convinced him that the two most important words in the English language for any legislator were "yes" and "no." It required little intelligence for an honest representative to say " 'no' to the repeal of the excess profits tax, 'no' to lowering taxes on millionaire incomes, and 'no' to turning back the railroads to private management with a guaranty of earnings before we had passed through the reconstruction period."[26]

This special election was taken seriously by both sides. Governor Preus, Johnson's opponent in this as well as in the previous year, felt that the time was ripe for a test of sentiment, and put himself up as a candidate instead of appointing a Republican to fill out the unexpired term in the Senate. Preus, in this campaign, made a round-about-face from the Republican stand on the tariff by repudiating the Fordney-McCumber Act of 1922, and literally banned the national administration, including the President, from taking an active role in the election. He also made a strong plea for cooperative marketing.[27]

The supporters of Johnson felt that the future of the farmer-labor movement was at stake. This was evident from the help that he received from progressives from out-of-state. They included Frazier, Wheeler, and three progressive congressmen from Wisconsin who were directed by Senator La Follette, who was in a Battle Creek sanitarium at the time. Phil La Follette, his son, went along with the Wisconsin delegation to present a personal plea to the Minnesotans from his father.[28]

The *New York Times* said that the Johnson victory was the result of a real farmer-labor coalition. ". . . Johnson defeated Governor Preus in the cities as well as on the farms. Thus both wings of the Farmer-Labor Party

26. "Magnus, The Unbluffable, of Minnesota," *Literary Digest*, LXXVIII (September 8, 1923), pp. 50–53.

27. *New York Times*, July 9, 15, 1923.

28. *Ibid.*, July 3, 9, 1923.

flapped together. Workingmen in St. Paul and Duluth and Minneapolis were just as emphatic in registering their verdict against the Republican party as were the grumbling farmers in the interior of the State."[29]

New fuel was added to the third-party flame by pronouncements that were made by La Follette shortly before his departure for Europe. This was late in July, 1923, less than two weeks after the Johnson victory in Minnesota. La Follette told a group of forty newspapermen that there would be a third party in 1924 if the two major parties nominated reactionaries, but if one of the parties nominated a liberal and the other a conservative, the need for a new party would diminish. If both parties did the unexpected and nominated liberals, the need for a new party would vanish. "Parties," said La Follette, "are not organized and made effective by resolutions passed by gentlemen who think there should be new parties. They come in response to public needs and public demands: they grow, they are developed. That rule will govern the question of a third party next year." La Follette, also true to the progressive tradition, minimized the interest of the American people in foreign affairs. He said that the people were chiefly interested in the problems that faced them at home and not in such issues as the League of Nations and the World Court.[30] No doubt the fact that La Follette had never been abroad before added to his insular approach.

His trip to Europe, the first in his long career, was expected to give him a first-hand opportunity to study the cooperative movement and labor conditions in Belgium, Germany, France, Italy, England, and several other countries. He was not expected to visit Russia, presumably because of the brevity of his trip. Upon his return, he was to take the stump again in behalf of the progressive cause.[31]

The Minnesota Farmer-Laborites, their appetites whetted by the victories of Shipstead and again by Johnson, accelerated the La Follette boom in November of 1923. This latest farmer-labor conference had been called together by Henry Teigan, the secretary of Magnus Johnson, and William Mahoney, a veteran St. Paul labor leader. The conference drew up resolutions that urged the Wisconsin senator to head a "Farmer-Labor National

29. *Ibid.*, July 19, 1923.
30. *Baltimore Sun*, July 28, 1923.
31. *Capital Times* (Madison, Wis.), July 27, 1923.

Party" or else a third-party ticket, and scheduled the holding of a national convention in the Twin Cities on May 30, 1924, for the nomination of candidates for the Presidency and Vice-Presidency of the United States. Invitations were sent out to farmer-labor groups in the Dakotas, Montana, Idaho, Washington, Nebraska, Wisconsin, and Kansas, to the National Farmer-Labor party, the Federated Farmer-Labor party, the National Progressive party, and to certain eastern groups that were eager to promote unity among the various liberal and progressive groups.[32]

By early 1924 the La Follette boom was also under way in the neighboring state of North Dakota. It was headed by Gerald P. Nye and John Andrews.[33] The following month a convention of Nonpartisan Leaguers asked La Follette to head a third-party ticket and also decided to find out where Senators Lynn Frazier, Henrik Shipstead, and Magnus Johnson stood on the question.[34]

Opinions regarding the future prospects of a new alignment varied. The Farmer-Laborites and progressives thought that the time to strike was near at hand. One eastern newspaper was ready to concede that La Follette had strength in the West, especially among the wheat growers, but felt that he had very little beyond that. His war record was considered a distinct handicap in the East.[35] In the spring of 1924 Governor Preus of Minnesota created a sensation in Republican and Democratic circles by stating that a third-party movement headed by La Follette had actually captured the West: "It is real and nothing is to be gained by ignoring it." Preus predicted that La Follette, if he lived, would carry Minnesota, Wisconsin, North and South Dakota, Montana, Nebraska, Colorado, and perhaps Iowa.[36]

In March La Follette set political leaders wondering by withdrawing his name from the ballot in the Republican primaries of North Dakota, Wisconsin, and Michigan. These withdrawals were accompanied by a statement to the effect that he had no hope of seeing a progressive nominated by the Republicans that June. This immediately brought to mind

32. *St. Paul Dispatch,* November 17, 1923.
33. *Wisconsin State Journal* (Madison), January 18, 1924.
34. *St. Paul Dispatch,* February 9, 1924.
35. *Christian Science Monitor,* February 12, 1924.
36. *Chicago Herald Examiner,* April 5, 1924.

the statement that La Follette had made to the forty newspapermen before he sailed for Europe in the summer of 1923.[37]

Meanwhile, the Conference for Progressive Political Action had its own ideas, which competed with what the Minnesota Farmer-Labor party had in mind. It also called for a convention of workers, farmers, and progressives to meet in Cleveland on July 4 to set in motion the machinery for the presidental campaign that year.[38] The expected elimination of William G. McAdoo as an acceptable Democratic candidate seemed to have paved the way for an independent party. McAdoo was very acceptable to the railroad men because of his handling of the railroads during the war years. The actions of the C.P.P.A. could hardly be overlooked, because it had taken a prominent role in the elections of 1922 that had sent Shipstead, Brookhart, and Wheeler to the Senate and also re-elected La Follette.[39] Here was a rival force with great influence which the Minnesota Farmer-Laborites could hardly ignore.

Despite this, representatives from forty political organizations in Minnesota, North and South Dakota, Montana, Nebraska, Illinois, and New York attended a conference in St. Paul in March to proceed with third-party plans. Originally, May 30 had been set as the date for the nominating convention, but many felt that it would be advisable to postpone the convention until after the Republicans had met and nominated their candidates. At this meeting it was stated that a delegation had visited La Follette and found that he had no objection to his being proposed as the leader of this third-party ticket. The idea that La Follette was too old and physically unfit to assume the responsibilities of President was cast aside. La Follette was their man.[40]

Meanwhile, La Follette men were reported to be greatly disturbed over the number of third parties that were springing up over the country. Especially did they show concern over the Minnesota call that had just been set for June 17. Reports had it that the majority of the members belonging to the committee sponsoring this call were members of the Workers' party, a recognized communist organization.

37. *New York Times,* March 3, 1924; *Wisconsin News* (Milwaukee), March 7, 1924.

38. *Christian Science Monitor,* February 12, 1924.

39. *Wisconsin News,* March 7, 1924; *Minneapolis Tribune,* March 17, 1924.

40. *Ibid.,* March 11, 17, 1924.

La Follette supporters were quick to accuse old-guard Republicans of conniving to pack this gathering with henchmen, disguised as radicals, to nominate the senator on an impossible platform and then follow through with a series of red speeches. This is what they said had happened at the Farmer-Labor convention in Chicago in 1920. Reactionaries had packed it with cronies of theirs, arranged for wild-eyed speeches, and then forced the adoption of a platform which they knew La Follette would never accept. The Minnesota convention of June 17 was predicted to become a repeat performance.[41]

Weeks before the June 17 meeting, stories were circulating to the effect that La Follette, although anxious to get the support of the Minnesota group, was "not out to receive the baptismal insignia of that assembly as the initial step. . . ." Progressives, in growing numbers, seemed to advise that their men had better avoid the St. Paul convention. Political suicide was predicted for those who took part in it. Samuel Gompers, quoted as describing it as a device of the Red "borers from within," urged organized labor to stay away from it.

This convention, like that of other liberal and progressive groups, was expected to go far in showing how wide the cleavages were within the Farmer-Labor ranks and how hard it was going to be to reconcile the political aspirations of the different groups. "Some labor sees red, some pink, some clear white. Of the farmers precisely the same thing is true. . . ."[42]

C. E. Ruthenberg, the secretary of the Workers' Party of America, announced that he would support La Follette if the Farmer-Labor convention in St. Paul nominated him. But at the same time he was going to destroy the illusion that La Follette represented the interests of the rank-and-file farmers and workers. He drew a distinction between the coming St. Paul and Cleveland meetings. According to Ruthenberg, the Cleveland meeting was dominated by dissatisfied wealthy farmers and small businessmen, while the St. Paul meeting was endorsed by the bulk of the workers.[43]

Speculation about whether La Follette was going to take part in the St. Paul convention finally ended with the publication of a letter written

41. *Labor* (Washington, D. C.), March 29, 1924.
42. *Minneapolis Tribune,* May 5, 1924.
43. *Milwaukee Journal,* May 7, 1924.

by the senator to Herman Ekern, the attorney general of Wisconsin, in which La Follette advised his supporters and friends to stay away from the June 17 meeting. He accused its promoters of conveying the impression that it had had his approval. He conceded that many who planned to take part in it were people who were anxious to promote the cause of "genuine democracy," but maintained that the Communist conspiracy which was so apparent made it impossible for most farmers, workers, and progressives to support it. The object of the Communists, said La Follette, was "to divide and confuse the progressive movement and create a condition of chaos favorable to their ultimate aims." They sought a dictatorship of the proletariat that was "repugnant to democratic ideals and to all American aspirations." The coming St. Paul convention was but one device for seeking their ends.[44]

La Follette's denunciation of the Reds is said to have sent his political stock soaring in the agricultural Northwest. Many believed that his declaration in behalf of the ballot box in place of Communist rifles strengthened the third-party movement.[45] La Follette For President clubs already had been reported springing up all over the country. A survey made by Chester C. Platt, the secretary of the Wisconsin Nonpartisan League, showed that conditions in 1924 were more promising than they had been back in 1912. The appalling political corruption that had been exposed in Washington was expected to be a great aid to the progressive cause.[46]

At the same time the position of the Minnesota Farmer-Laborites was weakened considerably. The La Follette warning was followed by similar ones from other groups. The American Federation of Labor warned all trade unions to be "on guard" and to have nothing to do with the St. Paul meeting. The Committee of Forty-Eight, one of the original sponsoring groups, officially pulled out of the convention and announced that it would be represented in the July 4 meeting.[47] *Labor*, the organ of the sixteen railroad organizations, also issued a statement that the June 17 meeting was Communist-infested and urged their members to stay away from it.[48]

44. *Wisconsin State Journal*, May 28, 1924.
45. *Chicago Herald Examiner*, May 29, 1924.
46. *Wisconsin State Journal*, May 10, 1924.
47. *Minneapolis Journal*, May 29, 1924.
48. *Pioneer Press* (St. Paul), June 17, 1924.

As expected, bitter protests poured forth from the sponsors of the St. Paul convention. The central committee accused La Follette of "gross misrepresentation" and of considering himself greater than the movement itself. His sincerity was open to suspicion. Once he was held to be the man best qualified to lead a movement that was greater than any single person, but his actions had erased all such beliefs. His charge that the Communists dominated the convention was a great exaggeration. The Communists made up only a small minority of the delegates. Furthermore, though their aims were well known, they were willing to cooperate in launching a third party. In the final analysis there was no more reason for doubting their sincerity than there was in questioning the motives of La Follette himself.[49]

William Mahoney, the temporary chairman of the convention, bitterly charged that the actions of La Follette were "cruel and unwarranted" and that he had been put up to it by the labor politicians in Washington. Again Mahoney pronounced this a movement that exceeded the interests of any single person. "This is not primarily a La Follette movement, but a working class movement with La Follette as an important factor." He related the visit to Wisconsin by a committee which found that while La Follette had not promised that he would run, he did nevertheless indicate that little was to be expected from the two major parties in 1924. La Follette showed no opposition to the St. Paul convention at the time and did leave the impression that he would become a candidate unless an unforeseen exigency arose.[50]

It had been stated that one reason why La Follette wanted to stage the third-party convention after, and not before, the Republicans met in Cleveland in June was that he wanted to come before the Republicans without a Farmer-Labor endorsement stamped on him. Besides giving him the position of an independent, it also would enable him to run on his own platform instead of being bound to that of the Farmer-Laborites.[51]

The La Follette supporters present at the Republican gathering in Cleveland were largely the Wisconsin delegates. The senator had given them instructions to refrain from presenting his name to the convention,[52] but

49. *Milwaukee Leader,* May 29, 1924.
50. *St. Paul Dispatch,* June 17, 1924.
51. *Minneapolis Journal,* March 18, 1924.
52. *Milwaukee Sentinel,* June 10, 1924.

he had made no similar pleas with respect to the Wisconsin platform. It was presented amidst an atmosphere of ridicule. Henry Cooper, congressman from Wisconsin's first district, temporarily brought the jeers of the delegates to a halt by reminding them that twenty-six of the thirty-one planks presented from La Follette's state since 1908 had been enacted into law. Both parties, he reminded the delegates, had adopted planks which they had originally branded as socialistic. But to no avail. The Republicans wanted none of La Follette. The platform presented to the delegates for approval, said Charles K. Warren, who introduced it, had the support of every state except Wisconsin. This "one-state" argument was repeated again and again, and each time was met with "hoots and jeers" for the La Follette men. Hisses also met the names of Norris and Brookhart.[53]

Despite the contempt with which the regular Republicans met the La Follette proposals, it was not to be denied that they were frankly worried over what he would do. The rejection of his proposals simply added to the rumors current to the effect that his campaign was going to be built around the organizations of the C.P.P.A., which functioned in thirty-two states and which were represented in the industrial centers of the East as well as in the Middle West.[54]

When the C.P.P.A. was about to meet in Cleveland, the Democratic national convention was still deadlocked. It was no secret that the third-party hopefuls wanted a conservative candidate like John W. Davis, fully expecting that this would enable La Follette to command a solid control over the radical and progressive votes. Such a turn of events also would enable the convention to denounce both the old parties in scathing language, and designate their candidates as agents of "Wall Street and the big interests."[55]

If there still was doubt about who was going to be the Democratic candidate, there was little doubt whom the C.P.P.A. was going to support. On the eve of the convention the national committee authorized the sending of a telegram to La Follette formally asking him to accept the nomination of the convention about to assemble. Little was to be expected from the two major parties, said this invitation; they were involved in

53. John M. Nelson, "The La Follette-Wheeler Candidacy," *Yale Review,* XIV (October 19, 1924), p. 43.

54. *Capital Times,* June 18, 1924.

55. *New York Times,* July 3, 1924.

"grave scandals and flagrant betrayals of the public trust." Needless to say, this was an unusual procedure for a group of progressives to follow, especially after they had denounced both of the major parties for high-handed methods. But that was what actually did happen.[56]

The convention that assembled, according to the *New York Times*, included, besides those insurgents who had been snubbed by the Coolidge convention,

> disgruntled farmers, business men, trade unionists, woman suffragists, progressives of the Roosevelt tradition, veterans of the World War and the usual contingent of freaks who pursue any new party as small boys follow a circus. . . .
>
> The delegates were well-dressed and serious-minded citizens. Long whiskers, windsor ties and other habiliments of those accustomed to pursue strange doctrines were conspicuous by their absence. The "communists" of the Foster-Ruthenberg type were excommunicated and the entire "Red" party was denounced. The convention represented those who seek political power by ballots and not by bullets.[57]

All in all, there were about twelve hundred accredited delegates.

On July 4 La Follette finally announced that he was going to be an independent candidate running on his Wisconsin program. This statement came in the form of a fifty-minute message, read to the gathering by young Bob, his son and secretary, who came from Washington for this very purpose.[58] To La Follette, "the one paramount issue of the 1924 campaign" was to "break the combined power of the private monopoly system over the political and economic life of the American people." This the American people could do by wresting the government from "the predatory interests which now control it. . . ." Uniting the people around the monopoly issue was the big hope of the country.

La Follette stated, with no hesitation, that the Sherman Act could have been an effective weapon in checking monopoly had it been employed when monopoly "was yet in its infancy," but small, powerful groups had united to resist its operation and to control markets and prices. "Each group dictates production and prices in its own field—in iron, coal, oil, steel, lumber, sugar, meats, clothing—in short, in mining, manufactur-

56. *Ibid.*, July 4, 1924.
57. *Ibid.*, July 13, 1924.
58. *Pioneer Press*, July 5, 1924.

ing, transportation and all important business enterprises. Through grain exchanges, elevator combinations and packing monopolies markets are manipulated and prices fixed on all products of the farm."[59]

One of the big problems before the convention was the question of actually forming a third party, and not merely confining the movement to the setting up an independent ticket without a formal organization. La Follette supporters, who knew that the senator did not want to be tied to a third party, at least at that stage, sought to have him endorsed immediately, but Morris Hillquit, head of the New York Socialist delegation, promptly objected on the grounds that the convention was not officially organized and that the chairman of the credentials committee had not yet made his report. The Socialists succeeded in postponing the endorsement, but they were not able to bring about the formation of the third party.[60]

The progressives fully understood the value of appealing to tradition. There followed in the convention the reading of the Declaration of Independence and of Lincoln's Gettysburg Address. Little time was lost in likening La Follette to Abraham Lincoln.[61]

The platform presented to the convention, a model from the standpoint of brevity, was drafted by La Follette himself and showed no evidence of control by either "Wall Street or Moscow." It was less than a thousand words in length and had in it fourteen specific pledges, ranging from the restoration of excess-profits taxes to public ownership of railroads and the repeal of the Esch-Cummins Law. The document was read by Donald A. Richberg, the general counsel for the railway brotherhoods and the chairman of the platform committee.[62]

The matter of nominating a vice-presidential candidate also confronted the convention. For a time, Louis Brandeis, long a personal as well as political friend of La Follette, was mentioned; the slate of "La Follette and Brandeis" was favored by some because it would link the East and the West and thus be geographically correct. Other vice-presidential suggestions included Huston Thompson, chairman of the Federal Trade

59. *New York Times,* July 5, 1924.
60. Kenneth C. MacKay, *The Progressive Movement of 1924* (New York, 1947), pp. 119–20.
61. *New York Times,* July 5, 1924.
62. *Ibid.,* July 6, 1924.

Commission, Burton K. Wheeler of Montana, George Norris of Nebraska, and Warren S. Stone of the Brotherhood of Railroad Engineers. The name of Charles W. Bryan also came forward, but this was turned down because he was "tainted with his party's ills."[63]

On the second day of the convention La Follette was endorsed by the delegates. There was no nominating speech, but there were four seconding speeches and a score of delegates were clamoring for recognition when the chairman, William H. Johnston, brought the speechmaking to an end. Likewise, the Wisconsin platform was "adopted with a whoop."

In the matter of the third party, the Socialists made known their desires. Hillquit made a seconding speech in behalf of La Follette but also declared for the formation of a third party. The La Follette men, however, were opposed; the senator wanted to conduct an independent campaign first and form the new party after the election, using the campaign organization as the nucleus. Some opposition also developed against vesting power in the national committee and the La Follette for President Committee to name a vice-presidential candidate.

Among those speaking from the convention platform were Edwin Markham, author of "The Man with the Hoe"; W. T. Raleigh of Freeport, Illinois; Andrew Furuseth of the International Seamen's Union; Attorney General Herman Ekern of Wisconsin; Representative Fiorello La Guardia of New York; and Senator Lynn Frazier of North Dakota.

The various organizations that were represented in Cleveland were estimated to have had a voting strength of 4,628,000. The principal groups represented were the Socialist party with an estimated membership of 1,000,000 voters, the Farmer-Labor groups with about 1,000,000 voters, and the Nonpartisan League with about 500,000. The progressive strength was unknown. A generous estimate would place the political strength of the third party at not more than 5,000,000.[64]

It was to be expected that barred groups would fire their blasts against the C.P.P.A. convention. Foster and Ruthenberg of the Workers' party, as was to be expected, did this very thing. They branded it as "the most reactionary political convention held this year." Its program, favoring a middle course that was based on trust busting and supported by small

63. *Ibid.,* July 3, 13, 1924.
64. *Ibid.,* July 13, 1924.

businessmen, and professional men, was ample evidence of this. La Follette talked of restoring democracy in government, but turned around, after the fashion of a dictator, to hand down a decision that he would run for President not as the candidate of a party but as an independent. "The king has spoken. The convention must swallow it." Workers and farmers, they said, had enough intelligence to rely on their organized strength rather than "upon the ukases of an individual even though he be Robert M. La Follette." His objective was "to lead the workers back to '76" and not forward. Socialization of industry was the sole hope of the farmers and workers, not trust busting.[65]

A couple of weeks after the C.P.P.A. convention La Follette re-emphasized the fact that he was going to run as an independent and not on a Farmer-Labor ticket in any state. He had received numerous telegrams from Farmer-Labor groups in several states asking him to run on that ticket to help them build up their organizations for future campaigns, but he refused. La Follette believed that his chances for obtaining Republican and Democratic votes in both states would be lessened if he ran as a Farmer-Laborite, and his managers had advised him that he would get the Farmer-Labor votes regardless of local politics. For instance, North Dakota was considered safe for La Follette, since four out of five of the Republican electors there had already declared themselves for him.[66]

The reasons for his refusal to associate himself with state Farmer-Labor tickets were several. First, he considered it bad politics to associate himself with any single element in the general movement that he headed. There were prospects of serious conflicts between the aims of the farmers and the railroad labor groups. His position would be weakened considerably if he were tied to platforms and organizations over which he had no control. Second, La Follette's strategy was to make it possible for Republicans and Democrats to desert their tickets and support him without placing themselves under the need for assuming the burden of a new party structure. Third, La Follette wanted to be a free agent after the campaign to move about as he pleased without the baggage and impediments which a hard and fast political party would bring. He did not want to be swallowed up by the independent movement. He wanted "to be the

65. *Ibid.*, July 6, 1924.
66. *Pioneer Press*, July 22, 1924.

independent movement." His earlier actions supported this. His attitude was that the independent movement needed him more than he needed it.[67]

Obviously, the position of La Follette toward agriculture was of prime importance to the farmers of the western Middle West. Traditionally, he was strong among the farmers of the upper Mississippi Valley. His attachment to their way of thinking was so strong that he could hardly shake himself loose from the agrarian arguments of the seventies. La Follette spoke of the importance of agriculture to the nation, of the relationship of the railroads to the farmers, of how the grain elevators were tied up with the railroad interests, and of how it was becoming impossible for the farmers to subsist on what they got for their products.[68] If anything, La Follette was more the inheritor of the Granger and Populist traditions than he was a natural ally of the Socialists.[69]

His position on the Esch-Cummins Act was one of unequivocal opposition. According to La Follette, it was "written for the railroads and the railroads, . . . and conferred upon the carriers special privileges as to rate making, freedom from state control, permission to combine and consolidate, such as no American corporation had ever before enjoyed or even dreamed of asking." [70] This surely was talking the language of the Grangers. In 1923 current gossip in Wisconsin had it that he was going to turn his political broadsides against the act in the campaign of 1924 and ask for its outright repeal. This, he felt, was a great political potential. He attributed his re-election in 1922 to many causes, but the significant thing was that he placed his stand against the act at the top of the list.[71]

His position on the tariff also was more in line with the arguments of the Grangers and the Farmers' Alliance than it was with the arguments of the McNary-Haugenites, but he was not consistent on this point. He voted for increases on agricultural products in the Fordney-McCumber Act of 1922, but no sooner were these tariff schedules passed than La

67. *St. Paul Dispatch,* July 21, 1924.

68. Louis F. Budenz, "Badgerdom; The Home of La Follette and the Socialists," *Labor Age,* XII (October, 1923), pp. 1–3.

69. *New York Times,* July 13, 1924.

70. Quoted in "The Progressives—What They Stand For and Want," *Saturday Evening Post,* CXCV (March 10, 1924), p. 165.

71. *Pioneer Press,* May 21, 1923.

Follette turned sour on them as effective protective agents for the farmers.[72]

> For more than a year, beginning in 1921, Washington was crowded with lobbyists, busily engaged in writing into the tariff law exhorbitant rates and special privileges for steel, cotton, wool, sugar and the thousand and one other industries which they represented. They were not required to produce their books and show their costs, nor was any attempt made to ascertain scientifically what tariff duties were necessary to promote the general welfare of the nation. The party majorities of the Ways and Means and Finance committees, sitting behind closed doors, simply asked them what they wanted and then gave them that, and sometimes a little bit more . . .[73]

La Follette did not take too positive a stand on the fixing of farm prices but said that he was not horrified by it as an invasion of natural economic laws, especially when he saw similar invasions committed daily by private groups and without protest from the conservatives:

> We have built up in this country an artificial business structure which throttles the natural law of supply and demand. The price of steel is fixed by private interests. The price of cloth is fixed by private interests. In virtually every line of manufactured commodities a few interests fix the prices. The conservatives, so-called, have nothing to say about that. They support it. But when it is proposed that the government fix prices to save from destruction the great agricultural industry, upon which the country is absolutely dependent, these conservatives throw up their hands in terror.

He justified his voting for the Norris Grain Corporation bill in Congress because he felt that it was the best measure before that body for the relief of the farmers. He admitted a reluctance to vote for price-fixing measures, instead of relying on natural economic laws and movements, because of the difficulty of making them work, but at times such actions were held to be the lesser of two evils.[74]

As election day approached La Follette came out with his farm program, which was nothing more than an attempt to harness the prevailing

72. *St. Paul Dispatch*, October 5, 1924.

73. Quoted in "The Progressives—What They Stand For and Want," *Saturday Evening Post*, CXCV (March 10, 1923), p. 165.

74. *Baltimore Sun*, July 28, 1923.

sentiments of the western Middle West and to restate his position on what ailed the American economy. Apparently, the releasing of such a program was prompted by uncertainties over what he was going to do for agriculture if elected.

He endorsed the principle of agricultural equality that was at the basis of the McNary-Haugen and the Norris-Sinclair measures. Originally La Follette favored the Norris proposal, but as election day neared he also came forward with an approval of the McNary-Haugen bill.

Other evidence of the omnibus qualities of his agricultural program was his insistence that legislation enacted give to the farmers their "cost of production plus a reasonable profit," and also that the government extend aid to the farmers to build a national cooperative-marketing program. La Follette promised to give agriculture equality by appointing as secretary of agriculture a man who was in full sympathy with cooperative marketing, buying, and credit—an implication which, to say the least, was unjustified in so far as Secretary Wallace was concerned. The farmers were in need of adequate representation on the Federal Reserve Board, the Federal Farm Loan Board, the Tariff Commission, and the Interstate Commerce Commission.

Outright repeal of the Esch-Cummins Law was asked for, and also the return of railroad rates to prewar levels and the basing of evaluations of railroad properties on the actual prudent investment. The development of waterways was held a means for bringing down transportation costs. Legislation was needed to protect the farmers from fraudulent branding and advertising of seeds, feeds, and fertilizers that were sold in interstate commerce. Tariff schedules that were framed by "the highly paid attorneys and technical experts" had to come down; figures were cited to show that farmers paid out more dollars for every dollar that the tariff brought to them. Honest enforcement of the Packers and Stockyards Act and the Grain Futures Act was urged. Employees in government posts who owed their appointments to special groups should be driven from their posts. Above all, farmers should make common cause with the wage earners, who also were at the mercy of monopoly interests.

La Follette cited his progressive record in Wisconsin as proof of what the farmers could expect from him if elected president. The Progressives there were largely responsible for legislation to protect the dairy farmers from the competition of imitation dairy products—filled milk and cheese, oleomargarine colored like butter, and the use of deceptive trade names—and also for the steps that were being taken to insure the production of high grade dairy products. Also beneficial to agriculture was the early encouragement that the Progressives gave to the cooperative movement and to the establishment of a railroad commission with power to make a physical evaluation of railroad properties, to reduce rates, and to compel the railroads to pay taxes that were based on the true value of their properties.[75]

The attempt made to bring about a political fusion of farmers and labor met "skepticism and even distrust" in certain quarters. A question asked time and time again was what conceivable common interests the two had. The La Follette campaign was a coalition of farmers, organized labor, Socialists, and other groups; but these groups had many points of conflict. Railroad men blackballed farm representatives who voted against labor legislation, and among those so censured were strong supporters of the McNary-Haugen bill. An alliance of this type, if it did actually take place, would simply serve to make "the farmer [the] catspaw extraordinary to industrial labor and the Socialist Party. As Mr. Dawes has put it, Senator La Follette is preaching high beef on the hoof and low beef on the table. Only one of these two desirables can be had. . . ." As proof of the predominance of labor in any proposed farmer-labor coalition, the Minnesota Farmer-Labor party was cited as a conspicuous example.

The McNary-Haugenites were especially grieved because of the stand that La Follette took against their pet measure. La Follette eventually came out for the measure, but only after the damage had been done. He was suspected of deliberately contributing to the defeat of the bill in order to keep the agricultural question and agrarian discontent alive until after the election. La Follette by so acting also enabled the critics of the farmers to charge that they were not united around a common program of action. The La Follette program was nothing more than "a loose jumble of the catchwords which are supposed to appeal to the farmer's fancy": this was a political program and not that of "the special protector of agriculture."[76]

75. *Equity News* (Madison, Wis.), October 15, 1924, p. 6.
76. *Pioneer Press,* October 19, 1924.

Besides banking heavily on labor and the farmers, La Follette sought the aid of the German-Americans and the votes of the recently naturalized citizens.[77] But this was all in vain. La Follette polled a total of 4,826,471 votes and thirteen votes in the electoral college, which was considerably less than Roosevelt received in 1912. He carried only his native state of Wisconsin and finished second in eleven others—Idaho, California, Minnesota, Iowa, North Dakota, South Dakota, Washington, Montana, Wyoming, Nevada, and Oregon.[78]

The causes for defeat were those with which any new political movement would be faced. For one thing, the progressive campaign needed organization, time, money, and a thousand things that could not be obtained within the short course of a single campaign.[79] La Follette failed to capture the agricultural vote in the numbers for which the progressives had hoped. Even though the farmers voted for him more than did any other group, he carried only Wisconsin, which had an urban population that equaled or slightly exceeded that of the rural areas; and his home state was even referred to as nothing more than "a La Follette pocket borough." In states like Kansas, Iowa, and Nebraska the La Follette collapse was even more complete. More prosperous times appeared to be on the way for the wheat farmers, whose support the progressives had counted on rather heavily. "The narrow escape of Senator Brookhart and the defeat of Magnus Johnson—both political leaders whose careers, like Mr. La Follette's, rest chiefly upon the farmers' desire for higher prices—merely add emphasis to the situation." Organized labor gave him some votes, but again not in the numbers for which the progressives had hoped. The Socialists also were of help, but their vote never was impressive. Progressive leaders like Norris of Nebraska and Borah of Idaho gave him little or no help.[80]

La Follette led the same type of movement in 1924 that he had been

77. "La Follette and German Americans," *New Republic,* XL (October 1, 1924), pp. 108–10; "La Follette and the German Vote," *Literary Digest,* LXXXIII (October 11, 1924), pp. 10–11.

78. Edgar E. Robinson, *The Presidential Vote, 1896–1932* (Palo Alto, 1934), p. 13.

79. *St. Paul Dispatch,* October 3, 1924.

80. "La Follette's Failure as a Candidate," *World's Work,* XLIX (December, 1924), pp. 118–19; MacKay, *The Progressive Movement of 1924,* pp. 195–96.

leading for the past quarter of a century. He scored the same victory, in the same region, and among pretty much the same people.[81] His greatest vote was in the old Granger states. The *St. Paul Dispatch,* no friend of La Follette, saw in the election a dire warning to the Republicans to accept a more western point of view. The party, it felt, had gravitated too much into the hands of men "who see with the eyes of Eastern industrialism. . . ." "If the west is to be held, it will be necessary to restore the balance within the party between East and West, and to re-establish the national character of its leadership." [82]

81. "The Future of the La Follette Party," *Literary Digest,* LXXXIII (November 15, 1924), pp. 10–11.
82. *St. Paul Dispatch,* November 5, 1924.

Chapter XIII

THE McNARY-HAUGEN MOVEMENT

STILL another phase of agrarian unrest that was typical of the western Middle West was the McNary-Haugen movement, which had hoped to make the tariff on agricultural products effective. The basic assumption behind this program was that the tariff which had been greatly responsible for the profitableness of certain manufactures and industries could be made to benefit the farmers also if only an effective wall, rather than the traditional one, was put around their commodities. Its sponsors felt, and with much justification, that in an era as dominated by the protectionist spirit as the decade of the twenties, it would be easier to put duties on "basic" farm commodities than to try to lower those on the goods and services the farmers bought.[1] This movement was in line with the trend toward self-sufficiency, which was a powerful force in a disillusioned postwar America; it also had the effect of focusing attention on the conflict between the interests of agriculture and industry, and even forced the Republican administration to give added encouragement to the cooperative movement—perhaps more than it would have liked to, but still with the hope that cooperatives would satisfy farmer demands and check any attempt to move the existing tariff structure in any direction other than upward.[2]

It was a foregone conclusion that the lower duties of the Underwood

1. George N. Peek, "Equality for Agriculture with Industry," *Proceedings of the Academy of Political Science,* XII (January, 1927), pp. 564–75; see also the editorial, "The Farmer and the Tariff," *Wallaces' Farmer,* XLV (October 22, 1922), p. 2469.
2. Wilson Gee, *American Farm Policy* (New York, 1934), pp. 32–38.

Tariff of 1913 would be revised upward when the Republicans took office in 1921. But for all practical purposes this revision would have amounted to nothing more than a gesture, because the lower schedules of the Underwood Tariff never had had a chance to operate. The war years not only had provided American industries with a type of protection that legislation could never have extended to it, but also had whetted the appetites of the protected groups, who clamored for more.[3] Their position was implemented by the fact that the war years saw the conversion of the United States from a debtor to a creditor nation and the growing desire of the indebted nations to meet their obligations through payments in kind.[4]

One could hardly say that protectionism was something that was confined to the United States alone, or that it was ushered in by conditions that were peculiar to it. This was a world-wide phenomenon. The war had thrown world trade and economies out of balance, and governments anxious to promote their interests placed embargoes on gold, which helped bring about wild fluctuations in exchange rates. For instance, France threatened that it would not permit the free importation of American goods unless their payment was arranged for in terms other than in the exportation of French gold. Likewise, it was obvious that Germany, a leading export and import nation before the war, was in no position to trade unless she could pay for her imports with goods that would compete with some of the industries in the United States. The possibility that European nations would return to their normal rates of production, and thus compete with the United States, was a fear that haunted many Americans, who began to feel, in increasing numbers, that unless tariff barriers were raised the nation would be flooded with foreign goods.[5] Among the recent converts were the western farmers, who preached the protectionist gospel with evangelical vehemence.[6]

The first links in the chain of agricultural protection were the emergency legislation of 1921 and the Fordney-McCumber Tariff of 1922. Both

3. F. W. Taussig, "The Tariff Act of 1922," *Quarterly Journal of Economics,* XXXVII (November, 1922), p. 3.

4. George Soule, *Prosperity Decade, From War to Depression, 1919–1929* (New York, 1947), pp. 252–59.

5. *Monthly Letter of the National City Bank of New York,* May, 1919, p. 4; *ibid.,* January, 1919, pp. 5, 10.

6. Taussig, in *Quarterly Journal of Economics,* XXXVII (November, 1922), pp. 3–4.

measures demonstrated their utter futility as price-raising or stabilizing influences, but they nonetheless were reflective of the thinking of many farmers who had become convinced that something more than the traditional tariff was needed to make protection work for them.

In the midst of the drastic price drops of 1920 and 1921, both farmers and their spokesmen seem to have recalled past arguments to the effect that the raising of duties would help to protect domestic producers. It was reasoning such as this that prompted President Harding, in his first message to Congress, to urge protection for the farmers as well as for industry. As a result, on May 27, 1921, an emergency tariff put high duties on wheat, corn, meat, sugar, and wool, with the proviso that these duties would remain in force for six months only. But on November 16 the measure was extended until otherwise provided for by law.

This act had great political significance. The agriculturists, by supporting it, committed themselves to a policy of high and ruthless protection and in return got a carte blanche right to fix duties pretty much as they pleased on their products. When it came to the duties on manufactured articles, they could not oppose them as they had done in 1909. Thus no moderating influence was of avail in the Sixty-seventh Congress. The net result was a tariff with rates higher than those of 1890, 1897, and 1909.

The duties provided for in the Fordney-McCumber Act of 1922 had in them economic jokers that were typical of past tariff legislation. Wheat had on it a duty of thirty cents a bushel as compared with twenty-five cents in the act of 1909; the ten-cent duty on rye was now fifteen, and corn also bore a tariff of fifteen cents a bushel; beef was taxed at three cents a pound and lamb at four as compared with one and a half and two cents in 1909. Then there was the usual list of petty and innocuous duties that ranged "from eggs to reindeer meat, peanuts to acorns."

Other concessions appeared on the free list. Agricultural implements such as plows, harrows, headers, reapers, cotton gins, even wagons and carts, were admitted duty free, duplicating in large measure the provisions of the act of 1913. These articles, in almost every case, were made cheaper in the United States than abroad, and only small quantities of foreign made machinery managed to find their way into the country.[7]

7. *Ibid.*, pp. 4–9.

Except for wool and sugar, it would have been difficult to find better proof of the failure of the customary tariff duties to serve as a check on declining prices. Despite the import duty of thirty cents on a bushel of wheat, the United States, during the fiscal year ending June 30, 1923, imported some 18,050,000 bushels of high-protein Canadian wheat. Again, over a nine-month period from July, 1923, to March, 1924, inclusive, the United States imported 23,498,000 bushels from Canada. Because of this, and also the growing clamor of the McNary-Haugenites, President Coolidge was prompted to raise the wheat duty from thirty to forty-two cents a bushel, effective April 7, 1924.[8]

The course that wheat prices took following this last pronouncement confirmed the utter futility of such measures. The President issued his proclamation on March 7; the day before that, May futures closed on the Chicago market at $1.11½ a bushel and July futures at $1.11¼. On March 26, May and July futures sold at $1.00½ and $1.02 respectively. Here was a drop of about ten cents in less than thirty days. True enough, wheat prices eventually did come back to the March 6 level, but this was due largely to the unfavorable crop reports that came in from Canada and other nations of the northern hemisphere. If anything, wheat prices should not have dropped as they did in March. The South American crop had already been harvested and marketed; American farmers had been reducing their acreage; winter wheat conditions were none too good; and the wheels of American industry had been moving into higher speed.

Obviously, in so far as the majority of the farm products were concerned, the traditional tariff was ineffective as a device to protect exports. The test of tariff effectiveness, according to the drafter of the first McNary-Haugen measure, was the ability of the domestic producers to determine prices behind tariff walls. Unless the price could be determined in this fashion, the American producers would have to content themselves with depressed world prices for their exports, as they had in past years.[9]

The event that drove farm leaders to search for more effective protective weapons was the fact that farm prices dropped faster and to lower levels than did the prices of the commodities and services that the farm-

8. Charles J. Brand, "The Price Balance Between Agriculture and Industry," *Proceedings of the Academy of Political Science,* XI (January, 1925), p. 168.

9. *Ibid.*, pp. 169–70.

ers bought. Here the farmers had the facts to support their charges as perhaps they never had had before. Freight rates, wages, taxes, farm implements, and the like, all of which went into the farmers' cost of production, remained high or came down via the stairway, while farm prices took the elevator.[10]

The McNary-Haugenites chose to consider agricultural prices from the standpoint of the purchasing power of the farmer rather than in terms of money prices received.[11] In these efforts they were amply facilitated by the work of statisticians of the United States Department of Agriculture, who had been compiling such figures. They found that "a suit of clothes which cost the farmers in North Dakota 21 bushels of wheat in July 1913, cost him 31 bushels in 1923, and a wagon which then cost him 103 bushels would cost him 166." "Average monthly farm wages for the United States on July 1, 1923 were 59 per cent above the 1913 level. Day wages at harvest time had increased even more. In Kansas the day wage in harvest was 82 per cent above 1913. . . . Wholesale prices of the more common farm implements were . . . from 45 to 59 per cent higher than in 1913, and retail prices were considerably higher. . . ." Tax burdens in many regions had become excessive. "Taxes on farm lands in Kansas increased 171 per cent between 1913 and 1921, in South Dakota, 129. . . ." "Since 1920 prices of wheat have fallen nearly to the pre-war level, whereas freight rates remain 45 per cent and more above pre-war rates." Granted that the price of wheat in 1923 was slightly above the prewar level, the costs of production were relatively much higher. And this was but one instance. The same was true of other commodities.[12]

Also included in this system which kept farm production costs high were such measures as the Adamson Law, the curbing of immigration, the Esch-Cummins Law, and the Railroad Labor Board. "These all tended to protect, stabilize and hold immune from world influence industry and

10. John D. Black, "The Progress of Farm Relief," *American Economic Review,* XVIII (June, 1928), pp. 252–55; see especially page 254 for a comparison of price indexes between farm and nonfarm products over the period 1910–27.

11. Brand, in *Proceedings of the Academy of Political Science,* XI (January, 1925), p. 163.

12. Henry C. Wallace, *The Wheat Situation,* U. S. Dept. Agri. (Washington, 1923), pp. 1–2, 21, 36–38.

labor, and to make effective the work of their organizations in holding up the prices of their commodities and services." [13]

During the early days of the farm bloc, agitation for protection received no more special attention than did measures to regulate the packers, to legalize cooperatives, and to extend more liberal credit facilities. It remained for two gentlemen, not farmers by vocation, George N. Peek and Hugh S. Johnson, who had seen their farm-machinery business wither away in the depression, to start the tariff on farm products on its way to popularity.

Peek and Johnson had become close friends during the war years while both worked on the War Industries Board. Peek formerly had been in the farm-implement business, but he had indicated that he had no intentions of returning to it when the war ended. Among his business associates was John Willys, the manufacturer of an automobile bearing his name, who recently had acquired the Moline Plow Company. Peek described the Moline Plow Company as "a terrible lemon"; it had failed to make money for years, and did not show the slightest indications of ever doing so. Willys, nevertheless, asked Peek to head his new company, which the latter finally consented to do, taking Johnson with him as his assistant and general counsel.

An inquiry into the financial status of the company revealed its actual impoverished condition. For a while the company was caught in the brief postwar inflation period, and was financed by Willys down to the beginning of the depression. However, when the depression came Willys, the Moline Plow Company, and all were caught in the impasse. Peek and Johnson soon became convinced that "there can't be any business until the farmer is on his feet. There is nothing we can do here—let's find out what is the matter with agriculture." [14]

Meanwhile, Peek and Johnson had written a pamphlet called *Equality For Agriculture*. It first apeared in 1922 as an anonymous publication, but later that same year a second edition was issued bearing the name of the joint authors and addressed to James Howard, the president of the

13. Peek, in *Proceedings of the Academy of Political Science,* XII (January, 1927), pp. 568–69.

14. Hugh S. Johnson, *The Blue Eagle from Egg to Earth* (New York, 1935), pp. 103–4.

American Farm Bureau Federation. The principal ideas in this pamphle soon captured the imagination of many farmers, their spokesmen in Cor gress, rural business groups, and vocal elements of the rural press, an one result was a "knock 'em down, drag 'em out fight" between the farm ers and the administration in Washington. Nowhere did their proposa gain more adherents than in the western Middle West.

The proposal of Peek and Johnson was based on the assumption tha agriculture as well as industry had to receive a "fair exchange value" fo its products if it was to survive. The fair exchange value of a particula commodity was defined as one which bore "the same ratio to the curren general price index as a ten year, pre-war average crop price bears to th average general price index, for the same period." Such a fair exchang value was to be reached not only by keeping the high tariff walls intac but also by implementing them with a mechanism that would enable th farmers to dispose of their surplus at world prices. What losses ther were suffered by selling on the world market would be recouped throug an equalization fee that would be assessed on those who sold for a highe price on the domestic market. In other words, this called for a two-pric system—a domestic and a world price, the first of which was expectec to be the higher one but with the added effect of raising general pric levels. Assessments on those who sold on the domestic market would b made by giving to them partial payment for their crop in the form of "scrip," the value of which would be determined after operation costs an losses had been determined. Theoretically, at least, those who lost by sellin on the world market would be paid back part of their loss by those wh sold on the domestic market.[15]

George Peek was one of the men who had been invited to attend Presi dent Harding's agricultural conference in 1922. One recommendatio made by the conference was that the President and Congress should "tak steps immediately to re-establish a fair exchange value for all farm prod ucts with that of other commodities. . . ." But for Peek the passing o a resolution was not enough. According to Russell Lord, "Peek grumblec that a big, sedate affair had not been his idea of a real conference," and for weeks he "kept coming to Wallace and his economists for a discussion

15. John D. Black, "The McNary-Haugen Movement," *American Economic Review*, XVIII (September, 1928), pp. 406–9.

about his further move toward Equality for Agriculture." He wanted a "conference about fair-ratio prices."

Finally, Wallace got permission from Harding to call the conference that met in the office of the Secretary of Agriculture. The list of conferees invited was "quite properly, nicely weighted with those who adhered to Hoover's ultraconservative view." In addition to Peek and Johnson, James R. Howard, president of the American Farm Bureau Federation, and Gray Silver, the Bureau's Washington representative, the conferees were Fred Wells from Minneapolis, General Charles G. Dawes from Chicago, Otto Kahn from New York, Judson C. Welliver, representing the President, and Julius Barnes, representing (as the Wallace element wryly put it) Herbert Hoover. Lord's account of the meeting says that ...

> the group exhibited a preponderantly hostile and critical attitude toward the Peek-Johnson proposal. As General Johnson said years later, "Harry Wallace was the only man at either of those first two price-ratio conferences who would give us as much as a pleasant look." Otto Kahn was more sympathetic than most of them; he granted that the plan had some merit but he urged that nothing be done for six months or so, in which time things might pick up. Howard and Silver played cagey. Julius Barnes said bluntly that he had his opinion of a Secretary of Agriculture who would take the time of busy men in considering such a plan.[16]

Herbert Hoover, the Secretary of Commerce, who was intent on building up American export trade, was strongly opposed to any plan which raised the cost of American industrial products. Hoover fought the equalization fee plan and clashed with Wallace over it.[17]

Peek and Johnson also took their plan to Congressman Sydney Anderson of Minnesota, who was serving at the time as chairman of the Joint Commission of Agricultural Inquiry, as well as of President Harding's agricultural conference. They proposed to Anderson that "the export surplus was the only controlling fact in the problem of farm distress. He frankly told us that if we tried to raise this point in that convention, he would steam-roller us—all of which he faithfully and artistically did."[18]

16. Russell Lord, *The Wallaces of Iowa* (Boston, 1947), pp. 238–40.

17. Black, in *American Economic Review,* XVIII (September, 1928), pp. 406–7; Johnson, *The Blue Eagle,* p. 105.

18. Peek, in *Proceedings of the Academy of Political Science,* XII (January, 1927), p. 569.

Little else was done after these preliminary attempts, but the plan loomed prominently in the mind of Wallace, as well as in those of Peek, Johnson, and others. In the fall of 1923 the North Dakota Bankers' Association endorsed the measure; and about the same time Wallace sent Henry C. Taylor into the Northwest to study the situation firsthand. Taylor found that the Peek-Johnson plan was being widely discussed and had much popular support behind it. On November 12 Wallace, in an interview with the Associated Press in Chicago, publicly endorsed it, as he did a couple of weeks later in his report to the President entitled *The Wheat Situation.*

Meanwhile, Charles J. Brand, a consulting specialist on marketing and former chief of the Bureau of Markets, was asked by Wallace to draft a bill embodying the chief features of the plan. Brand went to Illinois to obtain the assistance of Peek.[19] This preliminary draft, a very involved affair, was finally perfected with the aid of Senator Charles McNary of Oregon and Representative Gilbert N. Haugen of Iowa, under whose joint auspices this measure was to be introduced in Congress on January 16, 1924.[20]

The McNary-Haugen bill embodied the chief features of the original Peek-Johnson plan, including the price-ratio provision to determine fair prices, the selling of the surplus abroad at world prices, the equalization fee to recoup the loss by an assessment on the domestic price, and the scrip device to collect the fee. Hearings on the bill started on January 21 and extended through March 19, during which period representatives of labor, farm organizations, bankers, grain exchanges, farmers, and others were heard. Testimony was taken to the extent of 728 pages and more than a month was spent in reading the bill for amendment. The House Committee on Agriculture spent at least three months in daily session, in which all but two days were devoted to the bill.[21]

The first McNary-Haugen bill was endorsed by more than two hun-

19. Lord, *The Wallaces of Iowa,* pp. 253–54; Black, in *American Economic Review,* XVIII (September, 1928), p. 407.

20. Brand, in *Proceedings of the Academy of Political Science,* XI (January, 1925), p. 174; Black, in *American Economic Review,* XVIII (September, 1928), p. 407.

21. Report of the House Committee on Agriculture, *McNary-Haugen Agricultural Products Export Bill* (68 Congress, 1 session, House Report 631, serial 8228, Washington, 1924), p. 2.

dred farm organizations, including the American Farm Bureau Federation and numerous state farm bureaus, the National Board of Farm Organizations, which consisted of sixteen different associations, the national Grange, and countless other farm groups; commercial clubs, merchants' associations, Rotary, Kiwanis, and Lions' clubs; American Legion posts; the Chambers of Commerce of Seattle, Spokane, and other cities; the St. Paul Association of Public and Business Affairs; the Greater Des Moines Committee; the Greater St. Paul Committee; clearinghouse and state bankers' associations in Montana, North Dakota, Oregon, South Dakota, and Washington; the Iowa state legislature; Republican state conventions in Iowa and Minnesota; departments of agriculture for the states of Arizona, Montana, Oklahoma, and Utah; commissioners of agriculture, governors, college presidents, professors, railroad officials, bankers, and many others in all walks of life. In May, 1924, the House Committee on Agriculture had on file over ten thousand endorsements in the form of telegrams, letters, petitions, etc.[22]

The idea behind the first McNary-Haugen bill, as well as of the others that followed, was that certain "basic" farm products, were "selling out of line with other commodities." As a result, the farmers got too little for what they sold and paid too much for what they bought. It proposed to rectify matters by creating a board that was to find out the price at which these commodities were to sell and a government corporation that was to sell the surplus abroad. Operations were to be confined to wheat, flour, rice, corn, wool, cattle, sheep, swine, or any other food products derived from any of the three last-mentioned products, but only in the event that a special emergency existed; and such an emergency would be declared only if an exportable surplus existed and the ratio price for a particular commodity was higher than that of the existing domestic price.

The first big problem involved finding the ratio price. This was to be done by a mathematical formula which, no doubt, was "somewhat complicated to the ordinary mind" but perhaps "simple to the statistician." The ratio price for a basic farm commodity had to bear the same relation to the prewar average price of that same commodity as the current average price for "all commodities" bore to the prewar average of all

22. *Ibid.*, pp. 2–3.

commodities. The average prices, or price indexes, for all commodities were to be based on 404 different items.[23]

Obviously, this complicated mathematical formula was confusing to the average farmer, who preferred a blanket statement of how much he was going to get for his product. "But index numbers to the statisticians," someone suggested, "[are] like worms to a robin. They eat them up. And so the best way to deal with this feature of the bill is to assume that higher mathematics in the hands of experts will solve the problem of proper price and that it will be satisfactory to the producer. . . ."[24]

Since the current average price for all commodities was supposed to be a constantly changing one, the Secretary of Agriculture was assigned the monthly task of first determining the average price of all commodities before the current averages could be determined. The Secretaries of Agriculture and Labor jointly were to figure out the current average price for each of the eight basic commodities. The control of the giant organization which was to determine these prices was to be vested in four directors who were to be appointed by the Secretary of Agriculture with the advice and consent of the Senate.[25]

The next step consisted of the novel and ingenious scrip plan. As one contemporary put it:

> The corporation issues some engraved pieces of paper called scrip, just as the post office issues stamps, which will be sold for real money just as stamps are. A man who intends to buy wheat from a producer must first provide himself with the proper amount of scrip. He buys this from the post office which remits to the corporation which keeps the money to offset its losses. Then the buyer uses this scrip as cash in his purchase from the farmer. The corporation estimates its probable loss over a given period and decrees the use of scrip accordingly. If it thinks its losses will equal 10 cents on each bushel of wheat produced and to be on the safe side doubles its guess, it would declare that scrip must be purchased and used to the equivalent of 20 cents a bushel . . . every farmer who sells his wheat at $1.60 would receive $1.40 in money and 20 cents in scrip. The scrip would be worth nothing, except in the event that the losses of the corporation

23. "A Digest of the Provisions of the McNary-Haugen Bill," *Congressional Digest,* III (May, 1924), p. 266.

24. "The McNary-Haugen Bill and the Farmer," *The Independent,* CXII (April 12, 1924), pp. 191–92.

25. *Congressional Digest,* III (May, 1924), p. 266.

did not equal the estimates, in which event the farmer will receive upon his scrip what is euphemistically called a dividend, representing the difference.[26]

As expected, opponents of the McNary-Haugen bill called it a calamitous "price-fixing" scheme that would benefit the nonproducers instead of the farmers. The equalization fee provided for was excessive and would bring about higher living costs; the cooperative movement would be stifled, and agricultural production would be unduly stimulated. These charges were promptly denied by the McNary-Haugenites, who said that the measure was nothing more than an attempt "to restore rights inadvertently impaired by other legislation."

When the bill came up for consideration in the House on June 3, it was rejected by a vote of 223 to 153.[27] This vote followed geographic rather than party lines; the West and the Middle West were for it and the East and the South opposed.[28]

Meanwhile, the Republicans had been attempting to pacify the farmers as previously by sponsoring other legislation that was intended to deflect sentiment away from the McNary-Haugen proposal. For instance, in February President Coolidge called the Northwest Agricultural Conference in Washington, which led to the formation of the Agricultural Credit Company to help banks in the Northwest. It was during this conference that Coolidge expressed his approval of the Norbeck-Burtness bill, which offered credit to farmers who might wish to diversify their production. Then on March 7 the President announced that the tariff on wheat would be raised from thirty to forty-two cents per bushel. And in April the Capper-Williams bill, which provided for a farm board to be administered by the government and assisted by advising commodity groups, was introduced. Secretary of Commerce Hoover was said to have a hand in the framing of this bill.[29]

The rejection of the McNary-Haugen bill by the House, and the sponsoring of alternative measures by Republicans, failed to quiet the advocates of "equality for agriculture." J. F. Reed, president of the Minnesota Farm Bureau, an ardent McNary-Haugenite, said of the defeated measure: "It

26. *The Independent*, CXII (April 12, 1924), pp. 191–92.
27. *Congressional Digest*, III (May, 1924), pp. 267–69.
28. Black, in *American Economic Review*, XVIII (September, 1928), pp. 410–11.
29. *Ibid.*, p. 263.

was not a case of alignment by parties but rather a combination of East against West; of the city and business interests of the East against the principal agricultural regions of the country. Agricultural America supported the bill."[30] This first defeat led to the formation in St. Paul, on July 11 and 12, 1924, of the American Council of Agriculture, with George N. Peek as president, the avowed purpose of which was to pass the measure which had just been defeated. After this, the evidences of unrest appear to have waned somewhat. Wheat prices in particular showed some signs of rising, temporarily at least, and there was a noticeable adjustment in the exchange values of farm and nonfarm products.[31]

If anything, the number of votes that the defeated McNary-Haugen proposal got convinced the administration that the demands of the farmers could not be overlooked, regardless of the legislation that already had been passed in their behalf. At the close of the Sixty-eighth Congress on June 7, 1924, there were before the Senate and House Committees on Agriculture several proposals for cooperative marketing. They were the Curtis-Aswell, the Capper-Williams, the Smith, and the Tincher bills. During the summer of 1924 President Coolidge said that he proposed to appoint a committee to investigate and report to Congress measures that would be of help to the farmers in their marketing. This was their main need, in so far as he was concerned. In November Coolidge appointed delegates to an agricultural conference which he hoped would evolve a plan that would do something for the farmers comparable to what had been done for other segments of the economy. By March, 1925, this conference had made three reports to the President.[32]

This conference conducted hearings during the greater part of January, 1925. On January 14, in its first report, it recommended that a more liberal credit policy be adopted by the Federal Intermediate Credit Banks, and that a carefully administered leasing system for the grazing lands in the public domain also be put into operation. On January 28, the conference recommended the passage of a cooperative-marketing bill corresponding to the Capper-Williams bill; the placing of additional tariff duties on

30. *Minnesota Farm Bureau News* (Central Edition, Grand Rapids), July 1, 1924.
31. See chart in Black, *American Economic Review,* XVIII (September, 1928), p. 254.
32. "The President's Agricultural Conference," *Congressional Digest,* IV (October, 1925), pp. 265, 267–68; also *ibid.* (March, 1925), p. 194.

farm products; production to meet domestic needs "with only such foreign markets as shall be profitable"; and the extension of more aid to state experiment stations. On February 2 still another report recommended closer coordination between federal departments to prevent friction and duplication, and advised that the problems of agriculture were "complex, widespread and highly technical" and did not "lend themselves to any one remedy for any specific piece of legislation through which there may be found complete cure for many ills."[33] No bill before Congress was held to be adequate to solve the problem.[34]

During the course of the hearings the Capper-Haugen bill was introduced, embodying the recommendations of the conference; this called for the creation of a federal marketing board outside the Department of Agriculture, with the Secretaries of Agriculture and Commerce as two of the five members. This proposed board was to be empowered to register all sound cooperatives. In February the Purnell Act, which previously had been defeated, was passed authorizing an annual grant of $20,000 to each state agricultural experiment station conducting research in rural social and economic problems, with graduated sums to be added each succeeding year up to 1930. This, incidentally, was the only tangible result of Coolidge's agricultural conference, for the Capper-Haugen bill was defeated by the substitution of the Dickinson bill, which had been drafted by cooperative groups opposed to the conference proposal. The Dickinson bill also proposed to set up a marketing board in the United States Department of Agriculture, but omitted the provision for registering cooperatives proved to be sound.[35]

In March, 1925, a revised McNary-Haugen bill, dropping the cumbersome price-ratio feature, was favorably reported on by the House Committee, but it failed to come up for a vote in the Sixty-eighth Congress.[36] It was caught in the legislative jam of the closing days of the second session.

If the administration believed that added doses of cooperative marketing were going to soothe the disgruntled farmers, they soon learned other-

33. *Ibid.* (October, 1925), pp. 267–68; Black, in *American Economic Review,* XVIII (September, 1928), pp. 263–64.

34. *Congressional Digest,* IV (October, 1925), p. 267.

35. Black, in *American Economic Review,* XVIII (September, 1928), pp. 263–64.

36. *Ibid.,* p. 407.

wise. On May 11 and 12 a conference of farm leaders was held in Des Moines, Iowa, which led to the formation of the Corn Belt Committee. This conference had been suggested by Milo Reno of the Iowa Farmers' Union and was sponsored by the national body. Twenty-four farm organizations, representing chiefly the corn and hog belt, responded to a call which had as its slogan "cost of production plus a reasonable profit."[37]

Although the convention had been called by the Farmers' Union, it could hardly be interpreted to mean that the responding organizations had accepted the principle of "cost of production." What endorsement, if any, they might have given it was at best of a passive variety, the result of compromise and nothing else. The three planks adopted by the conference were not accepted unanimously. They asked for the construction of the farmers' own marketing machinery, including such terminal facilities as might be needed; "cost of production" for their crops; and the creation of an export corporation which would buy up the "available" surplus and would be administered by a board of farmers nominated by farm organizations. There were differences of opinion over this last point, and also over the government regulation of marketing and price fixing; these, however, did not obscure the fact that farm organizations had grown tired of farm-relief conventions that were dominated by nonfarm groups and wanted a greater voice in the shaping of farm-relief programs.

It was evident that three distinct trends had become apparent in the campaign for farm relief: (1) increasing sentiment of the western Middle West in behalf of the McNary-Haugen bill; (2) the growing opposition of the Republican administration to McNary-Haugenism as it turned instead to favor more liberal credit facilities and to sponsor an alternative program of cooperative marketing—a worthy long-time policy, but hardly one that would give instant relief; and (3) increasing hostility of farmers to farm-relief conventions that were dominated by bankers, railroad men, lawyers, politicians, and other nonfarming groups.[38]

One of the best evidences of the McNary-Haugenites' opposition to the administration program was the reception that Coolidge received at the annual convention of the American Farm Bureau Federation late in 1925.

37. *Des Moines Register,* September 9, 1928; *Minnesota Farm Bureau News,* June 1, 1925; *Iowa Farm Bureau Messenger* (Waterloo), June, 1925; *Farmers' Union Herald* (South St. Paul, Minn.), June, 1927.

38. *Farm Market Guide* (Minneapolis), June, 1925.

Many delegates there had hoped to hear Coolidge make a complete turnabout and state something favorable about the McNary-Haugen bill, but he did nothing of the sort. He remained consistent with the past by calling the bill a dangerous price-fixing device that would be dominated by the consumer, not the producer, and also be a menace to cooperatives. Coolidge informed the delegates that "the free list in the existing tariff was constructed especially to favor the farmer," and repeated his often-mentioned formula that cooperative marketing was the most dependable remedy they could find. When he finished, he was given a "cooperative luncheon" consisting of foods that had been cooperatively produced.[39]

The Coolidge speech was too much for the federation, which already had shown its unwavering support of the McNary-Haugen bill. It repudiated the administration program by defeating national president, O. E. Bradfute, the man who had invited Coolidge to make his coolly received address, and electing in his place Sam H. Thompson, a widely known advocate of the equalization fee principle.[40]

Other evidences of disapproval were found. A poll of newspaper sentiment found that Republican papers in general were satisfied with the speech of the President, while the Democratic press was especially critical of his statement that "the Republican tariff policy is just the thing for the farmer."[41]

Among the most ardent supporters of the equalization fee were the St. Paul papers, the *Pioneer Press* and the *Dispatch*. The *Pioneer Press*, which claimed that it had assumed the leadership among the metropolitan newspapers in the fight for equality for agriculture, drew parallels between the position of agricultural America and the England of the mid-nineteenth century. When England repealed its Corn Laws it did so because it had decided to become primarily an industrial nation.

Granting the wisdom of that decision for England, it was intelligent, albeit ruthless, to remove the protection from agriculture. It gave England cheap raw

39. *Literary Digest*, LXXXVII (December 19, 1925), pp. 10–11.

40. The statement of the *Minnesota Farm Bureau News*, January 1, 1926, was typical of the reply that met the Coolidge speech. It said: "His address failed to satisfy the most forward looking proponents of relief to agriculture and in the main failed to touch a responsive chord in the farmers of the nation." See also the *Capital Times* (Madison, Wis.), December 11, 1925.

41. *Literary Digest*, LXXXVII (December 19, 1925), pp. 10–11.

materials and it made possible the assumption by England of the industrial leadership of the world.

But America has been sliding into the submergence of agriculture without design, at least without the conscious wish of the population at large. The issue which has been before the country is whether America should become industrialized at the expense of agriculture, whether the farmer should become subservient to industry; or, on the other hand, whether agriculture and industry should be permitted to develop equally side by side. For a bitter period it has seemed that the Administration has thrown its influence on the side of industry. It resisted the efforts of the leaders of agriculture to obtain protection. Whereas in England the choice was between removing or retaining an existing protection, in America it is one between granting protection or forcing agriculture to do without. The consequence of the latter course inevitably will be the decay of the institution of the individual land-owning farmer, which is the foundation of our economic and political system, and the institution of something akin to peasantry. The trend in that direction has been unmistakable. . . .[42]

Meanwhile, events were rapidly coming to a head in Iowa. The war had all but wrecked agriculture in the state; farm land values had shrunk at least 40 per cent since the ending of hostilities; the farm income was placed at about a billion dollars less; and banks were still feeling the effects of the deflation. Farmers and the business interests alike had started to think more seriously than ever in terms of the farm problem; the bankers, among other things, wanted a greater turnover in land sales, higher prices, and the liquidation of mortgages "acquired in a period of free and easy banking," while militant farm and political leaders insisted that the government give them a free rein in shaping national agricultural policies.[43]

On December 21, the Corn Belt Committee in session in Des Moines restated its position in behalf of an export commission "to handle farm surpluses" in order to make the protective tariff effective. Shortly thereafter an "all-Iowa conference" called by Iowa bankers gave the impression that not everyone was satisfied with the work of the Corn Belt Committee. Many of the farmers felt that this action of the Iowa bankers had been inspired by the national administration to start a move in accordance with the program outlined by Coolidge before the Farm Bureau con-

42. *Pioneer Press* (St. Paul), December 28, 1925.

43. Eric Englund, "The Dilemma of the Corn Belt," *World's Work*, LIII (November, 1926), p. 48.

vention in Chicago. Differences developed, but in due time Governor Hammill became head of the conference and suspicion was allayed.[44]

On January 28, 1926, another convention, the Corn and Agricultural Area Marketing Conference, met in Des Moines. One hundred and forty delegates were present from Ohio, Michigan, Indiana, Illinois, Wisconsin, Minnesota, South Dakota, Nebraska, Kansas, Missouri, and Iowa. North Dakota joined the convention later. This conference granted that cooperative marketing was "a good thing," but in so far as the "present situation" was concerned it was only "a gesture," and asked that the government be either taken out of "other business," or else placed in "the farming business." Bill Hirth, president of the Missouri Farm Association, editor of the *Missouri Farmer,* and chairman of the Corn Belt Committee, warned that if the farmers did not receive protection, agriculture would turn its forces loose upon "the tariff itself." "The wheat country, the cattle-hog country and the cotton country will be driven to join in the common cause. There is enough dynamite in this to change the political map for the next fifty years."

Congressman Lester J. Dickinson and former Governor Frank Lowden of Illinois attended the conference and were warmly received. Dickinson explained his bill which was before Congress calling for the appointment of a commission to look after the surplus.[45] Frank Lowden, perhaps the most popular man in attendance, also spoke of the need for an effective tariff for farm products as a means for re-establishing the purchasing power of the farmer. He, likewise, stressed the need for an agricultural board to handle surpluses in periods of abnormally high yields. Both Dickinson and Lowden were of the opinion that cooperative marketing associations should be used in handling the surplus.

The conference, besides endorsing the essential features of the Dickinson bill, recommended the wider use of corn and appointed a Committee of Twenty-Two to press Congress for immediate action. The leaders of the

44. Henry C. Taylor, "The Iowa Movement," *American Review of Reviews,* LXXIII (March, 1926), pp. 271–72.

45. The Dickinson bill was a modified version of the McNary-Haugen bill that had been rejected in the House in June, 1924. This bill provided for the handling of the surplus by cooperatives wherever possible. *Nebraska Union Farmer* (Omaha), February 10, 1926, p. 3; Black, in *American Economic Review,* XVIII (September, 1928), p. 407.

conference also were again coming around to the belief that little would be accomplished without an alliance with either the South or the East. Many with strong party feelings hoped that cooperation would be forthcoming from the East to save the Republican party, while others spoke warmly of an alliance with the South that would bring together the agricultural interest that had been separated by the Civil War.[46]

Besides the McNary-Haugen bill and the administration-sponsored program, there was a third plan involved in the struggle for farm relief of the twenties—the export debenture plan. Its most ardent advocate was the Grange. It was proposed by Professor Charles L. Stewart of the University of Illinois. The plan was "an arrangement whereby exporters of those agricultural products of which we produce a surplus [would] receive from the Treasury Department certificates having a face value established by Congress and intended to represent the differences in costs of production between here and abroad, such certificates being negotiable and good for their face value in the payment of import tariffs on any articles later imported." This plan did not provide for the purchasing and storing of the surplus; it provided a bounty on agricultural imports; and its advocates called it simpler and more flexible to operate.[47]

Stewart had outlined the main features of his plan to his economics classes as early as May, 1924, and had been active in calling the attention of Congress to it. He framed a bill embodying the essential features of his plan, and Senator McKinley and Representative Adkins, both of Illinois, drafted similar bills and introduced them in their respective houses. Hearings were conducted late in March and early in April, 1926, but the bills never emerged from the committee rooms. The following November the national Grange endorsed the export debenture plan, and from then on it was to be its staunchest supporter.[48]

Meanwhile, word had got around that two of the most ardent disciples of McNary-Haugenism, George Peek and Chester C. Davis, had been

46. *Ibid.*, pp. 273–75; Englund, *World's Work*, LIII (November, 1926), pp. 43–44; *Pioneer Press*, January 29, 1926.

47. K. L. Butterfield, "The Farm Problem Made Clear," *Current History*, XXIX (November, 1928), p. 269.

48. Joseph S. Davis, *The Farm Export Debenture Plan* (Palo Alto, Calif., 1929), pp. 2–3.

carrying on a correspondence with Sir Josiah C. Stamp, the British economist, with Vice-President Charles G. Dawes serving as intermediary, over the relative merits of the McNary-Haugen proposal. As a result, Dawes was swamped with requests for the publication of their statements. Permission was obtained from Stamp to publish their views and shortly these found their way into the press. They were conspicuously presented in the St. Paul *Pioneer Press,* one of the most active supporters of the equalization fee.[49]

Southern farm leaders had shown little interest in the McNary-Haugen proposal; in fact, their representatives in Congress had voted against the first measure in June, 1924, and there was little evidence that they had supported the abortive measure of 1925. But by early 1926 they appeared to be in a more receptive mood. The cotton acreage had expanded considerably in 1925 and a surplus had accumulated to threaten the price of the 1926 crop; hence the idea of a South-West alliance was revived. A joint conference finally was held in Memphis in January, 1926, where both agreed to draft a measure modeled after the Dickinson proposal.[50] As a result of this maneuver, cotton leaders appeared in Washington before committees in support of the revised McNary-Haugen measure. Cotton and corn were included in this bill but with the proviso that no equalization fee was to be collected on either one for a period of three years. This period of grace was extended to cotton largely because the southerners were not ready for the fee portion of the program, but they were willing to content themselves with the benefits of the orderly handling of exports through the corporation.[51]

Meanwhile, the agitation for McNary-Haugenism continued unabated. Delegates representing the American Council of Agriculture, the Committee of Twenty-Two, the Farm Bureau, the Grange, the Farmers' Union, and others visited Washington and made known their demands for legislative aid.[52]

These McNary-Haugen demands became so loud and at times so threatening that the editors of the *World's Work* penned "An Open Letter to

49. *Pioneer Press,* January 6, 1926.
50. Black, in *American Economic Review,* XVIII (September, 1923), pp. 407–9.
51. *Pioneer Press,* February 9, April 6, 1926.
52. *Minnesota Farm Bureau News,* April 1, 1926.

the Iowa Farmers" in rebuke.[53] The editorial ridiculed the Dickinson bill as "mostly words" that signified nothing and informed the Iowa farmers that the national administration had nothing to offer them but the tariff, and that would not do them any good. The administration was opposed to the McNary-Haugen plan. Nor would farmers in other sections of the country "put their hands in their pockets to subsidize you." What did Iowa farmers ever do for the starved cotton farmer? Did Iowans ever subsidize nonfarm groups? Did Iowa farmers, for years among the most prosperous in the nation, ever help less fortunate communities? Also, the East had nothing to fear in the voting strength of the Middle West. Senator Wadsworth of New York represented four times as many farmers as did Senator McNary of Oregon. Senator Reed of Pennsylvania had 200,000 more farm constituents than did Senator Capper of Kansas. Senator Willis of Ohio had almost as many farm votes as did Senator Reed of Missouri and nearly 300,000 more than there were in Iowa. The farmers in these other sections did not have the same interests that the Iowa farmers had. Why should wheat producers in Pennsylvania agitate for lower freight rates so that Kansas wheat farmers shipping to Pennsylvania would have to pay no more freight on their products than would Pennsylvania farmers who had only a score of miles or so to send their produce? Why should cotton farmers feeding corn to their mules help keep up the price of Iowa corn? Escape from low prices there was, to be sure, but it was in a direction opposite that of the McNary-Haugen bill. Farmers had to organize to reduce general tariff levels and they also had to "squeeze" the water out of their land values.

William M. Jardine, the Secretary of Agriculture, proposed to deal with the surplus through a farm board, but without adopting the equalization fee plan, which he described as "an excise tax, put on necessities of life." This proposal was incorporated into the Tincher bill, which he endorsed but which was opposed by Peek, Frank Murphy, and other McNary-Haugen supporters who were bound and determined either to pass the equalization fee proposal or else to elect a Congress that would.[54] According to the equalization fee enthusiasts, about the only thing that

53. "An Open Letter to the Iowa Farmers," *World's Work*, LI (April, 1926), pp. 571–73.

54. *Kansas City Times*, April 8, 20, 1926.

the Jardine plan would do was to add "a few extra experts on cooperative marketing to the Department of Agriculture."[55]

As a further concession, the national administration in March raised the tariff on butter from eight to twelve cents. In April the National Industrial Conference Board, representing the business interests, stressed the need for farm relief, and the McNary-Haugen, the Curtis-Aswell, and the Fess-Tincher bills were reported to the House. Many compromises had been imposed on the McNary-Haugen bill by representatives who were uncertain how their constituents would receive it. Needless to say, the bill was defeated a second time in the House by a vote of 212 to 167. Both the Tincher and Aswell bills, which had been offered as substitute measures, also were rejected. In the vote the McNary-Haugen bill picked up sixteen votes in the South, but lost an equal number in the West and on the Pacific Coast.[56]

In mid-June, Secretary of the Treasury Andrew Mellon came into the fight. Mellon, in response to the requests of Representatives Haugen and Dickinson for his opinion on the measure, wrote that if the bill were to become law we would have "the unusual spectacle of the American consuming public paying a bonus to the producers of the five major agricultural commodities."[57] His statements were held to have been the position of the administration and gave the farmers of the corn and wheat belts an additional target at which to aim.

On June 24 the Senate rejected the McNary-Haugen bill by a vote of 45 to 39. The vote in the Senate showed even less southern support than did the vote in the House.[58] The following day President Coolidge endorsed the marketing bill of Senator Fess, which administration critics called "a scheme not for the relief of the farmer, but for the relief of a frightened administration. . . ."[59]

If the administration thought that it had squelched the McNary-Haugen

55. *Pioneer Press,* July 1, 1926.

56. Black, in *American Economic Review,* XVIII (September, 1928), pp. 264, 408–11.

57. *The New International Year Book,* 1926, p. 752; L. T. Beman, *Farm Relief* (New York, 1927), p. 170; a complete text of the letter is found here.

58. *The New International Year Book,* 1926, p. 750; Black, in *American Economic Review,* XVIII (September, 1928), pp. 264–65. The Fess bill authorized a revolving fund of $100,000,000 to handle the surplus.

59. *Pioneer Press,* July 1, 1926.

movement, it was mistaken, because the McNary-Haugenites struck back with even greater force. On July 19 the Corn Belt Committee reassembled in Des Moines and issued warnings to the "industrial bloc of the tariff coddled East" and to the administration by informing both that the fight for agricultural equality was "not over by any means." "Protection for all or protection for none" was the adopted slogan; Secretaries Mellon, Hoover, and Jardine were singled out for censure, and a demand was made to investigate the influences that were at work against placing agriculture in the protective system.[60] Appreciation was even expressed to the nonfarm groups interested in the farm problem, but a warning was also issued against "any movement of business organizations to initiate an agricultural program independent of farm organizations."[61] Another development in this meeting was the "cost of production" statistics presented by E. E. Kennedy of the Farmers' Union, which were considered altogether too high.[62]

A meeting of the Committee of Twenty-Two, now representing twelve northern states and including businessmen and farmers, adopted pretty much the same resolutions as did the Corn Belt Committee. The day following the Committee of Twenty-Two convention, the Iowa state Republican convention in Des Moines did the anomalous thing of both endorsing Smith W. Brookhart, an insurgent, and "commending and congratulating" the Coolidge administration. Apparently, wrote the *Literary Digest,* the corn belt farmers insist on relief, "especially tariff relief,—but are not ready to leave the Republican Party in order to get it." The *Lincoln State Journal* said that farm meetings "had the remarkable effect of uniting the extreme wings of the party" in Iowa and elsewhere. Clinton W. Gilbert, writing in the *New York Evening Post,* said that the action of the West raises the issue of whether the Republicans may divide, "the West being for a low tariff and the East for a high tariff." Mark Sullivan predicted in the *New York Herald Tribune* that "the Administration will

60. *Minnesota Farm Bureau News,* August 1, 1926.

61. Englund, in *World's Work,* LIII (November, 1926), p. 48. See also "The Third Knock-Out for McNary-Haugenism," *Literary Digest,* XC (July 10, 1926), pp. 5–7. The reactions of midwest farm leaders and newspapers are cited in the latter source.

62. E. A. Stodyk and C. H. West, *The Federal Farm Board* (New York, 1930), pp. 29–30.

pay no attention to the Des Moines meeting, and otherwise will do nothing about farm relief except to maintain its past attitude of encouraging farm cooperatives."[63] And he was right, for in July an act was passed appropriating $224,000 to set up the Division of Cooperative Marketing in the United States Department of Agriculture.[64]

In Minnesota the defeat of the McNary-Haugen bill was the signal for the formation of the Minnesota Council of Agriculture. This body was organized on July 22 as evidence that Minnesota was "enlisted in a finish fight to secure agricultural equality through national legislation. . . ."[65] Twin Cities labor leaders also enrolled in the fight to give protection to agriculture.

In challenging, melodramatic tones, and after a fashion recalling the sectional controversies of the antebellum period, the Minnesota Council of Agriculture resolved:

The people of the United States are facing today the greatest issue in American history since the civil war, the emancipation of agriculture. The common economic interests of the West, North and South, have for many years been seriously affected and are at this time threatened with complete destruction by the existence of a definite and indefensible maladjustment in the nation's economic system. Thirty-five per cent of the people who are engaged in agricultural pursuits and live in rural districts have become industrial serfs,—a situation forced upon them by the development of America's system of protection to groups.

The law of supply and demand has been supplanted by a law-made price fixing and economic system that compels the farmer to buy what he uses in a law protected market on a scale of prices more than one hundred per cent above the price levels prevailing in 1914, and at the same time compels him to sell his major products at the price levels prevailing in other countries, in competition with the lowest paid laborer in the world and with the peasants of other lands. Under the operation of economic conditions created and fostered by one-sided fiscal legislation, the American farmer has been denied the benefit of existing

63. "The New Iowa Idea," *Literary Digest,* XC (August 7, 1926), pp. 10–11.

64. L. S. Tenney, "The New Cooperative Marketing Law," *American Review of Reviews,* LXXIV (September, 1926), pp. 304–6.

65. The conference that led to the formation of the Minnesota Council of Agriculture was called by the American Council of Agriculture, the Corn Belt Committee, the Minnesota Farm Bureau Federation, the Farmers' Union Terminal Association, the Equity Cooperative Exchange, and the Minnesota Wheat Growers, Associated.

tariffs and compelled to operate at a cumulative loss so that the Eastern industrialist might continue to reap benefits in foreign trade. The West cannot withstand indefinitely the drain upon its capital resources by Eastern industry, and the waning purchasing power of the farmer must inevitably drag in its ruin western commerce and industry depending upon it. It is for that reason that Western business, banking and manufacture are vitally interested in the solution of the agricultural problem, and dare joining with the farmer in demanding prompt and adequate redress.

Eastern business has for years deliberately and systematically propagandized Western business, and is doing it now, and unfortunately the economic views of many Western business men have come almost entirely from Eastern sources whose interests are opposed to ours. These interests have branded as "economically unsound" any and all proposals to make existing tariffs effective for agriculture while they proclaim as inviolable the tariff advantages secured by Eastern industry with the aid of Western votes. It is to correct this cruel and demoralizing situation that the agricultural and business interests of the West, North and South are uniting in their demands that the protective system be extended to the farmer and that existing tariff schedules on agricultural products be now made effective for him. The time for a showdown in the West has come. The economic interests of the farmers and the business men in the West are the same. The farmer is fighting with his back to the wall for the preservation of his home and a square deal. The hour has come when Western business should familiarize itself with conditions as they are and make common cause with those who are contending for equal rights within the nation's protective system. The fight in which we are engaged must be carried on aggressively and admits of no compromise. If it is a wise policy to protect industry in the East it must be equally wise to protect agriculture in the West. If protection is not to be accorded to the West there is no reason why it should not [*sic*] be continued in the East. We demand for the West equal rights with the East, protection for all or protection for none.

In this, our struggle for equal rights, we demand of our representatives in the legislative halls more than passive support. We must have loyal and militant support of a type that will not hesitate to take the offensive, disregard party ties, resist administrative pressure, and carry on an aggressive fight until the principle for agriculture has been vindicated and established.[66]

The fall elections of 1926, however, showed that hardly a dent had been made in the Republican columns of the western Middle West by the McNary-Haugenites. In Nebraska Governor Adam McMullen, the Republican candidate to succeed himself, was re-elected by a narrow

66. *Minnesota Farm Bureau News,* August 1, 1926.

margin of 3,432 votes. In Minnesota the entire state Republican ticket and ten Republican congressmen were re-elected. In North Dakota the results were the same. In Iowa John Hammill and eleven Republican congressmen were re-elected. In Wisconsin the entire ticket—state and national—and Victor Berger, the Socialist, were swept into office. Only in South Dakota was the Republican candidate for governor defeated, and that because of opposition within his own party. A Democrat, W. J. Bulow, was elected along with Republican Senator Peter Norbeck and three Republican congressmen.[67]

Republican leaders, nevertheless, were still fearful of a possible alliance between the western Middle West and the South, for in 1926 the cotton crop was the largest in history and the prices very discouraging. On January 5, 1927, the New York Cotton Exchange quoted the price of cotton as 12.65 cents per pound, a figure considerably below the cost-of-production estimates of the *Analyst* of November 5, 1926. To stave off the imminent *rapprochement* between the South and the West, President Coolidge appointed a cotton committee headed by Eugene Meyer, director of the War Finance Corporation, and including Secretaries Mellon, Jardine, and Hoover. The task of this committee was to investigate the cotton market and to help disburse $30,000,000 to aid cotton producers store four million bales of cotton.[68]

The actions of the national administration, however, did not put to an end hopes for a southern alliance. On November 17, 1926, southern and western leaders met in a cotton and corn states conference in St. Louis where they again endorsed the principles of the McNary-Haugen bill. A bloc system in Congress was recommended "to express and work for the economic interests of agriculture." The need for southern help was apparent, but some southern representatives were reported "shying away from the principle of the bill on the assumption that it would commit them to a high tariff."[69]

Again a farm conference expressed the belief that programs intended to control surpluses should make use of the existing cooperative marketing associations. The farm board that former Governor Frank O. Lowden

67. *The New International Year Book*, 1926, 515–16, 487, 386, 782, 894.

68. "The Cotton Deluge," *Literary Digest*, XCI (October 23, 1926), pp. 5–6; *The New International Year Book*, 1926, p. 201.

69. *New York Times*, November 18, 1926.

of Illinois proposed provided for this and was similar to the McNary-Haugen bill last defeated in both houses. But the conference this time, instead of accepting existing tariff schedules on industrial products, sought a reduction of duties on aluminum, steel, and chemicals, which provided "shelter for price-fixing monopolies." Again it was suggested that Congress investigate those phases of agricultural legislation which had made it possible for industrialists, dealers, and speculators to take such a leading role in shaping and administering agricultural programs. Also, a permanent program was asked for cotton in place of the proposal that the President withdraw four million bales from the market, which was nothing more than a "temporary expedient."[70]

Late in November Senator McNary was in conference with farm heads in an effort to perfect details for a new measure that he was preparing to introduce when Congress convened in December.[71] About the same time Congressman Dickinson protested against the actions of the Industrial Conference Board and the United States Chamber of Commerce in their forming of "peripatetic" organizations "to find out how much some people don't know about the farm problem." He warned that the farmers were capable of changing the political complexion of the nation, if they were not given instant relief.[72]

If the leaders of the southern cooperatives, which handled about 10 per cent of the crop, favored the McNary-Haugen proposal, there were others like W. L. Clayton, the prominent cotton merchant, who believed that ". . . irrespective of [the] merits of the plan as applying to other agricultural products," especially for those of which 85 to 90 per cent of the crop was consumed domestically, "it must be abortive if applied in this way to cotton." About 55 per cent was exported and only 45 per cent was consumed at home. The best hope of the South was to buy the cotton surplus and remove it from the market temporarily.[73]

The louder the farm groups "yelped," the larger the dose of cooperative "medicine" that the Republicans gave to the farmers. In January, 1927, the Curtis-Crisp bill was introduced providing for the establishment of the Federal Farm Board. This board was to be allowed $250,000,000 to make

70. *Pioneer Press,* November 18, 1926.
71. *New York Times,* November 27, 1926.
72. *Ibid.,* November 29, 1926.
73. *Cotton Trade Journal* (New Orleans), February 19, 1927.

advances to cooperatives to enable them to withhold nonperishables from market whenever a surplus "above world requirements" threatened to depress prices below the level of "cost of production plus a reasonable profit."[74]

The revised McNary-Haugen bill again came up for a vote in February, 1927. The new measure provided for an equalization fee for cotton that was to apply at once to help in collecting funds for a "holding movement"; rice was added to the list of basic commodities, but cattle and butter were dropped; the operation of the plan was "dependent upon a vote in favor of it by representatives of a half of the product;" an advisory commodity council was to be set up for each of the commodities; and loans were to be extended to cooperatives to purchase and construct storage facilities. The bill passed both houses—the Senate by a vote of 51 to 43, and the House by 214 to 178.[75] On February 25 President Coolidge vetoed it.

The Coolidge veto message, though not unexpected, was a conglomerate mass of the charges that already had been advanced by the opponents of the measure. One Coolidge critic called it "a congeries of adverse opinions and objections from several different sources thrown together without definite sequence and with much repetition of points." His analysis was both shrewd and naïve. The McNary-Haugenites analyzed the President's message and proceeded to remove some of the objections "without sacrificing the essential equalization fee principle."[76]

But invective, sarcasm, bitterness came forth from the pens of farm journalists in a fashion that had seldom been equaled. No words were spared in attacking Coolidge. One farm columnist wrote:

On the day of his courageous act, he issued a proclamation increasing the tariff on pig iron 50 per cent. Who says that was not an exhibition of intrepidity, when he signed it—as all the world must know—that by the signing he increased the cost of every binder, every threshing machine, every tractor and farm implement; that it increased the cost of locomotives, rails, and steel cars and thus increased the freight rates to the farmer.

74. Black, in *American Economic Review,* XVIII (September, 1928), p. 265.

75. *Ibid.,* pp. 409–11.

76. *Ibid.,* p. 411. See the *Congressional Record,* 69 Congress, 2 session, Vol. LXVIII, Part 5 (1927), pp. 4771–73, for a complete text of the Coolidge veto message.

> Ah, the courage of Coolidge is vastly underestimated. He bares his breast to the arrows of outrageous fortune in defense of the steel trust and the banker with an unparalleled calmness and remains—Cool! There is none to make him afraid, for his prayer at eventide runs: "The Steel Trust giveth and the Steel Trust taketh away; blessed be the name of the Steel Trust." With such a faith who could know fear?
>
> Certain, serene—cool and calm are adjectives no longer good enough as Mr. Coolidge makes ready to visit the West for the summer and in a few nasal-toned speeches will convert the rabble to his view. The Western farmer needs only his persuasive drawl to fall down and worship. Could courage go to loftier heights? Could moral man exhibit greater self-reliance? He will come West and fish! He, who until last year, never threw a line into a stream—unless it was the muddy pool of politics. He, who posing as a farmer, has never been out of political office since maturity. He will come West and convert us to the Mellon notion that the West must raise food for Mellon's employees at less than cost.[77]

This same journalist added that for years the Bible circulated more freely than did any other book published, but now even that has to take "a back seat" for that "matchless piece of literature" known as the President's veto message.[78]

That summer Coolidge decided to spend his vacation in South Dakota. Farm spokesmen insisted that the President had decided to come there in order to learn firsthand the condition of agriculture and also to pacify the farmers, but even at that the St. Paul *Pioneer Press* was willing to admit that the farmers were not so angry with the administration as originally had been believed. Farm prices had been rising and the price of manufactured commodities had been dropping, which meant that some real progress was being made toward a favorable exchange ratio.[79]

McNary-Haugenite leaders, however, felt snubbed when the President failed to invite them to the summer White House to discuss the farm problem with him. Also taken as a rebuff was the unwillingness of the President to send a message to the farm conference that had been scheduled to assemble in St. Paul on July 12 and 13.[80]

This latest conference was expected to draw some 1,500 farmers from

77. *Farmers' Union Herald,* March, 1927.
78. *Ibid.,* May, 1927.
79. *Pioneer Press,* June 19, 1927.
80. *St. Paul Dispatch,* June 25, 1927; *Pioneer Press,* June 20, 1927.

Minnesota, Wisconsin, the Dakotas, Iowa, and Montana in a fight-to-the-finish battle for the equalization fee. This meeting was also expected to help the agricultural equality commissions of Minnesota and South Dakota come into contact with the different farm groups. Both these bodies had been created by the legislatures of their respective states to work out plans for state and national legislation and to cooperate with similar commissions that were to be established in other states. Pretty much the same personalities attended and the same arguments were heard. Also, a petition signed by 10,000 Montanans was exhibited asking Frank Lowden to run for President.[81]

In March, 1928, a broadened new McNary-Haugen bill, to include all types of farm products and surpluses, was reported to the Senate. This provided for the restoration of the equalization fee, but only if the buying and storage operations failed. The President was granted full appointive powers, and the appropriations were increased by an amendment in the House from $250,000,000 to $400,000,000. In April the Senate passed the bill by a vote of 58 to 23, and in May the House followed suit with a vote of 204 to 121. But once again Coolidge vetoed it. In a 51 to 30 vote the Senate failed to override the presidential veto.[82]

Although the second veto was not wholly unexpected, the finality with which it was accomplished stunned the farmers. This was taken to mean that American industry would not tolerate any attempt to tamper with the protective system.[83] Industry was the political and economic boss and it intended to remain thus. Henry A. Wallace, the son of the late Secretary of Agriculture and editor of *Wallaces' Farmer,* reminded sympathetic followers that the second Coolidge veto was further evidence that "Coolidge and Hoover stand for industrializing the United States" and that they were against giving farmers a fair share of the national income.[84] The editor of the *Prairie Farmer,* in a visit to the East after the second veto, reported that the average easterner was opposed to anything that would increase food prices. Agriculture was of no concern to him. "He

81. *Ibid.,* July 3, 1927; *St. Paul Dispatch,* July 12, 1927.

82. Black, in *American Economic Review,* XVIII (September, 1928), pp. 265, 412; *Des Moines Register,* May 26, 1928; *Des Moines Tribune,* May 4, 23, 1928; *Farmers' Union Herald,* April 1, 1928.

83. *Minnesota Farm Bureau News,* June 1, 1928.

84. *Des Moines Register,* May 24, 1928.

is simply not interested. He does not think in national terms, and the effect of a decadent and peasant agriculture on the nation's future is something entirely beyond his comprehension. . . . The real 'hicks' of America live along the Atlantic seaboard. They are far less well-informed than the average Middle-Western farmer, and their view point is far narrower."[85]

The Corn Belt Committee, in its April meeting, already had made known its intentions of fighting Herbert Hoover in the event that the Republicans nominated him for the Presidency.[86] Bill Hirth, chairman of the committee, in a warning that was typical of many of the militant proclamations that emanated from the Middle West, bluntly informed the Republicans that "as certain as they dare to nominate this man for President, the great Corn Belt states will bury him under an avalanche of votes that the Republican party will not forget for the next fifty years—and if there are those who think that I am talking through my hat, let them remember the cyclone that made Brookhart senator two years ago in the great erstwhile conservative Republican state of Iowa."[87] H. A. Wallace, a member of a family for years prominent Iowa Republicans, smarting under the defeat of his pet, the McNary-Haugen bill, which he espoused with almost evangelical vehemence, and remindful of the fact that Herbert Hoover was an archenemy of his father, was rapidly moving into the orbit of the Democratic party.[88] George N. Peek, as expected, denounced the Republicans and expressed the belief that farmers could "expect sympathetic action from the democratic nominee."[89]

In June some 2,000 farmers representing the Farm Bureau, the Farmers' Union, the Corn Belt Committee, the Committee of Twenty-Two, and lesser groups officially appeared before the Republican National Convention in Kansas City, where they reiterated their faith in the principles of the McNary-Haugen bill.[90] Shortly thereafter, farm groups visited the Democratic National Convention in Houston, Texas. On July 16 and 17 the Corn Belt Committee reassembled to review the attitudes of the two major parties. The Republicans were assailed for their failure to adopt

85. *Prairie Farmer,* quoted in *Minnesota Farm Bureau News,* July 1, 1928.
86. *Farmers' Union Herald,* April, 1928.
87. *Missouri Farmer,* quoted in *Farmers' Union Herald,* March, 1928.
88. See Lord, *The Wallaces of Iowa,* pp. 275–80.
89. *Des Moines Tribune,* July 16, 1928.
90. *Farmers' Union Herald,* June, 1928.

the program of "organized agriculture," while the Democrats were commended for what some McNary-Haugenites believed was a promise to do for the farmers what the Republicans had refused to do.[91] Notice was served that the 1,000,000 farmers behind the Corn Belt Committee were for Al Smith.[92]

Peek, a bitter-ender in his endorsement of Smith, created the impression that the Democratic candidate was for the McNary-Haugen bill.[93] But when Smith was pinned down to explain what he meant with his barrage of words promising to do something for the farmers, he admitted that he was not for the equalization fee. This put the Democrats in pretty much the same position as the Republicans. Both had told the farmers that controlling the surplus was necessary, but the equalization fee was not going to do it.[94] Meanwhile, Peek had described Hoover as the "agricultural adviser of the last two administrations" and accused him of being more responsible for the "continued depression in agriculture" than any other single person.[95]

Threatening as the language of the farm groups was, the Republicans appeared unmoved, and in November they scored the most decisive victory in the history of the Republican party. The Hoover vote totaled 21,391,993 —the largest ever cast for a Republican candidate—and it showed increases in every section of the country. He got five and a half million more votes than did Coolidge in 1924.[96] This was good evidence that neither the nation in general nor the farmers in particular were enraged over the twice-vetoed McNary-Haugen bill. In fact farm conditions had taken a turn for the better, especially over the period from 1926 to 1929.

91. *Ibid.*, July, 1928; Butterfield, in *Current History,* XXIX (November, 1928), pp. 269, 273.

92. *Farmers' Union Herald,* July, September, 1928; *Des Moines Register,* July 17, 1928; *Des Moines Tribune,* August 31, September 1, 1928.

93. *Kansas City Times,* August 6, 1928.

94. *Kansas City Star,* August 5, 1928.

95. *Kansas City Times,* July 30, 1928.

96. Edgar E. Robinson, *The Presidential Vote, 1896–1932* (Palo Alto, Calif., 1934), pp. 24–25.

Chapter XIV

FROM FARM BOARD TO FARM STRIKE

THOUGH defeated, the McNary-Haugen proposal, coupled with the farm depression, if nothing else had forced the administration to move more and more into the orbit of cooperative marketing and surplus control measures. Ample proof of this was first furnished by the passage of the Capper-Volstead Act in 1922, then by the enactment of the Co-operative Markeing Act in 1926, and finally by the Agricultural Marketing Act of 1929. As a result, the years 1929 to 1932 witnessed the launching of a federally subsidized farm program which up to that time had been unparalleled in relief annals. Millions were spent to marshal forth the resources of agriculture, to consolidate and coordinate the marketing activities of the cooperatives, and to engage in stabilization operations. But unfortunately the farm problem was further from solution in 1932, after three years of Farm Board activities, than it was in 1929 when the Hoover farm program was first announced. In short, the nationalistic policies of the administration fell far short of solving a problem that was of world-wide dimensions.

Once Hoover took office, he called for a special session of Congress to redeem two of the campaign pledges that the Republicans had made; these were farm relief and "limited" changes in the tariff.[1] Relief for

1. "President Hoover's First Message to Congress," *Congressional Digest,* VIII (May, 1929), p. 137.

griculture, to be sure, was a conspicuous part of the 1928 campaign, but ie same could hardly be said about the tariff which had so exasperated ie farmers.

Meanwhile, farmers and their spokesmen had assembled in Washing- on. Twice thwarted by the Coolidge administration, they met for the dual urpose of drafting what they felt should be essential parts of any farm rogram and of counteracting the charge that the farmers were at swords' oints over relief. Their demands, besides re-emphasizing the need for n effective tariff wall and for surplus-control measures, also sought ways nd means to check overproduction and to place in the hands of the armers the control of whatever marketing machinery was established. 'reference was given to the cooperatives already established, of course, as ie instrument of control.[2]

Hoover, in his first message to Congress, recited how heavy farm in- ebtedness, wasteful marketing methods, rising freight rates, growing oreign competition, overexpansion, shrinking domestic demands, and iounting taxes had contributed materially to the plight of the farmers, nd how relief from such conditions could be had through the reorganiza- on of "the marketing system on sounder and more stable and more conomic lines." With his characteristic faith in experts, technicians, and umbersome terminology, he felt that "the creation of a giant instrumen- ality clothed with sufficient authority and resources . . . would at once ransfer the agricultural question from the field of politics into the realm f economics and . . . result in constructive action. . . ."

It was advised that such an agency had to have finances to build and upport marketing associations, to obtain warehousing facilities, and to iake advances to cooperating farmers. According to Hoover, it also had have powers to conduct investigations, to make recommendations to armers, and to protect itself from "bureaucratic and governmental omination and interference." Likewise, this government agency was to e prohibited from buying, selling, and fixing the price of farm products.[3]

Obviously, the launching of this program was awaited with great nxiety. It remained to be seen whether the proposed marketing system vould bring about relief, whether it would be possible to divorce the

2. *American Farm Bureau Federation Weekly News Letter,* April 9, 1929, p. 1.
3. *Congressional Digest,* VIII (May, 1929), pp. 137–38.

economics from the politics of agriculture, whether farmers could remai
free from interference under such a superstructure, and whether the go
ernment actually would refrain from direct buying, selling, and oth
price-influencing operations.

The administration soon discovered that it had a real fight on its hand
Farm leaders and legislators, some Democrats and some Republican
apparently unwilling to resign themselves to defeat at the hands of th
administration, made plans for one last desperate attempt at placing th
"export debenture" on the statute books. This was resorted to either wit
the hope of embarrassing the administration or else in the belief that th
debenture plan was preferable to the Hoover proposal. On April 16 Sen
tor McNary announced the drafting of a new bill that provided for
farm board which would have discretionary powers in applying the debe
ture feature. On the same day the House Committee on Agriculture r
ported favorably on the Haugen bill that provided for a farm board wit
a revolving fund of $500,000,000 but without the debenture plan. Th
was the big difference between the two measures. By April 18 the questio
of farm relief was on the floor of both houses.[4]

The sponsoring of the proposal immediately drew a response fro
Hoover, who called attention to the divisions among the farmers and als
to the fact that the Republican platform had made no recommendatio
for export debentures. He wrote McNary that the debenture plan woul
bring disaster to the American farmers, but without success. The Senat
committee, in an eight to six vote, decided to retain the debenture featur
Senator R. S. Copeland, a New York Democrat, sought to replace it wit
the equalization fee, as did Congressman Clarence Cannon of Missour
but on April 25 the House bill was passed without amendment by a
overwhelming majority.[5]

In the Senate the debates over the debenture clause continued. Norr
of Nebraska, hoping that one of the major administration objectio
would be removed, introduced an amendment aiming to prevent ove
production in the event the debenture plan was adopted. But this was
little help because administration opposition persisted. The Senate was sti

4. *United States Daily News,* April 17, 19, 24, 1929. The debenture proposal wa
injected into the farm-relief debates largely through the insistence of the Grang

5. *Ibid.,* April 20, 22, 23, 25, 26, 1929; Chester H. Gray, "What Muscle Shoa
Means to the Farmer," *Congressional Digest,* IX (May 1, 1930), p. 139.

for the debenture proposal, while the House and the administration were against it. After continued debate the Agricultural Marketing Act was finally passed, without the debenture clause, and was signed by the President on June 15.[6]

This act called for the creation of a Federal Farm Board with eight members, to be appointed by the President with the consent of the Senate, but including the Secretary of Agriculture as an ex-officio member. The Board was authorized to extend loans to cooperatives and to conduct stabilization operations from a revolving fund of $500,000,000. Stabilization operations were to be conducted by corporations created for this very purpose; and in addition, the corporations were to serve as marketing agencies for the cooperatives affiliated with the Board.[7]

It was apparent that the Hoover program had much in common with farm programs functioning elsewhere in the world, but for the most part it was indifferent to the world situation aside from the possible markets that might be found for hard-pressed American farmers.

Granted that the 1920's were afflicted with world-wide epidemics to regulate production, prices, and surpluses, and also granted that our farm experts and advisers were fully aware of these developments abroad, there still were ample precedents in the United States for all phases of the Agricultural Marketing Act of 1929, including the Federal Farm Board, the subsidy, the stabilization features, and the proposed national marketing machinery. For instance, the farm board proposal was hardly a novel one. The Dickinson, the Capper-Haugen, the McNary-Haugen, and the Curtis-Crisp bills called for the creation of a farm board of one type or another before the Agricultural Marketing Act was placed on the statute books.[8] As for subsidies, the extension of them by the federal and state governments to railroads, canals and turnpikes, education, manufacturing, and agriculture are too well known to merit further comment.[9] Nor

6. *United States Daily News,* May 1, 2, 9, 10, 15, 17, 18, 27, June 7, 11, 12, 15, 16, 1929.

7. For a full text of the act, see *First Annual Report of the Federal Farm Board* (Washington, 1930), pp. 64–70.

8. John D. Black, "The Progress of Farm Relief," *American Economic Review,* XVIII (June, 1928), pp. 263–65.

9. For a convenient summary of this point, see Merle Fainsod and Lincoln Gordon, *Government and the American Economy* (New York, 1941), pp. 81–112.

were stabilization operations unknown. The Equity, the Farmers' Union and the Farm Bureau, as already observed, had on various occasions tried to reduce the size of the crop, to withhold crops from the market, and to control the surplus as means for stabilizing prices. The various commodity pools established during the twenties also had such objectives in mind. In 1926 Coolidge encouraged stabilization operations when he called on Eugene Meyer to head a cotton corporation for the avowed purpose of resisting further price drops. The presence of this giant government-sponsored corporation ready to step in and buy up cotton at a particular price was held to be a stabilizing influence.[10] It also was a means of keeping the cotton growers from being tossed into the open arms of the McNary-Haugenites, who were seeking their support.[11] Most successful in resorting to stabilizing practices were the manufacturers and industrialists, who had become the envy of farm leaders seeking to duplicate their production and pricing policies. One can hardly ignore the various foreign proposals to stabilize farm prices, but at the same time one must remember that stabilization operations were hardly foreign to the American scene; in fact, it appears that our farmers were perhaps more inspired by the practices of American industrialists.[12]

Precedents or no precedents, there were many questions to be raised about the operations and functions of the Agricultural Marketing Act. Was this widely publicized program of encouraging local cooperatives, building national marketing machinery, and engaging in stabilization operations just so much "window dressing" intended to pacify the farmers, or was the administration in dead earnest? If the administration was in

10. *New York Times,* November 18, 1926.

11. "How the New Farm Relief Law Will Work," *Literary Digest,* CII (July 6, 1929), p. 10.

12. Regarding stabilization programs abroad, see Bureau of Agricultural Economics, Agricultural Economics Bibliographies 12, *Government Control of Export and Import in Foreign Countries* (Washington, February, 1926), and 18, *Price-Fixing by Governments, 424 B.C.–1926 A.D.* (Washington, October, 1926). For a summation of some of these data, see the memorandum presented by Chester H. Gray of the American Farm Bureau Federation in William R. Sutherland's *A Debate Handbook on the McNary-Haugen Agricultural Surplus Control Act* (Lexington, Ky., 1927), pp. 160–96. See also the report of the Royal Institute of International Affairs, *World Agriculture, An International Study* (London, 1932), the portion dealing with "Stabilization Schemes," pp. 212–34.

earnest, the next logical question was who would control the machinery? Was it going to be the hand-picked candidates of the party leaders, or would it be the cooperatives with their years of experience behind them? Then there was the ever pressing matter of the relationship of the Farm Board to the existing marketing mechanism. Many commission firms and established cooperatives were uneasy over how they would fare with this new competition. Stabilization operations sounded good, but just what were they to be? If attempts at stabilization were resorted to and surpluses accumulated and prices failed to rise in spite of them, then what? Equally important, and hardly to be overlooked, were the attitudes of Congress and the farmers. Were they going to cooperate or show hostility?

Advance reports had it that Hoover would rely on the cooperatives for personnel and appoint practical and successful businessmen rather than accept the recommendations of the party leaders. These reports were confirmed when the make-up of the Board was announced. The chairman was Alexander Legge, the president of the International Harvester Corporation, an appointment that caused the lifting of many eyebrows; the other seven members (excluding the Secretary of Agriculture, an ex-officio member) were J. C. Stone, the founder and former president of the Burley Tobacco Growers' Cooperative Association; Carl Williams, Oklahoma, of the Farmers' Cooperative Association; C. B. Denman, Missouri, of the National Livestock Producers' Association; C. S. Wilson, professor of agriculture at Cornell University; William F. Schilling, Minnesota, of the National Dairy Association; Samuel McKelvie, former governor of Nebraska and publisher of the *Nebraska Farmer;* and C. C. Teague, of the California Fruit Growers' Exchange.[13]

Except for the cotton South, the selection of personnel was fairly well distributed geographically. The slight of the cotton interests was one of no small proportions, especially in view of the fact that Hoover was the first Republican since the Civil War to break into the solid South. This, many southerners believed, entitled the South to consideration; but the President ignored it first when he selected his cabinet, and then in selecting the Farm Board.[14]

13. R. L. Wilbur and Arthur M. Hyde, *The Hoover Policies* (New York, 1937), pp. 151–52.

14. "The Men Who Will Tackle the Big Farm Relief Task," *Literary Digest,* CII (July 27, 1929), pp. 8–9.

The appointment of Legge was bound to cause comment. It was hardly surprising that "friends of the farmers" looked upon him with suspicion. To some the fact that he was president of International Harvester and had several million dollars of his own had sinister implications. Others believed that Legge was more concerned about higher prices for plows and farm implements than he was about better prices for the farmers. His confirmation by the Senate was described as "an act of reluctant acquiescence."[15]

The ordeal to which the Board members were exposed before confirmation was indicative of the rough road over which the administration farm policy shapers were to travel. The Board was face to face with a hostile and suspicious Congress, "disappointed with the results of its farm relief legislation so far, differing in fundamental respects with the views of members of the Board regarding the policies the Board should pursue, and determined to exercise constant pressure determined to make the Board meet the Congressional view." It was even said that the legislation passed was "unsatisfactory to nearly everybody concerned" with farming. According to these critics, "The law was passed as a compromise and a sop to the farmer. . . ."[16]

The Senate hearings brought forth other interesting views. Some senators were still thinking in terms of an export debenture; others were skeptical over having the Board try to raise or fix agricultural prices by buying and holding staples off the market. Legge himself indicated that the Board would resort to buying and removing crops from the market and not confine itself strictly to the building up of cooperatives, while others believed that the Board program would be ineffective unless accompanied with a program to control production.[17]

First among the producers to receive the attention of the Farm Board were the grain growers. When it assembled for its first meeting on July 26 and 27, there were about four thousand local grain cooperatives, eight wheat pools, and twelve cooperative terminal agencies in operation. In attendance there were fifty-two delegates representing thirty-five associations, including the Farm Bureau, the Farmers' Union, the Grange, and

15. "Washington Notes," *New Republic,* LXI (December 25, 1929), p. 140.
16. "The Farm Board Faces the Future," *Business Week* (October 19, 1929), pp. 3–4.
17. *Ibid.*

the Farmers' Equity Union for the purpose of formulating plans for the creation of the national marketing agency.[18] The building of this machinery was in line with the views of Hoover, who as Secretary of Commerce had shown his dislike for wasteful methods of competition.[19]

The Farm Board took steps to aid the wheat growers even before the Farmers' National was incorporated. In August they were advised not to rush their wheat to market, and the Board indicated that it was in sympathy with the attempts being made by the cooperatives to hold their wheat for higher prices. Pending the organization of the Farmers' National, the Board announced that "duly qualified" cooperatives could obtain "supplemental loans" from the Board. But what aid was forthcoming went to a limited number of qualified cooperatives, which meant, of course, that relief was unavailable for the majority of associations.[20]

More of the problems facing the Board became apparent while it was in the process of organizing the Farmers' National Grain Corporation. For two months the groups represented were locked in heated debate over the form that the new national marketing agency was to take, over the policies to be adopted, over the reaction of the private commission firms, and over the future of the established cooperatives, which feared being absorbed by the super marketing organizations. It was not until October 29, the day of the serious stock-market crash, that the Farmers' National was incorporated.

It could hardly be denied that a fundamental conflict was anticipated with the private marketing agencies. Vast interests were involved. Obviously, many who favored the administration program did so with the hope that the federal powers would be employed either to help the cooperatives gain control of the private marketing facilities, or else to drive the private organizations from the field completely. Opponents of the program, on the other hand, charged that it was unfair to use public funds for cooperatives in competition with the established agencies.[21]

18. Federal Farm Board, *Cooperative Marketing Makes Steady Growth,* Bulletin 8 (Washington, 1932), pp. 8–9.

19. "Secretary Hoover Analyzes Wastes in Marketing," *Congressional Digest,* IV (October, 1925), pp. 262, 285; Edwin G. Nourse, "Hard Times for Farmers," *New Republic,* LXII (April 30, 1930), p. 288.

20. F.F.B., *First Annual Report,* p. 26.

21. *Business Week* (October 26, 1929), pp. 5–6.

Others like Senators Bob La Follette, Jr., Frazier, Brookhart, and Wheeler, normally sympathetic with the farmers, were skeptical about the prospects of a national marketing agency's stemming the tide of falling prices. La Follette, whose views were reflective of others, felt that cooperative marketing might work after long preparations in compact industries like dairying and fruit growing, but doubted that it would be of much aid to wheat growers, who were scattered far and wide and who lacked cohesiveness.[22]

In October the Board was faced with a serious demoralization of the stock market; this was the signal for the big depression that followed. Wheat prices dropped about fifteen cents a bushel over the period from October 15 to 25. On a single day—October 24—wheat dropped nine or ten cents. On October 26 the Board, hoping to check this drop, offered to make loans to cooperatives on various grades of wheat at values that were "approximately the closing prices of October 25 for these grades." For a while it appeared that this move was a successful one because wheat prices had recovered considerably by the end of the month.[23]

One of the first positive acts of opposition to the proposed national grain-marketing agency came from the spring wheat country. This appeared in the form of a proposed $6,000,000 rival corporation, the Cooperative Farmers' Northwest Grain Corporation, designed to take in about 225,000 farmers in Minnesota, North and South Dakota, and Montana. Its sponsors said that its purpose was to merge all grain associations into a unified corporation, as opposed to the existing system by which the wheat pools, sales agencies, and elevator associations would be able to retain their identities and work independently of each other.[24] To many this rival move was nothing more than a duplication of the Farmers' National, as well as the launching of a counteroffensive against it. A. J. Olson, the president of the Minnesota Farm Bureau Federation, replied instantly that this was the creature of the commission firms, working with the existing farmers' elevators for the purpose of either gaining control of the Farmers' National or else wrecking it.[25] The

22. *Pioneer Press* (St. Paul), October 11, 1929.
23. F.F.B., *First Annual Report,* pp. 27–28.
24. *St. Paul Dispatch,* October 15, 1929.
25. *Ibid.,* October 18, 1929.

sponsors of the rival agency denied that they were out to rule or ruin the Board proposal, yet admitted that they were opposed to it.[26]

The chances of this rival body were slim indeed. The resources of the Farm Board were too great. By mid-November, 1929, the Minnesota Wheat Growers at Minneapolis, the North Dakota Wheat Growers' at Grand Forks, the South Dakota Wheat Growers' representing the larger wheat pools, and the Farmers' Union Terminal Association at St. Paul were to turn over their selling facilities to the Farmers' National.[27]

In other quarters optimism and increased planting appear to have accompanied the unfolding of the Board program. Granted that it would be difficult to separate this optimism from the speculative craze that was characteristic of the times, there still were signs of it in the winter wheat region. In fact, banks in the corn and wheat states remarked about the revived interest in farm properties, and it was reported that chambers of commerce and state immigration commissions were inviting new settlers to take up farms that had been abandoned during the depressed twenties. One story told of "large scale upturning of virgin grazing land in western Kansas by speculative farm corporations using the latest mass production machinery—as well as the latest methods of selling stock. This speculative boom in wheat farming is supposed to be banking heavily upon Farm Board aid next year . . . rural banks have complained of withdrawal of deposits not for stock market speculation so much as for investments of this kind." It was difficult to point to tangible proof of these charges at the time, but the fact that the Farm Board did show ever increased acreages during the winter and early spring of 1930 indicated quite strongly that there was more truth than fiction behind reports about increases in the winter wheat acreages.[28]

The first far-reaching step of the Farm Board was taken on October 26, as indicated, when it offered loans through the Farmers' National to cooperatives up to stated amounts. This move had been prompted chiefly by the sharp decline in the stock market and the large-scale unloading of wheat. To some this move came as a surprise, especially those who had expected the Board to make outright purchases of corn and wheat.[29]

26. *Business Week* (October 26, 1929), pp. 5–6.
27. "The Farm Board Shows Its Teeth," *ibid.* (November 16, 1929), p. 42.
28. *Ibid.*, October 19, 1929.
29. F.F.B., *First Annual Report*, p. 27.

Several reasons were suggested for this action. One was that the authorities believed that the current prices were lower than the conditions of supply and demand had warranted. The situation was abnormal also in the sense that the farmers were bringing their crops to market earlier and in larger quantities than usual. Another reason, by implication, was that the Board would be in a better position to get farmers to join cooperatives associated with it. Nonmembers would be encouraged to join because they would be assured of ready cash and minimum prices. A third reason was that the Board would be better situated to discourage speculation. It was felt that since the incentive to speculate would be removed, the farmers would be in a better position to get prices equal to those paid on the market.[30]

It was shortly after this that the Farmers' National Grain Corporation was incorporated with an authorized capital stock of $10,000,000. It was to handle wheat, oats, barley, corn, buckwheat, flax, and grain sorghums in order "to centralize . . . cooperative marketing efforts, to unify the activities of all farmer-owned grain agencies, to minimize speculation, to avoid duplication of marketing machinery, to eliminate competition among grain cooperatives, and to enable grain producers to exert a stronger stabilizing influence on market prices."

The individual farmer linked himself with the Farmers' National by becoming a member of a pool, a grain dealers' association, or a terminal marketing agency which owned stock in the corporation. The Farmers' National lent money to cooperatives which it, in turn, had obtained from the Federal Farm Board, other government agencies, or private sources. Cooperatives were to lend money to the locals, which in turn lent it to the individual farmers; but in the case of the regional pool, the money was lent directly to the farmer.[31]

But extending loans was merely the beginning. After a further demoralization of wheat prices, the Farmers' National offered to buy wheat at loan prices. On December 21, at the start of the trading day, the bid of $1.18 for No. 1 hard winter wheat in Chicago was accompanied with rises of three and four cents on all markets; but despite this, there was little

30. "The Farm Board Takes a Chance," *Business Week* (November 2, 1929).

31. Federal Farm Board, *Farmers Build Their Own Marketing Machinery*, Bulletin 3 (Washington, 1930), pp. 7–10.

wheat forthcoming for sale. Newspaper stories had it that speculative sellers, who had been bears on the market, suddenly had become heavy purchasers to reverse their former position. Excitement also broke loose on the Minneapolis pit, where prices rose sharply on receipt of the news of the actions of the Farmers' National. Even the Liverpool market was said to have responded to this action and closed strongly before the American markets opened.[32]

If this latest move had what appeared to be a stabilizing influence on wheat prices, it had no such effect on the wrath of the private grain trade, which brought to a head a controversy that found Legge and Julius Barnes, both close friends of Hoover, on opposite sides. This latest flare-up gained farmer support for Legge, and caused many of the earlier skeptics to feel that the Board chairman probably had their interests at heart after all. The grain interests, through Barnes, made explicit their fears that Board actions such as that of December were likely to bring about their end. At one point, Barnes was quoted as saying that "the grain men are willing to be eliminated by an evolutionary process of fair competition, but not by unfair methods." If they were going to survive, there were certain things that the administration had to do: the cooperatives belonging to the Board had to be charged the commercial rate of interest instead of the low government rates they reportedly had been paying, and the private grain interests had to be consulted before the administration embarked on a new policy.[33]

After the elapse of several weeks the grain interests quieted down, but in the Minneapolis area the denunciation of the Farmers' National in terms of socialism and communism was strong. The attitude of the United States Chamber of Commerce was described as being one of "watchful waiting." The canners and packers also appeared greatly worried over what the Board would do next. It was empowered to aid the cooperatives gain control of processing facilities, and this was precisely what the processors did not want to happen.[34]

Early in 1930 the Farmers' National advanced its bid for No. 1 winter

32. *St. Paul Dispatch,* December 21, 1929.

33. "The Farm Board Finds a Fight," *Literary Digest,* CIV (January 4, 1930), pp. 5–7.

34. "The Farm Board Plans a Little Canning," *Business Week* (February 1, 1930), p. 6.

wheat on the Chicago Board of Trade from $1.18 to $1.20 a bushel, thus narrowing down the margin between it and spring wheat from seven to five cents. The price spread between the two varied widely in different years, depending largely on the protein content and the quality of the crop. As a rule, northern spring was worth from seven to nine cents more, but the difference in 1930 was narrowed down because of the unusually good quality of the winter crop that year.[35]

But the actions of the Farmers' National failed to check the price drops, and on January 17 it stepped up its buying orders in the principal markets, the purchases being made on the basis of the loan values already established.[36] Ardent Board supporters insisted that had it not been for the timely actions of the Farmers' National, wheat prices would have fallen to even lower levels.[37]

The acquiring and storing of wheat aroused further fears of price-depressing effects. Rumors on the Minneapolis market had it that there were between three and four million bushels of wheat held in store there that could be unloaded by the Farmers' National at any time that it chose to do so. The reports also were that line elevators and others were ordering what wheat they had stored at country points to be shipped to the terminal markets as soon as they could load it.

Still another question was whether the Farmers' National was going to continue its purchases. It was no more obligated to continue buying than were the private mills and operators.[38] The purchases continued, but these also failed to check the price drops. Early in February, after one of the heaviest trading days, prices dropped sharply.[39]

The Board, in making these purchases, again was prompted by the belief that wheat prices were going to advance that spring. Wheat was being stored with the intention of gaining a sufficient volume to exert some influence over prices. This prompted some to claim that the Board, by seeking to control the surplus, was putting into practice the McNary-Haugen idea, except that the losses incurred were shouldered by the government instead of by the farmers.[40]

35. *St. Paul Dispatch,* January 18, 1930.
36. *Pioneer Press,* January 18, 1930.
37. *Ibid.,* January 30, 1930.
38. *St. Paul Dispatch,* February 3, 1930.
39. *Pioneer Press,* February 4, 1930.
40. *St. Paul Dispatch,* February 5, 1930.

The next move was to establish the Grain Stabilization Corporation.[41] This corporation was supposed to have been brought into existence as a concession to those who had favored the equalization fee.[42] The belief was that neither Hoover nor Legge favored it, but that they moved in this direction only because they had been besieged by senators from the wheat and cotton states who were pressing for relief from the surplus. It was said that the administration, even though it yielded, had hoped "that stabilization would remain of only academic interest, like some other parts of the Act, never to be put to use or otherwise employed." But events moved too rapidly. The stock-market crash made the loan policy "look sick," hence the system of outright purchases was inaugurated. When this too failed, the Grain Stabilization Corporation was established.[43]

No sooner had the Grain Corporation come into being than it was discovered that some buyers "who earlier had purchased wheat from the farmer and hedged it were selling it to the . . . Corporation at an unwarranted profit." This brought a sharp reaction from the Farm Board. Thereafter, it was going to support the price of only that wheat held by the cooperatives and those affiliated with the Grain Corporation and none other.[44] This announced change immediately drew fire from the grain trade. It protested bitterly, but once again the protests made no difference. Legge, with his "apparent candor and prairie-forthrightness of speech," ruffled his critics all the more by denouncing them as "roll-top desk farmers."[45]

The actions taken by the Board in establishing the Grain Corporation showed that the administration was worried. Late in February Legge and others associated with the Board were called in by President Hoover for consultation, for the Republicans were worried over the possible effects that low prices were going to have in the November elections.[46]

It was claimed that the purchase of cash wheat and May futures helped to prevent a sharp break in prices in February and March. On the last

41. F.F.B., *First Annual Report,* p. 29.

42. A. C. Hoffman, "After Two Years of Farm Relief," *New Republic,* LXVIII (July 1, 1931), p. 169.

43. "Alexander the Goat," *New Republic,* LXVII (April 15, 1931), pp. 232–33.

44. F.F.B., *First Annual Report,* p. 29.

45. "The Farm Board Writes a New Subscription," *Business Week* (March 8, 1930), p. 4.

46. *St. Paul Dispatch,* February 25, 1930.

day of February, March wheat climbed up to $1.187. About this time the Board reversed its brief policy of supporting the price of only the wheat owned by cooperatives and those affiliated with the Board, admitting that actions by the government agencies had "interfered with the normal use of the futures market . . . and disturbed customary relations between wheat prices at different points." The grain trade, consistent with its past opposition, referred to this support policy as "the most advanced step, the most thoroughly socialized step ever taken in America in peace time . . . in dealing with a community."[47] One critic suggested that the government had found "a first class way of throwing good money into a bottomless pit."[48]

Besides being faced with the grim task of trying to support prices, the Grain Stabilization Corporation had an acute storage problem on its hands. In trying to cope with this situation, the aid of the millers was sought "to permit the Grain Stabilization Corporation to place wheat in positions where it would presumably be used rather than have it concentrate at terminal markets, such as Chicago. Cooperation under this agreement was an important factor in reducing the volume of wheat on which deliveries had to be accepted in Chicago in May, in preventing uneconomical movements of wheat and in averting threatened congestion at Chicago."[49]

Another proposal was to establish grain elevators up and down the Mississippi River, as far north as St. Paul and Minneapolis, from which a government barge line would carry wheat for cooperatives at considerable savings and in competition with the railroads. Much of the storage space provided up to this point had been financed by private groups, but now the Farmers' National was to announce a program for purchasing and erecting additional elevators through loans to cooperative associations.[50]

Others like Samuel McKelvie of the Farm Board believed that the situation could be relieved by having the farmers store their grain on their

47. F.F.B., *First Annual Report,* pp. 29–30; "The Fight to Save the Wheat Farmer," *Literary Digest,* CIV (March 15, 1930), p. 18.

48. "Uncle Sam, Plunger," *The Nation,* CXXX (March 26, 1930), p. 351.

49. F.F.B., *First Annual Report,* p. 31.

50. "Embattled Farm Board Sets Up New Fronts," *Business Week* (April 2, 1930), p. 6.

farms and in their own bins. Particular attention was called to the legislation enacted in Montana and North Dakota the past year, through the influence of the Farmers' Union, which had made possible advances running into the thousands of dollars on wheat that was stored on farms.[51] Still others proposed finding Oriental outlets, because the resistance to wheat imports in Europe was great.[52]

By early 1930 it was apparent that the Board was going to urge voluntary acreage reduction as a means to relieve the storage situation and raise prices. Since the winter wheat growers and those in the Pacific Northwest had already planted theirs, it was plain that the spring wheat growers were going to be the first to be asked to reduce their acreage.[53] Secretary of Agriculture Arthur Hyde, in facilitating this move, pointed to the evils of blind overproduction and the results of "competitive selling by 6,000,000 individual farmers," which gave the purchasers "a great advantage and the farmers a disastrously low price." The farmers were told in no uncertain terms that unless they curtailed their acreage there was very little that could be done by the Board about prices.[54]

One of the first problems posed by this drive for acreage reduction was the rivalry of the various wheat-growing sections. The protests of the spring wheat country called attention to this rivalry. Senator Peter Norbeck of South Dakota was skeptical of the proposal, as were others, and Brookhart of Iowa said that the Farm Board would "pretty near have to kill off 20 per cent of the farmers" in order to carry out its wheat-reduction program, and questioned the wisdom of not having a surplus available.[55] The St. Paul *Pioneer Press* felt that "To attempt to make the spring wheat growers stand the full burden of reduction for the whole industry, to penalize it for the action of the winter wheat branch, would be both unjust and futile, and would arouse a well-grounded resentment among the producers of the Northwest." Why should spring wheat be sacrificed for the benefit of winter wheat? Estimates had it that 7 per cent of the spring

51. *St. Paul Dispatch,* March 5, 1930.

52. "Farm Board Battles with Wheat as Carry-over Gluts Market," *Business Week* (April 16, 1930), pp. 11–12.

53. *St. Paul Dispatch,* January 7, 1930.

54. "Six Million Farmers are Pondering," *Literary Digest,* CIV (February 22, 1930), p. 17.

55. *St. Paul Dispatch,* January 7, 13, 1930.

wheat acreage would have to be eliminated in order to offset the 2 per cent increase in winter wheat.[56] Spring wheat spokesmen insisted that they contributed neither to the surplus nor to the export trade, but that the winter wheat area did.[57]

These protests hardly stopped the Farm Board with its acreage-reduction program. At the end of March a group of economists left Washington for the agricultural Northwest to explain to the farmers there how much better off they would be if they devoted some land to flax, barley, rye, oats, alfalfa, and sweet clover.[58]

Protests against reduction came from other quarters, too. The *Nation* was hardly enthralled by this latest proposal of the Board. It remarked that "As a farm reliever Mr. Legge is an incomparable machinery manufacturer," and suggested that Uncle Sam could well afford "to pay him an enormous salary to go back and work for International Harvester Company while we get any one of a hundred educated economists to run the Farm Board at say $10,000." It added that, "What big business men like Mr. Legge [who know nothing about economics and history] cannot get into their heads is that you cannot control production and prices among millions of farmers all over the world in the same way as among a half-dozen big machinery manufacturers."[59]

By midsummer the Farm Board was involved in a fight over acreage reduction that was as "hot as a July wheat-field in Kansas." In July wheat prices broke below the ninety-cent mark on the Chicago market, which simply added to the already confused state of affairs. There were some 60,000,000 bushels of wheat on hand; a new crop was coming on the market; the purchasing power of the farmers was low enough as things were; the Board was being challenged on all sides by conservatives and radicals alike; the Democrats were making political capital out of Republican misfortunes; and congressmen and senators were coming up for reelection. This created a pretty set of problems.[60]

More drama was lent to the campaign when Legge and Hyde toured

56. *Pioneer Press,* January 16, 1930.
57. *Literary Digest,* CIV (February 22, 1930), p. 17.
58. *Pioneer Press,* April 3, 1930; "The Battle of the Wheat," *Literary Digest,* CVI (July 26, 1930), pp. 7–8.
59. *The Nation,* CXXX (March 26, 1930), p. 351.
60. *Literary Digest,* CVI (July 26, 1930), pp. 7–8.

the winter wheat belt to urge compliance; this "quickly developed into a running debate with editors and officials, productive of epigrams, personal reflections, and sarcasm." The *Baltimore Sun* was quick to label it as the "Legge show," while the *Fargo Forum* went back to classical antiquity to come up with the term "anabasis" to describe the wanderings of the two gentlemen from Washington. Hyde told the farmers that a 25 per cent reduction in wheat acreage would put production on a domestic basis and would give to the farmers "the full benefit of the 42 per cent tariff."

There were other reactions to the acreage-reduction proposal. Some called attention to the emphasis that was being placed on wheat production in other nations; and it seemed strange that while Mussolini some years back had been urging increased production, Legge and Hyde should now be asking for a reduction. Governor Clyde Reed of Kansas felt that it would be wiser to use the facilities of the Board to feed the hungry people of Europe than to undertake a decrease in the acreage. Some felt that reduction appeared "logical and sensible," but others did not. Still others found it hard to understand why the government went to the trouble of encouraging reclamation projects like Boulder Dam, which made production increases possible, and at the same time urged the farmers to reduce their output.

The pleas of Legge hardly met the approval of the people of Kansas. He was quoted as telling its citizens that "The biggest hog will always lie in the trough. Kansas is now in the trough." Whether Legge actually said this is beside the point. Many Kansans believed it and were incensed. The *Wichita Beacon* demanded his resignation and an apology. Legge insisted that what he said was "Is Kansas in the trough?" and not what the papers quoted him as saying. When he was confronted with the demand for an apology and his resignation, he replied to the publishers of the paper, through a group of interviewing reporters, "You can present my compliments to Max and Louis, and tell them to go to hell."[61]

The Board had first become unpopular with the private interests, which feared that it would go far "in substituting cooperation for private business marketing, public credit for ordinary credit," and it had aroused the undying hostility of the United States Chamber of Commerce. Now it

61. *Ibid.*

was running into the opposition of the wheat growers themselves, who were hostile to its acreage-curtailment recommendations.[62]

The results of the acreage-reduction campaign were pretty much what one would have expected. The Board, by its own admission, conceded:

> The 1930 spring wheat acreage showed little, if any, effect of this campaign. The net reduction was only two per cent. Winter wheat plantings for 1931 as a whole were not reduced except in the soft winter-wheat areas. Spring wheat acreage for 1931 harvest was reduced 4,000,000 acres or nineteen per cent. Winter wheat came through the winter with only a four per cent loss from abandonment as compared with an average of eleven per cent and together with exceptionally heavy yields in the main winter regions, this resulted in a large crop in spite of reduced acreage, drought, and low yields for spring wheat.[63]

This statement tended to confirm the view that whenever general advice was given to reduce, many farmers actually increased their acreage with the full expectation that their neighbors would reduce their plantings.

In the spring of that year the United States Chamber of Commerce turned its guns on the Farm Board and met the equally deadly fire of its officials, including Legge and Hyde. Legge reminded his critics that chamber spokesmen had endorsed the agricultural act while it was being considered by a committee of the House of Representatives. He added that

> . . . there has been considerable evidence the past several months that entirely too many of your members were for the principle of cooperation so long as it did not work.
>
> I do not recall in years gone by of hearing you men making any such complaint against government aid that was extended to the manufacturing industry, to transportation and to finance. And these all played their part in adding to the disadvantages of the farmer, as did also the preferential treatment to labor through immigration and other measures.[64]

The general belief in many quarters was that these blasts had been engineered by the old-line grain interests and the chambers of commerce in those cities in which the grain trade influence was strong, and that they were going to solidify farmer sentiment in support of the Board.[65]

62. "The Farm Board Troubles," *New Republic,* LXIII (July 23, 1930), p. 274.
63. *Second Annual Report of the Federal Farm Board* (Washington, 1931), p. 63.
64. "Business Attacks the Farm Board," *Literary Digest,* CV (May 31, 1930), p. 9.
65. *Ibid.*

The American Farm Bureau Federation was among the first of the farmer groups to come to the defense of the Farm Board. Samuel H. Thompson, the national president, immediately sent a message to the 1,837 county farm bureaus across the country asking for "a united front against the forces which are seeking to undermine the effectiveness of the Federal Farm Board's activities."[66] That July, L. J. Taber, the master of the national Grange, announced that his organization would defer agitation in behalf of the export debenture plan until the Farm Board had had a sufficient trial. But to no avail. By November of that year opposition within the order had mounted and a resolution was forthcoming in the Grange's national convention asking the government to adopt the debenture plan. A group of delegates from the Middle West contended that since the Board had brought "no tangible benefits to the farmers" it should be abolished in the next session of Congress. The resolution was passed and once more the national convention endorsed export debentures, but shortly thereafter the national master announced that his organization would refrain from further agitation until Congress had convened the following year.[67]

Equally disheartening was the failure of the stabilization operations. On June 30, 1930, the Grain Stabilization Corporation held more than 65,000,000 bushels of wheat in store, but this was of no help in keeping up the price. Large Russian exports, the policy of selling regardless of price that was employed by Argentina, Russia, and other countries sorely in need of funds, and the continued industrial depression aggravated the price collapse. The prices on the Liverpool market dropped one-third between July and October of 1930. The Grain Stabilization Corporation, hoping to check further drops, made small purchases during the summer and early fall; and on November 15 it was authorized to purchase as much wheat as was needed in order to prevent a further decline, but with no satisfactory results. By July, 1931, the corporation had added 192,000,000 bushels to the 65,000,000 already acquired, thus bringing the total in store up to 257,000,000 bushels.[68]

The failure of the Board to achieve its objectives was obvious even to

66. *Commercial and Financial Chronicle,* CXXX (May 17, 1930), pp. 3467–68.
67. *New York Times,* July 19, November 16, 19, 20, 26, 1930.
68. F.F.B., *Second Annual Report,* pp. 64–66.

the most loyal. It had lent out huge sums and had acquired large quantities of wheat without success in holding up prices. Wheat production had not been curtailed; in fact, it was rising in the principal wheat-growing countries. Charges of speculation and price pegging continued to pour forth from all directions. One was inclined to agree with the chief economist of the Board when he said that its activities amounted to a "social-economic" experiment that was going to involve "large risks of loss of public funds."[69]

Equally turbulent was the career of the livestock machinery set up under Farm Board auspices. The organizational meeting for the livestock industry was held in October, 1929, in Chicago where sixty-six delegates assembled, representing chiefly the cooperative terminal sales agencies. Twenty-eight companies covering twenty-two central markets were represented, twelve of these being members of the National Livestock Producers' Association that had been sponsored early in the twenties by the American Farm Bureau Federation. Members of the national Farmers' Union, the national Grange, several college people, and two who did not fit into any of these categories also participated.

The Farm Board proposed the formation of the National Livestock Marketing Association, provisions for which were adopted unanimously after much discussion and some amendments. Charles E. Huff, the president of the national Farmers' Union, resolved that the acts and decisions of the meeting be taken only as recommendations and that a committee be created to prepare the articles of incorporation and by-laws. Charles B. Crandall, the president of the aggressive Central Co-operative Association, suggested that, on the basis of the business handled, "the Producers' organizations should have four representatives on the committee; the Farmers' Union three; the Central, one; and the Western Cattle Marketing Association, one." A three-man nominating committee made the selections on this basis.

A committee of nine, after prolonged debate, came forward with a plan that elicited slight enthusiasm from the National Livestock Producers' Association. Since the plan drawn up had made scant provision for certain activities already developed by the producers' group, the as-

69. C. P. Howland, "The Failure of Farm Board Stabilization," *Yale Review*, N.S., XXI (March, 1932), pp. 503–5.

sociation served notice that it would not come into any national organization that failed to include all these activities in its program in accordance with the Board plan submitted to the October meeting; and further, there was no specific provisions made for financing. In the end the Board took the matter out of the hands of the organizing committee and reassembled the sixty-six delegates of the October meeting for another consideration of the entire matter.

At a second conference held in Chicago on February 25 and 26, the Farm Board submitted another plan for organization, including articles of incorporation, by-laws, and controls. The plan submitted to this second conference was pretty much the same as that presented to the first, except that it did provide for the creation of the National Livestock Marketing Association as well as two subsidiary organizations, the National Feeder and Finance Corporation and the National Livestock Publishing Association.

An important part of the revised plan which led to much debate was the provision for a sales board. Fear was expressed that this plan would "bind all selling agencies to delegate their functions of bargaining on their respective markets to a single central price-determining agency which would . . . instruct them in what markets and in what manner to dispose of the stock entrusted to them." The larger terminal associations protested because there were no provisions made for additional representation for those organizations which had a membership in excess of the 2,500 carloads that were required for membership. Apprehensions were expressed both over the Feeder and Finance Corporation because there was no provision for direct loans to the livestock associations at low interest rates and over the feeder pools of the producers associations on the grounds that they were "neither co-operative nor commercially safe."[70]

The plan for the National Livestock Marketing Association was passed by a vote of 38 to 23 and was scheduled to go into effect as soon as two-thirds of the agencies handling livestock cooperatively marketed would formally approve it. There was, however, great opposition and it was believed that the producers' group, and few others, would accept it. But nevertheless on the ratification date, April 1, the plan was accepted.

70. Edwin G. Nourse and Joseph G. Knapp, *The Co-Operative Marketing of Livestock* (Washington, 1931), pp. 276–88.

Within a short time seven Farmers' Union firms, the Central Cooperative Association, and several others took issue with the National Livestock Marketing Association program. They insisted that control of the association should be based on the volume handled by the stockholders because that most closely followed "the accepted co-operative principle of 'one man one vote.'" The provision making the National Order Buying Corporation a subsidiary of the National Livestock Marketing Association was acceptable if participation in the order-buying corporation was assured to all members of the marketing association.

These suggestions were submitted to the Farm Board, but there was no reply forthcoming. The protesting groups attended the meeting called in Chicago by the Farm Board; but upon failing to secure amendments in conformity with their protests, they withdrew from the meeting, thus leaving a group of fifteen agencies, mostly of the producers' group, to proceed with the organization of the National Livestock Marketing Association and its two subsidiaries.

These were incorporated on May 7, 1930. Several days later the by-laws were amended to add four directors-at-large representing the American Farm Bureau Federation, the national Grange, the Farmers' Union, and the American National Livestock Association. Again invitations were extended to active livestock-marketing agencies to Join the National Livestock Marketing Association, but this and other bids failed to bring the outsiders into the fold.[71]

The dissenting groups met in Omaha on July 22 to launch another national agency, the Farmers' Livestock Marketing Association. Its members included Farmers' Union houses operating in Chicago, Omaha, Kansas City, St. Joseph, Denver, Sioux City, Wichita, and Sioux Falls; the Central Cooperative of St. Paul; the Farmers' Livestock Commission Company of East St. Louis; and the Missouri Farmers' Livestock Commission of Springfield. The general manager of the Central of St. Paul became the general manager of the new agency, which in turn applied to the Farm Board for help and was turned down because it was conducive to inefficient and wasteful methods of marketing.[72]

The Farm Board had a dairy program too, but it could hardly be said

71. *Ibid.*, pp. 276–95.
72. *Ibid.*, pp. 321–27.

that the dairy farmers were as hard hit as the others. Dairy production was pretty well within domestic demand and the farmers were in a somewhat better position to benefit from the existing tariff system than were the other producers.[73] The policy with respect to the dairy industry was to extend aid to the local cooperatives and the regional associations. Under this arrangement, five regional butter-marketing organizations were established, including two in the western Middle West—the Land O'Lakes Creameries, Incorporated, with headquarters in Minneapolis, and the Dairy and Poultry Cooperatives of Chicago. All dairy products shipped east of the Rocky Mountains or the Continental Divide by the western associations were handled by Land O'Lakes, and similar products shipped to the Far West were to be handled by the regional cooperatives on the Pacific Coast. In fact working agreements had been entered into by all these associations to help them minimize competition and give to them a greater influence on the markets. The National Cheese Producers' Federation at Plymouth, Wisconsin, was a regional sales organization owned and controlled by cooperative cheese factories in Wisconsin. This was a natural location because two-thirds of the cheese manufactured in the United States came from Wisconsin and adjacent territory.[74]

Shortly after the dairy program of the Board was announced, the advisory committee suggested that the farmers reduce the size of their herds in order to overcome the surplus in dairy products. They were asked to slaughter their low-producing and unprofitable cows. This was hardly taken in a welcoming manner. According to A. J. McGuire, the general manager of the Land O'Lakes, the problems of the dairy producers were due neither to too many cows nor to too many farmers. Rather, he said, "A protective tariff against coconut oil coming from the Philippines is the biggest need of the dairy men right now." McGuire also added that the difficulties of dairy farming were aggravated by the fact that there was one pound of oleomargarine produced in the United States for every pound of butter, and charged that too many farmers used substitutes which competed with their products. Farmers who sold their cream and used skim milk on their tables, or who sold their butter and spread their bread with oleomargarine, were doing their industry very

73. *Pioneer Press,* January 14, 1930.
74. F.F.B., *Cooperative Marketing Makes Steady Growth,* pp. 48–49.

little good. They owed it to themselves to consume more of their own products.[75]

The worries of the administration over the congressional elections in the fall of 1930 were fully justified by the results. It went down to defeat in the western Middle West as well as in other parts of the country. In Nebraska the insurgent George W. Norris was re-elected to the United States Senate by a substantial margin, and Charles W. Bryan, the Democrat, defeated the incumbent Republican, A. J. Weaver, for the governorship by a narrow margin. In Minnesota Senator Thomas D. Schall, a Republican, scored a close victory over Einar Hoidale, his Democratic rival; but far more significant was the gubernatorial victory of Floyd B. Olson, the Farmer-Laborite. Ten Republicans and one Farmer-Laborite were sent to Congress from Minnesota. In North Dakota the conservatives found themselves in complete control of the state for the first time since 1919; George F. Schafer was re-elected governor along with three Republican congressmen. In Iowa L. J. Dickinson, a Republican, defeated D. F. Steck, a Democrat, for the United States Senate, and Dan W. Turner, another Republican, was elected governor. The Republicans sent ten of their numbers to Congress and the Democrats one. In Missouri twelve Democrats and four Republicans won congressional victories, to give the Democrats a net gain of six seats. The lower house of the state legislature went Democratic, but the upper house remained Republican. In Kansas Arthur Capper, long active in agrarian circles, was returned to the Senate with an ample majority; while Harry Woodring, a Democrat, defeated Frank Haucke, a Republican, for the governorship in a close race. Seven Republicans and one Democrat were elected to Congress, while in the state legislature the Republican majorities were whittled down. In Wisconsin Philip F. La Follette, the younger of the brothers, was elected to his first term as governor on the Republican ticket. This was a repudiation of the Hoover Republicans in the state.[76]

Across the nation the rebuke to the Republicans was apparent. The Democrats elected seventeen governors as opposed to twelve elected by the Republicans, and a Farmer-Labor candidate and an independent Repub-

75. *Pioneer Press,* January 13, 1930.

76. *The New International Year Book,* 1930, pp. 526, 492, 572–73, 383, 495, 411, 810.

lican took two more gubernatorial seats. The make-up of the United States Senate consisted of 48 Republicans, 47 Democrats, and 1 Farmer-Laborite; in the House of Representatives there were 217 Republicans, 215 Democrats, 1 Farmer-Laborite, and 2 vacancies. The Republicans lost about 40 seats in the lower house, and in the Senate they lost ground in such states as Illinois, Kansas, Ohio, and South Dakota.[77]

If there was any farm organization that was split wide-open over the Farm Board, it was the Farmers' Union. The backbone of support of the Farm Board within the Union came from the northwest tier of states, whose membership comprised chiefly the area that formerly had been covered by the Equity Cooperative Exchange, while the opposition, bitter and aggressive, came mainly from the Nebraska, Iowa, and Oklahoma Unions.

The Nebraska Farmers' Union—frequently out of step with the more radical policies of the national organization and most of the state bodies, and sporting as it did its antistatist philosophy, which in turn asked for a decentralized economic order in which the cooperatives could hope to play a leading role—charged that the Farm Board would result only in "a great bureaucracy" controlled by "a political board, answering not to farmers, but to the exploitative masters of the government."[78] It was also charged that cooperatives affiliating themselves with the Board were placing themselves in a position where the enemies of cooperation could interfere with them.[79]

Equally strong in his anti-Farm Board pronouncements was the former president of the national Farmers' Union, Charles S. Barrett, who told the farmers that they were being "damn badly swindled" by the creation of the national marketing organizations. Milo Reno, the militant and colorful leader of the Iowa Farmers' Union, predicted that the Farm Board would be successful only in "peasantizing" the American farmers; the elevation of Alexander Legge to the Board, a man who "made millions exploiting the farmer," was advance notice of this. The livestock-market-

77. *World Almanac,* 1931, pp. 236–37.

78. *Nebraska Union Farmer* (Omaha), August 14, 1928, p. 4. No resolutions ever passed endorsing the Farm Board. The Nebraska membership was divided, but the editorial policy of the state paper was decidedly anti-Farm Board.

79. *Ibid.,* June 11, 1930, p. 4.

ing machinery established by the Board was described as totally inadequate to meet the surplus problems of the Middle West.[80]

The resolutions adopted by the Iowa Farmers' Union in 1930 amplified the position of Reno. They demanded that the Agricultural Marketing Act be repealed and that the essential features of the equalization fee be put into operation; also that, in view of the paradox that the state college of agriculture and the extension service were encouraging the farmers to raise more products, while the administration was asking them to restrict their production, appropriations to the county agents be withdrawn until "surpluses" had ceased to exist and the farmers were receiving "cost of production plus a reasonable profit."[81] The position of the Iowa Union was that the Farm Board had "not moved fast enough" or "been liberal enough to suit the more radical and militant."[82]

Among the most ardent of Board supporters were the states of the agricultural northwest, particularly North Dakota, Montana, Minnesota, and the adjoining spring wheat country. Their position was rather difficult to support, because these states were among the most bitter denouncers of the Republican party, especially after the second veto of the McNary-Haugen bill. To many this shift was nothing more than opportunism and political jobbery which could not be condoned, but Union leaders in this section defended their position on the grounds that there was no other possible course of action.[83] This group of Union states became very active in the grain-marketing functions of the Board, and also in shaping the policies of the Farmers' National Grain Corporation. The South St. Paul livestock firm also affiliated with the national livestock-marketing agency established by the Board, thus parting company with the other seven Union houses that denounced the arrangement.[84]

In 1930 the differences within the national Farmers' Union reached a climax with the defeat of C. E. Huff as national president and the elevation of John A. Simpson, a militant opponent of the Farm Board, to the presidency. Among the ten states voting for Huff and the Farm Board were Wisconsin, North Dakota, Minnesota, Missouri, and Kansas; but

80. *Des Moines Tribune*, September 17, 18, 1930.

81. *Ibid.*, September 19, 1930; *Iowa Union Farmer* (Columbus Junction), October 22, 1930.

82. *Farmers' Union Herald* (South St. Paul, Minn.), October 6, 1930.

83. *Ibid.*, November 3, 1930.

84. *Ibid.*, April 6, 1931.

the majority of the states were against the Board. The states that favored it made plain the fact that they wanted no part of the Simpson administration; in fact three of their representatives refused to serve on the national board of the Farmers' Union. This action, the bolting states said, was not to be interpreted to mean that they were leaving the organization but rather that they would refuse to sever their ties with the Farm Board. They even went to the extent of appointing Huff as their official representative in dealing with the Farm Board, Congress, and other legislative bodies. They emphasized the point that they would tolerate no interference with their marketing machinery and business operations by the national Farmers' Union.[85]

In Minnesota opposition to the Farm Board was gathering in other quarters, spearheaded by the Minnesota Farm Bureau and several independent commodity organizations and directed against the Farmers' Union in that state as well as against the national administration. Six Minnesota congressmen, officials of the Minnesota Farm Bureau, the Twin City Milk Producers', the Central Cooperative Livestock Commission Company, the Minnesota Cooperative Wool Growers' Association, and the Northwest Grain Association accused the Farm Board of wrecking regional cooperative institutions instead of building them up. The Farmers' National Grain Corporation was branded as not a true cooperative association, and the terms that it forced on associations affiliated with it were declared equivalent to placing "a gun" at their heads and ordering them "to give up their cooperative status or die."[86] Particular stress was placed on the past of the Farmers' Union Terminal Association, the largest stockholder in the Farmers' National.

The Farmers' Union Terminal Association was charged with being a cooperative "in name only," and with fraudulent dealings, the "Elevator M" case being cited as proof. Elevator M was a Farmers' Union elevator in Minneapolis containing grain samples that were said to have been "juggled" in such a way that inferior wheat was "graded out" as No. 1 Dark Northern. An investigation was under way when it was charged that Huff, the former national president of the Union and later

85. *Ibid.*, December 1, 1930; *Fargo Forum*, November 24, 1930; *Iowa Union Farmer*, May 20, 1931.

86. *Minnesota Farm Bureau News* (Central Edition, Grand Rapids), September 1, 1931.

president of the Farmers' National Grain Corporation, helped conclude a deal whereby the Farmers' National took over the properties of the terminal association, gave up the license for Elevator M and made it a private warehouse not subject to state regulation and inspection.[87] This was a development publicized in the press the truth of which had never been substantiated, yet it did serve to widen the gap between the pro- and anti-Farm Board factions. Union spokesmen there traced the charges to the doorsteps of the Minneapolis Chamber of Commerce, an inveterate foe of the grain cooperatives.[88]

When the Corn Belt Committee met in Chicago in May, 1931, differences among the farmer organizations had reached a new high. The apparent unity that characterized the workings of the body at the time of the McNary-Haugen movement was gone. A resolution passed in condemnation of the Farm Board, the Smoot-Hawley Tariff, and the Hoover administration in general caused the pro-Board groups to withdraw and form the National Committee of Farm Organizations in support of the Farm Board.[89] The majority of the Farm Bureau states and sympathetic commodity groups affiliated with these bodies and the conservative elements within the Farmers' Union supported the administration. The Nebraska Farmers' Union with its well-known antipathies toward state control and centralization condemned the program. The organizations remaining in the Corn Belt Committee comprised the radical wing of the Farmers' Union, the Missouri Farm Association led by Bill Hirth, and a number of independent commodity organizations.[90]

The bitterness of the latter groups toward the pro-Board factions was summed up by Milo Reno. He cited the bitter opposition reigning within the Farmers' Union after the second veto of the McNary-Haugen bill and queried whether the right-about-face made by some of the Farmers' Union states and their support of the Republican administration was the result of the bribes paid by the Farmers' National Grain Corporation and the "full belly" that followed. Reno wrote:

87. *Ibid.*

88. *Farmers' Union Herald,* September 7, October 19, November 2, December 21, 1931; *Fargo Forum,* November 11, 1931.

89. *Farmers' Union Herald,* May 18, 1931; *Des Moines Register,* May 6, 1931; *Minnesota Farm Bureau News,* June 1, 1931.

90. *Farmers' Union Herald,* May 18, 1931.

That this group of "bolters" have crossed the Rubicon and definitely and positively aligned themselves with the Farm Bureau, the County Agent, and the political machines known as agricultural colleges, goes without saying, and it is hardly understandable how they can further pose as Farmers' Union. They have definitely and positively aligned themselves with the Hoover administration, with the Mellons, with the Fesses, the Moses, in fact, with the powers that propose to industrialize the United States and absolutely and forever destroy the American farmer.[91]

By the end of 1931 the futility of the Farm Board program had been pretty well accepted by the heads of the three general farm organizations who met to form a common program of action. At a conference held in Washington in January, 1932, the leaders of the Farm Bureau, the Grange, and the Farmers' Union drew up a six-point program which they said they would support. It called for an amendment to the Agricultural Marketing Act to provide for an effective control of surpluses, an equitable federal tax program but not a general sales tax, a stable currency that would insure stable farm prices, tariff equality for farmers, speculation curbs, and independence for the Philippines as a means of stopping the importation of cheap substitutes for American farm products.[92] This program was broadcast over a national radio network with the three farm heads participating.

During 1932 farm organization after farm organization spoke out in critical vein against the Board. The Farm Bureau reverted to the equalization fee principle of the McNary-Haugen days, the Grange adhered to its export debenture plan, and the Farmers' Union, under the leadership of John A. Simpson, favored a price-fixing program that would insure the farmer his "cost of production plus a reasonable profit." In general, the only thing that kept these three bodies together was their opposition to the Federal Farm Board and not any agreement on the specific remedies to be applied.[93]

In its third and final report, the Farm Board conceded that the surplus

91. *Iowa Union Farmer,* May 20, 1931.

92. American Farm Bureau Federation, *Report of the Executive Secretary,* 1932, p. 6.

93. *Des Moines Register,* September 23, 1932; *Farmers' Union Herald,* December 21, 1931; *Milwaukee Journal,* March 13, 1932; *Minnesota Farm Bureau News,* April 1, 1932.

in itself was not the cause of the farmers' troubles. Low farm incomes were due to lowered consumer income, the shrinkage of the foreign market, the disorganization of world trade, unemployment, and reduced European purchasing power. The recovery of agriculture depended upon the recovery of domestic business, the recapture of the foreign market, reduced interest rates, taxes, freight costs, and other fixed charges the farmer had to pay, the expansion of cooperative facilities to give the farmer a greater share of the consumer's dollar, and a better adjustment between production and consumption.[94]

94. *Third Annual Report of the Federal Farm Board* (Washington, 1932), pp. 85–88.

Chapter XV

THE FARM STRIKE

THE FARM STRIKE—short-lived, dramatic, and unsuccessful—was another episode in the expression of agricultural discontent. It began in Iowa, and its leader was Milo Reno, the militant president of both the Iowa Farmers' Union and the Farm Holiday Association and aggressive advocate of "cost of production" as the basis for the farmer's price. This opposition had two stages: first the farmers resisted the state veterinarians who tested cattle for tuberculosis; and then as conditions worsened they applied the principle of the "bank holiday" to agriculture, hoping that this would encompass the nation unless relief was forthcoming to them soon. The strikers sought to restrain their members from shipping goods to market—first by persuasion if possible, then if that failed, by using force. But in these and other efforts they were no more successful in alleviating the burdens of the farmers than the Federal Farm Board had been. If it accomplished anything, the strike helped dramatize the plight of the farmer as few events did.

This movement had its incubation in Iowa, one of the wealthiest farm states. The years 1929 to 1933 were among the most trying in its history. As elsewhere, prices were dropping and debt burdens were high; hence farmers who had purchased their land and equipment at inflated prices found themselves face to face with bankruptcy. What had made the situation especially acute was the fact that the Iowa farmers had been so prosperous.[1]

1. Staff of the Department of Economics at Iowa State College, *The Agricultural*

Milo Reno was hardly an untried hand in farm movements. He had been a leader in the McNary-Haugen campaign and later hurled anathemas at the Federal Farm Board in a manner that few farm leaders could duplicate. In dramatic and vituperative fashion, he had attacked the Coolidge, Hoover, and the Roosevelt administrations, and with equal vigor he denounced the federal and state governments, the agricultural colleges, the county agents, the professors, and all those affiliated with groups he believed were exploiting the farmers. He burst into the national limelight as head of the Farm Holiday Association.[2]

Despite his unorthodox views, Reno had affiliations and ties that were quite conformist. For instance, he served as president of the Iowa Farmers' Union life and automobile insurance companies and was a director of the fire insurance company—positions which, according to one source, had netted him a total salary of $9,600 a year. This sum, plus a $10 per diem expense allowance while in the field for the fire insurance company, was cited as evidence that farm organization work was hardly unprofitable to Reno at least, despite all that he had to say about the machinations of the capitalist system. He was also listed as a member of the Masons, the Odd Fellows, the Christian Church, and the Republican party, yet he did not adhere strictly to party lines. In 1928 he supported Al Smith, and in 1932 he endorsed Franklin Delano Roosevelt.[3]

His best-known activities before the farm strike were in connection with the McNary-Haugen campaign of the twenties. He was credited with having suggested the idea that led to the forming of the Corn Belt Committee in 1925. In 1928 he broke with Senator Smith W. Brookhart of Iowa because the latter defended Hoover, and then reunited with him in 1932 when both joined in an attack on Hoover. In 1930 Reno called Alexander Legge, the chairman of the Federal Farm Board, a liar and disagreed with Governor John Hamill of Iowa over the creation of a state-wide livestock-marketing organization. When the Corn Belt Committee broke up in 1931, he sided with the anti-Farm Board faction.

Reno's attacks on agricultural colleges and professors were amusing

---

Emergency in Iowa (Ames, 1933). This is an invaluable study by experts, dealing not only with the situation in Iowa, but also with farm relief in general.

2. *Des Moines Tribune,* May 5, 1936.

3. *Ibid.,* August 18, 1932; May 5, 1936. See also Roland A. White, *Milo Reno* (Iowa City, Iowa, 1941), pp. 17–19.

and interesting but reflective of the sentiments of the type of farmer that he led. He accused the colleges of distracting the attention of the farmer "from the real solution of his problems," and of preparing him to accept "the lowly position of the peasant."[4] His main charge was that the colleges were "controlled by exploiters." In bitter vein, he attacked Iowa State College at Ames, taking exception to a particular set of instructions which "advised the farmers' wives how to make undergarments for their children out of feed-sacks." To Reno, the works of the academic theorists were not "going to be worth a damn in the next two or three years in solving the practical problems that confront us." For the "brain trusters" of the New Deal and the other dispensers of "collegiate farm relief" he had this piece of advice: try to run a farm of your own. The central theme in many of his farm speeches was that agriculture was the only basic industry, because "ever since man appeared on this earth, the procuring of food for humans to eat has been the only basic industry whether it was done by bow and arrow or by our modern methods of agriculture."[5]

In 1931 Reno and his followers burst into the public eye when farmers in southeastern Iowa resisted the state veterinarians who had come into that part of the state to test cattle for tuberculosis. This was in line with the recommendations that the United States Bureau of Animal Husbandry had been making for some time. Medical associations also had been crying out that a substantial percentage of all tuberculosis in children was traceable to milk from infected cows. Unfortunately, this tuberculin test was undertaken at a time when the morale of the farmer had fallen to a low ebb.[6]

Testing began in Iowa in 1917, when the first accredited herds appeared in the state. In 1919 the legislature appropriated $100,000 annually, a sum to be spent for testing in cooperation with the federal government. Two years later this appropriation was raised to $250,000 annually. In 1923 the "area-plan law" went into effect which provided that when a certain percentage of farmers in a county requested the test, it must be adopted by the county. This meant that testing was compulsory in many places. About 1929 the test was made compulsory in the state, one of its

4. *Iowa Union Farmer* (Columbus Junction), January 11, 1933.
5. *Des Moines Register,* January 27, 1934.
6. Walter Davenport, "Get Away from those Cows," *Collier's,* LXXXIX (February 27, 1932), p. 11.

most ardent supporters being the Iowa Farm Bureau, which for some years had been the most powerful state farm bureau in the nation.[7]

The cow-testing program appeared to have been proceeding fairly well as late as 1930; there were sporadic complaints but no organized protests. In part this was because the farmers got something for their condemned cows. For every infected animal slaughtered, the federal government assumed one-third the loss, the state one-third, and the owner the remaining third. As time elapsed the farmers began to feel that they were getting less for their animals; many felt that due to the impact of the depression, the state was "paring down its evaluation scale." The packers also were said to be giving less for the salvageable parts of the condemned animals.

Because of the known opposition in the southeastern part of the state, the authorities seem to have postponed the testing of cows there with the hope "that time would make them less scornful of urban laws and more amenable to general government."[8] Many of these farmers belonged to the Farmers' Union and the Farmers' Protective Association, a body formed to oppose the test. Their objections were based on several grounds: the test was "wholly unreliable; it did not protect the public health; it permitted confiscation in the name of the law; it provided meat packers with millions of pounds of good meat at condemned prices; and it furnished salaries to an army of workers at the expense of tax payers." "We appeal to the people of Iowa," pleaded a group of Cedar County farmers, "to help us place upon our statute books a law which will not permit confiscation of our property and establish a test which will be reliable, not a mockery in the name of public health."

The Iowa authorities took exception to these protests. They said that the test protected human life and in the long run gave the farmers healthier cattle and better prices. The Iowa test was upheld as "the same test that has universal approval. When another test is brought forward and wide use shows it to be an improvement, we shall adopt it in Iowa."[9]

Protesting farmers fought the compulsory test in two ways: one, by seeking legislation providing for an optional one in place of the com-

7. *Iowa Farm Bureau Messenger* (Waterloo), November, 1925; *Bureau Farmer* (Iowa Edition), May, 1931, p. 9; *Iowa Farm Bureau Messenger*, January-February, 1921; *ibid.*, April, 1922.

8. Davenport, in *Collier's*, LXXXIX (February 27, 1932), p. 11.

9. *Des Moines Register*, April 15, 1931.

pulsory measure; and two, by organizing committees to resist the state veterinarians when they attempted to apply it.

Typical of the methods employed in the latter instance were those used in Tipton, Iowa. On February 21 there were committees organized, one on every telephone line in the county, to notify farmers when the cow testers, or "cow squirters," as they were also called, started for the farm of anyone who objected to the test. Farmers who cared to chop wood, or pitch hay, were to go to the farm of the objector. State veterinarians, upon seeing these additional hands, would proceed with caution; either they would leave the farm peaceably or they would be subjected to force.[10]

In March farmers visited the state capitol in Des Moines to protest against the compulsory law; most of the farmers came from areas in which the test had been rejected by force and thus had brought about the jailing of some of their members. Reports that farmers would come to the capitol "armed with pitchforks" were disproved as the marchers moved through the downtown area. One placard read:

Fake, Fake, Fake
Vets condemn our cattle
And to the packers take
Fake, Fake, Fake
We oppose compulsory T. B. Tests
We demand justice.[11]

Reno used constitutional arguments in opposing the test, stating: "The real basis of the objection . . . lies in the fact that their property is no longer their own. Any little shyster who has come out of a certain college in the state can go on a farmer's property and conduct a test which is more apt to be wrong than right."[12] About that time a newspaper photographer and a veterinarian were forcibly ejected from the farm of one of the objectors in the Tipton area.[13] Shortly thereafter, word circulated that the state militia was being held in readiness.

These preliminary skirmishes resulted in a compromise between the

10. *Iowa Union Farmer,* February 18, 1931; *Des Moines Tribune,* March 10, 1931.
11. *Ibid.,* March 19, 1931.
12. *Des Moines Register,* April 13, 1931.
13. *Des Moines Tribune,* April 15, 1931.

objectors and the state. According to the terms agreed upon, the farmer were to be permitted to choose an accredited veterinarian to test thei cattle; assurances were made that the state officials would not be kept ir the protesting areas if the farmers gave evidence that they were going t comply with the law; and finally, the state legislators, not the governor were the ones who were empowered to bring the bill for the optional tes out of the "sifting committee" for a vote. The attempt made to bring th bill out for a vote failed by a vote of 80 to 22, which was good evidenc that public sentiment was not behind the objectors.[14]

While the governor restated his determination to enforce the testin law, farmers from Cedar County filed a petition seeking an injunctio to restrain the state from acting. The Iowa supreme court upheld the law however, when it reversed the decision of the lower court, and this tim the appeal went to the United States Supreme Court. The office of th attorney general of Iowa called this appeal frivolous, because there wa nothing in the state law that involved a federal issue; it did not deny du process of law because it was in the interest of public health and the gen eral welfare. As predicted, the United States Supreme Court failed to pas on the case because there was no federal issue involved.[15]

A somewhat embarrassing situation was created in the spring an summer of 1931 when the daughter of one of the Iowa farmers who ha had cows condemned was adjudged the healthiest girl in the Unite States. The recalcitrant farmers believed that here was a situation tha was going to help their protests, because she attributed her health to drink ing a quart of milk a day. Stories were circulating to the effect that all th cows of her father had been condemned, to which he replied that onl eight of his twenty-seven animals had been condemned and that th objectors were doing too much "yapping" and spreading of "maliciou propaganda." He further charged the objectors with opposing the law of Iowa, President Hoover, Iowa State College, the Red Cross, the Farn Bureau, and other "worth-while organizations." He added that he wa "mighty glad" that his cows had been tested.[16] By the once hopefu objectors, these utterances were taken with the greatest suspicion.

14. *Des Moines Register,* April 15, 1931.
15. *Ibid.,* April 19, 29, May 2, 26, 1931; *Des Moines Tribune,* September 22, 1931
16. *Bureau Farmer* (Iowa Edition), May, 1931, p. 11; *Iowa Union Farmer,* Jul 1, 15, 1931.

In the fall of 1931 hostilities broke out again when "armed agents" met the resistance of about four hundred farmers in Tipton. Governor Dan Turner was advised of the situation while he was in Washington attending a conference. He immediately declared martial law and hurried back to the scene of the disturbances.[17] Violence broke out, accompanied by the exchange of heated words, mud, clubs, and tear gas. The law was enforced, but at an estimated cost of about $2,500 per day—a heavy item to an administration that had committed itself to economy. Threats of staging taxpayers' strikes and of boycotting unsympathetic merchants were heard, but the veterinarians proceeded with their work and the cows were tested.[18]

The bulk of the Iowa farmers were not in sympathy with the objectors, yet the outbreak was indicative of the temper of certain areas of the nation, both rural and urban, which had been floundering in the depths of depression with slight evidence of relief in sight. The "cow war" also demonstrated the hostility of certain farmers to the far-reaching hand of the government, colleges, and other centralized agencies, especially at a time of falling prices. In addition, this outbreak furnished a precedent for the farm strike that was to gain more attention and for which the "cow war" had served as more or less a proving ground.

A "farm strike" was nothing new. It had been attempted with limited success during the first decade of the twentieth century by the Equity and the Farmers' Union. In 1920 shortly after the withdrawal of government guarantees, wheat farmers were talking in terms of striking and holding their wheat until they got $3.00 a bushel for it. Milo Reno favored such action at that time.[19] As time elapsed farm-strike sentiment appears to have been gaining headway among certain Farmers' Union leaders.[20] In 1930 one Union leader suggested that "if the farmers of the nation would band together and for sixty days neither sell nor buy from industry, the farm problem would be solved any way farmers wanted it solved."[21]

17. *Des Moines Register,* September 22, 1931; *Des Moines Tribune,* September 22, 1931.

18. *Ibid.,* September 24, 1931.

19. *New Farmer,* October 30, November 27, 1920; *Oklahoma Union Farmer* (Oklahoma City), December, 1920, p. 323.

20. *Des Moines Tribune,* September 25, 1931; *Des Moines Register,* September 27, 1931.

21. *Ibid.,* September 19, 1930.

In March, 1931, Reno was reported sounding out the head of the Iowa Farm Bureau on the prospects of joint action in such a move, but there was very little encouragement extended.[22]

At the annual Iowa Farmers' Union convention in 1931, a resolution was passed asking for "a farmers' buying, selling and tax-paying strike" to be called unless the necessary remedial legislation was forthcoming. The convention instructed the president to name a committee of three to confer with a similar committee that was expected to be selected by John A. Simpson, president of the national Farmers' Union, to launch the movement. The Iowa convention described an acceptable farm program as one that included the following five points: inflation of the currency, increased graduated income taxes, higher inheritance and gift taxes, restrictions on federal borrowings, and the confiscation of wealth in times of war.[23]

By March, 1932, some progress was reported in getting the farm strike under way. Mass meetings had been scheduled for Grinnell, Webster City, Fort Dodge, Harcourt, and other places, and progress in organization was in evidence in Harrison, Cedar, Hamilton, and Marion counties. A farmers' convention held in Des Moines on May 3 voted to launch a strike beginning on July 4, the date selected apparently being to give a patriotic touch to the movement. The slogan for the campaign was "Stay at Home—Buy Nothing—Sell Nothing." The name "farm holiday" was adopted because the term "holiday" had been chosen by the banks which had closed and made it impossible for farmers to withdraw their money. If the bankers were entitled to a "holiday," so were the farmers.[24]

Come, fellow farmers, one and all—
We've fed the world throughout the years
And haven't made our salt.

We've paid our taxes right and left
Without the least objection
We've paid them to a government
That gives us no protection.

22. *Iowa Union Farmer,* March 9, 1931.

23. *Des Moines Register,* September 9, 1931.

24. *Ibid.,* March 11, 1932; *Iowa Union Farmer* (Columbus Junction), May 4, 1932; *Farm Holiday News* (St. Paul), February 20, 1933.

Let's call a "Farmers Holiday"
A Holiday let's hold
We'll eat our wheat and ham and eggs
And let them eat their gold.[25]

When the movement was first considered in 1932, the purpose was simply to withhold products from market, especially if they sold below the cost of production. The movement was expected to last a month. By the fall of 1932, however, state units were in existence in Minnesota, South Dakota, North Dakota, Iowa, Montana, and other states; but at no time was it a cohesive, well-directed effort. From the start it appears to have been nothing more than a mob affair which first sought to keep farmers from marketing their products by peaceful means but next assumed the aspect of a group of angry, resentful men who wanted revenge against those of their kind who marketed their goods while they "picketed and struck."[26]

In August, 1932, when the strike officially began, farm prices were reported as follows: eggs, 22 cents; oats, 11 cents; butter, 18 cents—all of which were far below the cost-of-production levels named by the Farmers' Union. The farmers' cost of production, according to the Iowa group, had to take into account several items: 5 per cent on his real estate investment, 7 per cent on his personal property and equipment, and $100 per month for the farmers' own labor and management. The average farmer operating a 160-acre farm, in order to obtain these returns, had to receive 92 cents per bushel on corn, 49 cents per bushel on oats, $11.25 per hundred on hogs, 35 cents for eggs, and 62 cents for butterfat.[27]

The earliest attempt to launch the strike was made in the Sioux City area, where trouble resulted immediately. Roads were blockaded, fist fights broke out, arrests were made, and gun toting, exhortation, vituperation, picketing, storming of jails and capitol buildings, and stopping of trains and automobiles were among the other events that took place. In some places the old Populist cry of "Raise less corn and more hell" was heard; in others, Hoover was likened to Louis XIV, and the actions of

25. *Iowa Union Farmer,* March 9, 1932.

26. *Farm Holiday News,* February, 1933.

27. D. R. Murphy, "The Farmers Go on Strike," *New Republic,* LXXII (August 31, 1932), pp. 66–67.

the strikers were compared to those of the Boston Tea Party and William L. Garrison.[28] A patriotic tone was given when the Khaki Shirts of America, former members of the Bonus Expeditionary Force that had marched on to Washington, took the lead in blockading the Des Moines highways.[29]

Governors Bryan of Nebraska and Turner of Iowa both refused to call out the militia, thus leaving the matter of preserving peace to the local authorities. Businessmen, however, kept appealing to the governors for action. Finally, Governor Green of South Dakota announced that he had a plan for a conference of the fifteen chief executives of the agricultural states to promote an "orderly, practical, legal, and non-violent program for raising farm prices."

Criticisms against the strikers came from various sources. The liberal *Nation* referred to them as "rebels without ideas."[30] The Minnesota Farm Bureau, like other groups, conceded that the strike focused attention on the plight of the farmers, but charged that it failed to take into account factors that were of fundamental importance in determining prices, such as the tariff, purchasing power of the consumers, the monetary question, world competition, and the effects that the strike would have on the existing marketing machinery.[31]

What the strike achieved in the way of national publicity was offset by the lack of accomplishments; two victories scored by the milk producers in the Omaha area were erased shortly after it had ended. The *New York Journal of Commerce* said that as "a demonstration of the intensity of the economic depression . . . the revolt of the farmers is deserving of serious consideration"; but "as a plan for raising farm prices . . . it betrays a pathetic ignorance of the causes and the possible remedies for inadequate prices."[32]

When the governors' conference was set for September 9 in Sioux City,

28. W. T. Davis, "The Farmers' Holiday," *New Republic,* LXXII (September 21, 1932), p. 156.

29. "The Farmers' War for Higher Prices," *Literary Digest,* CXIV (September 10, 1932), p. 9.

30. "Rebels Without Ideas," *The Nation,* CXXXV (August 31, 1932), p. 184.

31. *Minnesota Farm Bureau News* (Central Edition, Grand Rapids), September 1, 1932.

32. Quoted in *Literary Digest,* CXIV (September 10, 1932), pp. 9, 11.

Reno ordered a temporary truce, but the farmers persisted in blockading the roads.[33] Before the governors met, there was a meeting of the strikers in Des Moines which drafted a plea asking the executives to endorse the food embargo.[34] About that time, George Shafer, the governor of North Dakota, refused a plea to declare an embargo on wheat with the aid of the state militia, charging that he had no constitutional authority to do so. Governor Floyd B. Olson of Minnesota, however, offered to declare an embargo on farm produce with the aid of state militia, providing that the governors of the neighboring states joined hands with him.[35] On September 9 representatives from nine farm states met in Sioux City to draft a program calling for tariff equality, currency expansion, more agricultural credit at lower interest rates, a moratorium on debts, and surplus-control legislation.[36]

This failed to quiet the holiday association. On September 18 its executive council called upon the grain and livestock farmers of the South and Middle West to declare a holiday; and if prices failed to reach a cost-of-production level within thirty days, then the strike would be extended to perishable products as well. At this time, the League For Independent Political Action, sponsoring a third-party movement, warned that the farmers of the Middle West were determined "to have relief either by ballots or by violence."[37]

Meanwhile, Reno and his associates were planning a parade of farmers in Des Moines for October 4, the date that President Hoover had selected to open his campaign for re-election.[38] Stories circulated to the effect that the Republican national headquarters were worried that hostile demonstrations would break out, and it was felt that the proposed American Legion escort ought to be strengthened by adding companies of regular army soldiers stationed near Des Moines.[39] Democratic leaders also were fearful lest hostile demonstrations against the President hurt the Democratic party; hence Iowa leaders were asked to discourage any such moves.

33. *New York Times,* September 1–3, 1932.
34. *Ibid.,* September 7, 9, 1932.
35. *Fargo Forum,* September 8, 1932.
36. *New York Times,* September 10, 12, 1932.
37. *Ibid.,* September 19, 1932.
38. *Ibid.,* September 25, 1932; *Minneapolis Journal,* September 26, 1932.
39. *New York Times,* October 1, 1932.

On October 4, a few hours before the speech, an estimated crowd of two thousand farmers paraded through the downtown area in protest against Hoover. Among the paraders was Senator Smith W. Brookhart, who had supported Hoover in 1928. Although the demonstration was peaceful, anti-Hoover sentiment in the traditionally Republican state of Iowa was very strong. Some of the placards read: "In Hoover we trusted; now we are busted"; "Cost of production only will save our homes"; "Mr. Curtis: We are not so damned dumb in 1932. Signed Mr. and Mrs. Iowa Farmer"; "Hoover, Hyde, Hell and Hard Times. The Republican 4-H Club." [40]

Angry mobs of farmers must have had some effect on the politicians and others who dared break the strike lines, but there is no evidence that the low prices were cowed by them. In a few regions there were increases in fluid-milk prices; but in other areas the tendency was to flood the market with goods and hence depress prices. For instance, livestock shipments into the Iowa markets were slowed down, but those flowing into the Chicago area were increased and prices lowered. Also, farmers and railroads in the nonstriking areas captured the business of those in striking communities. Truckers who had purchased their trucks on the installment plan stopped their monthly payments because of the strike; some had their trucks taken away and even lost their equities. In Minnesota stories of connivance on the part of holiday leaders were reported. Some were said to have hurried their produce to market before the lid was "clamped down." Market quotations were also lower after than before the strike.[41]

Strike activities slowed down, or else were modified, as 1932 turned into 1933, presumably for the purpose of allowing the new administration to show what it was going to do, and also because of the passing of the marketing season.

One major exception was in the state of North Dakota. There prominent political figures—Congressman Bill Lemke, Usher L. Burdick, later elected to Congress, state legislators, and Farmers' Union leaders—took part. In a convention held in Bismarck early in 1933 strongly worded resolutions urged the farmers to organize councils of defense in each county

40. *Ibid.*, October 5, 1932; *Iowa Union Farmer*, October 5, 1932.
41. *Minnesota Farm Bureau News*, October 1, 1932.

. . . to prevent foreclosures, and any attempt to dispossess those against whom foreclosures are pending if started; and to retire to our farms, and there barricade ourselves to see the battle through until we either receive cost of production or relief from the unfair and unjust conditions existing at present; and we hereby state our intention to pay no existing debts, except for taxes and the necessities of life, unless satisfactory reductions in accordance with prevailing farm prices are made on such debts.

Other resolutions passed requested farmers to boycott the sale of agricultural repossessions and asked for the enactment of the Frazier bill and the voluntary allotment plan, provided that the prices set were not below the cost of production. President Roosevelt was asked to appoint as Secretary of Agriculture John A. Simpson, whom the North Dakotans regarded as "beyond question agriculture's most fearless and outstanding leader," and a middlewesterner as Secretary of the Treasury. They declared war "on the International bankers and lesser money barons," and said with melodramatic eloquence that the farm home, "the granite foundation of this great republic," must be preserved, for if "that shall crumble, the Government itself must fall."[42]

On March 12 and 13, 1933, less than ten days after Roosevelt took the oath of office, the national convention of the Farm Holiday Association assembled in Des Moines.[43] The motto was "The Farmer Feeds the World and Deserves His Pay." When the convention was called to order, there were delegates present from Montana, North Dakota, Minnesota, Wisconsin, Iowa, Illinois, Ohio, Nebraska, and Kansas; representatives from Colorado, South Dakota, Oklahoma, and Texas were expected to arrive later, and still other states had reported that delegates had been selected but they could not arrive because the bank holiday had made it almost impossible for them to obtain funds to cover their expenses.

Resolutions again were passed calling for prices based on cost of production; moratoria on rural and urban properties; and the exercise of the right of eminent domain by the federal government to take away land from insurance and mortgage companies "on a fair basis of settlement" and to reopen this land for settlement by "actual home-owners" according to the provisions of the Frazier bill, which empowered the government

42. *Farm Holiday News,* February 20, 1933.
43. *Iowa Union Farmer,* March 8, 1933.

to "refund and refinance" land indebtedness, to assume broader control over the money system of the country, and to reach a common understanding with labor, for both were "exploited by the capitalistic owners of the means of production and distribution." These resolutions were accompanied by a warning to the nation's lawmakers that unless legislation was forthcoming in compliance with these demands by May 3, the Farm Holiday Association would prepare for a marketing strike within ten days after the expiration of that date.[44]

Early in 1933 the protestors dropped the farm-strike formula and resorted to the stopping of eviction sales and the waging of agitation to enact moratorium legislation. Forced sales were broken up in Wisconsin, Iowa, and Minnesota, where the holiday movement was the strongest, and also in Nebraska and South Dakota. On January 19, 1933, Governor Clyde Herring of Iowa issued a proclamation asking insurance and mortgage companies to cease making foreclosures until the state was in the position to act. Most of the important life insurance companies holding such mortgages replied that they had been pursuing a policy of leniency with "owner-operators who were willing to cooperate with them," but that they continued "to prosecute foreclosures in cases where the farm was operated by a tenant or where the premises had been deserted."

Violence and ugly tempers, however, continued to flare up. One writer observed that "It became virtually impossible for a life company to prosecute a foreclosure in counties where the Association was strong, no matter how undeserving of consideration the borrower might be. Some few borrowers took advantage of this situation, refused to make any payments, and dared the companies to take action." It is said that the life insurance companies had little trouble with the farm holiday group where "owner-operators" were involved, and that the association "was much less inclined to take up cudgels in defense of nonowner-operators in danger of foreclosure."

Some creditors at times were prone to try to prosecute foreclosures and met with consequent trouble. In one case the agent of foreclosing finance company was "escorted some distance away" and $800 worth of goods were bought for $14. A horse and an automobile were reported sold for ten cents apiece. In North Dakota some sheriffs continued to make forced

44. *Farm Holiday News,* March 22, 1933; *Des Moines Register,* March 13, 1933.

sales despite the warning from the governor to refrain from so doing; when the sheriffs refused to comply, the governor threatened to call out the militia to force them to abide by his proclamation.

The worst case of violence occurred on April 27 in Le Mars, Iowa, when some six hundred persons broke into a courtroom and demanded of the presiding judge that he sign an agreement not to execute any more foreclosure sales. "When he refused, his assailants dragged him out of his courtroom. Upon continued refusal, he was blindfolded, taken to a crossroads, severely beaten, and threatened with death. He did not sign the agreement." This outbreak placed the county under martial law. The assailants were arrested and sentenced, and no further serious outbreaks were reported.[45]

Other action was taken to alleviate the burdens of the farmers. In Iowa, besides the issuance of the proclamation urging mortgagors to refrain from pressing their claims, the millage tax rate was reduced by one-fifth, the period of grace for tax bills was extended and moratoria on property were provided. A study of the financial condition of the State of Iowa, conducted by the Brookings Institution and made public in September, 1933, had recommended a 10 per cent reduction in the direct property tax and increased levies on incomes, business transactions, tobacco, and theaters.[46]

In Minnesota farmers and businessmen informed Governor Olson that the taxpayers would refrain from paying taxes unless state expenditures were cut by one-fourth. During the regular session of the legislature, beginning in January and ending in April, a number of relief measures were passed, perhaps the most drastic of their kind in the nation. In February a proclamation was issued forbidding foreclosures on farms and homes until May 1; this, in turn, was superseded by the act of the legislature which declared a two-year moratorium, extending to May 1, 1935.[47] State direct property taxes were reduced; a tax on individual incomes was enacted ranging up to 5 per cent on incomes over $10,000 to make up

45. Archibald M. Woodruff, Jr., *Farm Mortgage Loans of Life Insurance Companies* (New Haven, Conn., 1937), pp. 101–6.

46. *The New International Year Book, 1933* (New York, 1934), p. 375.

47. *Ibid.*, p. 505; *ibid.*, 1934, p. 433; J. S. McGrath and J. J. Delmont, *Floyd B. Olson* (St. Paul, 1937), pp. 232–33; Woodruff, *Farm Mortgage Loans of Life Insurance Companies,* pp. 108–15.

for what was lost as a result of the reduction in property taxes; some 4,000 miles of roads were to be added to the state highway system to provide more public work; sweeping powers were given the banking commissioner to aid in reorganizing the state banks; the insurance commissioner was granted sweeping powers to regulate insurance company loans; a special levy was placed on chain stores to produce $1,300,000 for state aid to public school districts; a tax of ten cents per pound was imposed on oleomargarine sold in the state; and state appropriations for the next two years were slashed nearly 20 per cent.[48]

Legislation was enacted in other states, too. In South Dakota a tax was enacted on not net but gross income; grace was extended in the payment of taxes; the general levy for 1934 was eliminated; and the assessed valuation of properties was reduced by over $144,000,000. In North Dakota Governor Langer issued a proclamation forbidding the forced sale of farm properties and later that year declared an embargo on all wheat shipments until the cost-of-production level was reached. In Wisconsin legislation which required the governor to levy a state tax when the balance had fallen below the two-million mark was repealed, and the statutory time during which farmers could redeem their property was extended to three years; milk was classed as a public utility and the state department of agriculture and markets was authorized to fix the price paid for it.[49]

In the spring of 1933 Arthur C. Townley, a veteran of other farm campaigns, was asking that Congress adopt a plan which called for the issuance of $1,000,000,000 in scrip to be used in the exchange of products between farmers and organized labor. His plan also provided that workers operate idle factories and plants in which the products needed by the farmers would be produced; the farmers, in turn, were to be pledged to accept the scrip when it was offered them as payment by labor. Townley told his farmer listeners that they could win this strike "if you can provide a plan by which all of these people can pay you cost of production."[50]

As had been predicted earlier, the Farm Holiday Association was to call a national farm strike unless prices had reached the cost-of-production

48. *The New International Year Book*, 1933, p. 504.
49. *Ibid.*, pp. 758, 611, 844.
50. *Farm Holiday News*, April, 1933; *Iowa Union Farmer*, May 3, 1933.

level. This was slated to begin on May 13. But the day before it was to start Governor Olson advised Reno from his hospital bed that the strike was ill advised and that it "would create more unfavorable sentiment toward relief than favorable." After some deliberations, holiday leaders finally agreed to call the strike off with the note that farm prices appeared to be rising, that the farmers were too busy with spring planting to give much attention to it, and further that there was a "sagging of interest" among the farmers. However, the leaders announced that they would closely watch the actions of the Roosevelt administration.[51]

51. *Farm Holiday News,* April, 1933.

Chapter XVI

THE NEW DEAL FARM PROGRAM IS BORN

It was a foregone conclusion that the change in the national administration in 1933 would bring about sharp changes in the farm program. The Federal Farm Board conceded the need for this in its final report when it said that more drastic and far-reaching measures were needed. The farm strike also helped to dramatize the situation and to emphasize the desperate measures that some were willing to apply. Once the inadequacies of the Farm Board program had been demonstrated, the Farm Bureau renewed its campaign for the equalization fee; the Grange stepped up its demands for the export debenture plan; and the national Farmers' Union, under the leadership of John Simpson, sponsored a price-fixing scheme that aimed to guarantee the farmers their "cost of production." This revealed divisions in the ranks of the organized farm groups which prompted spokesmen for the incoming administration to inject themselves into the scene and bring about some semblance of unity. The result was the adoption of the A.A.A., a socio-economic experiment of far greater dimensions than anything that the Farm Board had dreamed of, and one in which the farmers of the western Middle West were to play a conspicuous role.

The domestic allotment plan that emerged as a rival farm-relief measure during the last year of the Hoover administration furnished a substantial base on which the New Deal farm-policy shapers were to build.

The origins of this plan, not to be confused with the price-fixing scheme of John Simpson which bore the same name, are traceable to the domestic allotment plan that was first proposed by W. J. Spillman of the United States Department of Agriculture in 1926 and then published the following year in his book, *Balancing the Farm Output*.[1]

Spillman, whom Henry A. Wallace once branded as the "philosophic father" of the Triple A, apparently had become convinced that the United States was going to remain a high-tariff nation for many years to come. Profitable and expanding foreign markets for the farmers were a thing of the past. But by this he did not mean to suggest that the United States should confine its productive powers merely to meet its internal needs. More than domestic requirements had to be produced and provisions had to be made to see that products raised beyond domestic needs were sold at an advantage.[2]

Spillman proposed to accomplish this through his "limited debenture plan," which sought to limit the amount of the product for which the grower was to obtain the benefit of the tariff. He made no proposal to control the output. There were to be created a central commission and local organizations which would collect data relating to acreages, yields, and the carry-over from earlier years, and he saw that the state agricultural colleges could play a part in carrying out the plan. Finally Spillman was convinced that if his plan was going to make the tariff effective on that portion of the product sold by the producer, changes had to be made in the allotments which would "make it impossible for a producer to profit by increasing his acreage of a protected crop."[3]

Among those to be influenced by the Spillman plan were John D. Black, a Harvard professor, and Beardsley Ruml. Black, who had received his doctorate from the University of Wisconsin, had gone to Harvard to teach farm economics after a highly successful career in the University of Minnesota. During the spring of 1929 he brought the "transferable-rights plan" to the attention of Congress in testimony that he presented to Senate and House Committees on Agriculture and also in his book,

1. W. J. Spillman, *Balancing the Farm Output* (New York, 1927).

2. Russell Lord, *The Wallaces of Iowa* (New York, 1947), pp. 190, 305–7.

3. Spillman, *Balancing the Farm Output,* pp. 84–104; Edwin G. Nourse, Joseph S. Davis, and John D. Black, *Three Years of the Agricultural Administration Act* (Washington, 1937), p. 13.

Agricultural Reform in the United States. Subsequently, this transferable-rights plan was acknowledged as having been originated by Beardsley Ruml, who was at the time the director of the Laura Spelman Rockefeller Memorial Foundation. According to Joseph S. Davis of the Food Research Institute of Stanford University, this resembled "an earlier plan presented unofficially by W. J. Spillman."

The transferable-rights plan, at least as applied to wheat, proposed

> to give to every grower a certificate expressed in bushels representing his pro-rata share, on the basis of his average production in some recent period of years, in approximately the amount of wheat domestically consumed for food. These certificates were to be salable to millers, who were expected to buy them at approximately the tariff rate per bushel; and they were to be required to surrender to federal officials, on the first sale of flour for domestic use, such certificates in amounts corresponding to the amount of wheat ground into this flour. Thus it was hoped that with no complex machinery, no disturbance of wheat production or marketing, no export dumping, no burden on the federal treasury, and little or no stimulus to production, the sale of their "transferable rights" in the "domestic allotment" would bring wheat growers a supplementary income sufficient to satisfy their ideas of "fair return."[4]

One of the most energetic converts to the domestic allotment plan was M. L. Wilson of the Montana State College faculty, who headed a group that came forward with a radically different version of the Ruml-Black transferable-rights plan. This Wilson version came to be known as the "voluntary domestic allotment plan."[5]

In 1933 Wilson said that his proposal took the international situation into account and had four basic points attached to it. (1) There was the tax to be collected at the processing point, be it the flour mill, packing house, or textile mill. One plan was that the tax collected was to equal the amount of the tariff, but another asked that the tax be sufficient to give the particular commodity its prewar purchasing power. (2) The government then would give the cooperating farmer a pro rata share of the funds collected, provided that he signed a contract not to increase his crop the

4. Joseph S. Davis, *Wheat and the AAA* (Washington, 1935), pp. 30–31.

5. "Bounty," *Fortune*, VII (February, 1933), pp. 117–19; Davis, *Wheat and the AAA*, p. 31; "The Voluntary Domestic Allotment Plan for Wheat," Food Research Institute, Stanford University, *Wheat Studies*, IX (November, 1932), pp. 23–62.

following year and, if necessary, to curtail it to bring about a better balance between production and consumption. (3) Since these benefit payments would be paid only to those farmers who cooperated with the government, the farmer who thought that his personal liberty would be interfered with by such a program would have the opportunity to go ahead and produce as much as he pleased. (4) Finally, the plan was to be as decentralized as possible, and the costs of operation were to be borne by those who benefited from it and not by the consumers.[6]

By 1932 the Wilson version of the domestic allotment plan had attracted the attention of a number of prominent individuals. Great strides had been made in propagandizing it since 1930, when he first began discussing certain phases of his plan with Montana farmers. Wilson is credited with having converted or interesting such men as George Soule of the *New Republic* and Joseph Knapp, head of the powerful Crowell publications. "He interested Republican and Democratic politicians, big landowners with money in distressed land, officials of farm organizations, members of board of trade. He almost converted Walter Lippmann, and he interested the extension force." Rexford G. Tugwell also became interested in domestic allotment and managed through Raymond Moley, it is claimed, "to outline Wilson's allotment plan at the meeting of the Brain Trust on the porch at Hyde Park." Roosevelt gave "a hearty reception" to the principle in his speech of acceptance. Wilson also has been credited with suggesting five of the six points that Roosevelt emphasized in his famous Topeka speech of September 14, 1932.[7]

The Wilson voluntary domestic allotment plan began to assume tangible form in the spring of 1932. On April 10 Wilson held a conference with a group in Chicago to discuss the plan at length. Taking part in this conference were George N. Peek; Henry A. Wallace; Louis S. Clarke, president of the Mortgage Bankers Association of Omaha; R. R. Rogers of the Prudential Life Insurance Company; Henry I. Harriman of Boston; W. R. Ronald, editor of the *Evening Republican* of Mitchell, South Dakota; and several agricultural and other economists. "Here for the first time," writes Joseph S. Davis, "were definitely incorporated the pro-

6. M. L. Wilson, *Farm Relief and the Domestic Allotment Plan* (Minneapolis, 1933), pp. 27–28.

7. Russell Lord, *The Agrarian Revival* (New York, 1939), pp. 147, 154.

duction control, farm contract, and cash benefit features that earlier plans had lacked." Wilson was given the task of appointing a committee to draft a bill and seek its passage.[8]

Shortly another farm-relief proposal, but by no means as important as the domestic allotment plan—the so-called Rainey bill—was brought to the attention of Congress. According to George Peek, Congressman Henry T. Rainey of Illinois, the Democratic House leader in the Seventy-second Congress, wanted legislation passed that would at least aid the farmers during the 1932 season. Rainey contacted Earl Smith, the head of the Illinois Agricultural Association, and asked him if an emergency measure effective for only one year could be drafted. Smith turned to Peek for advice and they in turn asked Fred Lee, a legal expert, to come to Chicago from Washington to help them draft a bill. After drafting a measure they asked "Chester Davis, Alexander Legge, Clifford Gregory and a few others whose views they respected" to pass judgment on the bill. Peek said they all approved it.

The Rainey bill contained a processing tax levied as an excise tax, at least according to Peek, and provided that benefit payments be made to producers on "the domestic percentage" of the crop. Senator Peter Norbeck of South Dakota introduced the measure in the Senate late on the evening of June 29, 1932, and it was then referred to the Committee on Agriculture and Forestry. Meanwhile the Farm Bureau prevailed upon President Hoover to use his influence to pass some farm-relief measure before Congress adjourned. Edward A. O'Neal, the president of the Farm Bureau, advised that the bill, "which undoubtedly will benefit prices on hogs, cotton, and wheat—three basic farm commodities of interest to the whole Nation—be enacted before adjournment." The measure was passed "on a day when a number of Administration senators were absent." It was brought up again in the Senate, reputedly at the request of the White House, and was defeated. No action was taken in the House.[9]

8. Davis, *Wheat and the AAA*, p. 31. For a lengthy account of the activities of M. L. Wilson, see Lord, *The Wallaces of Iowa*, pp. 292–311.

9. George Peek, *Why Quit Our Own* (New York, 1936), pp. 51–52; Nourse, Davis, and Black, *Three Years of the A.A.A.*, pp. 13–14 n. *Congressional Record*, 72 Congress, 1 session, Vol. LXXV, Part 13 (1932), p. 14358; *ibid.*, Part 14, p. 15194; *New York Times*, July 12, 1932; *Illinois Agricultural Association Record, 25th Anniversary Edition*, XIX (January, 1941), p. 29.

Of the two bills—the Fulmer-Walsh and the Hope-Norbeck—to come before Congress in the spring of 1932 embodying certain phases of the Wilson voluntary domestic allotment plan, it was the Hope-Norbeck bill which was the more important. On July 14, 1932, Congressman Clifford R. Hope of Kansas told his colleagues in the House that he had been interested in the theory behind the domestic allotment plan for years but that he could give no serious consideration to it because "it had not been worked out in practical legislative form until Professor Wilson and his committee gave it their study and attention." He commented on the great interest that it had aroused among the members of the House Committee on Agriculture and then discussed what he considered to be the outstanding advantages of the plan. Hope was convinced that the plan would release a large volume of new credit and place it in the hands of the farmers, which, together with the public works, productive credit, and relief measures that had been suggested in other proposals, would increase the use of credit in the country and "start the recovery from the long depression."

Two days later Senator Norbeck introduced two bills which he claimed were largely the work of M. L. Wilson. One of the bills sought "to amend the agricultural marketing act so as to make the tariff effective on farm commodities domestically consumed, and to provide a means of preventing undesirable surpluses and balancing production and consumption." The other sought "to amend the agricultural marketing act so as to make the tariff effective on that part of the production of specified farm commodities which is consumed within the United States, and to provide a means of balancing production and consumption." Norbeck added that he was convinced "that a voluntary allotment plan that will make the tariff effective is the key to the whole situation." Both measures were referred to the Senate Committee on Agriculture, whose chairman, Senator McNary, assured Norbeck that the bills would be given early consideration by the committee when Congress reconvened in December. No action could be taken at the time because Congress was about ready to adjourn.

The Hope-Norbeck bills were introduced in Congress at this time "not so much in the hope that they could be passed as in the desire to educate members of Congress and the country as to the nature of the proposal."

Events soon demonstrated that neither bill was going to emerge from the committee rooms. Later Wilson said that all the farm-relief measures to come before Congress during the spring and early summer of 1932 were incomplete.[10]

Since 1932 was a presidential election year, it was only natural for the major political parties to make some kind of a stand on the principles behind the domestic allotment plan. Some of the Republican party chieftains apparently were favorably impressed with it, because one of the planks in the platform read: "We will support any plan which will help to balance production against demand, and thereby raise agricultural prices, provided it is economically sound and administratively workable without burdensome bureaucracy." But Hoover in his speech of acceptance on August 11, 1932, indicated his opposition when he said: "There is no relief to the farmer by extending government bureaucracy to control his production and thus curtail his liberties, nor by subsidies that bring only more bureaucracy and ultimate collapse. I shall oppose it." [11]

Franklin Delano Roosevelt was fully aware of the disaffections of the farmers when he decided to open his campaign in the western Middle West. On September 14, in Topeka, Kansas, in the first of his projected twenty-one campaign speeches, he accused the Republicans of failing to understand the farm problem and came forward with a six-point recovery program. He asked that the producers of staples, in which there were surpluses, be given tariff benefits equivalent to those enjoyed by industry, but in a fashion that was different from anything that had been proposed previously. Such a program had to be self-supporting and of a nature that would not compel European nations to retaliate against the United States on charges of dumping. What machinery was erected to put this program in operation had to be as decentralized as possible, with authority resting chiefly with the locality rather than with a bureaucratic Washington machine, and be built as well as possible on the existing agencies. Roosevelt expressed approval of the idea that the program be put into

10. *Congressional Record,* 72 Congress, 1 session, Vol. LXXV, Part 14 (1932), pp. 15395, 15398, 15641. See pages 15641–43 of the *Record* for a statement by Wilson on the domestic allotment plan. Nourse, Davis, and Black, *Three Years of the A.A.A.,* p. 13; Wilson, *Farm Relief and Domestic Allotment,* p. 36.

11. Davis, *Wheat and the AAA,* pp. 32–33.

action only after it had the support of a reasonable majority of the producers of the exportable surpluses to which it was to apply. And the program had to be voluntary. Meanwhile, the cooperative movement was not to be lost sight of; it was to be given as much encouragement as possible.[12]

As Roosevelt advanced his campaign and appeared to be making considerable headway, Hoover tried to salvage as much support as he possibly could. As Iowa was preparing to receive Roosevelt, Hoover sent a telegram to Governor Dan W. Turner telling him that the administration had started another drive to bring immediate and practical relief to the farmers.[13] Hoover advised Turner of the efforts that were being made by some of the leading financiers of the country to bring help to the mortgaged farmers. Before this, it had been announced that arrangements had been made for feed and seed loans that would make it possible for thousands of farmers indebted to the federal government to pay only 25 per cent of their debts from their crop proceeds that year. There would be no pressure for payment of the remaining 75 per cent until Congress had had the chance to act.[14] Governor George F. Shafer of North Dakota, a Republican, said that this "seed moratorium" meant relief for 40,000 farmers in his state amounting to about $6,250,000.[15] Another move, a proposed fifteen-million-bushel wheat deal with China, intended to buoy prices in critical farm states before the election, ran into trouble first when the Reconstruction Finance Corporation asked for "adequate security" in financing it and then when the Farmers' National Grain Corporation showed an unwillingness to underwrite it.[16]

On October 4 Hoover fired "the opening gun of a home-stretch drive to reclaim the revolting West." It is significant that he chose Des Moines, Iowa, the state of his birth, as the place in which to start his campaign for re-election. According to the *Chicago Tribune,* Iowa was "the heart of the Republican disaffection and dissent." The *Literary Digest* poll gave

12. *Minneapolis Journal,* September 14, 1932.
13. *Ibid.,* September 29, 1932.
14. *Minneapolis Tribune,* September 29, 1932; William S. Myers, *The State Papers and Other Public Writings of Herbert Hoover* (2 vols., New York, 1934), II, 287–89.
15. *Minneapolis Tribune,* September 30, 1932.
16. *Pioneer Press* (St. Paul), October 15, 1932.

Roosevelt a 3 to 2 lead in the state, and the pro-Hoover *Des Moines Register* gave him a 5 to 3 advantage.[17]

In his Des Moines speech Hoover called attention to the economic storm "which embraces the whole world," ascribed it to "a terrific eruption in civilization itself," and then recited the efforts made by his administration to check industrial strife, unemployment, falling prices, foreclosures, and the drought and to balance the budget. His faith in the Smoot-Hawley tariff was as uncompromising as his belief in the gold standard. He felt it unfortunate that in 1930 the Democrats had gained control of the House of Representatives, and assailed the opposition party for its failure to place patriotism above party. The tariff, he repeated, was the "very basis of safety to American agriculture." [18]

The other parts of his twelve-point relief program for agriculture included the repeal of the stabilization features of the Agricultural Marketing Act, the adoption of a "sound" land-use program, advancement of the Great Lakes–St. Lawrence seaway, relief for drought-stricken debtors, a readjustment of land taxes, extension of short-term credits, loans to processors to enable them to carry their usual stocks, the extension of credits for the sale of farm products abroad, mortgage relief, recovery of world markets through disarmaments and peace, the use of "any annual payment on the foreign debt" for the expansion of the foreign market, and finally a reversal in the "process of deflation" to "bring things back to their real values."[19]

With Roosevelt elected President, the chances for the passage of some kind of domestic allotment bill grew brighter. Many were becoming more receptive to the plan. No doubt the "decisive November elections" helped make up the minds of those who were still hesitant. But much to the disgust of the new administration, the big farm organizations were still divided. Then something happened. "On December 12 and 13 'the most representative group of farm leaders ever assembled in the United States' met in Washington's Hotel Harrington and there behind locked doors conferred long and earnestly with Henry Morgenthau, Jr. . . . publisher of the *American Agriculturist,* and Roosevelt's right-hand man in

17. "Hoover's Fight for the West," *Literary Digest,* CXIV (October 15, 1932), pp. 7–8.

18. Myers, *Public Writings of Herbert Hoover,* II, 295–97, 301–6, 309.

19. *Ibid.,* pp. 309–17.

agricultural matters. When the doors were unlocked a political miracle had come to pass: the various farm organizations had come to an agreement. They would unite in support of Domestic Allotment."[20]

Apparently, these preliminary efforts were not without some results. Late in 1932 about 150 members of Congress were reported banded together to force through the short session of Congress a four-point program. According to E. A. O'Neal, president of the American Farm Bureau Federation, congressmen from both parties were backing an agricultural program which included expansion of the currency, devaluation of the dollar, the cessation of mortgage foreclosures, and the extension of equality to agriculture and labor.[21]

What appeared to be a major move in the renewed drive to bring relief to agriculture took shape when Marvin Jones, chairman of the House Committee on Agriculture, introduced a domestic allotment bill intended to serve as a temporary measure "pending more permanent adjustment of such burdens as the farm-mortgage situation, trade barriers, and taxes."[22] The House Committee on Agriculture began hearings on December 14 and continued until December 20. On January 3 Jones reported the bill to the House. The bill was a "production control measure on an allotment basis." It sought to foster "agricultural planning and readjustment to meet changed world conditions and to aid in restoring the parity between agricultural and other industries and correcting the inequalities between the prices of agricultural and other commodities." The Secretary of Agriculture was granted power to make allotments to each producer on the basis of "his domestic consumption percentage." Producers would receive payments if the acreage or production of a specific crop was below that of the specified period provided for in the bill. The President could by proclamation extend the operations of the act "from year to year for such commodities as the Secretary of Agriculture should recommend as necessary to correct 'inequality between the price of such commodity and other commodities.' " It was similar in many respects to the Hope-Norbeck bill; it was a compromise between the McNary-Haugen, export debenture, and domestic allotment plans.[23]

20. *Fortune,* VII (February, 1933), pp. 117–18.
21. *Pioneer Press,* December 21, 1932.
22. "Farm Rehearsal," *Business Week* (January 11, 1933), p. 3.
23. Nourse, Davis, and Black, *Three Years of the A.A.A.,* pp. 14–15.

When the bill was reported from the committee, it covered only four commodities—cotton, wheat, tobacco, and hogs. Those who favored limiting the bill to these four commodities did so on the theory that these four had a controlling effect upon prices for other agricultural commodities. On the floor of the House, spokesmen for the dairy interests fought to include butterfat. Once butterfat was included, the rice and peanut producers also lined up enough votes to have their products included. In amended form the bill passed the House by a vote of 203 to 150.[24]

Just who was responsible for drafting the bill and precisely what the attitude of the incoming administration toward it was at the time is not quite clear. George Peek wrote that "the bill was a composite of a variety of ideas contributed by Tugwell, Morgenthau, Ezekiel, M. L. Wilson, some other professors and economists and perhaps Henry Wallace. It was not the farmers' measure."[25] Senator Ellison D. Smith of South Carolina, upon his return to Washington from New York, where he visited Roosevelt and discussed the Jones bill, reported that Roosevelt approved of the allotment plan in principle but "felt its provisions should be confined to wheat and cotton."[26]

On February 20, 1933, the bill was reported to the Senate from the Committee on Agriculture and Forestry by Senator Lynn Frazier. The Senate committee amended the bill in a fashion that made it unacceptable to the farm groups that supported it in the House. The application of the bill was limited to wheat and cotton and the provision to control acreage was eliminated. There also were changes in the benefit payments proposed.[27]

Had the Jones bill been passed by the Senate, the chances are that President Hoover would have vetoed it. Hyde, the Secretary of Agriculture, opposed it because it "would not afford substantial relief to agriculture" and because it proposed "such drastic regulation as to be impossible of effective administration." Despite the generally acknowledged Republican opposition to the plan, the third and final report of the Federal Farm

24. *Congressional Digest,* XII (February, 1933), p. 33; *Congressional Record,* 72 Congress, 2 session, Vol. LXXVI, Part 2 (1933), pp. 1257, 1338–54, 1363–93, 1481–1545, 1582–1616, 1658–1710, 1714.

25. Peek, *Why Quit Our Own,* p. 71.

26. *Congressional Digest,* XII (February, 1933), p. 33.

27. *Ibid.* (March, 1933), pp. 89–90.

Board accepted some phases of the domestic allotment plan, the features approved being a self-sustained relief system to raise prices and the adjustment of production according to demand. Perhaps the importance of this last drive lay largely in the fact that it reflected another step in molding the rapidly forming opinion on agricultural relief.[28]

Despite assurances by Wilson and others that the costs for this plan would be shouldered by the producers and not the consumers, objections to it appeared soon. Liberal eastern publications hardly gave a welcome reception to it because it meant higher prices for the nonfarmers.

> The final excuse for the bill is that the manufacturer is already receiving a subsidy through the tariff, and that the farmer must now receive his through the parity plan. In other words, as the manufacturer is supported out of compulsory doles from the farmer, the farmer must now be supported out of compulsory doles from the manufacturer. This is Alice in Wonderland economics; the mythical islanders who lived by taking in each other's washing begin to seem relatively plausible. What is wrong with a drastic tariff reduction that would open the world's markets to the farmer's products and no longer make it necessary for him to endow the manufacturer?[29]

In similar vein the *New Republic* objected on the grounds that it would bring about higher living costs.

> Like a protective tariff, it aims to subsidize one section at the expense of another. How can such a device be of permanent or lasting benefit? . . .
>
> . . . Enthusiasts . . . speak of the stimulus which industry would receive if the farmers, selling their crops at higher prices, should come back into the market for industrial products. But what would be the net gain if industrial workers at the same time were compelled to restrict their purchases of industrial products because they had to pay more for food and clothing?[30]

One of the most pointed summations of the plight of the farmer and the need for taking prompt action appeared in the conservative *Business*

28. Nourse, Davis, and Black, *Three Years of the A.A.A.*, p. 15; Davis, *Wheat and the AAA*, p. 35.
29. "The Parity Plan," *The Nation*, CXXXVI (January 18, 1933), p. 54.
30. "The Consumer and the Farm Bill," *New Republic*, LXXIII (January 18, 1933), pp. 255–56.

Week, which depicted the farmers as "worn veterans" in the army of depression, alongside whom businessmen were but mere "raw recruits." Something had to be done quickly to relieve them. Out of the maze of proposals that were suggested there, appeared three alternative courses of action:

> . . . First is a blind way that disappears over the hills of hope. We may hope that with a return of prosperity, industry will expand so enormously that the migration from farm to factory will set in anew. Poorer farms will be abandoned, their occupants find work in the factories. Thus crop production will decrease. But it must be on a scale that will absorb from a fourth to a third of the population now on the farms. Presupposed also, the adjustment of industry to modern economic life wherein it is recognized that the workers' wage sets the ultimate limit of possible sales. Given adequate purchasing power, the ability of consumers to use goods has no easily imaginable limit. But food consumption is inelastic.
>
> The second road leads down hill. If industry does not revive on such a scale, our farmers, competing with peasants, and selling to peasants, must become peasants. The general advance in the use of agricultural machinery must be checked. Farms will be broken up into smaller units. The absentee landlord, who already holds half the farms, or nearly, will predominate; a tenant class will till the soil.
>
> Where the third road leads, nobody knows. It is the road of permanent subsidy. That is, we may tax the city dweller to maintain a decent standard of living on the farm. There can be no economic defense for subsidizing uneconomic production. It is social and political; there we may find strong justification. It might well seem important to us to preserve in our country the one large class of property owners, the greatest body of entrepreneurs, the one stable and rooted element. It might seem worth a high cost— and it might be cheaper than to add them to the breadlines of the cities. It is hard to visualize an America of the future should the stream dry up that steadily feeds us leaders in every walk of life.[31]

Among the specific remedies advanced, there were "taxes to be shifted from the farmers' backs; moratoria on tax, interest, and mortgage payments; writing down of mortgages; credit for crop production; stabilization of crop prices at higher levels. . . ."[32]

Obviously the man selected to serve as Secretary of Agriculture and to

31. "Three Farm Roads," *Business Week* (February 15, 1933), p. 32.
32. *Ibid.*

administer the program was of the utmost importance. Various names were mentioned, not many of which attracted too much serious attention. Among them there were Cully Cobb of Georgia; John Simpson, president of the national Farmers' Union; George Peek of McNary-Haugen prominence; Henry Morgenthau, Jr.; Henry A. Wallace; and others. According to a Farm Bureau version, Roosevelt had his heart set on Henry Morgenthau, "a fellow gentleman farmer and neighbor on the Hudson," as Secretary. According to this same source, "Midwestern, western and southern farm leaders could not see Mr. Morgenthau as head of the government agency that would play such a vital part in their anticipated agricultural program." Roosevelt is said to have demurred on Henry A. Wallace and yielded only after "continuing pressure." This same source observed that "when Wallace was finally appointed Secretary, Mr. Roosevelt gave Morgenthau the next most important agricultural post—head of the Federal Farm Credit system. He was later promoted to be Secretary of the Treasury." [33]

From all particulars—ideologically, geographically, and temperamentally—the appointment of Henry A. Wallace as Secretary of Agriculture was a logical one for the incoming administration to make. Iowa, "that kingdom of fat hogs and rank corn," was a center of unrest and agricultural thinking and it was strategically located. "The Middle West hailed the appointment; Iowa was loudly enthusiastic." Much of his thinking on the farm question had antedated that of the new administration. Wallace had favored inflation and a balanced production in agriculture; he had been waging a relentless campaign along these lines during the twenties. His most conspicuous efforts were in behalf of the equalization fee of the McNary-Haugen proposal.[34]

In his last column as editor of *Wallaces' Farmer,* just before assuming his post as Secretary of Agriculture, Wallace called attention to the differences in conditions when his father assumed the same post in 1921. In 1933 agriculture was in a far more desperate position than it had been in 1921, but he felt that he was to have the advantage of "working under

33. Orville M. Kile, *The Farm Bureau Through Three Decades* (Baltimore, 1948), pp. 186, 194; Lord, *The Wallaces of Iowa,* pp. 323–25.

34. *Wisconsin Agriculturalist and Farmer* (Madison), LX (March 4, 1933), p. 4; *Wallaces' Farmer and Iowa Homestead,* LVIII (February 4, 1933), pp. 4–5; *Business Week* (March 22, 1933), p. 13.

a chief who is definitely progressive, entirely sympathetic toward agriculture, and completely determined to use every means at his command to restore farm buying power." This, he believed, was no small factor, because it was incumbent upon the New Deal to "make up for twelve years of lost time"—to take marginal lands out of production, to reduce the output in the principal crops, and to lower tariffs over a period of one, two, or three years. He felt that agriculture had a fighting chance because the White House was in the hands of the farmers' allies. He granted that his new assignment was going to be a trying one, but said that ". . . I go down to Washington with real hope that something worth while can be done at once."[35]

Meanwhile there had descended on Washington "farm leaders representing every shade of opinion, every commodity, and every locality." Also there came "the forces of opposition—the grain dealers, the meat packers, the millers, the cotton converters, and the hundreds of business elements affected by farm legislation."[36] What objections there were to relief proposals were likely to be overlooked, for the time being at least, because of the need to do something for the farmers before the spring crops were planted.[37]

Judging from the preliminary efforts, statements, and the established views of the administration leaders, one required little insight to figure out in advance the nature of the new farm act. In graphic fashion, *Wallaces' Farmer* said of the proposed new bill:

> . . . It has more power than the old Goldsborough bill, the McNary-Haugen bill and all the land bank acts put together. As soon as the bill passes, three big horses will be ready to work for the farmer.
>
> The first horse is the section of the bill that provides for increasing farm buying power by paying farmers to reduce production to effective demand.
>
> The second horse is the section that cuts interest rates on many farm mortgages and makes possible the scaling down of the principal on many more.
>
> The third horse, led out last week amid farm cheers, is inflation.[38]

It was a foregone conclusion that inflationary measures were going to

35. *Wallaces' Farmer and Iowa Homestead,* LVIII (March 4, 1933), p. 5.
36. *Business Week* (March 22, 1933), p. 13.
37. "Idle Acres," *ibid.* (March 29, 1933), p. 3.
38. *Wallaces' Farmer and Iowa Homestead,* LVIII (April 29, 1933), p. 3.

be adopted by Congress. The American Farm Bureau Federation was waging a relentless campaign in behalf of inflation; Wallace had long been championing it through the columns of his paper; the national Farmers' Union was for it. Even the Hoover administration had given encouragement to it; the Federal Farm Board, the Reconstruction Finance Corporation, and the billion-dollar open-market credit-easing campaign of the Federal Reserve Board were inflationary in their tendencies.[39] The farm states were solidly behind the inflationary proposals. "But," *Business Week* pointed out, "anyone who supposes the demand comes solely from the rural sections is blind. There is strong Wall Street support for inflation, and advocates are not scarce in the ranks of Big Business. Nor does it pass unnoted that intellectuals—including the moderate-liberal Walter Lippmann—are saying the United States cannot avoid and should not try to avoid cheapening the dollar." [40]

By mid-April there were forty or more inflationary bills pending in Congress. Of the methods proposed, the old Populist formula, the free coinage of silver, was the most popular. In April, 1933, there were reported "16 pending bills asking for the purchase of silver, the issuance of silver certificates, or bimetallism at the ratio of 16 to 1. No other device has inspired so many money bills as this one which was the center of attention 37 years ago." But it was suggested that only two methods were being given consideration by the administration—devaluation of the dollar and a large public-works program.[41]

One of the most encouraging as well as curious developments several weeks before the A.A.A. became law was the advance in wheat prices. May wheat prices had advanced ten cents a bushel over a three-week pe-

39. *The Farm Bureau and Farm Recovery* (Chicago, n.d.) [booklet]; *Honest Money* (Chicago, 1932) [booklet]; *The American Farm Bureau Federation, 1933,* p. 10 [Annual Report of the Executive Secretary]; *Wallaces' Farmer and Iowa Homestead,* LVIII (February 4, 1933), p. 4, contains a short sketch of Wallace's inflationary views during the twenties. *New York Times,* January 26, 1933. John Simpson, the president of the national Farmers' Union, said that besides "a straight-out price-fixing measure on the basis of cost of production," inflation was needed. "What we need is the remonetization of silver, a good supply of paper money, and a sprinkling of counterfeit to take care of the situation." *United States Daily News,* April 8–15, 1933.

40. "Inflation Begins," *Business Week* (April 26, 1933), p. 3.

41. *United States Daily News,* April 8–15, 1933.

riod on the Chicago market—from 48 to 58 cents. This rise was attributed to the inflationary proposals, the imminence of the farm-emergency measures, and the poor conditions of the winter wheat crop. Another curious complication was the disparity between the domestic and world price. May wheat at 58 cents in Chicago was actually eight or nine cents higher than wheat in Liverpool.[42]

On May 10 the bill had passed both houses, and on May 12 President Roosevelt signed it.[43] The Agricultural Adjustment Act was an omnibus measure, possessing as predicted "all the earmarks of a document hastily drawn to the specifications of divergent and conflicting groups."[44] The essential features of the act provided for the refinancing of farm mortgages, the raising of farm prices by government controls, and the placing of greater powers in the hands of the President for the purpose of not increasing the quantity of money but decreasing the gold value of the dollar. These three measures were introduced at different times. The first two had the approval of the President, but not the third, which was intended to head off demands for money inflation that came especially from Farmers' Union quarters.[45]

Section two of the A.A.A. declared that its policy was to seek to establish and maintain such a balance between production and consumption as would re-establish farm prices at a level that would give farm commodities a purchasing power equivalent to that commanded over the base period. The original act applied to seven "basic" commodities: wheat, cotton, corn, hogs, rice, tobacco, and milk and its products; and the base period for all these, except tobacco, was the prewar period of August, 1909, to July, 1914. The base period for tobacco—August, 1919, to July, 1929—was selected because, due to the rapid changes in tobacco habits, the prewar period was no longer held to represent conditions in the industry.

Two sets of powers were conferred upon the Secretary of Agriculture, one dealing with voluntary production adjustments through contracts

42. "Wheat Prices," *Business Week* (April 19, 1933), p. 12; "Survey of the Wheat Situation," Food Research Institute, Stanford University, *Wheat Studies,* IX (September, 1933), pp. 369–70.

43. *The Public Papers and Addresses of Franklin D. Roosevelt* (9 vols., New York, 1938), II, 79.

44. *Business Week* (March 29, 1933), p. 3.

45. Davis, *Wheat and the AAA,* p. 30.

and benefit payments to farmers and the other with marketing agreements and licenses. Benefit payments were limited to the producers of the seven basic commodities who voluntarily agreed to adjust their production. These seven commodities were selected because the United States produced "an exportable surplus in nearly all of them, and also because changes in their price strongly influenced all commodities," and because of the belief that they could be regulated more easily in production and distribution since all of them had to go through some manufacturing process before they were ready for human consumption. Farmers who did not sign benefit contracts were at liberty to produce any commodity in any volume that they chose, but they had to meet their problems without direct government aid.

The other group of powers gave the Secretary the authority to enter into marketing agreements with processors. These agreements, inserted chiefly through the efforts of George Peek, could be entered into for all farm products, not merely the seven specified in the case of the benefit payments, and these agreements were to be exempt from the antitrust laws of the country. The agreement, with this exemption, could regulate trade practices, production quotas, prices, supply areas, and the many relationships among various branches of trade. To make effective the terms of marketing agreements, the act authorized the Secretary of Agriculture to grant licenses to processors and distributors and others handling agricultural products or any competing commodities and to revoke such licenses in the event of violation of the terms of the licenses. This is the part that George Peek contributed to the act. Funds were to be obtained to make benefit payments by levying a tax on the first processing of the product, the amount of which was to be equivalent to "the difference between the current farm price for the particular commodity and the fair exchange value of the commodity."[46]

Another important phase of the New Deal program was the establishment of the Farm Credit Administration, which knit together into one unit nearly all of the federal farm credit agencies. Various funds were to be made available to farmers, the money to be provided by the issuance

46. *The Public Papers and Addresses of Franklin D. Roosevelt,* II, 176–79. For data on "Tax Collections and Refunds" for 1933–35, see U. S. Dept. Agri., Agricultural Adjustment Administration, *Agricultural Adjustment, 1933 to 1935* (Washington, 1936), pp. 291–94; Davis, *Wheat and the AAA,* pp. 36–37.

by the Federal Farm Loan Banks of two billion dollars' worth of long-term tax-exempt 4 per cent bonds. As soon as the Farm Credit Administration was created, new credit programs were set up to extend financial aid of one type or another.[47]

By the Thomas amendment, the President could direct the Secretary of the Treasury and the Federal Reserve Banks to purchase federal government bonds in the open market to the extent of $3,000,000,000; the Secretary of the Treasury could issue greenbacks up to the sum of $3,000,000,000 to meet federal obligations that could be retired at a 4 per cent rate of interest; the President could devalue the gold content of the dollar by 50 per cent; and finally, silver could be accepted by the United States Treasury from foreign debtors at fifty cents an ounce up to $200,000,000. Silver certificates could be issued against it in equal amount.[48]

The big difference between the program finally adopted by the administration and the McNary-Haugen and export debenture proposals was that it felt the need for production control. The allotment plan was accepted as "a recognition of the principle that a tariff does not benefit farmers who produce a commodity of which there is an exportable surplus." Since the United States was committed to a high tariff "and since foreign countries [had] turned to almost every conceivable form of restriction—export bounties, licensing systems, import quotas, mixing regulations, importing monopolies, etc.—the domestic allotment plan [was] developed to give the American farmer the benefits of protection for that portion of his produce used domestically." Like the Farm Board, it was nationalistic and its sponsors were willing to concede that economic nationalism had victimized the farmers in the past. Still, nationalism was a world-wide phenomenon and the A.A.A. was looked upon as "a means for equalizing the social costs of adjusting the agricultural plant of the United States to this situation."[49]

47. *Congressional Digest,* XII (June-July, 1933), p. 184; William G. Murray, *Agricultural Finance* (Ames, Iowa, 1941), pp. 191–92.

48. Broadus Mitchell, *Depression Decade* (New York, 1947), pp. 137–38; *Federal Reserve Bulletin,* XIX (June, 1933), pp. 336–37; James D. Paris, *Monetary Policies of the United States, 1932–1938* (New York, 1938), p. 43.

49. Theodore W. Schultz and A. G. Black, "The Voluntary Domestic Allotment Plan," in Staff of the Department of Economics of Iowa State College, *The Agricultural Emergency in Iowa* (Ames, 1933), p. 104.

Chapter XVII

THE NEW DEAL: FIRST PHASES

ONCE the A.A.A. had become law, the United States embarked on a program of unprecedented proportions. Production controls were the most novel—no doubt the most conspicuous—part of it, but inflation, marketing agreements, trade treaties, commodity loans, and cheaper credit facilities were also part of the program. Before the year was over, "pictures, literature by the ton, moving pictures, thousands of columns of newspaper information, hundreds of speakers were used in appealing to millions of farmers" in the largest program ever presented to American agriculture.[1]

The legislation having been passed, the next step was to erect the machinery needed to put the program into action. In this, time was of the essence. Wallace wrote that the passage of the A.A.A. on May 12 left very little time for effective action on 1933 crops. For personnel to man the new machinery, "crude and untried" as it was expected to be, the administration went to those who for "many years had fought for the right to build such machinery." Wallace said, "Soon after the bill was introduced I had sounded out George Peek for the post of administrator, and for other positions of importance, Charles J. Brand, who drafted the first McNary-Haugen bill, Chester C. Davis, first lieutenant to Peek in the farm fight, and M. L. Wilson, the successful evangelist of the domestic allotment plan."

Peek was selected as administrator of the A.A.A. largely because of his experiences as a businessman, his sympathies for the farmers, and his

1. *Minneapolis Journal,* December 31, 1933.

known "aggressiveness." Brand was named coadministrator because of his "familiarity with many agricultural trades, and his encyclopedic knowledge of the processing and distributing as well as production of farm products." He was expected to concern himself especially with marketing agreements and codes. Chester Davis was considered the logical man to have charge of the other principal function—the adjustment of production by agreement with farmers. Finally, M. L. Wilson, because of his intimate knowledge of the wheat problem and the domestic allotment plan, was an immediate choice for the head of the wheat section.

Once the matter of personnel had been decided upon, the next thing to do was to fit together the new machinery. In the process, "the corridors of the Administration Building were crowded with farmers, farm leaders, processors, and reporters, each with dozens of insistent questions, few of which could be answered then and there. . . ." "Those were hectic days," said Wallace. "Somehow we got through them though it was a rare day when an irresistible desire didn't crash into an immovable fact, with heavy damage to frayed nerves." Meanwhile, milk experts and lawyers were drafting marketing agreements, and the wheat and cotton sections prepared for action in their respective areas.

One charge made against the A.A.A. was that it would lead to "gouging" the consumers. Hence, to protect them, "the Adjustment Act had specified that the farmer's share of the consumers' dollar might not exceed the share he got in the base period, 1909–14." To carry this out, the Secretary of Agriculture was to make public his findings concerning the effect of the processing tax on both producers and consumers. Fred C. Howe was appointed as consumers' counsel to keep the public informed of the relation of price increases to increased costs.[2]

The extension system, with the well-known activities of the county agents, became an integral part of the A.A.A. program. The work performed by these agents can no more be minimized than can the support that the American Farm Bureau Federation gave to the national farm program. In fact the functions of these different agencies became so interlocked that it was difficult to distinguish one from the other. Some farmers spoke of the county agent, the A.A.A., and the Farm Bureau as though they were one and the same thing.

2. Henry A. Wallace, *New Frontiers* (New York, 1934), pp. 168–70, 173.

The work of the county agents varied. Much of it was promotional in nature. In many states they "assumed administrative responsibilities for federal programs which not only provided large benefits for farmer cooperation but also provided definite penalties to insure cooperation." They helped to inaugurate the A.A.A. and to see to it that it continued to function. They helped to explain and interpret the act and the constant stream of administrative rules sent from Washington. In some sections the agents added to, and in others they "almost completely replaced, the old type of scientific agricultural projects and readjusted individual farm management work in accordance with a planned agriculture on a national scale."

Once these preliminary meetings had been held, the agents set up the local machinery which administered the program. In carrying out the corn-hog and wheat programs, the county agents often were responsible for the appointment of temporary county committees which in turn either appointed or else made provisions for the selection of township or community committees. At times spokesmen for the Democratic party advised in the appointment of these committees.

These temporary committees were the ones which, under the guidance of the county agents, staged the "sign-up" campaigns and the elections of permanent township committeemen. "The county agent attended most of these election meetings and was responsible for seeing that they were conducted according to Washington rules which not only provided for election by secret ballot but also for the tedious process of nomination by secret ballot." Also, the county agent often served as secretary of the county allotment committee, presumably because of his natural position of leadership. This was not the case, however, in those states in which this was against the policy of the state extension service. Where the sentiment against the Farm Bureau was strong, bitter struggles were waged over the election of the county secretary. Frequently the county agent was made secretary for the sake of economy. Some of the agents used the franking privilege freely in the commodity program. This practice created problems, especially when the material that was sent out by the agents was of a noneducational character.[3]

3. Gladys Baker, *The County Agent* (Chicago, 1939), pp. 69–73; Russell Lord, *The Agrarian Revival* (New York, 1939), pp. 161–66.

Wheat is the crop one normally thinks of first when speaking of the western Middle West, and it became an immediate concern of the A.A.A. The situation called for drastic action, with a wheat carry-over three times normal size and a new crop coming on, with no hope for exportation of this surplus and prices far below parity. One proposal, therefore, was to remove from use in wheat growing enough of the wheat land to be cultivated in the 1933 crop to keep the carry-over down. When the wheat producers and the representatives of the processing and consuming organizations came together to set up their program, there were sharp differences of opinion. Of the proposals presented, the domestic allotment plan was the one that met with the least opposition.

But events soon showed that drastic curtailment methods would not have to be used for 1933. Bad weather indicated that there was going to be a sensational reduction in winter wheat prospects. As expected, the proposal that finally was adopted was the domestic allotment plan for "making payments to each wheat producer on the basis of his proportionate share of the national production that was domestically consumed. In return . . . the producer would agree to reduce his wheat acreage in the 1934 and 1935 crops by such percentage, not to exceed 20 per cent, as the Secretary of Agriculture should determine."

Because bad weather had left thousands of growers with little or nothing to sell from their 1933 crop, it had been decided to make the first payments equal to about two-thirds of the total payment and make them as early that fall as possible. That summer the administration and extension workers began the considerable task of acquainting the growers with the details of the wheat program.[4]

The livestock program lagged behind that for wheat and cotton, chiefly because the latter crops were beginning to mature and prompt action had to be taken. Also, the A.A.A. had a good idea of what to do about commodities like wheat because of the earlier campaigns over the domestic allotment plan, but such was not the case with respect to corn and hogs. There were differences of opinion among administration leaders. Wallace

4. Wallace, *New Frontiers,* pp. 171–72; U. S. Dept. Agri., Agricultural Adjustment Administration, *Agricultural Adjustment, A Report of the Administration of the Agricultural Adjustment Act, May, 1933, to February, 1934* (Washington, 1934), pp. 47–52.

believed that steps had to be taken to relieve the surplus, while Peek thought that the shrinking foreign market and high distribution costs needed attention first. Even though the Wallace viewpoint prevailed, the fact is that these differences delayed the launching of the corn-hog program. Another cause for this late start was that there was no producers' organization to spearhead the indoctrination work in the corn belt; hence time was lost in "orienting" these producers.[5]

Wallace, while on an earlier trip through the Middle West, had suggested that there be developed an agency to work closely with the administration in applying the A.A.A. program to the corn and hog producers. Not much later committees were set up in Iowa, Kansas, Nebraska, South Dakota, Minnesota, Ohio, Illinois, Wisconsin, Indiana, and Missouri which came together in a national meeting in Des Moines on July 18. The job of this conference was to select a national committee of corn and hog producers consisting of twenty-five members, twenty-one of whom were to be selected from the states mentioned and the remaining four by the presiding officer. The delegates said that the farmers were in favor of curtailing production as a means for obtaining parity prices, and to get such a program under way it was agreed that representatives of the Des Moines meeting would confer with agents of the processors in Chicago on July 20.

When the Chicago meeting came together the processors stressed the need for marketing agreements and the finding of new markets. They opposed the processing tax out of fear that a production-adjustment program would tend to depress prices. In fact they looked with disfavor on curtailment of corn and hog production until all chances for enlarging the home and foreign markets had been exhausted.

More conferences led to the adoption of a compromise program. As a concession to the processors, it was agreed that marketing agreements would be encouraged at home and reciprocal trade agreements entered into with foreign countries. As a concession to the producers, it was agreed that two billion pounds of hogs would be taken from the regular market channels and also that controls would be applied in the production of corn and hogs.

Of the ways discussed for reducing the hog tonnage in the 1933–34 mar-

5. D. A. FitzGerald, *Livestock Under the AAA* (Washington, 1935), pp. 52–55.

keting season, the one that asked for the buying up of unfinished pigs and sows soon to farrow carried much favor. This was an unknown practice in the United States, but "pig-buying programs" such as these had been carried out with some success in recent years in several of the European countries, particularly in the Netherlands and Denmark.

It was decided to buy up several million pigs weighing less than a hundred pounds and about one million sows due to farrow in fall. The sows bought were to weigh not less than 275 pounds. As a result of these purchases, it was expected that hog supplies would be reduced from 10 to 15 per cent. The packers were to process and otherwise handle the animals for the Secretary of Agriculture, who, in turn, was to dispose of them as he saw fit.

On August 18 Wallace approved of the plan in an address in Chicago and announced that it would be put into operation on August 23. The authorized processors were to make the purchases and continue to do so until October 1, but the buying could end sooner if the maximum of pigs and sows had been reached. In so far as practicable, the sows were to be converted into salt pork and be distributed among the unemployed by the Federal Emergency Relief Corporation. Pigs weighing more than eighty pounds were to be processed into dry salt pork, and those weighing less than that were to be processed into the inedible products of grease and fertilizer tankage.

As announced, the emergency buying program began on August 23 in six of the principal livestock markets of the Middle West: St. Paul, Sioux City, St. Joseph, Kansas City, Omaha, and Chicago. Buying was to start on other markets as soon as practicable. On the first day the shipments were relatively moderate—about 30,000 pigs and sows—but on the second day there were received more than 100,000 hogs. This was an unusually heavy load. In fact the administration had expected heavy shipments to the six designated markets and hence it had urged farmers who normally did not ship to these points to await the opening of their own markets. These admonitions were of no use. The number of hogs reaching the markets taxed the capacities of the processors to the point of bringing a temporary halt in shipments, at least until they had had the time to dispose of the excess shipments. To check similar future developments, the administration stated that henceforth the shippers would have to obtain permits from the proper authorities before shipments could be made.

No sooner had the surpluses been disposed of and the markets resumed their buying operations than new difficulties were faced. There was a limited number of permits available for each market, and this gave speculators an opportunity to profit: many farmers conceivably could be made to sell at discriminatory terms to dealers who had obtained a large number of permits.

Some farmers lost out for other reasons. There were those who were ignorant of the existence of such a program even after it had been announced. Then there were those who knew nothing of the program that was being devised, and so they sold their hogs at low prices to dealers who bought them in large quantities and disposed of them later at the higher prices provided by the emergency program. But except for some troubles involved in regulating shipments and the control of dealers who bought pigs from farmers at unwarranted prices, the program went off in a fairly satisfactory fashion.[6]

Administration leaders believed that the emergency corn-hog measures adopted would do the producers more harm than good unless a program for production control was adopted. There was little difficulty involved in agreeing on a program for corn reduction through acreage rentals, but differences developed over the methods of curtailing the hog output. Finally, the A.A.A. decided to reduce hog production by requiring each contracting farmer to decrease the number of hogs for sale in 1934 litters to 25 per cent below the number so raised in the average of the 1932 and 1933 litters. On October 17 the main features of the corn-hog program for 1934 were announced.[7]

In the fall of 1933 two supplementary measures were initiated: one consisted of corn loans, prompted chiefly by the sharp decline in corn prices and the agitations of governors in the Middle West who began pressing for price-fixing measures; a second called for the purchase of "fat" hogs for distribution among the needy, a proposal which became feasible when the Federal Surplus Relief Corporation was established in the fall of that year.[8]

6. U. S. Dept. Agri., A.A.A., *A.A.A., May, 1933, to February, 1934*, pp. 103–18.
7. FitzGerald, *Livestock Under the AAA*, pp. 57–59.
8. *Ibid.*, pp. 59–61.

The problems of the dairy producers were also among the most difficult to come before the A.A.A.; the complexities of the industry and the differences of opinion over the remedies to be applied simply added to the confusion.

In May, 1933, a committee of the Bureau of Agricultural Economics that had studied the various means by which the dairy producers could be helped said that the best immediate prospect for helping them was in the marketing of fluid milk. No branch of the industry appeared to favor production-control measures. A committee that had been appointed to study the subject said that "voluntary and individual adjustment through educational methods was preferable, perhaps accompanied by efforts to increase consumption." Marketing agreements were given much attention, but there was little thought given to production-adjustment measures.

By August, 1933, new difficulties faced the administration. The prices of butter and cheese had dropped sharply and action was necessary to keep them up. Late that month a committee representing milk producers and creamery and cheese-factory representatives met with leaders of the administration for this very purpose. Even when faced with this crisis, leaders of the dairy industry were reluctant to advocate production control, preferring instead the stabilization methods that had been used by the Federal Farm Board. This might have been satisfactory to the dairy industry, but it was nothing of the kind in so far as the administration was concerned. The administration favored a program of production controls, but it held the plan in abeyance while the various producers, distributors, and manufacturers arranged their marketing agreements.[9]

By mid-September the administration was knee-deep in troubles. To many what prospects there had been of re-establishing the "Arcadian parity of 1909–1914" had vanished. Among wheat, hog, and dairy producers the problems were pretty much the same. Wheat prices had been rising altogether too slowly to please the growers, while the prices of the goods they bought were going up fast. The corn and hog producers had their troubles too. For a while they had deluged the market with pigs and sows, but when this was over it developed that they had held back "piggy-sows" and had thus endangered the entire program with the probability

9. U. S. Dept. Agri., A.A.A., *A.A.A., May, 1933, to February, 1934,* pp. 152–59.

of a surplus the following year. And the dairy producers had their difficulties. Besides the low prices for cheese and butter, the marketing agreements were being challenged in the courts. The prices that they were getting for milk had gone up, but so did the margins that the distributors received.

The administration was beset with other troubles. At the outset it had conceded that the job it was undertaking was a vast one, faced with numerous obstacles, but there were those who insisted that the administration had promised miracles, as though solving the farm problem were merely a matter of rubbing Aladdin's lamp.[10]

The prices received and paid by the farmers furnish a good barometer of agrarian discontent and the difficulties which faced the administration in 1933. In February of that year the general level of farm prices and their exchange value had dropped to the lowest point on record, 49 per cent of the prewar average. In March the new legislative program was launched. Farm commodity prices improved slightly in March and substantially in April and May. In July there was a sharp speculative advance followed by a reaction. Speculation in wheat, cotton, and other commodities and purchases by mills, consumers, and others accelerated business activity, and prices rose. The sharp business recession came after the middle of July. Still, from mid-March to mid-October there was a net gain of 47 per cent. There was, however, a gain of only 22 per cent in the exchange value of farm products from March to October, somewhat less than had been hoped for because the prices paid by the farmers had advanced considerably.[11]

This rise in nonfarm prices caused the administration no end of trouble. The increase was attributed in large measure to the National Recovery Administration, which was accompanied with rising costs of production for manufactured goods. In September, 1933, the farmers complained that they paid more for their overalls than they did before, that flour cost more, and that one of the big mail-order houses had put into effect a horizontal increase of 20 per cent on farm implements. In South Dakota a good portion of the crop had been laid waste by grasshoppers, and in other states the crops had been cut by the drought. In Nebraska and

10. "Farm Troubles," *Business Week* (September 16, 1933), p. 16.

11. U. S. Dept. Agri., *Yearbook*, 1934, pp. 13, 58; Joseph S. Davis, *Wheat and the AAA* (Washington, 1935), p. 53.

North Dakota the governors came out openly against the N.R.A. and the way it operated there. Hugh S. Johnson, the administrator of N.R.A. admitted that in some instances, particularly in textiles, retail prices had advanced faster than had purchasing power.[12]

Facts substantiated the complaints of farmers that nonfarm prices were rising faster than those for farm products. In many industries wages per hour rose as much as 50 per cent. The manufacturers naturally tried to pass the increase on to the consumers, which included the farmers, and in most instances this is precisely what happened. Between March and October the average advance was more than 17 per cent. Urban wages also rose, and farm wages had to follow suit if the farmers were to compete with city wages. Briefly, agriculture failed to make the progress expected in reducing the disparity between agricultural and nonagricultural prices.[13]

One of the widely heralded objectives of the A.A.A. was to raise commodity prices sufficiently to enable the borrowers to repay their debts "in the same kind of dollar which they borrowed." Monetary reform was considered an essential part of any such recovery. Judging from the series of events which took place, one could have had good reason for expecting this goal to be attained. The abandonment of the gold standard, the prospect of a small North American wheat crop, political pressure for inflation, "a confident spirit from the White House," and a mounting hope on the part of the masses contributed to speed up industrial activity and encourage speculation in various farm commodities, hence to raise prices. But the pronounced business recession which followed after the middle of July caused many to believe that the next big demand of the farmers was going to be for more inflation.

Wallace, however, made it clear that the carrying of inflation beyond the point of establishing parity prices would create fresh injustices. In the fall of 1933 the Secretary cautioned that to depend exclusively on a monetary policy to restore farm incomes was insufficient, because depreciation of the dollar reacted differently on different farm products. Wallace claimed that depreciation of the dollar raised the prices of the export or

12. *Milwaukee Journal*, September 17, 1933; *Christian Century*, L (November 1, 1933), pp. 1355–56.
13. U. S. Dept. Agri., *Yearbook*, 1934, p. 13.

peculative commodities such as wheat, cotton, and corn much more than t did the prices of milk, hogs, beef cattle, poultry, and other nonspecula- ive commodities that were sold primarily on the domestic market. Then here was the fact that inflation raised the prices of things the farmers ought. If anything, the farmers could expect "controlled inflation" to aise farm prices and in this way to lighten the burden of debt and taxes, ut this by itself could not close the gap between agricultural and non- gricultural prices.

The depreciation of the dollar had some significant effects on commodi- ies like cotton, tobacco, and grain, which were influenced by the foreign narket, but hardly any on those that were governed chiefly by local con- litions. Late in October the American dollar was worth only 64.4 cents n terms of French, Dutch, and Swiss moneys. Speculation in commodities ike wheat and cotton, along with the depreciation of the dollar, had a rief stimulating effect on wheat and cotton prices. During the brief reces- ion the prices of these items dropped sharply, but they resumed their up- vard climb in September and October. On the other hand, the prices of roducts sold chiefly in the domestic market did not advance greatly, ex- ept in cases like potatoes in which the supplies were greatly reduced. In October, 1933, beef-cattle prices were about as low as they were in March, nd in terms of gold and purchasing power they were decidedly lower.

The domestic price of wheat reacted differently from that which was ased on the British currency. Beginning early in April and continuing nto the third week of July, the price of wheat in Chicago in terms of he dollar rose 84 per cent. Wheat prices in Chicago during the fourth veek of October were 48 per cent higher, in terms of the dollar, than hey had been during the first half of April, but in Liverpool they were 1 per cent lower than they had been during that same period.

In 1933 Wallace had something to say about raising the price of gold nd the likely effects of such a policy on farm prices. It would not, he felt, ave any great effect for some time on livestock and dairy prices, which lepended more on payrolls in the United States than on foreign markets. Still, he ventured to predict that raw-material prices would rise to the xtent to which the gold in the dollar was reduced. Also, he believed that vhat favorable influence our monetary policy would have on cotton and vheat could not continue if the foreign countries reduced the gold content of their currencies as rapidly as did the United States. Currency policies could stimulate foreign trade for a brief period, but they could not create the foreign demand that the reduction of tariff barriers could.[14]

Among the severest critics of the administration was the Farm Holiday Association, which appeared to have had a degree of influence on some of the lawmakers of the western Middle West. Its leaders were so taken up with the ideas behind the N.R.A. that they wanted them extended to agriculture; in fact, leaders of the movement had been busy drafting a code to submit to the directors of the holiday association, who were to assemble in Des Moines on September 22. This code was based on the "cost of production" demands of the association, which would seek to establish a net income for farmers, reduce their working hours, eliminate destructive trade practices, and adjust general farm prices to living costs. One Farm Holiday spokesman was quoted as saying that "if N.R.A. has moved in to stay, I'm going to fix up a room for A.P.C.—Agricultural Production Cost. If the industrialist is entitled to cost of production, and the law says he is, so is the farmer."[15]

In North Dakota opposition to the A.A.A. and the attempt to get cost of production for the farmers took a not unexpected turn. In mid-October Governor William Langer announced that because of the sudden drop in wheat prices and the rise in prices of commodities that the farmers bought, he would act in accordance with the recently enacted law which empowered him to declare an embargo on any commodity selling below the cost of production. Notice was served upon the President, Wallace, and Johnson that this embargo would go into effect immediately unless minimum prices were fixed or unless more effective measures were taken to lift prices. In this fashion Langer had hoped to tie up some fifty or sixty million bushels of wheat, and even threatened to call out the troops to enforce the embargo on this and other commodities.[16]

Langer, hoping that the embargo would spread to other states, sent letters to a half-dozen other governors asking them to join him, but the replies that he received were hardly encouraging. Olson of Minnesota questioned both his authority to declare such an embargo and the effective-

14. *Ibid.*, pp. 59–60.

15. Quoted in the *Milwaukee Journal*, September 14, 21, 1933.

16. *Pioneer Press* (St. Paul), October 16, 17, 1933; *St. Paul Dispatch*, October 16, 1933.

ness of such action, yet said that he would not hesitate to join in such a move if the other governors did. Governor Tom Berry of South Dakota expressed sympathy, but refrained from so acting because he lacked the authority. Governor Clyde Herring of Iowa said that he had no intention of proclaiming an embargo, and Governor Charles Bryan of Nebraska declined to comment after his attorney general said that he lacked the authority.

The Langer embargo placed the railroads in a quandary. If they defied it, they would be in for a first-class legal and political battle with the state administration and a large faction of the farmers who supported Langer; besides they would be accused of playing the game of the grain trade, which was so roundly hated in the state. On the other hand, if the roads sat back and awaited action by the grain trade to break the embargo, their yards would be choked with blocked cars, liabilities for delayed shipments would arise, and a mass of litigation would result.[17]

It was hard to see just what good such an embargo would bring, other than to focus more attention on the well-known plight of the farmers. After all, wheat was a standard world crop and the withdrawal of the ouput of one state would have little effect on prices. It was estimated that about 45 per cent of all the wheat already had been sold for the season and that North Dakota was likely to be in for more difficulties because it did not have a large enough local market to absorb its crop.[18]

Meanwhile, the presidents of the four railroads shipping wheat notified Governor Langer that they would be forced, under the Interstate Commerce Act, to accept wheat for shipment and to transport it despite the embargo. In fact North Dakota wheat was beginning to move into Minnesota when the adjutant general's office started to make plans to use the national guard.[19]

About a month later North Dakota lifted its ban on out-of-state shipments of durum for a period of six days, but the embargo on spring wheat continued. The reason given for this action was that durum prices had risen to the point at which the Canadian product could be shipped into the United States, even with the tariff of forty-two cents on it, and still be

17. *Pioneer Press,* October 18, 1933.
18. *Ibid.,* October 17, 1933; *St. Paul Dispatch,* October 17, 1933.
19. *Ibid.,* October 19, 1933.

able to compete with that of the North Dakota producers. Concern over this had forced commission firms and millers to threaten to buy the Canadian product. This, plus other troubles, had caused many North Dakotans to want to sell their wheat. But at the same time that the ban on durum was taken off, Langer announced that he was willing to extend the embargo to livestock, poultry, and other commodities if the other governors would join him.[20]

As was expected, the legality of the embargo was tested in the federal courts. The defense for the State of North Dakota charged that the legislative act authorizing the embargo was based on the police power, but to no avail. Early in 1934 the United States District Court declared that the embargo had the effect of regulating interstate commerce and hence was unconstitutional, because that power rested with Congress and not with the individual states.[21]

Opposition to the A.A.A. took still another form early in November when five governors from the western Middle West appeared in Washington and submitted a program calling for price fixing and immediate inflation. The governors unanimously favored the licensing of farmers, processors, and distributors to bring about higher prices, and also to strengthen the production-control program. Governor Olson of Minnesota recommended that agriculture be "handled as a public utility, as voluntary action to curtail production cannot succeed as long as a substantial number of farmers do not voluntarily join in the program."[22] Milo Reno and his followers endorsed the proposals of the governors and threatened to take drastic action if the administration failed to respond to their recommendations. Reno was willing to place the blame for whatever happened on Wallace and roundly denounced the A.A.A. as a plan that sought to "make dole takers and mendicants of the farmers."[23]

After three days of conferences between the governors and the President and the Department of Agriculture, the White House issued the following statement:

20. *Ibid.*, November 17, 1933.
21. *Ibid.*, January 15, 1934.
22. Quoted in the *Milwaukee Journal*, November 2, 1933.
23. *Ibid.*, November 4, 1933.

The governors wish the federal government immediately to license all handlers and processors of agricultural products to pay fair exchange value, a price which on the average is 70 per cent above that now prevailing. To enforce the immediate adoption of such a price, in view of the inability of the city consumers to take present quantities of farm products at such a price, the governors advocated compulsory control of marketing so that each farmer would have a definite quota to sell each month, thus backing up on the farm the products which could not be sold at fair exchange values.[24]

The governors, it was said, wanted to put over "a program which amounts substantially to the licensing of every plowed field and marketing by a ticket punch system of all grain and livestock."

The administration felt that if the farmers of the western Middle West were willing to accept a type of regimentation that was under the combined leadership of the federal and state governments, there was no certainty that the proposal would be acceptable in states such as Ohio, Pennsylvania, and New York, where large quantities of food were also produced and where the large city population would make it very difficult to deliver the cooperation that was needed to make such a plan successful. Then there was the question of whether the eastern and southern farmers would be willing to submit to the regimentation proposed by the five governors, who were anxious to extend the plan to other crops.

Frankly, the administration was worried over these demands, but it was of the opinion that the flow of cash into the corn and hog belt would quiet down the farmers. "There has been no opportunity as yet to send out checks to the corn and wheat regions of the west and northwest. The wheat checks are now beginning to move and the corn-hog benefit checks will begin to flow out into the country about January. Corn loan money will become available within a few weeks. . . ."[25]

Once the federal administration had rejected the demand of the governors for "cost of production," the leaders of the Farm Holiday Association ordered a major offensive. About that time the administration advised that Secretary of Agriculture Wallace make a "peace-making" tour in behalf of the N.R.A. and the A.A.A.[26] On November 11, 1933, Wallace spoke in Des Moines, Iowa. There he admitted that farm prices had

24. *Ibid.*, November 5, 1933.
25. *Ibid.*
26. *Ibid.*, November 6, 1933.

failed to reach the desired levels; still he felt that some progress had been made, even though the improvement was not uniform and the rate of progress in many areas was inadequate to prevent acute distress. The farm holiday group, "the hell-raising boys" with whom he had "never seen eye to eye," he tossed into the same obstructionist category as the "reactionaries." Wallace said that one reason why he had come out to Iowa was to determine whether the farmers of the corn belt were ready for production and marketing controls.

If they are, new legislation will be necessary; the existing laws, I am quite convinced, will not permit the methods the governors have in mind. It would be necessary, apparently, to declare agriculture a public utility, and then to begin the truly staggering task of deciding which farmers should have certificates of public convenience and necessity, of telling farmers whether they would be permitted to farm at all, what crops they might grow, how they might plant, and how, when and where they might market them; of requiring from each of the six and one-half million farmers in the United States detailed, periodic reports of receipts and expenditures and inventories; and finally, of checking up on each of these reports with appropriate frequency. That sort of thing is involved in all public utility regulation, and I presume agriculture could not be any exception.[27]

In place of this the administration offered its corn-hog and monetary programs and announced the forty-five-cent per bushel loan on wheat.

By early December cash started to roll into the Middle West under the corn-hog program. The forty-five-cent loans per bushel on corn stored on the farm were being made at the rate of $100,000 a day, and the prediction was that this soon would rise to $1,000,000 a day. Such loans were advanced only to farmers who agreed to sign for corn and hog reductions.[28]

Late in December, the program was moving along at a rapid pace. Loans were being made in volume in states such as Nebraska, Illinois, Minnesota, and South Dakota which had warehouse laws and which permitted borrowing on corn stored on the farm. Missouri was reported in the process of taking action to establish a farm-warehouse system. As a result, the corn market stiffened and cash actually was flowing into the corn-belt states. Curiously enough, this program was giving the farmers

27. *Wallaces' Farmer and Iowa Homestead,* LVIII (November 25, 1933), p. 5.
28. *Ibid.* (December 9, 1933), p. 3.

a chance to borrow at more than the market price on corn and still retain their corn to sell at a higher price in the event that the acreage-reduction program succeeded.[29]

More difficulties were in store for the administration when late in 1933 a smoldering revolt that had been going on within the A.A.A. broke into the wide-open. It involved Administrator George N. Peek and his brain-trust wing headed by Assistant Secretary of Agriculture Rexford G. Tugwell and Jerome Frank, an urban liberal and counsel for the A.A.A. Peek, whose protests found wide support among the conservative opponents of the New Deal, was a man who had no use for abstractions, no stomach for theories. He wanted facts. Some believed that because he was "a connoisseur of facts," he furnished a valuable balance to Wallace, "the professors and the economists." Peek also had been an implement manufacturer and this no doubt had much to do with his seeing the problems of the farmers as being largely those of finding a market. While Wallace surrounded himself with "the professors and the economists," Peek surrounded himself with farm lobbyists from the Middle West. Much of the lack of sympathy between the two men stemmed from this fact. The chief complaint by Peek was that the liberal wing was delaying the approval of all marketing codes and was insisting on making it "field day" for socialism and social planning. The breach between Peek and the Tugwell-Frank group had been mounting ever since June, 1933, when Wallace sided with Chester Davis and M. L. Wilson in favor of controlling production.[30]

Wallace, himself, was skeptical over arbitrary code and marketing agreements.

Codes are all right for industry, business and wages. The NRA codes will work, but in meeting problems of the farmer and the consumer of foodstuffs, we are faced with the fundamental law of supply and demand. By imposing these agreements on the production of foodstuffs which force prices out of line with supply and demand, we are exerting the same kind of pressure that the prohibition law did and we are creating the same bootlegging condition.[31]

29. *Ibid.* (December 23, 1933), p. 3.
30. Edwin G. Nourse, Joseph S. Davis, and John D. Black, *Three Years of the Agricultural Adjustment Administration* (Washington, 1937), pp. 81–82; *Minneapolis Journal,* December 6, 1933; *Fortune,* IX (January, 1934), p. 61.
31. *Minneapolis Journal,* December 7, 1933.

It was the emergency that had forced Peek to accept the curtailment program, which he did very reluctantly. His instincts, like those of most farmers, rebelled against the destruction of foodstuffs. His heart was not in it. An old McNary-Haugenite, he turned to codes and marketing agreements through which prices and trade practices would be regulated. Peek believed that the government should maintain prices at home and help the farmer dispose of his surpluses in the foreign market.

As the A.A.A. began to establish its machinery, various groups submitted codes concerned with the food industries. More than four thousand of these had been filed when the President decided to transfer from the A.A.A. to the N.R.A. all codes save those which had to do with the first steps in processing. In connection with these, differences had arisen over the degree of governmental participation in enforcing them and also over whether the agreements would have the desired effect of keeping up the price paid the farmer for his product. Wallace, Peek, and Tugwell all had a hand in formulating the agreements, but Peek had most faith in them.

A sharper conflict arose over the question of governmental control, notably in the meat-packing agreement. The Tugwell group, it was said, wanted the packers' books kept open for federal inspection, to which Peek agreed, provided that they were kept open only for the verification of reports and not for the staging of "fishing expeditions" in that or any other industry. This conflict stirred up "the battered ghost of 'rugged individualism' and the degree to which business men should be permitted to 'run their own business.' "[32]

As 1933 turned into 1934 the A.A.A. found more difficulties tossed into its lap. No sooner had the forty-five-cent loans on corn been made than "the rash broke out in new spots. Trying to feed 45¢ corn to $3 hogs or to $5 beef cattle and come out even was a headache in itself."[33] Beef-cattle men had opposed having their industry included among the basic commodities when the list was drafted in the spring of 1933, partly because they feared that a processing tax would react against the market price; but now they had undergone a change in heart.[34]

32. *New York Times,* December 17, 1933; see Nourse, Davis, and Black, *Three Years of the A.A.A.,* pp. 44–45, 218–19.

33. "The Sorrows of the AAA," *Business Week* (December 23, 1933), p. 18.

34. *Minneapolis Journal,* January 2, 1934.

The dairy industry was in a bad way. Curtailed milk consumption had forced conversion of big surpluses into butter, and prices had fallen to the lowest levels in years. This forced the A.A.A. to deal with the butter problem in the manner of the deceased Farm Board. Butter had dropped to fifteen cents by mid-December, when Wallace finally disclosed that 46,000,000 pounds had been purchased and bids were in for 15,000,000 more by December 28. At the same time, the dairy interests continued their protests against the competitive products—particularly coconut oil, and other vegetable, animal, and marine oils—which were coming in duty free and were "hogging the market." They said that it was futile "to reduce butter production by the various proposed schemes when the American consumer can readily turn to a cheap and adequate substitute." This created a difficult position for Wallace, who believed in a low tariff so that foreign nations could be put into a position to pay for our agricultural products, for here he ran squarely into the opposition of the butter interests, who favored not only the retention but also the extension of the protective system.[35]

In March, 1934, the governors of Wisconsin, Iowa, and Minnesota attended another farm-relief conference held in Des Moines. Inspired by the Farmers' Union and the Farm Holiday Association, they repeated that the A.A.A. program was a failure and that a more realistic approach to the farm problem was necessary. Again, "cost of production" was asked for all commodities, and compulsory production controls were demanded for all as soon as a majority of the farmers had signed agreements. Governor Olson of Minnesota was designated to present the demands of the conference to the administration.[36]

Early in the spring of 1934, before the drought began, sharp differences developed over the administration's plan to remove unprofitable lands from cultivation. This move was in effect a criticism of past practices which had encouraged people to farm submarginal lands. It seems that the government was beginning to put into operation what the Indians had known many years earlier: "where nature had eliminated the tall grasses very little profitable farming could be done." This was the beginning of a program to transplant farmers from submarginal, or unprofit-

35. *Business Week* (December 23, 1933), p. 18.
36. *Pioneer Press,* March 12, 1934; *Minneapolis Journal,* March 12, 1934.

able lands to new and profitable ones which were irrigated or else had ample rainfall and sufficient tall grasses.

This was no mean program. Obviously, the government would have to buy out the poor land before the farmer could be induced to move from it. But once the farmer had sold his land, the question was where would he go? Then, too, if the government purchased his land, what would it do with it?

Opposition to such a program was to be expected. Some western newspapers had already started a campaign of opposition, charging that if the government went ahead and purchased this kind of land in states like South Dakota, there probably would not be enough people left in some of the counties to continue with the county form of government. Then there was the matter of taxation after these submarginal lands had been taken out of cultivation; where would the revenues that these lands formerly contributed come from? Also, there was bound to be a strong psychological reaction on the part of the people involved. These people "despite the lack of rainfall, lean prices and the devastations of grasshoppers [had] through the years managed somehow to build towns, obtain homes and educate their children," and probably would be unwilling to leave the regions to which they were sentimentally attached.[37]

After one year of the New Deal, it came as no surprise that critics began to pass judgment on the accomplishments and the shortcomings of the A.A.A. It was observed that many who cooperated with the A.A.A. were for it, but there was a very strong undercurrent of resentment evident on the part of a sizable number of others. Many who were opposed to it did not criticize it openly, partly on the theory that they did not want to handicap the administration in its experimental efforts until a sufficient amount of time had passed "to demonstrate the futility or the success of attempting to legislate prosperity into agriculture." Others were open and more pointed in their criticisms. Some farmers who had been practicing soil fertility on their own were being penalized because they were curtailing the output after their own fashion and not after that prescribed by the A.A.A. Complaints were also registered that benefit payments were going to the large speculative farmers who were in part responsible for the excessive production, while the small producers were carrying the

37. *New York Times,* April 1, 1934.

brunt of the program. Likewise, the plan for taking millions of acres out of cultivation was not accepted as a sound one, because by better and more intensive methods of cultivation of the land being planted, the anticipated effects from acreage curtailment could easily be offset. The question was also raised whether the curtailment program would lead to an increase in the number of unemployed in the rural areas who would of necessity be thrown onto the already overburdened relief agencies. Others felt that the costs of the program were excessive and that the heavy taxes that were being imposed to finance the New Deal would retard recovery.

One would be uncharitable indeed to deny that the A.A.A. had something constructive to offer, because it did, and along lines that were novel and difficult to measure. It helped make farmers a little more conscious of conditions in other parts of the country and the world; it sought to impress the farmers with the need for keeping farm records, a not insignificant effort; it helped increase the amount of land converted to pasturage and soil-building crops; it gave the farmers some additional insight into the intricacies of marketing; and it demonstrated the value of cooperation in the realm of public affairs.[38]

Meanwhile, the county agents, who had played such a big role in carrying out the provisions of the A.A.A., were being subjected to a barrage of criticism. Such protests came not merely from farm groups who in later years contemptuously referred to this alignment as the "Farm Bureau-Extension Axis," but from others as well who opposed the multiple activities that the agents engaged in. Very early in the New Deal program, one caustic critic observed:

> The county agent, created for a good and laudable purpose, has been revamped into a tool for politicians. His original duties have been forgotten and today, in addition to being the local representative of political machines, he is in many instances the active competitor of the local elevator, the retail feed dealer, the retail coal merchant and practically every other merchant and enterprise in the community. He is the advance guard of every type of farm relief measure and an educator has been turned into that of a rural ward-healer [*sic*]. . . .[39]

38. *Weekly Kansas City Star*, May 15, 1934.

39. *Co-operative Manager and Farmer* (Minneapolis), XXII (April, 1933), p. 11. For an added attack against the county agent system, see *ibid.*, pp. 14–15.

Likewise, it seems that rivalry between farm organizations broke out anew because of the launching of the A.A.A. In the states in which the rivalry was keen, "it was generally assumed that the county agent was at least morally supporting the side of the active county farm bureau." Some idea of the extent of the influence of the farm organizations may be gathered from the fact that in states like Iowa, Illinois, and New York about 85 per cent of the township and county committeemen were members of the Farm Bureau. The large-scale farm bureau representation was attributed to the claim that the more capable members belonged to the organization. Where the influence of the Farm Bureau was great, it was usual for it to claim "considerable credit for the enactment of the A.A.A. In these states nonfarm bureau members often felt a moral obligation to become members and promoters of the county farm-bureau organization."[40]

During the summer of 1934 the *Christian Science Monitor* carried a series of articles based on interviews with undesignated representatives—presumably professors and extension workers—from agricultural colleges in the Middle West. These academicians tended to substantiate and amplify the findings of the newspapermen. Marked differences were noted on the matter of restricting the output and taking land out of cultivation. Those who upheld production controls felt that they were needed to give the farmers security and also to make the necessary adjustments to the shrinking foreign demand for our products. Others were skeptical, and presented these objections: such controls involved too much compulsion, the danger inherent in political direction, too much dependence on government, introduction of bureaucracy into farming, a danger of food shortage, and the denial of necessities to millions; the program was futile; it made for national isolation and was too expensive; and in addition the idea of the artificial creation of scarcity was a fallacy. One professor hastened to remind the interviewing reporter that nothing in the past had hastened the reduction of output as much as did low prices; they were a slow but an effective way of bringing it about.

The proposal for a national land-use program found much support; but, as in other matters, there were differences over how this was to be

40. Baker, *The County Agent*, p. 73.

put into operation. One professor pointed out that planning needed much educational effort behind it if it was going to work—to the point of educating the planners themselves on the matter of planning. But once such a plan had been put into operation, there would be abundant information available. More nearly accurate information would be available on the kind of products needed, the amounts and grades needed of each, and the areas in which these products could be produced to best advantage. Such a plan would go a long way toward working off the ill effects of a national land policy that had been concerned only with the transferring of land from public to private ownership as rapidly as possible, with no thought being given to distributing land in units of sufficient size to establish an economic enterprise and no attention being devoted to the use which the settlers would make of this land.[41]

Perhaps nothing better demonstrated the barriers that faced the A.A.A. than did the severe drought of 1934, which blanketed nearly three-fourths of the country and was described as being of unprecedented proportions in the history of the nation.[42]

> Vegetation refuses to grow. Streams have stopped running. Springs, never before failing in the memory of early settlers, are dry. Trees, with leaves blighted, shriveling and falling with every gust of furnace hot air, produce little or no shade.
>
> Cattle, starved for proper nourishment, refuse to put on flesh. Clouds will not form in the skies, or, if they form, refuse to disgorge any moisture. Soil, turned to dust, drifts over once fertile grazing lands, unrestrained by grass roots that are brittle and crumbling.
>
> Only the sun refuses to strike and he works overtime, producing almost unbelievable heat. Some idea of it can be gained from Wednesday's announcement of the Topeka (Kans.) weather observer, who said that only twice in 27 days has the temperature failed to reach 98 degrees, only four times has it fallen below 70 degrees at night.
>
> And if you consider the last week alone the average daily maximum temperature has been 107 degrees. Temperature maximums in scattered communities have been 114 degrees often, sometimes as high as 117 degrees.
>
> The produce truck has been replaced on the highways by the waterwagon.

41. *Christian Science Monitor,* August 9–12, 1934.

42. U. S. Dept. Agri., Agricultural Adjustment Administration, *Agricultural Adjustment in 1934, A Report of Administration of the Agricultural Adjustment Act, February 15, 1934, to December 31, 1934* (Washington, 1935), pp. 17–19.

There is little produce to ship but farmers are trying feverishly to keep stock alive. And many are failing.[43]

The western Middle West was in the very midst of this. The first stage of the drought centered about the Dakotas and Minnesota and was the nadir of a series of downward trends in the rainfall in the area. For North Dakota, South Dakota, Nebraska, and Minnesota, the five-year average of rainfall, up to the end of 1933, was 19 inches, while for the five years ending with 1909, at the time of the last maximum phase in this area, the average was 24.1 inches, or 27 per cent greater. Early in May, 1934, in North Dakota "29 counties reported the 'drought of 1933 not yet broken'; 17 counties reported 'crops destroyed'; 34 counties reported 'dust storms' seriously affecting crops and livestock; 32 counties reported 'no feed'; and 13 counties reported 'stock dying.' Other counties reported 'crops suffering'; 'seeding stopped because of windstorms'; 'insects ravaging crops'; and 'dire need for human food.' Similar reports came from Minnesota, South Dakota, and eastern Montana, and later from many other quarters." By late fall of 1934 the wheat crop was only half the average size, the corn crop was the smallest in forty years, the barley crop the smallest in thirty-four years, and the production of oats, rye, and buckwheat the smallest in more than half a century.[44]

One of the first worries of the farmers was the replenishment of seed stocks. A large part of the surplus from the previous year had moved into commercial channels, or was being fed, before it was realized that on many farms the 1934 crop would not return even the amount of seed planted. More acute was the feed and water shortage, which made it impossible for many farmers to carry their cattle any longer. Water had to be shipped in, new wells were dug, and old ones were sunk deeper with the aid of the Federal Relief Emergency Adminstration to meet the water needs of the farmers. The feed situation was such that the farmers either had to rush their stock to market in unfinished condition and without regard to prices, or leave the animals to die of thirst and starvation. Some farmers had hoped that the drought would be broken and that it would not be necessary for them to disburse their stock. This was in vain. "In the areas where conditions were most acute, many of the cattle were so

43. *Milwaukee Journal,* July 19, 1934.

44. U. S. Dept. Agri., A.A.A., *Agricultural Adjustment in 1934,* pp. 17–19.

thin and emaciated that they could not withstand the shipment to market. Even if it had been possible for them to get them to market, they would have been condemned as unfit for human food because of their extreme emaciation." This forced liquidation of meat animals reached a great volume and forced down the prices of all animals.[45]

In some communities special prayer days were set aside by church and government officials. In South Dakota and North Dakota frantic farmers were reported moving their cattle by railroad, truck, and hoof into Minnesota, thus crowding out Minnesota livestock, much to the dismay of the authorities of that state, who ordered the national guard to check all such shipments. In the neighboring state of Wisconsin, farmers complained that Minnesota farmers were doing the very same thing that the farmers from the Dakotas were doing.[46] In Emporia, Kansas, the city fathers put into effect a "four-inch bath" decree.[47] Tragic though the results were, the *Milwaukee Journal* well pointed out that "the drought is doing what the agricultural program apparently was failing to do. . . ."[48]

One thing that aroused the ire of the agricultural authorities in Washington was the fact that some farmers were being led to believe that the drought came in retribution for the human destruction of the crop.[49]

Fortunately, this serious crisis found the United States better prepared for such eventualities than ever before in its history, because there had been established emergency agencies with broad and flexible powers to meet any critical situation that arose. The broad policy of the A.A.A. was to maintain the farm income and buying power, not merely for the sake of the farmers alone but also for the general recovery of the nation. Farm production was to be kept in reasonable balance. As a result, drought-relief operations were well under way by the end of May.

As the emergency agencies were put into action, President Roosevelt and Congress prepared for additional action to carry the program through to a successful conclusion. Some $525,000,000 was voted by Congress to be distributed among the various agencies cooperating in the relief program. The President's Drought Relief Committee was appointed for

45. *Ibid.*, p. 20.
46. *Milwaukee Journal,* May 20, June 2, 3, 9, 1934.
47. *St. Paul Dispatch,* August 11, 1934.
48. *Milwaukee Journal,* June 1, 1934.
49. *Minneapolis Journal,* July 30, 1934.

this purpose. The participating agencies included the A.A.A., the F.C.A., the F.E.R.A., and the C.C.C. The responsibilities entrusted to these agencies ranged all the way from the purchase of surplus livestock, feeds, and seeds, the continuation of rental and benefit payments, and the modification of acreage contracts to the granting of emergency loans, reforestation, and other measures "to conserve moisture, prevent wind erosion, and to minimize the effects of future drought."[50]

Of the more than $102,744,455 spent in the United States at the end of 1934 for the emergency purchase of cattle, almost half the sum was spent in the western Middle West. The hardest-hit states in the area were North and South Dakota, Missouri, Kansas, Nebraska, and Minnesota, in the order mentioned. The only state to exceed North Dakota in cattle purchases was the giant state of Texas, whose wealth exceeded that of North Dakota by many times.[51]

The effect of the weather on production was well shown during 1933–34. For instance, in 1933 acreage reduction for wheat was unnecessary because the unfavorable weather had already restricted the crop.[52] At the end of 1934 the problem of oversupply had disappeared for the time being for wheat, tobacco, corn, and hog products. The wheat carry-over for 1935 was not expected to be much beyond the normal 125,000,000 bushels as compared with the almost 400,000,000 bushels at the start of the 1932–33 season. Hog production, because of the drought, was lower than planned under the A.A.A. This adjustment was not a controlled adjustment, admitted the A.A.A., because there was no regulation of the acres brought into cultivation, but rather an adjustment that was brought about by the weather, over which man had little or no control.[53]

One of the features of the 1934 wheat program was the development of a compliance-checking plan whereby it would be possible to determine whether the farmers were complying with the terms of their adjustment contracts. This task was accomplished through the wheat-allotment committees that were established in each of the counties. Each county committee checked and certified the compliance of the cooperating farmers in its own county. Farmers and other local people in each county were

50. U. S. Dept. Agri., A.A.A., *Agricultural Adjustment in 1934*, pp. 20–23.
51. *Ibid.*, p. 31.
52. *Ibid.*, p. 4.
53. *Ibid.*, p. 13.

named as supervisors to measure fields, the measurements in turn being subject to sample checks by trained surveyors; but the major portion of the work was performed by the cooperating farmers.

The weather again affected the 1935 crop. There was a severe outbreak of black-stem rust in the spring wheat area in July, which during that month alone reduced the prospective crop by more than 100,000,000 bushels.

The acreage reduction for 1935 was set at 10 per cent in the fall of 1934, and the winter wheat producers cooperated on this basis. By March 20, 1935, the A.A.A. had to announce a modification of the 10 per cent planting restriction because drought and dust storms had hit the winter wheat areas severely. "Growers under contract were permitted to plant up to 165 per cent of their base acreage for 1935 under the terms of a supplementary agreement in which the farmers agreed to make corresponding reductions in their plantings for the 1936 crop." This arrangement affected the spring wheat growers in particular.

The first wheat-adjustment program had been planned on a three-year basis. As the end of the period approached, a nation-wide referendum was held among the wheat growers on May 25 to determine whether they wanted to follow up the first program with another one when the 1935 crop year was over. The poll was preceded by a series of discussion meetings among farmers in all communities where wheat was grown on a commercial basis. The vote was open to all farmers who had signed contracts. Of the 466,720 farmers voting, 404,417 voted in favor of continuing the program. Better than half of the ballots cast were from the states of the western Middle West, where the overwhelming majority of the farmers voted for a continuation of the program. The greatest popularity of the program was in North Dakota. Kansas cast more votes against the program than any other single state.[54]

Referenda were also held among the corn and hog growers at the end of the 1934 and 1935 contract periods on whether to enter another year of the program. Of the 389,139 corn-hog farmers voting in October, 1934, 67 per cent favored continuing it. One year later, with cheap and abundant feed and with small or no increase in the number of livestock on

54. U. S. Dept. Agri., Agricultural Adjustment Administration, *Agricultural Adjustment, 1933 to 1935* (Washington, 1936), pp. 153–56.

hand, the corn-hog producers were 6 to 1 in favor of the program. Some 816,891 votes were for and 127,091 against. The bulk of the total vote was cast by the farmers of the western Middle West, and the states having the largest vote both for and against the program were also found in the area.[55]

The New Deal farm credit program began with the creation of the Farm Credit Administration by an executive order submitted to Congress by the President on March 27 and made effective on May 27, 1933. This measure called for the consolidation into one organization of "the powers and functions" of all the federal agencies dealing with farm credit. These included absorption by the F.C.A. of the functions of the Federal Farm Loan Board and the Federal Farm Board (except those relating to the stabilization operations), those duties of the Reconstruction Finance Corporation that related to the management of the regional agricultural credit corporations, and the functions of the crop-production and seed-loan offices of the United States Department of Agriculture. The Farm Credit Act of 1933, along with the Emergency Farm Mortgage Act, increased the resources of the existing lending agencies and provided for the creation of new ones.[56]

The Farm Credit Administration had two important functions to perform: one was to cope with the emergency that faced the farmers, and the second was to create a permanent but complete unified system of farm credits to meet the needs of the farmers at the lowest cost consistent with sound business practices. Farm-mortgage relief was provided. Long-term loans were to be obtained as previously "by first mortgages on farm real estate for amounts not in excess of 50 per cent of the appraised value of the land plus 20 per cent of the appraised value of the permanent insured improvements." For cases involving special risks and the refinancing of indebtedness too large to be covered, there was provided a supplementary fund of $800,000,000. The extent of the refinancing job undertaken by the F.C.A. was made evident by the fact that 905,299 applications were made for mortgage loans between May 1, 1933, and December 31, 1934. These applications were equivalent to about one-seventh of all the farms

55. *Ibid.*, p. 176.
56. *First Annual Report of the Farm Credit Administration, 1933* (Washington 1934), p. 4.

in the United States.[57] Of this number better than 360,000, or more than one-third of the applicants, were from the nine states of the western Middle West. The greatest number of applications from any single state were filed by the farmers of Iowa—52,299. This figure even exceeded that of Texas, where the applications numbered 50,188. Next in order were Minnesota with 45,754; Wisconsin with 45,335; North Dakota, 45,239; Kansas, 41,593; and Illinois, 38,177. On the basis of applications filed, the farmers of the western Middle West were definitely among the most numerous as well as the hardest pressed.[58] About 90 per cent of the total amount actually lent was used to liquidate prior indebtedness.[59]

Help was also extended to indebted farmers through agreements to reduce the amount of their claims. From May 1, 1933, through December 31, 1934, there was an aggregate scaling-down of Federal Land Bank loans that amounted to about $75,000,000. There were also interest reductions, extensions, and deferred payments on Federal Land Bank loans. The F.C.A. encouraged the state governors to set up farm-adjustment committees to handle cases of excessive indebtedness that were submitted to them either by debtors or creditors; settlements were negotiated without resorting to foreclosures. Committees were organized in more than 2,700 counties in forty-four states and handled successfully over 40,000 cases involving about $200,000,000 of principal indebtedness. Short-term credit was provided, and production-credit associations were organized to serve all parts of the United States and to take the place of the twelve regional agricultural credit corporations set up in the fall of 1932. Emergency crop and drought loans were made available to farmers who could not offer adequate security.[60]

Besides these emergency financing measures, there was developed a complete and permanent credit system for farmers. These lending institutions were divided into three groups: long-term credit, short-term production credit, and credit for farmers' cooperative buying and selling organizations. Long-term loans were secured by first mortgages on farm real estate, and were available through the twelve Federal Land Banks

57. *Second Annual Report of the Farm Credit Administration, 1934* (Washington, 1935), pp. 2–3.

58. *Ibid.*, p. 92. These figures are from Table 2 in the appendix.

59. *Ibid.*, p. 3.

60. *Ibid.*, pp. 4–6.

and more than 5,000 national farm-loan associations. These had been organized under the Federal Farm Loan Act of 1916 and were incorporated into the F.C.A. in 1933. Short-term credit was secured by chattel mortgages or crop liens through nearly 600 production-credit associations established in 1933. These local associations were organized and supervised by the twelve production-credit corporations. Finally, credit was provided the farmers' cooperative associations through the establishment of a central bank and twelve district banks for cooperatives. The banks for cooperatives extended long-term credit, and the Federal Intermediate Credit Banks extended short-term credit.[61]

During the summer of 1935 an unprecedented campaign was launched against the processing tax, especially after the N.R.A. was declared unconstitutional by the United States Supreme Court. Many lawyers had been arguing that the A.A.A. was equally unconstitutional. The lead in this opposition was taken by the food industries. Numerous injunction suits were being brought to court with the intention of tying up the tax revenues with which the government paid farm benefits. General Mills, Incorporated, of Minneapolis, reported to be the largest milling organization in the world, announced that it would challenge the right of the government to collect this processing tax. The company had more than a passing interest in this. In July, 1935, it was reported that its operating units had a daily production capacity of about 81,000 barrels, on which a tax of from $1.35 to $1.40 was assessed for each 196-pound barrel of flour. It was estimated that the tax paid the government by General Mills daily amounted to about $110,000. Early in July, 1935, fifteen huge milling concerns and five meat packers attacked the constitutionality of the processing tax. These recalcitrant firms refused to pay the taxes that were due on July 1 and asked the federal courts for permanent injunctions against their collection.[62]

It appeared that each succeeding year had brought new storms across the path of the A.A.A. In 1933 opposition developed because of the order to slaughter 6,000,000 pigs and to plow up every third row of cotton. In 1934 came the drought, which diminished production beyond all thoughts and desires of the A.A.A. and brought upon its head the wrath of many

61. *Ibid.*, pp. 6–10.
62. *Milwaukee Journal*, June 29, July 3, 9, 1935.

who blamed it for food scarcity and high prices.[63] As one critic said, "The Good Man up above never meant for anything to be killed."[64]

The next year hundreds of suits were instituted by processors to test the constitutionality of the act, and also to avoid payment of processing taxes, the backbone of the adjustment program.[65] That same year saw a "plowman's pilgrimage" being undertaken to Washington, in support of the A.A.A. It was led by a Texas corn-hog, cotton, and wheat raiser, and had a preponderance of southerners with a small delegation of farmers from the western Middle West. A.A.A. officials denied that they had anything to do with this march, which was so unlike those of the Bonus Army, the F.H.A. troop, and Coxey's Army, of "keep off the grass" fame. The leader of the demonstration, a Texan named Clifford H. Day, was aided by press agents from the A.A.A. information division, the convention facilities of the Washington Board of Trade, police officials, and hotel association chiefs. In contrast with older marches, this was a quiet, dignified, serious affair; the delegates went to see their congressmen, met in Constitution Hall to praise the A.A.A., visited Mt. Vernon, and then returned to their homes.[66]

According to the Gallup poll, the nation in general was opposed to the A.A.A.; what support there was for it was confined pretty much to the South and the states of Kansas, North Dakota, and Iowa. These results were published the day before the A.A.A. was declared unconstitutional.[67]

On January 6, 1936, in the Hoosac Mills case, the United States Supreme Court in a 6 to 3 decision held that the production-control activities of the A.A.A. were unconstitutional. This decision did not affect other activities of the United States Department of Agriculture under the act, such as marketing agreements, surplus-removal operations, and commodity loans.[68] True enough, the back of the original A.A.A. had been broken, but the court had not killed the farm problem. It was very much alive and kicking.[69]

63. *Christian Science Monitor,* January 8, 1936.
64. Minneapolis Tribune, January 5, 1936.
65. *Christian Science Monitor,* January 8, 1936.
66. *Pioneer Press,* May 13, 14, 16, 1935.
67. *Minneapolis Tribune,* January 5, 1936.
68. U. S. Dept. Agri., A.A.A., *Agricultural Adjustment, 1933 to 1935,* p. 35.
69. *Minneapolis Tribune,* January 7, 1936.

Chapter XVIII

THE NEW DEAL: LATER STAGES

EVEN before the A.A.A. had been declared unconstitutional, administration leaders had been laying plans for a new program to take the place of the old; in fact so calculated and speedy was their work that a new act was passed in less than two months following the invalidation of the old. In this as in other instances, speed was of the essence: the program, unlike that of the N.R.A., had much support among the farmers, and a presidential election was a matter of months away. Over the next three years such matters as soil conservation, the ever normal granary plan, crop insurance, aid to farm tenants, rural rehabilitation, a redirection of land use, crop-control revolts, revival of cost-of-production demands, trade treaties, flare-ups with organized labor, and the income-certificate plan came up for either periodic or fairly consistent attention. The congressional election of 1938, coming at a time of low prices, brought the New Dealers the greatest defeat that they had yet faced, but the outbreak of war in the fall of 1939 helped send prices skyrocketing.

The invalidation of the processing tax and production-control features of the A.A.A. was hardly to pass without notice. A *New York Times* correspondent, writing from Omaha, found some dismay among the farmers because of the court action; perhaps the biggest surprise came over the thorough manner in which the tribunal had acted.[1] Edward A O'Neal, the blunt and aggressive president of the American Farm Bureau Federation, a veritable pillar of support for the A.A.A., spoke in exasper-

1. *New York Times,* January 12, 1936.

ated terms over the decision. It was unbelievable that the agency that had been greatly responsible for raising farm income, the most important link in the chain for "economic equality," had been banned. Certainly the farmers had constitutional rights. If the Constitution in its existent form made it impossible for all groups to enjoy economic equality, steps had to be taken to amend it "so that the rights of all groups and of all citizens will no longer be jeopardized." William Green, the president of the American Federation of Labor, expressed regret over the unhappy turn of events, saying: "We had very sincerely hoped that the AAA would be sustained."[2] Within a week wheat prices had begun a downward move.[3]

No such regrets were voiced in the New England states. Spokesmen for that area said that the farmers and industries there had benefited little, if any, from the A.A.A. and were glad to see it go. The textile industry, operating on a narrow margin of profit, led the campaign against it after the fashion of a New England crusade. The most immediate effect that the decision was expected to have there was to bring about the return of some $12,000,000 in processing taxes that New England mills had been paying with protest since May 1.

The evidence is that the administration, despite its outward laments, was hardly unprepared for an adverse decision. Several days before the court decision, C. C. Davis, the A.A.A. administrator, had suggested the formation of forty-eight "little A.A.A.'s," under federal supervision, to administer the program in the event the court had decided against the act. Others, equally prepared for a reversal, felt that enough salvageable parts of the measure would be left to enable the administration to build a new structure.[4]

The court action put the administration in the same embarrassing position that it had been in when the N.R.A. was outlawed; again it was compelled either to give up its objective of economic planning or else to find a substitute. There was, however, one major difference between N.R.A. and the A.A.A. that cannot be overlooked. There was no demand from any source to revive N.R.A., except for a few in the administration

2. *Ibid.*, January 7, 1936.
3. *Minneapolis Journal*, January 12, 1936.
4. *New York Times*, January 12, 1936.

who sought to bring about economic planning for industry. "Neither big business nor little business nor the general public showed the slightest interest in further experimentation with the application of a government-controlled planned economy for the business world."

The same was hardly true of the A.A.A. There was strong support for it, despite the numerous protests that had been leveled against it. The administration was for the program, and so were many farmers. After all, it had been rewarding to those with little or no income, though hardly to the extent that it had been to the large operators with many acres to retire. The A.A.A. had meant some sort of a guaranteed income for many farmers whether their crops were harvested or not.[5] Hence the administration had to move with speed to avert any serious aftermath. New sources for revenue had to be found or else the contracts the government had entered into would go by default, which was something that the administration could hardly afford to have happen in an election year.[6]

Advance reports had it that Roosevelt had approved making the relatively obscure Soil Erosion Act of 1935 the vehicle for carrying out the purposes of the invalidated measure.[7] The liberal *Nation* wrote in caustic fashion: "The show was put into rehearsal by our White House Ziegfeld twenty-four hours after the court's decision was announced. . . ." It was suggested that what had been termed crop control in the original act would become soil conservation in the new measure. In other words the farmer, who under the old A.A.A. was paid benefits for retiring a certain number of acres, would be paid under the new measure not for retiring these acres, but for "turning them into pasture, woodland, or fertility-restoring legumes."[8]

5. "The New Soil Conservation Act—Substitute for AAA," *Congressional Digest,* XV (March, 1936), p. 68. This issue is devoted exclusively to the 1936 version of the A.A.A.

6. U. S. Dept. Agri., Agricultural Adjustment Administration, *Agricultural Conservation, 1936, A Report of the Agricultural Adjustment Administration* (Washington, 1937), pp. 2–4.

7. *New York Times,* January 17, 1936. This transition had been given serious consideration for some time before the Supreme Court decision. The court action simply hastened it. See Edwin G. Nourse, *Government in Relation to Agriculture* (Washington, 1940), p. 918.

8. Paul Ward, "The AAA Puts on False Whiskers," *The Nation,* CXLII (January 22, 1936), pp. 93–94.

Meanwhile funds had to be found to honor the contracts that originally were to be financed by the processing taxes. These revenues were provided when on February 11 the Supplemental Appropriation Act earmarked some $296,185,000 to be used by the Secretary of Agriculture for this very purpose.

As had been expected, the Soil Erosion Act of 1935, with amendments attached to it, furnished the basis for the new legislation. The act of 1935 had said that the policy of Congress was to provide "for the protection of land resources against soil erosion, and for other purposes," while the new measure, the Soil Conservation and Domestic Allotment Act, said that the policy of Congress was to promote "the conservation and profitable use of agricultural land resources."[9]

The original A.A.A. had been based on the theory that agriculture was overexpanded and that "a straight-forward drive" had to be made on production to reduce it. The Soil Conservation and Domestic Allotment Act, the new measure, was based on the contention that our land resources were being recklessly exploited and that it was necessary for farmers to shift from soil-depleting to soil-conserving crops.

There were other differences, too. The corn-hog farmers got no benefits as in the old program. The A.A.A. saw no way of getting at hogs except through keeping down the amount of corn raised through agreements, thus making less of it available to be converted into pork. As for administering the program, there were no contracts to be signed; county committees simply were to check on the "soil-building or conservation performance." Payday came once a year for those who took part in the program.

Strangely enough, about the same time that the soil conservation program was getting under way, dust storms were blowing in the Texas and Oklahoma panhandles, in eastern Colorado, and in western Kansas. Once more nature took a hand and once again was it to cast a strong influence over the course of action that the administration would take.[10]

No sooner had the new legislation been passed than voices of apprehension were heard from the Middle West. The farmers there were fearful lest the new act bring about increases in the production of feed, food

9. U. S. Dept. Agri., A.A.A., *Agricultural Conservation, 1936*, pp. 2–4.
10. "All Aboard For $470,000,000," *Business Week* (March 28, 1936), pp. 24–25.

crops, and meat animals in the Southeast that would deprive them of their former markets. Such a trend had been in evidence from 1929 to 1934, which, of course, had the effect of lessening dependence of the Southeast on the Middle West for feed and food crops. During 1935 the A.A.A. boosted the rate of increase with more legislation. Meanwhile, few food-processing plants had been built, which was accepted as pretty good evidence that the farmers in the Southeast were "using their home-grown meat animals, instead of importing meat from Midwestern plants."[11]

According to one source, the Supreme Court decision was acting as a boomerang in support of the farm program of 1936. Many had been led to believe that the end of processing taxes would bring about price drops, and it seems that this promise had been taken seriously. By late February, 1936, there were some drops which actually did take place, but these were hardly commensurate with the hopes of the more optimistic. Because prices did not drop as expected, grievances because of high prices that formerly had been directed against the farmers were now aimed at the manufacturers and processors, who before had charged that the processing taxes had been responsible for the rising living costs. On the basis of this reasoning, the Supreme Court had succeeded in creating more favorable sentiment in behalf of the A.A.A. than had the administration itself.[12]

The farm question was expected to play an important part in the presidential campaign of 1936, and the corn, hog, and wheat states were destined to become important scenes of political battle. It was largely because of assumed disaffections and the prospect of capturing votes there that Alfred M. Landon of Kansas became the Republican presidential nominee. If we are to believe *Business Week,* the Republicans nominated Landon because he was "their kind of person, possessing the homely Calvin Coolidge virtues, the old-fashioned, covered wagon, typical prairie state ideas of thrift and economy, recognition of property as well as human rights, etc." If this was the case, here is good evidence that in four long years the Republicans had learned nothing and had forgotten nothing.

Besides going into the heart of the farm belt for a presidential candidate, pressure was reported coming from Wall Street—"enemy territory," as

11. "Worried By Dixie," *ibid.,* pp. 25–26.

12. Morton Taylor, "The Middle West Answers The Court," *New Republic,* LXXXVI (February 26, 1936), pp. 71–72.

Bryan used to say—for the adoption of a "soft money" plank. The reasoning behind this strange turn of affairs was that the Republicans were so anxious to beat Roosevelt that "they were eager to sacrifice anything—almost—to be sure of winning. And they had been thoroughly sold on the idea that the West—the farm regions—would be afraid that a speedy return to gold would work toward lowering farm prices."[13]

As in 1932, the American Farm Bureau Federation supported the New Deal to the hilt and even went to the extent of recommending that crop controls, soil conservation, and a managed currency become parts of the Republican platform. O'Neal, its president, complained that the Republican platform of 1936, as finally drawn up, provided nothing that would enable farmers to control or adjust their production and nothing for the payment of commodity loans that would help farmers prevent surpluses from depressing prices. Earl C. Smith, the Republican element in the Farm Bureau high command, expressed disappointment on some points in his party's platform, yet felt that "a liberal interpretation of the plank . . . under a sympathetic administration" would make possible the development of an effective national policy for agriculture.[14]

O'Neal, though more enthusiastic about the Democratic platform, had some misgivings over the pledge it had made of "fair prices to consumers at a fair price to farmers." He felt that it would have been more advisable for the platform to promise "ample supplies to consumers with parity prices to farmers."[15]

The Farmers' Union by no means had the influence that the Farm Bureau did in political circles, but in 1936 it came forward with a crop-insurance proposal that was attractive enough to gain the attention of both presidential candidates. Its rival, the Farm Bureau, was sympathetic with the plan but went no further than to recommend a study of it. The demand for crop insurance, in view of the drought that year, was a very timely one.

Here was but another instance of the farmers' seeking to duplicate the practices of industry and business. Industry, it was apparent, was in a much better position to reduce hazards "by insuring plants and equip-

13. "Landon's Job To Win The West," *Business Week* (June 20, 1936), p. 27.
14. *New York Times*, June 24, 1936.
15. *Ibid.*, June 27, 1936.

ment against fire, flood, thefts, riots and strikes," but "nothing tangible [had] yet been accomplished toward modifying [the] risks of farming, one of the most speculative of enterprises."

Crop insurance was hardly a new proposal. Private insurance companies had given it serious consideration, but were very skeptical over its working because of past experiences. The United States Department of Agriculture, in a more optimistic frame of mind, had been studying crop insurance over a period of years and had backed bills in Congress that aimed to put such a program into operation, but nothing had ever come of them. The big difficulty facing the government, and the private companies as well, was the actuarial problem of determining the rates on acreages that were subject to drought, insects, and plant blights.

But this time the administration gave more than passing notice to the plan. Roosevelt believed that at first it would be wise to limit it to a few crops, possibly corn, cotton, or wheat. With this in mind, he appointed two committees: one to draft a crop-insurance program, and a second to work out a long-term drought-adjustment scheme. Wallace had hopes that the crop-insurance idea could be used in connection with the ever normal granary plan, which would be so constituted as to make it possible for farmers to save their surplus crops during the years of plenty to use during the lean ones. Surpluses such as these would be stored away not because the government went out into the open market to make direct purchases of them, but rather because the farmers would be able to pay their premiums in kind.

The idea of farmers' paying their premiums in kind was a novel one, if the plan for crop insurance was not. Friends felt that the plan was a doubly laudable one because it would cost the government little or nothing to operate and also because it would make everybody happy. But the big weakness, admitted by friend and foe alike, was that payments in kind would have to be limited to goods that could be stored over a long period of time.[16]

It would have been strange indeed had not Landon, in the course of the

16. "Rival Programs To Help Farmer," *Literary Digest,* CXXII (October 3, 1936), pp. 40–41; "Insuring Crops and Votes," *Business Week* (September 26, 1936), pp. 9–10. For a fuller discussion of crop insurance, see "The Question of Establishing a Federal System of 'All Risk' Crop Insurance," *Congressional Digest,* XV (December, 1936), pp. 289–320.

campaign, accused the Roosevelt administration of having failed to do anything for the farmers. He did all that and then turned around and promised the farmers pretty much the same thing that the New Dealers did. He would give them cash benefits equal to the tariff benefits enjoyed by protected industries, and that was talking the language of the McNary-Haugenites about ten years after the movement had reached its peak; he would seek an amendment to the Federal Warehouse Act to make it possible for farmers to borrow on feed reserves that were stored in their cribs; he would give full attention to crop insurance and any proposals designed to aid "capable farm tenants" in buying farms. And then he pledged himself to honor "all outstanding obligations made by the present Administration." In the final analysis Landon was simply telling the farmers, "Help put the Republicans in and we'll give you everything that the New Dealers ever promised, perhaps more."[17]

It was soon evident that no amount of criticism and promises that the Republicans could make could undo the grip of the administration on the farmers. The presidential election was a smashing triumph for the New Deal. This came as a great shock to John D. M. Hamilton and other Landon leaders, who had been counting heavily on farm opposition. The "Kansas Coolidge" failed to carry his own state, let alone capture the votes of other farm states in the Middle West. As the *Milwaukee Journal* wrote: "The farmers were voting for AAA. There is no other interpretation."[18]

Other phases of the New Deal program saw steps taken to combat farm tenancy, to provide additional relief in the case of dire emergencies, to seek to reduce the effects of the drought, and to adopt programs designed to redirect the use of marginal and submarginal lands. As a result, various agencies and committees were set up to investigate, to make recommendations, and to try to remedy conditions that for the most part in the past had been either ignored or else considered the special concern of the individual farmer.

The New Deal tried to provide for those farmers who were "clinging to the outside fringe of our economic system," and who, the belief was, if given "a boost," would be able to "get back on their feet." This type of

17. *Business Week* (September 26, 1936), pp. 9–10.
18. *Milwaukee Journal,* November 10, 1936.

aid was coordinated, so it was said, with other parts of the farm program such as soil conservation, crop loans, surplus-disposing facilities, and marketing agreements to make it possible for "the neediest, most handicapped farm families [to] get a new start toward self-support." Instead of the government's making grants of food or money to these people, as it was compelled to do in the earlier days of the New Deal, it would lend them the tools and livestock they needed, and thus help put into operation a system which, in the long run, would be cheaper economically and socially.

In 1935 the Resettlement Administration was set up to help the low-income farmers. The operations of this agency were expanded until in 1937 it was absorbed by the Farm Security Administration, which developed a major rehabilitation program in the face of bitter opposition to fight rural poverty.[19] But no matter how much was attempted or how good the intentions were, what was accomplished was a far cry from the actual needs of this distressed lot.

When a farmer applied to the Farm Security Administration for help, the first step taken by the local authorities was to find out why the farmer was in difficulties. Inevitably, this would lead into matters that not too many years back the average farmer would have considered no one else's business but his own. The F.S.A. would probe into such matters as whether the farmer had a satisfactory long-term lease, whether he was protecting his soil properly, whether he was faced with ruin because of one-crop farming, whether he had the tools and livestock that he needed, whether he was keeping his expenses down by raising his own food, whether his wife was canning enough vegetables to feed the family during the winter months, whether some neglected illness was keeping him from doing his best work, whether he needed more acreage in order to make a living, and whether he was making the best use of the land that he farmed. Once the answers to these questions had been found, the F.S.A. supervisors would sit down with the farmer and his wife and work out a plan to help the individual farm family out of its difficulties. No two cases were alike, because every low-income family had a different set of problems.[20]

19. U. S. Dept. Agri., Farm Security Administration, *Farm Security Administration* (Washington, 1941), pp. 9–10.

20. *Ibid.*, p. 10; for a typical criticism and liberal defense of F.S.A. activities in

The aid given to the low-income groups of the western Middle West was quite substantial, but hardly comparable in amount to the aid extended to the low-income farmers of the South. The farm-tenancy loans provided by the F.S.A. during 1938–39 to the southern states was somewhat greater than the similar type provided for the farmers of the western Middle West. The same, however, was not true with respect to rural rehabilitation aid over the period 1936 to 1939, when considerable sums were extended to farmers in Kansas, Missouri, North Dakota, and South Dakota.[21]

Unfavorable weather had great bearing on the New Deal. The drought years of 1934 and 1936 and the tragedies that followed, especially in the Great Plains, prompted the administration to take action to relieve a situation that over a period of years had grown progressively worse. Of the ten states falling within the Great Plains area, only portions of four fell within the confines of the western Middle West: North Dakota, South Dakota, Nebraska, and Kansas. Adequate data on farm incomes for this area are lacking, but figures available tend to show that such matters as low and variable incomes, poor living standards, abnormal indebtedness, rapid foreclosure increases, rising relief demands, and tax delinquencies had contributed materially to the misfortunes of the farmers there.[22]

In 1936 President Roosevelt appointed a special committee to report

> . . . not later than January 1 on a long term program for the efficient utilization of the resources of the Great Plains area. I am anxious that we leave no stone unturned in exploring and reporting on all the possibilities of this region, as one in which reasonable standards of living can be maintained by the largest possible population. We should face the fact that the climatic conditions make special safeguards absolutely necessary. I would like your report to include such recommendations for legislation as you may deem necessary. . . .[23]

This special task brought to mind the report that Major J. W. Powell

---

the field of rural medicine, see "Washington Notes," *New Republic,* XCVII (January 4, 1939), pp. 258–59.

21. Hearings before the U. S. Senate, Subcommittee of the Committee on Appropriations on H.R. 2481, *Agricultural Appropriations Bill for 1944,* U. S. Senate (78th Congress, 1 session, Washington, 1943), pp. 654–57.

22. Report of the Great Plains Committee, *The Future of the Great Plains* (75th Congress, 1 session, House Document 144, serial 10117, Washington, 1936), pp. 51–62 [also in plain-title edition].

23. *Ibid.,* p. 131.

had made to Congress in 1878. In this he presented a good account of the conditions that had to be met in order to colonize the Great Plains successfully. Unfortunately, the wisdom of his counsel was exceeded only by the general apathy with which it was met. At the time, Powell placed the extent of the arid region of the United States at more than four-tenths of the area of the entire country; he said that the "limit of successful agriculture without irrigation has been set at twenty inches [mean annual rainfall] . . . the extent of the arid region should by no means be exaggerated; but at twenty inches agriculture will not be uniformly successful from season to season. Many drouths will occur; many seasons in a long series will be fruitless; and it may be doubted whether, on the whole, agriculture will prove remunerative."[24] Powell said that in view of these conditions the farm unit should not be less than 2,560 acres.

Others also took an interest in the area. Warren Thornthwaite, in his *Great Plains,* had referred to that region as "an area where climatic conditions unfavorable to a permanent agricultural economy occur with irregular persistency." He said that farm operations were highly speculative and that the solution was to be found in a reversion to a pastoral economy, which would call for units too large to be handled by individual farm owners. Until that was done there were but two unhappy alternative courses for action: "permanent poverty and distress or permanent subsidy."

It was clear that the United States was seriously considering in 1936 what had been almost ignored since 1878. The more one studied the question the more it appeared that the problems of environment were intertwined with the many economic, social, and political factors.[25]

The Great Plains Committee, besides making an exhaustive investigation of the area as a whole, came forward with recommendations that called for "comprehensive action by government—Federal, State, and county—as well as by individuals."[26] The readjustments recommended were begun in some instances, but when distress persisted through 1937 and 1938, because of the depression and the continued effects of the drought, it was felt wise to take additional steps to better conditions. In April, 1938, a special committee was appointed, made up of members

24. Paul B. Sears, "O, Bury Me Not," *New Republic,* XCI (May 12, 1937), pp. 7–10.

25. *Ibid.*

26. House Document 144, 75th Congress, 1 session, p. 71.

of federal agencies, state planning boards, and local groups, to develop a program that would lead to more than temporary relief in the northern Great Plains. In October, 1938, a preliminary report of the findings of the committee was released. This revealed that the prevailing conditions had not come into being overnight:

Seven years of drought have disrupted the economy of the Northern Great Plains. The prevailing system of land utilization, hazardous at best, has failed. Tax delinquency, heavy real estate and chattel mortgages, and dependence on public relief are widespread. In North Dakota, for example, more than 70 per cent of all farms are listed as tax-delinquent; more than 75 per cent of the farms in representative counties are mortgaged; and approximately 35 per cent of all people are on relief.

Many factors contributed through the years to economic and social instability in the Plains, and helped to weaken resistance to the impact of recent droughts. The provisions of the Homestead Act, under which the region was settled, did not fit the semiarid environment—a quarter section of land was too small a unit for successful grazing or dry-land farming. Later legislation proved of little benefit. Most land holdings are too small. Settlement was without guidance. Homesteaders from humid lands in the middle and eastern interior encountered conditions in the Plains of which they had no knowledge. Farming practices that had served them well in their old homes were unsuitable, and the development of effective techniques proved a slow and difficult process which is still unfinished. From the outset of settlement, periods of adequate rainfall and of withering drought alternated.

In step with them, waves of immigration and of emigration succeeded one another. Within the Region, too, population shifted from one district to another. These restless movements and counter-movements reflected faulty and insecure adjustments of population to the land. Under the occasional stimulus of generous rains and high prices, wheat farming was carried far beyond its legitimate bounds into numerous areas physically unfit for it. The Region remains today a land of great risks, an unconquered frontier.

The history of settlement and land use in the Northern Plains indicates clearly that another period of normal or supernormal rainfall, however desirable, would not alone insure stability. The plague of dry years would presently return; crop failures would follow bountiful harvests; despair would again replace optimism. The future of the Region cannot be left safely to the unpredictable hazards of rainfall and the inadequate resources of individual farmers.

Generous public assistance has prevented extreme human suffering in the Northern Plains during the recent years of drought and depression. Food, clothing, and fuel have been furnished to all in need. Relief employment has been afforded to all certified applicants who were in towns and who were able to work. Farm Security Administration grants and loans, Agricultural Adjustment Administration benefit payments, Farm Credit Administration loans, and other types of aid have been extended to farmers.

Though the activities noted have attained their special objectives and have minimized suffering, they have not contributed to the permanent rehabilitation of the area to the degree that now seems possible through coordinated effort. For example, some farmers have been enabled to stay on their farms and to continue cultivating land suited only to grazing. Relief labor, naturally, has been used chiefly for such projects as roads and schools. The people would be little better equipped on the whole to cope with a serious drought next year than they were in 1930. To the greatest degree possible, relief should hereafter promote permanent rehabilitation.

Many families—perhaps 20,000 in all—have given up the fight during the recent years of distress and have left the Region. Most of the farmers hang on tenaciously with Federal aid, hoping that conditions will improve. Many have moved to the villages and the few cities, where, with Federal assistance, they await opportunities in other regions or the wet year that would enable them to return to their farms and produce a big crop.

Large-scale evacuation of the Northern Plains, were it practicable, would not solve the basic problems of the Region. Cheap land, the chance for speculative gain, the false promise of a few wet years, all these and more would lure new settlers likely to repeat the mistakes of earlier years with similar consequences. So far as can be foreseen, the economic and social life of the Region must always depend on agriculture. A type of agriculture suited to the climate, topography, soils, and natural vegetation, involving, in general, larger operating, units, a judicious combination of grazing and feed-crop production, and so far as practicable, supplemental irrigation, should replace the cash-grain and small-scale stock rearing type of agricultural development in the many areas where the latter has failed and cannot succeed. Locally, irrigation projects of considerable size are possible. In short, rehabilitation and stabilization can come only through fundamental readjustments in land utilization. Immediate action for rehabilitation is essential; continued action through years will be needed.

The committee conceded that what progress had been made in the area had been of limited extent and slow of execution, and expressed the fear that a prolonged European war would undo what progress had been made. "A sharp rise in the price of wheat, accompanied perhaps by the false promise of a series of generous rains, might tempt the Plainsmen again to overcultivate in the hope of speculative gain. Constant vigilance will be needed to safeguard the progress already made and to make continued progress possible."[27]

More attention was focused on the New Deal from another direction. Early in January, 1939, about one thousand sharecroppers from the seven "boot heel" counties of southeastern Missouri, economically and traditionally a part of the cotton South but geographically a part of the western Middle West, staged a protest against their lowly economic status. These "ragged, shivering sharecroppers, encamped along the rights-of-way of Highways 60 and 61," many of whom were women and children, most of them Negroes, were "ill-prepared" to face the winter months.

> Sewing machines, dressers, tables and beds were stacked along the roads in disarray. Groups took turns sleeping in dilapidated automobiles. Others slept on corn-shuck mattresses or blankets.
>
> A few had oil-barrel stoves and the familiar rural pot-bellied iron stoves to provide warmth and heat for preparing meals. Some of the more provident brought cooking chickens with them, but fat pork, bread and coffee was the fare for the majority of the refugees.
>
> Medical authorities, fearful of the danger of disease, expressed concern for the health of the farm families. Milk for infants was a pressing problem.[28]

More specifically this demonstration was in protest against mechanized farming and the growing practice in the South of abandoning sharecropping in favor of day labor. Leaders of the protesting group contended that some of the landowners had evicted the renters to avoid sharing crop benefits with them. Landowners, however, blamed the situation on the rapid growth of farm population in Missouri, the curtailment of the cotton acreage, the shift from manual labor and mule power to modern motorized farming, and losses suffered by some operators under the sharecropper system.

When Secretary Wallace was pressed for a comment on the remarks of tenants who charged that they had been evicted from their lands in order that the landlord might avoid sharing benefit payments with them, he stated categorically that such actions were contrary to the stipulations of

27. National Resources Planning Board, *Regional Planning*, Part IX, *The Northern Great Plains, A Progress Report, September, 1939* (Washington, 1940), pp. 3–4.

28. *New York Times*, January 12, 1939.

the law. Any landlord found resorting to such practices would have his benefit payments withheld. He had no advance information that some of the landowners had done that, but he made it clear that "under the act payments are made both to landlords and to sharecroppers, but it is provided that landlords cannot get during the year the payment normally going to the tenant if they evict him or change his status to hired man. The landlord further undertakes not to reduce the number of sharecroppers during the year for which he gets an AAA payment."[29]

Provoked landowners, in turn, demanded an inquiry, preferably by the Federal Bureau of Investigation, to determine what had brought this demonstration on. They insisted that it had been encouraged by "certain agitators who are telling the people that government will give them forty acres of ground, tools and teams," and that the demonstrators for the most part were neither sharecroppers nor residents of Missouri. Some Negroes were reported waiting for "Uncle Sam to give them a white house with a porch, a barn, well and a span of mules."[30] At the same time the landowners asked for an investigation of the supervisor of the Farm Security Administration resettlement project at La Forge, Missouri. This La Forge project, a 6,700-acre affair with one hundred families on it, was dedicated late in 1938 as a laboratory attempt to solve the problems of the sharecroppers. This project had appealed to many of the demonstrators, who reportedly demanded, "We want another La Forge."[31]

Another part of the program had to do with holding up prices by storing away during seasons of plenty surpluses that could be used in periods of lean crops. This was the main idea behind the ever normal granary plan, variations of which had been employed periodically during the early stages of the New Deal and even before. It attracted the attention of the administration from the start. In the fall of 1933 loans of forty-five cents per bushel of corn were advanced; this was one of the very first manifestations of the ever normal granary idea under New Deal auspices. By late 1934 some $120,000,000 had been lent on corn that was put under

29. *Ibid.*, January 12, 27, 1939. The latter issue gives an account of the effects of mechanization on the plight of the cotton producer. For a brief account of conditions there, see U. S. Dept. Agri., Farm Security Administration, *Southeast Missouri: A Laboratory for the Cotton South* (Washington, 1940) [mimeographed].

30. *New York Times*, January 17, 1939.

31. *Ibid.*, January 1, 13, 17, 1939.

government seal. Meanwhile, A.A.A. officials had been striving to get the individual states to pass uniform warehouse laws to facilitate the federal program. Once it was suggested that the federal government build granaries of one-thousand-bushel capacity on farms where grain pledged for loans could be held under seal, but it appears that the suggestion did not get very far.[32]

By late 1936 the ever normal granary plan was pretty much in the limelight, along with a growing demand for crop insurance. In pleading for the farmer, Wallace paid tribute to the earlier activities of Joseph in biblical times, citing the forty-seventh chapter of Genesis, to the works of Confucius and his followers in China, who had formulated a scheme known as the ever normal granary, and to the early Mormons in Utah. He also cited the storage operations of the Federal Farm Board, disillusioning as they were, as establishing further precedent. He appeared sensitive to critics who scoffed at his ideas as being nothing more than an attempt to regiment nature. Wallace replied, "We cannot regiment nature, but we do not have to let nature regiment us." In fact, he felt that it was about time that we took advantage of "the experiences of Joseph, the ancient Chinese and the Farm Board." The havoc brought upon the land by the droughts made such action mandatory.[33]

In the spring of 1937 a meeting of 5,000 farmers held in Sioux Falls, South Dakota, with representatives present from Minnesota, North Dakota, South Dakota, Nebraska, Iowa, Wisconsin, and Montana, asked for the adoption of a long-time farm program and the passage of a tenancy act that would make available long-term land purchases at reasonable rates. It was also maintained that easterners were endangering the A.A.A. program because of their economy demands. Because farm prices were up, the feeling among many was that there was no further need for such a farm program.[34]

When the Soil Conservation and Domestic Allotment Act became law in 1936, it was passed partly with the feeling that the conservation program had more to offer the farmer than did any other single proposal. But no

32. *Kansas City Star,* December 27, 1934.

33. *Congressional Digest,* XV (December, 1936), p. 299. For a critical analysis and historical background, see Joseph S. Davis, *On Agricultural Policy, 1926–1938* (Palo Alto, Calif., 1939), pp. 399–418.

34. *Pioneer Press* (St. Paul), May 22, 1937.

sooner had this become law than another serious drought hit the nation. This again confirmed the fact that the weather had a greater bearing on the output of the farmers than did the acreage-allotment and surplus-control features of the administration.

If the year 1936 was one of drought, the following two years were the very opposite of scarcity. Favorable growing conditions in 1937 and in 1938 again brought the farmers face to face with the surplus problem and low prices. Once more the administration was forced to reconsider its program. If only a broader one could be devised, one that would make it possible for farmers to control larger reserves through storage, the problems of surplus and drought would be met. This was the reasoning behind the ever normal granary plan that was incorporated into the A.A.A. of 1938.[35]

In February, 1938, President Roosevelt signed the A.A.A. of 1938, the ever normal granary bill which put on the statute books the first measure for which the special session of Congress had been called three months earlier. The law established a system of storing away surpluses of cotton, rice, tobacco, corn, and wheat during abundant years for use in times of lean years. Roosevelt, in signing the measure, said that this was part of the program to give farming a fair share of the national income, "to provide consumers with abundant supplies of food and fiber, to stop waste of soil, and to reduce the gap between huge surpluses and disastrous shortages."

> The nation is now agreed that we must have greater reserves of food and feed to use in years of damaging weather and to help iron out extreme ups and downs of price. We are agreed that the real and lasting progress of the people of farm and city alike will come not from the old familiar cycle of glut and scarcity, not from the succession of boom and collapse, but from the steady and sustained increases in production and fair exchange of things that human beings need.[36]

Under this act benefit payments would be paid farmers who withdrew acreages from production and employed soil-building practices, and loans would be made when the prices of corn, cotton, and wheat fell below cer-

35. U. S. Dept. Agri., Agricultural Adjustment Administration, *Agricultural Adjustment, 1937–1938* (Washington, 1938), pp. 17–18.

36. *Milwaukee Sentinel,* February 17, 1938.

tain levels; the law also authorized a crop-insurance plan, with some $20,000,000 set aside for wheat. The Secretary of Agriculture was the one to determine what the domestic and foreign needs would be and to set the acreages accordingly. If production exceeded certain bounds, marketing quotas would be invoked, provided they were approved by a two-thirds referendum. The administration of the act was to be handled by the thousands of local committees that were to be set up.[37]

The passage of the 1938 Agricultural Adjustment Act marked the third stage in the adjustment program. Administration spokesmen referred to it as occupying a sort of middle course between the A.A.A. of 1933 and the Soil Conservation and Domestic Allotment Act of 1936. The 1938 measure embodied the idea of "surplus control, that is, control of marketing in interstate commerce," in place of "the production-control approach of the original adjustment act." It was likewise believed that setting up the marketing and storage provisions for control of surpluses strengthened the conservation program that had been built up under the act of 1936. The new features of the 1938 act were the ever normal granary plan and the crop-insurance program for wheat.[38]

The year 1938 was a hard one for the New Deal. In the spring of that year, in the face of dropping prices, vigorous opposition, led by an aggressive minority of "old dealers" and supported by newspapers like the *Chicago Tribune,* began to mount against the acreage allotments of the 1938 act. This drive was spearheaded by small but very vocal and highly publicized bodies like the Farmers' Independent Council and the Corn Belt Liberty League, which demanded a free rein in agriculture and death for the farm law.[39] At a meeting held in Macomb, Illinois, plans were made to form county organizations and to call a meeting to assemble late in April with representatives present from seventeen western Illinois counties. Hope was expressed that the movement would spread into the entire Middle West. "The farmer doesn't want politicians telling him how to run his farm. He has been misrepresented and misquoted. Now he's going to have a chance to state his case." [40] Later, Governor Nelson G. Kraschel of Iowa, in a telegram to Wallace, urged the elimination of

37. *Congressional Digest,* XVII (April, 1938), pp. 97–98.
38. U. S. Dept. Agri., A.A.A., *Agricultural Adjustment, 1937–1938,* pp. 17–18.
39. *Chicago Tribune,* April 19, 1938.
40. *Ibid.,* April 20, 1938.

the "glaring inequalities" which he warned might "destroy the entire program" if they were not adjusted immediately. There was no denying that the activities of the Corn Belt Liberty League were rising and forcing top administration officials to take notice.[41] By May, 1938, the league had roots in Illinois, Kansas, Nebraska, Missouri, and Iowa.[42]

The administration, noticing that the situation was becoming worse, ordered state, county, and township committees affiliated with the A.A.A. to launch a counteroffensive against the critics. Claude R. Wickard, director of the north central division of the A.A.A., said that what inequities there were would be straightened out, but that the administration would not give an inch in the demands for a general increase in the corn acreage allotments. He accused them of fomenting unrest and misrepresenting the facts, and predicted that the "revolt" would die as fast as the facts could be relayed to the farmers.[43]

Congressmen were reported worrying over the protests about acreage allotments. The letters they were receiving were different from the typewritten complaints and telegrams that they usually received. "The letters I get," one legislator said, "are usually on cheap ruled paper and written in pencil. They are the kind of letters we pay attention to. One protest of that sort means more than a hundred letters on fancy stationery."

Wallace, in the face of mounting complaints, also told reporters that what injustices there were would be ironed out speedily and that the trouble would die down as soon as the program was better understood. He blamed much of the trouble on the late start that the program had, and the failure to perform the usual educational work among the farmers before launching it.[44]

Besides protesting against acreage allotments, these bitter critics of the A.A.A. cited other grievances. While the corn-belt farmers were being told to cut down their acreages, southern farmers who had been barred from raising cotton were being allowed to grow corn.[45] Dairy farmers

41. *Wisconsin State Journal* (Madison), April 29, 1938.

42. *Kansas City Star,* May 1, 1938; *Des Moines Tribune,* May 6, 1938; *Chicago Tribune,* May 7, 1938; and *Des Moines Register,* May 20, 1938.

43. *Wisconsin State Journal,* April 29, 1938. 44. *Chicago Tribune,* May 6, 1938.

45. See editorial, "Washington Moves the Corn Belt South," *Chicago Tribune,* May 23, 1938.

were discovering that producers who were being discouraged from raising soil-depleting crops were going into dairying with the aid of the federal government. Equally annoying was the campaign being waged by the A.F.L. and the C.I.O. to unionize farm labor.[46]

During the spring and early summer of 1938 elements from the spring wheat states also voiced their annual protests against the proposed acreage reductions for 1939. A strong complaint was prepared by a committee representing certain marketing and milling interests from North Dakota, South Dakota, Minnesota, and Montana, spearheaded by groups like the Greater North Dakota Association, the Greater South Dakota Association, the Montanans, Inc., and certain undesignated farm groups from Minnesota.[47] As in previous years, these elements demanded that sweeping reductions in acreage be confined to those wheat varieties of which there were surpluses, particularly the winter wheat types, and not be extended to the spring varieties, of which, they claimed, there never had been any surpluses.[48]

If these elements were serious, the administration was equally serious in its insistence that its recommendations be accepted. Official word had it that the government would refuse to reclassify wheat on the basis of these demands but would proceed to curtail the entire acreage on the basis of its calculations. It was said that the failure of the spring wheat growers to comply with the entire wheat program would bring about its eventual breakdown. H. R. Tolley, A.A.A. administrator, said that the request from these elements was studied by Congress and the administration and that the decision finally reached was that there could be no exceptions. The prices of all wheats, including the spring varieties, had declined sharply and united action had to be taken by all producers.[49]

By the fall of 1938 the question of low farm prices was as far from solution as ever. The great agricultural staples remained depressed, despite the frantic efforts that had been made by the administration to raise them. As expected, the critics had nothing to offer in place of the A.A.A. other than the usual medley of substitute proposals: more subsidies, price fixing, outright repeal, and currency inflation.[50]

46. *Milwaukee Sentinel,* May 13, 1938.
47. *Minneapolis Journal,* July 6, 1938.
48. *Minneapolis Tribune,* June 7, 1938.
49. *Minneapolis Journal,* July 6, 1938.
50. *Ibid.,* October 19, 1938.

This threw the administration all the more on the defensive. In October, 1938, Wallace told a group of listeners in Springfield, Illinois, to fight for the "best farm program agriculture ever had" and cautioned the corn-belt farmers to beware of the substitutes that were being offered. He granted that it was neither a perfect measure nor one that represented "a complete charter of farm equality," but maintained that it was capable of being improved on with experience. He credited the new act with preventing the big drop in farm income that many had expected, especially in view of the drastic reduction in factory employment and payrolls.

Most prominent among the measures intended to take the place of the A.A.A. was a price-fixing plan which favored setting the price of farm products at the "cost of production, or parity, or some other figure." Wallace made it clear that he was not opposed to price fixing in itself, but felt that any scheme proposing that a fixed price be paid on an unlimited quantity of goods was unsound. "No business organization anywhere has ever been able to fix a price while exercising no control whatever over production. Look out for price-fixing combined with unlimited production unless you want to get hurt." [51]

About that time there took effect a reorganization of the personnel in the United States Department of Agriculture, a shift that was referred to as the most drastic in a quarter century. These changes were announced by Wallace after a tour of the Middle West and Southwest during which he had personally studied the reaction of the farmers to the 1938 farm program. The reasons given for the reorganization was that it would facilitate coordination of the marketing and production-control features of the farm program that had been undergoing so much fire. The new arrangement was also expected to encourage the finding of new domestic markets.[52]

It was customary for farmers, like other groups, to blame the party in power for their ailments. Such was the case in Kansas, where the blame for the farmers' troubles was placed squarely on the shoulders of the federal farm program. But at the same time these grievances could hardly be taken to mean that the Kansas farmers were opposed to federal activities. They had been receiving millions of dollars in direct payments an-

51. *Christian Science Monitor,* October 10, 1938.
52. *Milwaukee Journal,* October 17, 1938.

nually, to say nothing of the higher prices they had gained from the program. If anything, the big complaint was against the way the program had operated and not against the principle of federal activities.

Of special interest to the Kansas Republicans was the fact that Senator George McGill, a New Dealer and joint author of the A.A.A. of 1938, "the allegedly distress-spreading law," was up for re-election. His Republican rival was former Governor Clyde Reed, who was shrewd enough not to attack either the New Deal or President Roosevelt too severely. He realized that both the President and the A.A.A. had a certain amount of popular support, and instead chose to speak of the "forward-looking" measures of the administration as proposals that had been first put forward by liberal Republicans like himself.[53]

The nearer congressional election time came, the more the A.A.A. was put under fire by the Republicans. Among its critics was none other than Senator Arthur Capper of Kansas, who a few weeks earlier had been defending his vote for it, but who now said that the farmers were worse off than they had been five years ago when the original measure was passed. Wallace, taken aback by Capper's reversal, reminded the senator that he had "helped load the gun" to shoot the farm problem, and repeated his previous point that the cooperating farmers were better off with the program than without it. This about-face by Capper was accepted by many as a sign that he believed that 1938 was going to be a Republican year.

Another development in the state was the adoption by the Kansas Farmers' Union of a resolution opposing the A.A.A. as a permanent farm program and asking for the substitution of the domestic allotment plan. This was a price-fixing proposal, not something to be confused with the original A.A.A., as a result of which parity prices would be obtained for the farmers on that portion of the crop that was used in the country. Briefly, the demand was for an American price, or parity, through price fixing. Such a move was hardly unexpected, especially when it came from certain quarters within the Farmers' Union, because price fixing at "cost of production" levels was an often discussed topic. Again, it was interesting to note that the Kansas group did not condemn the A.A.A. outright, but asked for a substitute measure.

53. *New York Times,* October 24, 1938.

The political situation in Iowa, on the other hand, presented a study in contrasts. While the Kansas Republicans were building up dissatisfaction with the A.A.A. as a means of defeating McGill, the Iowa Democrats were emphasizing its benefits with the hope of re-electing Senator Guy Gillette.[54]

It took very little investigating to realize that the wheat farmers had good reason to complain in the fall of 1938. Late in October the price of a bushel of wheat for December delivery on the Chicago market was reported stabilized at around 65.5 cents. This was the average at which the futures had been selling over the past three-month period. According to the brokers, stabilization had been brought about because of the government loans and the export subsidies. "Few professional operators [were] disposed to take a decided stand on either side of the market."

Granted that American prices were low, the fact is that they were higher than those in other countries. Prices in Winnipeg, Liverpool, Buenos Aires, and Rotterdam also were on the downgrade. Indeed the declines abroad were so severe that export sales of domestic wheat even with the subsidy program were far off the 100,000,000-bushel mark that had been set for the season by the United States Department of Agriculture. Over the past three months prices in Liverpool and Winnipeg had declined by about seventeen cents and in Buenos Aires by more than twenty cents. In brief the price of wheat in the United States at the time was the highest in the world, but also the lowest, domestically, since 1934.[55]

Because of low prices, the poor foreign market, and signs that bad export conditions would persist well into 1939, the Department of Agriculture forecast a sharply curtailed acreage for 1939. The department expressed hope that seeding would be confined to 55,000,000 acres as compared with the 81,000,000 acres harvested in 1939. But whether the farmers would adopt the wheat-reduction plan that the department had in mind was another matter.[56]

There is no denying that a campaign for price fixing was in full swing

54. *Ibid.*, October 30, 1938.

55. *Ibid.*, October 31, 1938; see also "The World Wheat Situation, 1938–39," Food Research Institute, Stanford University, *Wheat Studies*, XVI (December, 1939), pp. 113–203.

56. *New York Times*, November 1, 1938.

by election time. The reasoning behind this took a familiar turn. The farmers had grown weary in their campaign for satisfactory markets. If the existing legislation could only be replaced by laws that would direct the government to establish prices that would assure the farmers "cost of production plus a reasonable profit," conditions conceivably could improve. There was slight hope that the farmers could get profitable returns in a free market where the laws of supply and demand theoretically were allowed to determine price. It was agreed that price fixing ran contrary to "an economic system built on the theory of a free market and competition" but the "swing in industry and labor toward greater price regulation in recent years [made] it necessary that agriculture have corresponding price protection." As proof there was "governmental fixing of public utility rates, minimum wage and maximum hour laws, and the freedom of industry, as a result of concentration in large corporations, to influence the price of its products." The need of price fixing for agricultural products was also mandatory because of the many granaries, elevators, and warehouses that were bursting with grains and other commodities.[57]

When the ballots were cast and the votes counted, the results showed that the New Deal had suffered serious setbacks in the farm areas as well as in the urban and industrial sections of the nation. "Probably no New Dealer was more shocked by the election returns than was Mr. Wallace whose farm program had been thrown into confusion by heavy losses of supporting Congressmen in the corn and wheat belts." Wallace pointed out that the losses in Democratic House members were greater in the farm states than they were in the industrial areas, but on a percentage basis the losses in the corn and wheat regions were even greater. He took this as proof that the corn and wheat farmers wanted something positive done to help them, and said that he was open to suggestions for strengthening the program regardless of whether they came from Republicans or Democrats.[58]

It is significant to note that the co-authors of the 1938 farm bill—Senators James Pope, Democrat of Idaho, and George McGill of Kansas—both met defeat that year. Pope was defeated for renomination and McGill

57. *Milwaukee News Sentinel,* November 6, 1938; *Milwaukee Journal,* November 9, 1938.
58. *Christian Science Monitor,* November 12, 1938.

came out second best in his contest with Clyde Reed, his Republican rival.[59]

There was nothing in the tone of the Republican campaigners that indicated that there would be an end to farm relief when the new Congress took its place. The vote in 1938 was more against the low prices than it was against the federal farm program. The major crops around which the whole A.A.A. program was built were selling below the average prices of the five years preceding the New Deal. A *New York Times* correspondent predicted that the farmers, "instead of demanding an end to a national agricultural program, probably will insist that [their] leaders move on to bigger and better experiments." [60] If anyone did seek the outright repeal of the A.A.A., it was the Corn Belt Liberty League, which took the congressional defeats in the corn belt as a personal triumph.[61]

Besides sagging prices and a falling of industrial employment, the year 1938 saw the emergence of a growing tension between farmers and labor, perhaps far less in fact than the newspapers made many believe. Of the states in the western Middle West, perhaps in no other did these relations reach the stage that they did in Wisconsin. Here labor legislation had reached greater dimensions than it had in most other states, if not any other state, in the union.

The outbreak of labor troubles in two isolated farm areas of the state furnished the signal for a head-on assault against its labor laws and also the beginning of a big press campaign. First a strike broke out early in May at the Frank Pure Food Company, a canning concern near Racine, Wisconsin, and then there came another at the Richland Center Cooperative Creamery. Both became the focal point for an attack by the Wisconsin Council of Agriculture.[62]

What particularly hurt labor was the fact that both these strikes took place in a year of sagging farm incomes and at a time when the drift was

59. *Capital Times* (Madison, Wis.), November 9, 1938; "Farmers in the Election," editorial, *Christian Science Monitor*, November 12, 1938.

60. *New York Times*, November 13, 1938.

61. *Wisconsin State Journal*, November 22, 1938.

62. *Milwaukee Journal*, May 24, June 6, 1938; *Milwaukee Sentinel*, June 1, 11, 1938; *Kenosha Labor*, June 17, 1938; *Milwaukee Journal*, June 26, 30, 1938; *Capital Times*, June 28, 1938; *Labor Policy Adopted by the Wisconsin Council of Agriculture, August 6, 1938* [mimeographed].

definitely toward conservatism. As the *Christian Science Monitor* remarked, "In state after state, the combination of conservative city groups with the farmers appeared to nullify that balance of power which labor exercised two years ago." [63] The final upshot of the matter was the drafting of the Employment Peace Act, which the Wisconsin Council of Agriculture said had been designed to protect the interests of the employer, the employee, and the general public.[64] It became law in 1939 despite its opposition by progressives, liberals, union labor, and farm groups like the Farmers' Union, which had always taken a sympathetic stand with respect to organized labor.[65]

It seems that this law was placed on the statute books not because of any widespread labor disturbances in farm areas of the state, because there were only two involving farm labor, but because a well-organized group, traditionally opposed to labor, was able to capitalize on the conservative drift.

Trade pacts were another part of the New Deal effort to aid the farmers. The trade-agreements program was authorized on June 12, 1934, by means of an amendment to the tariff act of 1930, for the purpose of reversing the shrinkage of our foreign trade that had taken place during the depression years.[66] Between 1929 and 1933, the year before the Trade Agreements Act was passed, our total exports declined from $5,241,000,000 to $1,675,000,000. Proportionately our trade had fallen off more than had the international trade of the world as a whole.[67]

The reciprocal trade treaties were met with mixed feelings in the western Middle West. In 1936 they were attacked by the Republican opposition; Landon, in particular, assailed the Canadian treaty in Minneapolis, where it was quite unpopular. This attack was intended to attract the votes of dairy farmers in both Wisconsin and Minnesota, who believed that the increased imports from Canada had beaten down the prices of American cattle and dairy products.[68] Cordell Hull immediately took to the stump to defend his administration, heading straight for Minneapolis to speak

63. Editorial, *Christian Science Monitor,* November 12, 1938.
64. *Wisconsin State Journal,* March 2, 1939.
65. *Capital Times,* March 30, May 3, 1939; *Milwaukee Journal,* February 17, 1939.
66. *Congressional Digest,* XVIII (December, 1939), pp. 293–94.
67. *Capital Times,* December 1, 1938.
68. *Kansas City Star,* September 25, 1936.

from the same platform from which Landon had spoken. These treaties were unpopular along the American side of the Canadian border, yet Hull did not hesitate to uphold them. Said Hull, "Governor Landon was right. The American farmer has been sold out. But the Governor is mistaken as to who did the selling and when it occurred. The 'sell-out' took place during the Hoover administration, and it was the Smoot-Hawleyites who did the work." [69]

In 1937 Francis B. Sayre, the Assistant Secretary of State, told the Wisconsin Farmers' Equity Union that the trade program had not damaged the Wisconsin dairy industry as its critics had charged. He admitted that agricultural imports had increased since the fiscal year of 1933–34, but denied that the trade agreements made with the sixteen nations were chiefly responsible for this. The increase in farm imports since the fiscal year of 1933–34 was placed at $699,000,000, out of which only $83,000,000 was attributable to the trade pacts. He said that the boost in imports resulted from improved economic conditions and the droughts of 1934 and 1936. The trade treaties simply were "trying to clear the river of the debris, the agricultural wreckage with which it has been strewn since the passage of the Smoot-Hawley Tariff act." [70]

Hull, speaking before the National Farm Institute in Des Moines, said that the farm belt was the principal benefactor of his trade-treaty program. Unfortunately, the nation, he said, was being "subjected to a veritable barrage of sinister propaganda designed, for narrow and selfish reasons, to wreck the most important policy which our country can pursue to promote its economic well-being and peace." He warned the meeting against being misled into "helping predatory interests preserve their own privileged position under embargo tariffs—to the injury of the farmers themselves and of the nation as a whole." "Our great staple crops still definitely depend upon export outlets. So do our exceedingly important fruit-growing industry and various smaller branches of agricultural production." He reminded his listeners of the Smoot-Hawley tariff and the boomerang which it created in the mounting tariff walls abroad that it brought against American products.[71]

69. "Who Sold Out?" *Time,* XXVIII (October 19, 1936), p. 16.
70. *Capital Times,* November 3, 1937.
71. *Milwaukee Journal,* February 20, 1938.

In speaking before the same audience, M. L. Wilson said, "The really important problem is to discover a market for exports rather than to keep out imports. Among our largest markets for wheat during the present season have been The Netherlands, Belgium, and Sweden, with all of which we have concluded reciprocal trade agreements." [72]

John Vesecky, of Salina, Kansas, president of the national Farmers' Union, endorsed the principle of reciprocal trade, which he hoped would "gradually lower the trade barriers which are now blocking international rivers of commerce . . . , but in so doing care must be exercised to safeguard the farmer's interest." At the same time, he advised that we "all rid ourselves of the idea that our own special patent medicine is a cure-all for all our farm problems." [73]

E. A. O'Neal, of the American Farm Bureau Federation, urged the negotiation of pacts if they sought to provide new markets for American farm products and at the same time reduce "our excessive industrial tariffs." However, he voiced opposition to any action that would have the effect of lowering prices below parity price levels.[74] Allan Kline, vice-president of the Iowa Farm Bureau Federation, said that "a gradual lowering of tariffs undertaken in a studied way with the welfare of the whole people in mind and carefully administered would be an asset—should and will be an advantage." [75]

Louis J. Taber, the master of the national Grange, was not so sure that the trade agreements were doing for the farmers all that their spokesmen claimed for them. Why should labor and business be allowed to profit "at the expense of agriculture?" "We have a tariff policy, not because of agriculture, but because of industry. For more than a century, the farmer has paid tariff costs with little or no direct benefits. Now when industry wants to trade machinery, supplies, scrap iron, or printing presses for farm products to some other agricultural nation the farmer does have a right to complain. The government has not been fair to the producer of export crops during all these years." [76]

72. *Chicago Tribune,* February 19, 1938.
73. *Milwaukee Journal,* February 20, 1938.
74. *New York Times,* March 16, 1938.
75. *Ibid.,* March 21, 1938; Kline was elected president of the Farm Bureau in 1947.
76. *Chicago Tribune,* February 19, 1938.

During the summer of 1938 the Wisconsin cheese producers were faced with what was described as the greatest supply of cheese in the history of the state. Appeals were being made for new outlets, wider circulation of Wisconsin cheese, and even for a "cheese holiday." [77] The election that fall gave the opponents of the trade program the chance to lay the blame for the plight of the cheese industry on the trade treaties.[78]

Governor-elect Julius P. Heil of Wisconsin, whose respect for facts was generally exceeded by his ignorance of them, said, "I think it is a shame to allow farm produce from other countries to be sold in Wisconsin in competition with your milk, your cheese, your peas, your cherries. . . ." [79] He urged the citizens of Wisconsin to help the rural areas empty their warehouses by purchasing their products. "First we have got to look after our homes and fireside, and never mind the others." "If you want to send Christmas presents to someone, why don't you send something that will help the home state. Get a side of [Wisconsin] bacon or ham. Or, if you'd rather send Wisconsin cheese, God bless you, send that. We have got to get our warehouses empty." [80]

The Republican *Wisconsin State Journal* in similar vein wrote: "The only glimmer of light . . . is that this nation will not enter into any reciprocal agreements with Germany and that no opportunity will be given for the dumping through a barter exchange of cheap labor product from the Reich upon the people of the United States." [81]

Heil also was of the opinion that prosperity began not with the farme but with the industrialists. He made it plain that there could be no pros perity for either the farmer or labor unless it first came to the industrialist "It is so important that the industries be so busy so that the group of me that I represent may have orders and employ men. Can't you realize tha you farmers cannot be prosperous unless industry is prosperous?" [8

The following year Secretary Hull, speaking before the annual conven tion of the American Farm Bureau Federation, again reviewed the ec nomic dislocations that came after World War I, the disruptions in th

77. *Ibid.*, August 11, 1938.
78. *Capital Times*, November 22, 1938.
79. *Ibid.*, December 8, 1938.
80. *Ibid.*, November 28, 1938.
81. *Wisconsin State Journal*, November 21, 1938.
82. *Capital Times*, December 8, 1938.

normal channels of trade and finance, the maladjustments in agriculture and industry, and the pursuit by individual nations of "the perilous road of narrow nationalism." We witnessed an era of high tariffs, quotas, import licenses, exchange controls, barter arrangements, currency manipulation, and many other devices to choke off world trade. The American contribution to this dilemma was the Smoot-Hawley tariff, "one of the most ill-timed and costly pieces of legislation in the entire history of this country."

Hull said that the farmers had benefited from the trade program. Over the five-year period that these pacts operated, trade treaties were negotiated that accounted for "practically three-fifths of our total foreign trade." Hull pointed to the corn-hog industry as one that was becoming heavily dependent on export outlets again; barriers against American bacon, pork, and ham had been retained in ten countries; nine countries reduced their barriers on American lard, and three others agreed not to impose them; the removal of the burdensome duty by Britain was considered an achievement of first importance. Also, grain and grain products were reported flowing into foreign lands. According to Hull, American trade with trade-agreement countries had grown by almost 50 per cent, while that with nonagreement countries had either failed to increase or else had declined slightly. He held that the recovery of the foreign market was essential to the recovery of American agriculture, but it was apparent that the outbreak of the European war in 1939 confronted the nation "with severe new trade restrictions in many countries." [83]

Late in 1938 it was plain, even to the most casual observer, that a new frontal assault would be launched against the existing farm legislation with the avowed purpose of placing a new measure on the statute books when Congress convened in January. In order to speed up and encourage the drafting of the new measure, various farm organizations had already made known their plans for convening in Washington. It was then said that their aim was to pass a law "to free the farmers from restrictions on production and to increase their incomes."

Reports had it that administration leaders favored retaining the control features of the existing law but nevertheless welcomed changes, especially if they would make the program more effective. Wallace wanted processing taxes to raise the needed funds to finance the program and a

83. *New York Times,* December 6, 1939.

two-price system that would make it possible for families in the "depressed third" of the population to buy products at below the prevailing price levels. Wallace likewise hinted that lending rates on farm products should be lowered to a level that would promote sales in the export markets.

Regardless of what was said against the 1938 act, it was crystal clear that its critics had nothing to offer in its place other than the customary crop of proposals ranging from monetary reforms, export subsidies, and rigid government price fixing to subsidies on domestic consumption, unlimited production, and tariff revision. Numerous bills embodying these and other proposals had been prepared for introduction in Congress.[84]

When Congress convened in January, 1939, it was split four ways on the farm issue. At that time the long-expected "cost of production" bill was introduced, with the names of some eighteen United States senators and fifteen congressmen attached to it. This was the most radical of the proposed farm legislation; it called for the government to fix the prices of a number of farm products and to compel dealers and handlers of these commodities to pay a fixed price on the share of the crop that was sold in this country, the rest to be sold abroad for whatever price it would bring. This plan would discard all the production-control and marketing quota provisions of the administration program. When all was said and done, the appearance of this price-fixing bill had the effect of sharpening the lines of political battle and also of making the prospects of passing new farm legislation remote.

The list of senators supporting this bill was formidable and gave the impression to many that there was a good chance of its passing the Senate. The measure was sponsored by Senator Lynn Frazier and Representative Bill Lemke, both of North Dakota. Its supporters in the upper house included ten Democrats, five Republicans, two Farmer-Laborites, and one Progressive; the eight House members included four Democrats, three Republicans, and one Progressive, plus seven more who planned to join the group shortly.

The four camps into which the farm-relief advocates were divided were roughly these: (1) those who wanted to stand by the existing program, headed by Roosevelt, Wallace, and other top administration spokes-

84. *Ibid.*, December 4, 1938.

men, along with the head of the American Farm Bureau Federation, E. A. O'Neal; (2) those who wanted outright repeal of the existing farm program, including eastern Republicans, some conservative Democrats, and such inveterate foes of the New Deal as Dan Casement and C. C. Cogswell of Kansas; (3) adherents of the domestic allotment plan of paying subsidies and dispensing with production and marketing control; (4) the group backing the cost-of-production bill, including such senators as Frazier and Nye of North Dakota, Shipstead and Lundeen of Minnesota, La Follette of Wisconsin, Capper of Kansas, Gurney of South Dakota, and Burke of Nebraska.[85]

Senator Wheeler of Montana, also a supporter of "cost of production," said, "This country will not be able to maintain a democracy unless farmers get the cost of production for their products." Opponents insisted that it would be difficult to fix prices for a long list of farm products on millions of farms. Wheeler replied that the government already had made it possible for labor and industry to fix prices. "You can't have industry on a price-fixing basis as it is today and agriculture on a competitive basis." "If agriculture is destroyed with its vast purchasing power then industry will be destroyed."[86]

Keen interest was expressed by senators from the wheat states in the suggestion made by Secretary Wallace that the Frazier-Lemke cost-of-production plan might be tried on wheat alone as an experiment, especially if Congress was favorable to the idea. Senator Capper of Kansas was inclined to follow the suggestion to experiment with wheat. Senator Frazier said that it would be better than nothing, but hardly fair to the other farmers. At the same time he expressed surprise at the Wallace testimony that the domestic consumption of hogs and cattle would decline more than 50 per cent if prices on these products were raised to cost-of-production levels.

Two good reasons were advanced for suggesting that the plan be tried out with wheat first. One was that wheat consumption fell very little as prices went up, while with products like meat, consumption often fell as rapidly as meat prices rose. A second reason was that the support for price fixing was centered largely in the wheat areas.[87]

85. *Pioneer Press,* January 13, 1939. 86. *Ibid.,* February 9, 1939.
87. *Ibid.,* February 11, 1939.

On the eve of a vote by the House Agriculture Committee on the Frazier-Lemke price-fixing measure, a large group of Farmers' Union spokesmen from the spring wheat area and others representing the grain cooperatives in that region launched an unsparing attack on the measure. This group, led by Myron W. Thatcher of St. Paul and Glenn Talbott of North Dakota, demanded death for the measure in a letter to Representative Jones of the House committee.

This came as a great surprise, because the proponents of the measure had counted on the Farmers' Union for their strongest support. This meant that the organizations from the area for which Senator Frazier and Congressman Lemke purported to speak were aligned against the bill and that it was without the support of any major farm group. These spokesmen for the Farmers' Union said that no one in Washington was authorized to speak in favor of the bill in their behalf.[88] After a 15 to 6 vote against the bill, the committee pigeonholed it.[89]

Meanwhile members of the upper house began to gird themselves for action. A group of twenty western and southern senators sought passage of the proposal despite its overwhelming rejection by the House committee, which had acted in line with the wishes of the administration. This decision of the twenty senators also came in the face of a blistering attack from the Farmers' Union. This was proof that the Union had been split wide-open on a question that farm economists had long felt was unworkable and prohibitive in cost.

The Farmers' Union's statement was this:

> The police force necessary to enforce provisions for regulation and regimentation outlined in S570 staggers the imagination. How extensive bootlegging and policing would become is far beyond that envisioned by the proponents of the measure.
>
> The measure would centralize authority in the Secretary of Agriculture to a degree never hitherto contemplated nor proposed. Even a casual perusal of the provisions reveals that the powers accord[ed] to the Secretary are indeed amazing.
>
> While the Secretary of Agriculture has been accused on many occasions by leading proponents of S570 of exercising despotic powers over the American farmer, S570 in its practical operations would make him a dictator in both

88. *Ibid.*, April 20, 1939.
89. *St. Paul Dispatch*, April 25, 1939.

name and fact. The measure provides for an all-too-perfect pattern for authoritarian control of our agricultural population.

The degree and scope of regulation and regimentation necessary to make such a measure operative far exceeds anything yet proposed for a democracy and to the Congress. The ultimate operations of the measure would involve such sweeping bureaucratic control over all persons and agencies engaged in the production, marketing, processing and distribution of agricultural commodities as to require almost complete nullification of our traditional concept of democracy.

Simply establishing a price does not necessarily mean that buyers will be readily available with adequate purchasing power to absorb the volume needed for domestic consumption. Unfortunately, buyers cannot be coerced into buying when purchasing power is not adequate to meet the price demanded.

In other words, price alone constitutes only half of the problem in buying and selling transactions. S570 blandly ignores this obviously fundamental fact.

The measure fails to provide adequate and effective differentials as to the many grades and varieties of each commodity included in its sweeping provisions. The tendency to lump together with happy abandon all grades and varieties of each commodity and establishing a similar price for each is a wholly untenable position.

Inasmuch as S570 explicitly applies only to agricultural commodities actually entering into the channels of interstate commerce, intrastate traffic in such commodities remains outside the effective scope of the measure.

The obviously natural result of such an oversight would be the erection of forty-eight separate nations within the United States in so far as agricultural products are concerned. The most casual perusal of the provisions of S570 makes this fact self-evident.[90]

In the spring of 1939 an alternative proposal, "the certificate payment plan," supported by Myron Thatcher, described as "a balanced budget type" of farm program, came into the limelight with the apparent blessings of Henry Wallace. The virtue claimed for this proposal was that it combined the processing-tax feature of the original A.A.A. with the marketing-quota system, which recently had been upheld by the United States Supreme Court in a sweeping decision. It would furnish a continuous source of revenue for parity payments, functioning on a pay-as-you-go basis, and at the same time take the A.A.A. program out of the fire of the growing economy drive in Congress.

The plan had been worked out in some details with respect to wheat. It had two principal features: it would call for the payment of a process-

90. *New York Times,* April 27, 1939.

ing tax of from thirty to forty cents a bushel on all wheat milled for domestic consumption; and there would be issued to farmers complying with the A.A.A. wheat program tax certificates "to cover the proportion of their wheat marketing quota which, on the average, is consumed in the United States." Certificates would not be issued to farmers not complying with the program.

According to this plan, the flour millers would have no place to buy tax certificates except from the wheat farmers who complied with the program. The cooperating farmer would have certificates to cover his share of the domestically consumed portion of the crop. "That is, if a farmer had an acreage allotment of 100 acres and a normal acreage production of ten bushels per acre, and the domestically consumed share was put at 60 per cent of the total, he would get tax certificates on 60 per cent of 1,000 bushels, or 600 bushels."

This would make up the parity payment of the farmer, the major part, at least, of the difference between the current and the parity price. It would also act as a form of crop insurance, because in the event of complete or partial crop failure, the farmer would have the sale of his full quota of certificates as a source of income. The certificates would take the place of parity payments and the sum collected by the cooperating farmer would be had in addition to payments for soil conservation.

The farmer who failed to comply with the program would be forced to sell at the world price for export, or else buy tax certificates for all wheat sold on the domestic market, which, in turn, would furnish a strong incentive to cooperate with the program.

The plan was encouraged in Congress in opposition to the proposals for increases of $250,000,000 or more over the House appropriations for parity payments on the ground that the parity payments were piling up a big deficit and increasing the public debt. Wallace and other leaders had contended all along that the farmers would never have any assurance of permanence to their program until they recovered the continuous source of revenue which was lost to them by the adverse court decision in the Hoosac Mills case in 1936. The processing taxes had been yielding $500,000,000 or more a year.[91]

Very late in 1939 the income-certificate plan ran into opposition in

91. *Pioneer Press,* April 22, 1939.

administration circles. A lengthy conference of "an interdepartmental committee of top-fiscal officials" was called by direction of Roosevelt, Wallace, and his aides to get agreement on the plan. The Treasury Department looked askance upon the certificate plan and opposed it on the grounds that it was a tax. The opposition of Henry Morgenthau seemed to be causing the President to go along with that department instead of with Wallace. As was to be expected, additional opposition, and very weighty too, came from the processors concerned. The flour millers had been particularly opposed to it.

Support for the proposal came from Wallace, Senator Wheeler, and the Farmers' Union, especially in the spring wheat states. Wheeler not only supported it in public speeches, but also introduced a bill embodying the plan.[92]

Regardless of what grievances the farmers had had, and despite all efforts made by the administration to shape a long-range program, the outbreak of the European war in the late summer of 1939 had important effects on prices. Within a matter of a few days after the outbreak of hostilities, grain prices on the Chicago market soared as high as government and exchange rules would permit them to go.[93] "Trading came to a standstill. Rules which have been put into effect the past six years to curb runaway speculative markets met their first real test. Because they prohibited prices from going any higher than the daily limits amounting to 5 cents in wheat and rye, 4 cents in corn and 3 cents in oats, they throttled trade." Buyers with orders to buy millions of bushels were unable to fill them because there were few sellers who wanted to dispose of their holdings at the maximum prices. Only a few sales took place, the first time in exchange history that anything like this had happened.[94] Late in 1939 the Chicago market was described as "a seething caldron" that "bubbled over with the greatest flood of orders it has had to digest in months as prices skyrocketed in the wheat, rye and soy bean pits." At the same time grain prices on the Minneapolis market had closed sharply with wheat leading the way.[95]

92. *Ibid.,* December 10, 14, 20, 1939.
93. *St. Paul Dispatch,* September 5, 1939.
94. *Pioneer Press,* September 6, 1939.
95. *Ibid.,* December 19, 1939.

Chapter XIX

EPILOGUE

PERHAPS the one thing that stands out conspicuously among agrarian developments during the first two decades of the century is that the farmers were temporarily enjoying the fruits of prosperity. Even though these good times were not shared in by all farmers, and doubts were voiced whether they were good times, there were those who viewed the rising farm prices, incomes, and land values as proof that this was the "golden age" of American agriculture. When the war created heavy demands for food, these optimists found additional cause to believe that the need for our goods would give our farmers a profitable export market for many years to come. If there were any alarmists in their midst who dared to find some cause for alarm in the rising production costs, mounting debts, and overexpansion, or to entertain doubts about the future, they certainly were a meek and inarticulate group. Yet the truth of the matter is that these depressing times came much sooner than even some of the most pessimistic expected.

Many of the problems that faced the farmers, beginning in 1920, were like those of earlier times, except that this time they were more widespread and more aggravated, and had come swiftly upon the heels of a vanishing prosperity. The overexpansion of agriculture; the want of a program to aid the farmers convert from wartime to peacetime needs; sharp price drops; heavy freight, tax, and labor costs; high prices for farmers' supplies; and the lack of credit to tide them through the early months of the depression helped make their lot an unsatisfactory one.

Later events show that the two decades of relative good times were followed by almost two decades of depression and ceaseless agitation. During the first half of the 1920's, the farmers complained of the high prices they paid for what they bought and the low prices they received for what they sold. Beginning in about 1926 the tide shifted a little in their favor and they continued to enjoy these better times until the crash of 1929. But from then on until 1933 falling prices, crushing debts, the lack of foreign markets, heavy surpluses, and pleas for bigger and better farm programs became the order of the day. The forthcoming federal aids, coupled with bad weather and short crops, helped raise prices and farm incomes from 1933 to 1937. Then came the relapse of late 1937 and 1938, the New Deal defeat in the congressional elections of the latter part of the year, the outbreak of the European war in 1939, and finally the surging prices which temporarily drowned out many of the farmers' complaints.

The fact that agrarians from the western Middle West appeared as conspicuously as they did during these years can easily create the impression that the area was strictly an agricultural one. But the most cursory examination disproves this. The states in this area were neither the most rural nor the most urban part of the country; they occupied a sort of middle ground. As late as 1940 the total population accounted for less than 25,000,000 people, a figure that took in the city dwellers of Illinois and the substantial number of urban residents in Wisconsin, Missouri, Minnesota, and Iowa. The most rural states were North Dakota and South Dakota.[1]

Even though urbanism and industrialism made heavy inroads into the western Middle West, and granted that in 1939 this area was far from being exclusively an agrarian one, the fact is that it played a leading role in the agricultural thinking of the country. The bulk of its wealth consisted of wheat, corn, livestock, dairy products, and the various factors that went into production of these commodities. Depressed or not, it was the spokesmen for these groups who, through their legislators, farm leaders, and nonfarm sympathizers, took the lead in campaigns to get higher prices, to gain better credit facilities, to adopt surplus-control measures, to establish more efficient methods of marketing and purchasing, and to

1. *Statistical Abstract of the United States,* 1941, p. 7; *ibid.,* 1930, p. 46.

pass countless other measures designed to better the lot of the farmers. It was they who were most instrumental in laying down a barrage of charges against the industrial order in which agriculture found itself. They argued, and with much effect, that many, if not most, of the difficulties from which the farmers suffered arose from the subjugation of agriculture to the hegemony of the industrial state. Indignantly they warned the policy makers, and our industrial, financial and commercial leaders, that our entire social economy would suffer from maladjustments unless a better balance was established between agriculture, industry, and labor.

The role assumed by the agrarians poses a double-barreled question. First, why is it that this farm agitation reached the peak that it did in the western Middle West instead of in the South, which certainly was far more distressed, or in the New England and Middle Atlantic states, or for that matter on the Pacific Coast? Second, why is it that so much of the farm leadership came from these states?

Perhaps one reason why the New England and the Middle Atlantic states failed to furnish leadership in the fashion that led the western Middle West is that farming had been declining there for some years. Besides, several of the causes which made for this endless unrest were absent in these states. These farmers were close to the large centers of population, hence to the biggest consuming centers in the country. These conditions fostered an intensive as opposed to an extensive type of farming, such as dairying and vegetable and fruit growing, which contributed to keep the price of land and farm values low and in turn protected the farmers from the evil effects of inflation and tenancy.[2] The nearness of the market also meant lower freight costs for them; the lower land values meant lighter tax burdens, while the intensive methods of farming encouraged by these conditions yielded crops of greater intrinsic value. Such a state of affairs was neither conducive to an agitative spirit nor productive of an aggressive type of farm leadership. Perhaps the more complacent spirit that prevailed in these states helps account for the fact that the Grange—the conservative, ritualistic, rural Masonic order—made the progress that it did in these parts.

2. E. A. Goldenweiser and Leon E. Truesdell, *Farm Tenancy in the United States*, Bureau of the Census (Washington, 1924), pp. 23, 48, 50–51; Report of the President's Committee, *Farm Tenancy*, National Resources Committee (Washington, 1937), p. 96.

This does not mean that the eastern farmers were a submissive, docile lot. Hardly; they had their grievances and they spoke out in protest, but even in doing this they showed little affection for the farmers farther west, which goes a long way in explaining why they failed to support the McNary-Haugen measures. Some easterners with a dimmer view of the future felt that if they cooperated with the westerners they would be encouraging a type of competition which in the long run would work against their interests. Some of the older farmers in the East remembered quite well how in their earlier years the opening up of the cheaper, fertile lands of the West put them at a competitive disadvantage. They remembered that this had worked greater hardships on them than had the rise of manufactures and industry and the growth of commerce and finance, the agencies against which the westerners aimed some of their sharpest complaints.

As for the South, it seems that the reasons why it failed to assume this leadership are to be found in the demoralization and poverty which followed the Civil War, the complications that arose out of the race difficulties, and the prevalence of tenancy and production problems which differed from those in the western Middle West. Not to be ignored is the general suspicion and antipathy which still persisted in many quarters toward programs originating with the federal government.

The South, to be sure, supported federal programs like the A.A.A. as perhaps no other part of the country did. It also gave rise to its own farmer organizations and produced its own leaders. The beginnings of the Grange are attributed in part to the deplorable conditions that Oliver Hudson Kelley saw in the South after the Civil War; the Farmers' Alliance was partly southern in its origins and the Agricultural Wheel entirely so; while the Farmers' Union, which was organized in Texas and which spread across the South with amazing speed before it invaded the Middle West, was also the product of southern distress. Then, too, southern spokesmen were heard from in the halls of Congress. Farm leaders like Edward A. O'Neal and Charles S. Barrett, the heads of the American Farm Bureau Federation and the national Farmers' Union, both southerners, were influential in Washington. Yet when all is said and done, the fact remains that most of these organizations either were longer-lived or most influential among the farmers of the western Middle West.

At first the South seemed hesitant about supporting federal farm programs, at least when compared with the eagerness with which the agrarian western Middle West endorsed them. Nor was it on as strong a financial footing as the middle western area. Cotton still remained the number-one staple of the region, and its producers were far more dependent on the foreign market for the sale of their products than were the western wheat and livestock producers. When the southerners were invited to join hands with the western farmers, they were dubious, hesitant, skeptical—perhaps because they felt that their problems were different, perhaps because of a sense of apathy or surviving sectional tensions, or perhaps because of a combination of these and other reasons. When the southerners finally did consent to cooperate, they did so only because of much persuasion, and in the end their interest in the venture usually turned out to be a short-lived junior partnership.

The Pacific states can be disposed of more readily. To a considerable degree the farmers from this area were the victims of geography. They were isolated from the rest of the farming nation in many respects; the type of farming they engaged in was different from that of the more disaffected areas; and the influx of settlers from other parts of the country helped provide it with a flourishing activity that betrayed distress until the impact of the Great Depression.

If there were good reasons why farmers in other parts of the country did not take the leadership in farm action, there is at least one good reason why those from the western Middle West did. The most obvious is that the area had long been the scene of a great series of farm groups, some longer-lived than the others, but nevertheless all of them casting a strong influence over the thinking of the region. These states early had become the center for some of the bitterest of Granger battles, followed in turn by those of the Farmers' Alliance and the Populists. When the Grange shifted many of its activities to the states east of the Mississippi and advanced into the Middle Atlantic and New England states, and the Farmers' Alliance and the Populists started to disintegrate, new farm organizations arose to fill in the vacuum created by the decline of the older ones. The lengthy procession that followed reflected the farmers' agitable frame of mind. There were the various state farmers' grain dealers associations, the American Society of Equity, the Farmers' Union, the Farmers' Equity Union, the Nonpartisan League, the Missouri Farmers' Association, the American Farm Bureau Federation, the National Producers' Alliance, and groups like the American Council of Agriculture, the Corn Belt Committee, the Committee of Twenty-Two, the Farm Holiday Association, and scores of commodity associations, not to mention the abortive efforts made by minority groups to band farmers and labor together for joint political action.

One can hardly ignore the importance of these farm groups, whose demands met with greater approval than did the sober, well-meaning, and reasoned recommendations of some of our indifferent, unsympathetic, and cynical scholars. These bodies proved that, no matter how hard pressed the farmers were, they usually had in their midst leaders of some means and influence who could be counted upon to lead a campaign for relief. Organized farm campaigns were bound to be of influence in a "groupistic" society that was responsive to group pressures. This proved to be the case even when the farmers were not as closely knit together and as large in numerical strength as some of their leaders would have the country believe.

The first of the twentieth-century farm groups to take roots in the western Middle West was the American Society of Equity. Organized in Indianapolis in 1902, it soon spread into the adjoining states. From the tobacco fields of Kentucky and Tennessee, where it first attracted attention, it shifted its activities into Wisconsin, Minnesota, North Dakota, South Dakota, and Montana. It was in these parts that most of the years of its short-lived career were spent. It seems rather plausible to assume that the Equity banner became a convenient rallying point for discontented wheat growers; ex-Grangers, Alliancemen, and Populists; La Follette Progressives; the small shippers; and the economic radicalism of the Scandinavians.

Especially significant were the early Equity demands for controlled production, withholding products from market, and minimum prices. This is proof that the Equity was a pioneer in the parity price concept, and that its leaders had more in common with the agricultural thinking of the 1920's and 30's than they did with that of the 1870's, 80's, and 90's. One big difference, however, is that the Equity leaders sought their ends without the intervening hand of the federal government.

Another link to unfold itself in the Equity chain was the brief campaign staged by a small minority to encourage direct buying and selling between producers and consumers. This idea became the basis for at least two abortive attempts to get buyers and sellers to cooperate. Judging from the tone of the literature issued by the promoters of these ill-fated ventures, the success scored by the English consumers' movement appears to have been the great inspirational source.

A more lasting phase of the Equity appeared in the campaigns waged by it in behalf of cooperative marketing and purchasing associations. This phase received major attention, especially after the reorganization of the body in 1907. The Equity organized cooperatives in Wisconsin, Minnesota, Montana, North Dakota, South Dakota, and other states. It seems to have placed most stress on the marketing of grain and livestock, especially during the later years. Its more ambitious terminal-marketing experiences, pioneer efforts though they were, were hardly a flattering aspect of its program.

Next, the Farmers' Union invaded the western Middle West. The Union had several things in common with the Equity: it was born in a period of rising prices; it sought profitable prices for the producers of cotton, wheat, livestock, and other commodities; it attacked the boards of trade, chambers of commerce, cotton exchanges, and other organizations of middlemen.

From the South, where it was organized, it spread into Missouri, Kansas, and Nebraska rather early. After failing to absorb the Equity, its leaders launched a vigorous campaign for members in the same area in which its rival held forth. The Union made some progress in recruiting members here, but hardly to the extent that its leaders had hoped. Since its platform was militant and its leadership aggressive, and since it had a certain psychological appeal, it is not surprising that it eventually absorbed the remnants of the Equity, the National Producers' Alliance, and portions of the Nonpartisan League.

The Farmers' Union, like the Equity, passed through several stages before it placed main stress on cooperative marketing and purchasing. All the while it tried to put floors under prices by setting levels below which its members were asked not to sell; it advocated production controls and the construction of a system of warehouses to store products and to finance its minimum price efforts. Many members gave lip service to the formula of "cost of production plus a reasonable profit." Its program was buttressed by an educational program which revolved around such topics as farm credit, land tenure, and marketing.

The Farmers' Union appears to have suffered greatly from the want of cohesion. No doubt other farm groups had the same trouble, but these difficulties seldom broke into the open as often and as melodramatically as they did in the Union. Its spokesmen tried to palm off these outbreaks as being nothing more than the attributes of independent thought and action.

During the late twenties and early thirties, the Union seems to have been split three ways. One small group, conservative and aggressive, spearheaded by an element in the Nebraska Farmers' Union, did not stop with a protest against all forms of state and federal aid, political and central controls, but went further and demanded the return of a decentralized economic order in which cooperatives and small business would play a leading role. No special mention was made of how this decentralized economic order was to come into being. Suffice it to say that this element took its clues from the old-fashioned liberalism of Adam Smith and that it was out of step with the statist views of the majority in the Union. A second group, headed by the northwest Farmers' Union states—Minnesota, South Dakota, North Dakota, Montana, and Wisconsin—was equally enthusiastic about cooperatives, but perhaps it was just as enthusiastic, if not more so, about federal aids and the perfecting of legislative techniques to gain these aids. This tier of Farmers' Union states functioned with great proficiency in both these fields; the cooperatives which rooted themselves in these states were among the most successful in the country, and the legislative committee that represented them in Washington exerted an influence considerably beyond the numerical strength of its members. A third faction, headed by the Iowa Farmers' Union and including parts of the Illinois, Minnesota, Oklahoma, and other state bodies, reverted to the faith of "the founding fathers": "cost of production plus a reasonable profit."

By the very late thirties many Union members had become ardent supporters of parity, which is not surprising in view of the apparent break between the Farm Bureau high command and the administration on the one hand and the good relations existing between Union officials and the New Dealers on the other.

One of the most spectacular of farmers' political movements was the Nonpartisan League, which was organized in North Dakota in 1915. Its efforts, like those of its contemporaries, were facilitated considerably by the earlier activities of the Grange, the Farmers' Alliance, the American Society of Equity, and, hard as it may be for some to believe, by the Socialist party of North Dakota. The League placed considerable emphasis on the fact that the farmers of the state comprised the overwhelming majority of the population; hence they were entitled to a dominant influence in the state government. It argued that state ownership of warehouses, terminal facilities, banking institutions, and other agencies vital to the farmers had more to offer them than did an antiquated marketing system which catered to selfish, sordid interests or the cooperative marketing reforms of the Equity.

The League, by a strange blending of promotional techniques and state ownership, hoped to build a new political movement based on public ownership that was devoid of the Socialist label. It proceeded on the assumption that cooperative marketing and buying in themselves would never defeat the grain and milling trust, but that a farmer-controlled government could if it erected a state-owned industry on a scale that was big enough to have an effect on the market price.

The League program was helped considerably by the prosperity of the war and prewar years which made it possible for the farmers to pay dues, and also by the fact that its leaders had amassed one of the most artful groups of radical writers, speakers, and publicists that the nation had ever seen. As a result, the League had no sooner swept through North Dakota like a prairie fire than it began to look for new territory to conquer.

By 1918 the League was in complete control of the government of North Dakota, and the next year its industrial program, calling for state-owned warehouses, elevators, banks, mills, and other agencies, was enacted into law. Plans were also announced for extending this program into Wisconsin, Minnesota, Nebraska, Montana, and other states, but nothing substantial materialized. In 1920 a League-endorsed slate was elected in Wisconsin, but it was well known that this was nothing more than the La Follette Progressives riding into office under a new name. Only in

North Dakota was the League program put into operation, and there it met with varying degrees of success. Stalwart Republicans denounced it when out of power, but once they had been elected to office and were in a position to abolish the program, they did nothing of the sort because of the patronage opportunities that it provided them.

An evaluation of the League contributions is difficult. It stressed the role that the government could play in aiding the farmers, but at the same time it proved the futility of a single state's acting alone. We also know that for better or for worse, it brought into prominence political figures such as William Langer, William "Liberty Bill" Lemke (Father Coughlin's candidate for the Presidency in 1936), Lynn Frazier, and Henrik Shipstead. It also paved the way for the Minnesota Farmer-Labor party and the emergence of Floyd B. Olson and Elmer Benson. Worth investigating, yet hard to prove, is the claim that the League program helped to keep down the evils of land speculation and tenancy because of the extremist nature of its demands.

Another sign of the importance of the western Middle West in providing farm leadership for the nation was seen in the rise to power of the American Farm Bureau Federation, certainly one of the most powerful, if not absolutely the most powerful, farm groups in American history. Even though it planted itself firmly in other parts of the country, especially in the South, after the coming of the New Deal, the Farm Bureau perhaps reflected the legislative and economic demands of the western Middle West much more than it did those of any other part of the country. The fact that it championed cooperative marketing, in the face of strong sectional opposition, at the time that the national organization was founded, the election of an Iowan as the first national president, and the militant campaign that it waged, first in behalf of the McNary-Haugen plan and then for parity, are ample proof that it was concerned with western middle western interests. It is no secret that the Bureau, by endorsing the cooperative movement during its early years and giving to it the vigorous support that it did, alienated the support of many of its early patrons who preferred that it pursue an educational program dedicated to bigger and better production.

By 1920 some very obvious groupings were in evidence. The American Farm Bureau Federation, with the Iowa and Illinois bodies wielding tremendous influence, was a forceful agency. Amply fortified with funds, publicity, membership, and powerful nonfarm backing, it was highly reflective of the conservatism that generally followed in the aftermath of the war. It had much in common with the Grange, which no longer was the force that it once had been in this part of the country, but it was bitterly opposed by older groups like the Farmers' Union, the remains of the Equity, and the Nonpartisan League. The latter groups insisted, in fact do to this very day, that the Bureau was a stalking horse for the financial and industrial interests that were frightened by the upsurge of radicalism.

Farm Bureau members, cooperative buying and selling associations, and other activities of the organization were most numerous in the states of Illinois, Iowa, Minnesota, Indiana, and Ohio. As time elapsed the Bureau grew in Kansas and Missouri, despite the solid entrenchment of the Missouri Farmers' Association in the latter state, but little progress was made in North Dakota, South Dakota, and Nebraska, where the rival Farmers' Union enjoyed varying degrees of success. Likewise, Chicago remained the headquarters for both the national organization and the powerful Illinois Agricultural Association. Over the period from 1920 to 1939 three out of four of the national presidents came from the Middle West. Iowa, Ohio, and Illinois each contributed one, and Alabama the fourth.

The elevation of Edward O'Neal of Alabama to the presidency in 1931 was more an act of political expediency than it was a tribute to either the influence of the South or the state of Alabama. A smashing Democratic victory was anticipated in 1932, and the belief was that the Bureau stood a better chance to taking part in New Deal policy-shaping matters and in building up its membership if a life-long Democrat was made its national president. O'Neal's incumbency, though exceeding the combined tenures of the first three presidents by a number of years, is hardly an accurate index of Bureau membership in the South.

Earl Smith of Illinois, the second in command for a number of years, was more of a representative of the western Middle West. As a personality, he was hardly the dramatic and volatile type that O'Neal was, but many considered him the brains of the organization and he was once regarded as the logical successor to O'Neal when and if the Republicans again gained control in Washington. More specifically, Smith represented the corn-hog wing of the cotton and corn-hog alliance within the Farm Bureau. His formula for farm relief was "political pressure and co-operatives."

One of the most noteworthy contributions of the Farm Bureau was the campaign that it waged in behalf of cooperative marketing and purchasing. As a rule, cooperatives failed to attract the attention that they deserved because they provided less exciting materials for writers than did the legislative and political activities of the farmers. Some of the associations failed to come up to the standards generally prescribed for cooperatives, while in the early years the Bureau incited antagonism because it established cooperatives in areas already organized by older farm groups. Still, the successes scored by it more than offset the failures and the work of associations of dubious cooperative standing.

Originally, the Farm Bureau placed much faith in cooperatives and commodity-pooling programs, but beginning in about 1924 its leaders came around to the view that something more was needed. At this time it went all out for "tariff equality," the need of "a fair exchange value" for the farmers, and the equalization fee. When the Farm Bureau saw that the McNary-Haugen measures had been defeated, it opportunistically endorsed the program of the Federal Farm Board, and when that failed it became a bulwark of support for the A.A.A. and parity. Meanwhile, the Bureau interest in cooperatives continued, but this was overshadowed by the more dramatic campaigns waged in behalf of "tariff equality" and parity.

The Bureau is best observed in a pressure-group setting. Legislative pressure was a byword in Bureau circles from the time of its inception, and even more so after the New Deal had taken office. Bureau leaders could hardly have been expected to overlook the encouragement given the farmers by the new administration to come to Washington with their own programs. Farm leaders had early discovered that having something over which to agitate kept up the interest of members, attracted new converts, and impressed legislators. Legislators and administrators also became convinced that the Bureau was a force with which to contend; they sounded it out on important legislation, compromising with it on occasions or yielding to its demands. The Bureau was represented in many important hearings, even those which remotely affected agriculture.

Critics of the Bureau were heard to say that the hue and cry that the organization raised over parity was due not to an implicit faith in it, but rather to its potentialities as a bargaining device. It could be used as a club to force tariff increases on some farm commodities, obtain government subsidies for others, abolish some of the corporate and labor controls, and perhaps some day bring the major nonfarm groups back within hailing distance of the free competitive system under which the farmers claimed that they wanted to operate. If nothing else, the Bureau could justify its right to exist.[3]

Besides the Equity, the Farmers' Union, the Nonpartisan League, and the American Farm Bureau Federation, there were lesser bodies: the short-lived National Producers' Alliance, the Missouri Farmers' Association (a body of considerable substance), and numerous independent commodity groups like the Land O'Lakes Creameries, the Central Cooperative Livestock Association, the business agencies of the Farmers' Equity Union, the state farmers' grain dealers' associations and numerous other agencies. What they advocated and accomplished was hardly different from that sought by the other bodies.

Among the political spokesmen for the region were Arthur Capper of Kansas, Henrik Shipstead of Minnesota, Lynn Frazier of North Dakota, the La Follettes of Wisconsin, George Norris of Nebraska, Peter Norbeck of South Dakota, and others. The senior La Follette helped hand down the torch of Grangerism and Populism to the succeeding generations, and kept it alive after much of its effectiveness had expired. Norris, who also was a carry-over from the insurgency period of the years before World War I, managed to hold office until after the New Deal had ended and played a big role in much of the farm legislation that was passed. Capper, Shipstead, and Frazier, on the other hand, were products of the agricultural unrest of the postwar era. Capper was the most orthodox spokesman of the lot. But both Shipstead and Frazier, however, were representatives of political and economic unorthodoxy when elected to office. Frazier remained faithful to this minority point of view, but Shipstead, with the passing of years, moved more into the orbit of conformity.

3. Theodore Saloutos, "The American Farm Bureau Federation and Farm Policy: 1933 to 1945," *Southwestern Social Science Quarterly,* XXVIII (March, 1948), pp. 313–33.

The campaign for more efficient marketing methods reached its peak during the 1920's. During the first flush of enthusiasm of the early twenties, it had the backing of the American Farm Bureau Federation. Part and parcel of this better marketing campaign were drives to get farmers to sign iron-clad contracts to sell their particular commodities through the same organization for a period of years, usually five, by pooling and withholding their products from market if necessary. The reasoning behind this movement was based on the premise that the plight of agriculture could be alleviated if the benefits of consolidation and combination which were so well known to industry and business were applied to the marketing of the farmers' products.

Another segment of farmers, split into two schools of thought, placed considerable emphasis on political action. The conservative wing, the farm bloc, spearheaded by the American Farm Bureau Federation, transcended partisan lines. There was nothing ideological or theoretical about its demands. Incensed over the failure of Congress to pass legislation designed to help the farmers, the farm bloc thwarted the efforts of the stalwarts to adjourn Congress and launched a vigorous counteroffensive for legislation to regulate the packers, to liberalize credit facilities, and to encourage cooperatives. Another group, supported by liberals, progressives, and elements in the Farmers' Union, the Equity, and the Nonpartisan League, wanted to go beyond this and build a new party committed to a broad program for social and economic reconstruction. Inspired in part by the work of the British Labor party, spokesmen for this group hoped to do on this side of the Atlantic what the liberals were doing on the other. Differences within, personal ambitions, and the conservative drift of the postwar years kept their program in abeyance for a time. Frustrated in their first bid for votes in 1920, they gained courage from the congressional elections of 1922 and entered the presidential campaign of 1924 with some hope. This new alignment, steeped in the best traditions of Grangerism and Populism, went down to defeat, but only after it amassed the largest third-party vote on record.

Long before these latest hopes of the third-party enthusiasts had been quashed, agrarian attitudes toward the tariff had been crystallizing. For years many farmers voted for a tariff, expecting that it would bring them larger markets and higher prices; but instead of gaining these ends they found themselves face to face with surpluses, vanishing foreign markets, and higher prices for what they bought. Crops like cotton and wheat were especially vulnerable to violent price fluctuations over which the domestic producers had little or no control. In other words, the agrarians, whether justified or not, came to feel that the tariff system as it operated brought them greater burdens than benefits, and they became determined to right the balance.

The critics of American tariff policy had been advancing several proposals: one was to lower the tariff schedules to a point that would encourage a freer flow of trade between nations and would bring down the prices of goods the consumers bought; a second called for a "scientific tariff" that would be based on equal costs of production; and a third sought tariff equality for agriculture.

The campaign for "tariff equality" had special appeal. This approach appeared more expedient. In a decade that had gone all out for high tariffs, the agrarians reasoned that they had a better chance for relief by seeking to be placed under a more effective system of protection than by trying to gain this relief through a diametrically opposite drive for tariff reduction.

As someone wrote, "The term 'tariff equality' had a Delphic vagueness: to practical politicians it meant sufficient concessions to the West to hold them to their traditional party loyalty, but it soon developed that realistic spokesmen for western agriculture meant by the term something very different from a few almost meaningless duties." As a result leaders from the corn belt believed that "agriculture must have a subsidy . . . to offset the subsidy in the form of a tariff which was given to the eastern manufacturers. The East rebelled against what it termed the 'unsound' policy of paying a subsidy to agriculture. . . ."[4]

The drive for McNary-Haugenism was of great significance. This effort to make the tariff effective for agriculture, coming in an era when protectionism reached the highest point in history, came closer to giving the farmers a sense of unity than did any single farm campaign up to that time. It appears certain that the vigorous drive waged in its behalf forced the Republicans to give greater support to the cooperative move-

4. Frank W. Fetter, *The New Deal and Tariff Policy,* University of Chicago, Public Policy Pamphlet No. 7 (Chicago, 1937), pp. 18–19.

ment, perhaps more than they would have liked, because they looked upon it as the lesser of the two evils. Administration opposition forced the McNary-Haugenites to band together into bodies like the American Council of Agriculture, the Corn Belt Committee, and others for the purpose of coordinating their activities. Said the *St. Paul Dispatch,* "Unless agriculture enjoys the same American price standard as transportation, finance, labor and manufacturing, a permanently fair exchange value between the products of the soil and those of the shop, between the East and West cannot exist. That means the decline and submergence of agriculture, and transformation of the independent, land-owning farmer into something like a peasant."[5]

Another thing the McNary-Haugen movement did was to bring to the surface conflicting interests within agriculture. One of the best proofs of this is furnished by the failure of the corn-hog and wheat leaders to bring the South into the equalization fee fold. Southern cooperative leaders, to be sure, gave lip service to "tariff equality" but at no time did they ever represent a very substantial part of the farmers of their area. History reveals that southern tradition militated against the adoption of any programs that threatened either to increase the power of the federal government or to extend the principle of protection which jeopardized the foreign market for cotton. Experience seems to have taught many of the southerners that their cotton economy could be better aided by federal programs that looked toward the purchase of surpluses, the temporary removal of them from the market, and the implementing of these efforts with an acreage-reduction program. Many southerners also felt that they had to guard their position as consumers. They were led to understand that an equalization fee would "boost the price of flour, meat and meal, the very things that the southern farmers purchase[d] in largest quantities." Such a program would force up the price of mules because a rise in corn prices would make the rise in the price of mules inevitable. "Cotton interests would be short-sighted indeed," wrote the *Cotton Trade Journal,* "to accept this gift horse from the farm bloc Republicans of the midwest whose troubles originate[d] in inflated land values due to postwar speculation rather than in low grain prices."[6]

5. *St. Paul Dispatch,* January 16, 1925.
6. *Cotton Trade Journal* (New Orleans), January 15, 1927.

Potentially, industrialists and consumers were against the equalization fee. Those industrialists who were eager to recapture as much of the foreign market as they possibly could were opposed to any program that threatened to raise the price of food for labor and that of raw materials for industry. It is obvious that the lower the production costs of industry were, the better the chances for American manufacturers to tap the foreign market. Theoretically, millions of consumers also were opposed to any program that threatened to raise their cost of living, but curiously enough their case was presented not by an organized group of their own representatives but by spokesmen of industry and commerce who were hypocritically posing as defenders of the consumers' interests.

By the spring of 1926 the export debenture plan, another farm-relief proposal, entered the arena of farm politics. It was proposed by economist Charles L. Stewart of the University of Illinois, while its most ardent convert was the national Grange. Supporters of the plan called it a simpler one to operate than the McNary-Haugen proposal. It did not provide for the purchasing and storing of surpluses, but it did provide for a bounty on agricultural products. It was an arrangement which promised to make it possible for exporters of those agricultural products of which we produced a surplus to receive a certificate from the Treasury Department. This certificate represented the difference in production costs here and abroad and was to be used "in the payment of import tariffs on any articles later imported." Representatives in Congress drafted bills embodying the chief features of the export debenture plan and introduced them in their respective houses. Hearings were conducted, but the bills never emerged from the committee rooms.

At the same time that the campaign for "tariff equality" reached its peak, the cooperative movement, under Republican encouragement, also was making tremendous strides. In fact, this is one major constructive contribution made during a decade that usually is decried as one of corruption and reaction.

Meanwhile, Calvin Coolidge was telling the farmers that agriculture was about to "resume normalcy" and that what was most needed was cooperative associations for the farmer and higher tariffs for industry. If these Coolidgean exhortations were reassuring to the industrialists, they certainly were nothing of the sort to the organized agrarians. The net result was a widening of the breach between them and the administration. Meanwhile, Republican aid to the cooperatives continued. The Capper-Volstead Act of 1922, the Intermediate Credits Act of 1923, the Purnell Act in 1925, another measure creating the Division of Cooperative Marketing in 1926, another passed in 1927 to prevent discrimination by boards of trade, and finally the Agricultural Marketing Act of 1929 which created the Federal Farm Board were among the important measures having deep roots in the western Middle West.

For the Republicans, the often-referred-to handmaidens of the industrial and financial interests, to sponsor cooperatives and to pour out federal funds for the purpose may appear strange and inconsistent. In fact, there is good reason to have expected the opposite. But for the Republicans to ignore the farmers, whose votes they had counted upon so regularly in the past, would have been a mad piece of political strategy. If anything, the cooperative movement appeared less offensive than did that of the equalization fee. The Republicans also must have realized that cooperatives should be a part of any long-range policy for agriculture, though they were hardly adequate to bring instant relief, and they must have seen that building the efficient marketing bodies for which the cooperatives' most enthusiastic supporters had hoped would be a long-drawn-out process rather than an overnight affair. The Republican stand was that if the farmers were not as well off as they should be, their position at least had improved, and it was but a matter of time before the farm depression would lift completely. But in 1929 when the general economic situation took a turn for the worse, the Republicans, already committed to cooperatives, could do nothing more than offer the farmers larger and larger doses of them and throw stabilization operations in for good measure. Even though this was not what the organized farmers wanted, it also was far more than some of the ardent supporters of the Republican party had bargained for.

In 1928 organizations like the American Farm Bureau Federation, the Farmers' Union, and an undesignated number of commodity associations were on record as being opposed to all forms of farm relief short of the equalization fee. But by 1930 sharp differences were in evidence: the rival farm groups had aligned themselves into Farm Board and anti-Farm Board factions. Hence, elements that were hostile to Republican farm relief in 1928 had become staunch defenders of it by 1930. For instance, the Farm Bureau did a complete about-face when its national president, Sam Thompson, formerly an outspoken McNary-Haugenite, asked the members to close their ranks against the foes of the Farm Board. The Farmers' Union, on the other hand, was badly torn with dissension over the issue. A smoldering controversy broke into the open in 1930 when John A. Simpson, a bitter opponent of the Farm Board, was elected national Union president. His election, however, did not stop the Union's pro-Farm Board faction, which had a strong following in the wheat-growing section, from giving further support to the administration agency. Similar difference broke out in the Corn Belt Committee and reached a climax when administration supporters withdrew to form the National Committee of Farm Organizations.

At least two phases of the Farm Board program—withholding crops from market and acreage-reduction proposals—are noteworthy because they were adopted by the New Dealers and carried to even greater lengths. Withholding operations were engaged in by the Farm Board when it made loans and provided ways and means to withhold crops from market, especially after they could not be sold at the government-sponsored price. In 1933 the Farm Board came to the conclusion that acreage restrictions were indispensable to the success of any farm program. The Board gave special emphasis to these two phases of its program in two sections entitled "Surplus Control Methods" and "Production Adjustment Involves Land Utilization" in its third annual report.

Meanwhile, there had emerged in the state of Iowa the farm holiday movement led by Milo Reno and other elements in the Farmers' Union. They favored a program that would provide the farmers with "cost of production plus a reasonable profit" with the element of force injected into it. This represented an act of desperation in one of the most critical periods in history, an act which gained a few members in the adjoining states, attracted nation-wide attention, and dramatized forcefully the plight of the farmers. Foreclosures were to be checked and farmers were to be persuaded, if necessary by force, not to ship their goods to market unless prices rose to the "cost of production" level designated by its leaders. John A. Simpson was recommended for Secretary of Agriculture. Finally, when the administration failed to accept its price-fixing proposal, the holiday movement directed a bitter campaign against the New Deal and the "college professors." This group also seems to have had a degree of influence on some of the midwest governors, who during the late summer and early fall of 1933 urged the administration to adopt more effective measures to raise prices. Reno wanted the principles of N.R.A. extended to agriculture.

The over-all objective of New Deal relief was to preserve individual farm ownership wherever possible and to provide help for those who had lost their farms or had never owned one. Administration strategists were of the belief that these objectives would be achieved, at least in part, if the farmers got a "parity price." This was a price that would give the producers of a particular commodity a purchasing power equal to that which they enjoyed during some base period in the past, generally from 1909 to 1914. Parity was expected to bring about that better balance between agriculture, industry, and labor to which its supporters gave so much lip service.

Production controls, buttressed by processing taxes, were but one way by which it was promised that the farmers would receive parity; they were the chief means to this end from 1933 to 1936. Other methods included the payment of commodity loans, soil-conservation payments, trade pacts, marketing agreements, export subsidies, rural rehabilitation and electrification programs, inflationary practices, debt adjustment, mortgage relief, and more liberal credit facilities. When the first A.A.A. was declared unconstitutional, the emphasis shifted from production control to soil-conservation practices, and except for the processing tax, most of the other means, with variations, were retained and even added to. For instance, there were more aid for farm tenants—insufficient though it might have been—the ever normal granary plan, and the "all-risk" crop-insurance idea.

Dissatisfaction with the A.A.A., low prices, a drop in city employment, and a large wheat output brought serious New Deal casualties in the congressional elections of 1938, the heaviest losses being registered in the corn-hog and wheat states. In 1939 a new farm-mortgage emergency arose in the dairy, wheat, and beef-cattle states from Minnesota and Iowa westward. The administration sought to handle this crisis by making the Farm Credit Administration a division of the Department of Agriculture rather than the independent agency that it had been. One of the first acts of the F.C.A. in 1934 was to halt foreclosures on defaulted mortgages, but its nonforeclosure policy had relaxed by 1939.

Farmers coming from the western Middle West protested when the A.A.A. failed to operate to their liking. The national Farmers' Union and the Farm Holiday Association poured their wrath on the New Deal because of its opposition to the cost-of-production formula which they sponsored. Opposition was also leveled against the administration because the N.R.A. had forced up the prices of the goods which the farmers bought at a pace faster than the A.A.A. raised the prices of the products they sold. Complications and protests arose over the hog-sow purchases and the slaughter of these animals, and over the delays that the farmers met in obtaining the advances that they had been promised earlier in 1933. This spurred on the "cost of production" enthusiasts to attack Wallace bitterly and force him and other administration spokesmen to come out into the corn-hog states on good-will missions. In North Dakota Governor William Langer, an A.A.A. foe, tried unsuccessfully to put an embargo on those farm products which sold below the "cost of production."

Parity served as an integrating, focalizing, synthesizing force, and was somewhat a form of economic appeasement to the farmers who, for the most part, had been unsuccessful in adopting the restrictive devices that the industrialists and the manufacturers had used in order to keep up the prices of their commodities. As Equity leaders once said, high tariffs for industry and low tariffs or none at all for agriculture, "corporate controls and agreements," and "labor monopolies" kept industrial wages up and prices high, but they inevitably meant higher production costs for farmers.

If parity promised the farmers better prices and higher living standards, they promised no equivalent benefits to the millions of unorganized consumers, the countless white-collar workers, school teachers, pensioners, widows, and others who lived on more or less fixed incomes and who had to pay higher prices for what they bought because of parity schedules. Nor did it promise to make possible a very effective use of our natural resources.

Local action was of the utmost importance in putting farm programs into operation. The Great Plains Committee conceded that much when it said that the success of "a long-time plan for essential readjustments . . .

will depend on local action even more than on Federal or State action. The Federal agencies may advise, assist, and coordinate, State agencies may administer permissive or mandatory legislation, but in the end local attitudes, policies, and actions are bound to be decisive. These can be guided and influenced—indeed, they must be if the downward trend is to be stopped—but they cannot be coerced."[7]

In 1939 the states of the western Middle West still held the lead in cooperative activities. There were at the time some 1,364,402 farms in the United States that reported doing business with cooperatives. Of these, 589,205 were located in the western Middle West. The Pacific Coast states —California, Washington, and Oregon—were a strong second. Individually and on a percentage basis, Minnesota ranked first with 66.0 per cent, Wisconsin was second with 48.3, Iowa third with 45.3, Idaho fourth with 43.3, New York fifth with 39.9, and North Dakota sixth with 39.8. On the basis of the number of farms doing business with cooperatives, Minnesota also led the field with 130,261, Iowa was second with 96,639, Wisconsin was third with 90,261, Ohio fourth with 71,599, and Illinois fifth with 70,296. Michigan, sixth with 61,199, was followed closely by New York with 61,088.[8]

Both Republicans and Democrats paid tribute to the western Middle West when it came to appointing a Secretary of Agriculture. At no time was this recognition greater than during the twenties and thirties. Over the period from 1921 to 1939, except for one temporary appointment, this cabinet post was filled by a representative from the western Middle West. Warren G. Harding called upon Henry Cantwell Wallace of Iowa to fill this post, which he did until his death in 1924; Calvin Coolidge chose William M. Jardine of Kansas, who served until 1929; Herbert Hoover gave the post to Arthur Hyde of Missouri, who served through the darkest years of the depression; and in 1933 Franklin Roosevelt appointed Henry Agard Wallace, also of Iowa, who held the position until he was elected Vice-President of the United States.

Both Hoover and Roosevelt realized the importance of the western

7. Report of the Great Plains Committee, *The Future of the Great Plains* (75 Congress, 1 session, House Document 144, serial 10117, Washington, 1936), p. 10 [also in plain-title edition].

8. *Statistical Abstract of the United States,* 1941, p. 704.

Middle West in 1932. The former opened his campaign for re-election in Des Moines, Iowa, and the latter chose Topeka, Kansas, as the place to lay down the six points that he held essential to any sound approach to the farm problem. In 1936 the Republicans hoped to capitalize on farm unrest in this area and went to the state of Kansas for their candidate.

The western Middle West was also a pioneer in state rural credits. Specifically, the states of North Dakota, South Dakota, and Minnesota, unhappy though many of their experiences were, set up state-financed rural-credit systems to furnish long-time loans on rural real estate. These three systems were built largely in the belief that the private credit institutions were incapable of meeting the credit needs of the farmers. "Although these three [states] were not the only ones which tackled the problem, they went farther than any other states."[9]

Progress was also made by these same three states in state warehouse supervision. Preliminary efforts along these lines had been made by Dakota Territory as early as 1887. In 1917 North Dakota, as a result of Nonpartisan League influence, passed drastic warehouse legislation. Legislation was also passed by South Dakota, Minnesota, and other states. One or two of these other states provided warehouse supervision as good as that in the three spring wheat states, or even better. Most states, however, found that the staff available to supervise the laws was altogether too small and the turnover in personnel was high. On the whole, the experiences of the states indicated that local efforts were not enough.[10]

While the agrarians organized, protested, and drafted their own formulas of relief, the evidence is that agriculture declined in its relative importance to the American economy. Agriculture still remained very important as a source of food and raw materials; but from the standpoint of the numbers engaged and the amount of capital invested in it, it certainly did not occupy the position that it formerly held.

One scholar points to this declining importance of agriculture as an

9. William G. Murray, *Agricultural Finance* (Ames, Iowa, 1941), pp. 312–15; Gilbert W. Cooke, "The North Dakota Rural Credit System," *Journal of Land and Public Utility Economics,* XIV (August, 1938), pp. 273–83; Gilbert C. Fite, "South Dakota's Rural Credit System," *Agricultural History,* XXI (October, 1947), pp. 239–49.

10. Geoffrey S. Shepherd, *Marketing Farm Products* (Ames, Iowa, 1947), pp. 438–40.

irresistible force in the progress of civilization. He argues that as society advances, the demands for "foodstuffs and materials for clothing," the satisfaction of which has been one of the main tasks of the farmers, fall off and other needs far more elastic arise in their place to be met. He further adds that with the growth of commerce, trade, and industry, there inevitably follows a rise in living standards; the professions and the service callings increase; and the importance of agriculture wanes as that of non-agricultural activities grows. Wrote this same economist:

> . . . Every progressive nation shows this. Even unsatisfactory data for a century or more, such as those for Great Britain and the United States, bear eloquent testimony to it. The forces at work are well-nigh irresistible; the trends they cause can be reversed, if at all, only at terrific cost. Where farmers still constitute a high proportion to the total population, as in China, India, Bulgaria, and the USSR, this is a symptom of a retarded civilization and a backward agriculture.[11]

No doubt the highly accelerated industrial order in which the farmers operated was bound to affect them adversely in various respects. One of the big agrarian complaints of the twenties was that the interests of the farmers either were "ignored or evaded by those responsible for the direction of national policies," and that the government, because it had fallen into the hands of these elements, provided them with "a mechanism through which special groups under the guise of law exploited those less strategically placed." Professor E. R. A. Seligman, a leading economist in his day, wrote:

> If there were no tariff on industrial products the farmer could secure many of his articles, both of production and consumption, at a lower price; if there were no restrictive immigration law he could secure his farm labor at a cheaper rate; if there were no adherence to outgrown methods of taxation he would not have to suffer the unfair burdens which now rest upon him; if credit conditions were as satisfactory in agriculture as in business he could secure his capital more cheaply; if freight rates were so adjusted as to put the emphasis still further upon value than upon bulk, his outlays would be reduced.[12]

11. Joseph S. Davis, *On Agricultural Policy, 1926–1938* (Stanford, Calif., 1939), pp. 439–40.

12. E. R. A. Seligman, *The Economics of Farm Relief* (New York, 1929), quoted by Cassius Clay in *The Mainstay of American Individualism* (New York, 1935), pp. 58–59.

Still another economist, Edwin G. Nourse, who had more appreciation for history than did most of the economists of his day and who wrote at a little earlier time, carried this point further. He observed that at the turn of the century "American agriculture stood in just the same subservient position to American industrialism that the colonies occupied toward England a century and a quarter earlier."[13]

It is certain that, no matter what the causes for the farmers' unrest were and no matter how divided they were over the program to be adopted for their relief, there was one central thought that many could not forget. For years they had been told that they were the backbone of the nation, that their calling was the most important, the most deserving, the most fundamental of all, the collapse of which would bring down the pillars of civilization itself. Of the farmers of the nation, those from the western Middle West appear to have been among the most tenacious in holding to these beliefs and among the least willing to accept a status of inferiority in our economy. This is why their leaders spoke at length of the need for "tariff equality," "a fair exchange value," "parity prices," and a better balance between agriculture, industry, and labor. Their demands marked the beginning of a reconsideration or recasting of past formulas and the creation of new ones. The farmers, instead of putting their emphasis on trust busting with the hope that this would either preserve or restore what they believed would be a healthy state of competition, tossed such thoughts out the window and proceeded to build restrictive devices patterned to a great degree after those of industry. If tariff walls were beneficial to industry and the traditional walls built for farmers, especially for those who depended on the foreign market, were not, then new ones had to be built that would work. If industrialists controlled their production to influence prices, it was conceivable that the farmers could also control theirs. If business profited from better marketing methods, agriculture could also benefit from the same. Again, if industry could be insured from hazards, conceivably agriculture, one of the most speculative of enterprises, could also be protected by the adoption of a plan for crop insurance.

13. Edwin G. Nourse, "The Place of Agriculture in Modern Industrial Society, II," *Journal of Political Economy,* XXVII (July, 1919), pp. 565–70.

Index

INDEX